MW01147212

In Dominico Eloquio

IN LORDLY ELOQUENCE

Robert Louis Wilken

In Dominico Eloquio

IN LORDLY ELOQUENCE

• •

Essays on Patristic Exegesis

IN HONOR OF

Robert Louis Wilken

Edited by

Paul M. Blowers,
Angela Russell Christman,
David G. Hunter, and
Robin Darling Young

WILLIAM B. EERDMANS PUBLISHING COMPANY
GRAND RAPIDS, MICHIGAN / CAMBRIDGE, U.K.

© 2002 Wm. B. Eerdmans Publishing Co.
All rights reserved

Wm. B. Eerdmans Publishing Co.
255 Jefferson Ave. S.E., Grand Rapids, Michigan 49503 /
P.O. Box 163, Cambridge CB3 9PU U.K.

Printed in the United States of America

07 06 05 04 03 02   7 6 5 4 3 2 1

Library of Congress Cataloging-in-Publication Data

In Dominico eloquio = In Lordly eloquence: essays in patristic exegesis
in honor of Robert L. Wilken / edited by Paul M. Blowers . . . [et al.].
        p.   cm.
Includes bibliographical references.
ISBN 0-8028-3882-0 (alk. paper)
1. Bible — Criticism, interpretation, etc. — History — Early church, ca. 30-600.
2. Fathers of the church.   I. Title: In Lordly eloquence.   II. Wilken, Robert Louis, 1936-   .
III. Blowers, Paul M., 1955-   .

BS500 .I5 2002
220.6′09′015 — dc21

                                         2001040679

www.eerdmans.com

Contents

CONTENTS

II. The Development of Patristic Exegesis

Contents

Abbreviations

Primary Sources

ACW	Ancient Christian Writers
ANF	Ante-Nicene Fathers Library
BA	Bibliothèque augustinienne
CCSG	Corpus christianorum, series graeca
CCSL	Corpus christianorum, series latina
CPG	Clavis patrum Graecorum
CPL	Clavis patrum Latinorum
CSCO	Corpus scriptorum christianorum orientalium
CSEL	Corpus scriptorum ecclesiasticorum latinorum
CWS	Classics of Western Spirituality
FOTC	Fathers of the Church
GCS	Griechischen christlichen Schriftsteller
GNO	Gregorii nysseni opera
LCL	Loeb Classical Library
NPNF	Nicene and Post-Nicene Fathers Library
PG	Patrologia graeca
PL	Patrologia latina
PO	Patrologia orientalis

Abbreviations

PS   Patrologia syriaca
SC   Sources chrétiennes

Secondary Sources

AugStud   *Augustinian Studies*
ChHist   *Church History*
HTR   *Harvard Theological Review*
JECS   *Journal of Early Christian Studies*
JThS   *Journal of Theological Studies*
OC   *Oriens Christianus*
ParOr   *Parole de l'Orient*
SP   *Studia Patristica*
ThS   *Theological Studies*
VChr   *Vigiliae Christianae*

A Tribute to Robert Louis Wilken

In a career that has taken him to professorships at the Lutheran Theological Seminary (Gettysburg), Fordham University, the University of Notre Dame, and now the University of Virginia, where he holds the William R. Kenan, Jr. Chair in the History of Christianity, Robert Wilken's contribution to the study of early Christianity is both substantial and multifarious. His pioneering work in the social and intellectual history of the early Church is well known and widely acclaimed. His monograph *The Christians as the Romans Saw Them* (1984), a *tour de force* on pagan criticism of emergent Christianity, and his essays on religious pluralism in the Greco-Roman world have forged a significantly deeper understanding of the whole dynamic of Christian self-definition in relation to Roman religious idioms and pagan caricatures of the Christian movement. Wilken's *John Chrysostom and the Jews* (1983) painted a vivid portrait of the attractiveness and resilience of Judaism in late antiquity and provided a fresh interpretation of the complexity of the disengagement of Christianity from Judaism. And in a work born of deep personal as well as scholarly interest in *Eretz Israel*, his *The Land Called Holy: Palestine in Christian History and Thought* (1992) provided the first comprehensive account of how a uniquely Christian idea of the Holy Land was shaped through centuries of Christian presence in Palestine.

These studies, and an abundance of other works on the life of the early churches,[1] have hardly been one-dimensional exercises in historical description. Wilken's history-writing is characterized by a deep sensitivity to the whole complex of factors that lend a religious tradition — especially Chris-

---

1. See the comprehensive bibliography of R. L. Wilken below, pp. 427-38.

tianity, but also Judaism, Islam, and each of the significant religions of the Roman Empire — its integrity and viability, and that give credence to that religion's claims to human devotion. Theological reasoning, the language of faith, sapiential instruction in the life of virtue — these do not float above the surface of the "real" story of a religion but remain inextricably interwoven into that story, demanding the historian's attention. Thus, for example, Wilken has chosen to depict the clash between Christianity and paganism in antiquity essentially as a "conflict between two *religious visions*,"[2] a struggle of whole competing constellations of religious conviction and understanding, and not simply an alienation driven by sociological factors, however important those might be. In a bold statement as president of the American Academy of Religion in 1989, Wilken strongly lamented the tendency of the guild of historians and scientists of religion, broadly speaking, to create a forum of absolute detachment, an illusive autonomy in relation to their subject matter, as if religions were to be treated as invariably fideistic and sectarian or simply as having no real future in human culture. Wilken is particularly qualified to have leveled such a criticism, having taught not only in the context of a theological seminary and two major Roman Catholic universities, but for the last fifteen years in a secular university's department of religious studies.

For Wilken, methodologically speaking, no account of Christianity is adequate that does not consider two developmental principles, principles that ultimately qualify each other in the historical interpretation of the Christian tradition. First — and here one may note the impact of Wolfhart Pannenberg on his thinking — the Church is a historical community called to an ever *future* mission, an eschatological vocation, in which straightforward reduplication of the thinking or action of the past is always impossible. Christianity "is" what it ultimately will become, not merely an enduring clone of what it was in the first century of the Common Era. Wilken made this point especially forcefully in his early book *The Myth of Christian Beginnings* (1971), and he has refined it elsewhere as well. Second, the Church, as a community in history, nonetheless always carries its past with it in a vital collective memory. In his own words, "the church is a living community that is the bearer of ancient traditions received from those who have gone before."[3] Thus it has conscientiously to engage the resources of its past as it moves into the unpredictable future. Its prospective vision is invariably tied up with its retrospective vision.

2. *The Christians as the Romans Saw Them* (New Haven: Yale University Press, 1984), p. 201.
3. "Memory and the Christian Intellectual Tradition," in *Remembering the Christian Past* (Grand Rapids: Eerdmans, 1995), p. 168.

This conviction about the collective Christian memory and the traditioned character of Christianity has been especially pronounced in Wilken's work since his reception into the Roman Catholic Church in 1994, and it stands out powerfully in his diverse collection of essays *Remembering the Christian Past* (1995) and in his more recent essays on patristic biblical interpretation.[4] Both within the principal academic sphere of his scholarship, the "guild" of early Christian history and patristics, and in the context of his long-time involvement in pastoral ministry and in ecumenical initiatives, Wilken has been, unashamedly, a historical *theologian*.[5] In his judgment the Church can ill afford to ignore the rich legacies of theological and spiritual instruction mediated through creed, through finely articulated theological language, through liturgy and the devotional practices of the Christian faithful, and certainly through the ongoing discipline of biblical interpretation in all its manifold modes. These are the very lifeblood of the Christian religion. I can say with confidence, however, that the classical forms of patristic (and medieval) exegesis of the Bible have come to occupy an especially prominent place in Wilken's constructive reengagement with the time-tested traditions and intuitions of the ancient Church.

Speaking from experience, I well remember a group of nervous first-year doctoral students sitting quietly around the table in a seminar room in the Hesburgh Library of the University of Notre Dame in the fall of 1983. It was the opening session of the Christianity and Judaism in Antiquity area seminar. Our professor entered and with few words proceeded to distribute, to each of this anxious lot, an enormous stack of photocopied excerpts of Greek patristic commentaries on Romans. While his exact words cannot be recalled, the sense of it, *quasi ad litteram,* was this: "Translate these. Then we'll talk." Little more was said, other than a few words of introduction setting out the parameters of the seminar. Class was dismissed and the first-years, I among them, scrambled to their Smyth's *Greek Grammar* and their Lampe's *Patristic Greek Lexicon* to begin the onerous task of translation, with vivid images of having their lowly renderings of the patristic commentators submitted to the careful scrutiny of their professor and the upper-level doctoral students. Our baptism in patristic studies at Notre Dame had begun.

---

4. See especially his "In Defense of Allegory," *Modern Theology* 14 (1998): 197-212; reprinted in *Theology and Scriptural Imagination,* ed. L. Gregory Jones and James Buckley (Oxford: Blackwell, 1998), pp. 35-50.

5. One need merely look at his study *Judaism and the Early Christian Mind: A Study of Cyril of Alexandria's Exegesis and Theology* (New Haven: Yale University Press, 1971) to observe that his interests in historical theology developed early in his work.

As I look back, that seminar was formative for me and for others. In that year we caught something of Robert Wilken's contagious passion for reading the Fathers, or better still, reading the Fathers *as readers*, as the pioneering Christian interpreters, in their scholia, homilies, and commentaries, of the "language of the Lord," the divine oracles of Holy Scripture. Indeed, the exegesis of Romans provided a particularly fertile entry into the world of patristic hermeneutics since so many themes from within the Bible and from the history of Christian thought intersect in that great text. Wilken led us to discover that it wasn't just Augustine (and Luther and Barth after him) who probed the depths of this, Paul's theological manifesto; indeed, a broad array of ancient commentators, including the likes of Origen and Theodore of Mopsuestia, also offered profound insights into the epistle's timeless questions of the economy of salvation, the providence of God, grace and human freedom, faith and righteousness.[6]

Those who have worked closely with him know that for Robert Wilken, the study of patristic biblical interpretation is much more than a historical reconstruction of the hermeneutics of the early Church, however important that may be. Sharing a kindred spirit with David Steinmetz, the late Henri de Lubac,[7] and others, Wilken views it also, crucially, as a labor of retrieval, of *ressourcement*, a living engagement that brings the ancient exegetes into conversation with the science of contemporary biblical commentary. The Bible, as he never tires of reiterating, is the Church's Book, demanding not only the most exacting historical-critical scholarship but also a keen attention to the whole historical continuum of its interpretation, the trained insights of centuries of theological interpreters, and to the power of the scriptural Word to speak in an ever contemporary way to the people of God. Patristic exegesis has remained exemplary for Wilken precisely because he has found in the Fathers a model wherein the Bible is *read* with a view to the immediate *hearing* of the Word and, what is more, an *envisioning* (θεωρία) of the Word in its full spiritual and ecclesial scope. "Context," writes Wilken in a reflection on the patristic use of allegory, "needs to be understood to embrace the Church, its liturgy, its way of life, its practices and institutions, its ideas and beliefs. Without the Bible these things would not have come into being, and without

---

6. A fruit of that seminar was Wilken's essay "Free Choice and the Divine Will in Greek Christian Commentaries on Paul," in *Paul and the Legacies of Paul*, ed. William Babcock (Dallas: Southern Methodist University Press, 1990), pp. 123-40.

7. See Wilken's foreword to the recent English translation of de Lubac's classic on patristic and medieval biblical interpretation, *Medieval Exegesis: The Four Senses of Scripture*, vol. 1, trans. Mark Sebanc (Grand Rapids: Eerdmans, 1998), pp. ix-xii.

the Church and its life as a commentary the Bible is a sealed book for Christians."[8]

The set of essays that follow comes from a group of colleagues, scholarly associates, and former students of Robert Wilken, many of whom share his passion to uncover the riches of early Christian biblical interpretation. Scholarly discussion of the "future" of patristic exegesis has been enhanced for many of us through the forum provided by the North American Patristic Society, of which Wilken is a past president and a continued strong advocate for collaborative study of patristic exegesis. Several contributors to this Festschrift are in fact involved now in a large-scale project under Wilken's editorial supervision to be entitled *The Church's Bible*, a multivolume collection of translated patristic commentary on biblical books, due to be published by the William Eerdmans Publishing Company.

On behalf of the other editors, Angela Russell Christman, David Hunter, and Robin Darling Young, and all of our contributors, I can say that it is with genuine gratitude and friendship that we offer these essays to one whose love for the "lordly eloquence" of Holy Scripture and for the grand tapestry of patristic biblical interpretation has so greatly broadened and deepened the field in which we carry on our work. Like one of his own heroes, Origen of Alexandria, Robert Wilken has, in the words of Gregory Thaumaturgus, "hoed, dug, watered, done everything he could, applied every skill and solicitude he had"[9] to advance us in the true Christian *philosophia* and the interpretation of the superabundant Word, the Church's Bible.

PAUL M. BLOWERS

---

8. Wilken, "In Defense of Allegory," p. 209.

9. Gregory Thaumaturgus, *Address of Thanksgiving to Origen*, trans. Michael Slusser, in *St. Gregory Thaumaturgus: Life and Works*, FOTC 98 (Washington: Catholic University of America Press, 1998), pp. 106-7 (slightly altered).

Contributors

Gary A. Anderson
Professor of Old Testament
Harvard Divinity School

Paul M. Blowers
Professor of Church History
Emmanuel School of Religion

J. Patout Burns
Edward A. Malloy Professor of
    Catholic Studies
The Divinity School
Vanderbilt University

J. David Cassel
Associate Professor of Theological
    Studies
Hanover College

John C. Cavadini
Associate Professor of Historical
    Theology
University of Notre Dame

Angela Russell Christman
Associate Professor of Theology
Loyola College in Maryland

Michael Compton
Adjunct Assistant Professor of Classics
University of Richmond

Brian E. Daley, S. J.
Catherine F. Huisking Professor of
    Theology
University of Notre Dame

Joseph M. Hallman
Professor of Theology
University of St. Thomas

Sr. Nonna Verna Harrison
Visiting Lecturer
Institute for Orthodox
    Christian Studies
Cambridge, England

Susan Ashbrook Harvey
Associate Professor of Religious
    Studies
Brown University

Michael J. Hollerich
Assistant Professor of Theology
University of St. Thomas

David G. Hunter
Monsignor James A. Supple Professor
  of Catholic Studies
Iowa State University

Charles Kannengiesser
Catherine F. Huisking Professor
  Emeritus of Theology
University of Notre Dame

Judith L. Kovacs
Assistant Professor of Religious Studies
University of Virginia

Richard A. Layton
Assistant Professor of Religious Studies
University of Illinois, Urbana-
  Champaign

Joseph T. Lienhard, S.J.
Professor of Theology
Fordham University

Frederick W. Norris
Dean E. Walker Professor of Church
  History
Emmanuel School of Religion

Richard A. Norris, Jr.
Professor Emeritus of Church History
Union Theological Seminary,
  New York

Robert D. Sider
Professor Emeritus of Classical
  Languages
Dickinson College

Joseph W. Trigg
Rector, Port Tobacco Parish
La Plata, Maryland

Robin Darling Young
Associate Professor of Theology
Catholic University of America

I. Exegetical Themes

The Resurrection of Adam and Eve

GARY A. ANDERSON

Aristotle's god, whose clearest characteristic is his indifference, would not have been moved by such an egoistic and human argument. But a God who turns toward man and is interested in man's destiny and in man's reaction to His commandments leaves Himself open to such intimidation. We have two choices: Either an indifferent God who does not reveal Himself through a prophetic revelation because He Himself is devoid of personality and feeling, or a personal God presenting a full blown personality who is worried about what the nations of the world will think. It is the same God, according to Ezekiel, who cannot stand the argument of the nations, namely "If these are God's people, why have they left their land?" (Ezek 36:20). This God cannot tolerate even the shadow of a doubt that His power may not be sufficient to save the day. Such a doubt is, after all, a desecration, "a dirtying" of His name. In this scenario, God is obliged to sanctify, even though they do not deserve this redemption according to strict justice. Divine need is the decisive factor. The biblical God is anthropomorphic. He who strips God of His personal quality distorts the true meaning of scripture.

Yochanan Muffs, "Who Will Stand in the Breach?:
A Study of Prophetic Intercession"

There is no disagreement that the greatest work of Dante, the great Florentine poet of the thirteenth century, was his epic poem *The Divine Comedy*. This enormous work was a progressive tour of those realms that lie beyond the

3

grave. He began in the Inferno, moved to Purgatory, and then ended in Paradise or Heaven. Though much of the work has a somber and eerie atmosphere — how could a conversation with those condemned to the Inferno be otherwise? — it was aptly titled a "Comedy" because it moved inexorably toward the redemption of humanity. His purpose was not to satisfy the curious about the nature of the hereafter; the goal was moral and spiritual. Working under the inspiration of his near contemporary St. Thomas Aquinas, he wanted to trace, in narrative form, how the life of virtue was to be lived and would be rewarded.[1] At the very beginning of the work, when he enters the shadowy abyss of Limbo, he meets the greatest of all Latin poets, Virgil. Virgil's masterful epic about the founding of Rome, the *Aeneid*, was well known to Dante as it would have been to any educated medieval person, and the work as well as the poet were highly esteemed. Yet Virgil lived just prior to the advent of Christ and therefore was not privy to the preaching of the gospel. "For such defect and no other offense," Virgil confesses to Dante, "We are lost, and only so far amerced; That without hope we languish in suspense." Dante was greatly grieved at this discovery but hastened to press an urgent question to this esteemed man:

"Tell me, my Master, tell me, Sir!" I said,
　　Seized with a longing wholly to be assured
　　Of that faith wherein error cannot tread,
"Did ever any of those herein immured
　　By his own or other's merit to bliss get free?"

The question appears cryptic to modern readers, but those of Dante's day knew exactly what the subject was. According to a widespread and quite ancient tradition, Christ was thought to have descended into Hades during his three days in the grave and to have retrieved the righteous dead among the Israelites. Virgil, already a denizen of Limbo when Christ was crucified, provides Dante with the objective confirmation he seeks,

And he, aware what meant my covert word,
Answered: "I was yet new in this degree

---

1. On the importance of Dante's narrative to the Thomistic enterprise see A. MacIntyre, *Three Rival Moral Versions of Moral Inquiry* (Notre Dame, Ind.: University of Notre Dame Press, 1990). On p. 142 he writes: "What then would it be for the sequences of the *Summa* . . . to be mirrored in the enacted dramatic narratives of particular human lives lived out in particular communities? Aquinas himself does not supply an answer to this question, but Dante does."

> When I saw one in power crowned appear
> On whom the signs of victory were to see.
> He took from us the shade of our first sire;
> Of his son Abel, and Noah of that same seed. . . .

In Limbo the holy name of the redeemer is not pronounced, but there can be no doubt that the "one in power crowned" was Christ. He had entered Limbo and restored Adam ("the shade of our first sire") along with other worthies from the Old Testament. "And I would have thee know," Virgil divulges, "that before these,//There has been no human soul that he atones." The crucifixion was a cosmic turning point among the dead. Only at the descent of Christ was anyone redeemed.

Dante has drawn on a long-standing tradition, widespread in both Eastern and Western Christianity, of Christ's descent to the underworld to redeem Adam. In the West, this tradition is best known in dozens of apocryphal narratives about "the Harrowing of Hell." Perhaps the most well known and influential of this genre was a tale called *The Gospel of Nicodemus.*[2] In this story, the righteous dead are awakened during the last moments of Christ's life by the noisy and desperate efforts of Hades and Satan to prevent Christ from storming their door. They had bickered endlessly as to whether they should finally kill this figure on the cross. Hades feared his death would do them more harm than good. Satan was resolute; he demanded that his life be taken. Yet at his death both had to concede they had made a colossal mistake. Like the centurion at the foot of the cross, they recognized that this was no ordinary man; he was the son of God. Quickly they attempted to bar the gates and reinforce their stronghold. Christ arrived at the door and demanded to be let in: *"Lift up your heads, ye gates, and let the King of Glory enter!"* The famous words of Psalm 24 became the libretto of this final operatic act. Satan replied: *"Who is this king of glory?"* To whom an answer was quickly returned: *"The Lord strong and mighty, the Lord mighty in battle."* Then straightway the gates of brass were shattered, the bars of iron were ground to powder, and the dead were loosed from their chains. The King of Glory entered the realm of the dead, Sheol, and retrieved his bounty, Adam and Eve.

This tradition was so deeply woven into the traditions of Easter that it informed numerous liturgical celebrations.[3] To this day in many Orthodox

---

2. Wilhelm Schneemelcher, ed., *New Testament Apocrypha* (Louisville, Ky.: Westminster/John Knox Press, 1992), vol. 1, pp. 501-36, esp. 521-26.

3. See the fine discussion of the liturgical developments in H. A. Kelly, *The Devil at Baptism* (Ithaca, N.Y.: Cornell University Press, 1985).

services in the East, the congregation gathers outside the doors of the church at the service of the Easter Vigil and knocks on the doors demanding that the King of Glory be ushered in. The celebration of Easter is founded on a dramatization of this moment of infernal combat. As testimony to its importance in the West, one need only point to the way Handel used this Psalm in his Easter Oratorio, "Messiah." He set this Psalm exactly in between the account of the crucifixion and the ascension into heaven. Handel's audience would have known very well why this Psalm was placed precisely in this location, a detail that is lost on nearly every modern listener.

For all the importance of this tradition in the West, its true place of origin was the East, and it is there that the tradition still enjoys a receptive and knowledgeable audience. No small part of the explanation for this is the high value put on religious iconography in the East. Eastern religious iconography possessed more than mere "artistic" or aesthetic qualities; the image was vested with revelatory content. Icons were canonized just as Scripture was, and those authoritative images were a necessary part of church architecture; they were not mere decoration. In the East, one studies and prays to these icons; they are to be venerated and kissed, not merely viewed. They are the "image" of those who are beyond image.

Of signal importance in the iconography of the East was the depiction of Christ's despoliation of Hades, entitled the *Anastasis* in Greek, meaning "the Resurrection." In the Church of Christ at Chora in Constantinople (fourteenth century), there is a spectacular rendering of this image on the vault of the apse.[4] The enormous figure of Christ strides toward Adam while grasping the hand of Eve. The hands of both are pulled into the mandorla of light that surrounds Christ. We can tell by their postures that they must be pulled from their graves. Christ is the active agent in this drama; Adam and Eve enjoy the benefits. The righteous dead watch in wonder as Christ lifts Adam and Eve out of their respective sepulchers and tramples on the gates of Hades. The bolts and bars used to block his entry, as well as Hades himself, lie scattered below.

The Theology of the *Anastasis*

It is easy to be mesmerized by the beauty and power of this image and miss the subtleties of its message. In his masterful book on the three last days of Christ, *Mysterium Paschale,* Hans Urs von Balthasar rues the florid develop-

4. M. Zibawi, *The Icon: Its Meaning and History* (Collegeville, Minn.: Liturgical Press, 1993), fig. 77 (p. 102).

ment of the tradition of Christ's descent on the grounds that it obscures the most important aspect of Holy Saturday, that Christ's body lies *dead*. "The first vantage point to be taken up," he writes, "is that of the solidarity of the Crucified with all the human dead. The careful description [in the Gospels], free of all apologetic tendencies, of the taking down from the Cross, of the treatment bestowed on the cadaver, and of the burial testifies in simple fashion to this solidarity. The body simply *must* be put into the earth."[5] The East has erred, he writes, when it puts undo emphasis on the victorious *actions* of Christ during this period. This was only possible, he argues, "by an anticipatory interpolation of the Easter event into the time of Holy Saturday, and by the transformation of a victory which was objective and passive into one that is subjective and active."[6] For von Balthasar, Christ gives his body up to death on behalf of mankind, and in honor of this perfect sacrifice the Father raises him up. To make Christ the active agent would be to efface the central trinitarian element of the Easter mystery: the Son *offers* his life to the Father, and the Father in turn restores him. Christ does not simply transform himself into the victor. In addition, von Balthasar notes, the liturgy itself testifies to Christ's human death, for on Holy Saturday the Eucharist is not celebrated nor is the alleluia chanted as part of the Church's liturgy and prayer. The Church mourns because the hope of Israel is no longer. If this was not sufficient proof, then one need only point to the silence of the Gospels themselves about the state of Christ while he lay in the grave. "We are grateful to them for this," he concludes.[7]

These arguments are certainly weighty, but they lean more heavily against the popular apocryphal literature of the West than against the iconography of the East, for it is in the West that so much emphasis was placed on the *descent* of Christ. It is striking to note that the icon of Christ's retrieval of Adam and Eve is not titled "descent" *(katabasis)* in the East, but "rising again" *(anastasis)*. In fact, one of the earliest surviving inscriptions ascribed to this image is "Christ raises Adam out of Hades."[8] Art historians had once imagined that the entire iconographic cycle of the *anastasis* was derived from the literary pattern found in the *Gospel of Nicodemus*. In her aptly titled book, *Anastasis*, Anna Kartsonis shows this to be impossible. The *dramatis personae*

---

5. Hans Urs von Balthasar, *Mysterium Paschale: The Mystery of Easter*, trans. Aidan Nichols (Grand Rapids: Eerdmans, 1990), p. 160.

6. Von Balthasar, *Mysterium Paschale*, p. 180.

7. Von Balthasar, *Mysterium Paschale*, p. 148.

8. Anna Kartsonis, *Anastasis: The Making of an Image* (Princeton, N.J.: Princeton University Press, 1986), pl. 44a.

or central narrative figures are completely different between the two. The *Gospel of Nicodemus* distributes the benefits of Christ to several key figures: Adam, Seth, Isaiah, and John the Baptist. The *anastasis* tradition does not so distribute the benefits. Adam and Eve are the primary beneficiaries; David and Solomon are commonly portrayed as witnesses to the salvific moment. The most important aspect of the image, Kartsonis argues, is not the rising of Christ. "This aspect of the miracle of the Resurrection is taken for granted," she writes.[9] "However, in both instances the opposite is true of the raising of Adam. The recognition of Adam by homilists as 'the first created . . . and the first dead amongst men' makes his raising from the dead an act of re-creation on the part of the Logos (The Divine Word)." The redemption of Adam is a guarantee of the work of redemption begun by his death. Hades thought he was taking another in Adam's train, but, truth be told, by taking Christ he was undoing his very hold on the human race.

Although this image cannot do justice to the sacrifice Christ has offered his Father, it does display, in the boldest manner, the immeasurable salvific power of the *crucified* savior. This power becomes manifest only in *weakness*. The emphasis of the iconography, to paraphrase the words of Luther's close friend and fellow reformer Melanchthon, is to highlight Christ's benefits. "The iconography of the Anastasis was not . . . designed to be a visual reproduction of the chronicle of Christ's spoliation of Hades," Kartsonis concludes, "[but] a metaphor of the salvation realized at the moment of the raising of Adam-Everyman following the defeat of Death."[10] In contrast to the fears of von Balthasar, the image does not efface the sacrificial value of Christ's death; it merely puts the spotlight on its effects. As Abdiel confessed to Satan in *Paradise Lost,* the universe is ordered such that obedient subjection and humility will, in the end, redeem and glorify.[11]

The earliest image of the *anastasis* we possess dates to the early eighth century and is located in the Chapel of the Forty Martyrs of the Santa Maria Antiqua Church in Rome.[12] In this early version of the tradition we see just three

9. Kartsonis, *Anastasis*, p. 5.

10. Kartsonis, *Anastasis*, p. 76.

11. In *Paradise Lost*, Book V, Christ is elevated over the entire angelic host. Satan refuses to give Christ the adoration that is his due and retires to the northern sector of the heavenly realm to plot his revolt. His argument to his prospective band of rebels is that genuflection toward this figure will result in their loss of status in the kingdom of heaven. Abdiel, who had accompanied Satan unaware of the plans for rebellion, objected strenuously to this claim. "All honor to [Christ] done," he declared, would return "our own" (lines 844-45).

12. Kartsonis, *Anastasis*, pl. 14b.

actors: Adam, Christ, and Hades. Because Adam represents every man, the artist felt no need to include the figure of Eve. If Adam, from whom the human race descends, was raised, then *all* will follow. Christ is the dominant figure of the image; enveloped in a mandorla of light he strides to the left and reaches down to grasp the waiting hand of Adam. The mandorla is noticeably broken at two points. Adam's hand has been pulled within this glorious light, and Christ's foot stands outside it, trampling on the figure of Hades. This trampling of Hades recalls the threat made to the snake in Genesis 3:15: "the seed of the woman shall trample upon your head." Christians had long understood this punishment of the snake as a compact and ironic prophecy of redemption. Christ, the seed of Mary, would trample the serpent, the cause of death. Hades is a dark muscular figure who appears bent on maintaining his kingdom at all cost. Like Satan of *Paradise Lost,* he is unbowed by the power of the redeemer and desperately reaches forward in attempt to retain his grasp on Adam. Kartsonis makes the intriguing suggestion that the foot of Christ stands outside the mandorla to inform the viewer that it is Christ's *humanity* that restores Adam. Hades is not vanquished by divine fiat; it is the human vigor of the savior that does him in. In addition, she argues that Adam's hand within the mandorla hints at the eventual return of Adam to his stature as God's image. "God had become man," Athanasius had once said, "so that man could become [like] God." The entire mystery of the incarnation is encapsulated in terse form within this image.

Christus Victor

The *anastasis* presents a compelling picture of the victory of Easter, but due to its iconographic form it cannot supply the total picture of what early Christian thinkers imagined took place at the resurrection. Our story will not be complete without considering what patristic authors and apocryphal writers thought about it, and on this event they had much to say and were in considerable agreement. In the words of Gustav Aulén, the main outline was clear:

> The work of Christ is first and foremost a victory over the powers that hold mankind in bondage: sin, death, and the devil. These may be said to be in a measure personified, but in any case they are objective powers; and the victory of Christ creates a new situation, bringing their rule to an end, and setting men free from their dominion.[13]

13. G. Aulén, *Christus Victor: An Historical Study of the Three Main Types of the Idea of Atonement,* trans. A. G. Hebert (New York: Macmillan, 1951), p. 20.

Aulén aptly characterized this perspective of Christ's atoning work as *Christus Victor*, and this model was hardly rare. It dominated Eastern thought from the time of Irenaeus of Lyons to John of Damascus (second century through the seventh) and was equally vibrant in the West, including such figures as Ambrose, Ambrosiaster, Augustine, Leo the Great, and Gregory the Great.

The picture of *Christus Victor* must be spelled out in narrative terms. To describe it simply as a battle over death and the devil will hardly do justice to the complexity of ideas it represents. In brief the narrative runs as follows: Adam and Eve sin and bring into creation the penalty of death. Unlike other acts of malfeasance, this penalty does not fall on the perpetrators of the trespass alone; because all humankind descends from this couple, all bear the marks of their punishment whether deserved or not. At their expulsion, the powers of sin and death are quickened and the kingdom of the underworld is founded. From now on, Hades has the *legitimate* right to take each and every human being. Some writers prefer to identify Hades as Satan himself, whereas others identify Hades with Death; this is no small difference, as we shall see. God must acquiesce in some respects to this tragic picture. The death of each and every man and woman is the just outcome of the command and penalty he had imposed in Eden. Yet the love that God feels towards his most favored creatures and the power of his merciful nature will not allow him to stand by idly as all creation meets its ignominious end. He must devise a way to retrieve man from Hades in such a way that the just claims of Hades over all humankind are respected. In order to accomplish this he decides to send his son in human flesh into the world. The divine son, born of the virgin Mary, does not fall under the legal terms of Hades' contract. He is entitled to all those descended from Adam and Eve, not to a God-man born of a virgin. Hades is puzzled during Christ's entire earthly life as to who he is. His miracles, especially the raising of the dead, are those of a divine being. Yet his experience of hunger, need for sleep, his weeping over the dead, and his sweating of blood in Gethsemane indicate a human being subject to the various and sundry passions of this mortal life. Hades could not resist the temptation; on Good Friday he took him. Yet as Christ was put to death his power was revealed, a power that was activated through weakness. Hades is not entitled to take him; he has overreached the terms of his contract over human life. As a result, his just claims are abrogated, and man, through the figures of Adam and Eve, can be redeemed.

This perspective on the atonement has been enormously popular and abhorred at the same time. No doubt the popularity stems from its sense of drama. God enters history to engage and destroy the forces of death that threaten each and every human life. The medieval theory of the atonement advanced by Anselm of Canterbury — as is commonly thought — put too heavy an emphasis on the concept of "satisfaction" of God's wrath; that is, the idea that God himself was dishonored by human sin and required a perfect sacrifice to appease his vindictive anger.[14] Here God stands over against his creation as a stern but *just* arbiter of human affairs. How much more attractive, Aulén argued, is the idea that God's *mercy* stands with us over against the stern but implacable sense of justice of Hades. Yet the theory of *Christus Victor* comes at some cost. As Jaroslav Pelikan notes in his introduction to Aulén's book, moderns have "disliked intensely the 'mythological language' of [the idea]" and "the realistic, often undeniably grotesque imagery, in which the victory of Christ over the devil, or the deception of the devil, was depicted in lurid colors."[15] Can the atonement be a respectable idea if it is founded on deceit?

I would like to hold the moral problem for later. A more pressing problem for the moment is the mythological dress in which the entire tradition is robed. As von Balthasar has noted, the Gospels themselves evidence a loud silence about what happened the setting of Jesus' corpse in the grave and his miraculous appearance on Easter. Shouldn't this silence be respected? The problem here is that the Gospels are loath to ascribe any cosmic significance to the death of Christ. If all we possessed was the Gospel of Mark, we would know that no one, save the centurion at the foot of the cross, knew who Christ was. Christ's messianic office was to become manifest in his suffering. On this point Mark is crystal clear, but he takes no pains to describe *how* this was so. The passion of Christ is the defining moment in his life — on this point all the Gospels are clear — but if we wish to proceed further to clarify its more general theological content, we must turn to the epistles of Paul and other early Christian writings.

Perhaps we could make one exception, that being the Gospel of John. It is not by accident that Clement of Alexandria (second century) called this book the "spiritual Gospel," for it took extra care to set the actions of Jesus in a cosmic context. John eschewed the somber, terse tones of Mark's presentation. Instead he described the victory wrought by Christ's passion in warmer, more positive hues. His death on the cross was not the result of some tragic miscalculation on the part of the Jews or Romans; it was the desired outcome of his incarnate ministry. Indeed, on the eve of Christ's gruesome death John

---

14. This common perspective on Anselm has been justly challenged by D. Hart, "A Gift Exceeding Every Debt: An Eastern Orthodox Appreciation of Anselm's *Cur Deus Homo*," *Pro Ecclesia* 7 (1998): 333-49.

15. Aulén, *Christus Victor*, p. 10.

announces (John 12:31), "Now is the judgment of this world; now the prince of this world shall be cast out."

For Chrysostom, John's theology of the passion was encapsulated in these two brief clauses.

> It is as if Christ said, "now shall a trial be held, and a judgment be pronounced. How and in what manner? He (the devil) smote *the first man,* because he found him guilty of sin; *for it was through sin that death entered in.* But he did not find any sin in me; wherefore then did he fall on me and give me up to the power of death? . . . How is the world judged in me? It is as if the devil was addressed in a court of law, 'Thou didst smite them all, because thou didst find them guilty of sin; wherefore then didst thou strike Christ? Is it not evident that thou didst this unjustly?' *Therefore the whole world shall become righteous through him.*"[16]

Chrysostom has drawn nearly the entire tableau of the myth of *Christus Victor* into his interpretation of John 12:31. Yet this is no innocent exposition of the Gospel. The picture drawn here is dependent on the theology of St. Paul, particularly Romans 5:12-21 and Colossians 2:14. In Romans, Paul argues that it was through the death of the first man, Adam, that sin had entered the world. Through him all men and women will die, but Adam's sin was undone by the arrival of the second man. His death secured the release of the first Adam's progeny. Through the death of the second Adam all would become righteous. Yet Romans does not supply the mechanism for how the rule of death was overturned. It only sets in bold relief an antinomy: through Adam death — through Christ life. Colossians, however, provides the crucial missing link. According to Colossians 2:14, God redeemed man through Christ by "erasing *the bond of indebtedness* that stood against us with its legal demands." What was this bond of indebtedness? According to Chrysostom, it was none other than the guilt of Adam writ large over all humanity.

The Bond of Adam

To appreciate this notion one must be aware of how sin was depicted in the biblical text. Sin was always concretized as some sort of physical burden. In the original Hebrew, the idiom for laboring under such a burden was "to bear a sin" *(nasa' 'avon).* Forgiveness was consequently understood as "physical re-

---

16. John Chrysostom, *hom. 67 in Jo.* (PG 59:372).

moval of the weight of sin."[17] Most sins were light enough that they could be borne for a while, at least until atonement was made; other sins were so heavy that they were lethal at impact. All sins, if left unattended, would gradually weigh on the back of any person and destroy him. During the time of Jesus, a conspicuous change occurred in the idiom for sin. The metaphor of "debt" replaced that of "burden." In rabbinic Hebrew and Aramaic one speaks of sin as an obligation to pay off some form of debt (*hova, hovta* in Aramaic). From this Jewish context we have the famous lines from the Lord's Prayer, *"forgive us our debts as we forgive our debtors."* The imagery of debt was very influential in how the early Church understood Paul. When Paul says, *"Christ erased the bond of indebtedness that stood against us,"* the thought naturally arose, Just where did this bond come from? How did it originate? The answer was as immediate as it was obvious: if death and sin derive from Adam (Romans 5), then certainly this bond of indebtedness must as well (Colossians 2).[18] Early Christian interpreters presumed that these letters attributed to Paul exhibited a consistent picture of the salvific act. We all die (Rom. 5:12-14) because of the enormous debt (Col. 2:14) that has accumulated in the wake of Adam's sin. The interest that has accumulated over centuries and millennia was such that no person could clear the account.

Through my discussion I have presented the patristic picture of *Christus Victor* as though it were a unitary phenomenon. Of course, in actuality, there was a myriad of differences. Though the overall dramatic character was the same, every scene and each character's lines would vary from one telling to another. It may be helpful to think of this teaching as a jazz tune; the key and simple melody were fixed, but each performance was a unique and often very creative event. Gregory of Nyssa, in his *Catechetical Oration*, emphasized God's justice in the entire affair. God could not redeem man by simple fiat because then the devil would possess a just cause of complaint. "Those who give up their liberty for money," he argued, "become slaves of their purchasers. By selling themselves, neither they nor anyone else can reclaim their freedom, even when those who reduce themselves to this wretched state are nobly born. And should anyone, out of concern for one so sold, exercise force against the purchaser, he would seem unjust in dictatorially freeing one legally acquired."[19]

17. See the fine treatment of Baruch Schwartz, "The Bearing of Sin in the Priestly Literature," in D. Wright et al., eds., *Pomegranates and Golden Bells* (Winona Lake, Ind.: Eisenbrauns, 1995), pp. 3-21.

18. See the discussion of E. Best, *An Historical Study of the Exegesis of Colossians 2,14* (Rome: Pontificia Universitas Gregoriana, 1956).

19. *Catechetical Oration* 22, trans. E. Edward R. Hardy, in *Christology of the Later Fathers*, Library of Christian Classics 3 (Philadelphia: Westminster, 1954), p. 299.

Christ became incarnate to rectify this situation. When the devil saw the miracles that he performed "he recognized in Christ a bargain that offered him more than he held. For this reason he chose him as the ransom for those he had shut up in death's prison." Yet knowing that the devil could not gaze directly upon the divine nature, Christ clothed himself in the very flesh Satan "already held captive through sin." Concealed under the cover of our nature, Christ deceived the devil; "just as it is in the nature of things for the bait of flesh to attract greedy fishes, so too was his divinity the hook." In Nyssa's view, it is not so much that Satan overreaches the terms of his contract as that he becomes greedy for an even larger quarry. He is willing to give up all humanity for Christ, but in the end loses Christ as well.

Narsai, a fifth-century Syriac theologian, presents the encounter of Christ and the devil in even more dramatic terms. Like an apocryphal storyteller, he fills in the gaps left by the terse biblical picture. As Christ threatens to undo his kingdom, Satan more vehemently argues his case:

> He recalled the transgression of God's command in paradise;
>   upon this offense he based his case. [. . .]
> The signature of Eve and Adam he showed him, saying:
>   "Behold! Your parents have sealed and delivered this over.
>   Read and understand it.
> A bond Adam wrote me in Eden, because he succumbed to sin;
>   because he did not repay it, he pledged his sons as interest.
> From the beginning, I have possessed authority over mortals;
>   not in secret were they enrolled and enslaved as debtors."
>   *(Hymn on the Resurrection)*[20]

In this view, Adam and Eve are said to have signed a legal document as a result of their violation in Eden. Though Satan had dictated the terms of the document, the ground for those terms had been set by God: *"If you eat of this fruit, you shall surely die."* Satan chastised Christ for thinking that he can violently abrogate a legal deed. Christ is able to work within this legal framework by presenting himself to Satan as a mere mortal, someone who should fall within the legal framework set by Adam and Eve. As it turns out, Christ is no mere mortal; as the God-man who knew no sin, he stands outside this bond of indebtedness. Christ exclaims,

---

20. *Narsai's Metrical Homilies on the Nativity, Epiphany, Passion, Resurrection, and Ascension,* ed. and trans. Frederick G. McLeod (Turnhout, Belgium: Brepols, 1979), p. 141.

He thinks that [Adam and his progeny] were given as hostages;
    I will cancel the bond of his lordship over mortals.
By death, he sealed the bond of mankind's debts;
    and through death upon a tree, I will tear it up.
In the sight of spiritual and corporeal beings, I will void
    that sentence of condemnation about which he boasts as conqueror.

When Christ descends to Hades he shouts, "Let the Gates of Sheol raise up its head before me." This allusion to Psalm 24 recalls vividly the image of Christ astride the gates of Sheol while he reaches down to hoist Adam and Eve from the abyss of death.

There were countless other versions of the tale as well. In spite of their many differences in detail they were united on several key points. God's love toward humankind is so extraordinary that he cannot simply stand with hands clasped as the human race is led "justly" to its death. Yet to act simply by divine fiat would be equally unfit. God must solve the problem from within, by taking on human flesh, not from without, by simply wiping the slate clean. Had he done otherwise, John of Damascus wrote, "the tyrant (Satan) would have had cause to complain." Yet the hold of death on humankind was not altogether rational. Even within the penalty imposed on Adam there were the signs of injustice. According to Romans 5:12-13, when Adam sinned, sin and death entered the world. *"Sin was indeed in the world before the [Mosaic] law, but sin was not reckoned when there was no law. Nevertheless, death exercises dominion over those whose sins were not like the transgression of Adam."* This peculiar retelling of Israel's history distinguishes between the sin of Adam, the sin of those after Adam but before Moses, and the sin of those after Moses. Why the interest in the category of those after Adam but before Moses? Although the text is not entirely clear, the reason appears to be this: both Adam and the generation after Moses had received publicly given commandments from God that threatened death if they were violated. The death of Adam and those who lived after Moses was due to the faults of the individuals so named. Yet it was not so for those who lived in between. They were not given the benefit of such law giving, yet they paid the penalty nonetheless. Death then does not exercise his office with complete fairness; he has already overstepped his bounds. *His rule is like that of a tyrant.*[21]

---

21. On the theme of Death's tyrannical rule and its relation to Romans 5, see G. Anderson, "The Status of the Torah in the Pre-Sinaitic Period: St. Paul's Epistle to the Romans," in *Biblical Perspectives: Early Use and Interpretation of the Bible in Light of the Dead Sea Scrolls. Proceedings of the First International Symposium of the Orion Center, 12-14 May 1996*, ed. M. Stone and E. Chazon (Leiden: Brill, 1998), pp. 1-25.

The notion that Adam's sin had inaugurated a period of tyranny was not lost on patristic writers. Indeed, Romans 5:12-14 is one of the most frequently cited texts in patristic writings, and on nearly every occasion death's dominion is glossed in despotic terms. Irenaeus is particularly perceptive in this respect. He argues that the revelation of the law had two purposes. On the one hand, it made human beings responsible for their sins. On the other, it showed that Death was truly a robber and a tyrant for he took human life even without justification:

> But the law coming, which was given by Moses, and testifying of sin that it is a sinner, did truly take away his (death's) kingdom, showing that *he was no king, but a robber;* and it revealed him as a murderer. It laid, however, a weighty burden upon man, who had sin in himself, showing that he was liable to death.[22]

St. Ephrem went a step further than this. He argued that Abel's violent death at the hands of Cain — which was the first death to be visited upon the world — was unjust, and thus that the rule of Death himself was founded on tyrannical grounds. Had Adam been the first to die, all would have been different. The establishment of Death's kingdom would have been just and God — because he is Justice himself — could have done nothing to redeem Adam. "For if Adam had been the first to enter [into Sheol], *which was his deservedly,* it would have been meted out to him to remain there forever."[23] This surprising interpretation becomes more intelligible if we realize that Abel's death was considered a type of the crucifixion itself. The undeserved death of Abel as an innocent victim foreshadows the innocent death of Christ. Abel, in the form of Christ, provides the necessary and just grounds upon which those imprisoned in Hades will be freed.

Does God Deceive?

Aulén's work on the problem of *Christus Victor* is masterful and exerted a tremendous influence on recent thinking about the atonement. A strong element of his argument was to show a line of continuity between this dominant patristic idea and the heart of the gospel message in the thought of Martin

---

22. Irenaeus, *haer.* 3.18.10.
23. *Commentary on the Diatessaron,* trans. C. McCarthy (Oxford: Oxford University Press, 1993), p. 339.

Luther. The Reformation marked a return to this classic idea that had animated the life of the early Church. However we understand this historical account of Aulén, it must be conceded that his arguments have not convinced all. Aulén readily conceded there were logical problems with the patristic approach, but he also argued that "it may be doubted whether . . . this demand for rational clearness represents the highest theological wisdom. . . . God in Christ overcomes the hostile powers that hold man in bondage. At the same time these hostile powers are also the executants of God's will. The deliverance of man from the power of death and the devil is at the same time his deliverance from God's judgment."[24] This last line was particularly annoying to Frances Young. In her view, the question was whether the theology of *Christus Victor* was in the end insightful or incoherent. "Surely we can only charge [all the fathers] with the latter," she concluded.[25] God is love or God is wrath; one cannot combine the two without involving oneself in hopeless self-contradiction.

First of all, it must be kept in mind that most patristic thought about the atonement was set in the context of Christ's passion, a feast identified in the East as *Pascha*, that is, Passover. The primary Old Testament reading was that of Israel's first Passover, the victory of God over Pharaoh. Because this event was construed as a cosmic battle in both Judaism and early Christianity, it was only natural that the victory of Christ at his crucifixion was patterned on the earlier victory of the God of Israel over Pharaoh. The Easter Hymn, the *Exultet,* makes this identification quite clear, and the hymns of Ephrem on the crucifixion and resurrection are often nothing more than lengthy comparisons of God's vanquishing Pharaoh and Christ's defeat of Satan.[26] The theme of a battle over an external enemy was demanded by the readings of the liturgy. In the words of Christopher Seitz, "the theological horizon of the Old Testament determined that of the New."[27] Or to put it in the reverse: What the New left unsaid could be filled out from the Old.

Another argument for the coherence of Aulén's position can be made on purely historical grounds. The resurrection of Christ represented a mo-

---

24. Aulén, *Christus Victor,* p. 59.

25. Frances Young, "Insight or Incoherence: The Greek Fathers on God and Evil," *Journal of Ecclesiastical History* 24 (1973): 113-26, 124.

26. See the introduction to and translation of St. Ephrem's *Hymns on Fasting, Unleavened Bread, The Crucifixion, and Resurrection* by G. Anderson, S. Griffith, and R. Young (Leiden: Peeters, forthcoming). For the text of the Syriac, see E. Beck, *Des Heiligen Ephraem des Syrers, Paschahymnen,* CSCO 248 (Louvain: Secrétariat du Corpus SCO, 1964).

27. C. Seitz, *Word Without End* (Grand Rapids: Eerdmans, 1998).

ment of cosmic healing in the thought of early Christianity. The healing of humankind naturally lent itself to metaphors of medicine. It is a well-known fact that the Greeks were intrigued by the Janus-faced property of many drugs used to heal. Administered improperly, these elixirs could kill as quickly as heal. Indeed in Greek, it is one and the same term, *pharmakon*, that identifies both the poison and the drug; only literary context will notify the translator how to render the term in English. The physician, Gregory of Nyssa argued, was very similar to the conspirator who wishes to poison. "The conspirator," he writes, "and the one who cures the victim both mix a drug with the man's food. In the one case it is poison; in the other it is an antidote for poison. But the mode of healing in no way vitiates the kindly intention."[28] This very same contrast defines the mystery of salvation. Satan mixed a poison *(pharmakon)* in the food he fed Adam and Eve; in contrast God mixed a drug *(pharmakon)* within the flesh of Christ that Satan consumed. The former we condemn as a conspirator, the latter we praise as a healer.

A more important argument can be made for the model of *Christus Victor* than an appeal to the ancient Greek conception of medicine. I would like to argue that *Christus Victor* worked and continues to be employed in much contemporary hymnody and preaching because it is deeply biblical. In order to make this point I would like to consider the theme in its Jewish dress.

Middat Ha-din u-Middat Ha-rahamim — Mercy and Justice in Judaism

It is well known that the rabbis imagined the character of the God of Israel to have two constituent parts: the principle of justice *(middat ha-din)* and the principle of mercy *(middat ha-rahamim)*. In many texts these two parts were presumed to characterize the double name of God, the Lord-God that appears so frequently in the Bible. The generic term for deity *(elohim)* identified his just nature, whereas his personal name (YHWH) that he revealed to Moses and then all Israel represented his mercy. When God answered prayer or issued judgment, he weighed each and every case against these two principles before issuing his answer or edict. Yet it has also been observed that this double aspect of the divine personality could also be externalized in the figures of his attending angels. One group would represent justice, the other mercy, and God would be the arbiter between the two. Frequently, the display of mercy

---

28. *Catechetical Oration* 26, trans. E. Hardy, in *Christology of the Later Fathers*, Library of Christian Classics 3 (Philadelphia: Westminster, 1954), p. 303.

was not the obvious outcome of a particular situation, and the unruly forces of justice would have to be tamed or somehow silenced in order for a favorable verdict to result. These contests almost always involved the situation of penitence, that is, when sinful persons turned to God for mercy when they were clearly undeserving. It is striking that these penitential moments are invariably scenes of heavenly conflict in which God must put down the objections of rightly angered subordinates. Consider the infamous case of King Manasseh *(y. Sanh.):*

> (When King Manasseh was being led in chains to Assyria as an exile [2 Chron. 33:11]), he saw that his troubles were great and there was no form of idolatry in the world that he had not tried. When none of this proved useful, he said, "I remember my father (the righteous King Hezekiah) would read to me in synagogue the verse, '*When you are in distress and all these penalties come upon you, at the end of days you shall return to the Lord (YHWH) your God, and obey his voice. For the Lord your God is a God of love. He will not abandon or destroy you; he will not forget the covenant he made with your fathers* (Deut. 4:30-31).' So I now shall call to you, if he answers me then it will be fine; if not then this God and that of the idols are the same [i.e., of no value]."
>
> Then the ministering angels closed the portals of heaven so that the prayer of Manasseh could not ascend to the Holy One, blessed be He. The ministering angels said before the Holy One, blessed be He, Lord of the World, "Will you accept the repentance of a man who has practiced idolatry and set up idols in the Temple?" He answered them, "If I don't accept his repentance, then I shall close the door before all penitents!" What did the Holy One, blessed be He, do? He bored a hole beneath the throne of his lordship and heard his prayer. That is what is written, "He prayed to him and the Lord consented. He heard his prayer and returned him to Jerusalem and his kingdom" (2 Chron. 33:13).

King Manasseh had become famous in the postbiblical period for his act of penitence.[29] This particular midrash demonstrates the power of penitence

---

29. Consider the well-known penitential prayer of the late Second Temple (or perhaps early Christian) period, "The Prayer of Manasseh." This work had its origin in the remarkable tradition found in 2 Chron. 33:1-14 that Manasseh had repented of his idolatrous ways and was forgiven by God. In the parallel text found in 2 Kings 21:1-15, Manasseh is a brazen, unrepentant sinner who is single-handedly responsible for the Babylonian exile.

in the most extreme fashion imaginable. King Manasseh does not really turn to God with a contrite heart; he is a man who will try any religious act with the hope that it might work. He returns to the religion of his father only because all other avenues have been closed and solely as a calculated gamble. If it works, great; if not, no harm done. Yet the text he recalls emphasizes that the biblical God (YHWH) is defined by mercy and bound by his obligation to his chosen people. The angels naturally take umbrage at even the thought that this villain will be heard, and they attempt to block his prayer. The power of mercy does not contest the position of the angels; it is conceded by the terms of the story. The angels are not defeated by argument but by a ruse.

The same sort of story could be told about Satan, the archnemesis of Israel. Consider the tale found in *Pesiqta Rabbati:*

> *"An instruction of David. Happy is the one whose wrongdoing is borne away, whose sin is covered over"* (Ps. 32:1). This is what David means: you have borne away the wrongdoing of your people, all their sins you have covered up.
>
> Once, on the Day of Atonement, Satan came to accuse Israel. He detailed her sins and said, "Lord of the Universe, as there are adulterers among the nations of the world, so there are in Israel. As there are thieves among the nations of the world, so there are in Israel." The Holy One, blessed be He, itemized the merits of Israel. Then what did he do? He took a scale and balanced the sins against the merits. They were weighed together and the scales were equally balanced. Then Satan went to load on further sin and to make that scale sink lower. What did the Holy One, blessed be He, do? While Satan was looking for sins, the Holy One, blessed be He, took the sins from the scale and hid them under his purple royal robe. When Satan returned, he found no sin; as it is written, *"The sin of Israel was searched for, but it is no longer"* (Jer. 50:20). When Satan saw this, he spoke before the Holy One, blessed be He, Lord of the World, *"you have borne away the wrongdoing of your people and covered over all their sin"* (Ps. 85:3). When David saw this, he said, *"Happy is the one whose wrongdoing is borne away, whose sin is covered over"* (Ps. 32:1).

As Peter Schäfer has noted, Satan is not a figure of complete evil here. He represents the principle of justice and wants to make the claim that Israel does not deserve forgiveness. "In this midrash," Schäfer argues, "the principles of justice and mercy are evenly balanced — the one personified in Satan, the other concretized in the robe of God — and justice was overtaken by mercy."[30] God atones for Israel's sin by "bearing it away" and "covering it up." These two clauses from the Psalter are not morally neutral; God has deceived Satan.

The theme of angelic rivalry is hardly rare in rabbinic literature as Schäfer's massive catalog of examples demonstrates. In some stories the angels must be punished; in others they must be deceived. Whatever narrative turn is taken, it must be conceded, Schäfer argues, "that the angels speak for God himself when they represent the principle of divine retribution. . . . Even though the Rabbis never express this problem abstractly, nevertheless it cannot be doubted that they make clear that in all of the polemic against the angels' arguments, the argument in the end is grounded in God himself."[31] Mercy would have no value unless it was calibrated against a strict measure of justice, yet a world that is just through and through would allow no room for man. God must "deceive" himself because to do otherwise would be to denigrate and falsify the claims of justice. Yet this doctrine cannot be stated in unvarnished form for fear of tarnishing the deity. To preserve the mystery of God's *unknowable* being and his unfathomable rulings the midrash avails itself of the closest alternative: it tells a *story* of how God's mercy can be *likened* to the deceit of a just, but overly zealous prosecutor.

This exposition of the mystery of God's ways with sinful humanity is not the creation of the rabbis or the Church Fathers. It is deeply rooted in the Bible itself, especially in those narratives that concern repentance.

The paradigmatic moment in the Bible when God's wrath is turned toward mercy occurs immediately after Israel has begun to worship the golden calf. Moses is at the end of his forty-day sojourn at the peak of Mt. Sinai, and God has just finished revealing to him the details of the tabernacle in which the Israelites are supposed to house God's divine glory on earth. The irony of what has happened should not be lost on the reader. As this heavenly structure is being revealed, Israel is already in the midst of erecting her own counter-temple, a shrine to a lifeless golden calf. "I am the Lord your God who brought you out of Egypt," God had announced from the heights of Sinai as the people trembled below (Exod. 20:1); "These are your gods, O Israel," Aaron had responded after the calf had emerged from its mold, "who brought you up out of the land of Egypt" (32:4). The irony, or better the hubris, was not lost on God. "Go down at once," he commanded Moses, "*Your* people, whom *you* brought up out of the land of Egypt, have acted perversely."

---

30. Peter Schäfer, *Rivalität zwischen Engeln und Menschen: Untersuchungen zur rabbinischen Engelvorstellung* (Berlin: de Gruyter, 1975), p. 187.

31. Schäfer, *Rivalität,* p. 222.

Wasting no time, Israel's God in his ire came right to the point: "I have seen this people, how stiff-necked they are. Now let me alone, so that my wrath may burn hot against them and I may consume them, and of you I will make a great nation." The entire mystery of election was poised to unravel: no longer was YHWH the God of Israel; the people of Israel belonged to Moses ("*your* people, whom *you* brought up"). Furthermore, this very God who had promised never to send a flood again to destroy all mankind was now on the brink of destroying an entire nation and rebuilding their foundation from the person of Moses. Perhaps the promise to Noah was not being broken — the world at large, after all, was in no danger — but the parallels to the flood were ominous indeed. Would God destroy an entire people only to refashion them from the likes of a single righteous man?

Moses clearly perceives the seriousness of the situation, both the gravity of Israel's sin and the burning rage of divine wrath. Yet as God's chosen prophet he does not simply acquiesce to the script that lies before him. He does not kneel in obedience to the whims of the deity. He stands in the breach between God and his people and attempts to make amends. "O Lord, why does your wrath burn hot against your people," he begins, echoing the words of God himself, "whom you brought out of the land of Egypt with great power and with a mighty hand?" These are not my people, Moses counters, they are *yours*, those whom *you* led out of Egypt. Moses does not stop there; this is not a matter of linguistic precision about the status of the elected nation. He launches a frontal attack on the very character of God. "Why should the Egyptians say, 'It was with evil intent that he brought them out to kill them in the mountains . . .'? Turn from your fierce wrath; change your mind, . . . Remember Abraham, Isaac, and Israel, your servants, how you swore to them by your own self saying to them, 'I will multiply your descendants like the stars of heaven, and all this land that I have promised I will give to your descendants and they shall inherit it forever.'" With this Moses rests his case. And the verdict? "The Lord changed his mind about the disaster that he planned to bring on his people."

The audacity of Moses' words should not be minimized. He appeals to the stature of God among the nations ("What will the Egyptians say? You led this people to the desert simply to kill them?") and the promises made to the patriarchs ("you swore to give the land to their descendants"). With Moses' response, the proposal to destroy the entire elected nation was tabled.

The Bible, it should be remembered, does not frequently deal in theological abstractions. As Hans Frei has so well reminded us, the Bible teaches theology through the medium of narrative. In the stories about God and his prophets we learn of the mysterious workings of the divine psyche. There is no higher level of reflection on the principles of justice and mercy; there is no detailed account of how the heavenly host adjudicates the affairs of mankind. These will turn up later in rabbinic and patristic writings. However, we can infer the very same processes in the relationship between God and prophet. As Yohanan Muffs has observed, the prophet's moral perspective is not lobotomized by the strong hand of God.[32] Quite the contrary, God raises up prophets for just this task: to press the case in favor of the accused. If the prophet must use what looks like moral blackmail ("What will the nations think?"), so be it. This is how the Bible has chosen to represent the battle between mercy and justice. For those not familiar with prophetic narrative, the idiom of intercessory prayer may appear barbaric. "Aristotle's god, whose clearest characteristic is his indifference," Muffs observes, "would not have been moved by such an egoistic and human argument [as that of Moses]. But a God who turns toward man and is interested in man's destiny and in man's reaction to His commandments leaves Himself open to such intimidation."[33]

What is striking is the necessity of a human interlocutor in the rendering of divine judgment. God does nothing, Amos informs us, *"without first revealing his plan to his servants, the prophets"* (Amos 3:7). The reason is clear: the prophet is charged with the task of communicating God's plan to the people; he is also to argue its merits with the deity. In the divine law court, Mercy and Justice must jostle and even fight. The rabbis certainly were attuned to this dimension and castigated Elijah for taking the word of condemnation toward Israel literally. God himself demands that Elijah, who fled to Sinai to avoid the coming wrath, stand before him and argue Israel's case. He should have said, "Lord of the Universe, behold, Your children, the sons of Abraham, Isaac, and Jacob, have done what you wanted" (*Yal.* 2.217). Instead, Elijah was silent, and God chose to replace him with Elisha. In the figure of Ezekiel, the contours of the prophetic vocation are inscribed in the starkest of terms, *"I searched for a man, a fencemender, somebody who would stand in the breach against Me on behalf of the land, that I not destroy the land. But I did not find one, and I poured out My wrath upon them"* (Ezek. 22:30-31). Through the intercession of the prophet, the fiery hand of God's just decree could be stayed. Yet the more profound point is the identity of the enemy. The breach has been opened by sin. As a result Israel faces imminent destruction. Yet as Muffs so astutely observes, "the enemy is not the army of the gentiles (King Nebuchadnezzar and his Babylonian legions) that is placing siege around Je-

---

32. Y. Muffs, *Love and Joy: Law, Language, and Religion in Ancient Israel* (Cambridge, Mass.: Harvard University Press, 1992), p. 11.
33. Muffs, *Love and Joy,* pp. 12-13.

rusalem. *The Lord Himself is the enemy,* the warrior who is setting His face against Jerusalem to destroy it."[34] Unlike postbiblical Judaism and Christianity, the Old Testament knows no developed demonology. The figure of Satan, on those rare occasions when he makes an appearance, is not yet the font and source of all human evil. The monotheism of the Bible is more narrowly conceived; God is author of all things. *"I am the Lord, and there is no other,"* the prophet Isaiah declares, *"I form light and create darkness, I make weal and create woe; I the Lord do all these things"* (45:6-7).

The theological tensions inherent in a strictly monotheistic system are enormous. Unlike the religions of the ancient Near East, the harsh vindictive wheels of history could not be steered by diverse divine figures. The god Enki took pity on humankind when the gods met in council to debate the flood. When the decision was made to destroy all human flesh, Enki deceived his colleagues by informing his servant Atrahasis about the plan. An ark was built and mankind survived. In the Bible, God's vindictive nature cannot be run over roughshod. He is a just God and must punish in accord with sin. Yet his mercy and love toward humankind is stronger still; he is bound by his promises to the patriarchs. However wayward Israel might become, the being of God is tethered by his former obligations. By creating man and electing Israel, God has become inextricably bound to the created order. The tension that results is immense, and it is the burden of biblical and postbiblical narrative to do justice to it.

At the heart of Christian theories of atonement is an examination of the divided inclinations within the Godhead. The deceit of Satan, when abstracted from this biblical context, appears silly if not downright immoral. Yet if Satan is understood, in part, as an externalization of an essential part of God himself, then his deceit is, to paraphrase Peter Schäfer, an act of self-deceit.

Satan as the Externalization of God's Justice

Satan as an externalization of the deity himself? If this is not heretical, what would count as heresy? In order to get a handle on this problem, it would be best to step back from the individual personalities of *Christus Victor* and focus on the overall narrative shape of the teaching. Even Frances Young concedes the power of the narrative when freed from explicit invocation of the figure of Satan. Recall the image of the jazz bar-line that I invoked earlier. The simple yet dramatic plot line of *Christus Victor* is shared by all, but each pa-

---

34. Muffs, *Love and Joy,* p. 31.

tristic writer offers his own unique improvisation on the theme. Young prefers the arrangement in Athanasius because his version is relatively free of demonology. The problem of human wickedness foists a profound dilemma and nearly intolerable tension upon God. He had granted this favored creation a portion of his own being (the word or *logos*) and could not simply allow an aspect of himself to perish forever. Creation involved a commitment on the part of God. God had to salvage his integrity yet be true to his love and obligation toward man. In Young's summary of Athanasius, the sacrifice of Christ becomes the solution: "it was a sort of 'self-propitiation,' offered by God to God, to make atonement for the existence of evil in his universe."[35]

This brings us back to the point Schäfer made about the midrash. Fundamentally the critique of the angels toward God was a critique of God himself. The forgiveness of men and women necessitates God's own "self-propitiation." Yet in my view, a far more illuminating figure is Ephrem the Syrian. Unlike Athanasius, Ephrem's theology takes the form of a recast narrative. He expounds the mystery of the passion of Christ by weaving into the story the cosmic dimension that the writers of the Gospels ignore. He is well aware of the limits of this approach but believes it is fair to the subject matter.

> Our Lord tore asunder [the forces of] Error in Sheol
> > So as to teach through the visible *(galya)*, what was hidden *(kasyah)*.
> For as he visibly tore asunder Sheol,
> > So he burst open Error in hidden fashion.
> Many saw the graves ripped open,
> > They did not see that Satan was defeated.
> By what is close at hand he demonstrated
> > what is hidden [and] far away.
> > > (*Hymns on the Unleavened Bread* 4:3-7)[36]

His reference to graves that were ripped open refers to what the Gospel writers claim was an objective and clear historical event. *"At that moment [when Christ breathed his last] the curtain of the temple was torn in two, from top to bottom. The earth shook, and the rocks were split. The tombs also were opened, and many bodies of the saints who had fallen asleep were raised"* (Matt. 27:51-52). Through this visible event, Ephrem concluded that Error, or Satan as he

---

35. Young, "Insight or Incoherence," p. 125.

36. From the forthcoming translation of Ephrem's Pascha cycle, by G. Anderson, S. Griffith, and R. Young (see n. 26).

is more often called, had been defeated. Christ's resurrection was anticipated on the cross through the raising of some of the just. The workings of Sheol are like the molten lava that lies below the earth's crust. Though invisible to the naked eye, its existence is proven whenever there is a volcanic eruption. Thus for the kingdom of Hades. The ripped-open tombs were tangible evidence of the cosmic victory over the kingdom of death.

It is natural that the curiosity of Ephrem, like that of any geologist studying the composition of molten lava, was quickened. What did this surface eruption tell us about the nature of the kingdom that lies below? As we have seen, the figure of Hades could be developed in different ways in early Christian thought. The iconography of the *anastasis* left this ambiguity in place. Patristic writers were not afforded this luxury. The moment pen was set to paper, the identity of this figure had to be revealed. For Gregory of Nyssa (and the majority), the foe to be defeated was Satan. For Ephrem, the foe was Death. In his view, Death was the one who meted out justice in accord with Adam's sin, and he discharged the affairs of his office with utter resolve and fairness. "I despise the money of the rich," he asserted, "their gifts cannot bribe me. . . . A hater of persuasion I am called by all men; I do only what I am commanded."[37] Satan, however, was an immoral figure; but even this characterization has its limits. In fairness to his person, we should recognize that he was charged with the task of testing human virtue. "I am an oven of testing for mankind," he boasts; "by me, their thoughts are put to proof."[38]

When Ephrem tells the story of Christ's life and passion, he follows a well-trod path. Death and Satan are fooled by the signs of Christ's human nature. As he lies dying on the cross, Death cries out:

> If you are God, show your strength;
> If you are man, test our strength.
> If it is Adam that you seek, be gone!
> He is bound for his sins here.
> Neither Cherub nor Seraph can pay his debt.

(Carmina Nisibena 36:2)

Though Death and Satan remain puzzled to the end, they decide to risk all on the grounds that Christ sweat blood in the garden of Gethsemane (*Carmina*

---

37. St. Ephrem, *Carmina Nisibena* 36:5, from a forthcoming translation by G. Anderson (and Ed Mathews). For the original Syriac see E. Beck, *Des Heiligen Ephraem des Syrers, Carmina Nisibena*, CSCO 240 (Louvain: Secrétariat du Corpus SCO, 1963).

38. *Carmina Nisibena* 40:7.

Nisibena 35:18). Only a man beholden to his passions would behave in this fashion. On this miscalculation, they put Christ to death.

When Christ descends to the gates of Sheol, Death — not Satan — recognizes that he has made an enormous mistake. Unlike Satan, Death was not a disobedient rebel opposed to the reign of God. He was installed as king over Sheol due to Adam's sin, and he paid no respect to persons as he executed his duties there. "It is God that I serve," he confesses (38:3), "for there is no partiality before him." He complains that though his acts have been good, his name has been otherwise. His conscience, however, can rest in truth; in God he takes consolation. Satan, Death concedes, has been an obstinate rebel. In him Death puts no trust (38:5):

> Concerning Satan who is enraged
> May seven woes be uttered. Though the Son of Mary had trodden
>   on him,
> His spirit is exalted. He is the serpent who perseveres though bruised.

As for himself, Death will follow a different course. Though his name was besmirched by virtue of his office, his character was redeemable. In contrast to Satan he declares (38:5):

> It is better for me to fall prostrate
> Before Jesus, this one who has vanquished me by his Cross.

The capitulation of Death before the entry of Christ into the gates of Sheol is remarkable. More remarkable still are its grounds. As Christ enters his kingdom he need not break down its doors. Death runs forward to open his gates and announce the arrival of the Messiah just as John the Baptist had done several years earlier. "I am your servant forever," he promises (38:6). Though he reviled Christ because of his body that had "veiled [his] divinity," he begs mercy on the grounds that he opened and closed the doors of his kingdom at Christ's command. Like John, he concedes that though he came first he was really last. It was Christ who was the true firstborn, and through him everything in creation had its ground. Others had been raised prior to Christ, but Christ was still the true "first-born of Sheol" (38:7):

> Those who were first have become last,
> The recent-born have become first-born. If Manasseh was the
>   first-born,
> How did Ephrem assume his rights?

27

If a child born later could precede him,
How much more should the Lord and Creator be first at resurrection.

The Christological confession of Death is as surprising as it is unexpected, but its true significance cannot be grasped unless we compare it to the story of Satan's fall told in the *Life of Adam and Eve*. In that tale, Satan refused to worship Adam on the grounds that Satan was the true firstborn and that Adam should prostrate before him, not the other way around.[39] Ephrem has moved this tale from creation to crucifixion. This puts the exaltation in a clear Christological matrix; there is no question of Adam *qua* Adam receiving such tribute. More importantly it gives the exaltation scene a passion context. At Christ's *death,* his true status is revealed.

In this respect Ephrem's treatment of this tradition parallels that of Milton. Neither author was comfortable with an exaltation scene that focused on Adam alone. Adam's glory must be a reflection of Christ's. This latter point Ephrem drives home through the confession of Death. For when Death concludes his words of praise toward Christ, he then turns to address the person of Adam. Like Christ, Adam's cause "was older than the other created things which were created for him" (*Carmina Nisibena* 38:9). Though Adam's physical being came into existence on the sixth day, all of the rest of creation was brought into being solely on his account. Though last, he was truly first. Death had been granted a contract or bond over Adam and his progeny (48:9).

> Adam returned to his earth, he made a pact [cf. Col. 2:14];
> He signed the contract and many became liable to sin and death.

Death overreached the terms of the contract in taking Christ, and in compensation the terms of Death's contract are rewritten. Death gives up Adam as a pledge that at the end of time all humanity will return in bodily form to their maker (*Carmina Nisibena* 48:9):

> Death rewrote the contract, Sheol stood as surety
> All they had snatched and plundered would return at the resurrection.

The overcoming of Death was not, strictly speaking, the vanquishing of a purely external enemy. In the figure of Death, we have represented an aspect

---

39. For a full development of this theme, see G. Anderson, "The Exaltation of Adam and the Fall of Satan," *Journal of Jewish Thought and Philosophy* 6 (1977): 105-34.

of the divine itself. This can be clearly shown by observing other portions of Ephrem's writings where the figure of Death is replaced by the principle of Justice. Let us reconsider his interpretation of Abel, the innocent son slain by Cain and identified by Ephrem and nearly all Christian interpreters as a type of Christ:

> In your mercy you entrusted Abel as the first into the depths of Sheol. [This was] in order that it would be compelled *in justice* to cast him forth from its depths, so that, on his account, the door which had closed up everyone might be opened, and the bosom which was enfolding them might be emptied bare. For, if Adam had been the first to enter [Sheol], which was his deservedly, it would have been meted out to him to remain there forever.[40]

This remarkable text dispenses with the externalizations of Satan, Death, Error, and the other countless characters that Ephrem is so fond of animating and giving voice to. Unlike the highly charged drama of the *descensus,* the issue at hand is the conflict between mercy and justice. Abel, through a vicious murder, dies first in order that the *just* decree imposed on Adam not rest on a just foundation. Had Adam gone to Sheol first, he could never have been redeemed. Ephrem delights in the irony of this self-deception; since the innocent Abel dies unfairly, Adam will justly be cast forth from Sheol. Indeed in this text, Ephrem's use of the categories of justice and mercy look strikingly similar to their use in rabbinic literature. They mark out different sides of the Godhead.

Baptism and the Exaltation of Adam

It is very important not to lose sight of the *liturgical* context in which the story of Adam and Christ was retold, interpreted, and expanded. As we learn from the homilies of Chrysostom on the first three chapters of Genesis, the context for this material was Lent. It is easy to work on the myriad of early Christian sources on Adam and Eve and forget this essential fact. Indeed, I had read the homilies of Chrysostom several times through before considering the importance of context.

One important consequence of this liturgical context is the very idea of the *felix culpa,* or happy fault. Because the coming redemption of men and

---

40. *Commentary on the Diatessaron,* p. 339.

women is the defining feature of the Lenten season, the elaboration of the sin of Adam and Eve is never meant to lead to despair. Quite the opposite; it underscores the audacious mercy shown toward mankind. In light of Christ, the sin of Adam leads to exaltation, not condemnation. Another key concept to bear in mind is that crucifixion is not a one-time moment limited to the figure of Jesus of Nazareth; in the liturgy of Easter, it is continually reappropriated in the life of the Church. Paul says that baptism is our participation in the glory of the cross, *gloria crucis* — *"Do you not know that all of us who have been baptized into Christ Jesus were baptized into his death? Therefore we have been buried with him by baptism unto death, so that, just as Christ was raised from the dead . . . so we too might walk in newness of life"* (Rom. 6:3-4).

At baptism, the Christian descends to the dead in order to reclaim the high calling for which he was created. This liturgical cycle had profound impact on how the Church understood Christ's own baptism. According to the Gospel of Matthew, the baptism of Christ was questioned by John the Baptist. *"Shouldn't I be baptized by you?"* he asked. To which Christ replied, *"Let it be so for now; for it is proper for us in this way to fulfill all righteousness."* In the life of the Church, the baptism takes on even deeper importance; it anticipates the passion; and if baptism is an initiation into Christ's death, early Christian thinkers reasoned, then Christ's own baptism must have foreshadowed this death. Proof of this is evident in an iconographic cycle in Cappadocia dedicated to the life of Jesus.[41] The cycle narrates the life of Jesus in chronological sequence with one exception: the baptism of Christ is placed after the resurrection. This does not comport well with the life of Jesus, but it fits perfectly with how that life was appropriated within the Church. At the Easter Vigil service, the catechumens who had studied the life and teaching of Jesus were now initiated into his passion. At the moment of his resurrection, they were baptized. A similar juxtaposition of baptism and resurrection can be seen in the Baptism-Anastasis icon found at Sinai.[42] At the top of this image Christ descends into the waters at his baptism; at the bottom he descends to Hades to redeem Adam and Eve. The icon draws no line between the two scenes; the descent is a single one. Similarly there are numerous reliquaries of the cross that portray the baptism on one side and the *anastasis* on the reverse.[43] Going slightly further afield, there are a number of murals in Slavonic churches of the sixteenth and seventeenth centuries that show Christ holding the "bond

---

41. See Kartsonis, *Anastasis,* pl. 65 and the excellent discussion of the entire problem on pp. 173-77.

42. Kartsonis, *Anastasis,* pl. 63.

43. Kartsonis, *Anastasis,* pl. 25a and b, 26a, b, c, d and e.

written against Adam and all humanity" as he descends into the waters of the Jordan.[44] According to Colossians 2:14 this bond was destroyed on the cross; in these murals the destruction begins at baptism.

At baptism the entire cosmic cycle of redemption is compressed within the individual life of the catechumen. As Theodore of Mopsuestia makes clear in his account of the Church's liturgy, it is at baptism that the full stature of men and women as creatures made in the image of God is restored.[45] It is for this reason, Theodore asserts, that Satan appears on the scene and offers such resistance. The baptismal liturgy begins with the exorcisms because Satan represents the claims of justice waged against the power of God's mercy. Our image should not be the young girl in the movie *The Exorcist,* vomiting green spittle across the room; rather, the image should be any one of those numerous midrashim and apocryphal tales that detail how mercy must outwit justice in order for true human personhood to blossom and flourish.

Baptism, in the early Church, began at the start of Lent with the candidates coming forward to register their names with the priest at the church. Theodore likens the moment of enrollment into the catechumenate to a census in which you are about to establish "legal title to a land fertile in corn and rich in good things, in which there is much happiness to those who are registered for it."[46] Previously this land had belonged to an enemy who envies you the happiness he once enjoyed. He appears before you, arguing that you have no rightful claim to this land. So, Theodore concludes, "it behooves [you] who are about to be registered . . . to go to a magistrate and make use of the title which he possesses, and show the supposed owner of the land . . . that he is desirous of bringing the matter before a judge." Thus is the drama of Baptism. When Satan hears of the pending enrollment of the catechumen, he shows the same hostility he had formerly shown toward the exaltation of Adam and the resurrection of Christ. "[He] tries and endeavors to bring us to the judgment hall as if we had no right to be outside his ownership. He pleads that from ancient times and from the creation of the head of our race we belong to him by right; he narrates the story of Adam, of how he listened to [Satan's]

---

44. See the excellent studies (and plates found therein) of L. Kretzenbacher, "Hunger treibt Urvater Adam zum Pakt mit dem Teufel," in *Teufelsbünder und Faustgestalten im Abendlande* (Klagenfurt: Rudolf Habelt Verlag, 1968), pp. 42-53; and "Jordantaufe auf dem Satansstein," in his *Bilder und Legenden* (Klagenfurt: Rudolf Habelt Verlag, 1971), pp. 49-72. The illustration above is pl. IV in the latter work.

45. *Commentary of Theodore of Mopsuestia on the Lord's Prayer and on the Sacraments of Baptism and the Eucharist,* ed. and trans. A. Mingana, Woodbrook Studies (Cambridge: W. Heffer & Sons, 1933).

46. *Commentary of Theodore of Mopsuestia,* p. 26.

words and by his will rejected his Maker and preferred to serve [Satan]; of how this kindled the wrath of God, who drove [Adam] out of Paradise [and] pronounced the sentence of death upon him."[47]

Having pledged to resist Satan, the candidates were urged to "stand with outstretched arms in the posture of one who prays, and look downwards and remain in that state in order to move the judge to mercy. And you take off your outer garment and stand barefooted." In some contexts the catechumens stood on animal skins while they prayed, symbolizing the taking off of the garments of skin they had inherited from Adam.[48] By stripping themselves of this mortal skin, they were preparing to put on those heavenly garments with which humanity was first clothed.

This drama of Satan's ire toward the catechumen is almost exactly identical to the rage he shows toward Christ during his passion. In Narsai's account, after Christ's baptism but just before his death, Satan holds forth adamantly about the justice of his claim over all humans. He shows Christ the bond on which appears the handwriting of Adam and Eve. "Behold," he charges, "your parents have sealed and delivered this over. Read and understand it." The similarity of Narsai's depiction of the passion to the liturgy of baptism is striking. Indeed, it would be hard to determine what was the direction of influence. Did the account of the passion derive from the libretto of the liturgy, or did the liturgy simply act out the denouement of the passion? In the affairs of Adam and Eve, the lines between liturgical enactment and historical reconstruction become blurred.

In short, the passion of Christ was not a one-time affair. It was continually relived in baptism. It has long been observed that the doctrine of creation is subject to two different descriptions in the Bible. According to Genesis 1, the creation of the world appears to be a single and once-in-a-lifetime action. The foundations were laid and creation was set in motion. No further maintenance was required — thus the teaching of *creatio ex nihilo*, "creation out of nothing." Yet alongside this we have numerous examples, especially in the Psalms, of an ongoing battle on the part of God to uphold creation.[49] The forces of evil wage war against the divine will, and creation must be continually shored up against these onslaughts. This notion of *creatio continua*, "an ongoing creation," is most at home in the Psalms, the prayer book of ancient

47. *Commentary of Theodore of Mopsuestia*, p. 27.

48. See the article of J. Z. Smith, "The Garments of Shame," *History of Religions* 5 (1965/66): 217-38.

49. This theme is the subject of Jon Levenson's book, *Creation and the Persistence of Evil: The Jewish Drama of Divine Omnipotence* (San Francisco: Harper & Row, 1988).

Israel. In the liturgy, God's creative task is never at an end. The same analogy holds for the passion. In the Gospels and creeds it is presented as a single moment in historical time, but at baptism the drama comes to life time and again.

At baptism, the envy of Satan toward the status God wishes to confer on men and women returns with a vengeance. This reveals an aspect of angelology that is not often appreciated. The angels serve as an important category that marks off human life from the divine. One might expect that the hierarchy that emerges would be a simple pyramid with men and women on the bottom, angels in the middle, and God at the top. For both Jews and Christians this was not the case. One of the functions of the angelic host is to be supplanted by man! We saw how the rabbis described Israel's election as God's choice of Israel over the other nations and over the angels themselves. It is not surprising that the angels contested this election and had to be put down for their efforts. As a consequence of this election, the angels in heaven must begin their praise of the deity *after* Israel. Israel does not mimic the liturgy in heaven; the liturgy in heaven mimics Israel. Similarly in Christian writings we have seen that the angels were commanded to prostrate themselves to Adam and Christ. Some angels resisted this command, and they were eternally damned for their efforts.

What I would like to underscore is that this angelic resistance toward the election of Israel or the resurrection of Christ *persists*. Earlier we examined a midrash in which God thwarted the designs of Satan by removing the sin of Israel from the scales and hiding it within his robe. What I did not emphasize then was that the occasion of this encounter was the Day of Atonement, the day in which Israel repents before her God and is restored to the status she had at Sinai prior to venerating the golden calf. This restoration of Israel to her former glory enrages Satan, and the midrash begins with his calling into question the fairness of Israel's election itself. Satan asks God whether Israel's sins are any fewer than those of the nations of the world. Nothing about Israel's moral capacity would seem to warrant the favors God has cast their way. As in many other (but not all) traditions about the election of Israel, the moral question is left unanswered. Israel is not chosen because of her moral nature; she is chosen solely by the grace of God. Christian baptism shows striking similarities to the Jewish Day of Atonement. Both rites are penitential, both restore man to his status before the fall, and both stimulate the renewed contest between the justice and mercy of God.

The story of Adam and Eve begins with sin in Paradise and ends with redemption on Easter Sunday. The Orthodox churches saw the redemption of Adam and Eve from Sheol as of such consequence that they canonized this image, the *anastasis,* and so made it a permanent witness to the work of Christ. What the Gospels had omitted the iconographer restored. Yet this story of Adam and Eve was never narrated as a simple objective account of human beginnings, as though the story could take its place alongside modern theories of the "Big Bang" or evolution. The story of Adam and Eve was always subject to liturgical enactment. It derives its meaning from the world of penitence and restoration. A more pertinent parallel than Darwin would be the parable of the prodigal son, a favorite gospel reading in the Lenten season. The story of the fall had value in the early Church because every Christian was called to situate his life in between the contours of Adam and Christ as well as Eve and Mary. The arc that extends from Adam to Christ forms a horizon defined by mercy. Adam is unintelligible apart from Christ, and Christ is unintelligible apart from Adam.

Exegetical Transformations:
The Sacrifice of Isaac in Philo, Origen, and Ambrose

JOHN C. CAVADINI

I would like in this paper simply to trace the history of one strand of exegetical tradition, namely, Philo's treatment of the *aqedah* (Gen. 22:1-19), examining first Philo's own exegesis, and then the reception and transformation of that exegesis in two later Christian exegetes, Origen and Ambrose. Although I believe the evidence suggests that these texts are related by a line of descent, with Origen having read Philo's exegesis, and Ambrose having read both earlier sources, it is not the intention of this paper to demonstrate dependence, nor do the conclusions of this paper depend on such a demonstration. The paper examines the transformation of an exegetical idea, recognizably itself as it is nevertheless exhibited and developed in three very different contexts over the course of time.

Philo's treatise *On Abraham* is the first (or second, depending on the placement of the *de opificio mundi*) treatise in his *Exposition of the Laws*. Philo explains that before his treatment of particular laws, it is necessary to treat the patriarchs, whom Holy Scripture advances as "living laws, endowed with reason" (ἔμψυχοι καὶ λογικοὶ νόμοι, *On Abraham* 1.5)[1] whose lives serve as the "archetypes" (ἀρχετύπους προτέρους, 1.3) of which the particular laws are only copies. In a kind of reverse typology, the laws later established serve as no more than "reminders of the life of the ancients" (ὑπομνήματα . . . βίου τῶν παλαιῶν, 1.5), summaries of their virtuous character and their piety to-

---

1. The text is that of Cohn and Endland as presented by F. H. Colson, *Philo*, vol. 6 (Cambridge, Mass. and London: Loeb Classical Library, 1935). Generally I have offered my own translations, but in some cases I have relied on Colson's.

wards God. Among these Abraham holds pride of place as "the first, the founder of the nation," whose love for God and, especially, whose faith (πίστις, 46.268) or trust in God qualifies him as "the law itself" (νόμος αὐτὸς, 46.276, or, following F. H. Colson's more conservative translation, "himself a law and an unwritten statute"). His life is an "unwritten law-code" (θεσμὸς ἄγραφος, 46.276); one is tempted to say, in the language of later Christian exegetes, it is the spirit of which the law itself is the letter. It is probably for this reason that Philo is very careful to pay full attention to the literal story of Abraham's life, alternating allegory with lengthy literal expositions of prominent episodes in the Genesis text.[2]

After a preliminary consideration of a trinity of antediluvian heroes (Enosh, Enoch, and Noah), Philo turns (10.48) to Abraham as the first of the greater triad, Abraham-Isaac-Jacob (the treatises on the latter two are lost). Philo pauses, noting (10.49) that it must be emphasized that these three are "all of one house and family" (τούτους . . . μιᾶς οἰκίας καὶ ἑνὸς γένους, 10.50), the latter two the son and grandson, respectively, of the first. He then goes on to make a striking statement, namely, that in view of their status as "God-lovers" and "beloved by God" (φιλοθέους . . . καὶ θεοφιλεῖς, 10.50), God deigned to join his own proper name (ἴδιον ὄνομα, 10.51) to theirs, thus relativizing, in the strict sense, God's own absolute identity, making it a term of relation (πρός τι, 10.51) instead of an absolute term. Philo underscores the graciousness of God's act, "for God does not need a name," yet, in order to provide humankind with recourse to prayer and the benefit of hope, God graciously gave (ἐχαρίζετο, 10.51) to the human race his own name (κλῆσιν οἰκείαν, 10.51). Thus the relation of the three patriarchs — father, son, and

---

2. It is hard to keep track of precisely what is literal and what is allegorical. Samuel Sandmel, speaking of Philo's treatment of Abraham, and of the division between literal and allegorical that Philo sets up, notes that Philo "is by no means rigid about the division, and the commentator who would separate these strands too sharply can find himself doing inadvertent injustice to Philo's thought. . . . [T]here is a literal Abraham in Philo and there is an allegorical Abraham. The literal Abraham is the historical character of the simple biblical account . . . ; it is the Abraham who migrated from Chaldea, to Haran, and then to Palestine, who was the husband of Sarah; who rescued Lot; who begot Ishmael and Isaac; and who ultimately passed away in good old age. The allegorical Abraham is the historical character who abandoned pantheistic materialism and went on to the cognition of the true God by a process of freeing his soul from domination by the body" (Samuel Sandmel, *Philo's Place in Judaism: A Study of Conceptions of Abraham in Jewish Literature*, augmented ed. [New York: Ktav, 1971], p. 96). Both the literal and the allegorical Abraham are the historical Abraham. To put it another way, both are interpretive analyses of the narratives about Abraham.

grandson — is modified as well, for their names are joined now not only as father, son, and grandson but as united in and to God's name, as "lovers of God and beloved of God." God's act of self-identification, gracious and prompted by no need on God's part, becomes the basis of their identity as well, relativizing what would otherwise be the absolute claims of kinship structure.

It is precisely these claims on his identity that Abraham is depicted as always ready to renounce, in the first instance at his departure from Chaldea at God's call. He leaves his home at God's command "not as though leaving home for a strange land but rather as returning from amid strangers to his home" (14.62). Philo elaborates on the strength of our natural desire for the delights of kin (συγγενῶν, 14.63) and country, something that makes banishment a fate worse than death (14.64) and that makes many return home with business unfinished (14.65). Abraham leaves home virtually alone, "taking no thought for fellow-clansmen . . . schoolmates, comrades, or blood relations on father's or mother's side, or country, or ancestral customs, or community of nurture or home life," overpowered by heavenly love (ἔρωτος οὐρανίου, 14.66).

Yet Abraham's "greatest deed" (32.167) for Philo is the story reported in Genesis 22, the sacrifice of Isaac. The story is recounted by Philo with a kind of tenderness and pathos that makes it genuinely moving.[3] Philo reminds the reader that this is the "beloved and only" (32.168) son born of his wife Sarah, of great physical and spiritual beauty, and that the command to sacrifice him came suddenly, as a shock (32.169). Abraham does not hesitate, does not pale or waver, and "mastered by his love for God" (32.170) overcomes "all the names and charms of kinship" (συγγενείας ὀνόματα καὶ φίλτρα, 32.170). We are reminded here of the opening passage where God was said to join his own name to Abraham's, Isaac's, and Jacob's. In the sacrifice of Isaac, recapitulating Abraham's departure from kin in Chaldea, we begin to see in Abraham's character what it means to have one's identity bound up in God's. It means that even Abraham's relation to his son becomes defined by that identity as he has to leave the "names and charms" of kinship behind. Philo emphasizes the poignancy, too, of the dialogue between father and son, when Isaac says, "My father, behold the fire and the wood, but where is the victim?" (Genesis 22; 32.173). Abraham does not break into tears, but responds (in Philo's paraphrase) that "with God all things are possible," that even in the open desert a victim will be found (32.175). He seizes his son, but God the Savior (ὁ σωτὴρ

---

3. "Discret et pathétique" (Jean Gorez, in his translation of the treatise: Philo, *De Abrahamo*, vol. 20 of *Les Oeuvres de Philon d'Alexandrie* [Paris: Éditions du Cerf, 1966], p. 14).

θεός 32.176), calling the father twice by name (ὀνομαστὶ καλέσας δὶς τὸν πατέρα, 32.176), stops the deed mid-action, and Isaac is saved (33.177).

The story is over, but Philo now spends four times as long reflecting on Abraham's action in a kind of *apologia* to unnamed "quarrelsome critics" (33.178) who would deride Abraham's act. The apologetic tone is familiar to readers of his *Life of Moses*, where he notes that, out of bad will or envy, Hellenic pagan detractors have completely overlooked the Jewish sages, and Moses in particular (*Life of Moses* 1.1). Here the criticism comes from just these educated, Hellenic quarters, who point out, presumably with such persons as Agamemnon in mind, that "among the Greeks" (Ἑλλήνων, 33.180) others have sacrificed their children with little or no thought or reluctance, and among barbarians child sacrifice is an accepted and sacred custom (34.181). Why praise Abraham (34.183)? Philo scrutinizes the motivation of Abraham to see if any of the motives — "custom, love of honor, or fear" — common among the examples raised apply to him. One by one he rules them out, noting, for example, that it could not have been love of praise, since Abraham went off virtually alone and then left even the two servants he had brought behind (34.190). Further, Abraham's obedience to God was consistent with his character in the past (35.192), and he knew nothing of the sanction of custom (35.193). Isaac, too, was his only son in the truest sense of son, so his affection for him was higher than chaste loves and friendships (35.194), and as a son begotten in Abraham's old age he was not likely to be replaced. To give up one's only and darling son is an action beyond words (λόγου παντὸς μεῖζον ἔργον, 35.196). Abraham "concedes nothing to the tie of relationship," to the οἰκειότητι (35.196) that he had, in a preliminary form, already given up when leaving Chaldea. Further, unlike Agamemnon and others, he did not pawn the job off on others but did it himself, this most affectionate of fathers with this best of sons (35.197-98). Philo again emphasizes that this is an act beyond language (παντὸς λόγου κρεῖττον, 35.199), thus recalling his description of Abraham as the unwritten, living law, as it were, the spirit of the letter. His "piety" (εὐσεβείας, 35.199 and passim) is extraordinary.

It is only after this lengthy exposition of the "narrated and open" (ῥητῆς καὶ φανερᾶς, 36.200) sense that he goes on to what we might recognize as an allegory, although Philo does not use that word here. "Isaac" signifies laughter or a higher joy, which the sage must sacrifice to God. This suggests that such joy belongs properly only to God, who gives it back once it is sacrificed, once it is "acknowledged" as proper to the condition of God and not to the condition of humanity, once it is acknowledged to be a free gift by God to human beings (36.200-204). In other words, the sage knows that his joy is only in God, and that God freely deigns to share with the sage what is properly only God's. The careful connection of this allegory with the literal sense of the text is obvious. Abraham has placed all of his joy in God, and his identity is transparent to that sacrifice, in which he has refused to absolutize any of the claims that even kinship would have on that identity. Such is the "first and greatest" of the unwritten laws.

Turning to Origen, we find his most sustained treatment of the sacrifice of Isaac in a homily, the eighth on Genesis, delivered at Caesarea probably around 240[4] and preserved in the Latin translation of Rufinus. Crouzel singles it out, and Louis Doutreleau characterizes it as "très belle, . . . toute frémissante d'émotion."[5] Origen uses the homiletic setting to heighten the pathos of the story, at one point directly addressing the fathers in the congregation, advising them to take the faith of Abraham literally as an example in situations of tragedy affecting their children (*Hom.* 8.7, SC 7 *bis:* 224.13-226.38), and the homily as a whole is shaded with allusions to the martyrdom to which any person in the congregation was still liable (*Hom.* 8.8, SC 7 *bis:* 226.1-230.55). In fact the homily functions partly as an exhortation to martyrdom, or at least to readiness for martyrdom, taking as its pivot Abraham's readiness to sacrifice even his own son. Origen draws into this new context Philo's focus on Abraham's identity, rendering the poignancy of Philo's account, if possible, even more pointed (perhaps due to his own father's martyrdom?). As in Philo's text, there is a long exposition of the narrative sense, which is followed by a brief allegorical application based on the meaning of "Isaac."

4. As dated by Pierre Nautin, *Origène: sa vie et son oeuvre* (Paris: Beauchesne, 1977), pp. 401-5. Text is that of Louis Doutreleau in Origène, *Homélies sur la Genèse,* SC 7 *bis* (Paris: Editions du Cerf, 1985). I have used the translation of Ronald E. Heine, *Origen: Homilies on Genesis and Exodus,* vol. 71 of *The Fathers of the Church* (Washington: Catholic University of America Press, 1982).

5. Doutreleau's comments are at SC 7 *bis:* 212, n. 1. Henri Crouzel remarks that it is "one of Origen's finest homilies in terms of literary merit" (Henri Crouzel, *Origen: The Life and Thought of the First Great Theologian,* trans. A. S. Worrall [San Francisco: Harper & Row, 1989], p. 44). Crouzel, appealing to the comments of Erasmus, notes that Origen "keeps almost throughout on the literal and moral plane" (p. 44; see p. 44, n. 32 for the citation of Erasmus). In section 10, Origen takes Gen. 22:14, *The Lord saw,* as an exhortation to see the account "in the spirit," as the Lord sees things, and thus "just as there is nothing corporeal in God so also you might perceive nothing corporeal in all these things." Heine takes this statement as leaving "no place for a literal interpretation of the account" (p. 146, n. 62). That two such opposite interpretations of the homily can be reached by experienced commentators (one of them no less than Erasmus) is probably an indication that we do not yet have sufficiently fine categories for talking about "precritical" exegesis (so-called). Sandmel's comments about Philo's Abraham, cited in n. 2 above, seem to me a good way to think of Origen's Abraham as well.

It is significant that Origen leaves behind Philo's description of Abraham as unwritten law, as well as Philo's discussion of God's alliance of God's proper name with Abraham, Isaac, and Jacob. Instead, Origen focuses immediately upon, and develops, the issues of identity Philo had raised regarding Abraham. He begins by noting that God calls Abraham twice by name, and indeed, by the name that God had given him (*Hom.* 8.1, SC 7 *bis:* 214.13-15), and reminds his hearers that God had given him this name when God promised to make Abraham "the father of many nations" (*Hom.* 8.1, SC 7 *bis:* 214.20-21, citing Gen. 17:5). Origen, in a brilliant evocation of biblical irony, suggests to his hearers that God's very use of Abraham's name here is a part of the temptation, for the use of the name is an invocation of God's promise to him, and the demand that Abraham sacrifice the son that was the fruit of that promise seems like its nullification. To ask "Abraham" to sacrifice Isaac is, seemingly, to unname Abraham. Specifically, it is Abraham's very identity as a *father* (Gen. 17:5), and in particular the father of Isaac, that is the bearer of the promise, and thus Abraham's attachment to Isaac is not simply an affectionate attachment to his son but an attachment to his own identity precisely as a father and precisely insofar as that identity is the bearer of God's promise: "[God] had kindled his soul, therefore, in love for his son not only because of posterity, but also in the hope of the promises" (*Hom.* 8.1, SC 7 *bis:* 214.24-25). Like Philo's Abraham, Origen's Abraham is about to learn what it means to have one's identity bound up with God, and here, specifically, with God's promises. It is important to note the continuity of theme here: Philo's Abraham learns that God's aligning God's own proper name with himself as father and grandfather qualifies those relations and the identities predicated on them; likewise Origen's Abraham learns that God's tying God's promises to his paternity qualifies the identity based on it.

In an uncharacteristic rhetorical apostrophe, Origen evokes Abraham's temptation to despair:

> What do you say to these things, Abraham? What kind of thoughts are stirring in your heart? A word has been uttered by God which is such as to shatter and try your faith. What do you say to these things? What are you thinking? What are you reconsidering? Are you thinking, are you turning over in your heart that, if the promise has been given to me in Isaac, but I offer him for an holocaust, it remains that that promise holds no hope? (*Hom.* 8.1, SC 7 *bis:* 214.30-36; trans. Heine, p. 137)

Origen cites "Paul" to help his hearers think about what Abraham is thinking: "By faith Abraham did not hesitate, when he offered his only son, in

40

whom he had received the promises, thinking that God is able to raise him up even from the dead" (Heb. 11:17, 19; *Hom.* 8.1, SC 7 *bis:* 216.46-48; trans. Heine, p. 137). While Origen's invocation of this passage from Hebrews might seem to have the effect of mitigating Abraham's temptation, it actually may be intended to have the opposite effect, for Origen aligns Abraham's temptation with that of the Christian facing possible martyrdom. The Christian has faith not only in the future resurrection of Isaac but also in the (past) resurrection of Christ; he or she should have it easier than Abraham did. Is it possible, Origen implies, that Abraham's faith is greater than our own, for we (as he notes later in the homily) not only are reluctant to follow Christ's injunction not to value family ties over the gospel (*Hom.* 8.8, SC 7 *bis:* 230.48-52) but also grieve when our children die, despite our faith (esp. *Hom.* 8.7, SC 7 *bis:* 226.25-38)? After all (recalling Philo's *apologia* for Abraham's superlative motivation), we have not been asked actually to sacrifice our sons ourselves, as Abraham was, nor did Abraham have the advantage of knowing Christ's resurrection. Origen the homilist brilliantly evokes the Christian hearer's own experience as a locus for understanding the text, and for letting the text, in the person of Abraham's faith, challenge the hearer.

He will later note, commenting on God's concluding words in the story ("For now I know that you fear God," Gen. 22:12):

> But these things are written on account of you, because you too indeed have believed in God, but unless you shall fulfill "the works of faith" (2 Th. 1.11), unless you shall be obedient to all the commands, even the more difficult ones, unless you shall offer sacrifice and show that you place neither father nor mother nor sons before God (cf. Mt. 10.37), you will not know that you fear God nor will it be said of you: "Now I know that you fear God." (*Hom.* 8.8, SC 7 *bis:* 226.10-16; trans. Heine, p. 143)

In case his hearers missed the biblical allusions to martyrdom, he specifies further:

> For example, I intend to be a martyr. An angel could not say to me on this basis: "Now I know that you fear God," for an intention of the mind is known to God alone. But if I shall undertake the struggles *(agones),* if I shall utter a "good confession" (1 Tim. 6.12), if I shall bear calmly all things which are inflicted, then an angel can say, as if confirming and strengthening me: "Now I know that you fear God." (*Hom.* 8.8, SC 7 *bis:* 228.29-35; trans. Heine, p.144).

Yet Origen immediately reminds the reader that these words were actually spoken to Abraham. Oddly, therefore, Philo's depiction of Abraham as an archetype of the law returns transformed. Abraham is a kind of archetype of faith, and this in a true Philonic sense, not as a type that needs fulfillment exactly, but as the original, definitive exemplar, whose faith Christians merely repeat or reenact when they are willing to believe in the resurrection of Christ, that is, to "spare not" their "son." We have seen that for Philo this meant that Abraham did not spare his identity as constructed on his kinship; following this, for Origen faith in the resurrection of Christ means a willingness to do what Abraham did, to predicate our identities on God's promises, to find our identity in the Gospel message. It is hard, but not as hard as what Abraham did; figuratively it *is* what Abraham did, since the point of continuity is the sacrifice of an identity, whether called to actual martyrdom or not:

> Who of you, do you suppose, will sometime hear the voice of an angel saying: "Now I know that you fear God, because you spared not your son," or your daughter or your wife, or you spared not your money or the honors of the world or the ambitions of the world, but you have despised all things and "have counted all things dung that you may gain Christ" (Phil. 3.8), "you have sold all things and have given to the poor and have followed the Word of God"? Who of you, do you think, will hear a word of this kind from the angels? Meanwhile Abraham hears this voice, and it is said to him: "You spared not your beloved son because of me." (*Hom.* 8.8, SC 7 *bis*: 228.46-230.55; trans. Heine, pp. 144-45)

Origen connects this explicitly to Romans 8:32, "where the Apostle says of God: *Who spared not his own son, but delivered him up for us all.*" He comments further:

> Behold God contending with humans in magnificent liberality: Abraham offered God a mortal son who was not put to death; God delivered to death an immortal son for humans. (*Hom.* 8.8, SC 7 *bis*: 228.40-43; trans. Heine, p. 144)

Abraham here is a kind of figure for God the Father in the drama of redemption to which Paul makes reference.[6] However, the figuration does not serve

6. Christian use of the *aqedah* as a type or prefiguration of redemption is actually at least in part a utilization of a pre-Christian Jewish theology of the *aqedah* that assigned atoning merit to Isaac's sacrifice. Isaac was understood to have suffered willingly. This is

to diminish or marginalize the "liberality" of Abraham. Rather, the point is that in Abraham we see, in a definitive and lasting way that cannot be superseded, what this Christian text means; we see what it means to base our identities on the good news of God's liberality; we come to understand that liberality. Isaac, together with the ram, prefigures Christ, but even this type is itself created by, and thus a testimony to, Abraham's faith or, following Philo, his love of God.

We must now turn briefly to Ambrose, who knows both the texts of Philo and of Origen,[7] to witness a final exegetical transformation. Ambrose's exegesis of the *aqedah* is in Book I of his *De Abrahamo,* a work that in its original form was probably a series of homilies (mystagogical?). What strikes the reader first is the way in which Ambrose echoes Origen's and Philo's depiction of the strength of Abraham's paternal affection and the ways in which all the details of God's command and the subsequent journey are meant to exac-

---

not a Philonic concept (see, e.g., Sandmel, *Philo's Place in Judaism,* p. 208) but goes back to the theology represented by the *Fragmentary Targum* and *Targum Neofiti,* and it was developed further by the rabbis. See Geza Vermes, *Scripture and Tradition in Judaism: Haggadic Studies,* 2nd, rev. ed. (Leiden: Brill, 1973), pp. 193-227; and also Jon Levenson, *The Death and Resurrection of the Beloved Son: The Transformation of Child Sacrifice in Judaism and Christianity* (New Haven: Yale University Press, 1993), pp. 171-233. Levenson points to Christian "revisioning of God in the image of Abraham" (p. 220), calling attention in particular to Rom. 8:32, among other texts. We can see that Origen is squarely in line with this tradition.

7. Ambrose has for the most part followed Origen's text, just as we might suspect he would given a choice between Origen and Philo, but there are several textual details Ambrose preserves that are found only in Philo, not in Origen: for example, that Isaac would be more beloved to Abraham since he was the son of his old age (see n. 8 below); and that Abraham himself was prepared to carry out the sacrifice, not to delegate it to others (Ambrose, *Abr.* 1.8.68; Philo, *On Abraham* 35.197). Also, that the conflict for Abraham was between his love for his son and his love for the precepts of God (*On Abraham* 1.8.67, "praecepta") is more characteristic of Philo (see Philo, *On Abraham* 35.192, τῶν προστεταγμένων) than of Origen, for whom the contest is between love of the flesh and love of God (*hom. in Gen.* 8.3, 7, although Origen does mention the "praecepta" of God as something anyone who would follow Abraham must prefer to all else, *hom. in Gen.* 8.8); and God's repetition of Abraham's name in Gen. 22:11 is commented on by Philo (*On Abraham* 32.176) and Ambrose (*Abr.* 1.8.76, cf. 1.8.67) but not by Origen. Ambrose's use of Philo's *On Abraham* was in general sparing (see Hervé Savon, *Saint Ambroise devant l'exégèse de Philon le Juif* [Paris: Études Augustiniennes, 1977], 1:175, 227-35, etc.; also Enzo Lucchesi, *L'Usage de Philon dans l'oeuvre exégètique de Saint Ambroise* [Leiden: Brill, 1977], p. 135), and it is not always easy to sort out direct and indirect dependence. For a good review of these studies, see David T. Runia, *Philo in Early Christian Literature* (Assen and Minneapolis: Van Gorcum and Fortress, 1993), pp. 295-311.

erbate the temptation it presents.[8] Yet equally striking is the omission of almost any hint of the identity issues that Philo so carefully raised and Origen so carefully developed. There is barely even a mention of God's promises. Far more prominent in Ambrose's text is the figure of Isaac, whose prefiguration of Christ receives more frequent and more protracted treatment. As Ambrose narrates it, the story almost becomes a Passion narrative in advance. When Isaac is mounted on the ass, he is a type ("typus," 1.8.71, *bis*) of Christ about to suffer his Passion (a detail not treated in Origen but given extended treatment by Ambrose); his carrying the wood of the sacrifice "commends the future events" of Christ's carrying his own cross (1.8.72).[9] The ram hanging by its horns in the bush is a figure of the way Christ would suffer, hung on the Cross, while the horn of the ram, being elevated, is also a figure of the elevation of Christ's horn (see Ps. 44:3) or stature over all others on earth, a more detailed and elaborate figure than Origen presents.[10]

Further, Abraham's function in Ambrose's text seems finally ancillary to the creation of this type. Origen, to be sure, emphasizes Abraham's prophetic vision, but always in the context of what the biblical figure Abraham could know from his historical vantage point. He has prophetic hope in resurrection but believes it is Isaac who will be resurrected. When he foretells, in answer to Isaac's question, that "God himself will provide for himself a sheep

8. In *Abr.* 1.67 (CSEL 32.1:546.14–547.5), God's instructions to Abraham not only name Isaac but exacerbate the trial by calling Isaac his "son" and also his "beloved son" (cf. Origen, *hom. in Gen.* 8.2); at CSEL 32.1:547.7-11, Isaac is the son of Abraham's old age (cf. Philo, *On Abraham* 35.195); at CSEL 32.1:547.13-15, the length of Abraham's journey to the place of sacrifice exacerbates the trial (cf. Origen, *hom. in Gen.* 8.3).

9. Compare Origen, *hom. in Gen.* 8.6, where Isaac's carrying the wood is said to be a "figure" *(figura)* of Christ's carrying his cross, while, apparently recalling this passage, at *hom. in Gen.* 8.9, Origen says that Isaac "bears the form of Christ" *(formam gereret Christi)* and the same expression is used of the ram found in the bush *(formam gerere Christi),* translated by Heine as "represents" (p. 145) and by Doutreleau as "figurait" (SC 7 *bis:* 231), thus losing some of the nuance of Origen's idea of "bearing the form of Christ."

10. Ambrose's picture of the ram as "hanging" *(suspensum, Abr.* 1.8.77) goes beyond the text of Genesis 22 (Ambrose's text of Gen. 22:13 reads *aries . . . haerens in virgulto, Abr.* 1.8.77); Rufinus translates Origen's text as *tenetur . . . aries in virgulto (hom. in Gen.* 8.9), but this was a common understanding of the passage in both Christian and Jewish circles (see Mark Bregman, "The Sacrifice of Isaac in Ancient Jewish and Christian Iconography," unpublished paper, delivered at the University of Notre Dame, April 1993). Origen does not picture the ram as "hanging," so the ram does not serve as a type of Christ on the cross. Rather, since the ram was slain, it "bears the form of Christ" insofar as Christ is human, in contrast to Isaac who was not slain and so "bears the form of Christ" insofar as he is the incorruptible Word *(hom. in Gen.* 8.9).

for the holocaust," Origen, in an uncharacteristic moment of self-revelation, stops to marvel at Abraham's prophetic insight. "Abraham's response," Origen observes, "sufficiently accurate and cautious *(satis diligens et cauta),* moves me." He continues,

> I know not what he saw in his spirit, for he speaks not about the present, but about the future: "God himself will provide himself a sheep." He responded to his son's inquiry about present things with future things. For "the Lord himself will provide himself a sheep" in Christ, because "Wisdom herself has built for herself a house" (Pr. 9.1) and "He himself humbled himself unto death" (cf. Phil. 2.8). And you will discover that everything you happen to read about Christ is done not by necessity, but freely. (*Hom.* 8.6, SC 7 *bis:* 224.22-28; trans. Heine, p.141)

Abraham's response, "sufficiently cautious," remains completely within the sphere of his historical purview. He does see something "in his spirit." He has an intuition of God's utter and sovereign freedom, which Christians know is revealed in the incarnation, and in that sense (and *only* in that sense) Abraham sees the incarnation.

Origen is moved at the depth of Abraham's knowledge of God, knowledge that is truly his and that is true in a way that is complete, if not specific; "accurate," if "cautious." Ambrose, by contrast, emphasizes that Abraham's prophecy is directly of Christ and as such absolutely unknowing. When he informs the servants that both he and Isaac will return, he "prophesies what he knows not" (*prophetavit quod ignorabat,* 1.71). It is the "Lord who spoke through his mouth," while Abraham's own intentions were to return alone to the servants after having sacrificed his son. His words were meant to calm the servants' fears and nothing more (1.71). This means that as a prophecy his words are completely divorced from both his intentions and his knowledge, that is, they are divorced from him as a character in the narrative and in fact almost make the prophecy dependent on an outright lie. Isaac too, when he asks Abraham where the victim is for the sacrifice, is prophesying "in word, not in knowledge" (*et hic prophetat sermone, non scientia,* 1.74). His prophecy is completely accidental to his intention; it is in the *sermo,* his word, not in his knowledge. Abraham responds *similiter,* that is, similarly in ignorance of what he is prophesying. He believes that the victim God will provide is Isaac.[11] Abra-

---

11. "Respondit denique similiter Abraham: *deus providebit sibi ovem in holocaustum, fili* (Gen. 22.8). Inflexibilis a studio devotionis minister vocare filium frequenter non timet. Ita erat intentionis soliditate fundatus et hoc se meliorem patrem putabat, hoc sibi in

ham's word, at least insofar as it is the bearer of prophecy, is being dislodged from the connection to Abraham as an agent, which Origen was so careful to preserve. It is thus reduced to a textual indicator to the Christian reader that it is a typology that is about to be enacted, and it functions as such precisely because Abraham does not know what he is saying. Abraham and all his struggles seem almost reduced here to the status of a textual cue.

When, at Genesis 22:13, Abraham sees the ram hanging in the bush, Ambrose comments on his "seeing" — he "sees in this sacrifice," represented by the ram, "His [Christ's] passion," as John indicated when he said, "Abraham saw my day, and rejoiced" (John 8:56). Abraham, however, doesn't know what he is seeing: his seeing it, as the final act of his struggle, serves to turn it into a type for the (Christian) reader. Unlike Origen's Abraham, whose vision is "in his spirit," Ambrose's Abraham is simply an onlooker. Abraham's struggle, so convincingly drawn on the basis of Philo's and Origen's elaboration of it, ultimately loses its self-referential meaning and comes to have meaning only as a reference to a type, as the vehicle by which Isaac and the ram are turned into types. In Ambrose, the focus has moved off Abraham entirely. He loses his identity, swamped under the weight of the typology that has, in a way, become the literal sense. Or, better, the literal sense vanishes as Abraham effaces himself by his seeing, becoming an onlooker only, serving to focus the reader on what is *seen*.

At one point in the text Ambrose echoes, although very distantly, Origen's impassioned apostrophe to the fathers in the audience. On account of the victim God provided, namely Christ,

> many fathers were to offer up their own sons and not be afraid to be separated from them in this world. Every day fathers are offering up their sons that they might die in Christ and be buried in the Lord. How many fathers, whose sons were put to death in martyrdom, returned from their tombs rejoicing![12]

---

perenne mansurum iudicabat filium, si eum immolaret deo" (1.74). Abraham concludes that he will be a better father if he sacrifices his son to God, and that in some sense he will not lose his son, at least to the extent that he will still be his son (in that case, taking *sibi* as a dative of possession). This is a curious passage. It cannot mean that Abraham believes Isaac will be replaced by an animal and will in that sense be present to him afterwards; otherwise he would not have planned on coming back "alone," as Ambrose has already remarked that he has (1.71; CSEL 32.1:549.11). Nor for the same reason can it mean that Ambrose believes Isaac will be raised from the dead after having himself served as the victim provided by God (and Ambrose does not cite Heb. 11:17-19). See n. 13 below for more on this passage.

12. ". . . propter quam multi patres offerent filios suos et separari in hoc saeculo a filiis non timerent. Cotidie offerunt patres filios suos, ut moriantur in Christo et

Ambrose has merged Origen's exhortation to the fathers in the audience to take heart from Abraham's faith when their children die, and his exhortation to martyrdom issued to all. For Origen Abraham's willingness to sacrifice his son meant his willingness to sacrifice his own identity as a father and the promises of God that were predicated on it. For Origen this became a paradigmatic exhortation for everyone to be ready to find their primary identity in Christ's call, and thus to be ready to give up all for Christ in martyrdom. Ambrose has removed the hortatory tone and literalized the example that Abraham offers to fathers. Because of Christ many fathers now offer their sons up in baptism or perhaps ascetic profession,[13] and many fathers in the past offered their sons up in martyrdom. Abraham's example is no longer archetypal; it is merely a foreshadowing of what certain people, namely, certain fathers, will be able to do after Christ comes, not an enactment and embodiment of what all Christians are called upon to do in the face of God's call. Perhaps as martyrdom faded into the past, in a time and place where conversion to Christianity did not mean such an identity crisis anymore, but perhaps even social gain, it is no accident that the exigency for retrieving the Philonic depiction of Abraham's *agon* recedes, just as Abraham himself recedes from view in his own story. In the story of the *aqedah,* that may be the most poignant moment of all.

*   *   *

The three interpretations of Genesis 22:1-19 examined above are all examples of a style of exegesis that, despite the work of scholars as diverse as Henri de Lubac and Hans Frei, is still often styled "precritical," an expression that actually implies "uncritical," "unsophisticated," and even "wrong." Ultimately the phrase "precritical exegesis" presents itself as a kind of oxymoron since it suggests that the various methods of ancient exegesis, including allegory and

---

consepeliantur in domino. Quanti patres occisis martyrio filiis laetiores ab eorum tumulo reverterunt!" (*Abr.* 1.8.74).

13. Baptism would not be a "separation" from the son "in this world" for a Christian father. That means that the father offering up the son to death and burial in Christ is more likely to be a reference to ascetic profession. Ambrose does at least at one other point connect Abraham's sacrifice of Isaac with a father's offering his child (in this case a daughter) to a vow of virginity (*De virginitate* 2.6–3.10). He also points out to parents that pledging their daughters to virginity will in fact ensure that they do not lose their daughter (*De virginibus* 1.7.32). Thus, when Ambrose comments that Abraham will not lose his son by sacrificing him to God, he may be thinking more of the present application (advice to a parent of a would-be virgin) than the ancient narrative in its own right.

typology, are all finally forms not of exegesis but of eisegesis. The phrase implies, too, that whatever variations in quality or skill may be exhibited by the ancient exegetes, they are essentially insignificant for they are all variations on the common theme of error where interpretation of the text is concerned. In the last analysis, the ancient exegetes are not exegetes at all.[14]

Without denying and indeed while strongly affirming the gains in interpretation made by historico-critical methods of interpretation, there is no need to cast ancient and medieval exegesis collectively as their "precritical" shadow. This will mean not a uniform affirmation of ancient exegesis in place of a uniform rejection, but rather coming to have some sense of the variations in quality and success among the products of ancient exegesis, that is, coming to have an appreciation of the way in which ancient exegesis is critical. Ancient exegesis, one might say, is "differently critical" compared with our own methods, but not uncritical. Part of the job then of historians of exegesis would be to try to articulate the canons of criticism intrinsic to or appropriate for the ancient exegesis itself, to try to acquire a sense of the sort of sophistication proper to and characterizing these earlier forms of exegesis precisely as exegesis. For to say or to imply that there are no variations in quality — a mistake committed equally by admirers and detractors of the ancients — is the same as saying there are no canons for excellence or success in this body of literature and that it is indeed finally "pre-" (or at least "non-") critical.

Further, I would like to suggest that the above analysis of three "precritical" interpretations of Genesis 22:1-19 does begin to uncover some differences in quality of exegesis and so can serve as an example of the process of which I am speaking. The interpretation of Ambrose seems less successful than those of Philo or Origen, but *not* because it is typological, for Origen's is also typological, but because in his haste to create a typology Ambrose belittles or degrades the type. The valor of Abraham is described, but it has no bearing on the ultimate significance of the text. In fact Ambrose divorces the prophetic interpretation from the specific struggles, hopes, and fears of the character of Abraham as depicted in the narrative. Although it is an exaggeration, one could nevertheless say that Ambrose's reading of the text leaves one

---

14. A claim that persists even in the excellent and innovative study of David Dawson, who comments on the "misleading self-interpretation" of the ancient allegorists: "Although allegorical readers of scripture in ancient Alexandria sought to convince their audiences that they were interpreting the text itself, they were actually seeking to revise their culture through their allegorical readings." Must interpretation of texts (allegorical or otherwise) and attempts to revise culture be construed as mutually exclusive enterprises? Passages cited from David Dawson, *Allegorical Readers and Cultural Revision in Ancient Alexandria* (Berkeley: University of California Press, 1992), p. 235.

with no real reason for reading the Old Testament, apart from the desire to demonstrate its character as prophecy fulfilled. The Passion narrative can be read in more — and better — detail in the New Testament. However, Origen's setting up of a typology does not reduce the Old Testament text to a superfluity. His interpretation shows, on the contrary, that reading the New Testament without the Old is an impoverished reading, shorn of a richness of determinative insight and revelation that could come from no other source.

From Saul to Paul: Patristic Interpretation
of the Names of the Apostle

MICHAEL COMPTON

Robert Wilken opens his essay "Religious Pluralism and Early Christian Thought" by noting that "one task of the historical theologian [is] to remind others that issues debated in our times have been the subject of intellectual scrutiny in earlier times."[1] Those who will be reading this collection of essays in honor of Wilken no doubt already know this to be true, but truth often bears repeating: this is his point.

The present essay offers an example of the "intellectual scrutiny" of an earlier time, that of the patristic era. Patristic exegesis is all too often ignored by more recent scholars, some of whom appear to believe that their own historical-critical tools allow them to find previously unknown truths.[2] Dis-

---

1. Originally published in *Pro Ecclesia* 1 (1992): 89-103; reprinted in Robert L. Wilken, *Remembering the Christian Past* (Grand Rapids: Eerdmans, 1995), pp. 25-46.

2. I provide two examples: Most "critical commentaries" on Acts note that the story of Ananias and Sapphira in chapter 5 has parallels with the story of Achan ben Carmi in Joshua 7. Josh. 7:1 (LXX) and Acts 5:2 even use the same (somewhat unusual) verb, νοσφίζομαι. I have not yet, however, seen a commentary which notes that John Chrysostom, whose collection of fifty-five homilies on Acts constitutes our earliest complete "commentary" on that book, also cites this parallel in his *hom. 12 in Ac.* (PG 60:101).

W. Ward Gasque (*A History of the Interpretation of the Acts of the Apostles* [Peabody,

Earlier versions of this paper were presented at the AAR/SBL Southeast Regional Meeting, March 1997, and at the North American Patristics Society, May 1997. I would like to express my thanks to all who commented on the paper, and especially to Paul Blowers and to Angela Christman, who encouraged me to submit it for this Festschrift.

covering the value of patristic exegesis was one of the great (and, at first, quite surprising) joys of reading the Fathers while a graduate student under Wilken. I am grateful to Robert for introducing me to the thinking — and writing, and preaching, and praying — of the Fathers, and I am also greatly pleased to offer this essay as an expression of my thanks.

Let me hasten to add that I am under no illusion that my topic is as important as religious pluralism. Indeed, the question of the name, or names, of Paul may not seem to be a *theological* question at all. For the Fathers, however, it was often otherwise. My discussion will be thematic rather than chronological, and I will close with the comments of John Chrysostom, for two reasons. First, Chrysostom's interpretation is both a direct and, as I shall argue, indirect response to other views. Second, for Chrysostom the question is theological: he sees in the names of the Apostle evidence of divine *synkatabasis,* accommodation, for our sakes.[3]

The Problem

What *is* the name of the Apostle to the Gentiles? Everyone, it seems, knows the name Paul (Acts 19:15), which appears at the beginning of the thirteen epistles, Romans to Philemon, and which also is mentioned in 2 Peter 3:15. According to the Acts of the Apostles, however, Paul was also known by another name, Saul.[4] We are therefore dealing with Greek texts that preserve

---

Mass.: Hendrickson, 1989], p. 16) devotes one page to patristic exegesis (in a chapter titled "Pre-critical Study of the Book of Acts"). He suggests that Johann Albrecht Bengel (1687-1752) was the first to describe Acts as narrating "not so much the Acts of the Apostles, as the Acts of the Holy Spirit; even as the former treatise contains the Acts of Jesus Christ"; cf. p. 20. This is, however, almost exactly what Chrysostom says in the introductory section of his first homily on the entire book: "The Gospels, then, are a kind of history of what Christ did and said; but the Acts is a kind of history of what 'the other Comforter' said and did" (PG 60:21).

3. I am indebted to Robert C. Hill for the translation "accommodation," rather than the usual "condescension" for συγκατάβασις, which is an important theme with Chrysostom. See Hill, "On Looking Again at *synkatabasis,*" *Prudentia* 13 (1981): 3-11, and François Dreyfus, "Divine Condescendence *(synkatabasis)* as a Hermeneutic Principle of the Old Testament in Jewish and Christian Tradition," *Immanuel* 19 (1984-85): 74-86.

4. The name "Saul" never appears as a name for Paul in the New Testament outside of Acts. "Saul" is introduced in Acts 7:58; the name "Paul" does not appear for the Apostle until 13:9, after which the name "Saul" disappears (with the exception of 22:7, 13; 26:14, where the events of chapter 9 are narrated again). Some manuscripts, however, include the name Paul as early as 12:25. See Bruce M. Metzger, *A Textual Commentary on the Greek New Testament,* 2nd ed. (New York: United Bible Societies, 1994), p. 350.

both a Hebrew name, Saul, and a Latin name, Paul. As we will see, this linguistic datum is significant for our question: What is the relationship between these two names?

To many Christians (and non-Christians as well), the answer to this question has been and continues to be quite obvious. For them there is, in fact, no problem here at all: Saul the persecuting Pharisee received the name Paul when he converted to Christianity. I confess that this is the answer I was first taught, and I have met many who were taught likewise.[5]

Putting aside the question of Paul's "conversion" to Christianity, is there any evidence for this interpretation? It is true that Paul had at one time been a persecutor of Christians: this is the testimony not only of Acts but also of the Epistles.[6] Further, the name Saul is linked specifically with the act of persecution in Acts 9:4: "Saul, Saul, why are you persecuting me?" Finally, we see that after the events of 9:4 Saul stops persecuting and becomes a preacher of the gospel,[7] the "Paul" who is so familiar.[8] There seems to be, then, some support for this popular view.

As is so often the case, however, popular belief is at odds with the results of modern biblical scholarship. If one may dare use the term "consensus" when speaking of the latter, the consensus is that there is no change of names in Acts: "Paul had both names, and this from his childhood."[9] The classic exposition of this view is G. A. Harrer's article, "Saul Who Is Also Called Paul."[10] Harrer examines ancient Roman practices of naming and suggests

5. The note for 1 Tim. 1:12-14 in the *New Oxford Annotated Bible with the Apocrypha* for the RSV (New York: Oxford University Press, 1977), p. 1441, reflects (and perpetuates) this interpretation: "The Lord displayed his grace in making an apostle out of Saul the persecutor."

6. Gal. 1:13, 23; Phil. 3:6; 1 Cor. 15:9; 1 Tim. 1:13, where he describes himself as διώκων or διώκτης.

7. As Chrysostom puts it, ὁ διώκτης εὐαγγελιοστὴς γέγονεν: *hom. 3 in Ac. 9:1* (PG 51:139). See also Gal. 1:23.

8. And, as many early writers noted, the persecutor thus became the persecuted. In *Topographia christiana* (SC 159.321), Cosmas Indicopleustes, writing in the sixth century, puts it this way: ὁ ποτὲ διώκτης, νῦν δὲ διωκόμενος.

9. Gerhard Lohfink, *The Conversion of St. Paul*, trans. Bruce J. Malina (Chicago: Franciscan Herald Press, 1976), p. 116, n. 12.

10. G. A. Harrer, "Saul Who Is Also Called Paul," *HTR* 33 (1940): 19-33. For a recent summary, see Jerome Murphy-O'Connor, *Paul: A Critical Life* (New York: Oxford University Press, 1996), pp. 41-43. See both Harrer and Murphy-O'Connor, as well as most recent commentaries, for further bibliography. One treatment that is still quite valuable for its collection of primary data is by Johann Wessel (1671-1745): *Johannis Wesselii Dissertationes* (Leiden: Lugduni Batavorum, 1721), pp. 373-87, 388-408.

that "Paul" was the Apostle's *cognomen* while "Saul" was his *signum,* or infor-mal name. Harrer is, of course, working on a foundation built by others: Gustav A. Deissmann had already noted that it was common for Jews in the Roman Empire to have cosmopolitan names that were "more or less similar in sound to the native name." He offers, among other examples, the double names of Ἰάκιμ/Ἄλκιμος (Josephus, *Ant.* xii.9) and Ἰησοῦς/Ἰοῦστος (Col. 4:11).[11] It is plausible, then, that Saul, a Roman Jew, also had the name Paul from birth.

This conclusion, however, is far older than Deissmann. Harrer notes that Origen had already suggested that there is actually no "change of names" narrated in Acts.[12] In the introduction of Origen's *Commentary on Romans,* preserved by Rufinus in Latin translation, we see that he understands Acts 13:9, "Saul, who is also Paul," to mean that the Apostle had both names from an earlier time.[13] Origen may have been aware of the kind of supporting evi-dence that is cited by Harrer and others, but the only proofs he gives are from the Scriptures: he reviews the names of several biblical characters who have more than one name.

While Origen favors this interpretation, he records two others, which we will examine in turn. Each of these suggests that there *is* a change of name in Acts: the first interpretation argues for a change *from* Saul, based on Acts 9, while the second argues for a change *to* Paul, based on a reading of Acts 13:9.

A Change from Saul: Acts 9

In his treatise *On Prayer* Origen discusses the names Saul and Paul in connec-tion with Matthew 6:9, "Hallowed be thy Name." Origen argues that a "name" designates a person's character and shows from Scripture that, when one's character changes, so does one's name. His examples are Abraham, Peter, and

11. Gustav A. Deissmann, *Bible Studies* (Edinburgh: T & T Clark, 1901), pp. 314-15.

12. Harrer cites as his prime source for this material the article by H. Dessau, "Der Name des Apostels Paulus," *Hermes* 45 (1910): 347-68. See also the brief discussion in F. J. Foakes Jackson et al., *The Beginnings of Christianity, Part I: The Acts of the Apostles* (Grand Rapids: Baker Book House, 1965), 4:145, which begins, "Origen is the first writer to dis-cuss this question, and, as so often, is also the most intelligent."

13. Theresia Heither, ed., *Origen's Commentarii in epistulam ad Romanos,* Fontes Christiani (New York: Herder, 1990), p. 74: "evidenter non ei tunc primum Pauli nomen ostendit impositum, sed veteris appellationis id fuisse designat." The text is also available in PG 14:836.

Paul: "when the character of Saul, who persecuted Jesus, was changed, he was named Paul.[14]

Some writers further hold that Paul has the name Saul not only *while* he is a persecutor but *because* he is a persecutor. Jerome and Augustine, for instance, each note parallels between this Saul and King Saul of the Old Testament: not only are their names the same, but both were of the tribe of Benjamin (a detail recorded only in the Epistles, not in Acts).[15] Both men were also persecutors: King Saul persecuted David, while Saul/Paul persecuted Jesus. As we will see below, the name "Saul" inspired at least one other interpretation as well.

This ancient exegesis resembles the "popular" view mentioned above. The name Saul is again linked here with the activity of persecution, following Acts 9:4, and the inference is that, once Saul's persecuting ceases, the name Saul ceases as well. As with Peter and Abraham, the change is due to a divine action: his name *was changed* to Paul. The narrative in Acts does not explicitly support this conclusion; in fact, as we shall see, there is reason to think otherwise.

Nonetheless, this interpretation of the names Saul and Paul was quite popular in antiquity. While it is impossible to determine the age of this exegetical tradition, it was widely held by the second half of the fourth century. I will return to this point below; for now two brief examples must suffice. Epiphanius, in his *De Gemmis,* speaks in Paul's voice: "first Saul and now Paul: before I was a persecutor and now an apostle."[16] Gregory Nazianzen agrees: ". . . God transforms his zeal, and makes Paul out of Saul. . . ."[17]

---

14. PG 11:492: μεταβαλούσης γὰρ τῆς . . . τοῦ διώκοντος τὸν Ἰησοῦν Σαοὺλ [ποιότητος], προσηγορεύθη ὁ Παῦλος. Origen does not specify what aspects of the character of Abram or Simon were changed along with their respective names.

15. In Rom. 11:1 and Phil. 3:5; Acts 13:21, however, reminds us that King Saul was from the tribe of Benjamin. Epiphanius draws the following parallel: ". . . after all the apostles, there appeared as the chosen one Paul the apostle from the tribe of Benjamin: just as Benjamin was the last of his brothers, so was [Paul] chosen later" (no doubt an echo of 1 Cor. 15:8). Text in Robert P. Blake, *Epiphanius De Gemmis: The Old Georgian Version and the Fragments of the Armenian Version* (London: Christophers, 1934), p. 166, section 82.

16. Section 80 (Blake, *Epiphanius De Gemmis,* p. 168).

17. Or. 41.4 (PG 36:48): τὸν ζῆλον μετατίθησι, καὶ ποιεῖ Παῦλος ὁ πρότερον Σαῦλος ἀντὶ Σαύλων· It seems likely that the phrase τὸν ζῆλον μετατίθησι is meant to recall Paul's language in Phil. 3:6, κατὰ ζῆλος διώκων τὴν ἐκκλησίαν.

An Illustration of the Point

The popularity of this exegetical tradition is also attested by its appearance in art. The fifth book of Cosmas Indicopleustes' *Christian Topography* (written in the sixth century) records the lives of several biblical characters, including Paul. Two manuscripts of this work reproduce illustrations that are apparently taken from a now-lost illustrated copy of Acts.[18] One such illustration depicts the events of Acts 9. In the midst of these scenes has been placed a figure identified as ἅγιος Παῦλος, "St. Paul," who is pointing to a codex in his arm (see p. 56); this figure was "probably borrowed from the title picture in front of the Pauline Epistles."[19]

Given, then, that the figure of the epistle-writing "St. Paul" has been interposed among scenes from Acts 9, it is interesting to note *where* the figure has been placed. From left to right, we see five scenes: (1) Saul meeting with the chief priests;[20] (2) Saul and two men identified as his fellow travelers; (3) a voice from heaven, depicted as a ray of light coming from a cloud; to the left of the ray is the caption "Saul, Saul, why are you persecuting me?"; (4) a prostrate Saul, asking "Who are you, Lord?";[21] and (5) Saul accompanied by another man, with the caption "Ananias heals Saul."[22]

It is just before this fifth scene that the figure of "St. Paul" has been placed. Such a location is not for aesthetic reasons: it is not in the center of the drawing but to the right of center. (The Vatican MS, however, has removed the scene showing Saul with the high priests; as a result the figure of Paul is now in

18. Kurt Weitzmann, *Illustrations in Roll and Codex: A Study of the Origin and Method of Text Illustration* (Princeton: Princeton University Press, 1970), p. 142. The illustrations include events from both chapter 9 and from 7:58, the stoning of Stephen. Weitzmann discusses two manuscripts, Vatican Cod. gr. 699, which dates from the ninth century (see his fig. 130, which is from fol. 83v), and Mt. Sinai Cod. 1186, which dates from the eleventh century (see his fig. 192, which is from fol. 128v). Weitzmann (p. 187) suggests that, although the Mt. Sinai MS is later, it actually is a better witness to the original illustrated Acts. I offer further evidence for his conclusion below, where my discussion is based on the Mt. Sinai MS. See also the note in Wanda Wolska-Conus's edition of Cosmas's work (SC 159.320-27); a reproduction of the illustration from the Mt. Sinai MS is on p. 321.

19. Weitzmann, *Illustrations in Roll and Codex*, p. 142.

20. Although Acts 9:1 indicates only one chief priest, "chief priests" appears in Acts 9:14.

21. Acts 9:5; this question is, however, omitted in the Mt. Sinai MS. The answer to the question appears in both MSS to the right of the ray from the cloud, "I am Jesus, whom you are persecuting."

22. In the Vatican MS the caption identifies the Apostle by the name Παῦλον.

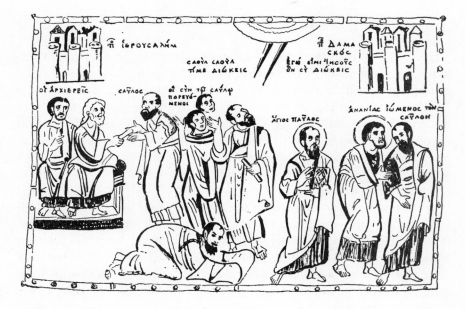

the center of the illustration.) That this location is an interruption of the original sequence is shown by the caption in the fifth and final scene: here Ananias is healing *Saul,* not Paul. (According to the text of Acts, this is anachronistic; there is no "Paul" until chapter 13. Ananias even addresses him as "Brother Saul" in Acts 9:17.) Further, the figure of "St. Paul" has a nimbus, while the figure of *Saul* with Ananias in the fifth scene does not (although Ananias himself does).[23] The location of St. Paul in the illustration, therefore, is deliberate, and reflects the exegetical tradition that Saul becomes St. Paul "on the road to Damascus" and immediately after the events of Acts 9:4.

In summary, one fairly early and widespread line of interpretation holds that there is a definite (if unrecorded) shift of name from Saul to Paul in Acts. This shift of name is linked to the shift in character from persecutor to preacher at the "Damascus Road" experience of Acts 9, and is often interpreted as a divine act, similar to the change of Abram to Abraham or of Simon to Peter.[24]

23. In the Vatican MS *every* drawing of Paul *and* Saul is accompanied by a nimbus!

24. Origen, *comm. in Rom.,* does note, however, that in the case of Paul there is no divine act of renaming: "Sed haec ex praecepto Dei legimus facta, nusquam vero erga Paulum invenimus tale aliquid gestum" (Heither, *Origen's Commentarii in epistulam ad Romanos,* p. 70). Cf. Jerome, *Philm.* (PL 26:603): "Quare autem e Saulo Paulus dictus sit, nulla Scriptura memorat."

A Change to Paul: Acts 13:9

Given that there is a change from Saul, a new question arises: What is the significance of the new name "Paul"? In the case of Simon Peter, of course, we have the statement in Matthew 16:18, "You are Peter, and on this rock . . . ," which links the name Peter to his confession of Jesus' identity as the Christ, the Son of the Living God. In a similar way, Genesis 17:5 explains the shift of name from Abram to Abraham, although readers of the Septuagint version were often baffled by this episode since neither Abram nor Abraham is a Greek name.[25] For "Paul," however, not only do we not have a "changing-name" episode, but we also are hard pressed to find what if any meaning this name denotes. To discover the answer to this question, we turn to the first appearance of Saul's other name, which is in Acts 13:9.

In the introduction to his *Commentary on Romans,* Origen notices the close proximity between "Saul, who is also called Paul" in Acts 13:9, and a Roman proconsul named Sergius Paulus in Acts 13:7.[26] Origen then reports that some conclude *(quibusdam visum est)* that, since Saul has conquered *(subiecerat)* Sergius Paul the proconsul, he now assumes *(sumpserit)* the proconsul's name. Note that the *Commentary on Romans* does not present this interpretation as Origen's own; as I have already indicated, he seems to prefer the view that Paul had always had both names. I suspect that it is not even Origen who is reporting it, but Origen's translator, Rufinus.[27] If this is so, the identity of those who hold this "triumphalist" view that Saul took the name Paul because of his first convert, Sergius Paulus, may become significant.

While we will probably never know the author of this triumphalist view, it is interesting that the earliest writer to offer it is Jerome, who records it

---

25. This did not, however, stop Greek-speaking Christians from attempting to make sense of these and other names in Scripture. Despite the (linguistically suspect) explanation in Gen. 17:5, Chrysostom, *serm. 9 in Gen.,* says that the name Ἀβρααμ is from a word he transliterates as ἄβαρ and translates as πέρα; as περατής Abraham's name means "traveler" (PG 54:628). Despite Chrysostom's admitted ignorance of Hebrew, this interpretation is not entirely his fault: here he is following the LXX of Gen. 14:13, where "Abram the Hebrew" is translated by Αβραμ τῷ περάτῃ, "Abram the traveler." (Chrysostom's *sermones in Gen.* are not to be confused with his series of sixty-seven *homiliae in Gen.* on the same book; further, the ninth *sermo* is actually part of the series, *hom. 1-4 in Ac. 9:1,* discussed below.)

26. The difference between these two names is only a matter of English translation; in Greek the names Sergius *Paulus* and *Paul* are the same.

27. Heither, *Origen's Commentarii in epistulam ad Romanos,* p. 75, n. 12, also doubts whether all of the discussion here is due to Origen.

more than once. While it is of course possible that Jerome is "borrowing" from Origen, it seems less likely he would borrow and elaborate on an explanation "Origen himself" rejects (according to the *Commentary on Romans*). Instead, it seems just as likely that Jerome is in fact the author of this interpretation, and that Rufinus reports it in the *Commentary on Romans* only to discount it by damning it with faint praise.[28]

In any event, Jerome includes this explanation in his *Commentary on Philemon*, as well as in his *Catalogue of Virtuous Men*, which I shall quote more fully:

> Paul, who earlier was Saul *(qui ante Saulus)* . . . was changed from a persecutor into an elect vessel *(in vas electionis de persecutore translatus est)*. Since Sergius Paulus Proconsul of Cyprus was the first *(primum)* to believe his preaching, he chose the name Paul *(sortitus est nomen Paulus)* because he had conquered him to faith in Christ.[29]

The historical work of Harrer and others has, of course, demolished this view: the expression Σαῦλος δέ, ὁ καὶ Παῦλος, "but Saul, who is also Paul," in Acts 13:9 introduces an alternate name, not a change of names. Jerome's interpretation did, however, pass into the Latin exegetical tradition. Augustine, for example, is aware of it *(Conf.* 8.4), and it also appears in the Venerable Bede's *Commentary on Acts.*[30]

Just as Augustine saw the name Saul as a fitting epithet, because Saul/Paul, like King Saul, had been a persecutor, so also Augustine regards Paul to be an epithet as well. Rightly observing that the Latin word *paulus* means "small," Augustine says, "When he was Saul, he was proud, exalted; when he was Paul, he was lowly and little."[31] Augustine then cites 1 Corinthians 15:9 *(ego enim sum minimus Apostolorum)* and Ephesians 3:8 *(mihi minimo omnium sanctorum)* to show that the name "Paul" is appropriate. Like Jerome,

---

28. "Quod ne nos quidem usquequaque evacuandum putamus" (Heither, *Origen's Commentarii in epistulam ad Romanos*, p. 72). Rufinus translated the *comm. in Rom.* ca. 406, after Jerome's works that include this interpretation, and after the friendship between the two had ceased.

29. *De viris illustribus* 5 (PL 23:615); see also Jerome, *Philm.* (PL 26:604).

30. "He obtained the name Paul from Sergius Paulus, the proconsul whom he conquered for the faith of Christ." Text in *The Venerable Bede: Commentary on the Acts of the Apostles,* trans. Lawrence T. Martin (Kalamazoo, Mich.: Cistercian Publications, 1989), p. 118.

31. *Tr. 8 in ep. Jn.* (SC 75:342): "Ergo quando Saulus, superbus, elatus; quando Paulus, humilis, modicus."

Augustine also holds that the change of name was Paul's *choice;* he repeats this claim in *On the Spirit and the Letter* 7.12.

It's All Greek . . .

Jerome Murphy-O'Connor dismisses Augustine's interpretation of "Paul"/ "little": it "has nothing to recommend it, except as an opportunity for rhetorical piety."[32] Whether we agree with Murphy-O'Connor that rhetorical piety is a fault, we should at least credit Augustine for recognizing that the name "Paul" is Latin. Greek readers of Acts often missed this point, with some interesting results.

I noted earlier that we are dealing with a Greek text with both a Hebrew name, Saul, and a Latin name, Paul. These names are not translated in Acts but are transliterated (this accounts for the variant reading Σαουλ for Σαῦλος in Acts)[33] and Hellenized: that is, they follow declension patterns familiar to readers and speakers of Greek.[34] This led some Greek Christians to interpret these names as Greek names and to try to make sense of them as such.[35]

Such a move was apparently widespread by the last half of the fourth century. In the so-called Euthalian Apparatus, a collection of materials dated ca. 375 and attributed, usually, to Euthalius the Deacon, we find a prologue to the letters of Paul.[36] After briefly narrating the earlier events of Paul's life, Euthalius describes the change from Saul to Paul by offering an etymological explanation:

---

32. Murphy-O'Connor, *Paul,* p. 44.

33. See the discussion by Harrer, "Saul Who Is Also Called Paul," pp. 24-26.

34. The following forms appear in Acts: Παῦλος, Παύλου, Παύλῳ, Παῦλον, Παῦλε; Σαῦλος, Σαύλου, Σαύλῳ, Σαῦλον.

35. I should add that Greek Christians are not the only ones to do this. Optatus of Milevis, *De schismate Donatistarum* (SC 412:244), for example, preserves an attempt to make sense of the Aramaic "Cephas" for Peter as a pun on the Greek word κεφαλή: he speaks of Rome, "in qua sederit omnium apostolorum caput Petrus, unde et Cephas est appellatus"; cf. Y. M.-J. Congar, "Cephas-Cephale-Caput," *Revue de moyen-âge latin* 8 (1952): 5-42.

36. See the study by J. Armitage Robinson, *Euthaliana. Studies of Euthalius codex H of the Pauline Epistles and the Armenian Version with an appendix containing a collation of the Eton MS of the Pseudo-Athanasian Synopsis* (Cambridge: Cambridge University Press, 1895), and, more recently, the study by Louis Charles Willard, "A Critical Study of the Euthalian Apparatus," Ph.D. diss., Yale University, 1970.

Because the blessed Paul experienced so great a change, he also changed his name, and proved true to his other name as well — for Saul used to "assault" *(esaleue)* the whole church, but Paul "paused" *(pepautai)* from further persecution and maltreatment of the disciples of Christ.[37]

Ancient etymologies are often suspect, and this example is surely no exception. Yet, once we agree with Euthalius to read these names as Greek words, we see that his explanation works quite nicely. The name *Paulos* is similar to the Greek word *paula,* which means "pause" or "rest" and is derived from *pauomai,* the verb Euthalius cites.[38] The name *Saulos* is identical with the Greek adjective *saulos,* which means a "shaking" and is derived from the Greek verb *saleuo.*[39] A similar (but less adequate) wordplay in English is that "Saul assaulted" the Church, but "Paul paused" his attack. It is tempting these days to sneer at interpretations such as this; G. W. H. Lampe's *Patristic Greek Lexicon* refers to it as a "fanciful etymology."[40] Murphy-O'Connor would likely call it another example of "rhetorical piety." It is perhaps surprising,

37. In this translation, which is my own, I have tried to preserve the wordplay of the Greek. Willard's translation ("A Critical Study of the Euthalian Apparatus," pp. 195-96) uses "shook" and "ceased"; the text is from PG 85:697. The closing phrase is καὶ [πέπαυται] λυμαίνεσθαι τοῖς Χριστοῦ μαθηταῖς, which is no doubt intended to recall Acts 8:3: Σαῦλος δὲ ἐλυμαίνετο τὴν ἐκκλησίαν. Willard notes in his appendix 3 that this explanation of the names is missing in more than half of the manuscripts he examined, which include the prologue to Paul's letters. Notice that Euthalius states that Paul changed his own name; he does not present it as a divine renaming similar to that of Peter or Abraham.

38. Gen. 5:29 (LXX) tells us that Noah was so named because διαναπαύσει, "he will give rest." This etymology was apparently known to some Greek speakers: Chrysostom, for example, tells us that the word Νῶε in Hebrew means ὁ ἀναπαύων and that the Syrian word Νία means ἀνάπαυσις: *serm. 9 in Gen.* (PG 54:628).

39. H. G. Liddell and R. Scott, *A Greek-English Lexicon,* new ed., rev. and augmented by H. S. Jones (Oxford: Clarendon, 1958), p. 1586a, states that the adjective is derived from σαυλόομαι; the *Scholia* on Aristophanes, however, interprets the word σαυλοπρωκτιᾶν (*Wasps* 1173) as σαλεύειν τὸν πρωκτόν. See also Chrysostom's interpretation below.

40. Liddell and Scott, *A Greek-English Lexicon,* p. 1054a. In a similar way, the historical-critical method has very little patience with the many parallels that the Fathers see between Joshua and Jesus, whose names are identical in Greek: Ἰησοῦς (for a partial list of these parallels, see the entry for Ἰησοῦς in G. W. H. Lampe, *A Patristic Greek Lexicon* [Oxford and New York: Clarendon, 1961], p. 672); to many scholars these parallels resemble the "parallels" that are sometimes drawn between Jesus and Elvis (for example, Jesus said, "Love thy neighbor"; Elvis said, "Don't be cruel"). I find this a good illustration for the limitations of the historical-critical method: while the method cannot establish such connections, the connections may nevertheless be made, sometimes quite fruitfully.

then, that this etymological interpretation is known, but rejected, by that paragon of patristic rhetorical piety, John Chrysostom.

John Chrysostom's Interpretation

Although Chrysostom takes up the question of the names of the Apostle in several places, his chief treatment is the series of homilies *On the Changing of Names,* preached from Antioch ca. 390.[41] Chrysostom preached these homilies directly after his series *On the Beginning of Acts,* which took up various introductory matters about the book.[42] Having concluded his introduction, Chrysostom moves directly to the narratives about Paul in Acts, which leads him to address the question, "Why was Saul's name changed to Paul?"[43]

Chrysostom first takes up the question in *On the Changing of Names* 2:

> Why then was he called Saul when he persecuted, but had his name changed to Paul when he believed? Some say that when he . . . shook (ἐσάλευε) the Church, he was called Saul, because of the very act of shaking (τὸ σαλεύειν) the Church, thereby taking the name from the deed. They also say that, when he abstained from this madness, and ceased the warfare, and stopped (ἐπαύσατο) persecuting, again his name was changed to Paul, because he paused (παύσασθαι).

41. *Homiliae in mutatione nominum* (= *hom. 1-4 in Ac. 9:1;* PG 51:113-56). In his *comm. in Gal.* (PG 61:627), Chrysostom does not take up the topic yet again but refers his readers and/or listeners instead to his written comments, surely a reference to the *hom. 1-4 in Ac. 9:1.* See the brief treatment of Chrysostom on this question in Margaret Mitchell, *The Heavenly Trumpet: John Chrysostom and the Art of Pauline Interpretation* (Tübingen: J. C. B. Mohr [Paul Siebeck], 2000), pp. 335-38.

42. *Homiliae in principium Actorum Apostolorum* (= *hom. 1-4 in Ac. princ.;* PG 51:65-112). This series should not be confused with Chrysostom's series of fifty-five homilies on the entire book of Acts: *Homiliae in Ac.* (PG 60). I discuss the *Ac. princ.* series and its relationship to the *Ac. 9:1* series in my study, "Introducing the Acts of the Apostles: A Study of John Chrysostom's *On the Beginning of Acts,*" Ph.D. diss., University of Virginia, 1996.

43. In fact, Chrysostom says he had intended to begin a *seriatim* exposition of the Acts of the Apostles but "Paul does not allow me to follow the narrative in sequence, but calls me to speak of himself and of his achievements. For I desire to see him traveling into Damascus, and being bound, not by an iron chain, but by a master's voice. I desire to see this great fish caught, who stirred up the entire sea, who raised up a thousand wounds against the Church. Yes, I desire to see him caught, not by a hook, but by a master's word": *hom. 1 in Ac. 9:1* (PG 51:117).

Now this is a silly explanation, and false as well; I bring it up just so you will not be led astray by specious etymologies.[44] First of all, his parents gave him this name: they were not prophets; they did not know what was about to happen. Next, if he was called Saul *because* he assaulted the Church, then it would be necessary for his name to be immediately changed when he stopped the assault. But, as it is, we see him ceasing his assault against the Church, and *still* called Saul. And lest you think I am leading you astray when I say these things, I will go through the passages from the start.[45]

Here Chrysostom reports the same etymologies recorded by Euthalius. Despite the obvious popular appeal of this explanation, Chrysostom rejects it. The most likely reason is that it does not accord with the narrative in the Acts of the Apostles, and Chrysostom is interested in teaching the *contents* of that book to his listeners.[46] Chrysostom often complains that his listeners do not know the Scriptures, and his complaints often include hyperbole, yet his comments on and his treatment of Acts seem to suggest that this book was (especially) unfamiliar to his listeners.[47]

Chrysostom therefore passes over the popular explanation in favor of showing what the text actually says. True to his word, he goes through the passages in Acts, one by one, showing that the name "Paul" first appears, not in chapter 9, but in chapter 13:

He begins to preach and to confound the Jews, and his name is not changed, but he is still called Saul. . . . He ministers to the saints, and is still called Saul. . . . He converts many, and is still called Saul. . . . He becomes a teacher and a prophet, and he is still called Saul. . . . Behold, he is set apart by the Spirit, and not yet is his name changed![48] But when he

---

44. Though his wording is less polite than that of Lampe, *A Patristic Greek Lexicon* (which does not cite Chrysostom's comments), Chrysostom agrees that this is a "fanciful etymology."

45. *Hom. 2 in Ac. 9:1* (PG 51:126-27).

46. See my discussion in "Introducing the Acts of the Apostles," pp. 141-50.

47. This likely accounts for a feature unique to Chrysostom's series on Acts: in fifty-three of the fifty-five homilies there is a recapitulation of the lection and of the exposition. Chrysostom does this for no other book. F. H. Chase suggested that the presence of these recapitulations arises from Chrysostom's wish to teach the contents of the book. See his *Chrysostom: A Study in the History of Biblical Interpretation* (Cambridge: Deighton, Bell, and Co., 1887), p. 149.

48. Compare Chrysostom's brief explanation in *hom. 28 in Ac.* (PG 60:209) that

came into Salamis, when he found the magician, *then* Luke says of him, "but Saul, who is also Paul, full of the Holy Spirit" (Acts 13:9). . . . *Here* is the commencement of the new name.[49]

Chrysostom therefore rejects the explanation preserved by Euthalius, which focuses on the change in Saul's character and the events of Acts 9. As I will now argue, in *On the Changing of Names* Chrysostom also attempts to refute the triumphalist interpretation preserved by Jerome and others, which focuses on the juxtaposition of Sergius Paulus with the first appearance of the name "Paul" for Saul in Acts 13:9.

Having demonstrated that the text of Acts shows Saul is not called Paul in chapter 9, Chrysostom must now explain two things: first, why is there another name at all, and, second, why does the name Paul appear for the first time in chapter 13? He answers both questions in the next homily, *On the Changing of Names* 3. Chrysostom frames his answer to the first question as follows:

> Let us finally take up the beginning of the narrative, "And Saul was still breathing threats and murder against the disciples of the Lord" [Acts 9:1]. Now in the Epistles he is called Paul; why then does the Holy Spirit change his name?[50] For this reason: just as a master who purchases a slave changes the slave's name, because the master wishes to teach him authority *(despoteian)*, so also the Holy Spirit did then [in the case of Paul]. For he took Paul captive, and he had only recently surrendered to this authority. For this reason [the Holy Spirit] changed his name, so that he might learn authority from this. For the placement of names is a symbol of authority. . . . This also happened in the case of the king of the Babylonians: [Nebuchadnezzar] did not allow Hananiah, Azariah, and Mishahel to keep their names but called them Shadrach, Meshach, and Abednego.[51]

Saul's name is changed (ἀμείβεται) to Paul "with his ordination, just as it was in Peter's case" (μετὰ τῆς χειροτονίας, ὅπερ καὶ ἐπὶ τοῦ Πέτρου γεγένηται). Chrysostom does not develop this interpretation, but the phrase μετὰ τῆς χειροτονίας must be understood loosely since the name Saul appears in Acts 13:7, after the "ordination" of 13:3. (In any event, Chrysostom's explanation here also counters the interpretation that the change occurred in chapter 9.) The discussion of patristic interpretations in Foakes Jackson et al., *The Beginnings of Christianity*, 4:146, includes Chrysostom's comments from *hom. 28 in Ac.* but omits this fuller discussion in *hom. in Ac. 9:1*.

49. *Hom. 2 in Ac. 9:1* (PG 51:127-28).

50. *Hom. 3 in Ac. 9:1* (PG 51:137); cf. a similar statement in his *hom. 1 in Rom.* (PG 60:395).

51. *Hom. 3 in Ac. 9:1* (PG 51:137). The closing reference is to Dan. 1:7.

Note that Chrysostom assumes that Saul's name *was changed* to Paul; it was not a personal choice. Already, then, Chrysostom's interpretation is at odds with the "triumphalist" view, which holds that Paul *chose* his name, taking it from his first convert.[52] Chrysostom also says, in *On the Changing of Names* 2 cited above, that Saul "converted many" before Acts 13:9.[53] Again, though, the triumphalist interpretation depicts Sergius Paulus as Paul's first convert.

Despite his desire to teach the contents of Acts to his listeners, Chrysostom omits any mention of Sergius Paulus in *On the Changing of Names*. In his recital of the appearances of "Saul" in chapters 9–13 of Acts, he stops with Acts 13:6: "But when he came into Salamis, when he found the magician, *then* Luke says of him, 'but Saul, who is also Paul, full of the Holy Spirit'. . . . *Here* is the commencement of the new name." By skipping from 13:6 to 13:9 Chrysostom ignores the appearance of "Saul" in Acts 13:7 and avoids any mention of Sergius Paulus; one wonders why.

It is also striking that Chrysostom uses victor-vanquished language in his explanation for the change of name, just as the triumphalist reading does, yet he reverses the roles exactly. Paul did not conquer, but was conquered. While this could of course be sheer coincidence, when put alongside the other factors just listed, it seems likely that Chrysostom is attempting to counter a second interpretation of the names of Saul and Paul, one that says Saul took the name Paul from Sergius Paulus.

That Chrysostom is attempting to refute the triumphalist reading of Acts 13:9 of course hinges on the assumption that Chrysostom was aware of this reading. If that interpretation is indeed as early as Origen's commentary, there is of course no chronological difficulty with this assumption; nor is there any real difficulty if it is actually from Jerome. The interpretation appears at least as early as Jerome's *Commentary on Philemon*, which is dated ca. 386. There is therefore no chronological reason why Chrysostom could not be responding to this interpretation in *On the Changing of Names*. I would further submit that it is possible that Chrysostom is in fact responding directly to Jerome. Any argument on this point must of course fail of demonstrating certainty, and so I must be content to argue from example, showing that Chrysostom elsewhere refutes an exegetical tradition preserved by Jerome.

---

52. The explanation in the Euthalian apparatus also suggests that Saul changed his own name.

53. Greek ἐπιστρέφει πολλοῦς (PG 51:127). This statement is apparently made in light of Acts 11:25-26, which does not explicitly state that Saul converted anyone.

In his *Commentary on Isaiah*[54] Chrysostom reports on Isaiah 6:1-8 as follows:

> Now *some say* that Isaiah had sinned in having failed to rebuke Uzziah when he dared enter the sanctuary, and for that reason wanted to make amends for his sin by a quick show of willing obedience in order to please God. This is the reason he said his lips were unclean, because of his lack of courage to speak. But I do not agree with those who say such things. Paul is more trustworthy than they, and he called Isaiah courageous when he said, "Isaiah is bold to say. . . ."[55]

Duane Garrett tells us that the view Chrysostom is rejecting here is held by Jerome: "Jerome explains the uncleanness of Isaiah's lips (6:5), by claiming that when Uzziah invaded the temple, Isaiah refused to rebuke him."[56] It may be objected that we cannot know whether Chrysostom is directly refuting Jerome, for Jerome is not named in Chrysostom's commentary. To make a conclusion either way on that fact is to argue from silence; it is worth noting, however, that in the Isaiah commentary Chrysostom never names any of his sources.[57]

One rather large obstacle for my theory is the belief that Chrysostom himself knew no Latin.[58] Yet this need not concern us, for this belief could be mistaken. As J. N. D. Kelly points out, Chrysostom's father has a Latin name

---

54. The *Interpretatio in Is. 1–8* ends with comments on Isa. 8:1; it is uncertain whether this is a portion of a longer work or whether Chrysostom stopped at this point. The commentary has been edited in SC 304; a study of the commentary and an English translation of it appear in Duane A. Garrett, *An Analysis of the Hermeneutics of John Chrysostom's Commentary on Isaiah 1–8 with an English Translation* (Lewiston: Edwin Mellen, 1992).

55. The translation is from Garrett, *Chrysostom's Commentary on Isaiah 1–8*, p. 132, though the emphasis is mine. The closing reference is to Rom. 10:20.

56. Garrett, *Chrysostom's Commentary on Isaiah 1–8*, p. 239; the citation is from Jerome, *ep.* 18 (PL 22:369).

57. Garrett, *Chrysostom's Commentary on Isaiah 1–8*, p. 238: "[Chrysostom's] Isaiah commentary, although manifesting an awareness of the views of other men [sic], never refers to another exegete by name. As a result, it is impossible to say which works he did or did not know or use." On the basis of references to and parallels with other sources, however, Garrett (*Chrysostom's Commentary on Isaiah 1–8*, p. 240) concludes that "the best two candidates for authors on Isa 6 read by Chrysostom are Eusebius and Jerome."

58. The only evidence I have seen cited for this is Chrysostom, *oppugn.* 3.5 (PG 47:357), which states that "those who know the Italian tongue may get preference at court."

(which "invites the guess that his father may have been of Roman stock"), as does his father's sister, Sabiniana.[59] Even if Chrysostom could not read Latin, however, he could read Latin exegetical work in Greek translation (or have it read to him). As I have shown elsewhere, Greek translation of Latin exegesis accounts for Chrysostom's comments regarding Philippians 1:18; he argues that it says "Christ is being proclaimed," *not* "Let Christ be proclaimed"[60] — a reading that reflects a retroversion into Greek of the Latin *Christus annuncietur* once the latter is removed from context.[61] I conclude, then, that Chrysostom's explanation for the shift in name is a deliberate refutation not only of the etymologies preserved by Euthalius but also of the triumphalist interpretation for the change to Paul preserved by Jerome.[62] (It is still to be determined, of course, whether Jerome is the author of this tradition, and, if not, who was.)

Finally, Chrysostom addresses the second question he must answer: why does the text say Saul's name was changed in chapter 13?[63]

But why did [the Holy Spirit] not change the name immediately, but rather allowed much time to pass? Because, if [the Holy Spirit] had

59. J. N. D. Kelly, *Golden Mouth: The Story of John Chrysostom: Ascetic, Preacher, Bishop* (Ithaca, N.Y.: Cornell University Press, 1995), p. 4. Kelly also points out that we know these names only through Chrysostom's biographers.

60. *Hom. 2 in Phil.* (PG 62:193): Χριστὸς καταγγέλλεται. οὐκ εἶπε, καταγγελλέσθω; see also his homily *de profectu evangelii* (PG 51:311-20), which treats this variation at length.

61. Michael Compton, "'Let Christ be proclaimed': Philippians 1:18 in Latin and Greek Patristic Exegesis," presented at the AAR/SBL Southeast Regional Meeting, March 1996. I am currently developing that paper into a larger study of Chrysostom's awareness (and often rejection) of Latin exegesis.

62. Jerome, of course, is no stranger to giving or receiving criticism; Kelly (*Golden Mouth*, p. 49) notes that Jerome's *ep.* 22.2 (CSEL 54:146) contains a "scarcely veiled criticism of John's extravagant ranking . . . of the faithful virgin with the Cherubim and Seraphim" in Chrysostom's treatise on preserving virginity: *fem. reg.* 6 (PG 47:527).

63. According to Henry J. Cadbury, *The Making of Luke-Acts* (London: SPCK, 1961), p. 225, the shift from Saul to Paul at Luke 13:9 shows Luke's "sensitiveness to style." That is, Luke deliberately shifts to the Roman name Paul in Acts 13 because this is where Luke begins to narrate Paul's activity among Gentiles. Cadbury likens this transition to the shift from "God-fearers" to "God-worshippers" (up to Acts 13:26 Luke uses φοβέομαι; beginning in 13:43 Luke prefers to use σέβομαι). He also notes that in Acts 9:4 and 22:7 the transliterated Σαουλ, Σαουλ appears; in 26:14, however, when Paul is relating this story to a Gentile, he adds τῇ Ἑβραΐδι διαλέκτῳ, as though apologizing for the barbarism; in a similar way, when Luke has Paul relating to Gentiles God's speech to him in Acts 27:24, God calls him Παῦλε rather than Σαουλ.

changed his name immediately, then Paul's change, and his turn toward the faith, would not have become known. . . . If, immediately upon leaving the Jews, he had come to us after changing his name, no one would have known that the persecutor himself was the evangelist. This was the amazing thing, that the persecutor had become an apostle.[64]

Chrysostom goes on to support this reasoning by citing Galatians 1:21-23:

"I came into the regions of Syria and Cilicia; but I was unknown by sight to the churches of Judea which are in Palestine," he says. And if he was unknown in Palestine, how much more so in other places. "I was unknown by *sight*," he says, not "by *name*." They had only heard that "the one who used to persecute us, now preaches the faith he once tried to destroy." They knew, you see, his earlier name, Saul, and so if, after his change, he was immediately called Paul, and then someone said, "Paul is preaching, the one who persecuted the church," they would not have known that it was he, because he was not called Paul, but Saul. For this reason [the Holy Spirit] allowed him for a time to keep the earlier name, so that [the change] might become clear to all the believers.[65]

I said at the beginning of this essay that Chrysostom's interpretation of the change from Saul to Paul was theological. Here we see that this is so: although Chrysostom does not use the word *synkatabasis* in this passage, the thought is there. The delay in the change of names, like the change of names itself, is a divine act. While the latter shows God's *despoteia*, the former shows God's divine consideration, or accommodation, for our limitations. For Chrysostom, the incarnation is always the prime example of *synkatabasis*, yet he finds other examples constantly, in both the story told in the text and in the text itself.

Chrysostom's interpretation, then, gets the better part of each of the two exegetical traditions discussed. On the one hand, there is a change from Saul to Paul, it is based on the events in Acts 9, and it is a divine act. On the other hand, Chrysostom is a close enough reader of the text to see that the name "Paul" is not introduced until Acts 13:9. There must be a reason for this, and through both a reading of the Epistles and his passion for seeing divine consideration, Chrysostom finds the explanation. The narrative of the

---

64. *Hom. 3 in Ac. 9:1* (PG 51:137; edited).
65. *Hom. 3 in Ac. 9:1* (PG 51:137-38; edited).

Acts of the Apostles should therefore lead us, says Chrysostom, to praise not Paul but God: Δοξάσωμεν τοίνυν τὸν μεταβαλόντα αὐτόν, "Let us glorify the One who changed him!"[66]

Conclusion

We have seen that the Fathers at times anticipate the work of later scholars. The view that Paul always had both names, which approaches a historical certainty, was put forward as early as Origen (or at least as early as Rufinus's translation). The popular view that Saul's name was changed to Paul "on the road to Damascus" (Acts 9) is by no means new, nor is its refutation: John Chrysostom took great pains to show that Scripture does not tell the story this way. In doing so, he declared, centuries before the judgment in the *Patristic Greek Lexicon,* that the popular view that "Saul assaulted" but "Paul paused" was based on a "fanciful etymology." Jerome (and others) note that the name "Paul" first appears in Acts 13:9, just after Sergius Paulus is named, and they decide this is no coincidence. More recent scholars agree that it is not a coincidence but disagree with the "triumphalist" exegesis. Against the triumphalist exegesis, Chrysostom and the scholars of today seem to have the better side of the historical argument: it is much more common for the vanquished to receive a name from the victor, not the other way around.

Few historical-critical scholars, however, would agree with Chrysostom's interpretation of the names Saul and Paul. I would say that this indicates not a flaw of patristic exegesis but a limitation of the historical-critical method. There is no substitute for solid historical-critical scholarship, but there is also need for more. The historical-critical method alone will not allow us to say what John Chrysostom is bold enough to say: Let us glorify the One who changed him!

66. *Hom. 3 in Ac. 9:1* (PG 51:143).

Why the Perfume Mattered:
The Sinful Woman in Syriac Exegetical Tradition

SUSAN ASHBROOK HARVEY

The anonymous Sinful Woman who washed the feet of Christ with her tears, wiped them with her hair, and anointed them with perfumed ointment was a favorite theme of Syriac homilists and hymnographers of late antiquity.[1] While the treatment often blended elements from all three Synoptic versions of the story (Mark 14:3-9; Matt. 26:6-13; Luke 7:36-50), it was the account in Luke 7, set at the house of Simon the Pharisee, which seemed most often to provide the homiletic material.[2] Syriac writers kept a distinction between this anonymous woman and Mary of Bethany, who, in John 12:1-8, performs a similar act that Jesus declares a preparation for his burial. Furthermore, they also did not confuse her with Mary Magdalene.[3] Rather, for Syriac writers the Sinful Woman

---

1. Though Syriac scholars have occasionally remarked upon the sizable body of surviving texts on the Sinful Woman, these texts have seen little scholarly attention apart from the publication of critical editions. For a recent exception, see Hannah Hunt, "The Tears of the Sinful Woman: A Theology of Redemption in the Homilies of St. Ephraim and his Followers," *Hugoye: Journal of Syriac Studies* [http://www.acad.cua.edu/syrcom/Hugoye] 1.2 (1998).

2. The Pharisee is not named as Simon until Luke 7:40 when Jesus addresses him by that name.

3. Victor Saxer, "Les Saintes Marie Madeleine et Marie de Béthanie dans la tradition liturgique et homilétique orientale," *Recherches de science religieuse* 32 (1958): 1-37. Eastern Christianity in general did not associate Mary Magdalene with the Sinful Woman, venerating her instead as one of the myrrh-bearing women who came to Christ's tomb and found he had risen. However, later copyists and editors of the printed editions often added subtitles to the homilies or hymns on the Sinful Woman, identifying her as Mary Magda-

with her alabaster flask of perfumed ointment merited attention in her own right. It is an interesting development in Syriac homiletic literature that, over the course of late antiquity, the center of attention when treating this gospel incident shifts from a focus on the figure of Christ or Christ's interaction with Simon the Pharisee to a focus on the Sinful Woman as a narrative character and, through her perfumed ointment, an approach to Christ.

Syriac treatment of the Sinful Woman raises the issue of literary genres and rhetorical forms in which exegesis might be presented. A number of these homilies and hymns take the form of dialogue poems *(soghyāthā)* or homiletic dramas — a homily or hymn mixing narrated action with substantial interludes of dialogue, whether internally within different characters or externally in exchanges between characters. Dramatic dialogue was a favorite Syriac literary device, and the dialogue poem *(soghîthā)* as a genre had deep roots in ancient Near Eastern tradition.[4] On the topic of the Sinful Woman, these dramatic presentations show significant literary overlap with contemporary hagiography on the popular penitent harlot saints. Here, the line between exegesis and hagiography blurs, and a mode of scriptural explication leads to striking narrative developments.[5]

---

lene (there is an allusion to "seven demons" having followed the woman in Jacob of Serug's homily, although the name "Mary Magdalene" is not mentioned: Jacob of Serug, *Homily 51*, in Paul Bedjan, ed., "On the Sinful Woman Whose Sins Our Lord Forgave," in *Homiliae Selectae Mar-Jacobi Sarugensis* [Paris/Leipzig: Otto Harrassowitz, 1905], 2:408, line 20). The tremendously influential tradition of Mary Magdalene as penitent harlot was a Western development, receiving its first real impetus in the sixth century from Gregory the Great. For an overview, see Susan Haskins, *Mary Magdalene: Myth and Metaphor* (New York: Harcourt, Brace & Co., 1994).

4. See, e.g., Sebastian P. Brock, "Dialogue Hymns of the Syriac Churches," *Sobornost/ Eastern Churches Review* 5 (1983): 35-45; idem, "Dramatic Dialogue Poems," in *Symposium Syriacum IV,* ed. H. J. W. Drijvers, R. Lavenant, C. Molenberg, and G. J. Reinink, Orientalia Christiana Analecta 229 (Rome: Pontificum Institutum Orientalium Studiorum, 1987), pp. 135-47; idem, "Syriac Dispute Poems: The Various Types," in *Dispute Poems and Dialogues in the Ancient and Mediaeval Near East: Forms and Types of Literary Debates in Semitic and Related Literature,* ed. G. J. Reinink and H. L. J. Vanstiphout, Orientalia Lovaniensia Analecta 42 (Leuven: Peeters, 1991), pp. 109-20.

5. Another instance of Syriac exegetical tradition demonstrating a distinctive contribution of its own can be seen in the patristic treatments of Genesis 22 on the sacrifice of Isaac. Here the narrative developments lie in the introduction of Sarah into the biblical episode. Jewish as well as Christian writers explore this gap in the Hebrew text and provide various imaginative scenarios of what her role would have been. As in the instance of the Sinful Woman, however, Syriac writers present a distinctive, and distinctly positive, rendering of Sarah's character and actions in the *aqedah.* See especially Sebastian P. Brock,

In this study, then, I would like to consider the Sinful Woman and her perfume in Syriac tradition from two vantage points, that of exegesis and that of narrative development. For the first, I will survey the homiletic materials with a view to the major exegetical themes that Syriac writers pursue on this topic. For the second, I will turn to the matter of the Sinful Woman and her ointment in Syriac homiletic texts: What is her story? How is she constructed, with what rhetorical features and what theological purposes? Who does she become in the hands of Syriac writers? Why did her perfume play such a prominent role in the homiletic dramas?

The Texts

While a good number of texts specifically on the Sinful Woman are extant in Syriac, the earliest sustained treatment is that of Ephrem Syrus in his magisterial *Homily on Our Lord*.[6] Ephrem has more to say about her elsewhere, but it is the *Homily on Our Lord* where he undertakes extensive consideration of this story.[7] His context is a tour-de-force presentation of Christ as the incar-

---

"Genesis 22 in Syriac Tradition," in *Mélanges Dominique Barthélemy,* ed. P. Casetti, O. Keel, and A. Schenker, Orbis Biblicus et Orientalis 38 (Fribourg, Switzerland: Éditions universitaires; Göttingen: Vandenhoeck and Ruprecht, 1981), pp. 1-30; idem, "Two Syriac Verse Homilies on the Binding of Isaac," *Le Muséon* 99 (1986): 61-129; idem, "Reading Between the Lines: Sarah and the Sacrifice of Isaac (Genesis, ch. 22)," in *Women in Ancient Societies: "An Illusion of the Night,"* ed. Léonie Archer, Susan Fischler, and Maria Wyke (New York: Routledge, 1994), pp. 169-80.

6. Edmund Beck, ed. and trans., *Des Heiligen Ephraem des Syrers, Sermo de Domino Nostro,* CSCO 270 and Scriptores Syriser 116 (Louvain: Secrétariat du Corpus SCO, 1966); English translation in Joseph P. Amar and Edward Matthews, *Ephrem Syrus: Selected Prose Works,* FOTC 91 (Washington, D.C.: Catholic University of America Press, 1994), pp. 269-332.

7. Hunt ("Tears of the Sinful Woman") treats an array of Ephrem's passages on this episode. Most important for the purposes of the present study, however, would be *Hymns on Nisibis* 60, for which see below n. 10; and the *Commentary on the Diatessaron* VII.18, X.8-9, for which see Carmel McCarthy, trans., *Saint Ephrem's Commentary on Tatian's Diatessaron,* Journal of Semitic Studies Supplement 2 (Oxford: Oxford University Press, 1993). For contrast, see Ephrem's treatments on Mary of Bethany in *Hymns on Virginity* 4.11 and 6.7, in Edmund Beck, ed. and trans., *Des Heiligen Ephraem des Syrers, Hymnen de Virginitate,* CSCO 223-24 and Scriptores Syriser 94-95 (Louvain: Secrétariat du Corpus SCO, 1962); English translation in Kathleen McVey, *Ephrem the Syrian: Hymns,* CWS (New York: Paulist Press, 1989), pp. 259-468. The pivotal homily, "On the Sinful Woman," attributed to Ephrem is discussed below.

nate Lord, fully human and fully God. With profound emphasis on the importance of bodily experience as a primary means by which humanity gains knowledge, Ephrem describes Christ as choosing incarnation so that we with our limited intellectual understanding would be able to know God and, further, so that death with its dependence on physical process could be defeated through its own activity. Ephrem follows the account of Luke 7, looking only at the events at Simon's house and emphasizing at all times the actions of Christ. Although Ephrem dissects the inner turmoil of Simon at length, playing upon the interior and exterior actions and conversations of the Pharisee, the Woman remains for the most part a shadowy figure. When highlighted, she is suddenly the shining counterfoil to Simon's lack of understanding, impoverished love, obstinacy, and blindness. She remains silent throughout the events, as in the gospel account, speaking instead with tears, gestures, and movement as she bears witness to the divinity of Christ.

If Ephrem's *Homily on Our Lord* was the first extensive and theologically sophisticated discussion of this episode to appear in Syriac literature, the most influential was a homily "On the Sinful Woman" attributed to him and extant in Greek translation as well as in Syriac; I will refer to it as the "Ephremic homily" throughout this study.[8] This homily was the direct source of a distinctly Syriac contribution to the exegetical tradition on this gospel story, subsequently influencing Greek and medieval Latin writers on the subject as well as other Syriac texts.[9] In the Ephremic homily, the scene shifts altogether, to the events preceding and leading up to the meeting at Simon's house — events placed outside the gospel story. The entire focus is the Sinful Woman, who speaks in the first person through much of the text. Hearing that Christ has

8. *Sermon 4*, in Edmund Beck, ed., *Des Heiligen Ephraem des Syrers, Sermones II,* CSCO 311 and Scriptores Syriser 134 (Louvain: Secrétariat du Corpus SCO, 1970), pp. 78-91; translated into Latin by idem, CSCO 312 and Scriptores Syriser 135, pp. 99-109; English translation by John Gwynn, NPNF 13:336-41. The authenticity of these sermons in general, and this one in particular, remains problematic. Beck's discussion of this sermon (CSCO 312/Scr. Syr. 135, pp. x-xii) demonstrates the uncertainty; cf. Brock, "Dramatic Dialogue Poems," p. 142. For the Greek version, which has important differences in content, see CPG III:3952; F. Halkin, *Novum Auctarium bibliothecae hagiographicae graecae,* Subsidia Hagiographica 65 (Brussels: Société des Bollandistes, 1984), p. 1162d-e.

9. On the medieval influence of this text, see A. C. Mahr, *Relations of Passion Plays to St. Ephrem the Syrian* (Columbus, Ohio: Wartburg, 1942); idem, *The Cyprus Passion Cycle* (Notre Dame, Ind.: University of Notre Dame Press, 1947), pp. 36-38, 50-52. An abbreviated version of the Ephremic homily "On the Sinful Woman" is still sung today by Syrian Orthodox Christians in the daily prayers (following the *Šḥīmo*) at the Soutoro ("Protection," or the office at the end of the day) for Monday. I am grateful to George Kiraz and Thomas Joseph for this reference.

come to dine with Simon, she repents with much inner soul-searching, changes her clothing, takes her money, and goes to the perfume shop to buy the ointment with which she will anoint Christ. At the shop, the perfume seller is shocked by her changed appearance and her extravagant purchase; their dialogue is the first attempt to dissuade the woman from her decisions. Satan then appears in the guise of a former lover and attempts to dissuade her in a heated exchange. Failing to deter her course, Satan hastens to Simon's house where he seeks to prevent her entrance by rousing Simon against her. Again, the woman will not be turned from her purpose. Finally, she obtains her entry and her goal, addressing Christ as she washes and anoints his feet. The episode is brought to an abrupt end with Christ offering praise and forgiveness to her, but reproach and the parable of the two debtors to Simon.

Subsequent Syriac homilies will follow one or the other of these patterns: that is, they will focus either on the episode at Simon's house following Luke 7 or on the events prior to that incident as imaginatively explored in the Ephremic homily "On the Sinful Woman." Often the homilies show influence from both of these patterns, exploring in detail differing moments out of what clearly became an entire narrative scheme that followed the Sinful Woman from the moment when she first heard that Christ had gone to Simon's house, through to the culmination of her redemption at his feet. No homily had to include the whole narrative, but its full course was implied with imagery or allusions that wove individual homilies back to the first two homilies and thence to the larger scheme. If we consider the homilies in narrative order, according to the overall story that developed, we can see how the skeletal gospel episode was filled out to become a mini-saga of its own, with the character of the woman gaining increasing depth and dimension.

Ephrem's *Hymns on Nisibis* 60 had presented a contribution to the story, with a first-person lament by Satan at the loss of those who had been his followers.[10] For the first ten verses, he weeps especially for the Sinful Woman, whose ways, appearance, actions, and understanding have all been changed by her conversion to Christ.[11] Two *soghyāthā*, or dialogue poems, fo-

---

10. Edmund Beck, ed., *Des Heiligen Ephraem des Syrers, Carmina Nisibena II*, CSCO 240 and Scriptores Syriser 102 (Louvain: Secrétariat du Corpus SCO, 1963), pp. 91-93; idem, trans., CSCO 241 and Scriptores Syriser 103, pp. 80-83; English translation by John Gwynn, NPNF 13:212-13.

11. Because of the echoes here with the Ephremic homily, Beck has argued that *Hymns on Nisibis* 60 is evidence for the authenticity of Ephrem's authorship of the homily (CSCO 312/Scriptores Syriser 135, pp. x-xi). However, the similarity in narrative content need not be an indication of authorship; a number of the texts discussed here show clear familiarity with other homilies on the same topic.

cus their action specifically on the exchanges between the Sinful Woman and Satan.[12] In these we find a dramatic presentation of the social and religious pressures that would deter such a conversion, voiced by Satan, as well as unequivocal confidence in the power of divine forgiveness, spoken by the woman steadfast in her decision.

Another homily, by "John," begins with praise for the woman's regeneration and rebirth through grace and then follows her purchase of the ointment and arrival into Christ's presence.[13] Here the homilist weaves back and forth between her transformation prior to her arrival at Simon's house, and her interaction with Christ. The stripping of her finery and putting on of penitential garb before she goes to the house are paralleled in the encounter with Christ by the cleansing and transformation of her soul as well as body that his forgiveness effects.

Jacob of Serug, Homily 51, and three anonymous homilies all focus exclusively on the events at Simon's house.[14] Although making no reference to what might have transpired earlier, these four show influence from the larger narrative scheme. Metaphors, imagery, and thematic patterns resonate with Ephrem's *Homily on Our Lord,* as well as with the Ephremic homily. Yet in sharp contrast to the *Homily on Our Lord,* these homilies place the woman herself at center stage in Simon's house. Her interior thoughts are explored at length, her actions elaborated and ritualized; sometimes she speaks to Christ with words, sometimes wordlessly. She is always the antithesis to Simon, with the contrast drawn along various themes.

Across these homilies, certain theological themes and patterns of imagery recur, although none more resoundingly than that of the power of repentance. Following the model of Ephrem's *Homily on Our Lord,* the authors of all these texts place tremendous stress on healing by Christ as the Divine Physician.[15] The forgiveness of the woman's sins is likened repeatedly to the healing

12. Edited and translated in Sebastian P. Brock, "The Sinful Woman and Satan: Two Syriac Dialogue Poems," *OC* 72 (1988): 21-62. Soghitha I, preserved in West Syrian liturgical tradition, probably dates to between the mid-fifth and seventh centuries; Soghitha II is preserved in medieval East Syrian liturgical texts.

13. Edited and translated in J.-M. Sauget, "Une homélie syriaque sur la pécheresse attribuée à un évêque Jean," *ParOr* 6/7 (1975/6): 159-94.

14. Jacob of Serug, *Homily 51,* in Bedjan, "On the Sinful Woman Whose Sins Our Lord Forgave," pp. 402-28. The three anonymous homilies: F. Graffin, ed. and trans., "Homélies anonymes du VIe siècle: Homélies sur la pécheresse I, II, III," PO 41 (Turnhout: Brepols, 1984), pp. 449-527.

15. A point stressed by Hunt ("Tears of the Sinful Woman"). While not unique to Syriac writers, the imagery of Christ as Divine Physician and Medicine of Life — a term

miracles Christ performed elsewhere: the healing of the blind man, of the paralytic, of the hemorrhaging woman. The healing of body and the healing of soul are thus presented as equivalent acts, both in terms of demonstrating divine compassion for human suffering and in terms of the miraculous power necessary to make them happen. Her sinful condition is rendered a bodily ailment, to be cleansed like leprosy or medicated or cauterized like ulcers.

The contrast between appearance and reality is played upon through multiple oppositions. Christ is seen as human by Simon and the guests, looking with the eyes of the body; but he is seen as divine by the Sinful Woman, who looks instead with the eyes of faith. Simon looks upon the woman and sees a harlot; Christ looks upon her and sees a penitent believer. Simon speaks aloud with respectful words to Christ, while his inner thoughts doubt and do not comprehend. The woman is silent, but by her actions she worships the divine Son. Simon worries about his reputation, and indeed the reputation of Christ, if such a notorious figure is allowed to have audience at his gathering; the woman comes without shame or regard for public opinion. Simon doubts; she is steadfast in her certainty. Simon offers a dinner table laden with rich food but a soul impoverished with lack of love or faith; the woman offers no food but a soul richly laden with love, faith, true virtue, and adoration. Simon thinks he knows who Christ is (a prophet, a human) and what the woman is (a sinner), but the woman truly knows Christ as God and thereby knows her own self to be forgiven, healed, cleansed, and made new.

Other late antique homilies on the Sinful Woman show similar interest in the gospel incident, but without any such narrative developments. John Chrysostom focuses on the account from Matthew 26 rather than Luke 7, so that the house is that of Simon the Leper and the criticism of the disciples is of the wasted money the ointment represents.[16] A Coptic homily attributed to Chrysostom shares with Severus of Antioch, Homily 118, not only the focus on the woman but also philosophical language about the passions and an allegorical reading of the perfume as the virtues of the soul — an interpreta-

---

also commonly used in Syriac for the Eucharist — is one of the most beloved in Syriac tradition. See Robert Murray, *Symbols of Church and Kingdom: A Study in Early Syriac Tradition* (Cambridge: Cambridge University Press, 1975), pp. 89-91, 199-203; Sebastian Brock, *The Luminous Eye: The Spiritual World Vision of St. Ephrem the Syrian*, rev. ed. (Kalamazoo, Mich.: Cistercian Publications, 1992), pp. 40, 99-114. Lynda L. Coon (*Sacred Fictions: Holy Women and Hagiography in Late Antiquity* [Philadelphia: University of Pennsylvania Press, 1997]) has argued that hagiographical texts about female saints particularly emphasize the healing aspect of Christ's ministry, while those about male saints stress the combative aspect of spiritual war against Satan.

16. John Chrysostom, *hom. 80 in Mt.*

tion of perfumed ointments traditional to Greek patristic thought but not otherwise found in the Syriac texts here under consideration.[17] However, the exquisite kontakion by Romanos Melodos on the Sinful Woman draws on the Ephremic homily for its narrative content, emphasizing events before the woman's arrival at Simon's house and engaging the storyline for its dramatic qualities.[18] In particular, Romanos develops the role of the perfume as instrument of agency, epistemological tool, and sacramental indicator. This is a

17. The Coptic homily is edited and translated in Y. 'Abd Al-Masih, "A Discourse by St. John Chrysostom on the Sinful Woman in the Sa'idic Dialect," *Bulletin de la Société d'Archéologie Copte* 15 (1958-60): 11-39. Severus of Antioch's *Homily 118*, "On the Woman Written About in Luke, that is, the Prostitute or the Sinful Woman," is extant only in Syriac (Maurice Brière, ed. and trans., "Les Homiliae Cathedrales de Sévère d'Antioche: Hom. 118," PO 26 [Paris: Firmin-Didot, 1948], pp. 357-74). For the Sinful Woman's perfume interpreted as the perfume of virtues in earlier patristic tradition, see Clement of Alexandria, *Paed.* II.8; and Origen, *Fragments on Luke* 113 (Joseph Lienhard, trans., *Origen: Homilies on Luke, Fragments on Luke,* FOTC 94 [Washington, D.C.: Catholic University of America Press, 1996]. p. 173). Severus, *hom. 118,* pp. 372-74, also interprets the incense of Exod. 30:23-25, 31 as a compound of virtues; so, too, Origen on sacrificial incense, *hom. in Lev. 9.8.* For the paradigmatic allegorical treatments of perfumes, see Origen's and Gregory of Nyssa's commentaries on the Song of Songs.

18. José Grosdidier de Matons, ed. and trans., *Romanos le Mélode: Hymnes,* vol. 3, SC 114 (Paris: Éditions du Cerf, 1965), no. XXI, pp. 13-43. The Ephremic homily circulated in Greek, as cited above in n. 8, but Romanos would also have been familiar with the Syriac themes from his upbringing in Emesa. There continues to be considerable debate about the relationship between Ephrem and Romanos, with polarized views on how much Syriac influence on the great Greek hymnographer there may have been. The most conservative arguments strictly limiting Syriac influence have been made by José Grosdidier de Matons, *Romanos le Mélode et les origines de la poésie religieuse à Byzance* (Paris: Beauchesne, 1977); the strongest case in support of such influence is by William Petersen, *The Diatessaron and Ephrem Syrus as Sources of Romanos the Melodist,* CSCO 466 (Louvain: Secrétariat du Corpus SCO, 1985), and idem, "The Dependence of Romanos the Melodist upon the Syriac Ephrem: Its Importance for the Origin of the Kontakion," *VChr* 39 (1985): 171-87. A perhaps more fruitful approach has been taken by Sebastian Brock, who stresses the fluidity of cultural interaction in a region so deeply bilingual as the late antique Syrian Orient; see his "From Ephrem to Romanos," in *SP* 20 (Leuven: Peeters Press, 1989), pp. 139-51; and idem, "Syriac and Greek Hymnography: Problems of Origin," in *SP* 16 (Berlin: Akademie-Verlag, 1985), pp. 77-81. Romanos was not the only Greek writer to draw upon the Ephremic homily; see ps.-Chrysostom, PG 59, cols. 531-36. R. J. Schork (*Sacred Song from the Byzantine Pulpit: Romanos the Melodist* [Gainesville: University Press of Florida, 1995]) provides a marvelous treatment of the dramatic mode in Romanos's kontakia. However, his discussion and translation of "The Sinful Woman" (pp. 20-21, 77-85) do not mention the Ephremic homily on which Romanos drew for the scene at the perfume seller's shop. See further the discussion below.

complex of functions fully consonant with what is found in the Syriac homilies but that stands in marked contrast to the allegorical language of the soul and its virtues. While his treatment is thoroughly his own, Romanos is here following the Syriac pattern of the larger narrative and thereby belongs in our discussion of this exegetical tradition.

Narrative Ritual, Narrative Knowledge

In the *Homily on Our Lord*, Ephrem's central concern is the reality of Christ's divine nature, made known to us and accessible to us through the tangible humanity of his incarnate person. Ephrem approaches Christ by recalling the experiences through which various biblical figures encountered him, but his primary attention is on Simon the Pharisee who repeatedly fails to understand the identity of his dinner guest. When the narrative focus turns to the Sinful Woman, it is her actions rather than a narrative character, or self, that Ephrem presents, in contrast to his portrait of Simon. What is important about her actions is that they reveal Christ to be who he truly is. Her actions identify Simon's dinner guest not as the prophet Simon had thought but rather as the Lord of Prophets, the Treasury of Healing present and at work in the very midst of Simon's earthly, worldly gathering. By her actions, the woman confesses her Savior:

> Streaming tears immediately announced that they were being shed as in the presence of God. Plaintive kisses testified that they were coaxing the master of the debt to tear up the bill. The precious oil of the sinful woman proclaimed that it was a "bribe" for her repentance. These were the medications the sinful woman offered her Physician, so that He could whiten the stains of her sins with her tears, and heal her wounds with her kisses, and make her bad name as sweet as the fragrance of her oil. This is the Physician who heals a person with the medicine that that person brings to Him![19]

Ephrem delineates the separate elements of her homage — tears, kisses, precious oil — as distinct actions, granting to the woman's behavior a ritual signification. While sequential usage of water (tears), veneration (kisses), and fine oil (anointment) would evoke strong liturgical associations for the audience,

19. *Homily on Our Lord* 44.1; translated in Amar and Matthews, *Ephrem Syrus*, p. 219.

Ephrem insists that the woman's actions superseded liturgical indication because they were offered directly to God's divine self and not, as in institutional religious expression, through the mediating structures of priestly efficacy: "that sinful woman . . . came to God, not to priests, to forgive her debts."[20]

In the Anonymous Homily I, the ritual sense of the woman's actions carried confessional significance as well as liturgical resonance. For by the deliberate ordering of her behavior, the woman confessed Christ to be God incarnate, to be encountered and experienced in both his natures, human and divine. In the words of her prayer, "You would not have become incarnate if You did not want us to know You."[21] As she knelt at Christ's feet, her actions declared the witness her prayer offered in words.[22] These actions the homilist renders into an explicit sacrificial act, with a play on Psalm 50[51]:16-17:

> I do not choose to offer you sacrifice because I know you do not delight in sacrifices. . . . Behold my heart contrite with sorrow: may it be a sacrifice for you; and my thoughts contrite with remorse: may they be acceptable as a whole burnt offering before you. . . . Myself in sorrow I sacrifice before you: receive me! Behold, in the place of my blood, my tears pour forth; in place of skin and hair with burnt flesh, here is the hair of my head spread over your feet, and my lips kiss your footprints. And in place of the priest, I myself make the offering to you.[23]

The force of seeing the woman's actions as ritualistic in a liturgical sense is

20. *Homily on Our Lord* 46.1; translated in Amar and Matthews, *Ephrem Syrus,* p. 322.

21. Anonymous Homily I, sec. 20; PO 41:160-61.

22. Anonymous Homily I, sec. 18-19; PO 41:158-59. In his *Commentary on the Diatessaron,* Ephrem offers a similar explication of the confessional significance of the Sinful Woman's actions. The woman offered her actions to Christ in his human presence with the purpose of seeking his divine blessing. In turn, Christ received her in both her physical and her spiritual conditions, accepting the exterior actions of her body while responding to the interior state of her soul.

> "His humanity was washed by her tears and refreshed, while his divinity granted redemption there and then for the price [of her tears]. Only his humanity was capable of being washed, whereas his divinity alone could expiate sins which were not visible. Through her tears she washed the dust which was on his feet, while he, through his words, cleansed the scars which were on her flesh. . . . He was cleansed of dust, and in return he cleansed her of iniquity." *Comm. Diatess.* sec. X.8; translated in McCarthy, *Saint Ephrem's Commentary on Tatian's Diatessaron,* p. 170.

23. Anonymous Homily I, sec. 22-23; PO 41:460-63.

made clear in the Anonymous Homily III, where the writer points out that the woman's approach to Christ lacked any other redeeming feature. That is, he declares that her love was offered to Christ without the "gifts" one would normally offer in approaching God: fasting, the practice of prayer, bodily penance, continual vigils, prolonged supplications, a life of asceticism and abasement, all of which might have made her pardon justified.[24] Devoid of the practices by which believers ordered their lives and their bodies into acceptable relationship with the divine, the Sinful Woman bypassed the standard mediating structures of religious behavior in an extraordinarily direct approach to the incarnate Lord.

For Jacob of Serug, the entire encounter must be seen as patterned into a eucharistic event. Carrying her perfume, the woman entered Simon's house with a fragrance heralding her holy purpose. Just as a church sanctuary is perfumed with the mingled scents of incense and holy oil (chrism), so did the woman transform the space of Simon's banquet from the mundane to the sacred by the aroma of perfume compounded with fervent intention: "With the fire of her love she kindled her tears like ointment/and the fragrance of her repentance was increasingly sweet."[25] Hence to the scent of ointment rendered holy by the very feet it would anoint the woman added the sacrificial odors of a love that burned so fiercely she herself was transformed into the dual role of sacrificer and sacrificed.

> Weeping was for her a pure censer, and she brought it with her,
> and with groans she kindled it to smoke in the Holy of Holies.
> She was for herself a priest who made petition for forgiveness,
> and willingly with contrition she made sacrifice for reconciliation.[26]

In Jacob's rendering, the fluid meanings of ritual activity are fully explored. In the process of washing Christ's feet, the woman's tears become the baptismal waters, consecrated with the chrism of the oil she had brought. As she herself washed and anointed Christ's feet, she entered into the "second womb of the Holy of Holies," finding herself baptized in the sea of Christ's love as he cleansed and purified her so that she might rise up pure and reborn.[27] Baptism and eucharistic sacrifice converge in Jacob's telling: "Before

---

24. Anonymous Homily III, sec. 53; PO 41:514-15.

25. Jacob of Serug, *Homily 51;* Bedjan, "On the Sinful Woman Whose Sins Our Lord Forgave," p. 411, ll. 20-21.

26. Jacob of Serug, *Homily 51;* Bedjan, "On the Sinful Woman Whose Sins Our Lord Forgave," p. 410, ll. 12-15.

27. Jacob of Serug, *Homily 51;* Bedjan, "On the Sinful Woman Whose Sins Our Lord Forgave," pp. 414-15.

the great flood of holiness she offered herself/And He poured upon her waves of His love that she would be absolved by Him./Her soul offered to the living fire the evilest body/and it kindled in the thicket of her soul and all of it was consumed."[28]

In the examples considered thus far, the perfumed ointment is cited as lending a liturgical air, quite literally, to the woman's actions in her approach to and service of Christ. The ritual associations allow the woman's actions to take on a collective significance, resonating with the liturgical rhythms of ec-clesiastical life whether in a simple village setting or in the grand ceremonial of an urban cathedral. The specific ritual meanings drawn by our homilists lift the woman's approach to Christ out of its unique situation as a gospel story. Instead, her actions are set into a narratively imposed ritual framework that assimilates them into the liturgical involvements of every believer, lay or ordained. She herself, priest and suppliant, prophet and penitent, fulfills mul-tiple roles that comprise the orchestrated interactions of religious practice for the Christian of late antiquity.

Yet what is the purpose of such a ritually oriented presentation of the Sinful Woman's story? Is it simply the commingling of biblical episode with liturgical structure, a frequent if important theme for patristic writers?[29] In the *Homily on Our Lord,* Ephrem had stressed that the woman's actions were significant because of their confessional force, that is, because they indicated and made clear Christ's identity as God incarnate. Thus the Sinful Woman engaged Christ's human existence even while paying homage to, worshipping, and seeking redemption from his divine person. From this perspective, the ritual elements of the woman's actions are important for what they reveal — and their revelatory capacity sheds light on the entire episode, its characters, setting, and actions. Through her ritualized activity, Simon and the Sinful Woman are revealed, and the dinner is shown to be not an occasion for the physical nourishment of the guests but a sacramental gathering for the salva-tion of believers.

In each case the ritual elements of the narrative sequence are held to-gether by reference to the woman's perfumed oil. The sweet scent of spices al-lowed the homilists to invoke the sacrificial image of incense burning, and in antiquity, sacrifice was above all a relational action, binding together human and divine participants, communities and domains both earthly and heav-

---

28. Jacob of Serug, *Homily 51;* Bedjan, "On the Sinful Woman Whose Sins Our Lord Forgave," p. 415, ll. 10-14.

29. The classic work by Jean Daniélou, *The Bible and the Liturgy* (Notre Dame, Ind.: University of Notre Dame Press, 1956), remains an excellent starting point.

enly. Moreover, with the image of fragrance pervading the room as the woman poured out her ointment, the vivid olfactory qualities of invisible yet tangible presence, of unseen yet physically experienced change, pervade the narrative as well. Throughout the ancient Mediterranean world perfume was a signifier of divine presence and transformation. By highlighting the woman's perfumed ointment, our homilists bring into play an imagery of complex associations for ancient peoples that is concrete in its referents yet fluid in its evocations.[30]

Perhaps the most original achievement in this group of homilies is the kontakion by Romanos the Melodist. Clearly drawing from the tradition both of Ephrem and of the Ephremic homily "On the Sinful Woman," Romanos offers a telling of this story that utilizes olfactory experience as its primary frame of reference. Thus he opens his kontakion with the image of the Sinful Woman begging that Christ will "receive this perfume as pleader" and grant forgiveness "from the slime" of her deeds. In his telling, it is in fact the odor of Christ that first attracts the woman:

> When she saw the words of Christ spreading everywhere
>> like aromatic spice
> As they dispensed the breath of life to all the faithful,
> The harlot hated the bad odor of her deeds.[31]

By this concise opening scene, Romanos draws on the whole array of symbolic meanings that smell evoked for the ancient Mediterranean. Sin, mortality, and fallenness are indicated by stench; purity, divinity, and para-

---

30. Béatrice Caseau, *Euodia: The Use and Meaning of Fragrances in the Ancient World and Their Christianization (100-900 AD)* (Ann Arbor: University Microfilms, 1994); Constance Classen, David Howes, and Anthony Synnott, *Aroma: A Cultural History of Smell* (New York: Routledge, 1994); W. Deonna, "EYΩΔIA: Croyances antiques et modernes: L'Odeur sauve des dieux et des élus," *Genava* 17 (1939): 167-263; Marcel Detienne, *Gardens of Adonis: Spices in Greek Mythology,* intro. Jean-Pierre Vernant, trans. Janet Lloyd, new ed. (Princeton: Princeton University Press, 1994); S. Lilja, *The Treatment of Odours in the Poetry of Antiquity,* Commentationes Humanarum Litterarum 49 (Helsinki: Societas Scientarum Fennica, 1972).

31. Romanos, "On the Sinful Woman," strophe 1; Marjorie Carpenter, trans., *Kontakia of Romanos, Byzantine Melodist* (Columbia: University of Missouri Press, 1970), 1:101. I will follow the translation of Carpenter throughout. However, two other fine translations of this homily into English are available: Schork, *Sacred Song from the Byzantine Pulpit,* pp. 77-85; and Ephrem Lash, *St. Romanos the Melodist: Kontakia on the Life of Christ* (San Francisco: HarperCollins, 1995), pp. 75-84.

dise are associated with sweet fragrance. In the "aroma" of Christ's words, the "fragrance of the knowledge of God" (2 Cor. 2:15) spreads abroad, pervading the consciousness of those near and far; in this, fragrance and the experience of it provide an exact analogy for the human experience of the divine — invisible yet tangibly known, uncontainable and ever mobile, transgressive across any boundaries humans might set or see.

Buffeted thus by aromas of competing moral states, the woman agonizes through an internal dialogue that brings her decision to seek her audience with Christ. Anticipating the liturgical pattern her approach will necessarily take, she explains the salvific purpose that brings Christ to Simon's house: "He sets up a table as an altar on which He is laid as a votive offering."[32]

The woman's decision to go is also a decision to take perfume, which she celebrates with the announcement, "as I breathe, I renounce the slime of my deeds" (strophe 5). Here and elsewhere in the hymn, Romanos plays upon the verb *emphuō*, to breathe upon.[33] The verb alludes to the baptismal liturgy in which the candidates renounce Satan as the priest breathes upon them, and also to the passage in John 20:22 when Christ breathes upon the apostles, filling them with the Holy Spirit. Directly, in the following strophe (6), the woman sets up a baptismal context:

> Therefore, I take the perfume and go forward.
>   I shall make the house of the Pharisee a baptistery,
> For there I shall be cleansed of my sin
>   and purified of my lawlessness.
> I shall mix the bath with weeping, with oil and with perfume;
>   I shall cleanse myself and escape
>   from the slime of my deeds.[34]

In a whirlwind, the Sinful Woman storms through the perfume seller's shop, purchasing his most expensive ointment. At Simon's house, she scandalizes the Pharisee into heated exchange with Christ, whose verbal chastisement is swift and fierce upon the obstinate host. Absolving the woman of her past, Christ admonishes, "Behold the harlot whom you see; consider her like the church/crying out: 'I breathe *(emphuō)* on the slime of my deeds.'"[35]

32. Strophe 2; Carpenter, *Kontakia of Romanos,* p. 102.
33. Discussed by Carpenter, *Kontakia of Romanos,* p. 103, n. 6.
34. Strophe 6; Carpenter, *Kontakia of Romanos,* p. 103.
35. Strophe 17; Carpenter, *Kontakia of Romanos,* p. 107.

With this his parting view of the woman, Romanos conjoins the language of exorcism and baptism, breath of life and rebirth, individual believer and ecclesiastical body.

Consider the olfactory sweep of Romanos's hymn: from the moral quality of stench, through the evangelical experience of the "aroma" of Christ's words, to the sacrificial altar, the perfume of love, the anointing of baptismal waters, the exsufflation of exorcism, the breath of life. All this Romanos conveys in the smells that attend the Sinful Woman's experience. In other homilies we have considered, the perfume has been primarily employed as an object that signifies the important ritual qualities of the encounter between the Sinful Woman and Christ. Here in Romanos's kontakion, the perfume matters not only to demarcate religious ritual from social etiquette but also, as a pedagogical tool, to instruct the audience. By attending to the variant qualities of olfactory experience as the homilist draws upon them, the audience is led to a richer understanding of Christ, of the divine-human relationship, indeed of the process of redemption — a process involving change both in one's inner person and in one's external behavior.[36]

With this kontakion, then, we see the perfume carrying an epistemological function as the woman learns of Christ, sees him, hears him, and also experiences him through an encounter that is physical — sensorily distinctive — as well as intellectual and spiritual. In the Anonymous Homily III, the epistemological function of the perfume is turned back onto the woman herself in relation to Christ. As she moves to anoint the feet of Christ,

> The ointment which had made her body sweet she changed, and by the means of Jesus' feet, she caused him to touch her soul and perfume it.
>
> . . . the fragrance of her perfume was sweet, and the repentance she breathed out in her thoughts was even more so, which, for Jesus, was sweeter than any scent.[37]

36. Greek Orthodox Christians sing the Troparion of the Sinful Woman at the Bridegroom Matins for Holy Wednesday during the week preceding Easter. The hymn is not the one by Romanos but that of the ninth-century hymnographer Kassia. For an edition, translation, and commentary see Antonia Tripolitis, *Kassia: The Legend, the Woman, and Her Work* (New York: Garland, 1992), pp. 76-79 (where the editor mistakenly names the Sinful Woman as Mary Magdalene, although the troparion and the service books leave her nameless). This troparion is generally referred to as the Kassiani. Kassia shares with the homilies considered here the tradition of having the woman speak in her own voice, but does not include any reference to the perfume seller or his shop.

37. Anonymous Homily III, sec. 16-17; PO 41:496-99.

Through fragrance the Sinful Woman had engaged her Savior and with rich scents expressed her devotion. So, too, for herself, the odor of her faith revealed her transformed condition, her cleansed spirit and now chaste bodily expressions of love. In these homilies we have seen ritual provide the channel, and perfume the medium, by which the human-divine encounter takes place.

Narrative Character: Exegesis and the Hagiographical Imagination

Thus far we have considered how the interpretive narrative of the Sinful Woman in its differing homiletic expressions provides us with both a ritual context and an epistemological result. There is, however, a more fundamental matter: the narrative character of the Sinful Woman herself, who enacts the drama and seeks to know. The homilies on the Sinful Woman are exactly that: homilies about her, and this narrative focus is what divides them from Ephrem's treatment in the aptly titled *Homily on Our Lord* and indeed from the gospel incident on which the story is based.

In this entire set of homilies, the method of exegesis lies in telling a story. Narrative itself — the playing out of the woman's story — becomes the didactic vehicle rather than the explication of symbols, terms, or the gospel text (as seen, for example, in the treatments by John Chrysostom or Severus of Antioch). From this perspective, we find the woman presented through two further ritual motifs, those of clothing (appearance) and of disputational dialogue (voice), and once again with perfume as the primary signifier of identity, process, and meaning.

As already noted, the Ephremic homily "On the Sinful Woman" is the text in which the woman emerges fully as a character on her own. The homily begins with her inner turmoil in response to the news of Christ's arrival at Simon's house. In a remarkable presentation of unmaking and remaking the self, the homilist then presents her dramatic change of clothing:

These things she inwardly said; then she began to do outwardly. She washed and put away from her eyes the dye that blinded them that saw it. And tears gushed forth from her eyes over that deadly eyepaint. She drew off and cast from her hands the enticing bracelets of her youth. She put off and cast away from her body the tunic of fine linen of whoredom, and resolved to go and attire herself in the tunic, the garment of reconciliation. She drew off and cast from her feet the adorned sandals of lewdness; and directed the steps of her going in the path of the heavenly Eagle.[38]

Her decision made, the woman sets out for the perfume seller's shop. The change in her appearance as well as the lavish sum of gold she presents him cast the perfumer into confused dismay. In consternation he addresses her:

What is this appearance *(schema)* that you show today to your lovers, that you have stripped off wantonness and clothed yourself in humility? Before today when you came to me, your appearance was different than today's. You were clothed in fine raiment and carried little gold, and you sought choice perfume to sweeten your wantonness. And now today, you have filthy garments and you carry much gold. I do not understand your change in how you are dressed. Either wear clothing like your perfume, or buy perfume like your clothing. For this perfume is neither fitting nor right for these clothes.[39]

The scene presents a marvelous confluence of visual and olfactory paradoxes. Previously, the woman had dressed in sumptuous finery, yet worn cheap perfume. Now, clothed in the "sordid weeds of mourning" as Satan describes her soon after (section 6), devoid of jewelry and barefoot, she asks of the perfumer his most exquisite ointment. What to believe: sight or smell? The woman will not be turned from her purpose; with her alabaster jar now filled with the finest scent, she sets forth for Simon's house.

The rhetoric of adornment was a favorite theme in both classical and biblical tradition. Bodily ornamentation was a topos explored at length, involving clothing, fabrics, colors, textures, hairstyles, jewelry, and fragrances variously applied with ointments, pomades, and perfumes. Philosophical tradition, especially Cynicism and Stoicism, had developed a discourse in which self-presentation — and therefore grooming and clothing — carried tremendous significance in the public realm as an expression of one's inner disposition and a life of virtue, adorned with simplicity and in accordance with nature; ornamentation of any kind represented moral depravity on an escalating scale. Early Christian writers turned this tradition to a decidedly gendered discourse, in which it was specifically the female body in its

---

38. "On the Sinful Woman," sec. 3; translated in NPNF 13:337.

39. "On the Sinful Woman," ll. 79-96 (my translation); Beck, *Des Heiligen Ephraem des Syrers, Sermones II,* p. 80 (cf. NPNF 13:337).

adorned state that represented the fallen human condition, fleshly temptations, and wanton lust. For these writers, the philosophical trope combined with profound biblical themes. Clothing was the material expression of Adam and Eve's sin (the "garments of skin" of Gen. 3:21, more often referred to by patristic writers as "garments of shame"). The lasciviously adorned (and perfumed) harlot was a favorite biblical image for the corrupt and faithless life. The frequency with which ancient writers, whether pre-Christian or Christian, employed this imagery only heightened its rhetorical efficacy. Our homilists could use the language of "cosmetic theology" as a concise yet vivid marker of the moral and ultimately salvific transformation in which the Sinful Woman was engaged.[40]

As several of our homilists go to great lengths to point out, every sin, every wrongdoing, every impiety of which humanity is capable is implicated in the crime of the Sinful Woman — that of lust, or desire wrongly directed.[41] The Sinful Woman is hence the greatest of sinners, and, in turn, once repentant, the most powerful measure of the miracle of the redemption possible through Christ's forgiveness. In our homilies, the change in disposition marked by the woman's change in clothing is, at the feet of Christ, rendered complete. For there the woman's body itself is made anew. As the homily by "John" described it, her eyes that had once turned every head now were purified by her tears; her hair that had been a snare for evil was now made new as she used it to wipe Christ's feet; her lips sullied by impure kisses were now sanctified by kissing holy feet; her heart once filled with impudence now poured forth saving penitence.[42]

Perhaps none of the homilies captures the visceral power of this trans-

---

40. Helpful discussions can be found in Marcia Colish, "Cosmetic Theology: The Transformation of a Stoic Theme," *Assays* 1 (1981): 3-14; Maria Wyke, "Woman in the Mirror: The Rhetoric of Adornment in the Roman World," in *Women in Ancient Societies,* pp. 134-51; Coon, *Sacred Fictions,* esp. chs. 2-4. For a typical example of how Syriac writers could combine both the philosophical and biblical rhetoric of clothing, cf. Aphrahat, *Dem.* 6, "On the Bnay Qyama," ed. I. Parisot, *Patrologia Syriaca,* vol. 1, ed. R. Graffin (Paris: Firmin-Didot, 1894), cols. 239-312; trans. J. Gwynn in NPNF 13:362-75. In Syriac tradition, clothing also provided important Christological imagery; see Sebastian P. Brock, "Clothing Metaphors as a Means of Theological Expression in Syriac Tradition," in *Typus, Symbol, Allegorie bei den östlichen Vätern und ihren Parallelen im Mittelalter,* ed. Margot Schmidt, Eichstätter Beiträge 4 (Regensburg: Friedrich Pustet, 1982), pp. 11-40.

41. Especially the Homily by "John," and Anonymous Homilies II and III. It is worth noting that the canonical gospel texts do not specify her sin.

42. "John," sec. 34-38; edited by Sauget, "Une homélie syriaque sur la pécheresse attribuée à un évêque Jean," pp. 180-81; translation on p. 169.

formation more sharply than Anonymous Homily III, when the homilist admonishes Simon the Pharisee directly for his inability to see the Sinful Woman with the eyes of faith.

> You [Simon] saw her as what she was, but [Christ] saw her as what she was not. You saw her as though in darkness, but he saw light while she was in darkness. He beheld her nothingness and made it something. He beheld her defiled and made her holy, in pollution and showed her purified, in prostitution and she became spotless, in debauchery and suddenly she became chaste. Depraved, she was ordered; scattered, she became collected. . . . Immediately when he saw her, he changed her and made her one thing instead of another, something instead of nothing.[43]

From the perspective of narrative character, the emphasis in these homilies lies on the processes by which the self is transformed. The solemn unclothing and reclothing of the Sinful Woman, the shocking change in the quality and purpose of her perfume, the moral renewal of her character as her love is purified by its changed focus — all are means and markers by which the audience, too, is led to see her with new eyes. If her change in clothing marks the first narrative ritual to signify her interior conversion to a life of faith, these homilies employ the literary form of dialogue as a further ritualized activity by which the transformation is wrought.

It is important to appreciate the weight that the narrative element of dialogue would carry in this instance: in every version of this gospel episode, the woman is silent. So, too, when these homilies portray the woman's encounter with Christ at Simon's house, do they emphasize her silence in Christ's presence in opposition to Simon's faithless and duplicitous words. Yet in the narrative expansion of the gospel episode, moving the story beyond the encounter at Simon's house, these homilies one and all grant the Sinful Woman a voice. She speaks repeatedly, first in interior dialogue with herself, then to persuade the doubtful perfume seller, then in argument with Satan in the guise of a former lover, and then in argument with Simon egged on by Satan. These dialogues are effective as mechanisms to enhance the drama of the story for they play every note of emotional and social scandal, paradox, and ultimate triumph this classic theme of epic romance offers — the fallen woman at last redeemed by true love.

These dialogues are also presented with a rigorous formalism that brings the dialogic process itself to the level of ritualized exchange. The woman, the

43. Anonymous Homily III, sec. 21-22; PO 41:500-501.

perfume seller, Satan, and Simon all speak as representatives of theological and social positions. The woman argues for conversion, the efficacy of repentance, the power of redemption, and the unshakable conviction of a faith that defies every rational objection. The male characters argue for the impossibility of such change: past actions and reputation will not allow the woman a new identity; the virtuous would have nothing to do with such a despised person; no one will believe her change; as harlot she had been showered with wealth and luxury — what more could she want? These are caricatured positions, variations on the debate between faith and reason. Although the speeches represent stock positions, they can be employed — as here, in the homilies on the Sinful Woman — with considerable emotional and theological force, an aspect of ancient dialogue or disputation literature well noted by scholars.[44]

In these homilies, the woman's voice in dialogue with herself and others presents the intellectual process to accompany the transformations marked through the sequences of her actions. Dialogic discourse in this instance allows a profound coordination between literary form, theological content, physical medium (certainly in the case of the two anonymous dialogue poems and the kontakion of Romanos, which would have involved antiphonal choirs), and the ritual location of their presentation in the liturgy where the homilist stands in interaction with choir, other clergy, and the congregation. Conflicting and perhaps even irreconcilable positions can be necessarily held together, in tension or in an evolving resolution, by the literary form of dialogic presentation and its ritual performance in the liturgical setting.[45] In the homilies on the Sinful Woman, the dialogues serve to convey the process of transformation — and thereby to enact the very nature of redemption — by their combined literary and ritual (liturgical) employment. In the narrative sequence, once the woman has made her decision to change, each dialogue is initiated in response to the sight of the woman carrying her alabaster perfume box. The perfume serves, repeatedly, to prompt the dialogues as a series of contests the woman must win to gain her entrance to Christ. From this perspective, what makes the perfume important is not its ritual associations

---

44. See above, n. 4; and further: Gregory W. Dobrov, "A Dialogue with Death: Ritual Lament and the [θρῆνος θεοτόκου] of Romanos Melodos," *Greek, Roman, and Byzantine Studies* 35 (1994): 385-405; Margaret Alexiou, *The Ritual Lament in Greek Tradition* (Cambridge: Cambridge University Press, 1974); Reinink and Vanstiphout, *Dispute Poems and Dialogues in the Ancient and Mediaeval Near East,* esp. Averil Cameron, "Disputations, Polemical Literature and the Formation of Opinion in the Early Byzantine Period," pp. 91-108.

45. A point made with particular clarity by Dobrov, "Dialogue with Death." Compare Alexiou, *Ritual Lament,* pp. 131-60.

or its epistemological significance but rather its cultural symbolism as marking immoral adornment or proper expression of love.

In developing the character of the Sinful Woman, these texts present a method of biblical interpretation that is much more closely aligned with hagiography than with exegesis, for they present yet another version of the penitent harlot story, a favorite devotional theme in hagiographical and monastic literature (as in biblical narrative).[46] In particular, the similarities between the Ephremic homily "On the Sinful Woman" and the tremendously popular vita of Pelagia of Antioch merit closer attention. The descriptions of the clothing of harlotry and the clothing of penitence and the sequence of dialogues (including the dialogue with Satan as a former lover) are strikingly parallel.[47] For these homilies, it is the narrative force of the story that provides the mechanism for explicating the meaning of the gospel episode. They offer us another form of narrative theology.

Yet if these homilies offer us exegesis by way of story, what is the story they tell? In a basic sense, they tell the story of the human capacity for change and the redemptive power of divine love. They tell a story that reduces to a threefold action: the woman's decision to repent, her approach to Simon's house, her confession of faith at the feet of Christ. Decision — approach — confession; or, conversion — rebirth — communion. Surely this threefold action is no more and no less than the sacramental process of Christian life, in which repentance leads to the renewal of the baptismal process, the casting off of the old self and putting on of the new, and the fulfillment of eucharistic worship in the reception of Christ's body. The Sinful Woman's story, then, was presented as every Christian's story in its simplest outline and its liturgical enactment. All this we know from the Syriac tradition on the Sinful Woman, a story in which perfume no less than person mattered.[48]

46. See the important discussions of this motif in Coon, *Sacred Fictions;* and Benedicta Ward, *Harlots of the Desert: A Study of Repentance in Early Monastic Sources* (Kalamazoo, Mich.: Cistercian Publications, 1987).

47. For the textual versions, see Pierre Petitmengin, ed., *Pélagie la Pénitente: Métamorphoses d'une légende,* 2 vols. (Paris: Études Augustiniennes, 1981). An English translation of the Syriac version may be found in Sebastian P. Brock and Susan Ashbrook Harvey, *Holy Women of the Syrian Orient,* rev. ed. (Berkeley: University of California Press, 1998). The legend of Pelagia may be based on a reference by John Chrysostom to a well-known prostitute of Antioch who reformed herself and ended her life as a penitent recluse; *hom. 67 in Mt.*

48. An earlier version of this paper was presented at Syriac Symposium III, University of Notre Dame, Notre Dame, Indiana, June 1999. I am grateful to the participants for their helpful discussion.

A Key for the Future of Patristics:
The "Senses" of Scripture

CHARLES KANNENGIESSER

A Preliminary Question: Is There a Future for Patristics?

The end of Western Modernity, as a historically defined period like the Latin Middle Ages, the Reformation, and the eighteenth-century Enlightenment, is marked by an orbital shift into what may be provisionally called "Globality." Benefiting from a planet-wide marketplace and an integrated communication system, "Globality" asks less that nations, countries, or individuals be turned toward their own past in self-centered affirmations of their identity than that they develop their capacity to communicate with each other. Instead of remaining focused on their origins, the contemporary identity quest is directed toward the future as the most promising horizon for an adequate reshaping of the inner self. It would be worth plumbing such basic considerations for their own sake, as a sort of postscript to the modern philosophy of the self, but here they form just a preamble to my remarks on the present and future status of patristics, for patristics, like Christian scholarship as a whole, testifies to the metamorphosis of the Western self-understanding at the start of a new millennium.

On the documentary level, patristics represents a discipline of historical inquiry with a wide-open future because so much still needs to be explored about the emergence of the foundations of Christianity. Despite the philolog-

This essay was suggested to me by Robert Wilken's delightful article "*In Dominico Eloquio:* Learning the Lord's Style of Language," *Communio* 24 (1997): 846-66. It also pays tribute to twenty years of fruitful scholarly companionship.

ical labor of nineteenth-century scholars together with the brilliant success of patristics, particularly in the second half of the twentieth century, a vacuum of critically established data is still encountered in all corners of the field of patristics. Indeed, while many editorial programs of primary sources are in full progress, as is the case for the Sources Chrétiennes series heading towards its five-hundredth volume, or for its German sister-series, Fontes Christiani, others are barely at their initial stages. Many projects of collective works are only now gaining momentum at this, the threshold of the information age. In short, the inner dynamic of patristic historical research in the field of late antiquity seems to warrant further substantial achievements in the next two generations of scholars. Hence, though dependent on the continuing quality of commitments in the present, the future of patristics is well secured.

On a more ideological level, preconceived options determine the very basis for documentary resources in patristics. The very goals of such studies are defined from ideological viewpoints. Hence, it looks as if today's experts are often entering upon uncharted territory. To venture a parallel, let me suggest that crossing into the twenty-first century of the Christian era is perhaps a more perilous adventure in regard to the ideological relevance of patristics than it was for the patristic traditions themselves entering the seventh century, where these traditions were to experience, in Averil Cameron's words, "the most profound crisis and transformation in their entire history."[1] In the seventh century, patristic scholarship was losing most of its imperial territory, due to the conquest of Byzantine provinces by Islam. In addition, it was undermined by political and religious dissent, and it was more and more cut off from its own classical foundations. On an even broader scale, the same seems to be happening to patristics at the start of the third millennium: it has lost the institutional territory of its traditional status; it has (or claims to have) given up any reliance on politico-religious apologetics, which served as a priority long before, and even more so after, the Reformation. Finally, patristics no longer has much of a direct access to the classical foundations of culture and church in which it is the most interested.

Yet here ends the parallel. Today's real crisis in patristic scholarship, in all countries and on all levels of its engagement, has to do with doubts about its own relevance. At the recent Patristics Conference in Oxford, August 1999, I had the irrepressible feeling of participating in an event still significant and spectacular (and certainly more costly than ever) but without a soul, without

---

1. Averil Cameron, "Byzantium and the Past in the Seventh Century: The Search for Redefinition," in *Le septième siècle: Changements et continuités,* ed. J. Fontaine and J. N. Hillgarth (London: The Warburg Institute, 1992), p. 250.

a vision that would have secured a common purpose for the hundreds of specialists gathered together. If such a purely subjective impression possesses a measure of truth, it might well be related to a distinctive feature of contemporary culture — a divorce from its own past, or an incapacity to assume that past and to integrate it into its own creative dynamics.

It may sound paradoxical to suggest that patristic scholars can be affected by such a deficiency, since their whole expertise is turned toward the past. However, they share with their contemporaries a common awareness of the end of Modernity, an end that entails a decisive distancing from the millennia-old inheritance of classical culture. In the life span of only one generation, they are witnessing the very end of the so-called Age of the Humanists, which, thanks to the pre-World War II curriculum of its secondary schools, had provided for Western boys and girls a genuine familiarity with classical antiquity. Again, patristic experts in the recent past have eagerly adopted electronic procedures for the treatment of texts and the analysis of written documents, quite aware of the fact that the new technologies may well cause people to dispense with the traditional art of extensive reading of ancient sources. In other words, there are sufficient grounds for the suspicion that even patristic scholars find themselves cut off from the very past on which they focus by profession. So great is the intellectual turmoil caused by the Western shift from Modernity to Globality that any form of historical inquiry needs to redefine its own relevance.

It was a challenge and a survival reflex for seventh-century scholars to fabricate *catenae* of patristic sources, those exegetical, theological, or spiritual *florilegia* illustrating the traditions behind them. In the same way, it is a fundamental challenge for scholars entering the twenty-first century (while continuing to process the patristic sources for their own sake, as has been done since the nineteenth century) to evaluate the significance of the *reception* of these same sources. Without such a study of tradition reception, the very motivation for studying the sources gets lost in the ideological context of today. A dramatic example of a contemporary retrieval of classical and postclassical antiquity is given by the gigantic Festschrift for Joseph Vogt of Tübingen, entitled *Aufstieg und Niedergang der römischen Welt*. Such monuments of scholarship, by their recapitulative mode, signal the end of postclassical times and illustrate the awareness of a common urge in today's intellectual culture to explain the ending of Modernity by summarizing Modernity's own past. Without such a critical retrieval, there should be no surprise if those same experts lacked vision and, hence, a real future.

Happily enough, most of them now avoid that narrow, erudite specialization of the kind that afflicted Byzantine scholarship, closing itself up in its own intensity and agonizing obsessively in its inner conflicts, when surrounded by the offensive of Islam. Such is not the case for patristic experts of today. Despite the broad disarray they share with large sectors of contemporary intelligentsia, patristic scholars not only turn the page on Modernity but, insofar as history-in-the-making gives them a chance to perceive it, they deliberately turn the *skopos* of their research toward the future.

The Outcome of the Twentieth Century

The study of the Fathers today generates many derivative trends of research, belonging to a variety of historical subdisciplines, such as the history of the arts in Late Antiquity, social history, feminism, and so forth. It may also limit itself to a strictly philological level; or it may give occasion to contextual studies of Late Antiquity in regard to politics, economics, philosophical ideas, religious institutions, and more. The vitality of a specific discipline of research always affirms itself in opening unexpected and highly diversified avenues of inquiry, in the same way as it benefits from the concern for its core interests shown by other intellectual disciplines. However, in all the ecclesiastical or secular settings where it operates, the proper science of patristics applies, by definition, to the thought and the fate of the so-called Christian "Fathers." Its essential purpose is to interpret that thought and to discuss that fate. Hence, even when some of its practitioners lack a Christian commitment, patristics needs to keep to its truth, and to be recognized as an ongoing interpretation of Christian origins. To give an account of such a complex phenomenon is in itself a formidable and fascinating challenge. However, to turn that account into a significant report or a message of hope for contemporary readers is even more demanding. It calls for a kind of militant response that is not always compatible with the objective serenity and the patient investigations needed for scholarly work.

In the twentieth century, patristics underwent a major transformation comparable only to the unprecedented initiatives taken at the same time in biblical studies. The collapse of traditional dogmatism in Anglican, Protestant, and Roman Catholic schools of theology rekindled in many Christian scholars a genuine interest in the study of traditional beliefs. From the standpoint of more empirical investigation, people and events linked with the early stages of the Christian movement were finally given a chance to speak for themselves. In reality, fewer preconceived categories were imposed on them than was the case with former dogmatic apologetics. The burgeoning success of patristic scholarship during the second half of the twentieth century is linked with the liberating effect produced by the receding tide of dogmatism. This sea change was also effected by patristic expertise becoming much more secular, instead of remaining monastic and clerical, especially within the Roman Catholic tradition. In the light of such structural changes in the discipline, close parallels between patristics and biblical studies need to be reconsidered. It has always been a central concern for people interested in the Fathers to understand how early Christians interpreted Scripture. For the sake of confessional apologetics, or simply to describe the doctrine of ancient authors, patristic exegesis was a top priority at all times, starting with the exegetical *catenae* popularized from the end of the sixth century.

My present focus is limited to examining which new trends conditioned the close encounter of patristic research with biblical studies in recent decades. How did the inherent reciprocity of these two disciplines exercise its inventive power during the twentieth century throughout the changes of methods and viewpoints in each of them? Some studies of intellectual history have appeared on that issue; more will certainly follow as ideological breakthroughs in the field display their full consequences. Here I shall only sketch a few salient aspects of the mental process by which experts in patristics and Scripture found themselves exposed to the same challenges, a fascinating process indeed. In my view this process should guide us to further possible contributions of patristics in the new millennium, on the three levels of reality on which theological identity has been tested during the twentieth century, namely, the levels of church, culture, and history. My conclusion will address what is, to my mind, the decisive issue at stake for the relevance, the dynamism, and the renewal of patristic studies in the future.

Church

On both sides of biblical studies and patristics, the canonical nature of Christian traditions has been a matter of lively discussions. Hans Freiherr von Campenhausen offered a clear summary of the patristic questions in the debate about "the Formation of the Canon."[2] Breaking its bonds with post-Hegelian and liberal Protestant views of the nineteenth century, as well as with the juridical and canonistic mindset of Roman Catholic scholasticism,

---

2. In the 1960s, in Strasbourg, he mentioned to me that he was proud to attend the regular meetings of Protestant biblical and patristic experts of Germany always held, as he observed with a twinkle in his eyes, in a *German* city. See von Campenhausen's classic study, *The Formation of the Christian Bible*, trans. J. Baker (Philadelphia: Fortress, 1972).

the very notion of the "canon" certainly deserved reformulation. After many debates, the notion itself was infused with a new sense of the vital link between Scripture and Church community. The codified sacredness of both scriptural testaments was no longer recognized as a mark of divine authority, supposedly imposed by an unverifiable, transcendent power; it was now linked more explicitly with the faith experience of the Church community. Historical clarifications, the result of decades of philological labor, emphasized the meanders, misgivings, dead-ends, but also the creative impulses and the ingenious continuity, through which second-century Christianity forged a biblical foundation centered on the gospel message.

Biblical scholars were quick to apply that same *Problematik* to the scriptural tradition in biblical Israel. Against the imposing background of Old Testament studies accomplished by former generations, mainly in Germany and Great Britain, they pressed beyond the research into the sources of biblical writings, explaining their composition and significance. They began to explore the reception of Hebrew Scriptures by subsequent generations of readers in biblical Israel and to analyze the process by which older writings gave birth to newer ones within the biblical tradition. The rhetorical procedures and the social modalities of a living tradition appeared at once conditioned by unpredictable circumstances, and at the same time enriched by a certain continuity of thought and language. Thus, on both sides, in biblical Israel or in the Church, the active role of the faithful community moved to center stage. One major divergent conclusion was expressed by Old Testament scholars who argued that there had never been a proper notion of a "canon" at work in biblical Israel, and that therefore such an authoritative notion needed to be considered as belonging exclusively to the Christian Church. More recently, Brevard Childs has reactivated the canonical debate with his strong affirmation of the significance of canonicity for the way Scripture is interpreted in the Church. His Barthian-style reaction also underlines the unavoidable connections between the question of the canon and patristic presuppositions concerning the very notion of Scripture itself. Childs' argument leads to the conclusion that the *canon* of Scripture, being organically bound to the life of the Church community, imposes on biblical exegesis a *canonical* interpretation, whose criteria would be determined by the communitarian Church consensus. On the very nature, or even the possibility of that consensus, all positions remain open.

In line with that ongoing discussion about the canon of Scripture, the next generation will inherit a notion of biblical exegesis rooted once again in a more ecclesiological awareness. For over two hundred years debates and controversies enclosed biblical studies ever more within the academia of the theological establishment in order to produce an adequate response to the rationalistic enlightenment of the seventeenth and eighteenth centuries. In recent decades, however, Christian academics themselves began to call biblical studies back home to the Church. As the hermeneutical criteria of "history of tradition" and "history of reception" were introduced into the study of Scripture, the link between writings and the community of readers was increasingly identified as part of the canonical value and the vital relevance of the writings. Such a renewed community awareness turned the attention of biblical scholars to the Church community itself, in which the Bible enjoys an innate familiarity with the traditions of its unique homeland.

Culture

In reaction to nineteenth-century schools of thought, like the school of "history of religions" from which Rudolf Bultmann took some of his views, or the trend of liberal Protestantism denouncing the loss of the genuine message of the gospel in the interaction between Church and pagan culture during the early stages of Christian history, Adolf von Harnack (d. 1930), a true giant as a patristic scholar, together with many of his contemporaries, such as Theodore Mommsen or Hans Lietzmann, concentrated on the problem of the biblical inculturation inside the Christian movement. Despite a negative prejudice inherited from the early days of the Reformation, by which they saw the "pure gospel" perverted and adulterated in its Hellenistic translation into the cultural idioms of pagano-Christian communities, these scholars inaugurated an extraordinarily fruitful line of research. To the present day, the program of "Antike und Christentum" has harnessed new energies. It has constantly widened its field and sharpened its critical treatment of the data under scrutiny. By integrating the comparative history of religions with a strict conformity to philological and historical criticism, and in contemplating any element of the Christian reality in the light of the cultural world of Late Antiquity, Theodor Dölger, with his collaborators and successors, down to the present-day team headed by Ernst Dassmann, secured a new basis for a fundamental debate about the truth of the gospel in the traditions of the ancient Church.

For in patristic traditions the truth of the biblical message exercised its power in two complementary directions: on one side, it effected, not without some amazing twists, its own "hellenization," which some leading historians of the early twentieth century deplored from their confessional viewpoint; on the other side, and much more obviously, it achieved a thorough "Christianization" of Hellenistic thought. The Septuagint, as received in the Church, was a Greek version of the Hebrew original (*pace* Jerome). A Hellenized Bible prevailed in Church traditions, not only on the linguistic level, including through early translations in Latin, Syriac, and other oriental languages, but, much more, on the interpretative level of systematic thought. What I have called "biblical inculturation" thus represents simultaneously a transfiguration of late antique culture in terms of the Bible, and a genuine metamorphosis of the truth of both Testaments in the discourse of Late Antiquity.

Any reception history of classical sources is by definition a history of culture. If the Bible represents the classic *par excellence* in the Judaeo-Christian tradition, its *raison d'être* can only be correctly identified as integrating Christian culture. In admitting "reception" as a hermeneutical category, biblical exegesis engages in a hundred and eighty degree turn from an etiological standpoint to a future-oriented study of Scripture. For instance, an exegete, *qua* exegete, would demonstrate how New Testament data anticipated Tertullian's teaching on baptism, instead of limiting his or her interest to water rituals inside the Transjordanian Baptist movement at the time of Jesus. The ecclesial relevance of Johannine and Synoptic traditions would enhance the exegete's conclusions in this matter. Probably more than one generation of experts will be needed, should such a U-turn happen on the highway of well-established academic exegesis. But, as I noted previously, that establishment itself is now in search of its reunion with the reality of community life in the Church. A positive and theologically inspiring identification of Christian faith, resting on its biblical foundation, but understood in cultural terms, remains a challenge for generations to come. The twentieth century has at least provided a preparatory stage for it.

History

In the twentieth century, history has been disrupted by two horrendous world wars. Again and again, history in its meaningful continuity was negated by massive slaughter, annihilating whole populations, from the Armenian genocide of 1917 to "ethnic cleansing" in the former Yugoslavia in the 1990s. In a gruesome materializing of apocalyptic imagery the atomic bomb of 1945 demonstrated the vulnerability of history. Philosophers speculated on the "end of history," and the systematic theologian Wolfhart Pannenberg insisted that the "end" had actually happened a long time ago with the resurrection of Jesus.

With even more conceptual vigor, Karl Barth, in what may well be considered the climax of all Christological investments in twentieth-century systematic theologies, proposed a notion of divine incarnation totally alien to the normal conditioning of history. His acute sense of the radical transcendence of the divine Logos (despite his abundant commentary on the divine incarnation) eventually ignored the humanity of Jesus as a humanity produced by history, making history, and at the same time being hardly aware of history.

To a younger generation, it soon became clear that history is more than an episodic staging for an affirmation of the incarnation of the Word. If Christian faith centers on such a mystery, it centers on a divine revelation operated within history itself, for in human reality one can hardly dissociate nature and history. God cannot have assumed nature, unless at the same time he assumed history. Thus history has replaced cosmology as *the* framing category for Christian faith, in particular for Christian exegesis of sacred Scripture. However, just as biblical studies needed to go a long way before overcoming the rationalistic historicism of the nineteenth century, so too patristic studies still linger in the painstaking analysis and discussion of data required by historicist scholarship. Current theology often appears still to ignore the need for a historical approach to its controversial issues. Nevertheless in the Western development of Christian theology, the twentieth century shall remain the century that introduced history into the very core of Christian thinking.

The immediate repercussions of that epochal change of mindset were especially dramatic in Old Testament and New Testament exegesis. After some admirable syntheses of so-called "biblical theology," produced by leading exegetes of the early twentieth century, works in which the groundbreaking advances of earlier philologists and historians reached a broader public, the time came for a critical deconstruction: the "Old Testament" was seen as an arbitrary imposition on Hebrew Scriptures; the New Testament was confiscated by the Jesus Seminar or atomized by similar methodologies. In systematic theology, the last Christological controversy of a traditional type occurred in the 1950s, when Hans Urs von Balthasar and Karl Rahner engaged in an intense debate on the burning issue of the day concerning the human and/or divine consciousness of Jesus. Rahner had the final word in stating that the debate was irrelevant and that speaking about a "divine consciousness" was an oxymoron! The subsequent Christologies "from below" and the "death-of-God" theologies only popularized the tacit admission by the experts of a general collapse of Christian dogmatism in the grand style.

Such a revolutionary shift could never have been imagined in earlier Christian traditions. It opened for patristics, at least in the Western Christian context, a unique chance to free itself from its academic confines as an auxiliary discipline subservient to the discipline of Church history. It challenged patristic specialists to participate again in the theological conversation on a broader systematic level. In tandem with biblical exegesis, which for a long time had already detached itself from any dogmatic superstructure, patristics allowed a new critical vision of the emergence and consolidation of such superstructures in the ancient Church, thereby sharpening an awareness of the transformative power of Scripture within the cultural model of Late Antiquity.

In regard to the dogmatic vacuum experienced by contemporary believers, patristics provided indispensable paradigms for new forms of creative thinking. Indeed patristic scholars emphasized that there has never existed anywhere else in Christianity a foundational dynamic comparable to what was achieved in Graeco-Latin Late Antiquity. The cultural and ideological figure of Christian reality resulting from that unique achievement may be called the "third temple," following the first temple of Solomon, and the second, postexilic temple. Just as the ruin of the first temple resulted in the written production of the Torah for the benefit of a new kind of Israel, obedient to the Law, and just as the ruin of the second temple was followed by the written production of the New Testament as a cornerstone for the Christian Church, so does the institutional death of dogmatism at the end of the second millennium of Christianity announce a new hermeneutical status for sacred Scripture.

Only in patristics are we introduced into the arena of creative interpreters of the Bible, whose work became foundational for the reception of the Bible for millennia. Paradoxically, only from the Fathers do we learn how to read Scripture in *our* own intellectual culture, as they learned to read it in *theirs*, and so now to reach within the Church a hermeneutical consensus based on a genuine creativity of our own. Such was their achievement, such will be the dream of future scholars, if only the new explorers of Christian origins follow the path traced out by biblical exegetes, heading toward the hermeneutical conversion needed for new foundations of Christianity.[3]

A Prospective Key: The Debate about "Senses of Scripture"

The key for a balanced prospective concerning the future of patristics lies in a proper appreciation of the true value of patristic hermeneutics. The cultural

3. These first two sections benefit from an oral presentation sponsored by Pauline Allen in 1999 at the Centre for Early Christian Studies, Australian Catholic University, Michelton, Queensland.

imagination and the peculiar logic of the Fathers paved the way for an under-standing of Scripture that contributed like no other factor to the birth of me-dieval and modern Europe. Despite modern materialism and consumerism, in its spiritual identity today the West continues to feed on values of a patris-tic origin, even if only a very few Westerners still know of the existence of the Fathers, and many reject those same values. Should scholars succeed in reach-ing the ground of the contemporary implications of the patristic interpreta-tion of Scripture, they would be in a position to emulate the creativity of the Fathers, that is, to articulate the truth of the Bible beyond the obsolete secu-rity of the "third temple."

The Debate over Henri de Lubac

Let us then focus on only one issue in that context, namely, the theory of the scriptural senses, brought to the worldwide attention of scholars by Henri de Lubac's work on Origen of Alexandria, *Histoire et esprit,* published in 1950.[4] In de Lubac's penetrating analysis it became clear not only that the "historical sense" of Scripture, namely, its literal meaning duly submitted to a text-critical revision and explored in its content, was compatible with a "spiritual" inter-pretation, capable of catching the universal message of the text interpreted, but also that the *littera* properly calls for the *spiritus,* and that no *littera* makes any sense without its intrinsic *spiritus.* Applied on a larger scale of reception history, de Lubac's initial intuition fructified in a multi-volume study of *Exégèse médiévale* published between 1959 and 1963.[5] I was privileged to be-come an indentured servant of de Lubac in the summer of 1958 to prepare the indices for the first two volumes of *Exégèse médiévale.* The immediate contro-versy surrounding de Lubac's ideas has faded away mainly because a younger generation has neglected to read his compact volumes. Should these volumes return to the limelight, undoubtedly they would again provoke strong reac-tions in the scholarly community, and the patristic theory of the senses of Scripture would reclaim its position as a central issue to be debated among specialists of ancient Christianity, as was the case from 1950 to 1970.

4. Henri de Lubac, *Histoire et esprit: L'intelligence de l'Écriture d'après Origène* (Paris: Aubier, 1950).

5. Henri de Lubac, *Exégèse médiévale: Les quatre sens de l'Écriture,* Théologie 41, 42, 59 (Paris: Aubier, 1959, 1961, 1964). The first volume has appeared in an English translation by Mark Sebanc as *Medieval Exegesis: The Four Senses of Scripture,* Ressourcement series (Grand Rapids: Eerdmans, 1998).

De Lubac convincingly demonstrated that the notion of scriptural senses pervades the whole commentary on Scripture achieved in the early Church. He pointed to Origen as the promoter of a form of exegesis that was to perdure through centuries, based as it was on the distinction between *histoire,* the historical narratives of the Bible in their historical content, and *esprit,* the spiritual power of biblical narratives endorsing Old Testament characters as "types" normative for New Testament exegesis. In de Lubac's perspective, allegorism was perceived as the indispensable requirement for the Christocentric reading of Scripture, causing no artificial distortion of the meaning of Scripture but offering the ultimate vision of why the very letter of the Bible had been written as it was.

A confrontation between different exegetical perspectives was inevitable because of de Lubac's emphasis on allegorism and contemporary biblical exegesis's exclusion of allegorism from the scientific compass. The same French Jesuit who, since before World War II, had strongly defied the neo-scholastic conservatism of Roman theologians in matters of systematic theology was now facing the quasi-unanimous disapproval of biblical scholars. In both cases his kind of avant-garde critical edge brought him into conflict with conventional thinking, but in the case of *Histoire et esprit,* his vision of Origen's exegesis prevailed, and a broad discussion developed around the notion of scriptural senses. However it was a debate that was heavily burdened by theological presuppositions, with the participants inevitably locating themselves in one or the other theological camp. Now that all passions in the matter have died down, one still appreciates the remnants of the past controversy, namely, the vast literature about the literal sense and the different aspects of the spiritual sense in patristic exegesis.

With the discussion following the publication of the first two volumes of *Exégèse médiévale* it also became more and more obvious that the very construct of patristic "senses of Scripture" was indeed a *medieval* product resulting from the Western *reception* of patristic exegesis in the monastic culture until the end of the Middle Ages.

The Theoretical Construct of the "Senses"

First, there is a need to stress two distinctive marks of the theoretical construct popularized during the past fifty years: (1) the conviction that "senses" are equivalent to methods of interpreting; and (2) the belief that such methods are imposed by Scripture itself.

In the 1950s a methodological approach was common to patristic and biblical scholars. The notion of *typos* and the method of typology were a matter of lively debate among biblical scholars before becoming a burning issue for patristic scholarship, with the effect that five times more publications on the issue came out of biblical-critical studies than out of patristic studies in this period. In a consideration determined by methodology, the focus is on the interpreter who generates and imposes given methods. Patristic authors are then questioned on their capacity to handle methods of interpreting and on whether they are consistent, inventive, or passively conformed to tradition. Interpretive traditions are identified over longer periods of time, bound to influential role models, or to local "school" requirements. The rhetorical and philosophical culture of Antioch inspired the local masters of biblical exegesis with a sense of the value of historical Old Testament narratives, which was different from the treatment of such narratives taught to Christian exegetes on the basis of Philo of Alexandria's legacy. In any case, the methodological study tends to focus on the procedures of patristic interpreters in a *descriptive* mode, as if the analytical deconstruction and reconstruction of ancient exegesis could give it a chance to come back to life.

In addition to establishing an equation between senses of Scripture and methods of interpretation, the theoretical construct of the past five decades, being a *theological* construct, included also the basic assumption that the "senses" were actually imposed by Scripture itself. In the case of the literal sense, the traditional canonization of the biblical text entailed an unshakable fixity of its literal content. To study the literal sense of a given passage was to pay tribute to that content: in other words, to verify its correctness by some text criticism, to make an inventory of its elements by etymological, grammatical, or historical inquiries, but only with the purpose of consolidating and clarifying its fixed literality in order to secure its right reception. When contemplating the spiritual sense, the patristic exegetes fundamentally shared the same attitude. Henri de Lubac, as much as Hans Urs von Balthasar or Jean Daniélou, found patristic exegesis legitimated by Scripture itself when dealing with the so-called spiritual sense. De Lubac polarized his whole understanding of the "senses" on Paul's observation ἅτινά ἐστιν ἀλληγορούμενα (Gal. 4:24). De Lubac claimed that Origen's paradigmatic construct of the spiritual senses of Scripture derived essentially from that Pauline observation. On his side, Jean Daniélou never tired of showing that patristic typology proceeded from an exegetical practice at the core of the New Testament itself.

The general view in the mid-twentieth century was that, far from betraying or corrupting the true meaning of Scripture, the patristic commentary actually magnified that meaning, so that, as Gregory the Great had suggested, the scriptural text never stopped growing in significance by its very reception. As a practical application of such a finding, many of the best students of patristic exegesis in the past fifty years ended by recommending a sort of mimetic appropriation of that form of exegesis. In such a conservative stance, in a modern critical guise, patristic exegesis was declared the only valid way to be faithful to Scripture throughout the millennia.

Back in the late 1960s, I was (and in the year 2000 still am) amazed by the turn to a past-oriented attitude adopted by many of my former masters and friends in patristic exegesis. I understand it as a logical step in line with their admiration for the consistent riches of that form of exegesis. However, as in any crisis of orthodoxy, I suspect that in this case also the projection of well-established values and truths becomes a pious utopia when these values and truths are perceived in an anachronistic way.

The patristic theory of the senses of Scripture can no longer be linked to apologetic paraphrase. Beyond their careful description of patristic claims, our distinguished predecessors of recent decades raised no real questions concerning the very nature of Scripture as the Fathers understood it. Let us raise such questions.

The Patristic Form of Christian Faith

De Lubac had offered a prodigiously rich analysis of the medieval reception of the patristic doctrine of scriptural senses in the Latin West. He made it clear that such a systematic theory of scriptural senses was not developed by the patristic authors themselves. Indeed neither Origen in Book IV of his *Peri Archōn* nor Augustine in his *De doctrina Christiana* articulated such a theory. Like many others they provided the essential elements for it, but they lacked the critical distance from the biblical text that would have allowed them to systematize their own hermeneutics. *Patristic authors lacked the critical space in which a hermeneutical theory would have blossomed in its own right.* Why so, if not because an all-pervading notion of God's revelatory initiatives occupied the whole horizon of their thinking? Their notion of God was such that the same God who nourished them with divine truths in the Bible was also the God who structured their minds for a proper understanding of these truths. Interpreting the sacred texts meant for them establishing a direct connection between the Spirit of God who was speaking to them in Scripture and that same Spirit who enabled them to become faithful recipients of Scripture. In other words, there was no space for a nontheological reference capable of providing a critical insight, such as happens with the scientific references imposed on us today by a secular culture. Also, because the Church was understood as instituted by divine power, and because the experience of Christian faith was authenticated by that Church alone, it was simply impossible for patristic interpreters *not* to become personally involved in their interpretation. They used Scripture as a mirror for reflecting their inner and corporate identity. Their reading of Scripture was for them a way of inventing their own language in order to tell the story of their spiritual ancestry and of their own spiritual journey. Their imposition of Scripture on their moral values and on their social regulations operated outside of any profane space and time in the immediacy of God's judgment as expressed in the sacred writings.

It suffices to delve briefly into the biblical religiosity of patristic authors in order to measure the shift of theological foundations between their generation and ours, a shift that separates them from any sound Christian thinker of today. In other words, a critical retrieval of the patristic form of Christian *faith* is indeed required if one tries to raise appropriate questions about the theory of the senses of Scripture.

Sometimes people wonder why such a theory is missing today. They neglect to admit that the patristic mind was shaped by a form of religious faith that was thinkable only in the context of a society and a civilization gone forever. On the threshold of the twenty-first century, *patristic faith* properly speaking is alien to our present way of thinking. One may only consider it as a historical datum, even if one should persist in clinging to the traditional Christian persuasion. The current relevance of that persuasion is not necessarily determined by the fundamental views of patristic faith. The exegetical revolution of the past two centuries demonstrated the obvious need and the validity of such a theological shift. Hence, the critical interrogation should rather be: How, in the post-Christian and posthumanistic society of today's Western world, should a Christian believer welcome the medieval theory of scriptural senses? The answer could well be: *by rethinking that theory in the light of the hermeneutical conversion characteristic of postmodern believers.*

The Hermeneutical Conversion

The cultural form of Christian faith inherited from the Fathers implies, first of all, in all Christian traditions, an objectivized notion of divine transcendence. The same generations of believers belonging to the Judaeo-Christian lineage of monotheism who, since biblical antiquity, opposed idolatry were also expressing their beliefs in a highly symbolic language. Anthropomorphism did not simply materialize for the common believer in magic and idolatry; for instance, in prophetic oratory *e contrario* it emphasized the transcendent being and acting of God. The more God's transcendence was celebrated in liturgies, the greater was the need for a wall of icons between the congregation and the liturgical ministers. Through the contemplation of the icons the faithful found an access in their hearts to the sacred mysteries performed during the liturgies. In the mind of patristic believers, such an access to divine transcendence itself was at once symbolic and objectivized in each comment they made on sacred Scripture. That highly imaginative representation of God in his almighty and salvific presence to them did not relieve Christian believers from facing extraordinary challenges in their intellectual creativity. What is usually called "Christian Platonism" imposed on the patristic mind more problems than it offered solutions. The attitude of patristic believers towards Scripture was dictated by the presuppositions of their more basic attitude towards divine transcendence.

The Western mind has undergone drastic changes that turn it towards a post-Kantian, or a post-Heideggerian, or a post-call-it-as-you-like horizon — in any case, towards a horizon that excludes any objectivized transcendence. The only kind of transcendence thinkable today is just as radical as the ancient one in being an intimate principle of the human subject itself. Hence the divine relevance of Scripture has shifted from the supracosmic Beyond evoked in it, and from the miraculous data reported in it, to the believing creativity of the communities that sponsored the production of biblical writings. The gospel stories are no longer seen as true and meaningful because of the wonders they so convincingly describe, but because of the consistent authenticity of the faith accounted for by their authors. Just as believers in the patristic age focused on divine incarnation in *biological* terms and fought a century-long battle for defining a metaphysical Christology, so do today's interpreters of the gospel elaborate a *hermeneutical* notion of divine incarnation. It was in the *mind* of the first disciples that the messianic presence, God Incarnate in the person of Jesus, was understood by John, Peter, Paul, and the others. Currently, the historical awareness, introduced into Christian theology for over a century, has matured into a theological openness to divine transcendence in history itself, specifically to the transcendent gospel event, actualized again and again by Christian believers. From an old dogmatic canon, people are called to a new perception of the divine covenant, the shift from an Old to a New Testament continuing to be, today as always, the central criterion of Christian authenticity.

Actualizing Patristic "Senses of Scripture"

After the use and abuse of historical-critical methods in biblical exegesis as a response to the rationalism of the eighteenth-century Enlightenment, and in the historical awareness of today, the "*literal* sense" of Scripture, which patristic authors understood in conformity with the rhetorical culture of Late Antiquity, now means that Scripture deserves to be scrutinized with all contemporary tools and methods at our disposal. The secular exploration of biblical writings, be it Jewish or Christian, like biblical archaeology, can only help the spiritual interpretation of the data under scrutiny. In recent decades, much has been published on the rhetorical infrastructure of patristic exegesis. The "senses" of Scripture were perceived in Alexandria and Antioch, and in the Latin West, as a *rhetorical* device applied by the Holy Spirit, declared the true author of the Bible. In the same way, Scripture makes sense today only if consistently interpreted in the frame of today's *hermeneutical* culture. This is especially true in regard to what patristic interpreters called the "spiritual" sense.

A proper interpretation centered today on the "spiritual" sense, in line with the patristic experiment, requires a relocation of the Bible on the religious map of the "Global Village," as Bultmann already insisted, for it was a quest for their religious identity that motivated the earliest theoreticians of the senses of Scripture. Today's Christian identity will receive due recognition only if validated by an interpretation of Scripture consonant with contemporary culture. That was Philo's challenge in the Jewish Diaspora of Alexandria. Philo pioneered a commentary on Scripture based on the "spiritual" sense. We try to invent the same kind of commentary in our own cultural setting.

More than its cultural dimension, it is the *ecclesial* dimension of the patristic "spiritual sense" that calls for a proper rethinking in the light of the current hermeneutical conversion. There is no doubt in my mind that the present state of New Testament exegesis, which has already thoroughly transformed our Christology, announces as well the burgeoning of a new type of Church life.

At last, the very definition of Christian *faith* itself is at stake in any attempt to actualize the patristic notion of scriptural senses. From a dogmatistic form of faith, bound to an institutional frame consolidated by ancient tradition, and leading to the cul-de-sac of confessional rigidity, the hermeneutical conversion in which our generations are involved leads to a belief in a nondogmatistic form of faith, in which faith itself generates its own newness, in the Apostle Paul's words ἐκ πίστεως εἰς πίστιν (Rom. 1:17), a newness of faith capable of integrating the legacy of past Christianity but also of welcoming the unpredictable and mysterious efficiency of the gospel event in a new millennium.

"As Yourself": A Least Love

FREDERICK W. NORRIS

During the twentieth century "historical exegesis" came to mean almost exclusively "historical-critical exegesis" in which insights into Scripture usually were limited to the Old and New Testament scholarship of that century. Everything else became labeled "precritical." The obvious result has been that commentaries on Holy Writ from any period other than Late Modernity have seldom been consulted. Few in New Testament studies beyond the magisterial J. B. Lightfoot (d. 1889) have continuously returned to the patristic period for clues to the meaning of biblical texts.[1] Even within heritages that highly value ancient tradition (Eastern Orthodoxy, Roman Catholicism, and Anglicanism) theologians have often found more important guides for their contemporary concerns in doctrinal treatises and conciliar decisions from Church

---

1. Lightfoot's commentaries on the Pauline epistles often turn on patristic interpretation. Sadly, however, his *St. Paul's Epistle to the Galatians,* 10th ed. (London: Macmillan, 1890) has almost no comment on 5:14 where "as yourself" appears. Some contemporary scholars are reappropriating earlier efforts. Ulrich Luz (*Das Evangelium nach Matthaeus,* Evangelisch-Katholisher Kommentar zum Neuen Testament, 3 vols., vol. 1 [Neukirchen-Vluyn: Neukirchener Verlag, 1985-97]) often relies on prior exegetes. In vol. 3, pp. 273-75, he notices the importance of Origen's and Augustine's interpretations of Matt. 22:39, the negative responses to their views by Calvin and Luther, significant points in favor of the patristic exegetes raised by Erich Fromm and Elizabeth Moltmann-Wender, a rejoinder by Dorothee Sölle, and further positive discussion by J. A. Bengel, Bernard Häring, and Kierkegaard. Every study of the passage should know of Luz's work. Luke T. Johnson (*The Letter of James,* The Anchor Bible [New York: Doubleday, 1995]) offers no specific patristic assistance on James 2:8, but he includes a healthy section on the history of interpretation of the entire book (pp. 124-61).

history than in historical commentaries or premodern treatments of specific scriptural verses. Protestants of many different persuasions have indeed looked to the Bible in their own ways, but only occasionally have they viewed ancient comments as helpful, let alone definitive. In spite of their persistent interest in preaching they have too seldom taken note of ancient sermons that serve as commentary on sacred books.

There is disdain for ancient interpretation of Scripture within the Academy and even within the Church because it is judged to be primitive, allegorical, and misguided. Although that disdain is deeply enmeshed in contemporary technical biblical studies and affects much of Church scholarship and life, it is itself misplaced. Forays into comments on Holy Writ from both times and regions other than our own can provide not merely interesting academic puzzles but also genuine guidance for congregations of believers. Such is the case for the rather troublesome and recurring biblical admonition to love our neighbors as ourselves.

The difficulty is a sensible one. Christian communities of all traditions have tried to be quite clear about the necessity of self-denial. Taking up one's cross and following Christ is at the center of Christian life together. Because the self can become so badly warped, its desires equated with its needs, the call for denial of self remains an overpowering issue. Yet as with much of the Church's teaching that is discovered by modern scriptural exegesis through a process wrongly understood as thoroughly objective, contextual, grammatical, and disconnected from the history of interpretation, wisdom about the meaning of the text is lost. What different ages and areas have already found in the text remains unknown. In my experience among believing and practicing conservative Christians, the phrase "as yourself" that forms the final words of the second commandment, becomes exceedingly problematic. Although it appears in each of the Synoptic Gospels (Matt. 19:19; 22:39; Mark 12:31; Luke 10:27) and in three epistles (Rom. 13:9; Gal. 5:14; James 2:8) and had occurred first in Old Testament law (Lev. 19:18), many find in it a contradiction to demands for self-denial. Careful, alert Christians worry that much present-day meditation on the phrase smacks of modern psychology at its worst. Informed either by great figures in that discipline from the nineteenth and twentieth century or the popularizers from that era — many of whom claim that self-esteem and avoidance of self-loathing are the basic building blocks of the good life — such interpretations go against the grain. Yet other careful, alert Christians are gratified that the great teachers of psychology in Western culture, as well as the popularizers, have been able to add modern depth to hoary scriptural insight.

Surely those attempting to love God with all their hearts, minds, and souls and their neighbors as themselves sometimes have reasons to be on guard against contemporary psychologies. Yet all insights of modern psychology are not entirely perverse. Perhaps what is often found to be most helpful within such insights was already in Christian tradition long before the evolution of present-day psychologies. Perhaps there was already a better principle undergirding the contemporary recognition that too many well-meaning Christian communities have produced a self-loathing guilt that has crippled people.

The point of this chapter, dedicated to Robert Wilken, who has insisted that we take classical interpretation with ultimate seriousness, is simple. Arguments pro and con about the merits of modern psychologies for understanding Christian self-love are moot. Had we paid attention to what the Church has taught us about this phrase "as yourself," we could have avoided numerous problems. Hidebound traditionalists might not be rejected for their rather ponderous inability to experience forgiving grace that liberates people from perpetual, debilitating guilt. Free cultural Christians might also not be viewed as frivolous because of the equally serious difficulties raised by the sense that humans are all fine once they understand that nothing really significant is wrong with them.

In order to gain access to premodern exegesis, we need not command all the ancient languages and know every place in the history of the Church where comments have been made about the verses in question. There are resources that can lead us into the treasure trove.[2] One remarkable place to look for early Christian interpretation of the phrase "as yourself" is Thomas Aquinas's *Catena Aurea,* a chain of comments on the four Gospels.[3] This profound theologian is noted for his *Summa Theologica,* a bench mark for systematics, and his *Contra Gentiles,* a manual of inculturation or contextualization be-

---

2. *Bibliographia patristica: Index des citations et allusions bibliques dans la littérature patristique,* vols. 1-6 and the *Supplement* (Paris: Éditions du centre national de la recherche scientifique, 1975-95), can help any student find where a particular biblical verse is referred to in patristic writings. The indices in some editions and translations of the Fathers also provide interesting leads.

3. Thomas Aquinas, *Catena Aurea in Quatuor Evangelia,* 2 vols. (Turin: Pontificia et Sacrae Rituum Congregationis, 1915). A reprint of the nineteenth-century English translation is available: John Henry Newman, ed., *Catena Aurea: Commentary on the Four Gospels,* 4 vols. (Oxford: John Henry Parker, 1841-45), in 8 parts, reprinted in 4 vols. with introduction by Aidan Nichols (Southampton, England: Saint Austin Press, 1997). In each citation I have adapted the translations. Because Aquinas was not always correct in his citations, I give the location in the original author of any quotation that I have been able to find.

fore we knew to use those terms. His *Catena Aurea* dramatically shows that he would not begin to plumb the depths of Holy Writ without the guidance of predecessors. We can employ his great learning, penetrating intellect, and wise soul to help us discover what the wealth of early exegesis about "as yourself" might be. John Henry Newman did not think it was proper to include this work of Aquinas in his "Library of the Fathers." When he had it translated, however, he hoped it would "be found as useful in private study of the Gospels, as it is well adapted for family reading, and full of thought for those who are engaged in religious instruction."[4]

Within the *Catena Aurea* we find what some teachers of the Church regularly taught about the two commandments Jesus mentioned. The first is to love God with everything that we humans are. These leaders knew that this first love must not be compromised in any way. They clearly saw that the second love is, as the scriptural texts say, like the first and not to be forgotten if the law and the prophets receive their proper honor. Love of God and love of the neighbor as ourselves comprise the great commandment and the one like it.

A number of these teachers, however, insightfully grasped that the second commandment, love of neighbor as yourself, included a proper love of self and was deeply implied in that first love of God. Theophylact perhaps represents the more general statement from which such inferences can be drawn. He insists that "these two commandments are in harmony with and contain one another. Whoever loves God also loves God's creatures. Because the best of God's creatures is man, whoever loves God ought to love all men."[5] The inference here unstated but rather difficult to exclude is that each person is a part of God's creation and thus that self-love of some proper type must be appropriate since the point is to love "all men."

Origen had earlier put it in a more explicit way:

> When the Lord adds, "This is the first and great commandment," we learn how we ought to consider commandments, that there is a great one and that there are less down to the least. The Lord says not merely that it is great but that it is the first commandment, not in order of Scripture, but in terms of value. . . . Neither did he teach only the first and great com-

4. Newman, "Advertisement," in idem, *Catena Aurea*, vol. 1.

5. Theophylact, *Enarratio in Evangelium Marci* 12 (PG 123:629); English translation in *The Explanation by Blessed Theophylact of the Holy Gospel of Mark*, vol. 2, *Bl. Theophylact's Explanation of the New Testament* (House Springs, Mich.: Chrysostom Press, 1993), Mark 12:28-34, p. 106, identified properly in Aquinas, *Catena Aurea*, 1:573, adapted from the English translation of John Dobree Dalgairns in Newman, *Catena Aurea*, 2:247, Mark 12:28-34.

mandment, but he also added a second like it: "You shall love your neighbor as yourself." But if "Whoever loves sin hates his own soul" (Psalm 11.5) is true, then it is clear that he does not love his neighbor as himself if he does not love himself.[6]

Gregory the Great appears to follow an insight like Origen's when he asks rather pointedly: "Since it is said, 'You shall love your neighbor as yourself,' how is someone merciful in being compassionate to another, who by unrighteous living is still unmerciful to oneself?"[7]

Both Origen and Gregory the Great interpret love of self through Psalm 11:5, Origen by quoting the insight and Gregory by referring to that thought in somewhat different language. The importance of the use of that Old Testament quotation lies in its clear understanding that people do hate themselves in ways that are quite destructive. Loving sin is hatred for one's own soul. People whose repeated behavior shows that they love ruinous acts are doing themselves irreparable harm. The reclaimed sentence from the Psalm, coupled with the "second commandment" from Jesus, suggests rather strongly that there is a type of self-love that is not only admissible, but clearly preferable. Self-hatred deeply damages.

Augustine has similar views, ones put in slightly different words at three places that Aquinas brings together:

> He who loves men should love them either because they are righteous, or in order that they may become righteous; and so he should love himself either for who he is or that he may become righteous. And thus without peril he may love his neighbor as himself.[8]

If a man loves his neighbor, it follows that he loves God also; for it is through the same affection in which we love God that we love our neigh-

---

6. Origen, *Comm. in Mt.* 1 and 3 (PG 13:1602C and 1604D) has sentences quite similar to those identified as from Origen (tractate 23) in Aquinas, *Catena Aurea*, 1:356, adapted from the English translation of Mark Pattison in Newman, *Catena Aurea*, 1:763, Matt. 22:34-40.

7. Gregory the Great, *mor. 19.23*, ed. Marci Adrien, CCSL 143A (Turnhold: Brepols, 1979), Book 19, section. 23, lines 94-97, not *Moralia* 20 or 14 as identified in Aquinas, *Catena Aurea*, 2:166, adapted from the English translation of Thomas Dudley Ryder, in Newman, *Catena Aurea*, 3:369, Luke 10:25-28.

8. Augustine, *trin.* 8.6 (CCSL 50:283-84) properly identified in Aquinas, *Catena Aurea*, 1:356, adapted from the English translation of Mark Pattison in Newman, *Catena Aurea*, 1:763, Matt. 22:34-40.

bor, except that we love God for himself, and ourselves and our neighbors for God's sake.[9]

Because the Divine nature is more excellent and higher than our nature, the command to love God is distinct from the one telling us to love our neighbor. But if you understand the "yourself" of the text as your whole self, both your soul and your body, and understand "your neighbor" in the same way, then nothing that is to be loved is left out of these commands. The love of God is first and the command is thus laid down for us in order to make all other loves center in that one; therefore nothing seems to be said about loving yourself. But then follows "You shall love your neighbor as yourself" so that love of self is not omitted.[10]

In each of these quotations Augustine insists on the importance of what one might call Godly love of the human self. Love of self cannot be left out of any inclusive consideration of love, but it is properly understood only when it exists in clear relationships with love of God and love of neighbor. Love of God is the first commandment because God's nature is above us; God deserves love beyond anything in his creation. When that first love sits in its proper place, we are then to love both our neighbor and ourselves for God's sake, either for what they and we already are, or for what they and we might become.

Bernard of Clairvaux died more than a century before Aquinas wrote his *Catena Aurea,* but he is not mentioned in that work where he might have been the most help. He does, however, show the influence of some of Augustine's insights within his treatise *On the Love of God,* ones that Aquinas would find so important. Bernard lays out four stages of growth in the spiritual life that eventually include proper love of self.

Love is one of the four natural passions [love, fear, joy, and sorrow]. . . . But because nature has become rather frail and weak, man is driven by necessity to serve nature first. This results in bodily love, by which man loves himself for his own sake. . . . But if that same love begins to get out

9. Augustine, *trin.* 8.8 (CCSL 50:288-89), identified as *De Trinitate* 8.7 in Aquinas, *Catena Aurea,* 1:357, adapted from the English translation of Mark Pattison in Newman, *Catena Aurea,* 1:764, Matt. 22:34-40.

10. Augustine, *doc. Chr.* 1.58 and 2.18, ed. R. P. H. Green, Oxford Early Christian Texts (Oxford: Clarendon, 1995), pp. 36, 54, are similar to what is identified as *doc. Chr.* 1.30 and 26 in Aquinas, *Catena Aurea,* 1:356, adapted from the English translation of Mark Pattison in Newman, *Catena Aurea,* 1:763, Matt. 22:34-40.

of proportion and headstrong, as often happens, and if it ceases to be satisfied to run in the narrow channel of its needs, but floods out on all sides into the fields of pleasure, then the overflow can be stopped at once by the commandment: "You shall love your neighbor as yourself" (Mt. 22:39).

But to love your neighbor with perfect justice, you have to be prompted by God. . . . You must first love God, so that in Him you can love your neighbor too (Mk. 12:30-31). . . . And so in that way it comes about that man who is a bodily animal (1 Cor. 2:14), and does not know how to love anything but himself, begins to love God for his own benefit, because he learns from frequent experience that in God he can do everything which is good for him (Phil. 4:13), and that without Him he can do nothing (Jn. 15:5). Man therefore loves God, but as yet he loves Him for his own sake, not God's.[11]

Man's frequent needs make it necessary for him to call upon God often, and to taste by frequent contact, and to discover by tasting how sweet the Lord is (Ps. 33:9[34.8]). It is in this way that the taste of His own sweetness leads us to love God in purity more than our need alone would prompt us to do. . . . And so it will not be difficult for the man who has had that experience to keep the commandment to love his neighbor (Mk. 12:31). He truly loves God and therefore he loves what is God's. . . . He who trusts in the Lord, not because He is good to him but simply because He is good, truly loves God for God's sake and not for his own. That is the third degree of love, in which God is already loved for His own sake.

Blessed is he who has been found worthy to attain to the fourth degree, where man loves himself only for God's sake. . . . I should call him blessed and holy who receives that experience even for a single instant, something that is rare indeed in this life. To lose yourself as though you did not exist and to have no sense of yourself, to be emptied out of yourself (Phil. 2:7) and almost annihilated, belongs to heavenly not to human love. And if indeed any mortal is rapt for a moment or is, so to speak, admitted for a minute to this union, at once the world presses itself on him (Gal. 1:4); the day's wickedness troubles him, the mortal body weighs him down, bodily needs distract him, he fails because of the weakness of

---

11. Bernard of Clairvaux, *L'Amour de Dieu,* ed. François Callerot, Jean Christoph, Marie-Imelda Haille, and Paul Verdeyen, SC 393 (Paris: Éditions du Cerf, 1993), ch. 8, pp. 116-18, 122-24; *On the Love of God,* chs. 8-9 in Gillian R. Evans, trans., *Bernard of Clairvaux: Selected Works,* The Classics of Western Spirituality (New York: Paulist Press, 1987), pp. 191-93. I slightly adapted Evans's translation in these quotations.

his corruption and — more powerfully than these — brotherly love calls him back.[12]

[To reiterate then], in the first instance therefore man loves himself for himself. He is a bodily creature and he cannot see beyond himself. But since he sees that he cannot be the author of his own existence, he begins to inquire after God by faith (Heb. 11:6) because he needs Him and because he begins to love Him. And so he comes to love God in the second degree, but still for himself and not for God's sake. But then when he begins to worship Him, and to keep coming to Him because he needs Him, God gradually begins to make Himself known to him through his thinking, reading, prayer, and obedience. By this growing familiarity God causes him truly to feel His sweetness. In this way, when he has tasted how sweet the Lord is (Ps. 33:9[34.8]), he passes to the third stage, where he loves God, not now for himself, but for God's sake. Truly he remains for a long time in that state, and I do not know whether the fourth stage, where a man comes to love himself only for God's sake, is fully attained by anyone in this life.

If anyone has experienced it, let him say so. To me it seems impossible. But I have no doubt that that is how it will be when the good and faithful servant is led into the joy of his Lord (Mt. 25:21) and intoxicated by the riches of the house of God (Ps. 35:9[36.8]). It will be as though in some miraculous way he forgets himself and as though going out of himself altogether comes wholly to God, and afterward holds fast to Him, one with Him in spirit (1 Cor. 6:17).[13]

There is a more developed view of the phrase "as yourself" here in Bernard's work than the one presented above from Augustine, and yet Bernard's treatise itself represents Augustine's own later distrust of human intent and attainment. Bernard clearly sees loving your neighbor as yourself in terms of a restraint against being carnally and excessively occupied with your own desires. The assumption is that love of self is natural but limiting. His biblical question is: "For who hates his own flesh?" (Eph. 5:29).[14] He further insists that the fourth stage, loving oneself only for God's sake — never for any other

12. Bernard of Clairvaux, *De diligendo Deo* 9 (SC 393:124-26), 10 (SC 393:128); Evans, *Bernard,* chs. 9-10, pp. 194-95.

13. Bernard of Clairvaux, *De diligendo Deo* 15 (SC 393:160); Evans, *Bernard,* ch. 15, p. 204.

14. Bernard of Clairvaux, *De diligendo Deo* 8 (SC 393:126); Evans, *Bernard,* ch. 8, p. 192.

reason — is perhaps reached at unusual moments in this life. Yet realistically it is impossible and attained fully only in heaven where one enters the Spirit of God. Bernard lacks the sense of potential that marked Augustine's earlier thought in which loving oneself for God's sake can be a goal of human life. For Augustine it is a possible ideal; for Bernard in this life it is probably not.

Part of the difference between Bernard and both Origen and Gregory the Great lies in the choice of the hinge scriptural passage. For Bernard the pressing insight is: "Who hates his own flesh?" (Eph. 5:29). For Origen and Gregory the more important point is that whoever loves sin hates his own soul (Ps. 11:5). The ambiguity raised by setting these two passages alongside each other is ours. Yet the different emphasis in terms of self-love may well be determined by that very decision.

Two things are clear from this received exegesis. First, "as yourself," that is, a love of self, is not considered a throwaway line that sadly appears with regularity in Scripture. Bernard at the very least sees it as a remarkable and necessary restraint against self-indulgence, while Origen, Gregory the Great, and Augustine view it as potentially significant when seen first and foremost from within the love of God. Too often in modern Christian exegesis a one-sided look at self-denial, mounted against what are perceived as modern efforts to minimize sin, has led to deep suspicion of the phrase "as yourself." Some have been on guard against the antinomianism of contemporary North America and Europe and have insisted upon attentive discernment of the distinction between real personal needs and dangerous individual desires. Others have been glad to find in Holy Writ the clear insights about self-worth that mark much of North American and European culture. What some classical exegetes like Origen and Gregory the Great bring to this discussion is the importance of Psalm 11:5 in recognizing a lack of mercy or love in those who continue in unrighteousness. They do not see themselves as children of God, highly valued.

Second, precisely and perhaps somewhat unexpectedly Augustine, who so often talks of a bound will and the power of sin to corrupt even infants, also calls on those who love a holy God to love themselves for God's sake. They should see in themselves a potential for good that can be realized only in God. The Cappadocians, indeed many of the Greeks, did not think that sin totally corrupted the ability of humans to respond to God's love. We expect from them some sense of righteous self-love. As Aquinas notes, Basil can insist that "the love of God cannot be taught":

> For neither did we learn to be happy in the presence of light nor to embrace life nor to love our parents and children; much less were we taught the love of God, but a certain seminal principle was implanted in us, that

115

has within itself the cause for humans clinging to God. The teaching of divine commands diligently cultivates that principle, attentively fosters it and carries it on to the perfection of divine grace.

For naturally we love good; we also love what is our own, what is akin to us. On our own we pour out our affections on our benefactors. If then God is good, but all things desire that good which is brought forth voluntarily, He is by nature inherent in us. Although looking to His goodness we are still far from knowing Him, yet from the very fact that we proceeded from Him, we are bound to love Him with great love because He, in truth, is akin to us. He is in the same way also a greater helper than all those who by nature we love in this life.

The love of God is therefore the first and chief command, but the second, as filling up the first and filled up by it, bids us to love our neighbor. And it follows "And your neighbor as yourself." We have an instinct given to us by God in order to perform this command. Who doesn't know that humans are kind and social animals? For nothing belongs so much to our nature as to communicate with one another, and mutually to need and love our relations. He gave us the seed of these things in the first place; He later demands the fruit.[15]

Chrysostom dreams of possibilities if we follow the second commandment with all our hearts:

If we diligently kept it, there would be neither slave nor free man, neither conqueror nor conquered (or rather, neither ruler nor subject), neither rich nor poor. The devil wouldn't even be known. Chaff would be more likely to withstand the touch of fire than the devil could stand against the fervor of love. The perseverance of love surpasses everything.[16]

15. Basil, *Regulae fusius tractatae* (PG 31:908C and 917A) contain the first and third paragraph. The second one I have not been able to identify. Similar thoughts but not the same language appear in 909B-C. In that section Basil also speaks of evil in human nature. This is one of the clearest indications raised within this study that Aquinas used some type of *florilegia* of the Fathers that put together quotations from various places or from manuscripts different from those used for our modern editions of the earlier Fathers. All three paragraphs are identified as from Basil in Aquinas, *Catena Aurea*, 2:165, adapted from the English translation of Thomas Dudley Ryder, in Newman, *Catena Aurea*, 3:368, Luke 10:25-28, where they are identified as Basil, *Reg. Fus. ad int.* 2.

16. Chrysostom, *hom. 32.6 in 1 Cor.* (PG 61:272), in Aquinas, *Catena Aurea*, 2:166, adapted from the English translation of Thomas Dudley Ryder, in Newman, *Catena Aurea*, 3:369, Luke 10:25-28, where the citation is given as *Homilies in 1 Corinthians* 32.

Such analysis by Basil and dreams from Chrysostom can strike us as less than sanguine. They had a deeper sense of sin than these lines suggest, but neither of them ever saw the image of God in humans as totally destroyed. Augustine, however, viewed it somewhat differently. Surely for him the realization of full human potential comes only through the acceptance of grace and the confession of one's inability to merit or to achieve salvation by oneself. Clay we are. Yet on his advice we must not be paralyzed by a sense of our dreadfulness into thinking either that God does not love us or that we are totally incapable of loving God. Our first love is to God who deserves more than we can give; the second love of neighbor, understood as loving that one for God's sake, includes loving ourselves for God's sake. "And thus without peril we may love our neighbors as ourselves."

These are truths that do not contradict what some Western psychologists have called to our attention. The Fathers' statements, however, are nuanced more carefully and count more deeply than either traditional misgivings about modern conceptions or contemporary acceptance of modern understandings. They clearly indicate yet again that we avoid fuller historical exegesis of Scripture not only to the endangerment of our squint-eyed scholarly careers but also to the rotting of our souls.

Early Commentators in Erasmus's
Annotations on Romans

ROBERT D. SIDER

Erasmus's first edition of the New Testament, published by Johan Froben of Basel in March 1516, was a single volume in three parts. In the first part Erasmus placed the dedicatory epistle to Pope Leo X, and several essays on hermeneutical principles. This was followed by the text of the New Testament both in Greek and in Erasmus's revision of the Latin Vulgate, the two texts being set side by side in two parallel columns on each page. The third part consisted of notes — the "annotations" — designed ostensibly to defend the text and justify the revisions Erasmus had made to the Vulgate.[1] Before Erasmus's death in 1536 four further editions were to follow, in 1519, 1522, 1527, and 1535. In these later editions Erasmus made substantial changes to the prefatory material and the text, but it is the changes to the annotations that most readily catch the modern reader's attention. Beginning with the second edition Erasmus's New Testament was published in two volumes, the second volume devoted entirely to annotation. Erasmus added material to the annotations in each new edition: in the first edition the annotations on the entire text required 400 relatively uncrowded pages, while in the final edition they extended over nearly 800 pages of closely printed text.

In the "Letter to the Reader" that prefaced the 1516 edition Erasmus de-

---

1. In his prefatory letter "To the Reader" (*Ep.* 373:14-16, 201-5 in Collected Works of Erasmus [hereafter CWE] [Toronto: University of Toronto Press, 1974-], 3:198, 204) Erasmus describes his Latin text as a revision of the Vulgate. In his 1519 and later editions the Vulgate base remains clearly visible, but the revisions are so radical as to form virtually a new translation of Erasmus's own making.

scribed the primary goal of his annotations. He wished, in the first place, to justify his revisions of the Vulgate. Further, where his revisions presupposed a different textual reading from that of the Vulgate, he felt obliged, at least for problematic passages, to cite the evidence of the Greek and Latin witnesses and to review the evidence offered by the citations of the Fathers. Moreover, he had endeavored by his revisions to the text to bring clarity to obscure passages: to punctuate in a way that would bring intelligibility to difficult sentences, to construe an extended passage so that the argument could be readily followed, to catch precisely the proper nuance of Greek words, and to render Greek idioms into their Latin equivalent. Such revisions often called for justification, for which the annotations were the appropriate place. Erasmus had also determined, as a particular aim of the annotations, to describe the efforts he had made to check against both the Hebrew and the Septuagint the passages in the New Testament that had been cited from the Old. For each of these endeavors the Fathers could contribute much.

Several important studies have shown how Erasmus attempted to achieve these goals in his annotations. These studies have, moreover, demonstrated the large place given to early commentators in the annotations, and they have sought to describe the role the commentators played in supporting Erasmus's endeavor to work out his stated aims.[2] The persistent reader will find, however, that Erasmus's annotations arouse an interest that goes beyond their historical value as a period piece of textual reconstruction and hermeneutics to focus upon their achievement as a literary artifact. Though Erasmus seems to have adopted the basic form for his annotations primarily from Lorenzo Valla (1407-57) (whose notes on the New Testament Erasmus himself discovered in 1504 and published in 1505),[3] Erasmus develops them into a literary creation stamped with his own particular genius. Annotations that appear to be simple are found to be deftly constructed to involve the reader in the process of reconstructing, interpreting, and responding to the biblical text. It is particularly Erasmus's instinct for projecting a sense of the dramatic that facilitates the process, the same instinct that made his *Colloquies* so successful. His sense of the dramatic appears at several levels: in the implicit evocation of images of colloquy, judgment scene, school, or congre-

2. See especially Albert Rabil Jr., *Erasmus and the New Testament: The Mind of a Christian Humanist* (San Antonio, Tex.: Trinity University Press, 1972), pp. 115-27; André Godin, *Érasme, lecteur d'Origène* (Geneva: Librairie Droz, 1982), pp. 141-97; Erika Rummel, *Erasmus' Annotations on the New Testament: From Philologist to Theologian*, Erasmus Studies (Toronto: University of Toronto Press, 1986), pp. 52-74.

3. But cf. Rummel (*Erasmus' Annotations*, pp. 13-18), who cautions against overestimating Valla's contribution to Erasmus's annotations.

gation;[4] in images that not only suggest scenes of debate but invite the reader to play an active role of assessment and evaluation as issues are debated; in the creation of *personae* for the commentators who enter into the debates, and whose presence is at times made to seem immediate and direct; and in the tension that comes from surprise, particularly the surprise that arises from the unexpected comment to which the notes are superbly adapted. The reader is also involved because Erasmus seems to actualize, with as much instinct as he had for the dramatic, the fundamental principle of rhetoric, that language artistically displayed has for its goals "to teach, to delight, to move," *docere, delectare, movere.* In order to achieve such effects in his annotations the eloquence of the Fathers was perfectly suited.

In this essay, therefore, I wish to show how the patristic writers contribute to the reader's engagement in the exegetical process undertaken in the annotations. To do so, however, it is essential to see how the early commentators enter generally into Erasmus's endeavor: in the first place, as he sought to achieve the goals he had explicitly defined; in the second place, as he acquired a constantly increasing knowledge of the Fathers; and in the third place, as he realized the potential of the patristic presence for engaging the reader. In short, this study seeks to be integrative — appreciation of Erasmus's literary achievement should emerge in the context of a descriptive overview of the development of the annotations and an analysis of their main characteristics. I shall limit the discussion to the *Annotations on Romans,* first, because Erasmus's use of early commentators is best viewed as particular to each New Testament book — availability of the ancient exegetes was not identical for every book, and Erasmus's knowledge of the early commentators grew over the years — and second, because it is only in the *Annotations on Romans* that sufficient scholarly groundwork has been done to make our present enterprise viable.[5] To reflect advantageously the development of the patristic influence on the *Annotations on Romans,* I shall pass in review each of the five editions in sequence.

---

4. Rummel (*Erasmus'* Annotations, p. 33) suggests that Erasmus addresses his readership as a "flock to be taught rather than a learned audience."

5. I refer to the publication of the *Annotations on Romans,* CWE 56, ed. Robert D. Sider, trans. and annotated by John B. Payne, Albert Rabil Jr., Robert D. Sider, and Warren S. Smith Jr. (Toronto: University of Toronto Press, 1994). Henceforth in this essay all translations of the text of the *Annotations on Romans* are taken from CWE 56.

Patristic Commentators in the
Annotations on Romans: 1516

For the edition of 1516, the chief patristic commentators were Origen, Jerome, and Ambrosiaster. Augustine is not entirely disregarded; otherwise, a single allusion to the Pseudo-Jerome of the *Breviarium in Psalmos* makes the roll call of patristic exegetes complete.

In this first edition the presence of Augustine is minimal. How well Erasmus knew Augustine at this time is open to question: his critics seem to have implied a lack of knowledge when they urged him to read the work of the great African bishop.[6] It is, however, certain that by 1495 he had read with great care, even memorized, parts of the *De doctrina christiana,* and knew as well the *Confessiones, Retractationes,* and *De civitate dei.* His letters confirm that he continued to read Augustine in the two decades that followed. Nevertheless, in the 1516 *Annotations on Romans* we find only one indirect allusion to the *Retractationes,* two references to the *De doctrina christiana,* and a brief citation from Epistle 196.[7] From the last of these Erasmus recalled the Latin word *recapitulatur* as a somewhat interesting translation for the Greek ἀνακεφαλαιοῦται in 13:9, better than the Vulgate's *instauratur,* though Erasmus himself rendered the Greek by *comprehenditur.* Both references to the *De doctrina christiana* (in the annotations on 8:33 and 9:30) merely note that Augustine commented on the sentence structure and style of these passages; they remain nothing more than that until 1527. Since Erasmus knew this work well, such curt dismissal of the *De doctrina christiana* may have been due to limitations of space, to Erasmus's early narrow conceptualization of the nature of his annotations, and to his failure to have seen at that time the rhetorical potential of fuller quotation from the Fathers.[8] However, Erasmus's

---

6. Their admonition may have been intentionally ironic, as Erasmus belonged to the order of Augustinian canons regular. For the evidence for Erasmus's knowledge of Augustine prior to 1516 see Robert D. Sider, "Erasmus, Influence of Augustine on" in *Augustine Through the Ages: An Encyclopedia,* ed. Allan Fitzgerald O.S.A. et al. (Grand Rapids: Eerdmans, 1999). For Luther's admonition (in 1516) that Erasmus should read Augustine, cf. *ep.* 501:55-58 (CWE 4:167); for similar advice from Johann Maier von Eck (in 1518), cf. *ep.* 769:107-13 (CWE 5:291-92).

7. Counting citations from and references to patristic authors in the Annotations has proven to be problematic; see Godin, *Érasme,* p. 143, n. 10, and p. 150, nn. 10, 11. In this essay my count generally approximates that of Rabil; I have usually (but not always) preferred to give approximate figures or relative estimates. In spite of the differences in particulars, relatively speaking the different counts yield much the same picture.

8. For Erasmus's occasionally negative evaluation of Augustine on account of his lack of Greek, see below.

instinct for the dramatic is already clearly evident: the allusion to the *Retractationes* reveals the quasi-colloquial setting assumed in the *Annotations,* for Augustine comes before us as a mute figure to which Erasmus points in a dialogue of two humanists: Erasmus challenges his "incomparable friend" Lefèvre, introduced here to the reader as a man of "unusual cordiality and affability," to reconsider a less than satisfactory interpretation of 1:15 and confides to the audience that "if Lefèvre reread his own work he would do occasionally what Augustine did in his books" (CWE 56:28).

Throughout the Middle Ages the text of the commentary of "Ambrosiaster" on the Pauline epistles had generally been included among the works of Ambrose, bishop of Milan.[9] Even as late as 1527 Erasmus himself included it in his edition of Ambrose, though he expressed doubts about its authenticity.[10] Erasmus's appeal to this text had distinct advantages. The text enjoyed the authority of its presumed author, the bishop of Milan, impeccably orthodox and one of the four great doctors of the Western Church. In addition, Ambrose was a Latin speaker who knew Greek well, and would therefore have been in a position to read the ancient Greek text. In fact, Ambrosiaster followed the Old Latin text and was therefore a witness to the Latin text prior to the time of Jerome's revision of the Gospels.[11]

From 1516 the *Annotations on Romans* reveals Erasmus's anxiety over the text of "Ambrose." In the annotation on 4:5 Erasmus notes that "Ambrose," like the Vulgate, reads words *(secundum propositum gratiae dei)* omitted by the Greek text and concludes that "it is clear he [Ambrosiaster] used a different witness," that is, he used a witness that diverged from that provided by Erasmus's Greek manuscripts. At another point Erasmus thinks there must be an "error in the books," that is, an error in the manuscript tradition of the text of Ambrosiaster. Elsewhere, Erasmus simply gives up: in the annotation on 1:4 Ambrosiaster supports Erasmus's reading by adding a couple of words, but, admits Erasmus, "I have no idea from where" (CWE 56:11). In spite of these uncertainties Erasmus used Ambrosiaster's commentary in

---

9. Cf. Henricus Josephus Vogels, ed., *Ambrosiastri qui dicitur commentarius in epistulas paulinas. Pars I. In epistulam ad Romanos,* CSEL 81. The *editio princeps* of Ambrosiaster's commentary, published in 1492 in Basel, also appeared among the works of Ambrose. Indeed, Erasmus was the first to challenge the Ambrosian authorship, but see the next footnote.

10. See CWE 42:7, n. 13. In spite of his doubts, Erasmus continued to designate the author as "Ambrose" even in the annotations of 1535.

11. For Ambrosiaster's text see Heinrich Josef Vogels, ed., *Das Corpus Paulinum des Ambrosiaster,* Bonner biblische Beiträge 13 (Bonn: Peter Hanstein Verlag G.M.B.H., 1957), pp. 13-15.

1516 chiefly as a support for his own readings and his construction of the text of Romans. He does so unpretentiously, typically with a brief formula, "so reads Ambrose" (4:20), "Ambrose reads" (5:16), "as Ambrose reads" (9:6). Once he goes further and actually records Ambrosiaster's construction: "And so indeed reads Ambrose: 'Therefore, as far as it lies in me I am ready, etc.'" (CWE 56:40 on 1:5).

Ambrosiaster is one of the least well-defined figures among the commentators who appear in the first edition of the *Annotations on Romans*. Even so, the name stands for something more than a script. In the first place, Erasmus's "Ambrose" comes before us as the possessor of an early, sometimes puzzling, text, and as a reader who on occasion unaccountably adds a pair of words. Moreover, a slight nuance can point beyond the commentary to the commentator. When Erasmus elucidates the textual difficulties of 5:14, he suggests that the "exemplarist" interpretation — that people sinned after the example of Adam — had been overlooked *not even* by Ambrose.[12] The emphasis subtly brings forward the authoritative figure of the bishop and theologian of Milan. Again, in determining the semantic value of Greek words, Erasmus not only places "Ambrose" in dialogue with himself, but even forces him into competition with the translator of the Vulgate, so revered by most, though frequently under attack by Erasmus: if "Ambrose" supports Erasmus's translation of ἀφθαρσία as *immortalitas* (2:7), he disagrees with Erasmus on the function of εἴπερ (8:9), and if he understands the force of συν-, his inelegant translation of συναγωνίσασθαι (15:30) "that you may share solicitude" makes him loser in this case to the translator of the Vulgate, "who has expressed it more correctly than Ambrose, at least in my opinion" (CWE 56:421).[13] Thus, Ambrosiaster also, like the other commentators, inescapably appears as a player in an act of textual construction.

When Erasmus returned from England to Paris in 1500, he resolved to edit the works of Jerome. It was at this point, and indeed, as an aid to his work in "restoring" Jerome, that he undertook to learn Greek.[14] Possibly from his early years, and certainly from his days in the monastery at Steyn, Erasmus had shared in the humanist cult of Jerome.[15] However, in 1501 he justified his

---

12. "Not even" seems to be the force of *nec* here as in similar constructions elsewhere in Erasmus; hence it is a necessary correction to the translation in CWE 56:164.

13. The Vulgate had rendered the expression by "that you help."

14. Cf. *epp.* 138:43-54 and 149:65-79. As both letters suggest, Erasmus also wanted to pursue biblical studies; in fact, for Erasmus "sacred literature" could include both biblical and patristic texts. However, in Ep. 149 he indicates that his immediate need for a tutor in Greek had arisen from his engagement in the Jerome enterprise.

15. Cf. the introduction to James F. Brady and John C. Olin, eds., trans., and annota-

editorial ambitions by expressing his desire that every reader "may come to recognize that the great Jerome, the only scholar in the church universal who had a perfect command of all learning both sacred and heathen, as they call it, can be read by anyone, but understood only by accomplished scholars."[16] In the immediately subsequent years other projects diverted him from his Jerome, but he returned to Jerome again when he was teaching at Cambridge (1511-14), and he was able in 1514 to join the great Amerbach project, begun in 1507, to publish Jerome's *Opera*. For this project, upon which several scholars were working, Erasmus became something like the editor-in-chief, and he himself contributed the first four of the nine volumes, volumes that included the letters, polemical treatises, and the spurious works.[17] During his Cambridge period and in their final stages of preparation Erasmus was evidently working on his New Testament and his Jerome edition at the same time. The New Testament was published in March of 1516, the Jerome edition in September of the same year.

These circumstances help to account for the fact that though we have no commentary on Romans from Jerome, Erasmus cites Jerome in his annotations on this epistle much more frequently in 1516 than he cites Ambrosiaster, and almost as often as Origen, finding in Jerome's extant commentaries citations from Romans or observations on biblical language and contextual problems by "the only scholar . . . who had a perfect command of all learning." Not only was Jerome's contribution to the study of biblical language undeniably immense, but allusions to his work in the *Annotations on Romans* reflected a poorly concealed agenda. In the early sixteenth century the Vulgate was commonly assumed to be Jerome's translation, and even before the publication of his New Testament text, Erasmus had been severely criticized for attempting to tamper with the Church's Bible, sacred for a thousand years.[18] Hence, whenever a citation indicated that Jerome himself either disagreed with or offered alternatives to what had become the Vulgate, Erasmus had implicitly demonstrated not only that the Vulgate could not in fact be "Jerome's translation" but also that his own undertaking rested upon the example and, therefore, the authority of Jerome, who himself appeared to be

---

tors, *The Edition of St. Jerome*, Collected Works of Erasmus 61 (Toronto: Toronto University Press, 1992), pp. xiv-xv. For an interesting effort to demonstrate Erasmus's deliberate attempt to cultivate a hieronymian image, cf. Lisa Jardine, *Erasmus, Man of Letters: The Construction of Charisma in Print* (Princeton: Princeton University Press, 1993); for a brief statement of Jardine's argument, see p. 5.

16. *Ep.* 149:72-75 (CWE 2:27).

17. See Brady and Olin, *Jerome*, pp. xix-xxix.

18. See *ep.* 304:90-163 (letter to Martin Dorp, September 1514) (CWE 3:20-22).

correcting the readings of the Vulgate. A few examples will illustrate the point:

> Jerome's *provocat* is preferable to the Vulgate's *adducit* (2:4);
> Jerome's *congemiscit* reflects the Greek prefix συν-, obscured in the Vulgate's *ingemiscit* (8:22);
> Jerome's *confido* represents the Greek πέπεισμαι better than the Vulgate's *certus sum* (8:38);
> Jerome rightly points out that *benignitas* is the correct translation of χρηστότης (11:22);
> Jerome repeatedly cites *inscrutabilia* rather than the Vulgate's *incomprehensibilia* (11:33).

In much the same way, Jerome's knowledge of Greek vindicated Erasmus's program embodied in the publication of his text of and annotations on the New Testament. Jerome's work demonstrated that Scripture must be understood in the first instance in the language in which it was written. The Latins, floundering over such critical words as "knowledge" and "predestination," were rescued by Jerome's ability to distinguish between ἐπίγνωσις and γνῶσις (1:28), and between ὁρίζειν and προορίζειν (1:4). Indeed, Erasmus would make his point about the critical value of Greek for biblical study even when he disagreed with Jerome, as in the subtle distinction Jerome made (without justification) between παράπτωμα and ἁμαρτία (5:13).

We can see, then, how the figure of Jerome becomes another source of the dramatic tension that energizes the *Annotations on Romans*. Jerome is the champion of the author in the latter's struggle, in 1516 still largely covert, against those who oppose the very conception of Erasmus's project. Tension arises also, in the 1516 edition, from the bold, if infrequent, attacks leveled against contemporary ecclesiastical customs and conditions, comments made more dramatic by the surprise their unanticipated appearance brings. In the 1516 *Annotations on Romans* Erasmus generally, on such occasions, sallies forth unshielded, but not quite always. Jerome provides cover, for example, when Erasmus attacks those who defend the burdensome multiplicity of feast days in the sixteenth century. Commenting on 14:5 ("some judge one day . . ."), he evokes the authority of Jerome: "To Christians . . . every day is equally holy: not that feast days should not be observed . . . but these are very few, namely, the Lord's Day, Easter, Pentecost, and a few others of this sort which Jerome recounts" (CWE 56:372).[19]

19. In the 1516 *Annotations on Romans* challenges to the status quo, though unques-

Augustine, Ambrose and Jerome all are Doctors of the Church. Origen, though prior to all of them in time, not only suffered condemnation by the Fifth Ecumenical Council (Constantinople, A.D. 553),[20] but was represented by highly questionable Latin translations, perhaps mistranslations.[21] Nevertheless, in the *Annotations on Romans* Erasmus's enthusiasm for Origen is manifest. It was an enthusiasm he had demonstrated first in 1501 while working on the *Enchiridion,* when he had come under the influence of Jean Vitrier, warden of the Franciscan convent in St. Omer and a devotee of both St Paul and Origen.[22] Later, the *editio princeps* of Origen's *Opera*[23] gave Erasmus easy access to Origen's *Commentary on Romans* in the preparation of his *Annotations.*[24]

Although in the *Enchiridion* Erasmus praises Origen for his skill as an allegorist,[25] one gathers from the annotations that it was rather the special qualities of Origen's mind that compelled Erasmus's attention.[26] In the *Annotations on Romans* Erasmus conveys to the reader his own admiration for Origen's intense intellectual energy and wide-ranging investigative curiosity, creating, as it were, an intellectual profile of the Alexandrian, who acquires thereby a *persona.* At almost the beginning of the *Annotations on Romans* Erasmus brings before us the image of Origen, the prodigious and untirings

---

tionably striking, are not especially frequent and are more or less limited to the following: the annotations on 1:1; 2:20, 24; 5:14; 8:33; 12:1, 21; 14:1; 15:5, 26; 16:7, 25. In later editions Erasmus modified his comments on some of these.

20. While the Renaissance humanists had, beginning in fifteenth-century Italy, done much to rehabilitate Origen, the old battle over the Alexandrian continued to rage in the early sixteenth century; see Godin, *Érasme,* pp. 4-9, 417-48.

21. Erasmus frequently complains about the quality of the translations of Origen; cf., e.g., CWE 56:94-95.

22. Cf. *ep.* 165:8-12 (CWE 2:54).

23. Origen, *Opera,* ed. Jacques Merlin (Paris: Josse Bade, 1512).

24. In 1501 Erasmus had apparently hoped to borrow a copy of Origen's *Commentary on Romans* from Vitrier's convent (see the reference to *Ep.* 165, n. 22, above). An edition of the commentary, under the name of Jerome, its assumed translator, appeared in Venice in 1506, but Godin notes that Erasmus used Merlin's edition for his *Annotations on Romans;* cf. Godin, *Érasme,* pp. 8, 165 n. 5, 168 n. 11.

25. Cf. the *Enchiridion,* trans. and annotated by Charles Fantazzi, in John W. O'Malley, ed., *Spiritualia,* CWE 66 (Toronto: University of Toronto Press, 1988), p. 69.

26. Cf. *ep.* 1844:42-45 in P. S. Allen, H. M. Allen, and H. W. Garrod, eds., *Opus epistolarum Des. Erasmi Roterodami,* 11 vols. (Oxford: Oxford University Press, 1906-47); index by B. Flowers and E. Rosenbaum (Oxford: Oxford University Press, 1958). Henceforth cited as "Allen." Rummel (*Erasmus' Annotations,* p. 66) cites this letter and notes that "[Erasmus] valued Origen for . . . his acute mind."

biblical scholar who produced the great Hexapla, and he wonders whether Origen could have gone beyond the Hexapla: Why did Origen, a Greek-speaker, cite the Latin witnesses on 1:4 ("who was predestined")? True, Origen's translator might have added the allusion on his own, but could it be, Erasmus wonders, that "Origen, not satisfied with so many [Greek] editions, tracked down not only the Hebrew sources, but with the same zeal scanned the Latin manuscripts as well?" (CWE 56:10). Origen's wonderful curiosity is also seen in the perceptive questions he raises, even on matters of fact. Thus, for example, the details of Romans 16 do not escape the questioning mind of Origen: he wants to know, as Erasmus observes, how Paul could send greetings to Prisca and Aquila now evidently in Rome (16:3), when Claudius had expelled the Jews from Rome, or how Paul could send greetings to Rome in the name of "all the churches" (16:16) when "all the churches" could not have been present at Corinth when Paul was concluding his letter (CWE 56:424, 429).

It is, perhaps above all, Origen's gift for recognizing distinctions that contributes to his intellectual identity. In the annotations, Jerome's definitions reflect a knowledge of Greek, but Origen's perceptive recognition of distinctions bespeaks an elegance of mind.[27] For example, Origen suggests a fancy distinction between "predestination" and "destination": the first word can be used of one who does not yet exist (i.e., a human being); the second, of one who already does exist (i.e., the eternal Christ) (1:4, CWE 56:11). Or, again, Origen distinguishes the various meanings of πρόγνωσις (8:29): we can "foreknow" in the sense of "predestine" — God foreknew even those who were to perish — or in the sense (customary to Hebrew idiom) of "embracing with affection" (CWE 56:226-27). Furthermore, Erasmus is manifestly pleased with the "elegant" manner in which Origen defines the distinction intended in 5:14 between Adam and Christ, which implies at once both a parallel and a contrast: "'generically alike,' says Origen, 'specifically contrary' — generically, in that as from Adam, so from Christ, something has flowed down to all; specifically, in that from Adam came death and sin, from Christ innocence and life" (CWE 56:168).

In yet one further respect Erasmus found in Origen a sympathetic

---

27. To say that allusions to Origen's fine distinctions enable Erasmus to project for Origen the image of an intellect that defines his *persona* is not to disallow the somewhat different vision of Godin (*Érasme*, p. 182), who sees Origen "comme un rhéteur posant des distinctions et définissant les termes. Dans une argumentation à dominante philologique, il semble jouer le rôle d'agent rhétorique qui réactive l'opération de décryptage grammatical."

mind. Like Erasmus, who lamented the sometimes virtually unintelligible constructions of the Vulgate, Origen, it appeared, could rest content only when the text of Scripture made sense in its context, when, that is, the text had been properly construed. Erasmus records Origen's complaint "that the Greek style [in Romans] is involved, obscured by hyperbata, and that due to Cilician idioms some parts are scarcely Greek."[28] Even where there are no hyperbata, an unpunctuated text can be ambiguous. Wherever, therefore, the arrangement of words brought ambiguity to the text, Erasmus sought clarification, and turned to Origen from time to time to illustrate the clarity Origen's fine mind could bring to the text. I cite three illustrative examples:

1. Origen has noted the hyperbaton in 1:13-15, "but he believes the sequence of language can be restored as follows: 'Just as I have had fruit in other nations (I am debtor to Greeks and barbarians, to the wise and foolish), likewise, insofar as it lies in me, I am ready, if it be permitted, to preach the gospel also to you who are at Rome'" (CWE 56:38).
2. Origen concurs with Erasmus in 2:7 in making "eternal life" the object of "he will give" — "to those seeking immortality he will give eternal life" — though the Greek permits one to understand, "to those seeking eternal life he will give immortality" (CWE 56:76).
3. Origen finds two ways to read the passage beginning in 5:12 with a subordinate clause for which there appears to be no main clause, that is, a sentence without an apodosis. On the one hand Origen finds an apodosis "after a considerable interval" in 5:15.[29] He suggests, on the other hand, that Paul might deliberately have left the sentence incomplete, for if he had finished it with a contrasting parallel — "so through one man righteousness came into the world, and through righteousness life was passed down to all" — "there was the danger that some, on hearing this, would become quite unconcerned and negligent or would begin to expect even now what will come later" (CWE 56:137).

The last example indicates how readily Erasmus could represent the agile mind of Origen leaping from the construction of the text to hermeneutics, from arrangement of words to the moral and theological significance of Scripture. Indeed, the articulation of biblical texts within the annotations, sometimes in a fresh arrangement of words, sometimes as paraphrase, held

28. CWE 56:30; on "Cilician idioms" see CWE 56:30 n. 6.
29. Modern scholars generally hold that after a long interval the apodosis begins in 5:18; cf. CWE 56:128 n. 3.

considerable potential for both capturing the rhetorical power of a biblical passage and suggesting its significance for life and doctrine. The impact is heightened when the text thus rendered is heard from the resonant and authoritative voice of one of the Fathers. In the 1516 *Annotations on Romans,* however, Erasmus offers in this respect only a foretaste of what will follow in later editions. He was, after all, confined to a single volume for prefatory material, text, and annotations. It is likely, moreover, that it was through the successive editions that he realized more fully the power of citation — whether of the biblical text or of the commentators' extrapolations upon it — "to instruct, to delight, and to move." We have seen that he dismissed some outstanding passages of Augustine on the style of Paul with merely a reference to the *De doctrina christiana.* In 1516 he similarly dismisses Origen's interesting reconstruction of the sequence of thought in Romans 1:24-31 with the comment, "Since I cannot comment on this briefly, and it does not really belong to the present undertaking, I have noted it in passing, and anyone who wishes can turn to the author himself" (CWE 56:70 and 70 n. 1). Later editions will trace out carefully the thought of both Augustine and Origen in the respective passages.

Patristic Commentators in the
Annotations on Romans: The Later Editions

The Edition of 1519

The decision to devote an entire volume to annotations minimized in 1519 the constraints of brevity. Further, it is reasonable to suppose that Erasmus had become alert to the various effects he could achieve by more numerous and more extensive quotations from the Fathers. Certainly, the *Annotations on Romans* in this edition is marked by a vast expansion of patristic allusions. Nevertheless, the four early commentators of the 1516 edition remain the almost exclusive source of the patristic allusions in 1519. While Jerome offers fewer new allusions than in 1516 (just over a dozen references), Augustine provides over forty new ones, references to Origen triple, and those to Ambrosiaster quadruple. Three other patristic authors just barely find a place: Erasmus makes a single reference to Athanasius's *To Serapion;* another to Didymus the Blind's *On the Holy Spirit,* a treatise translated by Jerome and included therefore in the *Opera* Erasmus had published in 1516;[30] and one to

---

30. Cf. Brady and Olin, *Jerome,* p. xxix.

Hilary available to Erasmus in the edition of Robert Fortuné.[31] Cyprian is cited five times, twice for his translation, otherwise as a textual witness. It is open to question how far the citations from Cyprian reflect Erasmus's preliminary work on his edition of the *Opera* of the Carthaginian bishop, published in 1520. The project for an edition of Cyprian edited by Erasmus was most probably conceived in the summer of 1518, but since the second volume of the 1519 New Testament (the *Annotations*) was printed first, and before September of 1518, it may well be that the references were recalled from earlier reading.[32]

It was apparently in 1517 that Erasmus accepted Froben's invitation to edit the works of Augustine.[33] Although Erasmus at first displayed relatively little enthusiasm for the project — indeed, the publication of the edition was completed only in 1529 — one gathers from the many allusions to the work of Augustine in the 1519 *Annotations* that Erasmus must have begun a vigorous program of reading for his prospective edition.[34]

It is Erasmus's ambivalence towards Augustine's knowledge of Greek that especially arrests our attention in the citations from his work in the 1519 *Annotations on Romans*. Erasmus obviously admired the *De doctrina christiana,* but if he regarded the work as something of a model text for the Christian humanist, he was less pleased with the image of the author himself, for Augustine was short on Greek.[35] In fact, nowhere in the 1519 *Annotations on Romans* does the *persona* of Augustine more dramatically confront the reader than when Erasmus hands to the saint one of his most stinging rebukes. In the annotation on 14:5 ("judging the day") Erasmus gives Augustine's reading of the passage, then adds,

31. Cf. the introduction to *ep.* 1334 (CWE 9:245).

32. For his own edition of Cyprian Erasmus used three earlier editions, those published in Rome in 1471, in Deventer in 1480, and in Paris in 1512; cf. Jacques Chomarat, *Grammaire et rhétorique chez Érasme* (Paris: Société d'Édition "Les Belles Lettres," 1981), 1:458. For the date at which Erasmus began work on his edition see the introduction to *Ep.* 1000 (CWE 7:25-26).

33. Cf. Sider, "Erasmus."

34. In the *Annotations on the New Testament* (taken as a whole) Erasmus cites from more than forty different works of Augustine in 1519, in contrast to less than half a dozen in 1516; cf. Sider, "Erasmus."

35. This circumstance no doubt played a part in the somewhat faint presence of Augustine in the annotations of 1516; cf. Rummel, *Erasmus'* Annotations, p. 59. It becomes a factor in Erasmus's interesting comparison of Augustine and Jerome in his letter to John Eck, *ep.* 844:133-291 (CWE 6:31-35).

But I am embarrassed by [Augustine's] interpretation of this same passage, which he by no means would have written if he had consulted the Greek. . . . I will add his own words: "In want of a better idea, I think that this speaks not of two persons, but of man and God. He who judges different days is man . . . he who judges every day is God. . . ." I ask you, reader, does he not seem to be living in some other world when he writes this? . . . this error on the part of so great a man should convince us that we must not neglect to consult the Greek volumes.[36]

In the light of this image of Augustine, it could be unexpected that in 1519 Erasmus frequently acknowledges in Augustine's work an authentic reflection of the Greek text of Romans. If, however, Augustine appears to receive the credit, Erasmus would no doubt assume that in many cases a Latin translation lies behind Augustine's citations. The following references indicate the manner of allusion:

> Augustine cites 4:17 (not according to the Vulgate but) according to the original Greek in his exposition of Psalm 104 (CWE 56:119).
> Augustine's translation of 9:10, however bad the Latin (with ablatives absolute), reflects exactly the Greek text (CWE 56:258).
> Augustine catches the appropriate image of "dough" in the word φύραμα (9:20) (CWE 56:276).
> Augustine's *bona voluntas* in 10:1 attempts to render εὐδοκία literally (CWE 56:276).
> Augustine's *glorifico* is just right for the Greek δοξάζω in 11:13 (CWE 56:304).
> Augustine's expression, "consecrating," in 15:16 expresses the meaning of the Greek ἱερουργοῦντα more nearly than the Vulgate's "sanctifying" (CWE 56:404).

There is, however, no ambiguity when the 1519 annotations recall Augustine, once a teacher of rhetoric, whose skill in the recognition of figures and the analysis of style becomes exemplary. The ancient rhetorician opportunely confirms Erasmus's exposition at various points:

> To call Abraham's body "dead" was a figurative way of saying that it was "worn out" — Augustine says something of this sort (on 4:19; CWE 56:123).

36. CWE 56:371-72.

The expression in 7:3 that "a woman is *to* a man" is a figure for "is married to a man"; Augustine includes this figure in his work on biblical expression (CWE 56:185).

In 8:3 the expression "in the likeness of the flesh of sin" contains a double figure: "likeness" implies a kind of play-acting, while "flesh of sin" is idiomatic for "flesh subject to sin." So Augustine understands (CWE 56:201).

Augustine understands the proper way to read 8:33-34 by distinguishing between two figures: an "enquiry" and a "question" (CWE 56:231).

In both 13:8 and 13:14 Augustine has pointed out the figured pattern of the prose (CWE 56:362).

The last two passages just cited provide a gauge by which to measure Erasmus's developing conceptualization of the annotations. In 1516 he had merely pointed to Augustine's comments on style;[37] now, in 1519, he cites Augustine with relatively brief explications; we must await the edition of 1527 for a full account of Augustine's demonstration of the pleasure and the force, and hence the power, of the Pauline style to captivate the hearer or the reader.

Erasmus's "Ambrose" remains somewhat faceless in the 1519 annotations on Romans, though he is characterized as a "follower of Origen," and his assumed identity with the bishop of Milan, who was fluently bilingual, puzzles Erasmus when the supposed Greek-speaker admits that he himself had not consulted the Greek texts.[38] Yet "Ambrose" contributes significantly to Erasmus's developing conceptualization of the annotations, for Erasmus learns how in the more expansive notes of 1519 to extend citations from his "Ambrose" so that the bishop of Milan becomes a mouthpiece for Erasmian thought, engaging the reader, therefore, in theological and moral discourse not only with Erasmus but with "Ambrose," too. One can, for example, sense Erasmus's own emphasis upon active faith and individual moral responsibility as he records and explicates the "readings" of Ambrosiaster in the following:

Regarding the intended referent for the phrase "according to the flesh" in 1:3: Ambrose gave us to understand "that . . . not even Abraham himself would have gained anything 'according to the flesh' . . . if he had not pleased God by the merit of his faith" (CWE 56:105).

37. Cf. the annotations on 8:33 and 9:30 discussed above.
38. For "Ambrose" as a follower of Origen see CWE 56:151 n. 2, 168, 266. For Ambrosiaster's failure to consult the Greek, see the annotation on 12:11 (CWE 56:334).

On the sense of ἀμεταμέλητα in 11:29: Ambrose took advantage of the Vulgate's *sine poenitentia* to understand that sin is freely remitted in baptism without the need for any good works, but only a heartfelt profession (CWE 56:312).

In 13:8 "Ambrose adopted the sense . . . '[Paul] wishes us to have peace if possible with all, but with our brothers love [as well]'" (CWE 56:353).

In the *Annotations on Romans* in both 1516 and 1519 Erasmus sought the resources of Jerome to facilitate his study of the Old Testament in the New. For some of this work Erasmus may have relied chiefly on friends in Basel, particularly the Hebraists Johannes Oecolampadius and Wolfgang Capito; occasionally, also, he turned to Origen and Augustine.[39] In any case he refers to Jerome less frequently for this purpose than we might expect.[40]

Indeed, in spite of Erasmus's apparent love for Jerome, the 1519 *Annotations on Romans* are marked by a recurrent criticism of him. In the annotation on 1:1 Erasmus actually mocks him: ". . . as to Jerome's point that in Hebrew Paul means 'wonderful' — it is a wonder to me," says Erasmus, "that [Jerome] commits the very fault he elsewhere criticizes in others who sought the etymologies of words from a different language" (CWE 56:3). He deplores those who "twist the words of Scripture in any way at all to gain a victory . . . [which] Jerome appears to do in his struggle against Jovinian" (CWE 56:165). In 1519 Erasmus still assumed that Jerome was the translator of Origen, and he did not hesitate to scold him for preferring "to allow incorrect language rather than to express inadequately Paul's meaning" (CWE 56:191). Like Augustine, Jerome does not escape the sharp tongue of Erasmus, with a similar effect upon the character of the annotations, for the implicitly personal attack seems to place the ancient writer on the stage before us.

In the many new references of 1519, Origen continues to play roles assigned to him in 1516: he is a witness to the Greek text of Romans, he en-

39. Cf., e.g., the annotations on 10:8, 16, 21; 11:9. Erasmus began the study of Hebrew but soon abandoned it and generally relied on others for citations from the Hebrew Scriptures.

40. In 1516 in more than fifteen annotations on Romans in which Erasmus studies citations from the Old Testament in the New, he appeals specifically to Jerome only three times; see the annotations on 1:17; 2:24; 11:33. For 1519 compare the annotations on 3:14 and 8:15. It seems likely that in some other cases when Erasmus speaks of the "original Hebrew," he is relying on the translations in Jerome's commentaries, or even in the Vulgate, without specifically crediting Jerome; cf., e.g., the annotation on 10:2 (CWE 56:289; "I have found . . .").

riches the exposition of the text by the explication of images and verbal nuances, and he remains the exegete of fine distinctions.[41] Yet just as Ambrosiaster had become in 1519 the vehicle for an effective rhetoric of theological and moral discourse, so Origen also became such a vehicle, and nowhere more decisively than when Erasmus cites his construction of the text. The annotation on 2:1 offers a splendid example: in 1516 Erasmus had, due to limitations of space and the nature of the undertaking, been obliged to dismiss Origen here with a brief acknowledgment that the latter had in fact explicated the sequence of thought in the extended passage from 1:24–2:1. The 1519 addition explores Origen's construction fully. In the thrice-repeated "God handed them over" the Apostle pointed to three dreadful forms of human evil that had become the ground for the action of God, whose terrifying justice could be felt to reverberate in the repetition of the phrases: "since human beings changed the glory of God . . . and since they corrupted the truth . . . and since they did not wish to acknowledge God, therefore God handed them over to the desires of their hearts . . . he handed them over to shameful affections . . . and handed them over to a reprobate mind" (CWE 56:70). What purports to be a record of a patristic endeavor to construe the text becomes in fact, for the reader of the annotations, a vivid and moving representation of the Pauline moral vision.

In the 1519 *Annotations on Romans* Origen receives a greatly enlarged role as an interpreter of the epistle. To construct the text is, of course, as we have seen, to interpret it. In 1519, however, Origen is invited not only to construe the Greek; he comes before us as a devoted hermeneut with a highly creative mind, indeed, in the first instance, as an exegete whose imagination fascinates and wins our admiration even while it does not convince. In these passages there is a typically Erasmian ambiguity. On the one hand, Origen in 1519 will be subjected to the criticism of Erasmus, as were Augustine and Jerome in the same edition, for the annotations, as I have noted, constitute a sort of colloquy in which no speaker is exempt from the scrutiny of his own words. On the other hand, Erasmus appears to recognize in Origen's fanciful interpretations little jewels of imagination that will enliven his own annotations by their vivacious sparkle, as well as by the attractive luster of the mind that shaped them; thus, they are worthy of record if not of trust. Hence in the following annotations:

41. Cf., e.g., the citations from Origen in the annotations on 3:25 (on ἱλαστήριον); 7:3 (on "sinning sin"); 6:11 (on the verb λογίζεσθαι); as well as the 1519 addition to the distinction between predestination and destination (1:4) and the distinction between "sign" and "seal" (4:11).

On 1:20 Origen (once again) distinguishes "with shrewdness and erudition, no doubt" between the "called" (those summoned to a particular service) and the "chosen" (those who faithfully complete it). Erasmus does not explicitly reject such an interpretation but notes that "in divine literature the simplest and least forced interpretations are more satisfactory" (CWE 56:6).

On 11:13 Origen thinks Paul's phrase "as long as I am an apostle of the Gentiles" may imply that after Paul's death he will be an apostle "to the invisible beings in heaven," an interpretation Erasmus finds "harsh" (CWE 56:303).

On 13:1 Origen, interpreting "soul" in terms of Platonic psychology, considers soul inferior to spirit. Thus the soul that is to be subject to inferior powers represents the person not entirely free from the things of this world, an interpretation Erasmus regards as "more clever than true" (CWE 56:346).

Even if Origen's inventive mind was capable at times of excess in the hermeneutical endeavor, the 1519 *Annotations on Romans* also represents Origen as in some respects a model exegete. Erasmus continues to be impressed by the untiring curiosity Origen brings to his task: "Who can sufficiently admire the care of Origen in examining sacred literature? This, too, exercised the man" — how Paul (in 1:8) could say "first" when no "second" followed. Just as, in 1516, Lefèvre was invited to learn humility from Augustine, so in 1519 Erasmus himself seeks to learn diligence from Origen. The great exegete, unwilling to overlook even the absence of a syllable, wondered why Paul wrote "Abraham" (4:13) since the Apostle was referring to the patriarch at a time when he was still called "Abram." Erasmus comments: "I certainly praise the man's diligence, and am ashamed of my own slackness" (CWE 56:107). On another occasion Erasmus creates the explicitly dramatic *mise en scène* of a contest between two ancient exegetes to show his esteem for Origen. In the annotation on 15:18 both "Ambrose" and Origen place their interpretations before the reader, while Erasmus plays the role of judge, expressing his preference for Origen's, not only because his interpretation is "more modest and fits better with what follows . . . but also because I do not see how the sense that Ambrose wants can be gathered from the Greek." The good judge then declares the winner and awards the prize: "I give the palm to the interpretation of Origen" (CWE 56:407).

The Edition of 1522

In contrast to the 1519 edition of the *Annotations on Romans,* which so greatly enlarged the first edition, in the edition of 1522 the revisions and additions were minimal. Accordingly, one finds few additional citations from the early commentators, and those added are generally brief citations offering an additional witness to the text or a comment on imagery and language. Ambrosiaster receives three new citations, Jerome and Origen two each, Cyprian one, while the only reference in all five editions to Bede (in the *Gloss*) appears in this edition. Augustine is cited nearly a dozen times, but nine citations are from a single work, the *Contra Faustum Manichaeum,* which may suggest recent reading in that work in preparation for his edition of the *Opera.*[42]

The Edition of 1527

New additions considerably enlarged the edition of 1527 beyond those of 1519 and 1522. Nevertheless, only two patristic authors, Augustine and Chrysostom, make a significant impact on the development of the *Annotations on Romans.* The citations added from other early commentators are generally brief, as in the edition of 1522: they offer additional evidence to establish the text, or they attempt to shed light on the language of Romans. Origen and Jerome provide three new citations each, Ambrosiaster offers two, though an additional reference to the commentary on Luke by the bishop of Milan makes three for Erasmus's "Ambrose." From Hilary, cited once in 1519, now come five new allusions, a reflection, perhaps, of Erasmus's work on his edition of Hilary, published in 1523. We meet Tertullian for the first time in the *Annotations on Romans* in two citations, though the *editio princeps* of the African's work had been published by Beatus Rhenanus in 1521. Likewise for the first time in the *Annotations on Romans* Erasmus introduces in 1527 Pseudo-Jerome, whose commentary on the thirteen epistles of Paul has been shown to be the work chiefly of Pelagius.[43] Erasmus refers to him only twice in 1527 in our annotations: once as "the man

---

42. *On the Merits and Remission of Sins* and *Against Maximus the Arian* are each cited once.

43. Cf. Alexander Souter, *Pelagius's Expositions of the Thirteen Epistles of Paul,* 3 vols., Texts and Studies 9 (Cambridge: Cambridge University Press, 1922-31): vol. 1, *Introduction* (1922); vol. 2, *Text and Critical Apparatus* (1926); vol. 3, *Pseudo-Jerome Interpolations* (1931). Souter has shown that the commentary of Pseudo-Jerome was in fact written by Pelagius with interpolations by a Pseudo-Jerome.

whose scholia we have on all the Pauline epistles, a learned man," but to whose work an "imposter has added a preface, pretending the author was Jerome — to make the work more saleable" (CWE 56:152); a second time as "he whose scholia we read under the name of Jerome" (CWE 56:164). Thus, apart from the allusions to Augustine and Chrysostom, the *Annotations on Romans* of 1527 offered an unimpressive list of new citations from the Fathers.

The citations from Augustine in the 1527 *Annotations on Romans* are important because they indicate Erasmus's constantly increasing commitment to read the Bible as literature — as a text able to inspire and motivate — and they reveal his confidence in Augustine's support for doing so.[44] In 1516 Erasmus had merely referred to the *De doctrina christiana;* in 1527 he reviews, cites, and paraphrases extensive passages from it. These passages provide him with something like a manifesto that articulates and justifies his commitment in the face of opponents who despise his endeavors as work for grammarians, unworthy therefore of theologians. The drama of such a background is not lost upon the reader in the annotation on 5:5, where Erasmus reviews the "figures" Augustine pointed out in 5:4-5: the gradatio, the rhythmical clauses, and the periods, all of which effected the "structural grace" of the passage. Erasmus concludes with Augustine's acknowledgment that these efforts were not sought by Paul, "but that eloquence was of its own accord a companion to wisdom, and wisdom does not disdain such a companion" (CWE 56:132).

The intensity of drama may also be felt in the contagious enthusiasm that leads Erasmus to extravagant comparisons in three further additions of 1527 designed to record and develop the thought of Augustine on Pauline style. Augustine speaks in the annotation on 8:35, where the rhetorical brilliance of the whole passage from 8:29-39 is set out on display. The passage is a "model of artistic prose that combines force . . . with ornament," and the "phrases make the speech elevated, because Paul, breathed upon by the divine power, says nothing in the low style." Erasmus concludes, "What did Cicero ever say that effected more fully the grand manner?" (CWE 56:233-34). Two further passages exemplify, according to Augustine, the "middle style." Through Augustine Erasmus describes the "fine touches" in the figures of 13:12-14. He notes also the "mannered diction" of 12:6-18. "Certainly there is scarcely another passage in Paul better ordered and, so to speak, more patterned, . . . a passage so modulated . . . that no song could be more pleasant" (CWE 56:344).

44. See my article, "Erasmus on the Epistle to the Romans: A 'Literary Reading,'" in *Acta Conventus Neo-Latini Torontonensis,* Medieval and Renaissance Texts and Studies (Binghamton, N.Y.: Medieval and Renaissance Texts and Studies, 1991), pp. 129-35.

Though for parts of the New Testament, Latin translations of Chrysostom's homilies had been available in the West throughout the early to the late Middle Ages, Erasmus had no access to the *Homilies on Romans* until he was able to obtain a copy of these in Greek.[45] Indeed, it was only in August 1526 that he indicates he had received these homilies in a copy that had apparently been made for him from a manuscript found in the library of Johann von Dalberg in Ladenburg, near Heidelberg.[46] It may be, therefore, that Erasmus had insufficient time fully to absorb these homilies, for the fourth edition of his New Testament was published in March of the next year. It is at least noteworthy that of the approximately seventy allusions to the homilies in the 1527 edition, the vast majority are brief citations providing the textual evidence offered by the manuscript. Indeed, in many cases Erasmus merely adds the name of Chrysostom to reinforce the witness of a commentator already cited in an earlier edition, saying, for example, that "Origen *and Chrysostom* read . . ." From such references it is unlikely that an effective *persona* would emerge for Chrysostom. Other allusions, however, point to a coherent set of intellectual qualities that mark the saint: his sensitivity to language, his knowledge of rhetoric, and his contempt for the wisdom of this world.

Though in the 1527 *Annotations on Romans* Erasmus seldom calls upon Chrysostom for the denotation of Greek words,[47] he recognizes his ubiquitous efforts to explicate *emphasis*, understood as a rhetorical term designating the special significance a word or construction may be intended to convey. Thus Erasmus cites Chrysostom for the implications of ὀψώνιον "wage" in 6:23 (CWE 56:181), of ἀνεξιχνίαστοι "untraceable" in 11:33 (CWE 56:317), and even of the arrangement of words in 12:15 (CWE 56:338). Chrysostom's rhetorical knowledge and skill also find a place in these annotations. Following Chrysostom, Erasmus notes the rhetorical "ethos" in Paul's letter when he introduces himself to the Romans (on 1:12; CWE 56:37). He cites Chrysostom to identify rhetorical figures, such as the "antithesis" or "counter-proposition" in 9:16 (CWE 56:261), or the "intensification" or "amplification" of 11:33 (CWE 56:317-18). In one of only three 1527 additions that constitute an extended ci-

---

45. Cf. my article, "'Searching the Scriptures': John Chrysostom in the New Testament Scholarship of Erasmus," in *Within the Perfection of Christ: Essays on Peace and the Nature of the Church*, Essays in Honor of Martin H. Schrag, ed. Terry L. Brensinger and E. Morris Sider (Nappanee, Ind.: Evangel, 1990), p. 90.

46. For the manuscript, see Allen, *Epp.* 2258: n. 6 and 1736:23-24. Dalberg was a patron of humanists; see Peter G. Bietenholz and Thomas B. Deutscher, eds., *Contemporaries of Erasmus: A Bibliographical Register of the Renaissance and Reformation* (Toronto: University of Toronto Press, 1985), 1:474.

47. Yet for exceptions see the annotations on 6:23 (ὀψώνια) and 9:3 (ἀνάθεμα).

tation from Chrysostom[48] are we shown Paul's admirable rhetorical skill — in "closing in upon the self-righteous sinner" of 2:1 (CWE 56:68).

We have seen that as early as 1519 Erasmus had effectively used Ambrosiaster as a mouthpiece for his own opinions. Two additions in 1527 reflect an appeal to Chrysostom to authenticate the Erasmian polarization of simple faith and sophistic reasoning. The first, in the annotation on 1:5, is particularly interesting because Erasmus merely adds in 1527 the stamp of Chrysostom to his own expression of 1516: "By 'obedience of faith' [Paul] means, *as Chrysostom explains,* that [faith] is not obtained by a painstaking process of logical reasoning but by simple obedience and quiet compliance" (CWE 56:27). Erasmus continues the theme in the next annotation ("for his name," also on 1:5) with a short concluding sentence: "[Chrysostom] explains: 'I [Paul] was not sent to spin out syllogisms, but to perform the task committed to me'" (CWE 56:28). A third addition is worthy of note for its Erasmian emphasis on Christian moral responsibility, where the long series of rhetorical antitheses cited from Chrysostom effects a claim upon Erasmus readers: "[Paul, says Chrysostom,] did not say merely . . . 'share,' but 'bountifully and eagerly'; nor did he say . . . 'care for,' but added . . . 'zealously.' He did not say . . . 'show mercy,' but . . . 'love,' and that without hypocrisy . . ." (12:11; CWE 56:335).

The Edition of 1535

In the *Annotations on Romans* of 1535 Erasmus went far beyond anything he had previously written, largely, it appears, in response to the criticism from theologians leveled against his biblical scholarship and its perceived challenge to theological and ecclesiastical tradition.[49] Hence, in the 1535 edition, not only were short additions made to correct and clarify earlier comments, but some annotations were completely rewritten, lengthy remarks were added to others, and some entirely new annotations were composed. Of additions ex-

---

48. For the second cf. CWE 56:250-51, the annotation on 9:5, where the rhetorically effective language of Chrysostom arouses in Erasmus's reader a certain sense of exaltation appropriate to a benediction; for the third (annotation on 12:11), see the next paragraph.

49. In each of the editions subsequent to 1516 Erasmus countered his critics, but after the completion of his *Paraphrases* on the New Testament in 1524, and as the Church felt itself threatened ever more seriously by the "schism" of the Reformers, Erasmus became increasingly embattled with the theologians, in spite of his overt break with Luther in 1524. Erasmus's later controversies are described in Erika Rummel, *Erasmus and His Catholic Critics,* II, *1523-1536,* Bibliotheca humanistica reformatorica 45 (Nieuwkoop: DeGraaf Publishers, 1989).

tending to a page or more in length, one finds six in 1519, only four in 1527 (of which two are devoted to Augustine on style), but eleven in 1535.[50]

In spite of the vastly increased text of 1535, there are few new voices from the Fathers. Though Erasmus had prepared the (Latin) *editio princeps* of Irenaeus, published by Froben in 1526,[51] and had directed the publication of the (Greek) *editio princeps* of Basil of Caesarea (1532),[52] each author provides only one citation for the 1535 *Annotations on Romans,* like Paulinus, whom Erasmus did not edit. Of voices already heard in previous editions, Cyprian returns with a single new allusion, Hilary with four, and Pelagius/Pseudo-Jerome with five. Erasmus keeps to his favorites: Origen and Ambrosiaster, Jerome and Augustine, and now, above all, Chrysostom. The presence of Augustine is felt with particular force, his *persona* dramatically conceived, in the annotation on 5:12, where his authority, though exercised with bold and unremitting insistence in the early Church, is shown to have been utterly disregarded by the inheritors of the tradition, including Erasmus's critics (CWE 56:149-50).

Perhaps the most striking feature of the 1535 *Annotations on Romans* is Erasmus's highly systematic and extended appeal to patristic exegetes in defense of his position in theological debate. In 1535 it is frequently not a matter of a brief supporting comment from one or more of the Fathers; the Fathers are summoned systematically, in sequence, one after another, while the reader, led through their expansive comments, sentence by sentence, seems to hear the living voice of the ancient commentator evoked by their "Hermes," Erasmus. The most decisive example is found in the annotation on 5:12, completely rewritten for the 1535 edition, and the longest of all on Romans. Erasmus undertakes to show that the ἐφ' ᾧ of 5:12 does not necessarily imply a doctrine of original sin but permits an exemplarist view, that human beings sin after the example of Adam. A long preliminary discussion defines the terms of the debate and reviews the characteristic use of the preposition (CWE 56:139-41). Then Erasmus turns to the early commentators. First, "he whose scholia . . . bear the name of Jerome" is summoned. Erasmus guides the reader through Pelagius's every turn of phrase until the reader hears Pelagius say at the crucial point, "They sin through the example of Adam" (CWE 56:141-42). The words

50. The "page" is that of CWE 56. These major additions will be found as follows: for 1519, in the annotations on 2:1; 7:1; 8:33; 14:6; 15:18; 16:25; for 1527, in the annotations on 1:7, 32; 8:35; 13:14; for 1535, in the annotations on 4:12; 5:1, 12; 8:18; 9:5; 11:11, 31; 12:2; 15:4, 7, 24.

51. Erasmus had only Latin manuscripts for this edition. He confesses that he did not know whether Irenaeus wrote in Latin or in Greek (cf. Allen, *ep.* 1738:73-75).

52. For Erasmus's participation in the project see Allen, *ep.* 2611, introductory note.

of Origen are then passed in review over nearly two pages (CWE 56:142-44); two further pages record the exegesis of "Ambrose," whose ambiguity Erasmus attempts to eliminate with an imaginative scenario from the world of finance, dramatically posing the question, "Who would suppose, if talk were about loans, that the reference would be to the deposit?" (CWE 56:145-46). Chrysostom comes before us last of all. Erasmus offers a direct quotation of more than half a page, so that Chrysostom, referring to himself in the first person, seems to be speaking directly to the reader rather than to his audience of late antiquity: "Some think the Apostle had in mind the time before the Law was given . . . but it seems to me that what I [i.e., Chrysostom] am about to say is a more probable [interpretation]. . . . I think he means . . ." (CWE 56:146-47). In these words Chrysostom in his own person is made to stand before us.

The Erasmian technique in citing the Fathers reaches here what is perhaps its most sophisticated level. The sense of the drama is implicit throughout. In this annotation the Fathers are not in debate among themselves but speak with an overwhelming unanimity in the debate between Erasmus and his critics. Their force lies not only in the voices speaking in unison, but also in an implicit authority that is successfully explicated, as it were, through the power of their presence on the stage before us, as well as in the weight of the massive and systematic quotation that seems to crush the opponents.

It remains to note more specifically the contribution of Chrysostom to the *Annotations on Romans* in this edition. We have seen that for the 1527 edition Erasmus had at hand a manuscript of Chrysostom's *Homilies on Romans* that had been copied for him. In 1529 the "Verona" edition of the homilies on the Pauline epistles was published in three volumes under the direction of John Matthew Giberti.[53] The availability of the published text and, no doubt, of the additional time needed to absorb the homilies enabled Erasmus in the 1535 annotations to give to the homilies a place even more prominent than in 1527.[54] The citations continue to offer textual evidence, but they are more remarkable for their contribution to the *Annotations on Romans* in three other respects.

First, in 1527 Chrysostom had been cited, but sparingly, for his defini-

---

53. Erasmus attests his use of this edition; cf. CWE 56:377 and 378 n. 17.

54. Some sixty new citations from Chrysostom appear in 1535, only a few less than in 1527. By way of contrast, Origen and Ambrosiaster each receive approximately twenty-five new citations in 1535. Indeed, while Origen and Ambrosiaster are cited in all five editions, just over 140 and 130 times, respectively, Chrysostom receives a little more than 130 citations in the last two editions alone.

tions of Greek words. In 1535 Chrysostom plays a much larger role in explicating Pauline language, for, as Erasmus specifically points out, Chrysostom "spoke Greek" (on 14:21; CWE 56:385). Thus Chrysostom is able to give us authoritative definitions of the denotations and the special connotations of Greek words: εἴπερ for "since," "seeing that" (CWE 56:206); λογίζομαι in the sense of "consider," not "suppose" (CWE 56:215); παρίστημι properly used of those who furnish war-horses to military commanders (CWE 56:320); στέργειν, which is something more than φιλεῖν, since it is the spontaneous love of relatives, whom we cherish even when they are disagreeable (CWE 56:332); προσκόπτω in the sense of "scandalize" (CWE 56:385); φιλοτιμεῖσθαι "to act for the sake of glory" (CWE 56:409); λειτούργησαι "to minister" (CWE 56:417), to mention just a few!

Second, Erasmus continues to criticize, if somewhat more cautiously, the contemporary ecclesiastical scene, taking cover under the name of the Fathers, nowhere more strikingly than when Chrysostom becomes his mouthpiece to attack an episcopal authority based on externals: Erasmus concludes the annotation on 15:19 by tautly noting a dramatically vivid contrast: ". . . in this passage Chrysostom seems covertly to censure certain bishops who claim authority for themselves on the basis of their mitres, staffs and robes, while Paul proves that he is an apostle by arguments far superior — by the greatness of his miracles and the success of the evangelical doctrine" (CWE 56:408).

Finally, as in earlier editions, quotations from the early commentators, even when cited in support of a textual reading, often have an effect that goes beyond their ostensible objective. Chrysostom's "golden stream" of rhetoric can bring to the annotations the evangelical fervor of devotional literature and the sense of moral urgency intended by the homiletical endeavor. In the 1535 edition the devotional intensity and the moral gravity are enhanced by the expansive room given to quotation. The annotation on 13:12 (CWE 56:359-60) may exemplify the effect. Erasmus cites Chrysostom to support his reading, "the night has advanced" (in contrast to the Vulgate's "has preceded"). "'Accordingly,' says Chrysostom, 'if the night is ending . . . let us do those things which are of the day. . . . For when we see the night hastening towards the dawn and hear the swallow singing, we rouse our neighbors . . . casting aside our dreams, shaking off sleep, so that the day will find us prepared.'" If in the first instance we listen to the words of Chrysostom to verify a textual reading, it is, in fact, the music of the language in this passage that haunts us, challenging us to the moral endeavor that Chrysostom demands.

Erasmus's annotations are a very complex literary undertaking. To understand them it is essential to begin with his own stated aims. Yet in the course of our evaluation of the place of the early commentators in the *Annotations on Romans,* we have come to see that the abiding value of this work lies not only in the witness it brings to the solid work of Erasmus in constructing the text of Romans, or to the expression of his theological convictions, or to his commitment to reform within the Church. The Fathers are also part and parcel of a literary endeavor — to create a genre that attracts the reader to, and involves the reader in, the process of hermeneutics. The annotations do so, in the first instance, by creating a pervasive expectation of "drama" and "the dramatic" in the course of the reading experience. To this the early commentators contribute much as they acquire *personae* and as they debate among themselves or join Erasmus in his debates with his contemporaries, and, particularly (but not exclusively) in the longer quotations, insofar as the Fathers seem to address the reader directly in them. Further, the ancient commentators are made to confront the reader with the compelling immediacy of their presence and their commanding authority, so that the reader cannot easily escape their gaze. Finally, their bold imagination delights, their confident knowledge instructs and persuades, and their rhetoric inspires. Thus in the *Annotations on Romans* they have played a very considerable part in bringing the Bible before the reader as a living book.

II. The Development of Patristic Exegesis

Servant of Christ and Steward of the Mysteries of God: The Purpose of a Pauline Letter according to Origen's *Homilies on 1 Corinthians*

JUDITH L. KOVACS

Introduction

Origen "stands out in splendid isolation at the fountainhead of the tradition of Greek exegesis." So Maurice Wiles characterizes Origen's exegesis of Paul.[1] The most influential exegete of the ancient Greek Church, Origen wrote commentaries on at least ten of the Pauline epistles and homilies on at least six of them.[2] Yet today Origen's exegesis of Paul is largely unknown.[3] In part, this is

---

1. Maurice Wiles, *The Divine Apostle: The Interpretation of St. Paul's Epistles in the Early Church* (Cambridge: Cambridge University Press, 1967), p. 6.

2. I use the term "Pauline" to refer to the fourteen letters attributed to Paul by the early Church. According to Wiles, Origen seems to have written commentaries on all the Pauline epistles during his Caesarean period (*Divine Apostle*, p. 6). Pierre Nautin cites evidence that Origen wrote commentaries on Romans, Galatians, Ephesians, Philippians, Colossians, 1-2 Thessalonians, Titus, Philemon, and Hebrews and homilies on 1 Corinthians, 2 Corinthians, Galatians, 1 Thessalonians, Titus, and Hebrews (*Origène, sa vie et son oeuvre* [Paris: Beauchesne, 1977], pp. 243-45, 253-54, 385-86). Nautin estimates that the homilies on Paul were written around 239-42, and the Pauline commentaries in 243 (pp. 386, 408-11). Carolyn Bammel ("Origen's Pauline Prefaces and the Chronology of the Pauline Commentaries," in *Origeniana Sexta: Origène et La Bible*, ed. Gilles Dorival and Alain le Boulluec [Leuven: University Press, 1995], pp. 495-514) argues that Nautin's dating is pure guesswork and suggests that the Pauline commentaries were composed over a longer period of time.

3. The only full-length study of Origen's interpretation of Paul is Francesca

due to the accidents of transmission. Of Origen's works on Paul, only the commentary on Romans survives, in an abridged Latin translation.[4] From the rest we have only fragments of the commentaries on Ephesians and Galatians, and of the homilies on 1 Corinthians.[5]

Another reason we know so little about Origen's interpretation of Paul can be traced to the Reformation. Luther said of Origen: *In toto Origene non est verbum unum de Christo* — "In all of Origen there is not one word of Christ."[6] According to Wiles, what Luther really meant was "that Origen did not teach the same doctrine of justification by faith alone which [Luther] found in the writings of Paul."[7] The influence of this kind of negative judgment is still felt today. The idea persists that Origen is more a Greek philosopher than a serious interpreter of the Bible,[8] and his exegesis is often discounted because of his use of allegory.[9]

Cocchini, *Il Paolo di Origene: Contributo alla storia della recezione delle epistole Paoline nel III secolo* (Rome: Edizioni Studium, 1992). See also her article, "Paolo in Origene nel periodo alessandriano," in *Origeniana Quinta*, ed. Robert J. Daly (Leuven: University Press, 1992), pp. 165-73.

4. Carolyn Hammond Bammel, ed., *Der Römerbriefkommentar des Origenes: Kritische Ausgabe der Übersetzung Rufins*, 3 vols. (Freiburg im Breisgau: Herder, 1990, 1997, 1998): vol. 1, *Bücher 1-3;* vol. 2, *Bücher 4-6;* vol. 3, *Bücher 7-10.* A fragment of this commentary (on Rom. 3:5–5:7) also survives in a Greek papyrus published by Jean Scherer, *Le Commentaire d'Origène sur Rom III,5–V,7*, Bibliothèque d'Étude 27 (Cairo: Institut français d'archéologie orientale, 1957). On the relation of the two versions see Henry Chadwick, "Rufinus and the Tura Papyrus of Origen's Commentary on Romans," *JThS* new series 10 (1959): 10-42. Chadwick argues that Rufinus's translation is generally reliable.

5. "*Commentary on Ephesians* (fragments)," ed. J. A. F. Gregg, *JThS* 3 (1902): 233-44, 398-420, 554-76; "*Homilies on 1 Corinthians* (fragments)," ed. Claude Jenkins, *JThS* 9 (1908): 231-47, 353-72, 500-514; *JThS* 10 (1909): 29-51. Fragments from *Commentary on Galatians* in J. A. Cramer, *Catenae Graecorum Patrum in Novum Testamentum*, vol. 6 (Oxford: Oxford University Press, 1838).

6. Dr. Martin Luther's *Tischreden* (Weimar edition, vol. 1), 136.22, quoted in Einar Molland, *The Conception of the Gospel in Alexandrian Theology*, Skrifter utgitt av det Norske Videnskaps-Akademi i Oslo II: Historisk-filosofisk Klasse I Bind (Oslo: I Kommidjon hos J. Dybwad, 1938), p. 170, n. 2, and in Wiles, *Divine Apostle*, p. 6.

7. Wiles, *Divine Apostle*, pp. 134-35.

8. See, e.g., Hal Koch, *Pronoia und Paideusis: Studien über Origenes und sein Verhältnis zu Platonismus*, Arbeiten zu Kirchengeschichte 22 (Berlin: de Gruyter, 1932), esp. pp. 180-205, 315-17.

9. See R. P. C. Hanson, *Allegory and Event: A Study of the Sources and Significance of Origen's Interpretation of Scripture* (London: SCM, 1959). Hanson speaks of Origen's using allegory "as a panacea for all Biblical intransigence" (p. 371). Origen, he says, "was gener-

The time is ripe for a reassessment of Origen's reading of Paul as part of a more general reexamination of the role of the Bible in his works. The publication in 1950 of Henri de Lubac's study of Origen, *Histoire et esprit,* provided a strong argument that Origen is above all a biblical theologian[10] — a view that has found ample support in a series of studies by Henri Crouzel.[11] The one Pauline commentary that survives *in extenso,* that on Romans, has begun to receive belated attention,[12] including translations into German and Italian.[13]

Despite this interest in Origen's interpretation of Romans, the fragmentary evidence of his interpretation of the other Pauline letters remains largely unexplored.[14] There is not one study, for example, of the seventy-three pages

---

ally speaking not seriously restrained by the Bible; he knew very little about the intellectual discipline demanded for faithful interpretation of biblical thought; his presuppositions were very little altered by contact with the material in the Bible, though he was perfectly willing to accept the ideas of the Bible when they did not conflict with his presuppositions." For a concise summary of scholarly discussion of Origen's allegory, see Karen Jo Torjesen, *Hermeneutical Procedure and Theological Method in Origen's Exegesis* (Berlin: Walter de Gruyter, 1986), pp. 3-12.

10. Henri de Lubac, *Histoire et esprit: L'intelligence de l'Écriture d'après Origène* (Paris: Aubier, 1950), esp. pp. 69-77 on Origen and Paul. De Lubac says of Origen: "C'est aussi qu'il a vraiment, depuis sa plus tendre enfance, 'vécu dans la Bible'. Quoi qu'il en soit des autres sources de sa pensée, c'est vraiment d'elle qu'il a tiré la moelle de sa théologie" (pp. 73-74). For criticism of de Lubac, see Hanson, *Allegory and Event,* pp. 185-86, 188, 213-14, 224, 255-58.

11. See especially Henri Crouzel, *Théologie de l'image de Dieu chez Origène* (Paris: Aubier, 1956); idem, *Origène et la "connaissance mystique,"* Museum Lessianum, section théologique 56 (Paris: Desclée de Brouwer, 1961); and the essays collected in *Les fins dernières selon Origène* (Brookfield, Vt.: Variorum, 1990). See also Robert L. Wilken, "Origen's *Homilies on Leviticus* and *Vayikra Rabbah,*" in *Origeniana Sexta,* pp. 81-91.

12. See Carolyn Hammond Bammel's text-critical study, *Der Römerbrieftext des Rufins und seine Origenesübersetzung* (Freiburg im Breisgau: Herder, 1995); idem, "Origen's Pauline Prefaces"; Theresia Heither, *Translatio religionis: Die Paulusdeutung des Origines in seinem Kommentar zum Römerbrief,* Bonner Beiträge zur Kirchengeschichte 8 (Vienna: Böhlau, 1990); Peter J. Gorday, *Principles of Patristic Exegesis: Romans 9–11 in Origen, John Chrysostom, and Augustine,* Studies in the Bible and Early Christianity 4 (New York and Toronto: Edwin Mellen, 1983); idem, "Paulus Origenianus: The Economic Interpretation of Paul in Origen and Gregory of Nyssa," in William Babcock, *Paul and the Legacies of Paul* (Dallas: Southern Methodist University Press, 1990), pp. 141-63, 350-58.

13. German translation by Theresia Heither, *Origenes, Commentarii in Epistulam ad Romanos,* 5 vols. (Freiburg im Breisgau: Herder, 1990-96); Italian translation by Francesca Cocchini, *Commento alla lettera ai Romani,* 2 vols. (Casale Monferrato: Marietti, 1985-86).

14. The one full-length study is the unpublished Ph.D. dissertation of Richard Layton, "Origen as a Reader of Paul: A Study of the Commentary on Ephesians," Univer-

of fragments from Origen's homilies on 1 Corinthians, which Claude Jenkins collected from medieval catenae and published in the *Journal of Theological Studies* in 1908-9[15] — aside from a brief article by C. H. Turner on textual matters.[16] This is surprising given the prominence of texts from 1 Corinthians in Origen's works. The *Biblia Patristica* lists 3,572 references to 1 Corinthians, not far behind the 3,827 references to Romans, the most-cited Pauline letter.[17]

---

sity of Virginia, 1996. Layton studies the catena fragments of Origen's *Commentary on Ephesians* in relation to Jerome's working on Ephesians, demonstrating that Jerome's commentary is largely plagiarized from Origen. See also the general study of Cocchini, *Paolo di Origene*.

15. See n. 5. Jenkins describes his text-critical principles in "The Origen-Citations in Cramer's Catena on 1 Corinthians," *JThS* 6 (1904): 113-16. He has recollated the sixteenth-century manuscript Paris gr. 227 used by Cramer in *Catenae Graecorum Patrum in Novum Testamentum,* vol. 5 (Oxford: Oxford University Press, 1838), and compared it with the eleventh-century Vatican MS gr. 762, which he thinks is the original from which the Paris manuscript was copied; he also adds some readings from a catena preserved on Mount Athos (MS Pantocrator 28).

16. C. H. Turner, "Notes on the Text of Origen's Commentary on I Corinthians," *JThS* 10 (1909): 270-76. Turner emphasizes the importance of Jenkins's work: "I do not think that the *Journal of Theological Studies,* in the nine years of its existence, has published any contribution to theological learning more solid and more valuable than the edition of the fragments of Origen on St. Paul's epistles to Ephesus and Corinth. . . . Any fragments of the original Greek of Origen's work on the New Testament are worth all that we can devote to them of loving and patient study" (p. 270). Although several scholars refer to the 1 Corinthians fragments, no one has focused on the homilies as a whole. Some works that discuss individual fragments are collected essays of Henri Crouzel, *Les fins dernières selon Origène* (especially: "L'exégèse origénienne de I Cor 3,11-15 et la purification eschatologique," 2:273-83; "La doctrine origénienne du corps ressuscité," 6:175-200, 241-66; "Les critiques adressées par Methode et ses contemporains à la doctrine origénienne du corps ressuscité," 6:679-716); idem, *Virginité et mariage selon Origène* (Paris: Desclée de Brouwer, 1962); Wiles, *Divine Apostle;* Carolyn Bammel, "Die Prophetie in der patristischen Exegese zum ersten Korintherbrief," *Augustinianum* 29 (1989): 157-69; Reimer Roukema, "La prédication du Christ crucifié [1 Corinthiens 2.2] selon Origène," in *Origeniana Sexta,* pp. 523-29; Cocchini, *Paolo di Origene,* pp. 82-88.

17. *Biblia Patristica: Index des citations et allusions bibliques dans la littérature patristique,* vol. 3, *Origène* (Paris: Éditions du Centre National de la Recherche Scientifique, 1980); I follow Gorday ("Paulus Origenianus," p. 351, n. 2), who has counted up the number of references. See Gorday's suggestions about how these references are to be studied: "What matters, aside from sheer frequency (which is not to be ignored), is how one *weighs* these citations and allusions: in what context do they appear, across how many works are they scattered, how central do they seem to be to an argument, with what other texts are they combined? . . . We still need an adequate hermeneutic of the use of texts in order to understand what writers like Origen make of scripture."

If we adjust for the fact that the commentary on Romans has survived, whereas we have only fragments from the homilies on 1 Corinthians, it would seem that 1 Corinthians had even more influence on Origen than Romans did. This is suggested by Joseph Trigg's observation that many of the main themes of Origen's theology have a basis in this letter:

> Origen's enthusiasm for Paul may appear curious in light of the issues that have dominated Western Christian interpretations of Paul. . . . We should remember that the same Paul who wrote Romans also wrote 1 Corinthians. In the latter book Paul appears as a person much like Origen: an allegorist who understands the secrets of the Bible and expounds them discreetly, a stern ascetic who counsels celibacy and the expulsion of a sinner from the church, a charismatic leader who relies on the self-authenticating power of the Spirit, a spiritualist who seeks to correct a fleshly understanding of the resurrection, and a visionary who expects a cosmic redemption which will culminate when God is all in all. Origen also relied heavily on Paul's Christological ideas and on his understanding of providence.[18]

The remarks that follow represent a first foray into a subject that deserves much longer treatment. My main focus here is on what Origen says about the letter as a whole — how he understands its purpose and audience, and its relation to other Pauline letters. I treat primarily the fragments from the *Homilies on 1 Corinthians,* which, despite their brief and incomplete nature, contain the most promise for reconstructing Origen's understanding of the whole letter. I also consider a few references to 1 Corinthians in *On First Principles* and the *Homilies on Exodus.*

A Key to Origen's Reading of 1 Corinthians: The Corinthians and the Ephesians (Comments on 1 Corinthians 1:2; 4:1-5; 4:15)

There are various difficulties in assessing the fragments of Origen's homilies on 1 Corinthians. In addition to their incompleteness and the fact that we cannot know how reliably they have been transmitted,[19] we have no preface

---

18. Joseph Trigg, *Origen: The Bible and Philosophy in the Third-century Church* (London: SCM, 1983), p. 173.

19. On the general reliability of Jenkins's attribution of comments on 1 Corinthians to Origen, see Crouzel, *Virginité et mariage,* pp. 10-11. It is difficult to know, however, to

to clue us into the main lines of Origen's interpretation. Approaching these comments for the first time is a very different experience from setting off into the extensive homilies on 1 Corinthians of John Chrysostom, which were preached a century and a half after Origen's.[20] Before beginning his commentary on individual chapters, Chrysostom provides the reader with a roadmap, prefixing a lengthy ὑπόθεσις which summarizes the contents and purpose of the letter.[21] In the case of Origen's homilies, we are plunged *in medias res.*

The first comment treats 1 Corinthians 1:2: *to the church of God which is in Corinth, to those sanctified in Christ Jesus, called holy,*[22] *with all those who call upon the name of our Lord Jesus Christ.* As he often does, Origen begins his exegesis with a close analysis of specific phrases:[23]

> If all the hearers are included in the word *church,* what further need would Paul have to add *with all those who call upon [the name]?* If all *call upon [the name]* in the same fashion, what need was there to write [not only] *to all who call upon [the name]* but also, in addition to these, *to the church of God?* We have shown that only those who deserve praise ought to be called *church,* whereas those who deserve blame, even though they are not apostates who have grown old in sin but are still *calling upon [the name],* nevertheless are not the *church.* Let us then be eager to ascend from *calling upon [the name]* to become the *spotless* and *blameless* (Eph 5.27) *church.*[24]

Faced with a double description of the addressees of the letter, Origen does not explain it in terms of geography — by saying, as a modern exegete might, that the second phrase *(all those who call upon the name)* serves to broaden

---

what extent the catenists have transmitted Origen's actual words. In the case of the fragments of the commentary on Ephesians, Layton ("Origen as a Reader," pp. 119-22) shows that Origen's comments have been edited in light of the Origenist controversies, especially through omission.

20. PG 61:9-382. English translation by H. K. Cornish and J. Medley, revised by T. W. Chambers, in NPNF 12:1-269.

21. Chrysostom sees the unifying theme of the letter in the action of Satan, who causes divisions and all sorts of other problems.

22. Unless otherwise indicated, all translations from Greek are my own. The NRSV translates this as "called to be holy," but Origen does not seem to read the phrase this way.

23. For a discussion of Origen's use of the methods of Greek philology, see Bernard Neuschäfer, *Origenes als Philologe,* 2 vols. (Basel: Friedrich Reinhardt, 1987).

24. *Comm. in I Cor.* I.7-13 (*JThS* 9 [1908]: 232). Words and phrases from the biblical text are printed in italics.

the audience of the letter to include Christians in other locations.[25] Instead he gives a moral interpretation, seeing in this verse a distinction of two types of Christians. From the very beginning of the letter, Origen asserts, Paul wants to encourage the less perfect among the Corinthians to make progress on the road to perfection.[26] As he will do again and again in these homilies, Origen then goes on to apply the lesson of the text to himself and his hearers: "Let us then be eager to ascend from *calling upon [the name]* to become the *spotless* and *blameless* (Eph 5.27) church.[27]

In the next fragment — a comment on what modern exegetes would call the "thanksgiving" section of the letter in 1:4-10 — Origen states that the church at Corinth was a mixture of sinners and righteous ones, and he admonishes his hearers to seek the spiritual gifts that the latter possess.[28] When Origen makes generalizations about this letter and its addressees, however, he tends to emphasize the unrighteous and blameworthy among the Corinthians. In a comment on 1 Corinthians 4:1, for example, he contrasts the way Paul teaches the Corinthians with his instruction of Christians at Ephesus:

> *Thus let a person consider us as servants of Christ and stewards of the mysteries of God* (1 Cor 4:1). The person who is not advanced in the teaching about the comprehension of the mysteries hidden in Scripture can be a *servant of Christ* but not a *steward of the mysteries of God*. For the one who is a steward has charge of the things entrusted to him (τὰ οἰκονο- μούμενα), and he *knows the mysteries of God* (1 Cor 13:2). Now perhaps the *servant of Christ* is understood as one who presides over the more common service, while the *steward of the mysteries of God* presides over the dispensation of mysteries that have been made known, in order that he not broadcast them in a haphazard way, nor transmit them without due consideration. But after he has performed preliminary purification, prepared the ground, and transported the one about to hear transcendent

25. See, e.g., Richard Hays, *First Corinthians* (Louisville: John Knox, 1997), pp. 16-17, and Gordon Fee, *The First Epistle to the Corinthians* (Grand Rapids: Eerdmans, 1987), pp. 34-35. Fee says Paul is referring to the universal Church in order to remind the Corinthians "that their own calling to be God's people belongs to a much larger picture."

26. In the apparatus to this text Jenkins notes that Origen repeats this exegesis in his *Commentary on John* and *Homilies on Luke.*

27. Note the allusion to Ephesians — a point to which I shall return.

28. *Comm. in I Cor.* II.1-9 (*JThS* 9 [1908]: 232). An interesting feature of Origen's comment on 1 Cor. 1:4-10 is the way he applies Paul's references to "speech" and "knowledge" to biblical exegesis. This focus on exegesis recurs at many points in the homilies.

teachings out of the world, then he speaks these things. *We,* Paul says, *are servants of Christ.* And the apostle devoted more time to the service of Christ than to *steward*ship of *the mysteries of God.* He administers *the mysteries of God,* for example, to Luke so that he might be able to write his gospel, and to Timothy so that he could rule over those in Ephesus (see 1 Tim 1:3), who had received more [extensive teaching], and so that he could administer *the mysteries of God.* And I make bold to say that in Corinth Paul was a *servant of Christ,* but in Ephesus he was a *steward of the mysteries of God.*[29]

In this passage Origen makes two main points: (1) the Corinthians are less advanced in their Christian training than the more spiritually mature Ephesians; (2) Paul, as a wise teacher, carefully adapts his teaching to the level appropriate for these different groups of hearers. As in his comment on 1 Corinthians 1:2, Origen bases this interpretation on a close analysis of the wording of the text.[30] Assuming that Paul is not merely being repetitious when he calls himself both *servant* and *steward,* Origen concludes that each term refers to a specific type of teaching.

This contrast between the Corinthians and the Ephesians is a significant clue to Origen's reading of 1 Corinthians. The first to compose running commentaries on the Pauline letters, Origen has already progressed far beyond his predecessors in thinking about the individual letters, and about the Pauline corpus as a whole. We know from the writings of Irenaeus, Clement of Alexandria, and the Valentinian Gnostics that the exegesis of specific Pauline texts was an important concern of theologians before the time of Origen. Origen, however, seems to have been the first to focus on the differences among the various Pauline letters and to pose the question of unity and diversity within the Pauline corpus. Rather like a modern exegete, he explains the diversity of the letters largely in terms of differences in Paul's addressees.[31]

Origen again contrasts the Corinthians and the Ephesians in his com-

---

29. *Comm. in I Cor.* XVIII.1-16 (*JThS* 9 [1908]: 354). Note how Origen uses data from Acts and 1 Timothy to elucidate 1 Cor. 4:1, alluding to 1 Tim. 1:3, which connects Timothy with Ephesus, and perhaps to Acts 20:17-34.

30. See Neuschäfer, *Origenes als Philologe,* 1:141-55, for a discussion of Origen's analysis of specific words, in relation to the practices of pagan grammarians.

31. In his preface to the *Commentary on Romans,* however, Origen explains the differences among letters as reflecting different degrees of Paul's own spiritual maturity. For a modern analogue, see J. C. Beker, *Paul the Apostle: The Triumph of God in Life and Thought* (Philadelphia: Fortress, 1980), pp. 94-108, 351-55. Beker explains the differences between Galatians and Romans in terms of differences in Paul's own situation.

ment on 1 Corinthians 4:15, *For if you have a thousand trainers (παιδαγωγοί) in Christ, you do not have many fathers.*

> These things seem to be quite obvious and not needing any interpretation. But they have a hidden sense. No man receives training (παιδαγωγεῖται) unless he is a babe, and imperfect. And Paul would not have written these things to the Ephesians, but to the Corinthians, to whom he says: *I gave you milk to drink, not substantial food, for you were not yet able to receive it and even now you are not able, for you are determined by the flesh. And I could not speak to you as spiritual people but as fleshly ones, as babes in Christ* (1 Cor 3:1-3).

Here Origen explains why Paul could not be a *steward of the mysteries* in Corinth by quoting 1 Corinthians 3:1-3. Because of their moral imperfection, their living according to the flesh, the Corinthians remain at an elementary stage, and are not yet ready to receive Paul's higher teaching.

The Corinthians and the Ephesians in *De principiis* IV.4.4 and III.2.4: Christology and Spiritual Combat

We know that the contrast of the Corinthians with the Ephesians was important for Origen because he repeats it in many different works, for example, in his *Homilies on Joshua*, his *Commentaries on Ephesians* and *Romans,* and his treatises *On Prayer* and *On First Principles.*[32] Numerous texts make clear that Origen understood 1 Corinthians 3:1-3 as a key for interpreting the whole letter. This is illustrated in two passages from *On First Principles.*

In Book IV.4.4,[33] in the context of a discussion of the incarnation, Origen makes a passing reference to the "weak" Corinthians:

> Therefore this *Word* (John 1:1) and this *Wisdom* (1 Cor 1:24, 30), through whose imitation we are said to be wise or rational, *becomes all things to all that He might gain all* (1 Cor 9:22). And because He was made weak, it is said of Him, *Although He was crucified in weakness, yet He lives by the power of God* (2 Cor 13:4). And for the Corinthians, who were weak, Paul

---

32. See, e.g., *hom. in Jos.* XI.4; *comm. in Rom.* VII.12; *comm. in Eph.,* fragments 8, 16, 33; *or.* XXIX.2; *Jo.* I.58; and *princ.* IV.4.4 and III.2.4, discussed below.

33. On the place of this chapter in the structure of *On First Principles,* see Charles Kannengiesser, "Origen, Systematician in *De Principiis,*" in *Origeniana Quinta,* pp. 395-405.

decided to know nothing among them except Christ Jesus and Him crucified (1 Cor 2:2).[34]

Here Origen uses Paul's words about his own practice of accommodation in 1 Corinthians 9:22 to describe Christ's incarnation. While he accepts the full humanity of Christ, Origen insists that the incarnation is not a complete revelation of the nature of the Word of God.[35] He says at the beginning of this section on Christology:

> Next we shall properly call to mind the corporeal coming and Incarnation of the Only Begotten Son of God. In it we must not take the view that the entire majesty of His divinity was shut up in the confines of one small body so that the entire Word of God and His wisdom and substantial truth and life were cut off from the Father or forced within the small compass of that body and contained by it, and He should be thought active in no other way than this.[36]

Origen interprets 1 Corinthians 2:2 to refer not only to the crucifixion but to the incarnation as a whole,[37] and he understands the text as a criticism of the Corinthians for a Christology that focuses too much on the human Christ, without a real understanding of his divine dignity.[38] What the Corinthians

34. In quoting from *On First Principles,* Book IV, I use the translations of Rowan A. Greer, *Origen,* CWS (New York: Paulist Press, 1979). Other parts of *On First Principles* are cited in the translation of G. W. Butterworth, Harper Torchbooks (New York: Harper, 1966). When passages quoted contain biblical texts, I print these in italics, instead of using quotation marks, as do Greer and Butterworth.

35. Clement of Alexandria makes similar statements about the incarnation; see Judith L. Kovacs, "Concealment and Gnostic Exegesis: Clement of Alexandria's Interpretation of the Tabernacle," *SP* 31, ed. E. A. Livingstone (Leuven: Peeters, 1997), pp. 414-37.

36. *Prin.* IV.4.3 (Greer, p. 207).

37. This is also true of other references to this text; see the discussion in Roukema, "La prédication."

38. On Origen's Christology, see Marguerite Harl, *Origène et la fonction révélatrice du Verbe Incarné,* Patristica Sorbonensia 2 (Paris: Éditions du Seuil, 1958), esp. pp. 255-59, 191-99; Crouzel, *Connaissance mystique,* pp. 470-74; J. A. Lyons, *The Cosmic Christ in Origen and Teilhard de Chardin* (Oxford: Oxford University Press, 1982). Lyons is especially interested in Origen's appropriation of "cosmic" Christology, which he explains as follows: "To refer to Christ as cosmic immediately suggests that he has a wider significance than God who becomes man in order to reveal himself to and to save human persons" (p. 1). It is interesting that the biblical texts where Origen sees "cosmic" Christology are drawn mainly from the Pauline letters.

fail to see is that the incarnation involves the condescension of a divine being who has taken on human form in order to reveal himself to human beings in a way appropriate to their limited understanding.

When Origen describes the exalted Christology that has eluded the weak Corinthians, he speaks of Christ as Logos and as Wisdom. The title σοφία, found in 1 Corinthians 1:24, 30, was an important one for Origen.[39] Reading 1 Corinthians 1–2 in light of the contrast between milk and solid food of 1 Corinthians 3, Origen discerns in these chapters a distinction between two stages of Christological teaching. Paul, he claims, alludes to the second, more advanced stage of Christology in 1:24, 30, when he calls Christ Wisdom, Power, and Righteousness. These are only allusions, however — in general Paul, the wise steward, sticks to a more elementary Christology when addressing the immature Corinthians.[40]

Origen repeats this interpretation of 1 Corinthians 2:2 in several other works. One example is found in the twelfth chapter of his *Homilies on Exodus*:

> To certain people whom he judged to be incapable, [Paul] says, *I decided to know nothing among you except Jesus Christ and him crucified* (1 Cor 2:2). To such people he did not say, *The Lord is Spirit* (2 Cor 3:17). He did not tell them that the Christ is *Wisdom of God* (1 Cor 1:24, 30). They were not able to recognize the Christ as *Wisdom,* but [only] in so far as he was *crucified.* Those, on the other hand, to whom he said, *But we do speak wisdom among the perfect, but not a wisdom of this age nor of the rulers of this age, who are perishing, but we speak a wisdom of God hidden in mystery* (1 Cor 2:6) — those had no need to receive the Word of God as *made flesh* (John 1:14), but as the *Wisdom hidden in a mystery.*[41]

Here the contrast between the Christology of 1 Corinthians 2:2 and that of 1 Corinthians 1:24, 30 is made explicit. In addition, Origen brings 1 Corinthians 2:6-7 into the discussion, interpreting *wisdom spoken among the perfect* as

---

39. See, e.g., *princ.* I.2.1; II.9.4 and the appreciative assessment of Origen's treatment of these verses in Wiles, *Divine Apostle,* pp. 115, 136. One reason these verses from 1 Corinthians are important for Origen is that they facilitate the application of Proverbs 8 to Christ.

40. In *princ.* IV.4.4 Origen's depreciation of the Corinthians is not accompanied by an explicit contrast with the Ephesians. However, he might have been thinking of texts such as Eph. 1:22.

41. *Hom. in Ex.* XII.4 (SC 321:366-69). See the discussion of this text, and of several others where Origen comments on 1 Cor. 2:2, in Roukema, "La prédication," pp. 523-29. See also Crouzel, *Connaissance mystique,* pp. 175, 75-76, 364.

another allusion to a higher Christology.[42] Elsewhere Origen understands the enigmatic passage 1 Corinthians 2:6-16 as a warrant for the spiritual exegesis by which the advanced Christian was led more deeply into the truths of the faith.[43]

Another reference to the Corinthians as beginners in the faith is found in *On First Principles* III.2.4:

> But in regard to the statement in the epistle to the Ephesians, *For our wrestling is not against flesh and blood, but against principalities, against powers, against the rulers of the darkness of this world, against spiritual hosts of wickedness in the heavenly places* (Eph 6:12), we shall be right in understanding the apostle's word *our* as meaning I, Paul, myself and you Ephesians and whosoever else has not to wrestle with flesh and blood; for these have their struggle *against principalities and powers, against the rulers of the darkness of this world,* as was not the case among the Corinthians, whose struggle was still against *flesh and blood* and whom *no temptation had taken but such as was human* (1 Cor 10:13).

This text further illustrates how Origen reads the whole of 1 Corinthians — not just chapters 2 and 3 — in terms of progress in the faith. Here his focus is on two stages of the moral struggle. In reading 1 Corinthians 10 — a chapter he cites elsewhere to justify his own spiritual exegesis of the Old Testament[44] — Origen's attention has been drawn to verse 13, a verse that is not

---

42. Roukema sees a contradiction between this text and Origen's frequent statements that the crucifixion is necessary as a foundation; see, e.g., *comm. in Mt.* XII.19, cited in Roukema, "La prédication," p. 526, n. 17. Yet *hom. in Ex.* XII.4 can be understood to imply that the believer who has advanced to understand the higher Christology *no longer* needs to focus on the crucified one. This is not to deny the importance of the cross in Christian teaching.

43. See, for example, *princ.* IV.1.7, which prepares for Origen's discussion of spiritual exegesis in IV.2: "Since we have been brought by a heavenly power, indeed by a more than heavenly, to faith and belief that we should worship as ours one God, the Creator of all, let us strive ourselves to advance earnestly by leaving the elementary doctrines of Christ, which are the first beginnings of knowledge; and let us go on to perfection so that the wisdom that is delivered to the perfect may also be delivered to us (cf. Heb 6:1; 1 Cor 2:6). For this is what the one to whom the preaching of this wisdom was entrusted promises when he says, *Yet among the perfect we impart wisdom, although it is not a wisdom of this world or of the rulers of this world, who are doomed to pass away* (1 Cor 2:6)." In his well-known description of the threefold sense of Scripture in *princ.* IV.2.4, Origen uses 1 Cor. 2:6 to describe the third, or spiritual sense.

44. Origen is particularly fond of verse 11; see, e.g., his use of this verse in *Jo.* XX.36. De

much emphasized in modern commentaries.[45] To follow Origen's reading of the verse one must look at the Greek. He does not understand it as did the NRSV translators: "No testing has overtaken you that is not common to everyone."[46] Instead Origen sees in the word ἀνθρώπινος an implicit contrast to a temptation that is *super*human — that is coming from spiritual powers. He has read the text in light of Ephesians 6:12, the verse of Ephesians that he cites more than any other one.[47]

These remarks about the Corinthians and the Ephesians are part of a long discussion of the "opposing powers" (*On First Principles* III.2.1-8).[48] Origen cites many texts from Scripture to show that spiritual powers are at work to influence the soul for both good and ill. Sins, he says, arise from natural desires of the body, such as hunger or thirst or sexual desire; but when a person, moved by these desires, fails to exercise temperance, the demons step in and incite him to greater sin.[49]

Lubac, *Histoire et esprit*, p. 73, notes similar interpretations of this verse in Hippolytus, Tertullian, and other early interpreters.

45. Fee, *Corinthians*, p. 460, remarks that "it is difficult to see how [verse 13] fits into the scheme of the present argument, especially since v. 14 follows vv. 1-12 so nicely." Fee notes further that this verse, taken out of context, has "served generations of Christians as a word of hope in times of difficulty."

46. RSV: "No temptation has overtaken you that is not common to man."

47. In *On First Principles*, for example, Origen refers to this verse in I.4.2; 5.2-3; 6.3; 8.4; III.2.1, 3, 4, 5, 6; IV.1.1. On Origen's treatment of Eph. 6:12 see J. A. Trevigano, *En lucha contra les potestades. Exégesis primitiva de Ef. 6,11-17 hasta Origenes* (Bilbao: Mensajero, 1973). On Origen's conception of the spiritual powers, see also Henri Crouzel, "L'anthropologie d'Origène dans la perspective du combat spirituel," *Revue d'Ascétique et de Mystique* 31 (1954): 364-85; Adele Monaci Castagno, "La demonologia di Origene: Aspetti filosofici, pastorali, apologetici," in *Origeniana Quinta*, pp. 320-25; G. S. Gasparro, "Eguaglianza di nature e differenza di condizione dei *logikoi*: la soluzione origeniana nel contesto delle formule antropologiche e demonologiche del II e III secolo," in *Origeniana Quinta*, pp. 301-19; J. A. Alcain, *Cautiverio y redencion del hombre segun Origenes*, Teologia Deusto 4 (Bilbao: Mensajero, 1973); Y.-M. Duval, "Jérome et Origène avant la querelle origéniste. La cure et la guérison ultime du monde et du diable dans l'*In Nahum*," *Augustinianum* 24 (1984): 471-94.

48. See *Princ.* III.2.1: "We must now see how, according to the scriptures, the opposing powers and the devil himself are engaged in a struggle with the human race, provoking and inciting men to sin." On the place of this section in the overall scheme of *On First Principles* see Henri Crouzel and Manlio Simonetti, *Origène: Traité des principes* (Paris: Éditions du Cerf): vol. 1 (SC 252, 1978), pp. 15-22; vol. 4 (SC 269, 1980), p. 55.

49. "[W]e derive the beginnings and what we may call the seeds of sin from those desires which are given to us naturally for our use. But when we indulge these to excess and offer no resistance to the first movements towards intemperance, then the hostile power,

Origen emphasizes that God does not *cause* the action of the evil powers, but he allows it and directs it for good. By divine providence the struggles against the powers are made to serve a pedagogical function in testing and purifying human souls and making them stronger. Origen describes this in the following chapter:

> For just as those who preside over the games do not allow the competitors to oppose one another indiscriminately or by chance in the contests, but after a careful examination match them in equal pairs according to size and years . . . boys, that is, with boys and men with men . . . so also must we understand in regard to the divine providence, that it treats all who descend into the struggles of human life with the most impartial care, according to the nature of each individual's virtue, which he alone knows who alone beholds the hearts of men. . . . For consider whether some such arrangement is not indicated by the saying of the apostle, *But God is faithful, who will not suffer you to be tempted above that ye are able* (1 Cor. 10:13), that is, each one is tempted in proportion to the degree and possibilities of the strength he possesses.[50]

In this providential scheme, struggles against the temptations of the flesh are more elementary than struggles against demonic temptation. The more one progresses in the spiritual life, the stronger the temptations permitted by God become.[51]

Origen's bringing together of 1 Corinthians 10:13 and Ephesians 6:12 is in itself an interesting piece of exegesis, and it seems to presuppose comparison of other parts of the two letters as well.[52] In *De principiis* III.2.4 (cited above) he draws on several verses from Ephesians besides 6:12 to describe the higher level of the battle: for example, the command in 4:27 not to *give place*

---

seizing the opportunity of this first offence, incites and urges us on in every way, striving to extend the sins over a larger field; so that while we men supply the occasions and beginning of our sins, the hostile powers spread them far and wide and if possible endlessly" (*Princ.* III.2.2).

50. *Princ.* III.2.3.

51. Crouzel and Simonetti (*Origène: Traité des Principes*, 4:66, n. 39) paraphrase Origen's thought as follows: "plus on s'élève spirituellement, plus les tentations permises par Dieu sont dures." On the struggle with demons see also *princ.* III.2.6 and III.5.8. In *princ.* IV.3.12 Origen interprets battles of the Old Testament as symbols of the struggle against demons, alluding to Eph. 1:20-22; 6:16; 1 Cor. 10:5-10; 15:24, 27.

52. In the *comm. in Eph.* XXXIII.28-36 (*JThS* 3 [1902]: 571) Origen makes a similar contrast between this verse and 1 Cor. 10:13.

to the devil, and the *fiery darts* of Ephesians 6:16.[53] Although Origen does not cite them here, it is easy to imagine texts in 1 Corinthians that led him to conclude that the Corinthians were struggling at a lower level.[54]

The Spiritual Banquet: Homily on 1 Corinthians 3:1-3

With these texts in mind, let us return to the *Homilies on 1 Corinthians*. Despite the fragmentary character of our evidence, it is possible to see that Origen has a clear, consistent, and quite creative interpretation of the letter as a whole. Given his fondness for denouncing the Corinthians, one might expect that 1 Corinthians would rank relatively low in Origen's personal canon, and it is perhaps surprising that it vies with Romans for the honor of being the most-cited Pauline letter. Of course this is partly accounted for by the fact that it contains a whole chapter on the eschaton — a subject that held considerable interest for Origen[55] — and that it played an important role in the development of his views on spiritual exegesis.[56] Yet there is another, more general, reason why this letter was valued by Origen. This is its role in the comprehensive divine pedagogy — God's plan for training all people up to himself.[57]

The idea of progressive training is particularly evident in fragment XII, which interprets 1 Corinthians 3:1-3. We have already seen that Paul's words on the "milk" and the "solid food" have influenced the way Origen reads the whole letter. Before Origen's time, this passage had already figured prominently in the

53. Origen understands the command in Eph. 4:27 not to "give place" to the devil as a warning that our actions might lead the devil to take possession of our souls or thoroughly pollute them. He understands the *quenching* of the *fiery darts* of Eph. 6:16 to refer to the process of perfection by which the Christian trains himself to be invulnerable to the attacks of the devil (III.2.4): "In rare cases, indeed, and by a few persons these *fiery darts* of his are *quenched,* so that they fail to find the place for a wound; that is, when a man has been covered with the strong and defensive *shield of faith*" (Eph. 6:16). For further commentary on the armor of Eph. 6:12-17, see *comm. in Eph.* XXXIII (*JThS* 3 [1902]: 571-72).

54. For example, Paul's discussion of discord in 1 Cor. 1:10-12 and of various sexual problems in chapters 5-7. For Origen's interpretation of Paul's advice in 1 Corinthians 7 as a lower level of morality, see "Concession and Challenge" below.

55. On Origen's eschatology see Crouzel, *Les fins dernières;* Brian Daley, *The Hope of the Early Church* (Cambridge: Cambridge University Press, 1991), pp. 47-60; Carolyn Walker Bynum, *The Resurrection of the Body in Western Christianity, 200-1336* (New York: Columbia University Press, 1995), pp. 63-71.

56. Especially important were 1 Cor. 10:11 and chapter 2; see above, n. 43.

57. On Origen's view of παιδεία see Koch, *Pronoia und Paideusis.*

debates between the Valentinian Gnostics and the emerging catholic[58] church. Clement of Alexandria devotes a long chapter of his *Paidagogos* to refuting Valentinian exegesis of 1 Corinthians 3.[59] The Valentinians, interpreting the text in light of Paul's distinction of the ψυχικός and the πνευματικός in 1 Corinthians 2, had claimed that the catholic Christian was the ψυχικός referred to in 2:14 and that 3:1-2 described the *childish* and *foolish* character of catholic teaching, that is, the basic doctrines of the catholic church. In the *Paidagogos* Clement goes to great lengths to refute this exegesis and to defend the Church's teaching. He uses both Scriptural and scientific arguments to show that *milk* and *solid food* are really one and the same, and that catholics, not the Valentinians, are the τέλειοι praised by Paul. In *Stromateis* V.10, 25-26, however, Clement adapts the Valentinian exegesis of 1 Corinthians 3 that he had rejected in the *Paidagogos,* now using the text in support of his idea of προκοπή, or spiritual progress. While the Valentinians had read the *milk* and *solid food* as a contrast between Valentinian and catholic teaching, Clement argues that they refer to two stages of catholic teaching, and he uses Paul's discussion of the *foundation* and *superstructure* in 1 Corinthians 3:10 in a polemical way, to show the continuity between πίστις and γνῶσις. Clement presents the Christian life as a pursuit of perfection that has two main stages, πίστις (elementary teaching that centers on the "rule of faith") and γνῶσις (mystical teachings and speculative theology). He quotes 1 Corinthians 3:1-3 as a justification of his γνῶσις and of the symbolic exegesis on which this γνῶσις is based.

Although Origen does not allude to this debate, his reading of 1 Corinthians 3:1-3 may well presuppose it. Origen was well informed about Valentinian teachings, and he often polemicizes against them.[60] His comments on 1 Corinthians 3, however, are not polemical, as Clement's are, but hortatory and pedagogical.

In his comments on 1 Corinthians 3:1-3, as in his discussion of 1 Corinthians 1:2, Origen points out that Paul is addressing a mixed congregation.

58. *Faute de mieux,* I refer to the emerging orthodox church in Clement's time as "the catholics." Clement himself usually refers to this group simply as "we"; see, e.g., *Str.* II.3, 10.1 and V. 1, 1.1, 5, where Clement is responding to Valentinian ideas.

59. *Paed.* I.6, 25-52. For further discussion of Clement's exegesis of Paul and of the Valentinian exegesis to which he is responding, see my forthcoming book, *Contending for the Legacy of Paul: Rival Interpretations of Paul in the Second Century.*

60. In *Gnosis als System: Zur Rezeption der valentinianischen Gnosis bei Origenes* (Göttingen: Vandenhoeck & Ruprecht, 1993) Holger Strutwolf argues that the basic structure of Origen's theological system is adapted from his Valentinian predecessors. Origen's polemics are particularly clear in the *Commentary on John,* which was written in response to the commentary written by Valentinus's pupil Heracleon.

Some of them are τέλειοι and πνευματικοί, while others are babes and σαρκικοί. He goes on to say:

> There is then a need for inferior lessons, for those who are less mature and who have not yet been *trained* (see Heb 5:14) in the holy Scriptures. Paul says these lessons are *milk*. For he says, *I gave you milk to drink. For you were not yet ready for it. And even now you are not ready.* Now among the spiritual foods, I think there is an upward progression (ἀναφορά):[61] *milk, solid food, substantial food* [62] (Heb 5:12), *true food* (John 6:55) — and also spiritual *vegetables* (Rom 14:2). Now I dare to say these things, in obedience to the Scriptures. For Scripture has not said that every spiritual food is *true food* (John 6:55), since it says: *My flesh is true food* (John 6:55).[63]

Origen, the spiritual gourmet, here interprets the *milk* and *solid food* of 1 Corinthians 3:1-3 in light of several other New Testament references to food.[64] This allows him to extend Clement's idea of two stages of Christian life (πίστις and γνῶσις) to many stages.

In the comments that follow Origen explains that there are different levels of both ethical teaching and mystical theology:

> As regards that which is *not solid food* (Heb 5:14), it is the more ethical teachings, and especially whatever of ethical matters is more elementary, spoken by way of concession and not as a command (1 Cor 7:6), being given because of the weakness of the hearers. As for those ethical matters which are a more perfect teaching, spoken among those who are eager to learn and ready to work, I would say that these things, in ethical matters, are the *solid food* (Heb 5:12): the teaching about perfect purity, about virginity or chastity, and about martyrdom. These are *solid food* (Heb 5:12).[65]

---

61. Alternatively, ἀναφορά could be translated "a higher reference." Does Origen see a definite progression from one of these "foods" to another, or is his interest here simply that Scripture refers to a variety of foods, all of which have a higher, symbolic meaning?

62. In English it is difficult to distinguish between the βρῶμα of 1 Cor. 3:2 and the στερεὰ τροφή of Heb. 5:12; both are rendered "solid food" in RSV. In general Origen seems to understand these terms to refer to the same thing, but in the present text he may intend to distinguish them, if by ἀναφορά he means "upward progression."

63. *Comm. in I Cor.* XII.5-10 (*JThS* 9 [1908]: 241).

64. Origen also treats different spiritual foods in *Jo.* I.20 (22), 119-24 and *hom. in Is.* III.3; on this theme, see Crouzel, *Connaissance mystique*, pp. 166-83.

65. *Comm. in I Cor.* XII.12-17 (*JThS* 9 [1908]: 241-42).

Here he introduces a theme central to his interpretation of 1 Corinthians, and a point dear to his own heart. As is well known, Origen was a rigorist in moral matters, who advocated celibacy and encouraged his followers to prepare themselves for the ultimate witness of martyrdom.[66] Confident that Paul shared his rigorist views, he assumes that 1 Corinthians was written both to discipline those who were still struggling with more rudimentary moral demands — such as self-control within marriage — and to challenge those who were ready to pursue a higher calling. In his comments on 1 Corinthians 4:1, he observes that Paul spent more time as a *servant* — an instructor of those on the lower level — than he did as a *steward of the mysteries* — a teacher of those on a higher level.[67] While most of 1 Corinthians is addressed to beginners, some verses do address the more advanced.[68]

In the continuation of his comment on 1 Corinthians 3:1-3 Origen goes on to give a second interpretation of the contrast of *milk* and *solid food*:

> But among the mystical teachings, *solid food* (στερεὰ τροφή) is the teaching about the Father and the Son. And in the same way the Law sometimes imparts *solid food* and sometimes inferior food. For example we come to the teaching about the snakes that were destroying the sons of Israel because of their grumbling (Num 21:6-9). If we read this on the simpler level, we say, *Do not grumble, as some of them grumbled, and they were destroyed by snakes* (1 Cor 10:10). But if the hearer is able to receive the mystical teaching, we say what the snakes are and who is the snake who was hung on the tree (see John 3:14; Gal 3:13), and how a person is saved when he looks on that snake — and in similar fashion for each spiritual text.[69]

Here Origen distinguishes two levels of teaching. The phrase "teaching about the Father and the Son" may refer to the kind of systematic, speculative theology that Origen attempts in *On First Principles*. He associates the two types of

---

66. See, e.g., his *Exhortation to Martyrdom*. In interpreting 1 Corinthians Origen emphasizes celibacy not only in his comments on 1 Corinthians 7 but also in his discussion of 6:12-20 (*Comm. in I Cor.* XXIX.1-12, *JThS* 9 [1908]: 370). Some examples of how Origen introduces the theme of martyrdom are his comments on 1:6, 27; 4:9 (*Comm. in I Cor.* II.31-40, *JThS* 9 [1908]: 233; *Comm. in I Cor.* VIII.41-45, *JThS* 9 [1908]: 237; *Comm. in I Cor.* XX.17-30, *JThS* 9 [1908]: 360).

67. Quoted in "A Key to Origen's Reading of 1 Corinthians," above.

68. See discussion of Origen's commentary on 1 Corinthians 7 in "Concession and Challenge" below.

69. *Comm. in I Cor.* XII.17-31 (*JThS* 9 [1908]: 242).

teaching with different ways of interpreting Scripture[70] and illustrates this by two interpretations of the story of the snakes in Numbers 21, both found in the New Testament. In 1 Corinthians 10, Origen says, Paul has drawn an elementary lesson from the Biblical text: it teaches Christians not to grumble. The same text, however, interpreted on a more advanced level, has a higher meaning. Apparently he is thinking of John 3:14, where the bronze serpent of Numbers 21:9 is used as a type of Christ on the cross.[71] In the homilies on 1 Corinthians, however, it is the two levels of morality that receive the most attention. I turn now to Origen's interpretation of 1 Corinthians 7, where this distinction is developed in the most detail.[72]

Concession and Challenge: Origen's Exegesis of 1 Corinthians 7

Paul's discussion of marriage and sex in 1 Corinthians 7 was important for Origen, both as an inspiration for his own ascetic practice and as a basis for his general theory of moral progress. In the fragments of the *Homilies on 1 Corinthians,* the comments on this chapter are by far the most extensive.[73] For Origen, the pivotal verse of this chapter is verse 6: *I say this by way of concession.* Modern exegetes have pondered the referent of τοῦτο in this verse: Does it refer only to the counsel of temporary abstinence in verse 5, or does it refer to the whole of verses 1-5?[74] To Origen it was quite clear that it referred to the entire treatment of sex within marriage in verses 1-5: by calling his instructions for marriage a *concession,* Paul indicates that there was a higher level of morality, that is, celibacy. Taking verse 1 *(It is good for a man not to touch a woman)* as Paul's basic view of the matter,[75] Origen thinks several

---

70. Compare the well-known description of three levels of meaning in Scripture in *princ.* IV.2.4 and the discussion of this text in Joseph Trigg, *Origen* (London: Routledge, 1998), pp. 33-34.

71. Jenkins lists no Scriptural allusions here, but the reference to John 3:14 is clear. Origen's use of the verb κρεμασθείς suggests that he is interpreting John 3:14 in light of Gal. 3:13 and Deut. 21:23.

72. See especially Origen's comments on 1 Cor. 7:6, 28, 34, 39. The distinction is mentioned at several other points in the homilies: for example, in the exegesis of 3:1; 4:6; 6:12-14; 9:12.

73. In Jenkins's edition of the fragments there are ten and a half pages on 1 Corinthians 7 (*JThS* 9 [1908]: 500-510), out of a total of seventy-three pages.

74. See, e.g., Fee, *Corinthians,* pp. 283-84.

75. *Comm. in I Cor.* XXXIII.13-25 (*JThS* 9 [1908]: 500-501).

parts of the chapter show that Paul allows marriage only as a *concession* to the weak. He interprets verse 5, for example, to mean that the prayers of the celibate are more effective than those of the married,[76] and he understands the δοῦλος of verses 21-23 as a reference to the married person.[77]

Origen also thinks that Paul indicates two levels of morality in 1 Corinthians 7:25: *Now concerning virgins I do not have a commandment of the Lord, but I give my opinion as one who has been given by divine mercy to be faithful.* Focusing on the word *commandment,* Origen distinguishes between those commandments that are necessary for salvation and those that go beyond what is "firmly ordained" and are fulfilled by our own choice.[78] Paul doesn't have a *commandment* from the Lord about remaining celibate because this is a matter of a more perfect morality, which transcends the minimum, obligatory commandments.

Origen does find some room for divine χαρίσματα within marriage. Relating 1 Corinthians 7 to Paul's censure of discord in chapter 1 and to the discussion of spiritual gifts in 1 Corinthians 12–14, he points out that a married couple has the opportunity to cultivate the spiritual gift of ὁμόνοια, or perfect concord.[79] He also adapts some of the general principles that govern Paul's ethical advice to address the situation of married people. For example, in giving advice to the married man who aspires to the higher calling of celibacy, he draws on Paul's advice to the *strong* in Romans 14:15, admonishing him to "beware lest your wife should perish, if she is not able to endure your purity, she for whom Christ died."[80] He also reminds the would-be celibate of what Paul says in 1 Corinthians 13:5: *Love does not seek*

76. *Comm. in I Cor.* XXXIV.1-7 (*JThS* 9 [1908]: 501-2).

77. *Comm. in I Cor.* XXXVII.10-14 (*JThS* 9 [1908]: 506); XXXVIII.1-7 (*JThS* 9 [1908]: 508). Commenting on v. 22 (*He who was called in the Lord as a slave is a freedman of the Lord*), Origen points out that the term ἀπελεύθερος — which he sees as a reference to the married "slave" — is less than totally free. See the discussion of these fragments in Crouzel, *Virginité et mariage,* pp. 127-28, 160-61.

78. *Comm. in I Cor.* XXXIX.1-23 (*JThS* 9 [1908]: 508-9). To support this interpretation Origen draws on several Gospel texts, including Luke 17:10; Matt. 5:27-28; 19:10-11. Compare Origen's comments on *not beyond what is written* in 1 Cor. 4:6; *comm. in I Cor.* XIX.8-13 (*JThS* 9 [1908]: 357).

79. *Comm. in I Cor.* XXXIV.40-54 (*JThS* 9 [1908]: 503). In this section Origen takes issue with Marcionites who forbid marriage on the basis of their teaching of two gods.

80. *Comm. in I Cor.* XXXIII.7-10 (*JThS* 9 [1908]: 500). Crouzel (*Virginité et mariage,* p. 165) comments on this passage: "Il y a là une idée profonde de la sanctification apportée par le mariage: un salut que les conjoints acquièrent l'un par l'autre. . . . Quelle que soit la très grande valeur qu'Origène donne à la chasteté, il n'en fait pas une fin en soi et met la charité au-dessus."

its own good.[81] Noting Paul's repeated use of the term ὁμοίως in verses 1-5, Origen concludes that the husband must not consider himself superior to the wife, but that the spouses have "similarity and equality" in relation to each other.[82]

Origen's aim is not to establish an elite group but to challenge *all* of his hearers to live more purely, to take seriously Paul's statement that they are the temple of God (1 Cor. 3:17). So Origen sees lessons in this chapter for Christians at all stages in their spiritual life. He challenges all to consider sexual abstinence but also warns of the dangers of this path. "Sometimes," he says, "in exceeding the rule, imagining that we are doing something better, we fail in the matter at hand."[83]

The fragments from his homilies on 1 Corinthians 7 illustrate very clearly the extent to which Origen interprets individual parts of 1 Corinthians in light of his understanding of the whole letter. I have already noted how Origen takes Paul's word *concession* in 7:6 as a key for interpreting other parts of the letter.[84] Conversely, he uses several other sections of the letter to elucidate 1 Corinthians 7. In addition to the examples already cited,[85] a particularly important verse is 1 Corinthians 4:1, with its contrast of Paul's roles as δοῦλος and as οἰκονόμος.[86] Origen sees in 1 Corinthians 7 a specific example of how Paul is a *wise steward,* in that he does not overdo either the teaching about virginity or the teaching about marriage.[87] In other words, Paul has successfully adapted his teaching for the mixed congregation that he addresses.

---

81. *Comm. in I Cor.* XXXIII.23-25 (*JThS* 9 [1908]: 501).

82. *Comm. in I Cor.* XXXIII.47-49. Crouzel (*Virginité et mariage,* pp. 152, 166) understands this to refer to equality in conjugal rights and in the duty of fidelity, within the context of hierarchical marriage. On Origen's view of marriage, see also Crouzel's discussions of "L'homme et la femme dans le couple" (*Virginité et mariage,* pp. 140-42) and "La misogynie d'Origène" (*Virginité et mariage,* pp. 135-39).

83. *Comm. in I Cor.* XXXIII.4-6 (*JThS* 9 [1908]: 500), a comment on 1 Cor. 7:1-2.

84. See, e.g., his exegesis of 1 Cor. 3:1-3 in *comm. in I Cor.* XII.12-17 (*JThS* 9 [1908]: 241-42), quoted in "The Spiritual Banquet," above.

85. See discussion above for Paul's use of 1 Cor. 3:17; 13:5; and chapters 1 and 12–14 in his comments on 1 Corinthians 7.

86. *Comm. in I Cor.* II.1-9 (*JThS* 9 [1908]: 232), discussed above, in "A Key to Origen's Reading of 1 Corinthians."

87. *Comm. in I Cor.* XXXIII.15-20 (*JThS* 9 [1908]: 500).

Conclusion

The *Homilies on 1 Corinthians* reinforce what Bernard Neuschäfer says in *Origen als Philologe*. Despite his reputation as an allegorical exegete, Origen was a careful philologist, who made use of the best critical methods of his day.[88] In many ways, Origen anticipates modern exegesis. Reading these homilies one cannot fail to be impressed by the remarkably detailed knowledge of Scripture that they exhibit, and the trenchant way Origen adduces texts from all parts of the Bible to illuminate the text of 1 Corinthians. Despite his conviction that all of Scripture is one, inspired whole, however, Origen is interested in 1 Corinthians as a distinct book, and in how this book relates to the other letters in the Pauline corpus.

For all his critical brilliance, Origen was not interested in philological or historical analysis for its own sake but in how it could serve a more important goal: the training of the soul so as to lead it back to God. In her book on Origen's exegesis, Karen Jo Torjesen emphasizes the importance of the idea of ὠφέλεια for Origen's understanding of Scripture:

> For Origen it is most of all the "usefulness" (ὠφέλεια) of Scripture which inspiration through the Holy Spirit guarantees. The divine intention of Scripture which the Holy Spirit underwrites is that the Scripture should benefit the soul.[89]

The books of Scripture, though inspired by one Spirit, contain a rich diversity, in order that they may benefit each individual who studies them:

> [T]he Logos in Scripture enlightens the eye of the reader, not in the unitary brilliance of his own light, but rather in the multiplicity and diversity of individual colorations which are all partial forms of the single light once it has been diffracted through the experience of the saints.[90]

---

88. A few examples, of many that could be cited from the *Homilies on 1 Corinthians*, are the word study of διακρίνω in the comment on 1 Cor. 4:6 (XVIII.28-37, *JThS* 9 [1908]: 354-55), the explanation of the odd use of the term ἡμέρα in 4:3 by reference to Isa. 13:9 (XVIII.37-41, *JThS* 9 [1908]: 355), and the discussion of whether Paul is referring to an earlier letter to the Corinthians in 1 Cor. 5:9-11 (XXVI.1-12, *JThS* 9 [1908]: 366).

89. Torjesen, *Hermeneutical Procedure*, p. 124. See also Wilken, "Origen's *Homilies on Leviticus*," p. 85, and the discussion of ὠφέλεια in Crouzel, "Le contexte spirituel de l'exégèse dite spirituel," *Origeniana Sexta*, pp. 334-37. Among other texts, Crouzel refers to *Jo.* XIII.5.26-30 as an illustration of this theme.

90. Torjesen, *Hermeneutical Procedure*, pp. 112-13.

Origen sees the Scripture both as a record of God's revealing himself to the saints in the past and as the locus of divine pedagogy in the present, the way the divine Logos addresses individual souls and gradually leads them up to perfection. Biblical books are designed in such a way as to be useful at various stages of moral and intellectual development:

> The contemporary pedagogy of the Logos which is mediated through Scripture is a pedagogy of the individual. As Origen understands it, the Logos discloses himself to each one in proportion to his ability to receive him. This capacity to receive the Logos is a function of growth. The more advanced soul is able to receive the Logos in greater fullness than the initiate. This means that for the individual the disclosure of the Logos is progressive.[91]

Torjesen shows how this idea of progressive training of individual readers determines the overall shape of Origen's exegesis of the Song of Songs, Numbers, Jeremiah, and the Gospels.[92] The texts I have examined in this essay suggest that Origen sees this same pattern in the Pauline corpus. When Origen contrasts the immature Corinthians with the spiritually mature Ephesians, he is not merely ridiculing the ancient Corinthians for the sake of rhetorical effect. Instead, he is locating the value of each letter as a guide for Christian life in the present. The ancient Corinthians may not be the model Christians, but Paul's first letter to this congregation has considerable usefulness in the pedagogy so providentially directed by the Spirit, especially for Christians who are nearer the beginning than the end of their spiritual progress.

A frequent theme in the *Homilies on 1 Corinthians* is how Paul "condescends" or accommodates his teachings for the benefit of the imperfect Corinthians. Paul, as a wise steward (οἰκονόμος), does not distribute the mysteries of God haphazardly but in a carefully considered way.[93] In this he follows the Logos himself, who in accord with the divine οἰκονομία, or plan for salvation, has condescended to take on human flesh.[94] In 1 Corinthians Paul

---

91. Torjesen, *Hermeneutical Procedure,* p. 123. For a discussion of similar ideas about divine pedagogy in Clement of Alexandria see Judith L. Kovacs, "Divine Pedagogy and the Gnostic Teacher in Clement of Alexandria," forthcoming.

92. See the section entitled "The Organizing Principle in Origen's Exegesis" in Torjesen, *Hermeneutical Procedure,* pp. 70-106.

93. *Comm. in I Cor.* XVIII.1-16 (*JThS* 9 [1908]: 354), quoted above, in "A Key to Origen's Reading of 1 Corinthians."

94. *Princ.* IV.4.4, discussed above, in "The Corinthians and the Ephesians." On the

spends most of his time addressing those who need counsel for their struggles against the temptations of the flesh. Yet the letter is also useful for those who are more advanced in their spiritual life. Paul gives glimpses of advanced theology for those who are able to discern them — for example when he calls Christ δύναμις and σοφία (1 Cor. 1:24, 30) and in his discussion of the consummation of all things in chapter 15. Paul addressed a mixed congregation in Corinth, and thus his exhortations can speak to all members of Origen's own congregation — from the beginner to the most advanced.

In interpreting 1 Corinthians, Origen makes frequent use of the hortatory subjunctive. For example he concludes his comment on 1 Corinthians 1:4-10: "Let us consider the grace exhibited by the praiseworthy among the Corinthians so that we may imitate it."[95] If we understand these first-person plural subjunctives as a rhetorical convention, appropriate to a preacher, we miss something essential about Origen's understanding of the letter. That is how he reads it as a personal address, and a challenge, to everyone — including himself. One example of this is his interpretation of 1 Corinthians 5:9-11, Paul's catalogue of the sins that disqualify a person for the kingdom of God. Noticing that Paul first mentions grave sins such as fornication and idolatry and then adds sins of quite a different magnitude (slander, drunkenness, and greed), Origen comments:

> As for the [graver sins] most of us have a clear conscience. But as for the sins Paul mentions after these, I am afraid also for myself, lest I somehow be guilty of them.[96]

He makes a similar observation in his comment on 1 Corinthians 3:10: *Let each one take care how he builds.* Origen applies this to his own activity as teacher: "Paul," he says, "speaks this also to me, in order that I not build up [the Church] in a careless fashion, since I know that on *that day the fire will*

---

theme of divine condescension, which appears frequently in Origen's works, see Joseph Trigg, "Divine Deception and the Truthfulness of Scripture," in *Origen of Alexandria: His World and His Legacy*, ed. Charles Kannengiesser and W. L. Petersen (Notre Dame, Ind.: University of Notre Dame Press, 1988), pp. 147-64. For Origen the condescension of the Logos also involves revealing himself in other forms, e.g., becoming an angel in order to instruct the angels; see *Jo.* I.31 (34), 217-18; *hom. in Gen.* VIII.8; and the discussion in Crouzel and Simonetti, *Origène: Traité des Principes*, vol. 4 (SC 269), pp. 254-55, n. 37. Divine condescension is also emphasized by Clement of Alexandria; see, e.g., *str.* V. 6, 32-40; VI. 15, 126.2-3; 132.2-4, and the discussion in Kovacs, "Concealment," pp. 425-26.

95. *Comm. in I Cor.* II.18 (*JThS* 9 [1908]: 233).

96. *Comm. in I·Cor.* XXVI.39-41 (*JThS* 9 [1908]: 367).

test the quality of my work."[97] Origen is convinced that Paul's letter to the Corinthians has a message for every Christian — including Origen the teacher and Origen the individual Christian soul, who for all his learning and rigorous moral discipline is still making progress on the way back to his creator.

97. *Comm. in I Cor.* XV.18-20 (*JThS* 9 [1908]: 244), commenting on 1 Cor. 3:13.

Hebrews, Jews, and Christians: Eusebius of Caesarea on the Biblical Basis of the Two States of the Christian Life

MICHAEL J. HOLLERICH

In the notes to his edition of the *Letter to Diognetus,* Henri-Irenée Marrou drew attention to the importance of a passage in Book 1 of Eusebius of Caesarea's *Demonstratio Evangelica (DE)* for the early Christian doctrine of the Church's relation to the world.[1] The passage describes the existence of two distinct modes of life within the Church. It is of interest not just for its content but for its timing: the *Demonstratio* was written in the tumultuous decade that saw the last persecution, the legalization of Christianity, and Constantine's emergence as co-ruler of the Roman Empire and a keen participant in the affairs of the Christian Church. Eusebius is our most important chronicler of these events, in which he also took an active part.

I am pleased to offer an examination of this text as my contribution to a festschrift in honor of Robert Wilken, whose first book made Eusebius's *Church History* a central object of its study[2] and who has ever since maintained a keen interest in the role the Bible played in Christianity's three-cornered conversation, and competition, with Judaism and Greco-Roman paganism. As is well known, Christians faced the fundamental task of proving to both Jews and pagans that the Jewish Scriptures were properly read in the light of Jesus Christ, that the Jewish leaders had therefore erred in rejecting Jesus' message,

---

1. *A Diognète,* ed. H.-I. Marrou, SC 33 (Paris: Éditions du Cerf, 1965), p. 167.
2. Robert Wilken, *The Myth of Christian Beginnings* (Notre Dame, Ind.: University of Notre Dame Press, 1980), originally published in 1971.

and that they, not the Jews, were the proper interpreters and custodians of the Jewish Scriptures. The task required proving, on the one hand, that the literal meaning of the Old Testament was in some sense inadequate and, on the other hand, that the literal meaning retained some degree of validity, no matter how provisional. Beginning with the New Testament itself, it became common practice to employ some form of typological interpretation as an exegetical expression of Christianity's profound convictions about God's revelation in Jesus Christ and its place in the history of the revelation to Israel. The "prodigious newness of the Christian fact" could not displace, in fact depended for its intelligibility on, its position in the revelation to Israel.[3] Eusebius's exegesis and apologetics are thoroughly taken up with the interpretive problem posed by Christianity's dialectical relationship to Israel.[4]

DE 1.8 is an especially intriguing example of his approach because of the way in which it touches on fundamental questions of Christian life and identity. Here is a translation of the text:

> The one [Moses] wrote on lifeless tablets, the other [Jesus] wrote the perfect commandments of the new covenant on living minds. And his disciples, accommodating their teaching to the minds of the people, according to the Teacher's will, delivered on the one hand to those who were able to receive it, the teaching given by the perfect Teacher to those who have transcended natural behavior. On the other hand, the teaching which they considered was suitable to men still in the world of passion and needing treatment, they accommodated to the weakness of the majority, to whom they handed it on to be kept, some things in writing and other things as unwritten ordinances.
>
> Two ways of life (δύο βιῶν . . . τρόπους) were thus legislated for the Church of Christ. The one is above nature, and beyond ordinary human society (πολιτείας); it has no place for marriage, child-bearing, property or the possession of wealth, but wholly and permanently separate from the common, customary life of mankind, it devotes itself to the service of God alone in its wealth of heavenly love. Those who follow this way seem

3. A phrase popularized, though not invented, by Henri de Lubac; cf. the first volume of the English translation of *Exégèse médiévale*, *Medieval Exegesis*, vol. 1: *The Four Senses of Scripture*, trans. Mark Sebanc (Grand Rapids: Eerdmans, 1998), p. xix. Chapter Five, "The Unity of the Two Testaments," remains a classic statement of traditional Christian exegetical understanding of this issue. I use the word "typology" in this paper in full awareness of de Lubac's reservations about the concept (*Medieval Exegesis*, 1:259).

4. See M. J. Hollerich, *Eusebius of Caesarea's* Commentary on Isaiah: *Christian Exegesis in the Age of Constantine* (Oxford: Clarendon, 1999).

to have died to mortal life: their bodies alone live in this world, while their souls have moved spiritually to the next. Like some celestial beings they gaze on human life, performing the duty of a priesthood (ἱερωμένοι) to Almighty God for the whole race, not with sacrifices of bulls and blood, nor with libations and unguents, nor with smoke and consuming fire and destruction of bodily things, but with right principles of true holiness, and of a soul purified in disposition, and above all with virtuous deeds and words; with such they propitiate the Deity and celebrate their priestly rites (ἱερουργίαν) for themselves and their race. Such is the perfect form of the Christian life (πολιτείας).

But the other form of life is subordinate and more human. It permits men to participate in chaste marriages and procreation, to undertake government, to give orders to soldiers who are fighting for a just cause; it allows them to devote themselves in a pious spirit to farming, to trade, and to civil affairs (πολιτικωτέρας ἀγωγῆς). For them fixed times of retreat and instruction, and days for hearing sacred things are set apart. A secondary stage (βαθμός) of piety is thus granted to them, in which they have exactly the kind of help such lives require, so that all men, whether Greeks or barbarians, have their part in the coming of salvation, and profit by the teaching of the Gospel.[5]

Let us begin by recalling that the *Demonstratio* is actually the second half of a twofold defense of Christianity, the first half of which, the *Praeparatio Evangelica*, had appeared not long before.[6] The *Praeparatio* had been directed against pagan criticisms of Christianity: for example, the charge that Christians were obliged to believe in their religion on the basis of authority alone, without the support of reason and intelligence. The immediate source of such criticisms is considered to have been Porphyry, but they had already been posed by others.[7] The *Demonstratio*, by contrast, was directed primarily at the Jews but also, by implication, against anyone who regarded Christianity as a religious apostasy from its ancestral traditions. How,

---

5. *DE* 1.8.1-4 (GCS 6:39.1-35). English translations are from *The Proof of the Gospel*, ed. and trans. W. J. Ferrar, 2 vols. repr. as one (Grand Rapids: Baker, 1981), 1:48-50 (partially altered).

6. Barnes dates the *Praeparatio Evangelica* to ca. 314–ca. 318, and the *Demonstratio Evangelica* to ca. 318–ca. 323. See T. D. Barnes, *Constantine and Eusebius* (Cambridge, Mass.: Harvard University Press, 1981), p. 278.

7. Cf. *PE* 1.5, among many places. The whole subject is well treated in Robert Wilken's *The Christians as the Romans Saw Them* (New Haven and London: Yale University Press, 1984).

such critics asked, could Christians continue to read and adhere to the Scriptures of the Jews, if they no longer accepted all of the religious injunctions, rituals, and institutions commanded and testified to in those Scriptures? Such a criticism could come not only from Jews or pagans but also from dualist Christians like the Marcionites, who wished to discard Christianity's Jewish origins altogether.

In the first book of the *Demonstratio,* Eusebius begins by repeating one of his fundamental apologetic themes: Christianity is no new revelation, nor a rebellion against an older, established revelation, but the restatement of the original religion of the human race.[8] He insists that

> . . . Christianity is neither a form of Hellenism, nor of Judaism, but . . . a religion with its own characteristic stamp, and that this is not anything novel or original, but something of the greatest antiquity, something natural and familiar to the godly men before the times of Moses, who are remembered for their holiness and justice. (*DE* 1.2.1).

This original religion of the human race is preserved for us chiefly among the descriptions of the "friends of God" found in the Bible who antedated the coming of Moses and the Mosaic "constitution," or πολίτευμα, as Eusebius likes to call it. These "pre-Mosaic" or "pre-Judaic" saints — he has in mind Enoch, Noah, and the patriarchs, but also Job — practiced a kind of ethical monotheism that rejected both polytheism and idolatry, although they did not observe the dietary, ceremonial, and cultic requirements of the Mosaic law, which had not yet been instituted. The fullest definition is found in *Praeparatio Evangelica:*

> You can define the difference between "Hebrews" and "Jews" this way: the latter take their name from Judah, the tribe from which the Jewish monarchy eventually arose, whereas the former are named after Eber [cf. Gen. 10:21, 24-25], who was an ancestor of Abraham. The scriptures thus show that the Hebrews preceded the Jews. As for their type of religion, Moses

---

8. Eusebius assumes his readers are familiar with the fuller development of the theme in *PE* 7.1-9 (cf. esp. 7.6) and 8.1-8. He had already employed it in the introduction to *Ecclesiastical History* (1.4). On this staple of Eusebius's thought, see Jean Sirinelli, *Les vues historiques d'Eusèbe de Césarée durant la période prénicéenne* (Dakar: University of Dakar, 1961), pp. 139-61; Guy Schroeder, "Introduction," in Eusèbe de Césarée, *La Préparation Évangélique: Livre VII,* ed. Jean Sirinelli and Edouard des Places, SC 215 (Paris: Éditions du Cerf, 1975), pp. 13-93; and now Jörg Ulrich, *Euseb von Caesarea und die Juden* (Berlin and New York: Walter de Gruyter, 1999), pp. 57-68, 79-88.

was the first to establish a legislation for the Jews: he passed down a day for the Sabbath, and the greatest possible observance of it, as a reminder of the study of the scriptures; the distinction between animals which could be eaten and those which could not; the calendar of religious feasts; certain other purifications of the body; and long periods to be understood more spiritually according to their symbolic meaning. The Hebrews were prior to Moses in time, and therefore were not bound by the entire Mosaic legislation. They practiced a free and unconstrained religion, and were marked by a life according to nature. Their extraordinary freedom from passion meant that they had no need of laws to rule them, but possessed a true knowledge of doctrines about God.[9]

Christianity, says Eusebius, is neither a form of Hellenism nor of Judaism but "something between the two, the most ancient constitution (πολίτευμα) for holiness, and the most venerable philosophy, only lately codified as the law for all mankind in the whole world" (DE 1.2.10). He even extends the substantial identity of the two stages[10] to include a mutual awareness of the divine person of the Word of God, whom he believes the pre-Mosaic saints knew and acknowledged (DE 1.5.10-21).

If the original revelation was true and right, why then the law? The general lines of his answer have long been recognized by scholars.[11] In this particular text, however, Eusebius makes an interesting exegetical move that adds a new aspect to the argument for Christianity's validity based on its antiquity.

First, the basic features of his case: Eusebius argues that the Mosaic law's provisionality is obvious from its geographical restriction to the temple in Jerusalem. He tries to demonstrate, by extensive citations, particularly from the book of Leviticus, that the law was incapable of fulfillment by anyone living even a moderate distance from the temple. The geographical locus of the law is proof that Moses foresaw its eventual replacement. Knowing that the Jews would be excluded from the city after the failure of the second revolt, he programmed the law's obsolescence by making its fulfillment absolutely impossible after Hadrian banned the Jews from Jerusalem (DE 1.6.37-39). In the long historical interval between Sinai and the Jewish revolts, however, the law had a provisional validity. Moses gave the law as a "nurse" or "governess" to a people that had succumbed to the low moral and religious level of the Egyptian people as a whole; as such, the law was a "lower and less perfect way of life to

---

9. PE 7.6.2-4 (SC 215:168-70), my translation.
10. "One and the same" in their way of life, he says (DE 1.5.3).
11. See works cited in n. 8 above.

the children of Abraham, who were too weak to follow in the steps of their forefathers" (*DE* 1.6.31). The law was to lead them back to God, a "first step (βαθμός) of holiness at the threshold and entrance to the Temple of the more Perfect" (*DE* 1.6.32). The next step would be taken much later, when Jesus called the Jews to ascend further via the stairs of the gospel. Following a paraphrase of chapter five of Matthew (*DE* 1.6.64-73), Eusebius has Jesus say in conclusion that the law was suited to the "hardness of heart of the mass of men and to those subject to the passions," making it "a form of religion reduced and inferior to the old [i.e., the religion of the pre-Mosaic saints]."[12]

Despite such frankly supersessionist language, Eusebius is at pains to present Jesus, whom he calls "the legislator of a new polity (πολιτεία)," *not* as a rebel but as one who willingly obeyed the precepts of the old law, thus fulfilling them, but not abolishing them. Had he rescinded the law, he could not have claimed to be the one foretold by Moses and the prophets (*DE* 1.6.76–1.7.3). In this way, Eusebius believes he can escape the double bind of critics who see Christians either as hypocrites for not obeying the customs of their forebears the Jews or as rebels who reject Judaism altogether:

> So then we are not apostates from Hellenism who have embraced Judaism, nor are we at fault in accepting the law of Moses and the Hebrew prophets though we do not live as Jews, but according to the way of life (πολιτεία) of the friends of God who lived before Moses. Instead, we claim that in doing so we authenticate Moses and the succeeding prophets, because we accept the Christ foretold by them, and obey His laws, and endeavor prayerfully to tread in the steps of His teaching. . . . And we heard just now what the ordinances of the prophet [Christ] were, which we must obey, their wisdom, perfection and heavenly character, which He thought fit to inscribe, not on tables of stone like Moses, nor yet with ink and parchment, but on the hearts of His pupils, purified and open to reason. (*DE* 1.7.18-19)

The foregoing analysis should explain why Eusebius placed his account of the two ways of life in the Church in this part of the *Demonstratio:* he uses it to show how Christianity really is the fulfillment of Judaism. This is demonstrated *both* in the form of Christianity's spiritual elite, "the ones who were able to receive it," who revive the lost spirituality of the pre-Mosaic friends of God; *and* in the form of the rank and file of the Church, "those still in the world of passion and needing treatment," which carries on the therapeutic

---

12. *DE* 1.6.72 (GCS 6:34.10-11).

and pedagogical work once performed for a resistant humanity by the Mosaic law. Eusebius's distinction between the written law of Moses and the perfect commandments of the new covenant, written not on lifeless tables but on living minds (cf. 2 Cor. 3:3), is a conventional Christian construal of Jeremiah's new covenant (Jer. 31:31-34; cf. Heb. 8:8-12). Eusebius goes on to say that the disciples of the master also passed on (παρεδίδοσαν) for others to keep "some things in writing, others in unwritten ordinances," as a discipline accommodated to the weakness of the majority.

Eusebius thus presents the distinction between two orders in the Church as a parallel to or a recapitulation of the historical distinction between the pre-Mosaic friends of God, the "Hebrews," and the Jews proper, who became a people only under the Mosaic covenant. The "Hebrews" adhered to a spiritual law fit for a moral elite, while "Jews" obeyed an authoritative legislation for the many. Mass Christianity therefore has something in common with Judaism's inclusion of larger numbers of people who were no longer equal to the high ethical demands of their "Hebrew" forebears. Like such "Jews," ordinary Christians are legally organized as a cultic collectivity: they are provided with written books and unwritten laws that fit souls still subject to the passions and in need of healing, just as the *Praeparatio* had described the Mosaic polity as "appropriate to their souls, prone to passion and diseased."[13] For the benefit of these humbler Christians a regimen of scriptural instruction served as a "secondary stage of piety" (δεύτερος εὐσεβείας . . . βαθμός). So too Eusebius had described the Mosaic polity as a secondary stage of piety (δεύτερον . . . εὐσεβείας . . . βαθμόν).[14]

DE 1.8 is thus a complex typology since it sublates two chronologically distinct stages of the divine economy into a unity that incorporates and perpetuates both of them. In that sense it is a typology based on analogy. Yet it also represents a typology based on contrast, for both the stage of "the Hebrews" and the stage of "the Jews" are raised to another level in their Christian fulfillment. It is the latter aspect that remains to be examined. We will look first at the case of mass Christianity and "the Jews," then at "the Hebrews" and the Christian spiritual elite.

---

13. The Greek shows the verbal parallel: τοῖς ἔτι τὰς ψυχὰς ἐμπαθέσι καὶ θεραπείας δεομένοις, said of the weaker Christians in the *Demonstratio*, and τὰς ψυχὰς ἐμπαθέσι καὶ νενοσηλευμένοις, said of the Jews in the *Praeparatio* (*PE* 7.8.39 [GCS 8, pt. 1:377.21]).

14. *DE* 1.8.4 (GCS 6:39.33-34); *PE* 8.1.1 (GCS 8, pt. 1:419.9-10).

Christians and "Jews"

As noted above, the new law is more spiritual than the old, even in the form of it adapted to weaker and humbler Christians. The Christian "polity for holiness" (*DE* 1.6.1) is not based on circumcision, dietary laws, purification rites, Sabbath observance or temple cult, but on a pure worship in spirit and truth that no longer depends on "symbols and types."[15] Rather, Eusebius says that the regimen appropriate to these ordinary Christians consists of regular Scripture readings and days for instruction.[16] At first glance it is curious that he makes no mention of Christian ritual life, above all, the Eucharist. He seems to want to portray the spirituality of ordinary Christians as shaped by a massive program in religious instruction, for which the laity in the world, so to speak, repair regularly to the Church for teaching and spiritual renewal. There is a parallel here with the Jewish practice of scriptural instruction every Sabbath.[17] Josephus's description of this practice is an interesting gloss on Eusebius's characterization of Christian worship:

> He [Moses] appointed the Law to be the most excellent and necessary form of instruction, ordaining, not that it should be heard once for all or twice or on several occasions, but that every week men should desert their other occupations and assemble to listen to the Law and to obtain a thorough and accurate knowledge of it, a practice which all other legislators seem to have neglected.[18]

Worship for ordinary Christians, then, is the Bible reading and instruction of the synagogue, but minus the temple cult, the dietary and purity laws, and so forth.

It is also noteworthy that Eusebius emphasizes the role of *tradition* in justifying this twofold differentiation of the Christian life. It is the *disciples*, he says, who differentiated between what the "perfect teacher," Jesus, taught for the elite, and what ought to be adapted to the level of the majority, though Je-

---

15. *DE* 1.6.42 (GCS 6:29.17-20). Book 1.10 argues at length the Christian case for having abandoned the sacrificial cult, on the basis of the vicarious sacrifice of Christ, a discussion that corrects the widespread impression that Eusebius devalued the atonement.

16. *DE* 1.8.4 (GCS 6:39.32-33). The ἀσκήσεως καιροί mentioned here must be scriptural study, not the special ascetical disciplines cultivated by perfect Christians. For ἄσκησις as scriptural study in Eusebius, cf. *HE* 6.2.15 (GCS 2:524.3) and *DE* 8.3 (GCS 6:393.13).

17. Cf. Acts 15:21.

18. Josephus *Against Apion* 2.175 (trans. H. J. St. Thackeray).

sus himself had authorized such an accommodation. Some of these accommodations were passed down (παρεδίδοσαν) in written form, some as "unwritten laws." Why does Eusebius make the distinction between "written" and "unwritten" tradition in presenting the disciples' "accommodation"[19] to the weakness of the majority? Considered in itself, the distinction was common enough; patristic writers both before and after Eusebius recognized that many aspects of Church order and usage depended on unwritten rather than written tradition, whether biblical or postbiblical.[20] Yet Eusebius is invoking the distinction to defend a development with exceptional relevance to the Church's new situation under Constantine, for his model of the Church asserts that there are, as a matter of course, two different forms of life in the Church — not just different levels of progress on the same path, but actually different states, which Eusebius gives no indication should be seen as temporary or transitional, but rather as a necessary state of affairs for as long as the Church existed in the world.

This does not appear the same as some other bipartite conceptions of the Church found in writers before Eusebius: for example, the distinction between clergy and laity, the distinction between simple believers, the ἁπλούστεροι, and Gnostic or mature Christians (cf. Clement and Origen, respectively),[21] or even the distinction between married Christians and those dedicated to virginity, although the last of these is certainly on the way towards Eusebius's categorization. Eusebius, however, goes much further in this direction by extending the distinction to cover virtually all of human life.

For purposes of contrast, compare Clement of Alexandria's use of the written-unwritten distinction in explaining the different levels of the Christian life. In his *Stromateis,* Clement appealed to unwritten apostolic tradition in defending the existence, not of moral concessions to a majority of Christians living in the world, but of a Gnostic elite that possessed a special unwritten knowledge from the apostles:

> If, then, we assert that Christ himself is Wisdom, and that it was his working which showed itself in the prophets, by which the gnostic tradition may be learned, as he himself taught the apostles during his presence; then it follows that the *gnosis,* which is the knowledge and apprehension

19. . . . συγκατιόντες τῇ τῶν πλειόνων ἀσθενείᾳ (*DE* 1.8.1 [GCS 9:39.9-10]).

20. See citations in G. W. H. Lampe, ed., *Patristic Greek Lexicon* (Oxford and New York: Clarendon, 1961), s.v. ἄγραφος and παράδοσις.

21. For Clement, e.g., *paed.* 1.6-8; for Origen, e.g., *Cels.* 3.49; *De princ.* 4.2.1; and *Jo.* 32.24.

of things present, future, and past, which is sure and reliable, as being revealed by the Son of God, is wisdom. . . . And the *gnosis* itself is that which has descended by succession to a few, having been handed down unwritten from the apostles (ἡ γνῶσις δὲ αὕτη ἡ κατὰ διαδοχὰς εἰς ὀλίγους ἐκ τῶν ἀποστόλων ἀγράφως παραδοθεῖσα).[22]

Eusebius's typological construction is thus appealing to unwritten apostolic tradition as a warrant for a significant expansion of the older idea that the Church comprised distinct orders or modes of life.

Christians and "Hebrews"

Where the two elite classes are concerned, the ancient "Hebrews" and the Christian perfect, a sharper and more conspicuous contrast is evident. Eusebius recognizes that the life of the spiritual elite diverges from the pre-Mosaic friends of God in its assertion of celibacy over procreation. The patriarchs were married, some of them to more than one woman. They saw the birth of children as a mark of divine blessing and barrenness as a curse. Yet Eusebius's spiritual elite have renounced marriage and procreation. Celibacy is only one of several renunciations that lack patriarchal parallels: besides sexuality and offspring, property and wealth are also rejected. Eusebius's allusion to Jesus' saying, "Let anyone receive this who can" (Matt. 19:12), suggests that his account of the life of the elite is based on the exhortations of Matthew 19, where the same four topics are found, and in the same order.[23] Perhaps this chapter of Matthew served as a convenient sketch of the ideal form of the Christian life.[24]

22. Clement of Alexandria, *str.* 6.7.61.1-3 (GCS 15:462.17-24, 28-30). Cf. also *str.* 5.10.62.1 (GCS 15:367.25-26 and 368.2): "For that the knowledge is not 'the possession of all' [cf. 1 Cor. 8:7], he [Paul] expressly declares [a quotation from Col. 2:2-3 follows]. . . . For some things were passed down unwritten, for example to the Hebrews . . . [a quotation of Heb. 5:12–6:1 follows]."

23. The four renunciations repeat Matthew's order of topics: γάμους (cf. Matt. 19:10, οὐ συμφέρει γαμῆσαι); παιδοποιίας (Matt. 19:13, παιδία); κτῆσιν (Matt. 19:22, κτήματα); and περιουσίας ὕπαρξιν (Matt. 19:23, πλούσιος).

24. Although Origen, in his treatment of Matthew 19 in his *Commentary on Matthew,* does not appear to take such an approach. See the extant parts of Book 15 in the *Commentary on Matthew,* which treat the saying on those who have made themselves eunuchs for the kingdom of God, the presentation of the little children to Jesus, and the story of the rich young man.

Nevertheless, Eusebius cannot rest content with the dominical injunctions since they run completely counter to the practice of the "Hebrews," which he has previously claimed is the authoritative biblical sanction for Christianity. To soften the contradiction, he offers several explanations in *DE* 1.9, immediately after the section we have been discussing. First, and apparently in his mind most decisive, is the eschatological justification for celibacy. The pre-Mosaic saints lived at the time of the world's beginning. Christians, however, live as it is nearing its end. As the former necessarily contributed to the increase of the race, so the latter thought this of no importance. They were waiting for the promised initiation of a new world, which was shortly to occur. A second reason is that the rough simplicity of the world in the earlier time made it easier to concentrate on religious and moral obligations. Now, in an advanced and decadent civilization, there was need of greater vigilance and withdrawal from the enticements of the world. (For both of these arguments he cites the authority of "the gospel teaching," by which he means St. Paul's counsel to the Corinthians.) Third, he says, the ancient friends of God were dedicated to founding a polity different from the world and, as a small company, were of necessity concerned to ensure their survival and increase by propagation. In contrast, Christianity was flourishing and spreading rapidly by conversion and therefore didn't need to worry about mere biological survival. Christianity could afford the differentiation of labor in the Christian polity that allowed some to have leisure for higher things and, in the process, to benefit a much larger number by their intercessory prayer than they could if they restricted themselves to the needs of family life. Finally, Eusebius argues that the pre-Mosaic saints were only provisionally committed to marriage and procreation and that, at key stages in their lives, they abandoned marital sexuality and dedicated themselves to continence (the examples of Enoch, Noah, Esau, Joseph, Moses, Aaron, and Melchizedek are all invoked). In the same way, he says, the bishops of the Church, though they may be married at the time of their consecration, cease to have sex with their wives: "Yet it is fitting that those in the priesthood and occupied in the service of God, should abstain after ordination from the intercourse of marriage" (*DE* 1.9.21); but, he hastens to add, Christians by no means reject marriage and procreation: "To all of those who have not been raised to the rank of this wondrous priesthood, Scripture makes an explicit concession when it proclaims, 'Let marriage be held in honor and let the marriage bed be undefiled; for God will judge the immoral and the adulterous' (Heb 13.4)."

Of this text I would make the following comments by way of conclusion: Eusebius has presented an exegetical rationale for the existence of two states in the Church that is an interesting and even notable defense of a development that was only going to intensify in the future. As the successor to Judaism, Christianity could not all at once leap into a new world and a new state of perfection for the race. Rather, God willed that it should advance in the gradual way that he had always educated humanity, accommodating his demands and expectations to what human nature was able to bear. The new situation created by the emperor's conversion to Christianity was not, therefore, one for which Christianity was entirely unprepared. The first argument in defense of celibacy is the one that in actuality is probably the best explanation for the primitive character of the ascetical and perfectionist impulse. Among modern students of asceticism, Erik Peterson (not otherwise an admirer of Eusebius's theology or apologetics) was the first to argue that Christian asceticism was not a dualist deviation foisted on the religion by an alien metaphysics but the behavioral deduction of the Christian message that in the life and death of Jesus, God was bringing a new world into being.[25]

Eusebius's account of the life of Christian perfection recognizes that the majority of Christians will live lives in the world, doing the necessary work of agriculture, commerce, government, and military service to see that human life flourishes and prospers. His perfectionist elite are not specifically said to renounce violence and bloodshed, but that is certainly implied. Presumably nonviolence is not mentioned explicitly because Eusebius's exegetical shorthand relied on Matthew 19, which did not mention the Sermon on the Mount's renunciation of the violent resistance against evil. The *Demonstratio Evangelica* was probably written not long after the Council of Arles (314), whose Canon 3 forbade Christian soldiers to throw down their arms in time of peace.[26] The bishops at the council, which Constantine had summoned and funded, were scarcely unaware of the empire's military needs or the emperor's role in ending persecution. Neither of course was Eusebius, who proudly reported in his *Church History* how the prayers of Christian soldiers miraculously saved Marcus Aurelius's army (*HE* 5.5.1-7). The division of labor in the Christian community liberated the ascetical elite from the duty of serving the empire in office and in arms. There is a notable contrast here with the situation analyzed by Origen less than a century before. Origen, it will be remembered, had responded to Celsus's condemnation of Christian pacifism by saying that Christians rendered the empire the greatest possible aid by

---

25. See the papers collected in Erik Peterson, *Frühkirche, Judentum und Gnosis* (Freiburg: Herder, 1959), especially "Einige Beobachtungen zu den Anfängen der christlichen Askese," pp. 209-20.

26. *De his qui arma proiciunt in pace, placuit abstineri eos a communione.* In *Concilia Galliae A. 314–A. 506*, ed. C. Munier, CCSL 148 (Turnholt: Brepols, 1963), p. 9.

praying for the emperor when he fought for a just cause.[27] In Origen's view, intercessory prayer was the work of the whole Church, which rightly claimed the same exemption from military service enjoyed by pagan priesthoods. Perhaps Eusebius's rationalization of the new situation, which he enthusiastically advocated, owed something to the exegetical scheme we have just described.

Finally, it is worth noticing that the ascetical elite do not seem identical with the clergy, even though interceding with God is one of their primary religious tasks. To that extent, Eusebius is simply continuing the legacy of Origen, who also made a distinction between the ascetical elite and the clergy. The clergy were certainly not obliged to renounce property, nor were they expected to be single men. Nevertheless, the adoption of the ascetical ethic has made significant headway since Origen's time because Eusebius presents it as normal that a bishop should abstain from the marriage bed after his consecration.

27. Origen, *Cels.* 8.73. See the whole discussion in 8.69-75.

Training for "the Good Ascent":
Gregory of Nyssa's Homily on the Sixth Psalm

BRIAN E. DALEY, S.J.

The exegesis of the book of Psalms always occupied a special place in early Christian biblical interpretation. Allusions to and quotations from the Psalms are woven into the works of the New Testament and into virtually all the letters, narratives, homilies, and apologies produced by Christian writers of the second century, as part of a fund of sacred texts with which their readers were presumably familiar. Attempts to interpret the Psalter in a Christian sense are as old as the practice of Christian exegesis itself. The first traces of this kind of interpretation are probably the fragments of introduction and commentary attributed to Hippolytus of Rome, from the first decades of the third century.[1] Between the mid-320s and the mid-350s, Origen — the first systematic Christian interpreter of the Bible — is said by Jerome to have commented on the entire Psalter, apparently in homilies, a learned commentary, and a set of briefer notes or *scholia*.[2] If one counts simply the works of Latin and Greek

---

1. The fragments on the Psalter attributed to Hippolytus were edited in 1897 by Hans Achelis (GCS 1:2.125-53). For modern discussions of the authorship and authenticity of these fragments, see Pierre Nautin, *Le dossier d'Hippolyte et de Méliton* (Paris: Éditions du Cerf, 1953), pp. 15-32, 99-107; idem, "L'homélie d'Hippolyte sur le Psautier et les oeuvres de Josipe," *Revue d'histoire des religions* 179 (1971): 137-79; Marie-Josèphe Rondeau, *Les commentaires patristiques du Psautier (IIIe-Ve siècles)*, vol. 1, Orientalia Christiana Analecta 219 (Rome: Pontificum Institutum Studiorum Orientalium, 1982), pp. 27-43.

2. Jerome, *ep.* 112.20; cf. *ep.* 33.4, and the prologue to his own *Commentarioli* (CCSL 72:177-78). See Rondeau, *Les commentaires patristiques du Psautier*, 1:44-63, for a full discussion of the evidence for Origen's exegetical work on the Psalms, and of the extant fragments.

185

Christian writers up to the end of the sixth century, commentaries on the Psalms easily exceed those on any other Biblical book in number, if not in sheer bulk. We still possess exegetical homilies or commentaries on some or all of the Psalms by at least twenty-one patristic authors — in some cases, such as Origen, Jerome, and perhaps Hesychius of Jerusalem, the remains of several different attempts by the same writers to expound the Psalter. Obviously, Christian interest in these ancient Hebrew prayers remained extremely high, and the difficulties that they posed to Christian religious understanding were perennially challenging.

One main reason for ancient Christian interest in the biblical Psalms was doubtless their familiarity. By the beginning of the third century, their regular use in Christian worship is unambiguously documented. Before this time, the evidence suggests that the songs Christians used in worship were more often hymns specially composed by Christian authors, and that the Psalms were normally considered a sacred prophetic text rather than as the material of hymnody. The proliferation of such original liturgical poetry in Gnostic communities, however, and its possibilities for conveying heterodox doctrine in an attractive way, seem to have prompted a new insistence, around the year 200, on using biblical texts as much as possible in Christian worship, including its sung portions.[3] A passage in a Greek fragment of the *Acts of Paul,* probably written in the last decade of the second century, provides what seems to be the earliest reference to the singing of the Psalms in Christian liturgy. During a visit of Paul to Corinth, a woman named Myrta is presented as prophesying during a Eucharistic celebration, predicting a good outcome of Paul's coming journey to Rome; "and immediately, when the Spirit that was in Myrta was at peace, each one took of the bread and feasted according to custom, amid the singing of psalms of David and of hymns."[4] In his *Apologeticum,* written probably in 197, Tertullian gives a detailed account of how Christians gather for worship; after describing the reading of Scriptures and the *agape* meal, Tertullian stresses that the celebration begins and ends with intense prayer, and adds: "After the washing of hands and the bringing in of lights, each person is asked to stand up and to sing to God, either drawing on the Holy Scriptures or on his or her own inspiration."[5] As-

---

3. For a brief description of this transition from original Christian hymn-texts to the use of Psalms in worship, see Balthasar Fischer, "Die Psalmenfrömmigkeit der Märtyrerkirche," in *Die Psalmen als Stimme der Kirche* (Trier: Paulinus-Verlag, 1982), pp. 19-20, with the earlier literature cited there.

4. E. Hennecke and W. Schneemelcher, *New Testament Apocrypha,* vol. 2 (London: SCM, 1974), p. 380.

5. Tertullian, *apol.* 39.

suming that the scriptural source for such Christian hymn singing would principally have been the book of Psalms, this text seems to reflect a period of liturgical development in which spontaneous, prophetic song and perhaps also specially composed Christian hymnody were in use alongside the Psalter, but the emphasis on the Psalms and other biblical poetry as the heart of liturgical music was to dominate almost exclusively in the next few centuries. By the mid-fourth century, the Synod of Laodicea could lay down a measure that seems to have been meant to regulate liturgical singing as well as reading: "It is not permitted that privately composed Psalms or non-canonical books be read out in Church, but only the canonical books of the New and Old Testament."[6]

Much of the interest, then, in interpreting the meaning of the book of Psalms must simply have been due to its use in Christian worship. With the meteoric growth of monasticism, especially, during the fourth century, the recitation and chanting of the Psalms grew to be the mainstay of Christian daily prayer, the prime vehicle for both private intercession and communal praise, the chief weapon against inner demons, and the medicine for diseased thoughts.[7] The desert monks seem to have learned large portions of the Psalter, or even the whole of it, by heart, and to have prayed the Psalms constantly as they worked, as well as using them in their weekly worship.[8] St. Athanasius, in his *Letter to Marcellinus* on the Psalms, extols the unique quality of the Psalter among the books of the Bible, both because of its contents and because of its intended use. On the one hand, he points out in the first section of the letter, the book of Psalms serves as a kind of summary of the themes and narratives contained in the rest of the Bible, pointing both backward to the story of Israel's origins, exodus, and exile, and forward to redemption in Christ: "Like a garden, it brings forth in song the fruits of all the books, which it bears in itself, and displays in addition the particular themes that it chants along with them."[9] On the other hand, in addition to its relationship to the biblical narrative, the Psalter acts, in Athanasius's view, as a kind of providential mirror for the whole range of human emotions and needs:

6. Synod of Laodicea, can. 59: E. J. Jonkers, *Acta et Symbola Conciliorum quae Saeculo Quarto Habita Sunt,* Textus Minores 19 (Leiden: Brill, 1974), p. 96.

7. See, for example, the *Sayings of the Desert Fathers,* alphabetical collection, Macarius the Great 33; Serapion 1.

8. On the use and understanding of the biblical text by the desert monks, see Douglas Burton-Christie, *The Word in the Desert* (New York: Oxford University Press, 1993), esp. pp. 107-33.

9. Athanasius, *ep. Marcell.* 2 (PG 27:12c.4-6).

The Book of Psalms also has a particular grace, an outstanding purpose, which is this: in addition to the other themes, in which it is related to the other books and which it shares with them, it also has this marvelous character peculiar to itself, that it contains the motions of each soul, their changes and the ways they are corrected, written out and portrayed within itself. As a result, anyone who wishes to take up and master the unlimited resources the book contains will be able to form himself just as is written there.[10]

A little further on, Athanasius makes the same point still more pointedly:

It seems to me that for the one who sings them, these works (λόγοι) become a kind of mirror, so that he may recognize himself and the movements of his own soul in them, and so proclaim them aloud as one who perceives himself.[11]

The reason one *sings* the Psalms, rather than simply reading or reciting them, Athanasius later explains, is both to give a fitting "breadth" and solemnity to the word of God by the use of musical sounds and to enable the image of ourselves contained in the Psalms to become — in the harmony of our singing — both the reflection and the cause of an inner harmony in the human soul, rooted in the harmonious working of the divine Logos in the whole of creation.[12]

Against the background of Athanasius's characterization of the Psalter, one can see more easily the extraordinary interest shown by Christian writers of the fourth century and later in reflecting on the meaning of the Psalms, so that the faithful who use them, and particularly the monks who use them almost incessantly, might draw full benefit from these healing incantations. Diodore of Tarsus, in the prologue to his own *Commentary on the Psalms*, written in the 370s, explains the importance of understanding the meaning of the texts one is singing, so that "the medicine begins to fit and to contain the

10. Athanasius, *ep. Marcell.* 10 (PG 27:20c.2-11). The Greek text of the last sentence appears to be corrupted in the Migne edition.

11. Athanasius, *ep. Marcell.* 12 (PG 27:24b.13–c.2).

12. Athanasius, *ep. Marcell.* 27-28 (PG 27:37d.5–40d.5). See also Hilary of Poitiers's prologue to his own homilies on the Psalms, written about 365, in which he compares the *psalterium* or harp with which David accompanied his prophetic songs to the body of Christ: both are instruments "by which the heavenly Spirit has spoken" (Prologue 7: CSEL 22:9.1-17).

disease to which it corresponds."[13] He has tried to explain the "subjects (ὑποθέσεις)" and the word-for-word meanings of the Psalms, he says,

> so that while they are singing them the brethren may not be simply swept along by the sounds or find their minds occupied by other things because they do not understand the text, but that by recognizing the sequence of meaning (ἀκολουθίαν) in what is said they may "sing with understanding" (Ps. 46:8b[47:7b]), as it is written, from the depth of their minds, and not simply from the top of their heads or the tip of their lips.[14]

To expound the Psalms, in other words, in the fourth-century Church, was not simply to comment on divinely inspired Scripture; it was to draw the mind of the believer more deeply into the process by which the Word of God, working in the deep recesses of the human heart and mind, continues to restore the harmony and health of creation.

My purpose in this essay, however, is not simply to reflect on the implications and purposes of ancient Psalm commentaries, but to examine more closely — and to offer in a new English translation — an unusual work in this genre, from the same period of growing interest in the Psalter, by one of the great theological and spiritual writers of the early Church: Gregory of Nyssa's *Homily on the Sixth Psalm*. This sermon, which has not received a great deal of attention in the scholarly literature,[15] stands by itself within Gregory's *oeuvre*. Although several of his festal homilies are mainly concerned with interpreting psalm-texts that were apparently part of the liturgy of those celebrations,[16] and although his treatise *On the Inscriptions of the Psalms* is in some respects a commentary on the Psalter through the focusing lens of their enigmatic titles,

13. Diodore of Tarsus, *Ps.*, Prologue 31-32 (CCSG 6:4).

14. Diodore of Tarsus, *Ps.*, Prologue 37-42.

15. There is a modern critical edition of the homily, by James A. McDonough, S.J., in GNO 5:187-93. Casimir McCambley has already published an English translation of the homily, with a brief introduction: "On the Sixth Psalm, Concerning the Octave, by Saint Gregory of Nyssa," *Greek Orthodox Theological Review* 32 (1987): 39-50; helpful as it is, however, this work needs both extension and correction. On Gregory's homily, see also Jean Daniélou, "La typologie de la semaine au IVᵉ siècle," *Recherches de science religieuse* 35 (1948): 394-97; Hans Christian Knuth, *Zur Auslegungsgeschichte von Psalm 6* (Tübingen: J. C. B. Mohr, 1971), pp. 36-41; Rondeau, *Les commentaires patristiques du Psautier* 1:114-16.

16. See his homilies on Easter (GNO 9.309-11), the Ascension (GNO 9:323-27), and Pentecost (GNO 10:2.287-92). Mme. Rondeau, following a suggestion of Joseph Paramelle, questions whether the so-called Ascension homily was really intended for that feast: *Les commentaires patristiques du Psautier* 1:114, n. 327.

Gregory seems never to have attempted a formal commentary on the book, and this homily is his only extant sermon on a single psalm.[17] Dating the works of Gregory of Nyssa is a notoriously conjectural business, and there are no reliable clues in this homily to its place within the sequence of his life and writings.[18] Brief as it is, his *Homily on the Sixth Psalm* can hardly be considered one of Gregory's major achievements; it clearly has a pastoral rather than a speculative character and seems to have been delivered either to a local community or, more probably, to a community of monks as an exhortation to carry on the laborious work of self-purification by confessing sins and taking on the works of penance. Its interest lies both in the clarity and economy with which it interweaves themes familiar from Gregory's other writings — the "ascent" to perfection, the purgation of "thoughts" that stand in the way of virtue, the gulf between the "age" in which we live and the "new creation" of eternal life — and in the ingenious way in which Gregory uses these themes, as well as the material of what was already an abundant and living tradition of psalm exegesis, to solve what appeared to him to be the principal riddles posed to the Christian believer by Psalm 6. In its own way, this elegant and deceptively simple homily is a classic example of how a major fourth-century theologian could work with a biblical prayer from a somewhat foreign religious and existential context, in order to enable the serious Christian faithful of his time to "sing it with understanding."

The Psalm Itself

The text of the psalm, in both the original Masoretic Hebrew and in the Septuagint Greek version that was normative for early Christian interpreters, can be translated as follows:

---

17. Gregory's attempts, at the beginning and end of the homily, to connect the content of Psalm 6 to that of Psalms 4 and 5, through their inscriptions, may suggest that this homily is part of a series — perhaps given during Lent since it is so directly focused on the confession of sins and penance. There is no other evidence, however, as far as I know, of the existence of such homilies.

18. Père Jean Daniélou, in an early article on Gregory's chronology ("La chronologie des sermons de Grégoire de Nysse," *Recherches de science religieuse* 29 [1955]: 368-71) suggests that all Gregory's writings on the Psalter are to be dated to 387 and 388; later ("La chronologie des oeuvres de Grégoire de Nysse," *SP* 7 [1966]: 160-62) he suggests the earlier date of 378. Mme. Rondeau suggests (*Les commentaires patristiques du Psautier* 1:115) that both his work *On the Inscriptions of the Psalms* and this homily are "oeuvres de jeunesse."

Psalm 6
Hebrew Text
(Revised Standard Version)

To the choirmaster;
With stringed instruments;
According to the Sheminith (lit.: to the Eighth);
A psalm of David.

1. O Lord, rebuke me not in thy anger,
   nor chasten me in thy wrath.
2. Be gracious to me, O Lord, for I am languishing;
   O Lord, heal me, for my bones are troubled.
3. My soul also is sorely troubled.
   But thou, O Lord — how long?
4. Turn, O Lord, save my life;
   deliver me for the sake of thy steadfast love.
5. For in death there is no remembrance of thee;
   In Sheol who can give thee praise?
6. I am weary with my moaning;
   every night I flood my bed with tears;
   I drench my couch with my weeping.
7. My eye wastes away because of grief,
   it grows weak because of all my foes.
8. Depart from me, all you workers of evil;
   for the Lord has heard the sound of my weeping.
9. The Lord has heard my supplication;
   the Lord accepts my prayer.
10. All my enemies shall be ashamed and sorely troubled;
    they shall turn back, and be put to shame in a moment.

Septuagint Text

To the end;
In hymns;
Concerning the Eighth;
A psalm of David.

1. O Lord, do not test me in your anger,
   nor correct me in your wrath.
2. Have mercy on me, Lord, because I am weak;
   Heal me, Lord, for my bones are troubled,

3. and my soul is very troubled;
   and you, Lord — how long?
4. Turn, O Lord, rescue my soul,
   save me for the sake of your mercy.
5. Because in death there is no one who remembers you;
   in Hades, who will make confession to you?
6. I have grown weary with my groaning;
   I shall wash my couch every night,
   I shall drench my bedding with my tears.
7. My eye is troubled by anger,
   I have grown old in the midst of all my enemies.
8. Depart from me, all you who work lawlessness,
   because the Lord has heard the sound of my weeping.
9. The Lord has heard my supplication,
   the Lord has accepted my prayer.
10. May all my enemies be ashamed and exceedingly troubled,
    may they turn back, and quickly be very much ashamed.

Modern exegetes tend to classify this psalm as a prayer of an individual in distress, usually as a "psalm of sickness and healing."[19] Other scholars point out that the specific problems of which the speaker complains in psalms such as this are characteristically somewhat vague; so here the speaker says that he or she is "languishing" (2) and near death (5), shaking with terror in body and soul (2-3), and that all of this is experienced as a sure sign of God's wrath (1) — yet he or she also complains of "enemies" as part of the cause of this "grief" (7). Patrick Miller has suggested this psalm as the kind of lament that would have been appropriate for a woman in the physical and social situation of Hannah, the mother of Samuel, in 1 Samuel 1:5-6.[20] Norbert Lohfink, moreover, has observed that its formulation of the human situation, like that in many other psalms of complaint, is multi-purpose and elusive.[21] In any case, like a number of other psalms of lament (e.g., 22, 41, 102), this psalm concludes with a declaration of thanks to God for having heard the speaker's

19. See, for instance, Hans-Joachim Kraus, *Psalms 1–59: A Continental Commentary* (Minneapolis: Fortress, 1993), pp. 160-61, who cites other literature.
20. Patrick Miller, *They Cried to the Lord: The Form and Theology of Biblical Prayer* (Minneapolis: Fortress, 1994), p. 238.
21. Norbert Lohfink, "Psalm 6 — Beobachtungen beim Versuch, ihn 'kanonisch' auszulegen," *Theologische Quartalschrift* 167 (1987): 280-81. Lohfink suggests (p. 284) that the real "situation" suggested by the psalm is probably persecution rather than physical sickness.

prayer (9) and with a lively petition for the further defeat of his or her enemies (10), a striking change of direction and mood that some suggest may be
a sign of an original cultic setting, with place before verse 9 for a priestly word
of reassurance.[22] The Septuagint text, in this psalm, follows the Hebrew
closely, differing mainly in the use of the future tense in the speaker's description of his weeping (6), in his first-person claim to have "grown old" rather
than simply to have become weak of eye (7), and in the transformation of
verse 10 into a clear prayer for the defeat of the speaker's enemies by God —
all details that play their role in the Christian exegetical tradition on this
psalm.

The Interpretations

Ancient commentary on Psalm 6 is fairly abundant. Comments on the psalm
from various sources in the rabbinic tradition — some of them attributed to
rabbis as early as the Amoraic period (third-fifth centuries c.e.) — appear in
the *Midrash Tehillim*, which is generally recognized to have been compiled
somewhere between the eighth and eleventh centuries of our era.[23] From
early Christian commentators, we have only a few reliably identifiable fragments on Psalm 6 from Origen's lost commentaries and homilies,[24] but more
substantial fragments — most of which seem, in this case, to be authentic —
from the commentaries of Eusebius of Caesarea,[25] Athanasius,[26] Didymus of
Alexandria,[27] and Cyril of Alexandria.[28] We also have complete sets of concise
and learned comments on this psalm by Diodore of Tarsus,[29] by Jerome in his

---

22. See Kraus, *Psalms 1–59*, pp. 163-64, and the literature cited there.

23. See the English translation of William G. Braude, trans., *The Midrash on Psalms,*
2 vols., Yale Judaica Series 13 (New Haven: Yale University Press, 1959), 1:93-100. For a
survey of the history of Christian interpretation of this psalm, see Knuth, *Zur
Auslegungsgeschichte von Psalm 6;* for Patristic authors, pp. 25-60.

24. See PG 17:602d.6–3b.6, a quotation in Pamphilus's *Apology for Origen;* the other
fragments are contained in various types of biblical catenae, most of which are not yet
published for this psalm. See Rondeau, *Les commentaires patristiques du Psautier (IIIe-Ve
siècles),* 1:55-62.

25. PG 23:120a.6–21c.5.

26. PG 27:76c.11–78c.7.

27. Ekkehard Mühlenberg, ed., *Psalmenkommentare aus der Katenenüberlieferung* 1,
Patristische Texte und Studien 15 (Berlin: De Gruyter, 1975), pp. 135-39; a partial and less
reliable edition of most of these fragments appears in PG 39:1173d–80a.

28. PG 69:744a–48c.

29. Ed. Jean-Marie Olivier: CCSG 6:32-36.

Commentarioli in Psalmos,[30] by the shadowy fifth-century African exegete Arnobius Junior,[31] by Theodoret of Cyrrhus,[32] and — in a more expansive and homiletic style — by Cassiodorus.[33] From Gregory of Nyssa, besides the present sermon, we have two passages commenting on the phrase "for the octave" or "for the eighth day" in the psalm's title, both from Gregory's treatise *On the Inscriptions of the Psalms*.[34] Augustine has left us an early *Enarratio* on this psalm;[35] John Chrysostom, a homily,[36] as well as substantial comments on the inscription in his second treatise *On Compunction*;[37] furthermore, there is a homily on this work in Asterius's homilies on the Psalms,[38] as well as a long, lone sermon on it — in two recensions — by the seventh-century theologian Anastasius of Sinai.[39] Although we cannot do more than summarize here, it would be useful to look briefly at the main contents of these other representatives of the ancient exegetical tradition on this psalm before we consider the particular characteristics of Gregory's own interpretation.

30. Ed. Germain Morin: CCSL 72:186-88.

31. CCSL 25:7-8. For a discussion of Arnobius's identity and probable date, see Rondeau, *Les commentaires patristiques du Psautier (IIIe-Ve siècles)*, 1:190-94.

32. PG 80:901b–5c.

33. CCSL 97:70-79.

34. Gregory of Nyssa, *Pss. kth.* 2:52-53 (GNO 5:83-84); 2:146-47 (GNO 5:121); for an English translation, see Ronald E. Heine, *Gregory of Nyssa's Treatise on the Inscriptions of the Psalms* (Oxford: Clarendon, 1995), pp. 136-37, 167-68.

35. CCSL 38:27-35. Augustine composed brief expositions of Psalms 1–32 as a young presbyter, in 392, which were probably never preached to a congregation. He later also delivered "live" interpretations of several of these early numbers of the Psalter, but his *enarratio* on Psalm 6 was apparently not one of them.

36. PG 55:71-80. See now the excellent English translation by Robert C. Hill, *St. John Chrysostom: Commentary on the Psalms*, 2 vols. (Brookline, Mass.: Holy Cross Orthodox Press, 1998), 1:95-110.

37. Chrysostom, *On Compunction II: To Stelechius* 4 (PG 47:415d–16a).

38. Marcel Richard, ed., *Asterii Sophistae Commentariorum in Psalmos quae supersunt*, Symbolae Osloenses, Supplement 16 (Oslo: Brøgger, 1956), pp. 81-92. Wolfram Kinzig has recently and convincingly argued that the author of these homilies on the Psalms is neither the mid-fourth-century Arian Asterius "the Sophist" nor the fifth-century preacher Asterius of Amasea, but another Asterius, Nicene in theology, who probably composed these homilies in West Syria (Antioch) between 385 and 410: *In Search of Asterius: Studies on the Authorship of the Homilies on the Psalms* (Göttingen: Vandenhoeck & Ruprecht, 1990).

39. PG 89:1077-116 (longer recension); 1116-44 (shorter recension).

The Inscription

Ancient interpreters of the psalms, Jewish and Christian, took the titles or inscriptions given to these prayers in the Bible very seriously. They were considered both integral to the text and revealing of what the subject or main point of the psalm was understood by the prophetic author to be. In the title of the present psalm, the detail that has puzzled and fascinated most interpreters is the phrase "for the eighth" (*'al ha-sheminith*), which also appears in the inscription to Psalm 12 (LXX 11). The original meaning of this direction is not clear. Hans-Joachim Kraus and other modern scholars, along with the Targum, Rashi, and Ibn Ezra, take it as referring to an eight-stringed harp, possibly to its eighth or lowest-toned string; supporting evidence for this is a description of levitical singing in 1 Chronicles 15:20-21, in which some musicians "play harps according to the *'alamoth*" (perhaps meaning "in a girlish voice" or in a high range), while others play "according to the *sheminith*" (which would then suggest a low timbre, associated with the eighth string).[40] Another important early medieval Jewish commentator and translator, Rabbi Saadya (ninth-tenth centuries), citing earlier rabbinic sources, identifies the phrase with the eighth musical mode.[41] Most ancient Jewish and Christian interpreters, however, assume the phrase has typological or symbolic significance. The *Midrash Tehillim*, characteristically, offers a variety of explanations: the phrase may refer to the seven obligatory prayers said each day, of which this psalm is not one; or to the "seal" of circumcision, which is performed on the eighth day after a male child's birth; or to the future "gathering" of Israel from the eight kingdoms into which it has been dispersed — in other words, to eschatological salvation.[42]

Early Christian interpreters, almost without exception, assume it is a reference to the "eighth day," doubtless because the Septuagint version of the phrase, περὶ τῆς ὀγδόης, easily suggests a reference to the word "day," ἡμέρας. As is well known, the eighth day of the week — the Sunday following a week of seven days, which begins a new week — was widely used from the early second century on to identify the Christian reason for worshipping on Sunday rather than on the Sabbath: to commemorate the day of Jesus' resur-

---

40. See Kraus, *Psalms 1–59*, p. 31; for the references to the Targum and Ibn Ezra, see Eric Werner, *The Sacred Bridge: The Interdependence of Liturgy and Music in Synagogue and Church during the First Millennium* (New York: Columbia University Press, 1959), p. 384. The designation *'al 'alamoth* actually appears in the inscription of Psalm 46.

41. See *Saadyas Psalmübersetzung* (ed. Galliner) 22, cited by Werner, *Sacred Bridge*, p. 379, n. 37. Ibn Ezra also offers this as an alternative explanation.

42. Braude, *Midrash on Psalms*, 1:93-96.

rection and to celebrate Christian hope in the beginning of an everlasting "day of salvation" with the resurrection of all the dead.[43] Commenting on the connection between the eighth day and the resurrection, Augustine writes to a certain Januarius, in 400, that the Christian celebration of Sunday as "the day of the Lord" does not annul the command of resting on the Sabbath, "but glorifies it" by giving that rest a new meaning;

> for the mystery of the eighth day was not hidden from our holy ancestors, who were filled with the spirit of prophecy. For a psalm was written "for the eighth day," and on the eighth day children were circumcised, and in Ecclesiastes (11:2) it is said, referring to the meaning of the two Testaments, "to these seven and to those eight."[44]

Augustine here reflects what has become by his time a familiar Christian *topos,* connecting this psalm inscription (and occasionally other texts, like Eccles. 11:2) both with the Jewish rituals of purification and circumcision on the eighth day and with Christian eschatological hope founded in the resurrection of Christ. A few decades earlier, Gregory of Nazianzus, in his sermon "On New Sunday" (*Or.* 44) — a festal oration celebrating both the local feast of St. Mamas and the octave of Easter as a day of Christian "renewal" — develops the point more elaborately still, observing that just as Easter itself, "the first Day of the Lord," marks the beginning of our salvation, so the celebration of its octave "clearly signifies our second birth":

> Just as the first creation takes its beginning from the Lord's Day (and that is clear: for the seventh day after that becomes the Sabbath, which is the day of rest from all labors), so the second begins anew from that day, being the first of what comes after it and the eighth after those before it,

---

43. See, for example, Barnabas 15.8-9; Cyprian, *ep.* 64.4, who also connects the Eighth Day with "spiritual circumcision." On the early Christian use of this symbol and its connection with the building of octagonal baptistries and churches, see Franz Joseph Dölger, "Zur Symbolik des altchristlichen Taufhauses: Das Oktogon und die Symbolik der Achtzahl," *Antike und Christentum* 4 (1934): 153-87; Jean Daniélou, "La typologie de la semaine," pp. 394-97; idem, *The Bible and the Liturgy* (Notre Dame, Ind.: University of Notre Dame Press, 1956), pp. 242-86; Reinhard Staats, "Ogdoas als ein Symbol für die Auferstehung," *VChr* 26 (1972): 29-52; Antonio Quacquarelli, *L'ogdoade patristica e suoi reflessi nella liturgia e nei monumenti,* Quaderni di "Vetera Christianorum" 7 (Bari: Adriatica, 1973).

44. *Ep.* 55.13 (CSEL 34:194-95). This letter to Januarius, along with *ep.* 54, is an attempt to answer a series of questions on liturgical practice.

more exalted than exaltation itself, more wonderful than wonder. For it looks towards a state of being that is above us, which holy Solomon hinted at, I think, in ordaining that we should "give a portion to the seven" — i.e., to this life — "and another to the eight" — i.e., to the life to come — referring to our good actions here and our restoration there. But the great David, too, seems to be referring to this same day when he sings the psalms about the Eighth Day, just as he is foretelling this day of renewal in another psalm, for the dedication of his house (Ps. 30 [LXX 29]): which we are, who have been found worthy to be, to be called, and ultimately to become the temple of God.[45]

In fact, virtually all the patristic commentators on Psalm 6 — including Gregory of Nyssa, as we shall see — identify the phrase "for the eighth" in the inscription with the whole range of biblical and eschatological significance traditionally associated with the eighth day of the week: circumcision and purification as types of Christian renewal, the resurrection of Christ, the beginning of a new and final "age" in human existence, and the start of a new creation, a "day" without end. The only exception is Diodore of Tarsus, who shows himself characteristically testy towards those interpreters who "give their readers gray hairs by wearing them out with speculations about odd and even numbers."[46] Diodore is even reserved about "those who think of 'the eighth' more reverently, saying it is both the first and the eighth day."[47] He himself prefers to remain agnostic about the inscription's meaning:

> But if this is so, I for one cannot understand why the Psalm does not have a hymnic content, but deals with public confession and the acknowledgement of sin, and is a plea for release from the troubles that hang over the speaker — even though the inscription reads, "a hymn; a

---

45. *Or.* 44.5 (PG 36:612c–13a). In his treatise *On the Holy Spirit,* Basil of Caesarea makes a similar reference to the Christian Sunday as a sign of "the true Eighth Day, of which the psalmist speaks in some of the inscriptions of the psalms; it reveals in itself the state which will follow this time, the day without end, without evening, without succession, that age which will never perish and never grow old" (PG 27:66).

46. CCSG 6:32.7-9. Diodore may be thinking of the fairly common patristic practice of connecting the phrase with Eccles. 11:2. He may also have more elaborate numerological speculations in mind; Augustine, for instance, writing in Latin twenty years after Diodore's commentary, argues that the number 7 refers to this life, in that the body is signified by the number 4 and the soul by the number 3, so that 8 suggests the new life of the resurrection.

47. CCSG 6:32.10-12.

psalm of David." For this reason, then, we will leave the whole inscription to those who want to hazard guesses about it, and will explain the true argument (ὑπόθεσις) of the Psalm. It is this: the psalms of accusation were spoken by blessed David concerning the sin he had committed with Bathsheba; in some passages they contain a confession and acknowledgement of his error, in others a plea for release from the misfortunes that have fallen on him as a result of his sin. . . . This Sixth Psalm, then, is one of these.[48]

Here, as so often, Diodore stands as one *cantans extra chorum.*

Exegesis of the Text

When one reads through the whole collection of extant ancient commentaries on this psalm, one cannot help but be struck by the relative uniformity of the interpretative tradition. Although each preacher and commentator tends to stress themes or aspects of the psalm of particular interest to him — John Chrysostom, for instance, making it into a treatise on the dynamics of conversion and repentance, in relation to the mercy of God, and Cyril of Alexandria seeing evidence in it that sickness and mortality are the result of human sin — most of the comments we find on this psalm in any one of our sources are remarkably similar to those in the others. One reason, of course, is that the content of this psalm, as opposed to its inscription, is fairly straightforward in meaning. Another is that all the early Christian interpreters, along with the midrash, are led by the first verse ("O Lord, do not rebuke me in your anger . . .") to take the psalm as dealing primarily not with disease or persecution but with the confession of sin and the experience of the mercy of God. None of them, as far as I can see, take any notice of the use of verse 8, "Depart from me, all you workers of evil," in the Sermon on the Mount (Matt. 7:23; cf. Luke 13:27), or of the application of it to Jesus' passion suggested by the echo of verse 3 in John 12:27, "Now my soul is troubled." Most patristic commentators, in fact, agree with Diodore in taking its original historical context to be David's repentance of his double sin of seducing Bathsheba and causing the death of her husband Uriah (2 Sam. 11:1–12:25) — just as the inscription of Psalm 51 identifies that prayer of repentance with the same event. For the later Latin tradition, in fact, beginning at least with Cassiodorus, Psalm 6 is listed as the first of the "seven penitential

48. CCSG 6:12-29.

psalms," along with Psalms 32, 38, 51, 102, 130, and 142.[49] The main problem raised by Psalm 6 for ancient interpreters, in fact, seems not to have been the theme of the text itself but the connection of its powerful language of repentance and divine judgment with the promise of resurrection and new creation that the inscription suggested was the psalm's real subject. Christian exegetes, almost without exception, solved the problem as Gregory of Nyssa does: by seeing the confession expressed in the psalm as an anticipation of the last judgment of Christ, and its confidence in God's mercy as a foretaste of eschatological salvation.

It is, of course, impossible here to set out the details of all the still extant ancient interpretations of this psalm, to illustrate either their particular emphases or the main lines of their common tradition. It is also clearly impossible to trace clear lines of influence, to say with certainty which authors read which predecessors or how much they drew on identifiable written sources. They stood in a tradition, they spoke an exegetical and homiletic vernacular that reached beyond boundaries of region, language, and theological "school," and that was even shared by Jews and Christians. It might be helpful, however, before we consider the distinctive and characteristic emphases of Gregory of Nyssa in his sermon, simply to list some of the main points of interpretation — beyond those I have already mentioned — on which several or most of the early commentators on this psalm agree.

v. 1: *"O Lord, do not rebuke me in your anger; do not chasten me in your wrath"*: Athanasius, Didymus, John Chrysostom (in *On Compunction II*), Jerome, Asterius, Theodoret, Cassiodorus — but not Gregory of Nyssa — stress that the Psalmist is not asking that he or she be free from divine judgment or even from healing punishment, but simply that God not do these things in anger. Didymus, Asterius and Chrysostom, too, consider it important to point out that language about God's anger is not to be taken literally, since God is not subject to passion. For Gregory, too, in the present sermon, the sense that God is angry is seen as part of the unavoidable perspective of one being

49. See Cassiodorus, *Expositio in Psalmum VI*, 1 (CCSL 97:71.43-47), the earliest listing of this group of psalms under the rubric of "penitential." Possidius of Calama, Augustine's biographer, tells us that Augustine, on his deathbed, "ordered that the Psalms of David — those few that deal with penance — should be written down; and as he lay in bed in the days of his illness, he gazed at the sheets of paper, attached to the wall, and read them, and wept constantly and plentifully" (*Vita Augustini* 31; PL 32:63). Possidius does not tell us which "few psalms" Augustine had chosen, but the passage suggests that already in his time some had been selected as particularly penitential in character. Psalm 6 may well have been one of them.

purged from sin by punishment: "for to those sentenced to the bitter training process (παίδευσις) of that dreadful punishment, judgment will be considered to be the product of anger and wrath."

v. 2: *"Be gracious to me, Lord, for I am languishing* (LXX: *I am weak)"*: Gregory of Nyssa here, along with Eusebius, Cyril of Alexandria, Theodoret, and Cassiodorus, points out that "the cause of evil" — presumably in the moral sense — "is not so much free choice as weakness of nature." The suggestion of the Hebrew text that the speaker is physically ill is taken in a more general and predominantly moral sense, as the "weakness" that is the root cause of sin.

"My bones are troubled": Most patristic interpreters take this metaphorically. Gregory, along with Eusebius, Augustine, Cyril of Alexandria, Asterius, Theodoret, and Cassiodorus, understands these "bones" to be virtues or moral strength: in Gregory's ascetical language, "the temperate trains of thought (λογισμοί) that hold up the soul," as bones support flesh.

v. 3: *"But you, O Lord — how long?"* With the midrash, most early Christian authors take this phrase as an expression of the intensity of the speaker's suffering, but there are a variety of nuances in their interpretation of the time-interval it implies. For Gregory, the Psalmist is asking how long it will take for the process of confession and repentance, guided by God's grace, to result in healing and renewal: "Why, then, O Lord, do you delay in healing me, he says; how long will you wait to show mercy? Do you not see how quickly human life fades away? Anticipate the crisis of our lives by correcting my soul, lest death come first, and all thought of healing come to nothing." This idea is echoed by Jerome, Asterius, and Theodoret. Eusebius, however, sees the question as referring to the time the speaker will need to practice penance, while for Cyril of Alexandria, the Psalmist is asking when Christ will come again, bringing resurrection and final salvation.

v. 5: *"In death there is no remembrance of you":* Like Gregory of Nyssa, most early Christian interpreters take this verse as meaning that repentance and healing will no longer be possible after death, for "the confession of sin has power on earth, but no longer exists in Hades." Athanasius, Eusebius, Augustine, John Chrysostom, Theodoret, and Cassiodorus all echo this line of thought, with Chrysostom explicitly ruling out the implication that the Psalmist is in any way denying human existence after death — "after all, he is aware of the doctrine of the resurrection!" Augustine, however, wonders if this interpretation can be right since the parable of Dives and Lazarus suggests that the dead can be moved to repentance; and Jerome insists that it is not impossible, but rare, that souls in Hell should praise God. Didymus, in fact, emphasizes that the holy dead are much more acutely conscious of God than they were during their bodily life, and he concludes that the "death" referred to in the verse must be the moral death of sin, "which cuts off the sinful soul from the life of virtue."[50]

v. 6: *"I am weary with my moaning; every night I flood my bed with tears"*: Almost all the early Christian commentators — including Gregory, Jerome, Chrysostom, Theodoret, and Cassiodorus — see this "moaning" and these "tears" as the necessary expressions of repentance. For Augustine, Asterius, and Cassiodorus, the "bed" signifies bodily pleasures, which are the object of the penitent's tearful regret.

v. 7: *"My eye is troubled by anger"* (Hebrew: *"My eye wastes away with grief"*): Several ancient Christian interpreters identify the "eye" in this verse with the mind (νοῦς) — so Athanasius, Eusebius, Chrysostom — or the heart *(cor)* — so Cassiodorus. Augustine and Diodore both suggest that the anger in question here is God's anger as experienced by the sinner, and that this makes us unable to see God (Augustine) or disturbs our "outlook" on things (ὀπτικόν: Diodore).

"I grow old because of all my foes": this phrase — slightly different from the Hebrew *("my eye . . . grows weak")* — is taken by Gregory as referring to the debilitating effect of the passions. For that reason, he clearly sees the anger mentioned here as the human passion of anger, which is a source of other passions and a fundamental cause of the "rot" of the soul.[51] Didymus, Augustine, and Jerome interpret this verse in the light of the injunction of Colossians 3:10 and Ephesians 4:24 to "put on the new person": the speaker describes his sin as a sliding back into the life of "the old man."

v. 10: *"All my enemies shall be ashamed"*: Gregory takes the "enemies" referred to in the psalm to be the vices or passions; Augustine sees them as both our own vices and the human companions that tend to confirm us in them. Most patristic interpreters, however, seem to understand this verse more literally, as

---

50. Didymus the Blind, *Psalmenkommentare aus der Katenenüberlieferung*, ed. Mühlenberg, 138.5-6.

51. Compare Evagrius of Pontus, *Praktikos* 11, where anger is said to be the most fierce of the eight fundamental passions or "thoughts (λογισμοί)" that deter the soul on its quest for God.

expressing both a sense of release from bad companionship and a prayer for the conversion of those who have, until now, been standing in the way of the speaker's conversion: so, for instance, Athanasius, Didymus, Jerome, and Chrysostom.

Gregory's Distinctive Theological Themes

Beyond these specific points of interpretation, in which Gregory generally fits well into a widely accepted ancient exegetical tradition with regard to this psalm, his homily, brief as it is, strongly emphasizes certain themes that are characteristic of his theological vision. For simplicity's sake, we can best group them under four headings.

Time and Eternity

Fully the first half of Gregory's sermon deals not with the verses of the psalm itself but with the perspective of eschatological hope suggested by its inscription. In fact, Gregory's exegesis of the text of the psalm, traditional though it is in most respects, tends to be summary rather than detailed, and to work by expansive, interpretative paraphrasing of the text rather than by close literal analysis. However, the opening paragraphs are an expansive meditation on the "mystery of the Eighth Day," as the typological fulfillment of the Jewish practice of circumcision and as a symbol of the radical change in existence promised to all rational creatures, when the "week" of time comes to an end and a "new creation," free from change and decay, takes the place of our present history.[52] It is precisely in the context of the biblical proclamation of this coming "Eighth Day" of our history, so different from the preceding seven, that the Sixth Psalm's call to confession and penance

---

52. For Gregory's understanding of the "closed" character of both temporal and spatial extension (διάστημα), in distinction from the stability and openness of the age to come, see Brooks Otis, "Gregory of Nyssa and the Cappadocian Conception of Time," *SP* 14 (1976): 327-57; T. Paul Verghese, "διάστημα and διάστασις in St. Gregory of Nyssa," in *Gregor von Nyssa und die Philosophie,* ed. Hermann Dörries, Margarete Altenberger, and Uta Schramm, 2nd International Colloquium on Gregory of Nyssa, 1972 (Leiden: Brill, 1976), pp. 243-60; Hans Urs von Balthasar, *Presence and Thought: An Essay on the Religious Philosophy of Gregory of Nyssa,* trans. Marc Sebanc (San Francisco: Ignatius Press, 1995), pp. 27-35; James LeGrys, "Names for the Ineffable God: St. Gregory of Nyssa's Explanation," *The Thomist* 62 (1998): 335-37.

finds its place, in Gregory's view — a point reinforced by the fact that the psalm that precedes it in the Psalter, according to the Septuagint, bears the title, "On the Inheritor." The inheritance of eternity is "for the worthy," and God's judgment, with its dreadful retributions, will stand as the barrier between the present order and the endless age to come. The task of the sinner, according to the rest of the sermon, is to anticipate that judgment now in confession and to make future chastisement unnecessary by the works of penance.

This understanding of eschatological judgment and salvation, explicitly connected with the notion of the Eighth Day and with the inscription of the present psalm, is given substantial treatment in two other passages in his works. One of these is the opening paragraph of Gregory's *Homily on the Eighth Beatitude* — the last in a series usually thought to have been delivered in the mid-370s. Here Gregory tries to explain the "mystery of the number eight," as associated with the Eighth Beatitude, by connecting it with Psalms 6 and 11 and with the Jewish practices of purification and circumcision,

> both of which, according to the Law, were to be observed on the eighth day. Perhaps this number has some affinity with the Eighth Beatitude, which, being as it were the summit of all the Beatitudes, is placed at the top of the good ascent (τῆς ἀγαθῆς ἀναβάσεως). For in the psalms the prophet signifies the day of the resurrection through the mystery of the number eight; the purification indicates humanity's return from defilement to natural purity; the circumcision means the casting off of the dead skins[53] which we put on when we had been stripped of the supernatural life after the transgression; and here the Eighth Beatitude contains the reinstatement in heaven of those who had fallen into servitude, and who are now from their slavery recalled to the Kingdom.[54]

Many ideas and phrases here, including the characterization of the life of faith and growth to perfection as "the good ascent," appear again — in considerably

---

53. The equation of the "garments of skin" (Gen. 3:21) — a dead thing — which Adam and Eve put on after the fall with bodily passion is a frequent theme in Gregory's work: see, for example, *On the Soul and the Resurrection* (PG 46:148c).

54. GNO 7:2.161.15–62.3; PG 44:1292a-b; Hilda C. Graef, trans., *St. Gregory of Nyssa, The Lord's Prayer and the Beatitudes*, ACW 18 (New York: Newman, 1954), p. 166 (modified).

greater fullness — in the first half of our homily and give some support to the suggestion that they were composed during the same period in his career.

The other passage dealing with the "mystery of the Eighth Day" and the title of the present psalm is found in Gregory's fifteenth and last homily on the Song of Songs, which is thought to be one of his last works, from the late 380s or early 390s. Here Gregory is explaining Canticles 6:8, "There are sixty queens and eighty concubines," discussing both numbers as tenfold multiples of 6 and 8. After dealing with six — and sixty — in terms of the perfection of virtue in those who keep the moral law (the last six commandments of the Decalogue), he turns to explain eight — and eighty — as signifying

> those who are taught by fear to keep away from all share in evildoing. For we have learned this in reciting the psalms, in which the Eighth Day is placed before us by means of inscriptions. The voices [of the speakers] here are obviously those of people being punished, and turn our ears to [God's] mercy by fear for the objects of our hope. For the speaker, gazing towards the Eighth Day, says to the judge, "Lord, do not test me in your anger; do not punish me in your rage. Have mercy on me, Lord, for I am weak; heal me, Lord, because my bones are shaken." And all the rest that follows he offers to that incorruptible judge by way of entreaty, where he laments that there is no memory of God in death. For how could it be possible for those who are condemned to weeping and gnashing their teeth to share in the delight that comes from remembering God? . . . The one who fears the Eighth Day, then, presents these and similar petitions, and so comes to realize that he shares in mercy; for he says, "You have heard the voice of my weeping." Since many blessed fears of this kind are revealed to us by the holy Scripture, there should be here — analogous to that of the six commandments — a tenfold multiplication of them, as well, so that a person may be taught by reciting the psalm how the fear of the Lord corrects us, teaching us first to lean away from evil and so to do the good.[55]

Here, as in the homily we are examining, Gregory emphasizes not just the promise hidden in the title of the psalm but the importance of the "blessed fear" of judgment for human growth towards perfection. It is our awareness of the greatness of our future, and of the demands for virtue that it brings with it, that is the strongest spur to moral reform.

55. *Hom. 15 in Cant.* (GNO 6:464.4–65.4; PG 44:1113d-16a).

Growth to Perfection

This leads us to a second theme characteristic of Gregory of Nyssa, which appears with emphasis in this sermon: the characterization of the Christian life as a constant "ascent (ἀνάβασις)" towards the Good, realized in ceaseless progress in virtue, self-control, and knowledge of God. Gregory's homily begins, in fact, not with a quotation of the psalm he is expounding, but with an allusion to Psalm 83, verses 6 and 8 (84:5, 7), in the Septuagint version: "Blessed is the man whose help is from you, Lord; he has accomplished ascents in his heart. . . . They will go on from strength to strength; the God of gods will be seen in Sion." For Gregory, the Sixth Psalm, too, is fundamentally about the conditions for making such an "ascent" towards the vision of God, characterized by increasing strength, through the reordering of our "thoughts" towards what is above. We have already encountered the phrase "good ascents" in the passage from his homily on the Eighth Beatitude, cited above, and Gregory speaks of spiritual progress as an ἀνάβασις in a number of places.[56] In addition, the first sentence of this homily also contains an allusion to another favorite phrase of Gregory's, the Pauline image of "reaching out (ἐπεκτεινόμενος) to what is ahead of us" (Phil. 3:13) — an expression that recurs especially in his description of human perfection as a voluntary and never-ending process of growth in virtue, in the homilies on the Song of Songs and the *Life of Moses*.[57] By incorporating both of these biblical images in the first sentence of this homily, Gregory makes it clear that he is speaking here, too, about human progress towards perfection through the vehicle of this psalm, which he understood to be *about* such progress — about its goal, in the endless fullness of God's new creation, and about the path towards that goal, in this life, through the

---

56. See, for example, *Pss. titt.* 2.16 (GNO 5:166.14; PG 44:597b); *hom. 5 in Cant.* (GNO 6:158.20; PG 44:876b); *hom. 8 in Cant.* (τὰς καλὰς ἀναβάσεις: GNO 6:246.13; PG 44:941b); *hom. 9 in Cant.* (GNO 6:280.8; PG 44:968c); *Life of Moses* 2.152 (GNO 7:1.82.4; PG 44:372c).

57. See especially *v. Mos.* 1.5 (GNO 7:1.3.14-17) and 2.225 (GNO 7:1.112.16-21), where Gregory again alludes to this Pauline verse. Daniélou took the nominal form of this verb, ἐπέκτασις, as the key concept in Gregory's understanding of perfection, even though that noun appears only once in his works (*hom. 6 in Cant.*: GNO 6:174.15; but see the whole passage: 173.1–74.20). See Jean Daniélou, *Platonisme et théologie mystique: Essai sur la doctrine spirituelle de saint Grégoire de Nysse* (Paris: Aubier, 1944), pp. 309-26; for other uses of this term in Gregory's works, see my article, "'Bright Darkness' and Christian Transformation: Gregory of Nyssa on the Dynamics of Mystical Union," in *Finding God in All Things*, ed. Michael J. Himes and Stephen J. Pope (New York: Crossroads, 1996), p. 229, n. 41.

conquering of anger and the other passions by confession of sin, by penance, and by the healing mercy of God.

The "Sequence" of Scripture

Since he understands human fulfillment and perfection not in static terms but as an ordered and endless movement of growth towards participation in the life and perfection of God, it is understandable that Gregory finds a constant invitation to that growth, and endless clues to its shape, in the Scriptures that embody divine and saving revelation. As Jean Daniélou and other scholars have pointed out,[58] one of the key features of Gregory's approach to biblical interpretation is a tendency to find in the books of the Bible a reflection of the ordered pattern or "sequence (ἀκολουθία)" of the "ascent" or growth of the soul that constitutes, in itself, its perfection. The narrative sequence of Moses' life, for instance, as it appears in the books of the Pentateuch, not only provides, in Gregory's view, a series of discrete types or images of salvation but also mirrors the ideal shape of human spiritual progress: "I think that for anyone who has been initiated into what this story suggests," he writes in his *Life of Moses*, "the sequence of growth in virtue, which the Scripture is sketching out, will be crystal clear from what we have said, provided one follows in their sequence the succession of symbols in the narrative."[59] This same notion dominates Gregory's approach to interpreting the Psalter, most notably in his treatise *On the Inscriptions of the Psalms*. In Gregory's view, the spiritual meaning of the Psalter is contained not only in each psalm separately but also in the arrangement of the whole collection, which mirrors the steps and challenges by which each reader of the Bible must "ascend" in virtue, knowledge, and holiness.[60] That same hermeneutical presup-

58. Jean Daniélou, "Akolouthia chez Grégoire de Nysse," *Recherches de science religieuse* 27 (1966): 219-49; see also Marie-Josèphe Rondeau, "Exégèse du Psautier et anabase spirituelle chez Grégoire de Nysse," in *Epektasis: Mélanges patristiques offerts au Cardinal Jean Daniélou*, ed. Jacques Fontaine and Charles Kannengiesser (Paris: Beauchesne, 1972), pp. 517-31; Mariette Canévet, *Grégoire de Nysse et l'herméneutique biblique* (Paris: Etudes Augustiniennes, 1983), pp. 269-72; Heine, *Inscriptions*, p. 9, and the literature cited there.

59. *V. Mos.* 2.39.1-4 (PG 45:337 A). For other references to the spiritual significance of the sequence of events in the text, see *Life of Moses* 2.33.3; 49.10; 54.1-3; 136.1-2; 148.1-3; 219.1-3.

60. For an analysis of Gregory's understanding of this sequence in the treatise, see Heine, *Inscriptions*, pp. 50-80.

position is evident in this sermon, especially in its opening and closing passages. Gregory begins, as we have mentioned, by reminding his hearers of the pattern of spiritual "ascent" hinted at in Psalm 83 (LXX), and of Paul's exhortation in Philippians 3:13 to keep "reaching out to what lies ahead." Turning then to the Sixth Psalm, he draws the conclusion that one must "keep an eye on the necessary sequence (ἀκολουθία) of its ordering" by connecting the title of the psalm with that of Psalm 5: in the Greek of the Septuagint, "On the Inheritor [feminine]." A psalm dealing with the conditions for sharing in the blessings of the Eighth Day makes perfect sense, in this view, as the sequel to a psalm on the inheritance that lies in store for the Bride of Christ. After he has explained the text of the Sixth Psalm, briefly but completely, Gregory returns to the larger issue of the ἀκολουθία: "This, then, is the sequence of the good ascent: the Fourth Psalm distinguishes the immaterial Good from bodily and fleshly goods (presumably in vv. 4-6), the Fifth prays to inherit such a Good, the Sixth hints at the moment (καιρός) of inheritance by recalling the Eighth Day." In the context of the whole Psalter, Gregory's interpretation of the psalm, traditional as it is in its details, takes on a wider significance that reflects his own distinctive theology of salvation and the spiritual life.

Confession and the Conquest of the Passions

Gregory's explanation of the actual text of Psalm 6 centers, as we have seen, on the salutary effect on weak human beings of the fear of divine judgment and punishment. So he connects his long explanation of the inscription with his briefer discussion of the body of the psalm by saying, "The prophet has skillfully begun his discussion of repentance (μετάνοια) by this allusion to the Eighth Day." The psalm's plea not to be "tested" and "punished" by God in anger, its description of the "weakness" and mortal illness of the anguished speaker, its promise (in the Septuagint's future tense) of penitential tears — all form part of a process of conversion and ascetical, perhaps even sacramental, self-correction by which the speaker, past and present, may best prepare himself or herself to share in the new creation. When the Psalmist dramatically speaks of his fear and distress, Gregory argues,

> he is saying: I do not wait for the correction of my hidden faults to take place in me, through the dreadful scourges that proceed from that [divine] anger, but I choose to experience beforehand, by my confession (ἐξομολόγησις), the punishment that manifests that wrath. For what pain produces in those who are scourged against their will, by revealing the

hidden aspects of lawlessness, free choice does on its own, scourging and punishing itself through repentance (μετάνοια) and publicizing the sin hidden in the remote regions of ourselves.[61]

Shame (αἰσχύνη), he will say towards the end of the homily, is an effective teacher; if one experiences the shame of public exposure and penance, one is not likely to sin so easily in the future.

Gregory seems to have in mind here the voluntary public acknowledgment of sins, before God and within the Church, that identified the sinner for a determined period as a member of the class of penitents, during which time they would be excluded from communion and be required to participate in the liturgy by prostrating themselves, kneeling or standing in various designated places in the church building.[62] Most of our evidence for the practice of public confession and canonical penance in Cappadocia in his time comes from the writings of Gregory's elder brother, Basil of Caesarea — especially from Basil's ascetical writings, where such practices are recommended for monks, and from his three "canonical letters" (*Epp.* 188, 199, and 217), where specific periods of penance are recommended for specific classes of sin. In these last-mentioned letters, the word "confession" (ἐξομολόγησις) is used as an apparent synonym for "penance" (μετάνοια), both seemingly referring to public classification as a repentant sinner within the Church community.[63] Gregory of Nyssa, however, does not often refer to canonical penance in his works.[64] In his treatise *On the Inscriptions of the Psalms,* however, he does comment on the use of the word "confession (ἐξομολόγησις)" in the title of Psalm 100 (LXX 99), noting — as Augustine so often does in his own *Confessions* — that it carries the double meaning of both the acknowledgment of our sin and the thankful praise of God. So Gregory remarks:

> Since the meaning of ἐξομολόγησις is twofold in the customary usage of Scripture, at one time denoting confession, and at another, praise, we are

61. GNO 5:190.27–91.8.

62. For a well-documented description of the development of public or canonical penance in the early Church, see Marie-François Berrouard, "La pénitence publique durant les six premiers siècles," *La Maison-Dieu* 118 (1974): 92-130; for the fourth century in the East, see especially pp. 116-120. Specifications of the various stages in the penitential process are reflected, for instance, in Basil of Caesarea, *ep.* 217.56-68, 73-84.

63. See, for instance, *ep.* 188.2 (both terms used); *ep.* 199.34 (μετάνοια); *ep.* 217.63, 65, 67, 73, 74 (ἐξομολόγησις).

64. One of the few passages where he does is *hom. 5 in Eccl.* (GNO 5:315.11; 328.16; 334.5).

herein led to the virtuous life by both thoughts. For confession produces departure and separation from evil things, and eagerness for praise causes grace from the benefactor to abound on those who receive the benefits with keen perception.[65]

This same double sense of "confessing" may be in Gregory's mind in this homily as he reflects on the intimate connection between voluntary penance and a grateful sense of God's healing forgiveness.

The object of this penitential process, however, as set forth in this homily, is not primarily the reconciliation of flagrant sinners to the community, but a much more interior growth in virtue: the penance of monks rather than the penance of people struggling to be Christians in the "public square." Gregory's interpretation of sober "thoughts" (λογισμοί) as the "bones" of the soul and his emphasis on the need for rooting out all the passions, especially anger, from the soul remind us of the ascetical psychology of Evagrius,[66] as well as Gregory's own treatise on Christian perfection, the *Life of Moses.*[67] In his *Homily on the Sixth Beatitude,* too, Gregory observes that our very begetting as human beings takes place in a context of passion, so that virtue is always hard-won for us. Yet he adds that even a passion like anger may be turned to good use, as a support in our battle with sin.[68] In any case, as he observes in his treatise *On the Soul and the Resurrection,*[69] the process of purification from passion is always laborious and painful but must take place either in this life or after death if one is to participate fully in the life of God. It is all the more important, therefore, that one undertake the labors willingly now, rather than undergo purification unwillingly — and more violently — later on.

In its main themes and arguments, then, this short homily fits well into Gregory of Nyssa's lifelong theological work. In fact, Gregory's deft use of exegetical *topoi* from the longer tradition of psalm interpretation really subordinates them to his own purposes, as he makes the psalm into a vehicle for preaching his own vision of Christian asceticism and Christian hope. It may be appropriate to ask, then, what typically Nyssene themes are noticeably missing from this work. I would suggest the following three:

---

65. *Pss. titt.* 2.6 (GNO 5:89.1-8; trans. Heine, *Inscriptions,* p. 141).

66. See, for example, *cap. pract.* 6-56; *or.* 4, 8-10, 62, 133-36.

67. See, for example, *v. Mos.* 2.90-94 (GNO 7:1.61.4–63.22), where he interprets the killing of the firstborn of Egypt as signifying our need to "destroy the first beginnings of evil" in ourselves, the passions that eventually lead to acts of sin.

68. GNO 7:2.144.14–47.17; see Graef, *St. Gregory of Nyssa,* pp. 150-52.

69. See especially PG 46:48c-64a.

a. There is very little reference to Christ in the homily: only the identification of him as the "rock" of purification prefigured in the "stone knife" with which Joshua circumcised his people, an allusion to the cleansing work of "the one who has purged us from our sins" and a reference to his "dreadful judgment" to come. It is surprising that there is not a greater emphasis here on the Christological foundation of human transformation since other works of Gregory — his treatise *To Theophilus, against the Apollinarians,* for instance, his *Antirrhetikos against the Apollinarians,* and his work *On Perfection* — present growth in virtue and the eradication of the passions as a process already modeled and begun for us in Christ's passage through death to transfigured life.[70]

b. Gregory makes no mention here of the idea he develops so powerfully in the *Life of Moses* that perfection for the Christian is never a state to be attained but is rather a never-ending process of growth towards greater union with and likeness to God.[71] In fact, in the third paragraph of the sermon on Psalm 6, he seems to be characterizing the blessed age to come in more traditional terms of stability and changelessness, an end to motion conceived in Aristotelian terms of "coming-to-be and passing-away."

c. Gregory also gives no hint, in this sermon, of the doctrine of ἀποκατάστασις πάντων, or universal salvation, which is carefully but unmistakably sketched out in a number of his other writings.[72] True, he presents God's punishment of the sinner primarily in terms of "training" (παίδευσις) or purgation; but he gives no hint that such a process may take place after death for the sinner who dies unrepentant, and in one passage he uses verse 5 of the psalm to rule out such long-term purgation:

---

70. See my article, "Divine Transcendence and Human Transformation: Gregory of Nyssa's Anti-Apollinarian Christology," *SP* 32 (1997): 87-95.

71. See especially *v. Mos.* 2.167 (GNO 7:1.88.13-24); 2.225-42 (GNO 7:1.112.16–18.2); cf. the end *of perf.* (GNO 8:1.212.17–14.6).

72. See, for instance, *mort.* (GNO 9:51.16-18); *anim. et res.* (PG 46:152a, 156b.12–57b.5); *hom. 15 in Cant.* (GNO 6:468.15–69.9); *v. Mos.* 2.82. See Jean Daniélou, "L'apocatastase chez Saint Grégoire de Nysse," *Recherches de science religieuse* 30 (1940): 328-47; Monique Alexandre, "Protologie et eschatologie chez Grégoire de Nysse," in *Arche e telos: l'antropologia di Origene e di Gregorio di Nissa: Analisi storico-religiosa,* ed. Henri Crouzel and Ugo Bianchi (Milan: Vita e pensiero, 1981), pp. 122-59; Brian E. Daley, *The Hope of the Early Church* (Cambridge: Cambridge University Press, 1991), pp. 85-89.

Do you not see how quickly human life fades away? Anticipate the crisis of our lives by correcting my soul, lest death come first, and all thought of healing come to nothing. For the one who, by the recollection of God, can heal the sickness rooted in himself through evil will no longer be able to do so in death; so the confession of sin has power on earth, but no longer exists in Hades.[73]

Explaining omissions, of course, is always a matter of speculation. One reason these characteristic doctrines of Gregory of Nyssa do not appear in this homily may be its date; although, as I have said, the chronology of Gregory's works is anything but securely established, some of these doctrines may have developed only later in his thought, and their absence here would confirm Mme. Rondeau's judgment that the homily is an early work. Another reason may simply be that the genre here is popular preaching or monastic exhortation rather than theological speculation; in such a context, it certainly makes better rhetorical sense to emphasize the traditional scheme of final judgment and retribution and to pass over arguments for the ultimate triumph of God's saving grace in every heart. However one explains these deviations from what other works of Gregory lead us to expect, the *Homily on Psalm 6* remains a powerful invitation, at once traditional and original, to engage us in the process of interior transformation and growth towards freedom that is, for Gregory, the very substance of salvation.

[What follows is a new translation of Gregory's homily, based on the critical edition by James A. McDonough, S.J. (GNO 5:187-93). I have corrected some of McDonough's biblical references. References in the homily to the text of Psalm 6 are given in italics.]

BY GREGORY, BISHOP OF NYSSA:

On the Sixth Psalm, concerning the Eighth Day

Those who are "progressing from strength to strength,"[74] according to the prophet's words of blessing, and who are accomplishing good "ascents in their own hearts"[75] first grasp hold of a good thought and then are led along

73. GNO 5:191.20-26.
74. Ps. 83:8 (LXX).
75. Ps. 83:6 (LXX).

by it towards a thought that is higher still; in this way, the ascent to the very summit takes place in the soul. So, "reaching out always to what lies ahead,"[76] a person never ceases to travel the good road upwards, always journeying through his lofty thoughts towards an apprehension of the things that are above.

I have said this to you, my brothers, to focus our attention on the Sixth Psalm and to keep an eye on the necessary sequence of its ordering:[77] how it is that a discussion[78] of "the Eighth Day" is offered to us after one "on the Inheritor."[79] Now perhaps you are not unaware of the mystery of the "Eighth Day." For it is inappropriate, after all, that some people's minds are distracted towards Jewish interpretations. Those who reduce the magnificence of the mystery of the Eighth Day to being concerned with the unseemly parts of our bodies say that the law of circumcision, and the purification rites after childbirth, and things such as that are signified by the number eight. However, since we are taught by the great Paul that "the law is spiritual,"[80] then even if this number is contained in the laws I have mentioned, legislating both circumcision for the male and a sacrifice on the day of purification for the female, we do not reject the law or receive it in a lowly way; for we know that the true circumcision, brought to realization through the stone knife,[81] genuinely does take place on the Eighth Day. For surely, through the rock that cuts away what is unclean, you recognize that "rock which is itself Christ"[82] — namely, the word of truth — and you understand that the flow of this life's affairs, which makes us unclean, will cease at the time when human life is transformed, in its elementary character, into something more divine.

So that it might be clear to everyone what is meant by these things, I will explain the work more clearly, as well as I can. The time in which we live this

76. Phil. 3:13.

77. Greek: τὴν ἀναγκαίαν τῆς τάξεως ἀκολουθίαν.

78. Here and elsewhere, Gregory refers to the psalm as a λόγος, which can mean a written work or treatise. Like most patristic writers except Athanasius, he is more concerned with the Psalms as prophecy, as a sacred text, than as something to be sung.

79. Gregory is referring to the fact that the title of the preceding Fifth Psalm, in the LXX, is ὑπὲρ τῆς κληρονομούσης, "concerning the one (fem.) who inherits." This title in the Greek Psalter seems to be a mistranslation of the Hebrew 'al hannehiloth, "for the flutes" — a phrase the Greek translator seems to have taken as coming from the root nhl, "inherit." Here and again at the end of his homily, Gregory connects this reference to our "inheritance" with the eschatology implied in the title to this psalm.

80. Rom. 7:14.

81. Josh. 5:2.

82. 1 Cor. 10:4.

life, in the first formative period of creation, has reached its completion in a week of seven days. The shaping of all that exists began with the first day, and the outer limit of creation came to its final form on the seventh. "For there was one day,"[83] Scripture says, in which the first stage of things came to be; similarly, too, the second stage took place on the second day, and so onwards in sequence until all the works of the six days had been completed. The seventh day, which came to define in itself the limit of creation, set the boundary for the time that is co-extensive with all the furnishings of the world. As a result, no other heaven has come to be from this one, nor has any other part of the world been added to those that exist from the beginning; creation has come to rest in what it is, remaining complete and undiminished within its own boundaries. So, too, no other time has come into existence alongside that time that was revealed along with the formation of the world, but the nature of time has rather been circumscribed by the week of seven days. For this reason, when we measure time in days, we begin with day one and close the number with day seven, returning then to the first day of a new week; so we continue to measure the whole extension[84] of time by the cycle of weeks, until — when the things that are in motion pass away and the flux of the world's movement comes to an end — "those things" come to be, as the apostle says, "which shall never be shaken,"[85] things that change and alteration will no longer touch. This [new] creation will always remain unchanged, for the ages to follow; in it, the true circumcision of human nature will come to reality, in the removal of our bodily life and the true purgation of our true uncleanness. Now uncleanness, in a human being, is the sin that is begotten along with our human nature — for "in sin my mother conceived me";[86] but the one who purged us of our sins cleansed us completely at that time, banishing everything bloodstained and filthy and uncircumcised from the nature of all that exists.

This, then, is the way in which we interpret the [biblical] law about the Eighth Day, the law of purification and circumcision: namely, that when the time that is measured in weeks comes to an end, an Eighth Day will come into being after the seventh — called "eighth" because it exists after the seventh, not because it is any longer capable of numerical succession. It will remain one day continually, never to be divided by the darkness of night. Another sun will bring it into being, radiating the true light; when once it "shines out" on us,[87]

83. Gen. 1:5.
84. Greek: διάστημα.
85. Heb. 12:27.
86. Ps. 50:7 (51:5).
87. Eph. 5:14.

as the apostle says, it will never be hidden by sunset, but, embracing all things in its luminous power, it will produce light continually for the worthy, without any succession of days, and will make those who share in that light into other suns. As the gospel saying puts it, "Then the just will shine like the sun."[88]

Since, then, [David] has conducted a discussion "about the inheritor" in the previous Psalm, and since the inheritance of the worthy is stored up in the Eighth Day, and since in it, too, the just judgment of God will take place, making return to each one according to his or her deserts, the Prophet has skillfully begun his discussion of repentance by this allusion to the Eighth Day. Who is there who will not be immediately torn apart in his own conscience,[89] when he takes up this allusion to the dreadful judgment of Christ — who will not be seized by fear and inner struggle, even if he should somehow be aware that his life is turned towards better things? Surely when one considers the exactitude of that judgment, in which even the most insignificant of our sins of omission will be subjected to investigation, he will be frightened by such a dreadful prospect, uncertain where the process of judgment, in his case, will reach its end. For this reason, keeping in view the dreadful judgments to come — what we call Gehenna, and the dark fire, and the unceasing "worm" of self-reproach that will constantly suck the soul dry with shame,[90] renewing its suffering by the memory of the evil deeds of its former life — [the speaker] now becomes God's suppliant, begging not to be delivered to that *wrath* for *testing*, and that the *correction* due him for the ways he has transgressed not be laid on him by that *anger* (v. 1). To those sentenced to the bitter training process of that dreadful punishment, judgment will be considered the product of anger and wrath.[91]

For this reason, speaking as if he were already in the midst of suffering,

---

88. Matt. 13:43.

89. Greek: συνειδός. This term was used by the Stoics, and by later Hellenistic writers on moral philosophy, along with its alternative form συνείδησις, to denote critical self-knowledge, especially knowledge of the ethical value of one's own actions. It is used in this sense in the Septuagint (Wisd. of Sol. 17:11) and in the New Testament (Acts 23:1; 24:16; 1 Cor. 8:7; 10:27-28; 1 Tim. 3:9).

90. Characteristically, Gregory interprets the details identified with punishment after death in the Synoptic Gospels (e.g., Matt. 8:12: "the outer darkness"; Mark 9:43-48: "unquenchable fire," "where the worm does not die") in a moral or spiritual sense. We have translated the word συνείδησις here as "self-reproach," but it can also mean simply "conscience"; see the previous note.

91. Gregory seems to feel obliged to justify the Bible's language about God's wrath: it does not suggest that God is subject to passion but describes the way souls undergoing purification will experience the process.

[the Psalmist] represents the voices of those in distress, to whom what is being done to punish the impious seems to convey anger and wrath. He is saying, in effect: I do not wait for the correction of my hidden faults to take place in me, through the dreadful scourges that proceed from that anger; but I choose to experience beforehand, by my confession,[92] the duress that manifests that wrath. What pain produces in those who are scourged against their will, by revealing the hidden aspects of lawlessness, free choice does on its own, scourging and punishing itself through repentance,[93] and publicizing the sin hidden in the remote regions of ourselves.

Having said, then, "*Do not test me in your wrath, nor punish me in your anger*" (v. 1), he next takes refuge in [God's] mercy, referring the cause of evil not so much to free choice as to weakness of nature: "Heal me by your mercy, for I have come to be in trouble"[94] — for I have come into passion out of weakness! What is this weakness? "My bones are disjointed,"[95] their harmonious connection with each other is destroyed. What he calls "bones" are the temperate trains of thought[96] that hold up the soul. "*Heal me, Lord, for my bones are troubled*" (v. 2b). He interprets the riddle of these words by adding to what has been said, "*My soul is very troubled*" (v. 3a). "Why, then, O Lord, do you delay in healing me," he says; "*how long* will you wait to show mercy?" (v. 3b). Do you not see how quickly human life fades away? Anticipate the crisis of our lives by correcting my soul (cf. v. 4), lest death come first, and all thought of healing come to nothing, for the one who, by the recollection of God, can heal the sickness rooted in himself through evil will no longer be able to do so in death (cf. v. 5a); and thus *confession*[97] has power on earth but no longer exists *in Hades* (v. 5b).

---

92. Greek: ἐξαγόρευσις.

93. Greek: μετάνοια. This word can have a variety of meanings connected with the process of repentance from sin: change of heart, conversion, the external acts of penance. Here Gregory seems to be referring to the whole process of public penance that involves acknowledgment of one's sin and participation in ecclesial and liturgical expressions of the need for growth in holiness.

94. As elsewhere in the homily, Gregory is paraphrasing verse 2 of the psalm here, rather than citing it directly.

95. Gregory here slightly changes the text of the psalm, which says: "My bones are disturbed (ἐταράχθη)." Gregory's substitution of "disjointed (ἐξηρθρώθη)" makes, of course, better anatomical sense.

96. Greek: λογισμοί.

97. Greek: ἐξομολόγησις. As we have seen above, Gregory observes in his treatise *On the Inscriptions of the Psalms* that this word can mean both praise of God and acknowledgment of sin. It seems to have primarily the second meaning here.

Next, as if someone had asked, "Why are you calling on God's mercy to heal your transgressions? How have you made propitiation to God?" he says: "*I have grown weary in my groaning,* and I wash the *bedding* of my sin with the water of *tears*" (v. 6). Why does he do this? "Because," he says, "*my eye was troubled by anger,* and therefore *I have become old* and decayed,[98] and the anger that has come to live in me because of *my enemies* has brought rot to my soul" (v. 7). Yet if anger alone instills such fear in the one who has sinned through it, how much more likely is it that they will despair of their saving hope who recognize in themselves not only the passions stemming from anger but all the effects of carnal desire, greed, arrogance, love of honors, envy, and the rest of the array of human vices? So he turns his speech towards every kind of enemy[99] and says, "*Depart from me, all you who do the works of lawlessness*" (v. 8a).

However, he shows, in the verse that follows, the good hope of correction that also comes to us from repentance, for immediately — almost in the same breath — he adds words about God's reaction to repentance, and, coming to an awareness of God's pleasure in it, he proclaims his gratitude aloud and rejoices in the gift, saying, "*The Lord has heard* the sound of *my pleading; the Lord has received my prayer*" (v. 9). Then, so that the benefit that has come to him through his repentance will remain permanently, and that his way of life will not need a second repentance later on, he begs that his *enemies be turned away,* punished, and *shamed* (v. 10). If a person who is ashamed of his involvement in evil uses that shame as a teacher, so that he is never again involved in the same deeds, he will refrain from similar experiences from that time on.

This, then, is the sequence of the good ascent:[100] the Fourth Psalm distinguishes the immaterial Good from bodily and fleshly goods; the Fifth prays to inherit such a Good; the Sixth hints at the moment of inheritance, by recalling the Eighth Day. The Eighth Day reveals the fear of judgment; the [thought of] judgment advises sinners such as us to anticipate its terrors by repentance; finally, the repentance that is appropriately offered to God promises us the reward that will accrue from it, saying, "*The Lord has heard the*

---

98. I have followed here the reading of manuscript P (= Vaticanus Pii II 4, of the eleventh century): εὐρωτιῶν — literally, "one who is becoming moldy" — as suggested by the most recent editor, James McDonough, instead of the more common reading, ἐρρυτιῶν — "one who is becoming wrinkled" — or related forms. McDonough observes that although the reference to wrinkles seems to fit better with the Psalmist's claim to have "grown old," the reading of P is better integrated into the whole sentence.

99. Gregory clearly identifies the "enemies" in the Psalm with the passions.

100. Greek: τῆς ἀγαθῆς ἀναβάσεως ἡ ἀκολουθία.

voice of the one who turns to him in tears" (v. 8b). When that has happened, in order that the Good might remain with us uninterruptedly for the rest of time, the Prophet asks that the thoughts[101] hostile to it might be made to vanish through shame, for it is not possible for a hostile, lawless thought to be vanquished in any other way, if shame over it does not cause it to vanish. Shame over the way we have acted badly in the past becomes a "great gulf fixed"[102] into the depths, walling off sin from a person simply by itself. Let us say, then, "*May all my enemies be put to shame* and utterly turned back!" (v. 10a). Now our enemies, clearly, are "those of our own household," which "come forth from the heart and defile a person."[103] Yet when they are *turned away* quickly by *shame* (v. 10 b), the hope of a glory that will never end in shame will take its place in us, by the grace of the Lord, to whom be glory for the ages.

Amen.

101. Greek: νοήματα.

102. Luke 16:26. Gregory's skillful allusion to this phrase from the story of Dives and Lazarus continues his general interpretation of the scriptural depiction of punishment for sin in typological and spiritual terms.

103. A paraphrasing conflation of Matt. 10:36 ("a person's foes will be those of his own household") and Mark 7:15 ("the things which come out of a person are what defile him").

Two Trees in the Midst of the Garden (Genesis 2:9b): Gregory of Nyssa and the Puzzle of Human Evil

RICHARD A. NORRIS, JR.

In the dedicatory letter with which he introduces his fifteen *Homilies on the Song of Songs,* Gregory of Nyssa offers the eminent virgin Olympias an apology for his practice of figural or allegorical exegesis. This practice is founded, he suggests, on the conviction that "the Scriptures say something for our profit by way of enigmas and below-the-surface meanings";[1] and at one juncture in the process of defending this practice — which he understands as an "anagogy" that leads from the corporeal realm upwards to the intelligible — he provides an illustrative list of Old Testament expressions or statements that seem to require such treatment. First among them, as one example of an "enigma" that requires especially thoughtful and energetic exegetical probing (θεωρία), he adduces Genesis 2:9b, where it is suggested that in the middle of God's Paradise there were two trees: the tree of life and the tree of the knowledge of good and evil.

This text stands out in Gregory's list of Old Testament examples: the other items in it are represented by brief allusions or quotations, but in the case of this particular verse he indulges himself in a brief discussion of it. He not only explains at some length why it counts as an enigma but also indicates its bearing. It has to do with one or another aspect of the problem of evil — the "whence" and indeed perhaps the "what" of evil.

This particular enigma, then, is important to Gregory. It is of course important to him because of the issues it implicitly addresses, which were a

---

1. *Hom. in Cant., praef.,* in W. Jaeger, ed., GNO 6:4.11-12: δι' αἰνιγμάτων τε καὶ ὑπονοιῶν εἰρῆσθαι.

subject of endless fascination to him; but it is also important to him on a more personal level because he seems to take a special delight at once in its difficulty and in the ingenuity of his solution to it. Most of the items on his list are accorded brief explications at one point or another in the *Homilies on the Song of Songs,* but, where this particular text is concerned, he inserts a comparatively lengthy discussion of it into his exegesis of Song of Songs 5:5, with which, at least at first glance and to the untutored mind, it has very little to do. The task of this essay will be to follow his interpretation of this text, to see what issues it raised or resolved for him, and to elucidate his explication of it by reference to discussions of the same matters in others of his writings. In this way we may hope to clarify the total effect and outcome of his discussion of it — and so his understanding of the difficult and perennial problem he discerned beneath the ordinary sense of its words.

I

Genesis 2:9b states that "in the middle of the Garden" the "tree of life" stood, "and the tree of the knowledge of good and evil." Even before he actually cites the words of this statement, however, Gregory summarily declines a literal interpretation of the second tree (and thus presumably of the whole statement). He gives two reasons for this refusal. The first is that the customary account of the tree's identity made little sense. "We are persuaded," Gregory writes, "that the tree which it was forbidden to eat of was not, as some have declared, the fig, nor any other fruit tree; for if the fig was a killer in those days, surely it would not be edible now."[2] Besides, the Lord himself had stated clearly that none of the things that enter in through the mouth can defile a person;[3] and clearly, for Gregory, this saying (itself treated as enigmatic in Matthew's Gospel) entails believing that the fruit of which Adam and Eve disobediently ate must represent something that transcends the corporeal plane.

There is a second reason, however, for Gregory's refusal of a literal interpretation here — and a reason that is equally if not, from his point of view, more persuasive. Taken just for what it straightforwardly says, Genesis 2:9b (LXX), as he sees it, simply makes no sense. It closes with the phrase: "and the tree of life in the middle of the Garden and the tree full of the knowledge of good and evil."[4] In Gregory's view, however, this expression proposes an im-

---

2. *Hom. in Cant., praef* (GNO 6:10.4-11).
3. Cf. Matt. 15:10; Mark 7:18.
4. In the text of the LXX: (καὶ ἐξανέτειλεν ὁ θεός . . .) τὸ ξύλον τῆς ζωῆς ἐν μέσῳ τῷ

possibility since it locates both trees in the same place, that is, at the geometric center of the Garden.

> And how can there be a pair of trees at the very middle (κατὰ τὸ μεσαίτατον) of the Garden — the tree of salvation and the tree of destruction? For the exact middle (τὸ . . . ἀκριβῶς μέσον) is surely at the single center-point (ἐν τῷ ἑνὶ κέντρῳ), as is the case inside the circumference of a circle. But if another center is set alongside the center, the circle must necessarily be shifted along with its center, with the result that the former center is no longer the midst. Since, then, the Garden in that place is one, why does the text say that each of the trees is to be treated as something separate, and that both of them are at the center, when the account which tells us that all the works of God are "very good" teaches that the killer-tree is no part of God's planting?[5]

Here we have, then, one of those texts that cry out for an anagogical or allegorical interpretation — or which, in Gregory's own words, "exhort us that we must examine the divine utterances, and devote ourselves to reading, and investigate in every possible way, to see if we can find a more elevated sense than the obvious one."[6] It is plain, furthermore, that in Gregory's eyes the issue that underlies this singularly oxymoronic text has in the end little to do with geometry. The problem, even at the literal level, lies not merely or even principally in the location of two different trees at the dead center of the Garden: rather it lies in the fact that God is said to have caused them to spring up (ἐξανέτειλεν) in this fashion — that is, that God is responsible for a situation in which the principles of life and of death are seen as somehow at one, even if not identical. "What sort of plants," Gregory tersely asks, "does the Father plant and tend?" More pointedly still: "Why does the text say that each of the trees is to be treated as something separate, and that both of them are at the center, when the account which tells us that all the works of God are 'very good' teaches that the killer-tree is no part of God's planting?" The enigma that is Genesis 2:9b is the problem of the nature and origin of evil. Hence he closes his discussion of this text with a tacit exhortation to the practice of spiritual exegesis: "Unless one takes the way of philosophy and looks more

---

παραδείσῳ καὶ τὸ ξύλον τοῦ εἰδέναι γνωστὸν καλοῦ καὶ πονηροῦ. Gregory does not seem to recognize the presence of the word γνωστόν in the text, which doubtless means that he draws the name of the second tree from Gen. 2:17.

5. *Hom in Cant., praef.* (GNO 6:10.17–11.5).

6. *Hom. in Cant., praef.* (GNO 6:10.1-4).

deeply into the truth of these matters, what is said will appear, to the inattentive, incoherent or fictional (ἀσύστατον ἢ μυθῶδες)";[7] and of course the biblical text is *ex hypothesi* neither of these things.

II

Gregory does not follow the "philosophical" way with this text in his dedicatory letter. He allows the problem of its meaning to stand as a question in his readers' minds until the twelfth of his homilies. There he is addressing the sense of the Bride's words at Song of Songs 5:5: "I have risen up to open to my kinsman: my hands dripped myrrh, my fingers choice myrrh"; and his understanding of these words provides the immediate context for his discussion of Genesis 2:9b.

The basic presupposition of his exegesis of Song of Songs 5:5 is that myrrh intimates death, and in particular the death of Christ considered both in itself and as shared by believers; but Gregory does not trouble to state this at the start of his discussion of the verse, for to him and, by the time they reach Homily 12, to his auditors or readers, it is a commonplace.[8] Furthermore, he also takes it for granted that his readers will instinctively recognize that the Bride's rising up "to open to" her kinsman[9] is a corporeal symbol of the entrance of the "living Word" into the soul — or, alternatively stated, the Bridegroom's causing the soul to dwell with him[10] — and, further still, that the Word's indwelling, or dwelling with, the soul is indeed the essential core of the meaning of "resurrection."[11]

7. *Hom. in Cant., praef.* (GNO 6:11.5-7).

8. For Gregory's explanation of the meaning of myrrh, see *hom. 6 in Cant.* (GNO 6:189.2-10) on Song of Songs 3:6 ("myrrh . . . and frankincense"): "Myrrh is appropriate for the preparation of bodies for burial, while frankincense is naturally set apart for the honoring of the divine. Hence the person who intends to dedicate himself to the worship of God will not be frankincense burned for God unless he has first become myrrh — that is, unless he mortifies his earthly members, having been buried together with the one who submitted to death on our behalf, and having received in his own flesh, through mortification of its members, that myrrh which was used to prepare the Lord for burial." See also *hom. 7 in Cant.* (GNO 6:243.17-19).

9. The Greek word here translated "kinsman" is ἀδελφιδοῦς, which strictly speaking means "nephew," and which the LXX employed to render the Hebrew word for "beloved." In Gregory's homilies the word undoubtedly carries strong overtones of the latter sense, but it is also used to convey the natural solidarity between the incarnate Word and humanity.

10. *Hom. 7 in Cant.* (GNO 6:342 *ad fin.*).

11. The Bride after all openly says ἀνέστην, "I rose up."

Once these assumptions are granted, it is no surprise that in interpreting this verse of the Song of Songs Gregory should have turned his mind immediately to Romans 6, with its discourse on baptismal death and resurrection. It is, he says, when "one removes the veil of the flesh by mortifying one's earthly members" that one "opens to the Word the door through which he makes the soul his home."

> This is apparent not only from the divine teachings of the Apostle, but also from what the Bride says in this text. For, says she, "I have risen up to open to my kinsman by making my hands founts of myrrh from which its spicy scent pours forth, and by showing my fingers to be full of myrrh." For by these words she states the way in which the door is opened to the Bridegroom: "I have risen up by being 'buried with him through baptism into death' (Rom. 6:4); for the resurrection does not become actual if it is not preceded by voluntary death."[12]

The word "voluntary" here adumbrates yet another matter that is central in Gregory's understanding of this text. He lays great stress on the requirement that this "death" (i.e., to sin) must flow from conscious choice. It must come from the soul itself and not be imposed by any external agency, for if it were accidental and involuntary, it could have no moral meaning or value. Song of Songs 5:5c itself intimates this requirement with its talk of hands and fingers; hands, as Gregory explains, signify "those motions of the soul that bring actions about," while fingers mean "activities that accord with virtue."[13] The proviso about choice, then, must be incorporated into any paraphrase of the meaning of the verse under consideration, as Gregory proceeds to do.

> Thus in sum the sense of what she says is this: "I have received the power of the resurrection by mortifying my earthly members, and the mortification of such members was effected voluntarily. The myrrh was not placed on my hands by another agent, but it flowed from my own choice, so that in all virtuous pursuits" — which she calls "fingers" — "a disposition of this kind is unfailingly discerned."[14]

Here, then, Gregory has, on the basis of the conjunction of myrrh and "rising up" in Song of Songs 5:5, moved from that text to the Pauline descrip-

12. *Hom. 12 in Cant.* (GNO 6:343.2-10).
13. *Hom. 12 in Cant.* (GNO 6:343-44).
14. *Hom. 12 in Cant.* (GNO 6:344.7-13).

tion of baptism as a participation in the dying and rising of Christ; and he has proceeded to apply this description of baptism to the Christian life as a whole, portraying it as a process by which, through a necessarily voluntary (and metaphorical) kind of death, a death to the flesh, to evil and to sin, the believer moves towards full sharing in the life of the divine Word. Baptism is thus both an event and, as lived out, a reproduction in the life of the individual of the way along which the humanity of the incarnate Word was brought to resurrection. So Gregory can speculate:

> Perhaps that is why the great Paul, who correctly understood the Lord's words to the effect that the plant cannot grow unless the seed has first been dissolved in death, declared to the church the principle [δόγμα] that death must precede life, so that life cannot find a place within the human person unless it make entrance by way of death.[15]

III

Having reached this point, however, Gregory is still not satisfied that he has sufficiently justified this "principle" or explained it, and so he offers a further argument in its favor — one that has little or nothing to do immediately with *Song of Songs* 5:5 and its wording. Rather it is a summary restatement of another commonplace of his thought, that is, his philosophical — and complex, not to say tortuous — anthropology, which of course is ultimately directed upon issues having to do with sin and redemption.

In human beings, Gregory says by way of opening, there is "a twofold nature. The one is fine and intelligent and light, while the other is coarse and material and heavy." This description implies that each of these "natures" has a dynamic "proper to itself and irreconcilable with the other." The former of the two tends upward, but "the heavy and material is ever borne, and ever flows, downwards."[16] In this particular passage, Gregory does not name these two "natures" with their differing impulses or tendencies. It seems obvious, however, that the first is the soul in its intellectual and rational character as

---

15. *Hom. 12 in Cant.* (GNO 6:345.6-11); cf. John 12:24 and 1 Cor. 15:36. It is not clear how Gregory thought the Apostle Paul learned of the saying attributed to Jesus in John 12:24.

16. GNO 6:345.11-17. For parallels to this theme in Gregory's own writings, see, e.g., *Beat.* 3 (trans. Hilda Graef, ACW 18:116); and *hom. 1 in Eccl.* (GNO 5:284). The same theme emerges in others of the *Homilies on the Song of Songs*: e.g., in Gregory's discussion of the maxim "Know thyself" (*hom. 2 in Cant.* [GNO 6:63-64]).

the creature made after the image of God, and while it is tempting to identify the second simply as body, that does not seem to be exactly what Gregory has in mind. To grasp his meaning, one must examine other works in which the terms of this duality are set out more carefully.

Consider, then, the sixth of his *Homilies on the Song of Songs.* There the picture of things presupposed by this anthropological duality is presented painstakingly. Its Platonist — even Platonic — origin is immediately apparent:

> The nature of being is divided, at the highest level of generality, into two categories. On the one hand there is that which is perceptible and material; on the other, that which is intelligible and immaterial. Now we reckon something to fall into the category of the perceptible to the extent that it is grasped by sense-perception; but we reckon as intelligible that which falls beyond the observation of the senses.[17]

As a Christian, Gregory must of course modify this scheme and adapt it to the polarity of Creator and creature. Thus the intelligible realm is also, on his account of the matter, divided into two. There is that which "is what it is eternally," being "in every respect self-identical" and beyond any change in its infinite goodness — that is, God — and there is the realm of intellectual and intelligible creatures who "by . . . participation in what transcends" them are on the one hand "preserved in the good" and are on the other "always being created as [they are] changed for the better by being enhanced in goodness."[18] It is in this second category that the human self is to be located.

From a passage in his earlier treatise *On the Creation of Humanity,* it is clear that the body is not — considered simply as a physical object in space — the opponent of this self (indeed he argues there that the body is so constructed as to reflect the nobility of the soul[19]), for it is not an agent or a dynamic but at most a source of needs and pleasures that can distract the soul.

---

17. *Hom. 6 in Cant.* (GNO 6:173.7-11). Gregory repeats this "principle" in many other places in his writings; it amounts to a recurring refrain.

18. *Hom. 6 in Cant.* (GNO 6:174.1-9). On the principle that the soul is ever-changing and cannot halt in its motion, see also *Virgin.* 6 (GNO 8/1:281.10-12).

19. See *hom. opif.* 8 (PG 44:145b-d), where "nature" seems to refer to the kind of life found in plants — i.e., the interior power of growth — and where this (Aristotelian) category is identified with the "body" of 1 Thess. 5:23 ("the part that nourishes for growth": "body" here is taken to denote a form or level of life). Gregory then further identifies it with the Pauline "flesh" considered not as a "thing" of some sort but as a principle of activity (*hom. opif.* 8 [PG 44:148a]).

In this work, then, the opposition seems to be between "nature" and soul, and the question is whether this nature that informs, shapes, and governs the body — a nature that is itself, when all goes well, an image of the divine image in the soul and thus a sort of projection or appendage or lower level of soul — has its "desire" (ἐπιθυμία; cf. Plato's ἐπιθυμητικόν)[20] focused on the excellence, that is, the goodness and beauty, of its original or, alternatively, upon "that which stands in need of a beautifier,"[21] that is, matter.

The question, then, is what Gregory intends to denote here by "nature."[22] The immediately plausible answer is that he intends the nature that Plotinus had understood as "an image of intelligence," which "since it is the last and lowest part of the soul has the last ray of the rational forming principle which shines in it," but which "for this reason does not know, but only makes."[23] One may doubt, however, whether Gregory intends to buy into all the presuppositions and implications of this Plotinian use of "nature." He merely wants to suggest (a) that what he has in mind is "the last and lowest part of the soul" and (b) that "nature" thus understood functions best when at its own level it reflects the divine image. Thus in his (later) dialogue with Macrina *On the Soul and the Resurrection,* he summarizes her teaching (which one may safely take as his own) about the soul in the following fashion.

Her argument (λόγος) insisted that the soul "is an intellectual substance, and that it creates in the organic body a power of life (ζωτικὴν δύναμιν) with a view to the activity of the senses" — a definition that owes

---

20. This is one of the two nonrational parts or dimensions of the soul as portrayed by Plato in his famous myth of the charioteer (reason) and his two horses (the desiring part [τὸ ἐπιθυμητικόν] and the assertive part [τὸ θυμοειδές]): see *Phaedrus* 246a-b; 253c-e; *Republic* 4 435b-e, & 9 580d-e. Aristotle (*De anima* 2.3 [414a29-b7]) associates these with the faculty (δύναμις) of perception and insists — as does Gregory — that their possession *presupposes* possession of the nutritive faculty characteristic of plants. But see *hom. opif.* 8 (PG 44:148a), where Gregory had associated the desiring part or faculty with a different level of the soul's operation, that is, the Aristotelian power of growth. His effort to conflate Plato's image of the charioteer and his two horses with Aristotle's analysis of the levels of the soul's activities, and both of these with the Pauline "body, soul, & spirit" formula (not to mention the heart-soul-mind formula of Mark 12:30) inevitably led him into some confusion of mind.

21. See *hom. opif.* 12 (PG 44:164b; 161-64).

22. For a use of "nature" (φύσις) similar to this, see *virgin.* 4 (GNO 8/1:274.16), where Gregory speaks of a life subjected "to the compulsions of nature" and characterizes nature as a "torrent" (GNO 8/1: 275-76).

23. Plotinus, *Enneads* 4.4.13 (trans. A. H. Armstrong). See J. N. Deck, *Nature, Contemplation and the One* (Toronto: University of Toronto Press, 1967), p. 65: "Nature is a mirror image of the soul, which the soul gives to the body."

more to Aristotle than to Plato.[24] It is this distinction — between an intellectual substance and the "power" to which it gives rise within a body — that seems most nearly to correspond to the opposed tendencies of which Gregory speaks in *Homily* 12 *On the Song of Songs;* and Gregory himself requests a clarification or elaboration of it when he inquires of his sister how the motions of desire and of assertiveness (i.e, "anger" or "spiritedness": θυμός) fit into this picture of the soul and its work.

Macrina's answer indicates with reasonable precision what Gregory had meant — or thought he had meant — in his treatise *On the Creation of Humanity* when he spoke of the duality of intellect (νοῦς) and the body's "nature" (ἡ τοῦ σώματος φύσις) with its "impulses" (ὁρμαί).[25] On the Christian principle that there is nothing in the soul proper to humans that does not reflect the divine image,[26] Macrina asserts that the motions of the nonrational sort of soul are not definitive of the human soul considered just as such.[27] The reason is that they are common to the rational and the nonrational "natures," and what is common to the two cannot be definitive of the former.[28] In fact, she is prepared to say that they are "from outside" and hence that they are affects or passions (πάθη) of the human soul and do not pertain to its being as such.[29] She hastens, however, in response to another of Gregory's leading questions, to explain what her use of the term πάθος here does and does not imply.

In this instance, Gregory's question is stimulated by two factors: first, his understanding that "passion" is a word that normally connotes something wrong or out of place in whatever is the subject of it; and, second, his belief that these motions of the soul — with which, Macrina has said, reason has a struggle (μάχη), and which she has characterized feelingly as "warts" on the

24. *Anim. et res.* (PG 46:48c). Cf. Aristotle, *De anima* 1.1 (402a5-7), where soul is said to be "the principle as it were of animal life (ζῴων)."

25. *Hom. opif.* 14 (PG 44:173d-e).

26. *Anim. et res.* (PG 46:52a). Macrina (and so Gregory) holds emphatically both to the principle of the unity of soul and to the principle that the specifically human soul is the intellectual and rational soul.

27. *Anim. et res.* (PG 46:52c-d): desire and "anger" or assertiveness are not to be considered as συνουσιωμένα τῇ φύσει. Again Macrina and Gregory echo Aristotle, who distinguishes between two classes of "affections" (πάθη) belonging to the soul: those that are proper to it, and those that belong to the body because of the soul's presence in it (*De anima* 1.1 [402a 8-10]).

28. One is bound to observe that "not definitive of," in the sense required for the truth of this statement, is after all not, as Gregory seems to suppose, synonymous with "not part of the definition of." A full definition must, on his Aristotelian principles, include species as well as difference.

29. *Anim. et res.* (PG 46:52c-56a).

intellectual soul[30] — can make a positive contribution to an individual's growth in virtue. Macrina hastens to affirm that the latter proposition is indeed correct, and gives a response to Gregory's question that tries to explain how, at one and the same time, these motions can on the one hand make regular, and indeed inevitable, trouble for the soul and on the other represent natural if not necessary or proper operations of the intellectual image of God.

> For we assert that the soul's capacity for insight and discernment and oversight belongs to it properly and of its very nature, and that she preserves within herself the image of the deiform grace by this sort of activity — for the reason that our thought reckons that the divine, whatever it be by nature, is to be found in these activities: i.e., in overseeing all things and in distinguishing good from ill. On the other hand, any functions of the soul that lie on her margins and incline towards one or another of the opposites in accord with their own nature — functions, I mean, whose outcome is determined by the use made of them, whether it be for the sake of the good or for that of its opposite, like anger or fear or any other such motion that occurs within the soul and apart from which there is no human nature to be observed: these, I say, we reckon to have gotten attached to the soul from outside, since no such characteristic can be found in the archetypal Beauty.[31]

These "affections," then, are certainly not proper to the intellectual soul, the bearer of the image of God; but, as Macrina's phrase "apart from which there is no human nature to be observed" suggests, they are essential to the human individual, that is, to the soul as embodied. Thus they can be said to belong to the soul, but only marginally. This is exactly what Macrina concludes. She reiterates what Gregory — drawing on Aristotle, to be sure — had already set forth at great length in *On the Creation of Humanity:* that the human being was created last of all because it was intended by God to embrace in itself every form of life, from the lowest to the noblest — the sort of life found in plants and in nonrational animals as well as that which pertains to intellect.[32] This explains

---

30. *Anim. et res.* (PG 46:52b-c, 56c).

31. *Anim. et res.* (PG 46:57b-c).

32. Aristotle makes no reference to the aims of a divine Creator, but, as Gregory in effect notes, his account of the soul's powers or faculties, like the Genesis narrative of creation, gives first place to the life of plants, and only then moves on to the life characteristic of nonrational animals (perception), and only after that to intelligence or reason. See Gregory, *hom. opif.* 8 (PG 44:144c-48b), Aristotle's discussion in *De anima* 2.3 (414a29-414b19), and above, nn. 19, 20.

why "everything that is proper to the non-rational level of life is blended in with that which is intellectual in the soul,"[33] and it also explains why these reactions of desire or anger have to be controlled by reason. They are passions, then, in the sense that they come to the intellectual soul from outside as modalities of nonrational life. They are not, however, passions in the sense that they are automatically to be counted as moral diseases or afflictions. "Such motions of the soul become instruments of virtue or of vice in accordance with the way in which our free choice (προαιρέσεως) makes use of them."[34] In themselves, therefore, these "passions" are morally neutral, and their moral valence depends not on themselves but on the way in which self-determining rational agents use them.[35] Macrina is in effect distinguishing two senses of "passion."

The principle, then, that Gregory is expounding in his exegesis of Song of Songs 5:5 — the principle that life for human beings is born through death, and death that is voluntary — becomes somewhat more comprehensible. The struggle in which human persons are caught up is that between the natural tendencies of the intellectual soul and those of the nonrational impulses that accrue to the soul in and through its association with the body. It is not a struggle between soul and body but a struggle between the essential or characteristic functions of the human soul and its marginal functions. Furthermore, while this struggle is perhaps inevitable, it is — at least apparently — not one whose aim is the abolition of the lower functions of the soul, but rather one that seeks to see all levels of human life focused on, reflective of, and indeed absorbed in the ultimate Good that the soul images.[36] The death in question, therefore, is a death to passion understood as the *voluntary alienation* of the intellectual soul from the Good that is not merely its archetype but the archetype of all goodness at every level of life, human and other. It is a death to passion understood as sin, then, and not a death to passion understood as the set of functions that the soul accumulates for itself by lending form to body. This at any rate seems to be the thesis of Macrina's argument in *On the Soul and the Resurrection* and the thesis that presumably underlies Gregory's use of Genesis 2:9 in his explication of the significance of the conjunction of myrrh and "rising up" in the Song.

33. *Anim. et res.* (PG 46:60c).
34. *Anim. et res.* (PG 46:61a).
35. *Anim. et res.* (PG 46:65c-68a).
36. On this point, see *virgin.* 12 (GNO 8/1:301.15-21): the "powers that dwell together with the soul," symbolized by the neighbors of the woman who searched her house for a drachma she had lost (Luke 15:8-9), will be aware of the joy and gladness of the soul that has recovered the divine image lodged within her and will reach out after the ineffable beauty of that image.

IV

Thus Gregory turns to the words of Genesis 2:9 in order — or so he suggests — to answer the question "how death raises us up from death," and at the same time to satisfy those "who seek to have our reasoning on this subject clarified further."[37] His first concern, however, is to reinforce his hearers' sense of the paradoxical character of this dogma — and, derivatively, of the enigmatic character of the statement that there were two trees in the midst of God's Paradise. To this end, he elaborates on the anthropological bearing of the statement in Genesis 1:31 to the effect that everything God had made was "very good." For the human being, he observes, a very special kind of goodness had been reserved: namely, to be "the likeness of the undefiled Beauty."[38] However, he argues, if all things were

> very good, and humanity was included amongst them or even set above them, there was assuredly no death in the human person. For humanity would not have been something good, if it had within it the melancholy mark of death's downcasting. But being the copy and likeness of unending life, it was truly good and very good, because embellished with the joyous mark of life.[39]

In confirmation of this judgment, there was the Paradise itself, which "teemed with life," and also the commandment that God gave to Adam, which was a commandment calculated to perpetuate the rule of life.

Life, then, is, one might say, normal, and death, by contrast, an intruder; and that reality is what is symbolized by the presence of the tree of life at the midpoint of God's Paradise. It is baffling, therefore, and even dismaying, to hear that there is another tree which is also at the center of the Garden, and that this is called "the tree of the knowledge of good and evil," the tree of which Adam and Eve ate — and died. It is here of course that Gregory first sets out the geometrical argument that he would repeat in his dedicatory letter: since the Garden, like a circle, could have only one center-point, there

---

37. *Hom. 12 in Cant.* (GNO 6:347.15-17). This may, as Franz Dünzl has suggested, be no more than a lame excuse for importing an exegesis of Gen. 2:9 into a context where it does not really fit (Franz Dünzl, *Braut und Brautigam: Die Auslegung des Canticum durch Gregor von Nyssa* (Tübingen: J. C. B. Mohr, 1993), pp. 171-82. However, Gregory's "dogma" of life-through-death, especially in the ascetic interpretation he gave it, may well have been questioned by some of his hearers.

38. *Hom. 12 in Cant.* (GNO 6:348.2).

39. *Hom. 12 in Cant.* (GNO 6:348.3-9). Cf. Wisd. of Sol. 2:23-24.

simply could not have been two trees "in the middle." The conclusion Gregory draws from this puzzle in the dedicatory letter is straightforward enough: if there did come to be such a tree at the center of the Paradise, it was — and could have been — none of God's doing. The reason for this judgment has nothing to do with anything said in Genesis 2:9b. The judgment seems rather to grow out of Gregory's belief, based on Genesis 1:26-27, that death was no part of God's purpose for the ἄνθρωπος made after God's image and hence that "the killer-tree is no part of God's planting."[40] In the body of *Homily* 12, the matter is stated somewhat differently, but the conclusion is substantively the same: "Life is the very center of God's plantation. Death, on the contrary, is in and of itself rootless and unplanted."[41]

<h1 style="text-align:center">V</h1>

From these two propositions, which for Gregory are merely two ways of saying the same thing, at least two central principles follow.

In the first place, there is, implicit in his assertion that "Death . . . is . . . rootless and unplanted," a proposition about the nature of evil. The proposition is a well-known commonplace of late Platonist philosophy, and it is no more peculiar to Gregory than it was, for example, to his younger contemporary Augustine, who discerned in it a key to the error of the Manichean dualism. In the text of *Homily* 12, this proposition, as we shall see, is only stated indirectly. In other works, however, Gregory states it and supports it explicitly. In his dialogue *On the Soul and the Resurrection,* for example, it is presented as an implication of what must be said about the divine "nature." That nature is "itself the fullness of all good things," and therefore beyond the neediness of the human creature. It "surpasses every individual good thing," and hence, when it looks within itself, "it wants what it possesses and possesses what it wants." There is, then, nothing that lies outside the Divine "save

40. *Hom. in Cant., praef.* (GNO 6:11.3). In the dedicatory letter, the question raised for Gregory by Gen. 2:9b, its "hidden mystery," is, What sorts of plants the Father plants and husbands (*hom. in Cant., praef.* [GNO 10:16-17])?

41. An earlier version of this thought is found in *virgin.* 13 (GNO 8/1:303.23–304.6): God's commandment was "to be in contact only with what is good, and to refuse the taste of evil, on the ground that out of unwillingness to be ignorant of evil, we might open ourselves to the chained sequence of evils. Hence too it was enjoined upon the proto-plasts not to take in knowledge of its opposite along with knowledge of the good, but to *keep away from the knowledge of good and evil,* and to take pleasure in the good in its pure and unmixed state when it has no share in evil." The emphasis is mine.

only evil, which — paradoxical though it be to say this — possesses being only in not being anything; for there is no way in which evil comes to be except by the negation (στέρησις) of what is."[42] This principle fits nicely with, and indeed follows from, Gregory's interpretation of Genesis 1:31. If God really did see that everything created was "very good," then it would seem to follow that the contrary of the good is also the contrary of whatever is. Hence he can say, in the course of his exegesis of Song of Songs 5:5 and Genesis 2:9, that death, being "rootless and unplanted . . . , has no place of its own," and certainly no place at the center of God's Garden.

A second principle essential to Gregory's understanding of the two trees is intimated by his assertion that death — the definitive instance, one might say, of negation or privation and so of evil — has no place in God's original plan for the human person. No sooner is this said than one is bound to ask whence evil and death derive if not from God, and Gregory's response to this question lays down what for him is a central assumption of his portrayal of the Christian way. He has already set it briskly forth at an earlier point in *Homily* 12: it appears in his justification of the line he takes in interpreting the Song of Songs' description of (the Bride's) hands and fingers as dripping myrrh. There he explained, as we have seen, that there is a "dual nature" in human beings, with contrary tendencies or dynamics. Of these two tendencies he asserts that there is indeed a conflict between them, such that

> it is not possible for the one to follow its natural course successfully unless the other has been weakened. But our self-governing faculty and choice, which is stationed in the middle between these, works both strength in the one that is sickly and weakness in the one that is strong; for it assigns the reward of victory to whichever side it takes.[43]

He proceeds immediately to explain that in the symbolism of the Gospels, the "faithful and prudent steward . . . represents our power of choice as it presides rightly over what goes on within us," while the "wicked slave . . . marks the flourishing of vice as over against the virtues."[44] The steward of the Gospels, then, is the rough symbolic equivalent of the Bride's hands ("motions of the

---

42. See *anim. et res.* (PG 46:92c-93b). The assumption of this argument is of course that what is not good is not-anything. The point however is not that evil is unreal in the sense that it does not "happen," but that it happens as a negation. It is real as the absence of something, and so wholly relative to that something, and hence nothing in itself.

43. *Hom. 12 in Cant.* (GNO 6:345-46). "Self-governing" here translates αὐτεξούσιος, and "choice" προαίρεσις.

44. Cf. Luke 12:45-51 with its parallel at Matt. 24:48-51.

soul that bring actions about") and her fingers ("virtuous pursuits"):[45] he is the human will caught in the very act of choosing the good. The wicked slave by contrast is the will electing the way of vice. Thus the originator — the "substantifier" — of evil is the human will. "Evil," says Gregory, "cannot exist outside of the power of choice";[46] and the curious implication of this proposition is (to use Gregory's metaphorical language) that the "killer-tree" exists only if and when it is chosen by a human agent[47] — or, more exactly perhaps, that the "killer-tree" becomes a killer only if and when it is chosen by a human agent.

VI

Does this picture of human choice as the sole source of the good's negation really work for Gregory?

To begin with, one must say that it is difficult to know how seriously to take Gregory's description of "our self-governing faculty and choice" as "standing in the middle" between the two rival tendencies. The characterization is reminiscent of a much earlier tradition that associated the power of choice with soul (ψυχή) as distinct from spirit and body (or perhaps flesh), which for their part represented alternative candidates for the soul's election. That Gregory does not intend this is indicated by his association of "soul" in the formula "body and soul and spirit" (1 Thess. 5:23) not with a separate species of soul from "spirit," but with the level of soul-function connected with sense-perception.[48] In fact Gregory sees choice as seated in the noblest

---

45. For these descriptions, see *hom. 12 in Cant.* (GNO 6:344.1.6-7).

46. *Anim. et res.* (PG 46:101a). This is a regular refrain in Gregory's writings. Compare *virgin.* 12 (GNO 8/1:299.12-14): "There is no such thing as evil outside the act of choice and available for inspection in the real world as an existent in its own right. For every creation of God is good. . . ."

47. Gregory certainly entertained this thought: see *virgin.* 12 (GNO 8/1:298.18-19), where Gregory says that Adam was "himself the inventor (εὑρετής) of evil, inventing something that did not come to be by God's agency." A bit later (*virgin.* 12 [GNO 8/1:299.6-12]), he explains in what such invention consists: it occurs when, having a world full of goodness and beauty in which to exercise his choice, the human being turns away from goodness and beauty — or alternately turns away from the light — and in that act of negation brings into being (δημιουργήσας) human acquaintance with evil. It is true that in this latter passage Gregory retreats slightly from a strict interpretation of his principle: he leaves Adam hanging from the hook of responsibility but suggests that his action is due to the intervention of the Devil.

48. Cf. *hom. opif.* 8 (PG 44:145c-48a). In setting free choice up as the arbiter between

dimension of soul, that is to say, in "spirit" or intellect, which is the seat of the divine image in the human person; in his view the primary element in that image "is to be free (ἐλεύθερον) from necessity and not to be under the yoke of any natural power, but to have a faculty of judgment that is self-determining (αὐτεχούσιον) where decision is concerned." The reason for this is the established principle that "virtue is a thing that is without master (ἀδέσποτον) and voluntary, and virtue cannot be necessitated or forced."[49] Free choice, then, stands "in the middle" only in the sense that at any given point it has the power to decide between the two alternative tendencies in whatever specific form they currently present themselves.

This would seem to imply, however, that there is in intellect's power of self-determination an intrinsic neutrality with regard to these alternatives. Certainly it is difficult to understand how it can at every point be able to strengthen the weaker tendency and to weaken the stronger (thus maintaining an appropriate balance of power) unless its own power is initially uncommitted at each successive point of decision. However, the gift of self-determination is itself one of the "goods" with which God has endowed the being created after the divine image, for, as Gregory observes, "there is in us the form of everything excellent."[50] Later, moreover, in his dialogue *On the Soul and the Resurrection,* he explicitly relates the human person's freedom to its possession of the other excellences (virtues) that pertain to the image. It is impossible, he suggests, that the human being should be adorned with the virtues unless it is self-determined and free, on the ground that, as long tradition had taught, virtue is "without a master." Conversely he insists that

---

the two contrary tendencies, Gregory seems to be echoing writers like Origen (see *hom. 2.2 in Lev.*), Irenaeus (*haer.* 5.12.3), and even teachers in the Valentinian tradition (cf. Clement, *exc. Thdot.* 56) who associated freedom of choice with soul exclusively and saw it as set, or as bearing the responsibility of choice, between "spirit" on the one hand and "body" or "flesh" on the other. Gregory seems at first glance to espouse this picture (which owes its wide dissemination, at least in significant part, to the trichotomous body-soul-spirit formula of 1 Thess. 5:23) at *hom. opif.* 8 (PG 44:148a), where soul is said to stand "in between vice and virtue, i.e., above the one but not unambiguously sharing in the other." In this passage, however, Gregory follows Aristotle in asserting the unity of the life-principle in the human person, and thus speaks of "powers" or "faculties" of the one soul (which he seems to imagine as successively layered levels of activity) rather than of different sorts of souls; and the levels of soul-activity associated with growth and sense-perception were not normally envisaged as the seats of choice and self-governance. See also above, n. 20.

49. *Hom. opif.* 16 (PG 44:184b).
50. *Hom. opif.* 16 (PG 44:184b).

all freedom (ἐλευθερία) is one in nature and has an affinity for itself. It follows that everything that is free shall be united with its like. Virtue, however, is without a master. Therefore whatever is free shall count as virtuous, since whatever is free is without a master.[51]

From this it is easy to see that in the end Gregory thinks that freedom — that is, the state of being self-determining and self-governing — is a gift that consorts most happily, indeed perhaps necessarily, with virtue: they are akin and attracted to each other as like to like. To be free is to be virtuous. Thus one might say that freedom as he understands it, far from being neutral or uncommitted, is positively, naturally, and powerfully prejudiced on the side of things good and noble. In that case, however, it is scarcely possible to say, on his principles, that free choice in and of itself, free choice left to its own devices, can be appealed to as the source of evil; and one is therefore bound to inquire what further factor enters into the picture.

VII

It is the enigma of the two trees that suggests Gregory's response to this problem — and in which Gregory sees his response adumbrated. Death, he had said, "exists as the result of a falling away from life" — a version, this, of the principle that evil is not a "something" but an absence of something normally present. Once one has grasped this, Gregory asserts, a thoughtful person

> can see why the One who has conveyed this principle to us in enigmas also says that the death-dealing tree — whose fruit, he says, possesses a power mixed together out of opposites — is also at the center. He has laid it down, in effect, that good and evil are one and the same thing, and in doing so hinted darkly at the nature of sin.[52]

The tree that represents death, and therefore the direct negation or privation of life, is said to be at the center of the Paradise along with the tree of life because the picture thus conveyed, though corporeally or literally absurd, nevertheless teaches something. It symbolizes a curious identity of some sort between good and evil; or rather, as it turns out, it symbolizes the goodness of evil.

51. *Anim. et res.* (PG 46.101d-104a).
52. *Hom. 12 in Cant.* (GNO 6:50.4-7).

The reader is bound to be puzzled, if not shocked, by such a suggestion and is therefore all the more eager to hear Gregory's explanation of this paradox. He gives it immediately if very briefly:

> Some pleasure or other is the instigator of all vicious actions that get carried out, and there is no such thing as sin that is disjoined from pleasure (whether the affects [πάθη] stem from assertiveness or desire). Hence the fruit is called "good" because of an erroneous judgment regarding what is good, for such it seems to people who identify the good with pleasure. Later on, however, it occasions sour digestion. . . .[53]

What Gregory means, then, by speaking of an identity of good and evil is a form of the traditional Aristotelian principle of the apparent good. He had already asserted this principle in an earlier discussion of "the tree of the knowledge of good and evil." Adverting to Genesis 2:16-17, he had written:

> Hence it is that the tree from which is gathered the fruit of a mixed knowledge belongs to the category of things that are forbidden. That fruit — which has the serpent hawking it — is produced by the mingling of opposites; and the reason for this may lie in the fact that evil itself, in its proper nature, does not lie exposed naked to our view. For vice would go unpractised if it did not turn something good to its own advantage — a good that has the effect of inducing someone who is deceived to desire it. As it is, though, the nature of evil is somehow a mingling: in its depth lies destruction, like some hidden snare, but in its outward show it deceptively manifests a certain illusion of goodness. . . . Since, then, most people judge of the good by the criterion of what is pleasing to the senses, one can see why desire for the evil as if it were the good is called "knowledge of good and evil" by the Scripture, given that "knowledge" means some sort of sympathetic affection and involvement.[54]

If one asks, then, whence evil comes, the answer is that it is the product of an error in judgment that consists essentially in taking pleasure as an infallible evidence of goodness (and presumably pain, of evil). Apart from such an error, it would be impossible to explain the intellectual soul's susceptibility to the blandishments of things that depart from the good precisely to the extent that they depart from stable being, but then — and Gregory is not unaware of

---

53. *Hom. 12 in Cant.* (GNO 6:350.9-14).
54. *Hom. opif.* 20 (PG 44:200a-b). Cf. Aristotle, *Ethica Nicomachea* 3.4 (1113a-b).

this problem — it is equally hard to imagine how the soul that is "after the image and likeness of God" could make such an error of judgment in the first place. Surely it might be expected to have a reliable if not infallible nose for what is good.

For just this reason, I suspect, Gregory resorts to more than one device to explain how the intellect's judgment in this matter is deceived; and the devices in question are not mutually exclusive. One of them is, of course, the appeal to pleasure. Another is an appeal to custom (συνήθεια), to whose power he devotes a long discussion in the eighth chapter of his early treatise *On Virginity*.[55] This appeal is plausible enough insofar as it seeks to explain the perpetuation and dissemination of the illusion that produces false judgment and so evil; it seems inadequate, however, to the task of accounting for the origination of the illusion whose continuance it assures. A further device is to plead the inability of the mind to grasp the transcendent Good — to "bring the Ineffable within the range of vision."[56] Such "weakness," however, like the power of custom, seems to presuppose the operative effect of the evil it wants to explain. More interesting, perhaps, is the personification of evil or vice (frequently, of course, as the serpent), which suggests that the error of judgment that lends substance to evil is a product of the intrusion of some alien energy into the human situation. In the end, Gregory assigns no great weight to the serpent in the origination of evil, but the appeal to the influence of an alien energy is fundamental to his vision of the human situation. There is, he thinks, something that is all but irresistible in the siren songs of the psychic "motions" or "passions" of desire and assertiveness or anger.

To be sure he continues to insist that these motions are not in themselves sinful passions: we have already seen him defending this proposition in his own and in Macrina's person. They are impulses or perhaps cravings (ὁρμαί), and not without an element of the compulsive about them; yet Gregory deliberately likens them to the "good seed" sowed by the householder in the Lord's parable of the wheat and the tares. "Each of them," he says in the person of Macrina, "if only it be cultivated with a view to the good, surely brings forth within us the fruit of virtue."[57]

This statement, however, initiates a treatment of the parable in question

55. GNO 8/1:286-88. See in particular 286.11-13, where he explains that custom has "an enormous power to draw and allure the soul and to present it with some imaginary picture of a good, by means of which a person possesses, as a result of habituation, a certain disposition or attachment." The sense Gregory assigns to "custom" seems to vary between what we might call "culture," on the one hand, and "fashion," on the other.

56. *Virgin.* 10 (GNO 8/1:289.16).

57. *Anim. et res.* (PG 46:64c).

that is interestingly odd. Gregory continues by rehearsing the story of how tares too were sown in the householder's field: "error as concerns our judgment of the good was sown amongst them [i.e., the good seed, the "motions" of the perceptive dimension of the soul], and the sole reality that is authentically good in its proper nature was obscured by the deceitful shoot that grew up along with them."[58] In this sentence, the distinction between wheat and tares is carefully maintained, but then, almost abruptly, Gregory begins to speak in strikingly different terms.

> For the faculty of desire (τὸ ἐπιθυμητικόν) did not grow and shoot up in the direction of that good-by-nature for whose sake it was sown. On the contrary, it redirected its shoot in the direction of the bestial and non-rational, since confusion (ἀκρισία) with regard to the good led the impulse of the faculty of desire down that path. In the same way, the seed of assertiveness (ὁ θυμός) did not train people for courage but armed them to fight their own species, and the power of love (ἀγάπη) turned away from intelligible reality and went mad for inordinate enjoyment of the objects of sense.[59]

In this passage, an interesting and significant ambiguity reveals itself in Gregory's thinking. The householder in the parable of the tares, following the narrator, states that the sower of weeds was "an enemy,"[60] but Gregory here sets this point aside, except to the extent that his use of the passive voice ("error . . . was sown") might be taken to imply the activity of an agent other than the householder (who presumably represents the Word). More important still, Gregory momentarily deserts the imagery of the parable. For the field he substitutes the soul with its several faculties or powers. Of these faculties or powers, some — the ones, presumably, that are associated with desire and assertiveness and their like — are (as Macrina had already argued) not proper to the intellectual soul as such but are additions to it; and these, as we have seen, are represented by the "good seed" sown by the householder. Nevertheless, in the passage just cited, it is precisely these, and not any alien tares, that figure as the subjects of confusion about the good and so as sources of error. Each of them somehow turns the wrong way and thus contributes to the leading of the soul astray.

In this particular section, then, of Gregory's treatment of the parable of the tares, nothing is said about the intellect's exercise of choice in connection

---

58. *Anim. et res.* (PG 46:64c-d).
59. *Anim. et res.* (PG 46:64d-65a).
60. Matt. 13:28; cf. 13:25.

with the sprouting of perversity: the rational soul is allotted a role only when Gregory returns to imagery of the parable itself — and indeed returns without noticing that in his psychological interpretation of it the good seed sowed by the householder had become, oddly and all unnoticed, the very source of the tares. In other words, the intellectual soul — the "heart" — is not explicitly assigned a role in the origination of evil, but only in its control and cure. The soul now, once again, becomes the "field,"[61] and this field "by means of the natural faculty which is lodged within it — I mean that of reasoning — dries up one set of shoots and makes the other fruitful and abundant." The distinction between two different sets of shoots, the acceptable and the unacceptable, is thus restored, but only to disappear yet again as Gregory dilates further upon the role of the rational will:

> So then if someone makes use of these [motions] in accord with reason's dictate, and they are kept in one's own power and not oneself in theirs, one has become[62] like a king that makes use of the many hands of his subjects as his ministers, and will attain the desired end easily and in accordance with virtue. On the other hand, if he becomes their property, as of a body of slaves that has risen against their owner, he will be reduced to servitude, having given in contemptibly to slavish notions; and should he become the property of those who are by nature his inferiors, he will by necessity be transferred to the pursuits to which he is compelled by the power of those who have authority over him.[63]

This picture of the enslavement of intellect to the "motions" of the lower ranges of the soul's activity represents a kind of summing up of Gregory's analysis of the human situation. It symbolizes, on the one hand, his unchanged belief that moral evil subsists only in the human will and its choices, and, on the other, his inability to imagine how that same will, image as it is of the eternal Good, can knowingly choose the worse except under the prevailing influence of some other power. That power, as it turns out, belongs to the psychic functions taken on in view of the soul's assignment to actuate the body's activities of sense-perception and growth or nutrition. It is their malfunction that originates evil: they are the good seed that (contrary to the par-

---

61. The word Gregory employs in this connection is ἄρουρα. The text of the Matthean parable has ἀγρός. The two terms are virtually synonymous.

62. Reading, with one MS, γενόμενος for ἀλλ' (which seems inconsistent with the syntax of the sentence).

63. *Anim. et res.* (PG 46:65c).

able) become tares. The intellectual soul's freedom of choice and self-determination are alluded to, but only in connection with their attempt to overcome, to shrug off, this domination and its consequences: that is, the "coats of skin" (Gen. 3:21), the state of a fallen humanity subject to the assaults of sinful passion. The soul proper — intellect — is not appealed to as the originator of this unhappy state. Hence, we have Gregory's interest in a metaphor that draws on human experience of the force of gravity. From that experience people learn that it requires less effort to let something go "down" than to lift it "up," and, says Gregory, "the pull of sin is a heavy, downward-dragging affair," which is therefore "stronger" than the opposite tendency; and so "the governing faculty of the soul is more likely to be pulled down by the weight of the non-rational element, than the heavy, earthen element is to be lifted up by the mind's elevating influence."[64] Here the origin of evil is discerned, for practical purposes, not in the free choice of the intellectual soul, with its natural prejudice in favor of the good, nor yet in the Devil's infiltration of the farmer's crop with a battalion of alien tares, but in the superior power of "the heavy, earthen element." That power supplies, presumably, the explanation why the apparent good of sensual pleasure is "stronger" — not rationally more persuasive, perhaps, but more compelling — than the upward pull of desire for the authentic Good that is God.

VIII

Gregory's interpretation of the phenomenon of the two trees, then, is, as he himself seems to have suspected, more than just a nice solution to a verbal enigma. The enigma indeed symbolizes — and at the same time illustrates — his own perception of the situation of a fallen humanity; moreover, it epitomizes his instructive but fruitless struggles with the question of the origin of evil.

In the first place, then, considered simply as a stab at explaining the *origination* of evil, Gregory's exegesis of Genesis 2:9b and the themes that inform and underlie it is a failure in the sense that it is, in the last resort, unintelligible; and it is unintelligible because at every point its plausibility depends on the one thing Gregory cannot allow: namely, the existence *apart from human choice* of some factor or reality that by its intrinsic magnetism or attractiveness deceives the mind, overwhelms the will, and so orients human loving away from the authentic Good. Moreover, the reason why Gregory

---

64. *Hom. opif.* 18 (PG 44:193c).

cannot allow this can be plainly enough stated: he is, when push comes to shove (as it does in any discourse about absolute origins), not in any significant sense a dualist. This is plain from the seriousness with which he takes the statement that "God saw all the things he had made, and behold! they were very good" — from which he inevitably draws the conclusion that "the killer-tree is no part of God's planting." Genesis 2:9b is not, then, to be interpreted as meaning that there was some evil lying about in God's creation for Adam to choose; and while it might make sense, in the abstract, to conclude that in that case the human will must have been the "inventor" of evil, it is difficult in practice to see what might have occasioned or motivated a choice that spontaneously desired and willed the constitution of an effectual nothingness — death. If Gregory then appeals to the "passions" — that is, the motions evoked by natural need — of the soul as it operates at the level of sense-perception and suggests that it is these that draw the mind down to love of things transient and material, and therefore away from the true Good, he nevertheless insists, in accord with his principles, that even these passions are not in and of themselves evil or vicious. Indeed he plainly holds that the true destiny and function of these passions is to have their dynamic incorporated within the motion of the will towards God. This refusal of dualism is, moreover, admirably illustrated and represented by one element — a strongly counter-intuitive element — in his reading of Genesis 2:9b. The two trees are said to stand together at the center of the Paradise because, in a sense, "good and evil are the same thing." It is the intrinsic goodness of the wrong thing that makes it attractive, and thus the existence of evil must either seem accidental or be attributed to a weakness or disease of the mind or will itself.[65] Adam may have summoned evil into existence by his choosing; but either he did not intend it (and by so much it is accidental), or else he could not help himself (and so the human will as God created it was defective — unfree *because* it was capable of choosing the worse).

In the second place, however, it is possible to read Gregory's reflections on Genesis 2:9b, and the whole cycle of problems it evokes for him, in a quite different way. It is possible, that is, to treat it as an analysis of the human condition or situation as that is presently observed or experienced — as the Nyssene equivalent of Paul's description of the conflict between "the law of [the] intellect" — that is, of the "inner self" (ὁ ἔσω ἄνθρωπος) that delights in the law of

---

65. It is this alternative that Gregory stresses in *hom. opif.* 16 (PG 44:184c), where it is human mutability and alterability that seem to ground the *possibility* of sin. Still, it is only a necessary and not a sufficient condition of humanity's turning the world upside down — to think otherwise would attribute the origination of sin to the Creator.

God — and the "law of sin which dwells in my members."[66] Read in this fashion, Gregory speaks as a dualist of sorts — a dualist who asserts that between the Good that is naturally sought by the intellectual soul and the material, evanescent goods naturally sought by the soul in the lower reaches of its functioning there is a contrariety *if and when the latter dynamic dominates.* This dualism is not less seriously meant because Gregory is forever hastening to qualify it in the interest of his abiding conviction that everything God has made is "very good." That conviction continues to reign, but not so much with an eye to origins as with an eye to the destiny that awaits all human wanting: that is, the cessation of the tug-of-war between life and death, being and nothing, and the refocusing of human seeking in all its dimensions on God.

In this perspective, the contrast of the two trees of Genesis 2:9b assumes a slightly different sense. The quasi-identity of good and evil steps into the background and what is emphasized is the contrast between the simplicity and integrity of unqualified life, on the one hand, and the ambiguity and uncertainty of an existence that is pulled in two directions at once, on the other; and it is the latter that represents human evil. Thus

> the fruit of the forbidden tree is not straightforwardly evil, since it is decked out in the good; nor yet purely good, for evil is hidden away in it; but a mixture of both, the taste of which, it says, leads those who touch it to death. Thus the Scripture all but shouts out its teaching that what is really good is by nature simple and uniform, foreign to any ambiguity (πάσης διπλόης) and to any mating with its opposite. Evil on the other hand is both variegated and much dressed up. . . . And knowledge of it — that is, the embracing of it in experience — is the principle and the ground of death and corruption.[67]

The contrast of the two trees, then, symbolizes the contrast between the purity and simplicity of the good and the deadly ambiguity of a "no-thing" parading itself as desirable. The implication of all this is that the symbol of the tree of the knowledge of good and evil represents the condition of the human person when torn between "the law of [the] intellect" and "the law of sin," while the tree of life represents not only the purity and simplicity of the true Good but also the human self's single-minded conversion, in all its several dimensions, to that Good, a conversion that is a death to death, a drenching of hand and fingers in myrrh (as the Bride says).

66. See Rom. 7:21-25.
67. *Hom. opif.* 20 (PG 44:200b-c).

Appropriating Genesis and Exodus
in Evagrius's *On Prayer*

ROBIN DARLING YOUNG

In some recent discussions of biblical exegesis, it has become common to observe that, in the ancient world, the Old Testament does not stand alone as a self-interpreting book, either in the synagogue or in the church. This observation reflects, in some sense, both the incomplete sum of the book and its innumerable interpreters.[1] Among Christians, the challenge of appropriating the covenant in the light of Jesus' life and teaching brought about an unwavering engagement with the Old Testament from the mid-first century forward. By the last decades of the fourth century, a host of Christian commentators had surrounded, in particular, the Pentateuch; even more did they gather around the books of Genesis and Exodus, directed by the newly posed questions of Christian faith and attracted to the biblical narrative of the first humans and their descendants and to its account of the world's creation, the establishment of the covenant with the children of Israel, and their voyage to the land of promise.

Due to its size, subject, expression, transmission as text, and interpretation (among, e.g., Philo and other first- and second-century interpreters), Genesis created a world of trouble for Christian thinkers, particularly since, as read in the liturgy, it required them to enter into a dialogue with the differing claims of their own, Graeco-Roman culture. Their varying approaches

---

1. For a concise discussion of the origins of interpretation beginning in postexilic Judaism, see James L. Kugel, *Traditions of the Bible: A Guide to the Bible As It Was at the Start of the Common Era* (Cambridge, Mass. and London: Harvard University Press, 1998), pp. 1-41.

could easily be illustrated by a comparison of the diverging exegeses of Theodore of Mopsuestia, Eusebius of Emesa, Ephrem the Syrian, Ambrose, Augustine, Jerome, Basil of Caesarea, and Gregory of Nyssa. Where Origen had been almost alone in devoting homilies and, earlier, a commentary to the book, 125 years later there was no solitude in the exegesis of the text — interpretation seemed to generate interpretation.[2] Exodus offered different problems, but it, too, required careful exposition as both the history of Israel and the ancient, typological charter for Christian worship.

Furthermore, these are merely the familiar names; other authors interpreted Genesis and Exodus on their way to discussing some other topic. One of these was Evagrius of Pontus, who began his literary life in Constantinople as assistant to the Nicene bishop Gregory Nazianzus and ended it in Egypt as the successor of Macarius the Great, training ascetics and composing letters, instructive works, and biblical exegesis in his monastic dwelling in Nitria. Evagrius is not usually thought of as a biblical interpreter, despite his four collections of scholia on biblical books. Yet the Scriptures form the backdrop for all his thought, which can hardly be understood without them. As a monk who instructed others in the various uses of Scripture, Evagrius was constrained to understand the text in its various levels of meaning. He had inherited a version of Origen's and Clement's interpretive technique through the intermediaries of Basil of Caesarea and Gregory Nazianzus as well as the Egyptian monastic heirs of those two original teachers.[3] This essay on Evagrius is offered to another teacher, Robert L. Wilken, as a token of friendship and in appreciation of his work as a scholar of the patristic intellectual tradition.

Evagrius understood the monk to be just as much an inhabitant of the biblical world as the characters who appeared in the text, with the important qualification that, since the incarnation, "Christ is the begetter of knowledge," and is the focus and mediator of investigation and contemplation.[4] He

2. The eastern dimensions of the enterprise are explored in Judith Frishman and Lucas Van Rompay, eds., *The Book of Genesis in Jewish and Oriental Christian Interpretation: A Collection of Essays* (Louvain: Peeters, 1997); for general discussions see, e.g., Gregory A. Robbins, ed., *Genesis 1–3 in the History of Exegesis: Intrigue in the Garden* (Lewiston, N.Y.: Edwin Mellen, 1988); and Adam Kamesar, *Jerome, Greek Scholarship, and the Hebrew Bible: A Study of the Quaestiones Hebraicae in Genesim* (Oxford: Clarendon, 1993).

3. See my article, "Evagrius the Iconographer: Monastic Pedagogy in the *Gnostikos*," *JECS* 9.1 (2001): 53-71, for a discussion of the influence of Clement's and Origen's exegesis upon Evagrius's instructions to monastic teachers.

4. *Scholion on Ecclesiastes* 1, in *Scholies à l'Ecclésiaste: édition princeps du texte grec, par Évagre le Pontique,* ed. Paul Géhin (Paris: Éditions du Cerf, 1993), p. 58.

regarded his monastic students as successors to the patriarchs, prophets, and apostles when they became adepts and instructors in the divine economy. They also participated in the selfsame understanding of the inner structure of created reality as had those earlier teachers, making them their virtual contemporaries. Hence they were supposed to resemble them by understanding the biblical text spiritually, as they had understood the events in which they were actors spiritually — by reading about them and accomplishing what they accomplished as contemplatives interpreting their own experience of God and creation, and making it intelligible, if obscurely, to the reader. For Evagrius, all biblical exegesis had as its goal personal appropriation.

The *Gnostikos* of Evagrius contains instructions and examples for interpreting the Bible in order to promote monastic teachers' participation in the divine pedagogy of Christ. In other works Evagrius also used examples to teach his readers how to expound the biblical text. The following essay explores how Evagrius included in one treatise, the *Chapters on Prayer,* instructions for approaching God through created beings, just as had the monk's predecessors in the Old Testament.[5] Such an ancient approach rested upon understanding the approach itself and also its environment. It required the monk to place himself in a pattern of ascent through creation understood as a pattern of intelligible realities, a code for recognizing the Creator by means of his signs in creation. It held out as a goal the contemplation of the Trinity. Always, the structure and matrix of such an ascent was liturgical, because the prayer of the monk occurred in the setting of the daily repetition of the Psalms.

Like his teachers, Evagrius was well aware of the limitations of the text of Scripture; of its obscurity he remarked: "That which is the contemplation of beings, the divine Book has not made known; but how one approaches it by the practice of the commandments and by true doctrines, it teaches in a clear fashion." Since the contemplation of beings is the penultimate goal of rational creatures, this seems like an omission on the part of the divine au-

---

5. Two differing Greek versions of the *Chapters on Prayer* are in print. They are the *De Oratione* attributed to Nilus of Ancyra in PG 79:1165-1200. Another version is included, also under the name of Nilus, in the *Philokalia* compiled by Nikodemos of the Holy Mountain and Makarios of Corinth (Venice, 1792). The first was translated by John Eudes Bamberger (Evragius Ponticus, *The Praktikos: Chapters on Prayer* [Kalamazoo, Mich.: Cistercian, 1972]), and the second was translated by G. E. H. Palmer, Philip Sherrard and Kallistos Ware (*The Philokalia: The Complete Text* [London and Boston: Faber and Faber, 1979], vol. 1, pp. 55-71); both translations appear under the name of Evagrius. A critical edition with translation has been prepared, but not yet published, by Simon Tugwell. All three translations were consulted, but translations where given are my own.

thor of the Bible, but Evagrius here reflects the intention of divine *paideia* in encouraging his readers to be led to the discernment of Scripture's meaning by means of its silences. At the very least, it can be said that Evagrius agreed with Origen when the latter referred disparagingly to those who were "enslaved by the letter [of Scripture]." When he went about the work of crafting a formal interpretation of Scripture, Evagrius developed an approach that inserted the letter of it into a proverb-like interpretation, so that it could be applied by his students to their own practice.

Here it will be seen that Evagrius devoted the prologue of the work to a recollection of the structure of the world based on his interpretation of Genesis, and he devoted the body of the work to a set of open-ended remarks placing himself as author in dialogue with the monk to indicate how the monk is like Moses, and even can surpass Moses in understanding the world and conversing with God. Throughout the work, Evagrius makes it plain that the path of such an ascent is the hazardous, complicated path of prayer, itself a constant repetition of the words of the Bible.

The Study of Evagrius's Interpretive Method

Unfortunately, the prevailing approach to Evagrius's biblical interpretation has been wanting, especially in general treatments of patristic exegesis. Yet Evagrius was one of the most interesting and intricate expositors of Scripture among Christians in the East in the late fourth century. However, among early Christian interpreters of the Bible, Evagrius is rarely considered significant. Although he composed scholia on distinct books of the Bible, as well as collections of *kephalaia* in the form of proverbs, and theological letters that depend on a comprehensive exegesis, these works have not been studied along with those of other patristic commentators. Even those scholars who have made him the sole object of study have only partially attended to his efforts as an exegete.[6]

This is odd, since Evagrius was constantly interpreting Scripture. Even

6. Evagrius goes unmentioned in the standard recent studies of exegesis: *The Cambridge History of the Bible,* vol. 1, ed. Peter R. Ackroyd (Cambridge: Cambridge University Press, 1970); Bertrand de Margerie, *Introduction to the History of Exegesis* (Petersham, Mass.: St. Bede's, 1991); Manlio Simonetti, *Biblical Interpretation in the Early Church: A Historical Introduction to Patristic Exegesis,* trans. John A. Hughes, ed. Anders Bergquist and Markus Bockmuehl (Edinburgh: T & T Clark, 1994); and Frances M. Young, *Biblical Exegesis and the Formation of Christian Culture* (Cambridge and New York: Cambridge University Press, 1997).

those scholars who have devoted an entire monograph to the thinker and have studied Evagrius as an integral or central part of some investigation into early Christian thought and practice seem to have been satisfied with the well-established custom of making a passing remark about his exegesis. John Eudes Bamberger, who provided one of the earliest English translations of Evagrius, included biblical citations in the notes to the volume but contented himself with remarking that Evagrius's description of contemplation included "penetration into the meaning of Scripture."[7]

Similarly, in a study of the ethical use of the Bible among the early monks of Egypt, Douglas Burton-Christie gives short shrift to Evagrius's interpretation. Although he discusses Evagrius's role as student and teacher in monastic communities devoted to appropriating and applying the instructions and prayers of Scripture, Burton-Christie's evaluation of Evagrius is incomplete because he limited his study of monastic exegesis to the *Apophthegmata Patrum* and, consequently, his mention of Evagrius to those places where he is mentioned in the *Apophthegmata*. In that document, however, a composition of the fifth century, Evagrius's own work is diminished, and his adroitness in interpretation disregarded.[8]

From a different angle, Elizabeth Clark does give a general description of Evagrius's exegesis. In her study of the fourth-century "ascetic interpretation" of the Bible, Evagrius appears among numerous other commentators who are said to have taken a text originally friendly to marriage, reproduction, and (in a limited way) sexual intercourse and read it against itself, making it by means of a particular type of exposition a kind of charter for Christian monasticism to the detriment of marriage and the establishment of families. She writes that Evagrius thought scriptural verses were useful to undergird certain monastic practices "if they were decontextualized and reapplied to the monastic setting." Like most scholars, Clark understands Evagrius's exegesis to be an heir of Origen's; as she writes:

And Origen, for his part, would find a worthy exegetical partner in Evagrius Ponticus, who also effects a transhistorical reading of the Bible that renders numerous passages of Holy Scripture, in allegorical guise, useful for Christian ascetics.[9]

7. Bamberger, *Praktikos*.

8. Douglas Burton-Christie, *The Word in the Desert: Scripture and the Quest for Holiness in Early Christian Monasticism* (New York and Oxford: Oxford University Press, 1993), pp. 58-59, 165.

9. Elizabeth A. Clark, *Reading Renunciation: Asceticism and Scripture in Early Chris-*

Clark's view of Evagrius's exegesis is part of a larger project — to show how, through the exposition of the Bible, asceticism was justified and promoted and ultimately triumphed as the preferred Christian way of life in Late Antiquity. One of the virtues of her approach is that it shows how, in early Christianity, the text of the Bible itself does not have one singular, stable meaning. Rather, Scripture belongs in its interpretive communities as a medium of interpretation but — because it was understood to be both inspired and alive — not the sole controlling agent of interpretation. However, *Reading Renunciation* does not treat Evagrius's work directly; in fact, it considers the ascetic teachers of early Christianity as a whole, concentrating on particular themes that most of them explored. Therefore, it does not distinguish between the communities and contexts that conditioned the work of any one author. Furthermore, Clark hints that Evagrius, along with other ascetics, wrenched the biblical text from its historical context and concealed its original meaning in a disguise — in spiritual readings, following the lead of Origen in distorting the meaning of the biblical text.

In recent discussion of Evagrius, monastic scholars have been almost the only scholars who have appreciated the particularly monastic character of his biblical interpretation. Gabriel Bunge, Jeremy Driscoll, Columba Stewart, and Luke Dysinger have called attention to the way in which exegesis grew out of the structure of the daily life of Evagrius and his monastic disciples. From Bunge, two works are particularly useful; these are *Das Geistgebet* and *Briefe aus der Wüste*.[10] The first book is a close examination of Evagrius's instructions on prayer as a constant dialogue or "conversation of the mind with God." Bunge regards the treatise *On Prayer* as a demonstration of the proper setting and disposition for monastic recitation of the Psalms. Therefore, the treatise should be understood as a kind of gloss on the Psalms. Bunge's earlier work is a translation of Evagrius's letters now extant only in Syriac. In the space of a few pages, he briefly makes clear the outlines of scriptural exposition as practiced by Evagrius. Taking his lead from the instructions to the monastic teacher contained in the *Gnostikos*, Bunge points out that while Evagrius shared the interpretive techniques and aims

---

tianity (Princeton, N.J.: Princeton University Press, 1999), pp. 132, 156. A careful, illuminating study of Evagrius's thought broadly considered can be found in her earlier work, *The Origenist Controversy: The Cultural Construction of an Early Christian Debate* (Princeton, N.J.: Princeton University Press, 1992), chapter two, pp. 43-84: "Image and Images: Evagrius Ponticus and the Anthropomorphite Controversy."

10. Gabriel Bunge, *Das Geistgebet: Studien zum Traktat "De Oratione" des Evagrios Pontikos* (Cologne: Luther-Verlag, 1987); and idem, *Evagrios Pontikos. Briefe aus der Wüste* (Trier: Paulinus-Verlag, 1986).

of Origen, the Cappadocians, and his older contemporary Didymus the Blind, he divided them into three areas specifically matching the states of the ascetic life — the practical, the natural, and the theological. In these three states the monk reads the Bible to benefit monastic practice, then to promote the contemplation of nature, and finally to attain the contemplation of the Trinity. Bunge remarks:

> Es mag hier genügen zu wissen, daß damit, grob gesagt, die Bereiche des praktisch-asketischen Lebens, der Erkenntnis des Geschaffenen und der Lehre von der Heiligen Dreifaltigkeit gemeint sind. Diese drei Bereiche sind aufs innigste miteinander verflochten, so daß man bei einem jeden die Dimensionen der beiden anderen mitsehen muß.[11]

Yet it is not Evagrius's interpretation for its own sake that draws Bunge's attention; he wishes to indicate in passing that the spiritual or allegorical exposition taken for granted by ancients and medievals, though strange to modern readers, was natural for Evagrius as a fourth-century teacher inspired by earlier Alexandrian exegesis — and that it has a continuing worth, not least for those who contemplate.

In a 1991 dissertation, Jeremy Driscoll gave more sustained attention to Evagrius's monastic exegesis. Because Evagrius often composed his works in the form of proverbial or gnomic *kephalaia*, Driscoll devotes a large portion of his commentary upon the text of the *Ad Monachos* to its setting in monastic culture. In particular, he considers the general significance of the proverb in "human culture," of the proverb in the Bible, and of the production of proverbs in a monastic world where teaching passed from experienced monk to beginner by means of proverbial instruction. Driscoll's approach, though, emphasizes the practical and ethical aspects of scriptural interpretation. He is particularly interested in how Evagrius's written responses to questions from his disciples, cast in proverbial form, provided a new genre in the Christian ascetical life; he distinguishes Evagrius's approach from that of the *Apophthegmata Patrum* by showing that the former was a more literary approach than the latter, which tried to reproduce the oral quality of spoken discourse. More importantly, Driscoll turns to Palladius's description of Evagrius's own practice, derived from Macarius of Alexandria, of praying daily one hundred prayers based on the Psalter and other biblical books. In addition, Driscoll points out, since Palladius relates that Evagrius slept only one-third of the night and spent the rest in meditation, prayer, and contem-

---

11. Bunge, *Evagrios Pontikos,* p. 114.

plation of the Scriptures, Driscoll concludes that Evagrius composed the *Ad Monachos* (and presumably other works as well) in the following way: "Evagrius at prayer or at work, the Scriptures ever on his mind, and a monk coming for a word."[12] Like Bunge, Driscoll thinks that the *Gnostikos* is the best source for Evagrius's theory, so to speak, of interpreting Scripture; and like Bunge, he wishes to set that practice firmly in the mainstream monasticism of late-fourth-century Egypt, which he does by showing its general similarity to the *Apophthegmata Patrum*.

Driscoll deliberately places his study of Evagrius's more philosophical doctrines after his study of the monk's appropriation and teaching of the Bible. In his first known writing, Evagrius, Driscoll notes, shows his desire for philosophy: "Who would become a Laban for me, free me from Esau, and guide me to the highest philosophy?" The historian Socrates had said that once Evagrius learned from Macarius the Great and Macarius the Egyptian, "he acquired from them the philosophy of deeds, whereas formerly he had been a philosopher only in word."[13] Without delving into the complicated history of the word "philosophy" as applied to theology among ancient Christians, or to the monastic life among writers about ascetics, it is still useful to note that even in the letter *On Faith* Evagrius pictures the philosopher as Jacob, an image he later used of the monk. Driscoll concludes that for Evagrius philosophy was a *psychagoge*, "a philosophical text in the ancient sense of spiritual exercises," in which scriptural exegesis was mingled with ethical proverbs and meditative guidance. His writing was intricate and obscure because

> he was in love with wisdom. He was philosophizing. He wanted to share this love and provoke it in others. He created a spiritual exercise. In it he created a literary shape that mirrored the shape of the divine economy whose outlines he had come slowly to discern in his own search for wisdom. He trusted this shape to take his disciples where it was taking him. It is the shape of faith leading to love and love leading to knowledge of the Holy Trinity.[14]

12. Jeremy Driscoll, *The "Ad Monachos" of Evagrius Ponticus: Its Structure and a Select Commentary,* Studia Anselmiana 104 (Rome: Pontificio Ateneo S. Anselmo, 1991), p. 341.

13. Driscoll, *The "Ad Monachos" of Evagrius Ponticus,* p. 361; Evagrius, *Letter on Faith* 1 (formerly Basil, *Letter* 8; Yves Courtonne, *Saint Basile: Lettres,* vol. 1 [Paris: Belles Lettres, 1957], p. 23); Socrates, *Ecclesiastical History* 4.23.

14. Driscoll, *The "Ad Monachos" of Evagrius Ponticus,* p. 383. Driscoll repeats these themes more compendiously in *The Mind's Long Journey to the Holy Trinity: The* Ad Monachos *of Evagrius Ponticus* (Collegeville, Minn.: Liturgical Press, 1993).

As intuitive as the foregoing is in broad strokes, it does not do justice to the frequent ambiguity, the slipperiness, and the obscurity of Evagrius's interpretation. For this aspect of Evagrius's gnomic teaching, his French translators Antoine and Claire Guillaumont and, more recently, Paul Géhin offer perceptive comments.

In their introduction to their critical edition and translation of the *Gnostikos,* the Guillaumonts write of the influence upon Evagrius of the rhetorical tradition and the form developed by ancient rhetoricians, the scholion. A tradition "à la fois païenne et chrétienne," the scholion was developed in order to allow and even to promote a kind of pedagogical esotericism whereby "the highest truths should not be exposed except in front of those who have the requisite disposition, i.e. are purified enough, to receive them, and those are few in number compared to the crowd."[15] Evagrius developed, following the traditions of Plotinus, according to Porphyry, and Clement and Origen, a kind of allegorical reading suited to a duplex interpretation. His method consisted in "inviting the capable of becoming gnostics in their turn, to research and discussion on δόγματα, i.e. points of doctrine left to free research, and on scriptural texts, which, according to allegorical exegesis, could be diversely interpreted."[16]

In the past decade, Paul Géhin has been producing critical editions of Evagrius's biblical scholia. In the introduction to his edition of the *Scholia on Proverbs,* he noted that Evagrius's fundamental exegetical principle was that the Bible was one harmonious whole, and thus the meaning of one passage is elucidated by another.[17] In his introduction to the *Scholia on Ecclesiastes,* Géhin devotes an entire chapter to biblical interpretation.

He discusses how Evagrius approached the book with the understanding that Christ is the "Ecclesiasticus," with the consequence that Ecclesiastes had to be interpreted as a testimony to the accurate description of nature and of beings. Treating the biblical book in this way, as a necessary locus for the *theoria physike,* Evagrius softened its pessimism and gave it "une lecture philosophique et spirituelle."[18] Géhin shows how Evagrius often inserts a paraphrase of a verse from Ecclesiastes to secure its reading as a philosophical book:

15. Antoine Guillaumont and Claire Guillaumont, *Évagre le Pontique: Le Gnostique, ou à celui qui est devenu digne de la science,* SC 356 (Paris: Éditions du Cerf, 1989).

16. Guillaumont and Guillaumont, *Évagre le Pontique,* p. 40.

17. Évagre le Pontique, *Scholies aux Proverbes,* ed. Paul Géhin (Paris: Éditions du Cerf, 1987), pp. 26-32.

18. Géhin, ed., *Scholies à l'Ecclésiaste,* p. 19.

Placée en début de scholie, l'incise en question a presque toujours le sens de "vouloir dire"; elle est associée à une récriture du verset qui rappelle ... la pratique des targums: l'exégète ne se contente pas d'élucider le texte, mais substitue aux termes bibliques importants leurs équivalents symboliques.[19]

Géhin's study of Evagrius's exegesis is the most thorough to appear in the *Sources chrétiennes* edition of his complete works. An even more ample study will probably appear in the long-hoped-for edition of Evagrius's *Scholia on the Psalms.*

Finally, three of the most recent interpreters of Evagrius have attempted to deal directly with his reading of distinct points of Scripture. Columba Stewart has pointed out that Evagrius's teaching on prayer is thoroughly situated in the expressions and narrative of the Bible. According to Evagrius, the monk's interpretation is a kind of "knocking on the door of Scripture with the hands of virtue." Scripture constituted the spiritual world of Evagrius, particularly in his description of the monk's ascent to the "place of God," a reinterpretation of the theophanies of Exodus 24:10-11 and Ezekiel 1:26 and 10:1. This explains Evagrius's teaching about the "sapphire light of the mind," as found in the *Skemmata* and elsewhere. Like Bunge and Driscoll, Stewart identifies Evagrius's exegesis as participating in the Alexandrian tradition; further, he points out that the very structure of the monk's life forced a concentration upon the Bible that required its exposition.[20] Luke Dysinger has examined Evagrius's understanding of the terms "providence" and "judgment" in relation to his interpretation of Scripture,[21] and William Harmless takes up the investigation of Columba Stewart in a description of what Evagrius meant by his assertion that the mind in pure prayer "sees its *katastasis* in a sapphire or heavenly [blue] color."[22]

It is important to understand Evagrius's biblical interpretation not only because it yields a fuller understanding of the varying patterns of exegesis in the fourth century but also because such studies allow Evagrius himself to be

19. Géhin, ed., *Scholies à l'Ecclésiaste*, p. 14.

20. Columba Stewart, "Approaches to Early Monastic Prayer: The Case of Evagrius Ponticus," paper delivered at the Thirteenth International Conference on Patristic Studies, Oxford, England, 1999.

21. Luke Dysinger, "The *Logoi* of Providence and Judgement in the Exegetical Writings of Evagrius Ponticus," paper delivered at the Thirteenth International Conference on Patristic Studies, Oxford, England, 1999.

22. William Harmless and Raymond R. Fitzgerald, "The Sapphire Light of the Mind: The *Skemmata* of Evagrius Ponticus," forthcoming in *ThS.*

seen, not as a relentless systematizer of Christian theology — which he most certainly was not — but as a monk always absorbed more and more by the levels of reality indicated by Scripture. The following is a brief example of how Evagrius handles a particular biblical text.

Scriptural Interpretation in the *Chapters on Prayer*

The treatise entitled *Chapters on Prayer* divides neatly into two parts. The first part is a prologue in the form of a letter written by Evagrius to a friend whom he considers his superior as a monastic teacher. The second, longer part consists of 153 short sentences, one-line "chapters" or "headings" meant to advise the monk in his daily work. Evagrius may have meant the treatise as an updating or adaptation of Origen's treatise by the same name, although he employs a very different structure and does not write a commentary on the Lord's Prayer itself. In any case, he provided a description of the hazards of prayer and instructions on the virtues necessary for prayer and indicated the signs of progress or deception in the monk at prayer.

Since the *Chapters on Prayer* appears to be a basic manual for the monastic life, it has been extensively commented upon by scholars of Evagrius. In 1960, Irenée Hausherr wrote a chapter-by-chapter commentary upon a French translation of the work.[23] *Les leçons d'un contemplatif: le traité de l'oraison d'Évagre le Pontique* confirmed, by cross-referencing themes and terms in the work to the more advanced theological works of Evagrius, that it was a genuine work of Evagrius, not of Nilus of Ancyra to whom it had formerly been ascribed, and that it reflected Evagrius's full teaching. About a decade later, John Eudes Bamberger provided the first English translation of the work, but his brief introduction confined itself to suggesting the most important points of Evagrius's views on prayer.[24] Finally, Gabriel Bunge has recently provided a study of six discrete themes in the treatise, connecting them with other locations in Evagrius's work where they are also discussed.[25]

None of these studies has examined the scriptural exposition Evagrius employed in composing the *Chapters on Prayer*. Therefore, in order to provide a fuller understanding of the treatise, the present essay concentrates on Evagrius's exegesis both in the body of the text and in its prologue. Because it

23. Irenée Hausherr, *Les leçons d'un contemplatif: le traité de l'oraison d'Évagre le Pontique* (Paris: Beauchesne, 1960).

24. Bamberger, *Praktikos*.

25. Bunge, *Das Geistgebet*.

would take too long to elaborate how each chapter is founded in a certain scriptural exegesis, an examination of one chain of chapters will serve to indicate the workings of the interpretation of the whole book. This chain has to do with the way in which the monk, says Evagrius, is an equal of the angels. In chapter 113, Evagrius writes: Ἰσάγγελος γίνεται μοναχὸς διὰ τῆς ἀληθοῦς προσευχῆς.[26]

Evagrius understands that the monk becomes an angel because he participates in the worship of which angelic worship is the prototype, and the worship of the patriarchs is the type. Here Evagrius uses a typological and spiritual exegesis to show how the monk is understood to be, by his prayer, participating in the same activity in which the patriarchs, most notably Moses, participated. Twenty-three chapters, spread throughout the work and interspersed with directions and examples, provide a pattern for this kind of interpretation.

Most notable, because they begin the body of the work, are chapters one through four. Anchored in the books of Exodus and Revelation, they place the reader squarely in the place of Moses before the tabernacle and the burning bush, making clear that this is the prototype, the *typos,* of monastic prayer. The first cites directions for Old Testament worship. The second offers advice on how to make the intellect firm. The third refers to communion with God. The fourth returns to Moses. This first cycle of proverbs seems to refer to the same cyclic movement of the intellect. They run as follows:

1. If anyone wishes to make fragrant incense, he is to mix clear frankincense, cinnamon, onycha, and oil of myrrh in equal proportions, according to the Law (Exod. 30:34-35). That means the tetrad of virtues, for if these four are complete and equally balanced, the mind will not be betrayed (or, perhaps, forsaken).
2. A soul that has been purified by means of the fullness of the commandments establishes for the mind a position of steadiness and makes it receptive to the stable condition that is required.
3. Prayer is a conversation of the mind with God. So what kind of mental state is needed if the mind is to be capable of reaching out unwaveringly toward its own Lord, to converse with him without any intermediary?
4. If Moses was stopped, when he tried to approach the bush that was burning on earth, until he had taken off his shoes from his feet (Exod.

---

26. See, recently, David E. Linge, "Leading the Life of Angels: Ascetic Practice and Reflection in the Writings of Evagrius of Pontus," *Journal of the American Academy of Religion* 68.3 (2000): 537-68.

3:2-5), do you think that you need not put off every passioned thought (νόημα) from yourself if you want to see him who is above all perception and all concepts, and converse with him?

Evagrius here makes the monk the equivalent of Moses, and also the superior to Moses, since he will later refer to the monk as "equal to an angel," who sees God not under a form, but in intelligible sight.

The next three passages underline the importance of the monk's prayer as worship in the spiritual temple. Evagrius anticipates the obstacles to this state, particularly in direct references to biblical passages about the temple or tabernacle. Chapter 21 states: "'Leave your gift before the altar and go be reconciled with your brother,' our Lord said — and then you shall pray undisturbed. For memory of wrongdoing blinds the reason of the man who prays, and casts a cloud over his prayer." In chapter 29, Evagrius writes, "Sometimes when you stand for prayer you will immediately start praying well, but at other times you will not attain your goal even after much toil. This is to make you seek all the more. . . ." In chapter 44, he refers to the exterior tabernacle: "If your mind is still looking around at the time of prayer, it has not yet realized that it is a monk who is praying; it is still a worldling, decorating the exterior tabernacle."[27]

Another chain of chapters begins after a discussion of the role of daemons, particularly in producing visions of light in the praying monk. Here the monk is seen as a fulfillment of the type of eschatological worship portrayed in the Apocalypse, receiving angelic assistance not only in his struggle but in the accomplishment of the liturgy.

75. The angel of the Lord comes and stops all our enemies' activity with only a word and stirs the mind's light to operate without deception.

76. When it says in the Apocalypse that the angel takes incense to add to the prayers of the saints (Rev. 8:3), I think this refers to that grace that is wrought by means of the angel. He implants knowledge of true prayer, so that thereafter the mind stands unshaken by listlessness and negligence.

77. The incense bowls that the twenty-four elders offered are said to be the prayers of the saints (Rev. 5:8). By "bowl" (φιάλην) we are to understand the friendship (φιλίαν) with God or perfect, spiritual love in which prayer is effected in Spirit and Truth.

80. If you pray truly, you will find great assurance and angels will accom-

27. The translation is Tugwell's; see n. 5 above.

pany you as they accompanied Daniel (Dan. 7:16), and they will enlighten you about the rationale of what is happening.

81. You should realize that the holy angels prompt us to pray and stand by
us, rejoicing and praying for us. Yet if we are negligent and accept inimi-
cal thoughts, we offend them greatly because, while they are striving so
intensely for us, we are not prepared even to supplicate God on our own
behalf, treating our own act of worship with contempt and abandoning
their Lord and God, in order to consort with unclean demons.

Not only, according to Evagrius, does the monk receive angelic assistance; he
also receives that assistance in order to enter their state. In chapter 141, he
writes, "The person who has moved away from all that is here to hold citizen-
ships in heaven (Phil. 3:20) the whole time, not just in mere words but in angelic practice and divine knowledge, he it is who desires to pray."

A final chain of chapters returns the end of the book to the theme with
which it began:

147. If God, who needs nothing and accepts no bribes, refused to receive the
man who came to the altar with his gift until he was reconciled with his
neighbor who was upset at him (Matt. 5:24), consider what degree of
watchfulness and discernment we need if we are to offer an acceptable
incense to God at the intellectual altar.

151. It is not simply quantity that makes prayer praiseworthy, it is rather
quality. This can be seen from the two men who went up to the temple
(Luke 18:10-14) and from the saying "When you pray, do not go gab-
bling on" (Matt. 6:7) and other such texts.

152. As long as you are paying attention to the appropriateness of your
bodily stance, as long as your mind is busying itself with looking after
the attractiveness of the tabernacle, you have not yet seen the place of
prayer; the blessed way of prayer is still far from you.

153. When you have joy beyond any other in performing your service of
prayer, then you have truly found prayer.

Here the monk has become prospectively restored to the angelic *katastasis* by
taking the path from the external symbols of incense, altar, and temple, as indicated in the text of Exodus and Revelation, to the internal state of conversation with God that is both his own goal and the goal of the divine economy.

If one series of chapters in the *Chapters on Prayer* shows the monk how
to participate in the prayer and contemplation of patriarchs, prophets, and
apostles, the prologue provides a justification, in the form of a letter, for com-

posing the chapters in the first place. Evagrius writes: "I was feverish with the flame of impure passions, and my mind was afflicted with shameful thoughts when you customarily revived me with the touch of your God-loving letters, happily (μακαρίως) imitating our great teacher and master." Here he refers punningly to Macarius the Great, but also to the way in which material letters had restored his own health. The next line gives the reason for their power: the unnamed recipient enjoys a superior status, for Evagrius compares him with the visionary patriarch Jacob: "And no wonder! for you have always been blessed like Jacob, whose share was 'the marked ones'" (Gen. 30:25-42). It is his desire that, like Jacob's, won Evagrius's health: "You have served well for Rachel; now that you have been given Leah and 'fulfilled her week,' you seek your well-beloved [Rachel], too" (Gen. 29:15-30).

Where his correspondent had been successful, though, Evagrius pretends to have failed; and he next employs the image of Peter as fisherman fishing at Christ's command to show that he stands in the position of apostle to his correspondent, who is like Christ. He writes in the next paragraph: "But I, I will not deny that I have worked all night and caught nothing (Luke 5:5-10), but when at your command I let down my nets (John 21:11) I caught a host of fish, not, I think, big ones, but 153 of them, and I am sending them to you in a basket (Matt. 5:15) of love, in an equal number of chapters, fulfilling your commandment."

Here, in the second paragraph, Evagrius has not only shifted scenes but has combined two separate events at the beginning and end of Christ's leadership of the apostles. The first is the calling of Peter and his partners James and John, "the fishers of men," and the second is Jesus' appearance after his resurrection, to disciples fishing at the Sea of Tiberias, where Jesus again instructs them how to catch fish — that is, to lure men into the net of the gospel. Evagrius hints, here, as he did in the first paragraph, that these texts have two meanings: the literal (the desire of Jacob, the fishing instructions of Jesus) and the spiritual (Leah stands for the exercise of the virtues in the *praktike* and Rachel stands for longed-for contemplation, while the apostle Peter and the fish signify a teacher who lures his students with hidden and spiritual meaning). Furthermore Evagrius has now elevated the position of his correspondent from Jacob, in the first paragraph, to Christ, in the second.

In the very next paragraph, Evagrius reveals the force behind these comparisons: it is desire that moves the disciple to imitate his master, and desire that moves the mind from considering an external sign to an internal reality; here Evagrius signals that there will be a spiritual interpretation of the 153 fishes. He writes:

> I admire and am very jealous of your excellent purpose in desiring these chapters on prayer. It is not just these external chapters that you want, which exist only thanks to ink on a piece of paper; you desire chapters fixed in the mind through love and the forgetfulness of injury (ἀγάπης, καὶ ἀμνησικακίας). Since "everything is twofold, one facing another," as the wise Jesus says (Ecclus. 42:24), receive these chapters in the spirit as well as in the letter. Furthermore, you must know that mind takes precedence in every way over the letter, because without mind there will be no letter. Likewise, the habit (τρόπος) of prayer is twofold, one active, the other contemplative.

To this description of the twofold (internal and external) quality of human activity, Evagrius adds a final line: "In the same way there is also the duality of number, the external surface, or quantity (ποσότης), and the significance, which is quality (ποιότης)."

Here Evagrius enters into a complex division of the number 153. The purpose of the division is to extract the quality, or symbolic meaning, of the number from its apparent meaning, which is merely arithmetical. At this point in the prologue, Evagrius humorously turns the tables on his respected correspondent, revealing that he is the one who feeds his correspondent with fish, thereby suggesting that he, too, plays the role of Christ in the exchange: "In dividing my book on prayer into 153 parts, I am sending you a morsel from the Gospels, to give you the pleasure of a symbolic number. . . ." Evagrius plays with the quantity of numeration, breaking the main number down into smaller proportions that have symbolic meaning, in order to arrive at its quality, which he here lists as "knowledge of the Trinity," "the delimitation of this world-order," "the tetractys of the virtues," "the wise knowledge of this world," and "the spherical nature of time." All together, 153 can signify the three levels of knowledge — faith, hope, and charity — and "gold, silver, and jewels."

Evagrius here depended on an already ancient theory of numeration that referred to the sums of certain patterns of numbers as triangular, square, spherical, and so forth. In addition, the episode of the catching of the 153 fish also attracted Jerome's interpretation.[28] Yet Evagrius's object here is not the deployment of a neo-Pythagorean numerology for its own sake, but a demonstration that the gospel itself means to signal its readers to look for the quality of its own numbered symbol. That quality had a curative effect, to judge by the last paragraph of the prologue:

28. See Bamberger, *Praktikos,* p. 54.

So much, then, for the number of the chapters. They are humble, but you will not be ashamed of them since you are familiar with both plenty and want and you have certainly not forgotten him who, far from rejecting the widow's two mites (Mark 12:44), welcomed them more than the wealth of many others. You know how to preserve the fruit of goodwill and love for your true brothers — so pray for me in my sickness, that I may become well and then take up my bed and walk (Mark 2:11), by the grace of Christ.

The twofold meaning of the Scripture has reminded Evagrius of the widow's two coins, and here he reminds his correspondent that his exegesis, though poor, has by implication also received the approbation of Christ. Evagrius may also here intend a reference to the poverty and humility of the monk. Quickly shifting scenes, Evagrius also portrays himself as the paralytic whose cure becomes one of the miracles of Christ. With this he concludes a prologue that has gathered images from different books of the Bible, emphasizing its unity; it has also alluded to the inner meaning of numbers and so attempted to point out the way in which space and time, those material realities defined by number, are seen to be of relative importance.

In this small example of monastic exegesis from one portion of one treatise, an entire world of interpretation begins to open up. Evagrius understands the trained and discerning monk to stand in the place of the patriarchs and in the place of Christ. In other works he will follow a similar procedure of exposition, right up to his contemplative interpretation of Genesis and the six days of creation as found in the *Kephalaia Gnostica*. A complete description of his exegesis, even of so limited a portion of the Bible as the book of Genesis, awaits further study, but it will be seen to be the foundation of both his mysticism and his monastic practice.

Women and the Image of God according to St. John Chrysostom

NONNA VERNA HARRISON

In discussions of women in Greek patristic theology, the views of St. John Chrysostom are among the most difficult to understand and interpret. This is partially explained by the vast extent and variety of his writings on the subject, but there are other reasons as well. Besides being a brilliant orator, he is primarily a pastor and a moralist. His genius as a teacher lies in showing how the principles of Christian doctrine and ethics he reads in Scripture can be applied practically in the daily life of his audience. Because the daily life of today is so different from that of the late fourth and early fifth centuries, and the social structure of our culture differs fundamentally from that of the Late Antique Mediterranean world, the pastoral import of his teachings cannot be adequately understood without a clear perception of their social context.[1] Another factor is his use of rhetorical techniques, which include exaggeration and the manipulation of commonplace cultural stereotypes, to build rapport with his audience and thus persuade them to repent and practice virtue. These techniques would have been easily recognized by Late Antique audiences, who may not have taken the stereotypes at face value. Robert L. Wilken's astute observations about how Chrysostom's anti-Jewish diatribes need to be read in light of these rhetorical practices apply equally to his denunciations of alleged feminine vices.[2]

---

1. See my review essay, "The Inevitability of Hermeneutics: David C. Ford on St. John Chrysostom," *St. Vladimir's Theological Quarterly* (forthcoming).

2. Robert L. Wilken, *John Chrysostom and the Jews: Rhetoric and Reality in the Late 4th Century* (Berkeley: University of California Press, 1983), pp. 95-127.

In addition, Chrysostom is an Antiochene exegete. Although his method of drawing profound ethical insights from the literal sense of the biblical text is distinctive, his underlying approach to the text is closest to the interpretive methods of his teacher Diodore of Tarsus and his friend and fellow student Theodore of Mopsuestia. Their ways of reading the human creation narratives in Genesis 1–2, and in particular their definition of the "image of God" in Genesis 1:26-27, differ markedly from the better-known interpretations of the Alexandrians and Cappadocians. John follows his Antiochene colleagues in interpreting this material, and this accounts for some features of his understanding of women, the divine image, and human identity that have baffled scholars. The Alexandrians and Cappadocians read Genesis 1:26-27 together with Galatians 3:28 and conclude that men and women alike are created according to God's image, a position that has become standard in subsequent Christian theology. In contrast, the Antiochenes Diodore and Theodore read Genesis 1:27b in terms of Genesis 2:18-24 and 1 Corinthians 11:3-12 and conclude that woman is not made in the image of God. Yet all are agreed that woman is fully human and of the same essence as man, is capable of the same virtue and sanctification, and hopes in Christ for the same eschatological reward.[3]

A full discussion of Chrysostom's views of women and human identity is beyond the scope of this brief essay, but I will attempt to elucidate two aspects of the topic in light of his Antiochene formation as an exegete. First I will consider the relationship of woman to the divine image in his *Homilies* and *Sermons on Genesis*. Then I will examine the place of gender in the communal dimension of human identity as described in his *Homily 26 on 1 Corinthians* and his *Homily 20 on Ephesians*.

The Divine Image and Likeness

Like Diodore and Theodore, John understands the "image" in Genesis 1:26 as referring to the authority of which the verse speaks, the human being's dominion over the earth and all its living creatures:

> In saying, "Let us make a human being in our image and likeness," he did not stop there, but through the following verse made clear for us what

---

3. For a detailed analysis of the views of Diodore, Theodore, and Theodoret of Cyrrhus on this issue, see my "Women, Human Identity, and the Image of God: Antiochene Interpretations," *JECS* 9.2 (2001): 205-49.

was the reason for choosing the word "image." What in fact does the text go on to say? "Let them have control of the fish of the sea, the birds of heaven, and all the reptiles creeping on the earth" [Gen. 1:26]. So "image" refers to the matter of control (ἀρχῆς), not anything else; in other words, God created the human being to have control of everything on earth, and nothing on earth is greater than the human being, under whose authority everything falls.[4]

Like his closest exegetical colleague Theodore, Chrysostom describes Adam as the king of the visible and material creation, for whom all of it was created, the sky and the luminaries as well as earth, sea, plants, and animals. He explains that this is why the human being was created last; God prepared Paradise beforehand like a palace for the arrival of its royal human master.[5] Theodore understands the divine image as belonging to Adam in his role as God's cosmic mediator and viceroy on earth, a unique function that is not shared with Eve and is ultimately fulfilled by the last Adam, the man Jesus.[6] Although Chrysostom does not develop the same theological speculations about the relationship between the human being and creation, his emphasis on Adam's kingship suggests that he probably has a similar conception of the divine image. This may explain why he never actually says that Eve shares the divine image, even before the fall, although she does share Adam's authority over the creation, as we shall see.

John next addresses the question why "image" refers to authority and not to the human form. His answer is that if it referred to form, the woman would also share it since she has the same human form as the man, that is, in effect, she is of the same species. In a parallel text he actually says "image" refers to authority, not to οὐσία, and he adds that men and women are one in type, imprint, and likeness (ὁ τύπος καὶ ὁ χαρακτὴρ καὶ ἡ ὁμοίωσις).[7] Yet, like Diodore and Theodore, Chrysostom says woman cannot be made according to the divine image because of 1 Corinthians 11:7, which for the Antiochenes

---

4. *Hom. 8 in Gen.* 3 (PG 53:72); Robert C. Hill, trans., *Saint John Chrysostom: Homilies on Genesis 1–17*, FOTC 74 (Washington, D.C.: Catholic University of America Press, 1985), p. 110. For the Genesis homilies I will cite the section numbers in PG, which differ from the paragraph numbers in Hill's translation.

5. *Hom. 8 in Gen.* 3 (PG 53:71).

6. See Theodore's discussion in a long fragment on Gen. 1:26 preserved in Theororet of Cyrrhus, *Questions on Genesis* (PG 80:109a-12a).

7. *Ser. 2 in Gen.* 2 (SC 433:192-94). Most of this paragraph closely parallels the text quoted below from *Hom. 9 in Gen.* 4.

provides the biblical key to interpreting the human creation narratives in Genesis.

> Listen to Paul's words: "It is not proper for a man to cover his head, being the image and glory of God, whereas the woman is man's glory" [1 Cor. 11:7]. One is in command, the other is subordinate, just as God had also said to woman from the beginning, "your yearning will be for your husband, and he will be your master" [Gen. 3:16]. You see, since it is on the basis of command (ἀρχῆς) that the image was received, and not on the basis of form (μορφὴν), man commands everything whereas woman is subservient — hence Paul's words about man, that he is constituted of God's image and glory, whereas woman is man's glory. If, however, he had been speaking about form, he would not have distinguished between them, man and woman being identical in type (αὐτὸς τύπος), after all.[8]

In speaking of the man's authority over the woman, John is surely thinking of 1 Corinthians 11:3, "the head of a woman is her husband," as he reads Genesis 1:26. It is odd that he cites Genesis 3:16 here, the sentence God imposes on Eve following her sin. This was not said to Eve from the beginning in Paradise. John could have made his case just as well by citing Genesis 2:18, where she is called the man's helper. This citation of Genesis 3:16 leads to confusion because two homilies later Chrysostom says that the woman shares Adam's authority, and elsewhere he adds that in Paradise she is equal to him, as we shall see. Here the female subordination of 1 Corinthians 11 is linked to the fall, though elsewhere John appears to link it to her creation and thus to her authentic human identity and God's original creative intention. Scholars have thus disagreed over whether Chrysostom implicitly affirms that women share the divine image since they share authority over the earth and animals,[9] whether Eve originally possessed the divine image but lost it through the fall, or whether woman as one created subordinate to man never had the divine

---

8. *Hom. 8 in Gen.* 4 (PG 53:73); Hill, *Saint John Chrysostom*, p. 111. Cf. Joseph Deconinck, *Essai sur la chaîne de l'Octateuque avec une édition des commentaires de Diodore de Tarse qui s'y trouvent contenus* (Paris: H. Champion, 1912), pp. 95-96 (frag. 9); and Theodore's fragment on 1 Cor. 11:7 in Karl Staab, ed., *Pauluskommentare aus der griechischen Kirche aus Katenenhandschriften Gesammelt und Herausgegegen* (Münster: Aschendorff, 1933), p. 188, mislabeled as a fragment on 1 Cor. 11:8.

9. Valerie Karras, "Male Domination of Women in the Writings of St. John Chrysostom," *Greek Orthodox Theological Review* 36 (1991): 131-39; David C. Ford, *Women and Men in the Early Church: The Full Views of St. John Chrysostom* (South Canaan, Penn.: St. Tikhon's Seminary Press, 1996), pp. 46-47, n. 28.

image.[10] Geoffrey V. Gillard states flatly that John contradicted himself on this issue.[11]

Chrysostom does not actually say that woman is created in God's image, and in this passage he says she is not. One wonders, then, how this can be consistent with his affirmations of her full humanity as well as her equality with Adam in Paradise and her sharing in the same cosmic authority. After all, he has defined the image as consisting precisely in this authority. To answer this question, we have to examine what Chrysostom says about Eve's creation, her relationship with Adam in Paradise, and how this relationship changes after the fall.

Like Theodore, John asserts that in speaking of "male and female" Genesis 1:27b is simply stating beforehand what God will do when he fashions Eve from the side of Adam in Genesis 2:21-22.[12] The Antiochenes' understanding of woman's identity is accordingly based primarily on the second creation account, to which we will turn shortly, not the first. Hence Chrysostom says that when God gives "them" in plural dominion over the earth and animals in Genesis 1:28 he is graciously extending this authority to Eve as well as Adam even before she is created.

> Behold the remarkable character of the blessing! I mean, those words, "Increase and multiply and fill the earth," anyone could see are said of the brute beasts (τῶν ἀλόγων ζώων) and the reptiles alike, whereas "Gain dominion and have control" are directed to the man and woman. See the Lord's loving kindness: even before creating her he makes her sharer in this control and bestows on her the blessing. "Have control," the text says, "of the fish of the sea, the birds of heaven and all the cattle, the whole earth and all the reptiles creeping on the earth." Did you notice the ineffable authority? Did you notice the great control? Did you notice all created things made subordinate to this being? No longer entertain casual impressions of this rational being (τοῦ ζῴου τούτου τοῦ λογικοῦ) but rather

---

10. Elizabeth A. Clark, *Jerome, Chrysostom, and Friends* (Lewiston, N.Y.: Edwin Mellen, 1979), p. 6; Frederick G. McLeod, *The Image of God in the Antiochene Tradition* (Washington, D.C.: Catholic University of America Press, 1999), pp. 198-205.

11. Geoffrey V. Gillard, "God in Gen. 1:26 according to Chrysostom," in *Studia Biblica 1978*, 3 vols., ed. E. A. Livingstone (Sheffield: Department of Biblical Studies, University of Sheffield, 1979), 1:149-56, 152. Astonishingly, Gillard refers to the issue of whether woman is included in the image as a "minor point."

12. See Theodore's fragments on Genesis in Robert Devréesse, *Essai sur Théodore de Mopsueste*, Studi e testi 141 (Rome: Cittia del Vaticana, Biblioteca Apostolica Vaticana, 1948), pp. 15-18.

realize the greatness of the honor and the Lord's benignity towards it, and be amazed at his love beyond all telling.[13]

Notice that in addition to emphasizing how she is honored and blessed by God and given cosmic authority, John declares her to be rational, that is, a fully human being in contrast to the nonrational animals. Elsewhere he draws a parallel between Adam's giving names to the animals, which shows that he possesses authority like that of a master naming his slaves, and Eve's fearlessness in conversing with the serpent, which shows her authority over it.[14]

Chrysostom asserts in *Homily 9 on Genesis* 3 that the human likeness to God in Genesis 1:26 consists in gentleness, mildness, and virtue. In what must be a reminiscence of the standard Alexandrian and Cappadocian interpretation of the authority over the animals, wherein this verse is read allegorically to mean mastery of the beasts within oneself, he says that we human beings can attain these virtues by controlling our passions. This control can be achieved through our reason, fear of God, and good will.[15] The likeness to God is thus a possibility for all human beings, including undoubtedly women, through God's grace and the right use of their human faculties of rationality and free choice. Thus, for Chrysostom the potential of divine likeness is linked to human identity as such, unlike the divine image, which refers specifically to Adam's cosmic authority. This leads to the seemingly odd conclusion, noted by Elizabeth Clark, that for John women can bear the divine likeness though not the divine image.[16] These distinct concepts of image and likeness are more understandable in light of the fact that Theodore of Mopsuestia understands these terms in the same way.[17]

This also shows why two Orthodox scholars with otherwise very different perspectives, Valerie Karras and David C. Ford, both conclude that Chrysostom must have affirmed the presence of the divine image in women. The standard Orthodox understanding of the image of God in the human person is that it is constitutive of human identity as such and comprises those human faculties

---

13. *Hom. 10 in Gen.* 4-5 (PG 53:86); Hill, *Saint John Chrysostom,* p. 134 (modified).

14. *Hom. 9 in Gen.* 4 (PG 53:79); *Sermon 3 on Gen.* 2 (SC 433:210-12).

15. PG 53:78.

16. Clark, *Jerome, Chrysostom, and Friends,* p. 6.

17. See Devréesse, *Essai,* pp. 13-14; Françoise Petit, "L'homme créé à l'image de Dieu: Quelques fragments grecs inédits de Théodore de Mopsueste," *Le Muséon* 100 (1987): 269-81; Frederick G. McLeod, "The Antiochene Tradition Regarding the Role of the Body within the 'Image of God,'" in *Broken and Whole: Essays on Religion and the Body,* ed. Maureen A. Tilley and Susan A. Ross (Lanham, Md.: University Press of America, 1995), p. 36; and my "Women and the Image of God: Antiochene Interpretations," pp. 217-30.

that enable us to practice virtue and enter into communion with God. Accordingly, the likeness is understood as the actualization of this potential for virtue and communion through our free choice and cooperation with God. The likeness is thus an intensification and fuller actualization of the image. This position, though it oversimplifies patristic anthropology, is often regarded as representing a consensus of the Greek Fathers. John of Damascus summarizes it in his comment on Genesis 1:26: "Intellect and self-determination manifest what is according to the image, and likeness in virtue to the extent possible manifests what is according to the likeness."[18] Given these definitions, it would follow that since Theodore and John affirm that woman shares the same human nature as man, possesses all the requisite human faculties, and can attain God's likeness through virtue, *a fortiori* they must have affirmed that she shares the divine image as well. The texts show that they did not affirm this because they defined the key terms differently. However, the Orthodox interpreters are right in the sense that Theodore and John do believe women possess everything the Greek Fathers are generally understood to include in the image and likeness of God.

The Creation and Fall of Woman

The story of woman's creation begins with God's declaration, "It is not good for the human being to be alone. Let us make him a helper like himself" (Gen. 2:18). Chrysostom, like Theodore, sees this verse as echoing the "Let us make" of Gen. 1:26. In both cases, as he understands it, God the Father is consulting solemnly with his eternal Son about the formation of a creature of great dignity, a human being. This contrasts with the way everything else is created by a simple command, "Let there be. . . ." Further, John observes that in contrast to the other animals, many of which provide great help to humankind, this helper is to be like Adam, to be of the same kind, to accord with him fully. In other words, her equality with him is precisely what enables her to provide him the fullest and most effective help. As Chrysostom observes, since she is fully human and rational, she is the man's comfort, his companion, his conversation partner, his full collaborator.[19] When surrounded by all the

18. *Expositio fidei* 2.12, in Bonifatius Kotter, ed., *Die Schriften des Johannes von Damaskos* (Berlin: De Gruyter, 1973), 2:76.

19. *Hom. 14 in Gen.* 4 (PG 53:116). See *Hom. 15 on Gen.* 3 (PG 53:122), where Chrysostom also says that, since Eve is created from Adam's side, she shares the same οὐσία as he. Contrast Augustine's comment that woman is created to help man specifically in procreation, since a man would be a better helper to a man for any other purpose: *Literal Commentary on Genesis* 9.5 (PL 34:936; CSEL 28/1:273).

nonrational animals Adam is still fundamentally alone, but with Eve he has genuine company. Thus after the naming of the animals, as Scripture says,

"For Adam, however, there proved to be no helper like himself," as if blessed Moses were teaching us in saying these words that, while all these animals were created and received from Adam the assignment of names, nevertheless none of them proved to be adequate for helping him. Accordingly he wants to teach us about the formation of the being about to be brought forth and the fact that this being due for creation is the one he was speaking about. "Let us make him a helper like himself," meaning like him, of the same essence (οὐσία) as he, worthy of him, lacking nothing that is his. Hence the words, "For Adam, however, there proved to be no helper like himself," by which this blessed author shows us that whatever usefulness these irrational animals bring to our service, the help provided for Adam by woman is different and immeasurably superior.[20]

Chrysostom agrees with the standard Greek patristic interpretation of Genesis 2:21-23 in affirming that the fashioning of Eve from the side of Adam makes her fully human, of the same nature as he is, and thus equal to him. Adam recognizes this himself when he declares that she is "bone of my bone and flesh of my flesh."

Notice, however, that their relationship remains androcentric and asymmetrical. God creates the woman for the man and her function is to help him, not the other way around. Chrysostom seems to view her entirely from her husband's point of view. Thus he says, "The loving Lord made it his concern to create a helper for him of his kind; having arranged everything with this creature of his in mind," namely Adam, "and for his sake brought forth all this visible creation, after all the other beings he creates also woman."[21] Because she is equal to him and shares all the same human faculties, she can collaborate with him in his own specific tasks, tending and overseeing the garden and ruling the earth and its creatures. She shares in his cosmic authority so that she can assist him fully in everything he does. Moreover, her equality frees him from loneliness by giving him a real companion and dialogue partner. In modern terms she is a person just as he is a person, capable of free, mutual interaction in love, not a mere object, puppet, or slave.

Although she is created for his sake, she is most helpful as a genuine collaborator, so for her to fulfill this function their relationship must involve

20. *Hom. 15 in Gen.* 1 (PG 53:120); Hill, *Saint John Chrysostom,* p. 197 (modified).
21. *Hom. 15 in Gen.* 2 (PG 53:120); Hill, *Saint John Chrysostom,* p. 197.

genuine mutuality. She will help her husband most if he also helps her, enters into dialogue with her, and respects her freedom and dignity. This is the implication of Chrysostom's descriptions of ideal marriages, such as that of Abraham and Sarah. He says that Sarah obeyed Abraham and called him "lord," but she was happy to do this because Abraham took the initiative to obey her, doing everything she asked of him.[22]

Chrysostom also emphasizes the unity between Adam and Eve, and in this context he again cites 1 Corinthians 11. He observes that "from the outset the man and woman are one, as Paul also says, 'the man is head of the woman'" (Eph. 5:23; 1 Cor. 11:3).[23] Later he notes that although the first woman was made from the man, subsequently "man will come from woman — or rather, not from woman but from the cooperation of the two, as Paul also says." Here he quotes 1 Corinthians 11:8-11, which emphasizes their unity and interdependence: "Man is not from woman, but woman from man; and man was not created for woman, but woman for man. . . . Yet man is not independent of woman nor woman of man," since a human being is born from man and woman together.[24] As Frederick McLeod has observed, the Antiochenes emphasize the communal dimensions of human identity.[25] Thus Eve in Paradise must be understood as fully united with Adam, in complete harmony with him. This unity and the shared identity and activity that flow from it have their center and foundation in him, since her being is derived from his and she has been created for him, as his helper. This picture is clearly androcentric, yet because of her unity with him and her derivation from him as an equal partner, she shares fully in his mode of existence, including his cosmic authority. She does not live apart from him, yet her help to him and participation in his life are so complete that he does not live apart from her either. The Pauline image of head and body, which is a favorite of Chrysostom, expresses the unity and interdependence inherent in their relationship as much as its asymmetry.

Their unity and the harmony and mutuality that go with it are shattered by the fall. As Chrysostom describes it, part of what goes wrong is the overturning of hierarchical order. This disruption begins when Eve enters into dialogue with a nonrational animal in place of Adam, her appropriate conversation partner. "After all," John says, "there was no need for her to get involved in conversation with him [i.e., the serpent] in the first place; she should rather have conversed with the person for whose sake she came into being,

22. *Hom. 20 in Eph.* 6 (PG 62:143-44).
23. *Hom. 14 in Gen.* 4 (PG 53:115); Hill, *Saint John Chrysostom*, p. 188.
24. *Hom. 15 in Gen.* 3 (PG 53:122-23); Hill, *Saint John Chrysostom*, pp. 201-2.
25. McLeod, *Image of God*, pp. 230-31.

with whom she shared everything on equal terms, and whose helper she had been made."[26] God, recognizing the human need for dialogue, for a companionship of equals, created community among humans by giving Eve to Adam. Thus he also gave Adam to Eve as a dialogue partner. As the whole of Hellenic culture recognized, dialogue is an activity of rational beings. The nonrational serpent belonged to a lower level of creaturehood and did not belong within the circle of human companionship. *A fortiori,* as an instrument of the devil he was even more deserving of exclusion. Instead of speaking face to face with her equal, Adam, Eve turned downward to look to an animal twisted by evil.

A little later Chrysostom explains in greater detail how her sin disrupts hierarchical order. Rhetorically he addresses his accusations to her directly.

> O woman, what have you done? . . . You put faith in the words of the serpent, you regarded its advice as worthy of greater heed than the instruction given you by the Creator. . . . Surely you are not, after all, of the same species (ὁμογενής) as the one who offered you the advice? He happened in fact to be one of those subordinate to you, one of the slaves placed under your authority. Such being the case, why did you disgrace yourself, departing from the one for whom you were created, as whose helper you were made, in whose dignity you had equal share, one with him in essence (ὁμοούσιος) and one in language?[27]

Of course the root of her error, the fundamental overturning of order, is that she transferred her trust from God to a creature. John adds that this creature was under her authority and again emphasizes her dignity and equality with Adam. He adds elsewhere that Adam in turn disrupted proper order by listening to his wife's bad advice instead of guiding her. Yet he takes care to add, citing Paul, that it is commendable if a wife leads her husband to faith and virtue through good advice.[28]

In Genesis 3:16 the divine Judge sentences her to a punishment that fits her crime. Since she has disregarded her own dignity in obeying the serpent and misled Adam instead of assisting him, she is now truly subjected to her husband's authority. Chrysostom presents God as giving her the following admonition.

> In the beginning I created you equal in honor to your husband, and my intention was that in everything you would share with him as an equal,

26. *Hom. 16 in Gen.* 2 (PG 53:127); Hill, *Saint John Chrysostom,* p. 210 (modified).
27. *Hom. 16 in Gen.* 4 (PG 53:130); Hill, *Saint John Chrysostom,* p. 214 (modified).
28. *Hom. 17 in Gen.* 9 (PG 53:145-46).

and as I entrusted control of everything to your husband, so did I to you; but you abused your equality of honor. Hence I subject you to your husband: "Your desire shall be for your husband, and he shall rule over you." Because you abandoned your equal, who was sharer with you in the same nature (φύσεως) and for whom you were created, and you chose to enter into conversation with that evil beast the serpent, and to take the advice he had to give, accordingly I now subject you to him in the future and designate him as your master for you to recognize his lordship, and since you did not know how to rule, learn well how to be ruled. "Your desire shall be for your husband, and he shall rule over you." It is better that you be subject to him and fall under his lordship than that enjoying freedom and authority, you would be cast into the abyss. It would be more useful also for a horse to carry the bit and travel under direction than without this to fall down a cliff. Accordingly, considering what is advantageous, I want you to have desire for him and, like a body being directed by its head, to recognize his lordship pleasurably.[29]

According to Chrysostom, woman is subordinate to man both in Paradise and after the fall, but in two very different ways. In Paradise she is his dignified, free, and equal collaborator. He is to take the initiative in their shared activity, but she assists him fully. As her head and the source of her being, he has the responsibility of grounding and maintaining their relationship as one of mutuality, a dialogue among equals and collaborative activity. Her task is to respond in kind, and clearly all this is based on love and the community of being and life named by the metaphor of one body. This mode of partnership is described further in Chrysostom's depictions of ideal Christian marriage, which must be understood to approximate as far as possible the way of life in Paradise.[30]

After the fall the husband is the master and the wife his slave. To a Late Antique reader sensitive to the nuances of social location in a community structured by hierarchical relationships of different kinds, the contrast between these two kinds of subordination would have been blatantly obvious. There is a vast distance between a free, dignified Roman matron and a despised slave.[31] Their quality of life and the character and degree of their obe-

---

29. *Hom. 17 in Gen.* 8 (PG 53:144-45); Hill, *Saint John Chrysostom,* pp. 240-41 (modified).

30. See *Hom. 20 in Eph.* and *Hom. 26 in 1 Cor.*

31. On the Roman matron, see Kate Cooper, *The Virgin and the Bride: Idealized Womanhood in Late Antiquity* (Cambridge, Mass.: Harvard University Press, 1996).

dience differ accordingly. Chrysostom has designated the nonrational animals as slaves to humans, and in this passage he compares fallen Eve to one of them. She is like a horse that cannot avoid falling off a cliff without the guidance of its rider, without the painful restraint of a bit in its mouth.[32]

A parallel passage makes the contrast between helper and slave explicit. In *Sermon 4 on Genesis* John names the subjection of woman to man as one of three kinds of slavery caused by humans' fallen condition, all of which he says have been established by God for their benefit. The other two kinds are the subjection of slaves to their masters and the subjection of the whole populace to the civil authorities. The text says that in Genesis 2 the nonrational animals are created as slaves, but not the woman. He notes that animals like the horse, ox, and donkey are helpers to human beings, but not in the same way as Eve was to Adam.

> For since, when [the biblical writer] introduced the non-rational animals as sharers in providing help for the many needs of our life, that we might not consider the woman also to be among the slaves, see how he makes the distinction clear. . . . For he did not say merely that [Adam] did not find a helper for himself, but "he did not find a helper like himself"; not merely this but "in accord with himself." This was the case before the sin, but after the sin: "Your desire will be for your husband, and he will rule over you."[33]

Significantly, he adds that a woman's husband is given her by God as her refuge, harbor, and security, so that in whatever dangers may befall she can turn to him and take refuge in him. The harshness of her slavery is also tempered by their mutual ties of love and desire.[34] So this is not, after all, the same as the menial condition of a household bondservant subject to corporal punishment from the master. Indeed Chrysostom condemns wife beating as equivalent to the unspeakable crime of parricide.[35] When discussing marriage in different rhetorical contexts, he explores the different gradations of subordination ranging from the role of a Roman matron, who is like an army's lieutenant general or a ship's first mate,[36] to the role of a lowly slave. A married

32. Real horses, of course, can watch their footing perfectly well without such restraints.

33. Laurence Brottier, trans. and ed., *Jean Chrysostome: Sermons sur la Genèse*, SC 433 (Paris: Éditions du Cerf, 1998), pp. 222-24.

34. Brottier, *Jean Chrysostome*, p. 224.

35. *Hom. 26 in 1 Cor.* 7 (PG 61:222).

36. *Hom. 20 in Eph.* 1 (PG 62:136); *Hom. 26 in 1 Cor.* 8 (PG 61:224).

woman is faced with both possibilities as she and her husband can choose between virtue and sin, fallenness and the journey back toward Paradise, as they move through life together.

These distinctions account for Chrysostom's apparent inconsistencies as to whether woman's subservience to man begins in their original creation or in the fall. Initially, Eve is Adam's helper but is intended to become his equal dialogue partner and collaborator. They are called to live together in such harmony and unity that their inequality fades into insignificance, and she shares all that is his including his sovereignty over the visible creation. Both, after all, owe worship and obedience to God. Sin is what pushes them apart and magnifies their inequality into a master's domination of a slave. Through a life of virtue in communion with Christ this distance can be overcome.

Father and Son, Man and Woman

A fundamental insight that has emerged in twentieth-century Orthodox theology and is now shared by many Western Christians is the affirmation that, for human beings, to be made in the image of God is to be made in the image of the Trinity. This means that human identity is intrinsically constituted as a communion among persons who are defined by their mutual interrelatedness.[37] It is often assumed that this concept originates with the Greek Fathers, or more specifically with the Cappadocians. Although they draw analogies between the three divine persons and three human persons, in contrast to Augustine who compares the Trinity to three distinct faculties within a single human soul, they do not conceptualize the human *imago Dei* by reference to an explicitly trinitarian model. After all, in the fourth century the doctrine of the Trinity is itself being articulated for the first time. Hence it is understandable that its anthropological implications will not become fully manifest until later. Nor do the Cappadocians think of the human image of God primarily in communal terms.[38] They think rather of the faculties that enable each hu-

37. See, for example, Vladimir Lossky, *The Mystical Theology of the Eastern Church* (London: J. Clark, 1957), pp. 114-34; John D. Zizioulas, *Being as Communion: Studies in Personhood and the Church* (Crestwood, N.Y.: St. Vladimir's Seminary Press, 1985); Kallistos Ware, "The Human Person as an Icon of the Trinity," *Sobornost* 8 (1986): 6-23; and idem, "The Trinity: Heart of Our Life," in *Reclaiming the Great Tradition,* ed. J. S. Cutsinger (Downers Grove, Ill.: InterVarsity, 1997), pp. 125-46.

38. Yet they do acknowledge the communal aspects of human identity. Basil identifies profound anthropological reasons for preferring cenobitic to eremitical monasticism

man person to attain a likeness to God, such as reason, free choice, and the capacity for virtue and communion with the Creator, though to be sure this involves love and hence interrelatedness with others. The biblical starting point for their anthropological reflection is Genesis 1:26, which speaks of a single human being as bearing God's image.

Like Augustine, Theodore of Mopsuestia and Theodoret of Cyrrhus discern a likeness to the Trinity in the relationship among faculties within the human soul.[39] Yet the Antiochenes highlight the communal aspects of human identity, and this is perhaps their greatest contribution to the articulation of Christian theological anthropology. Because John Chrysostom emphasizes Genesis 2:18-24 and 1 Corinthians 11:3-12 as starting points for his reflection about human identity, he develops a clear understanding of its interpersonal dimension as manifested in Adam, Eve, and their descendants. He sees in the relationship between man and woman a parallel to the relationship between Father and Son in the Trinity. He does not regard this parallel as revealing the divine image in human community, since he has defined the image narrowly as authority, a point noted above. Yet his discussion of these issues provides a firm patristic foundation for contemporary discussions of the human image of the Trinity. It might be worth investigating the extent to which his writings have influenced the Orthodox theologians who have developed this concept, though we cannot pursue such an inquiry here.

In 1 Corinthians 11:3, Paul says, "The head of every man is Christ; the head of every woman is the man; and the head of Christ is God." Here, as a post-Nicene Father like Chrysostom would inevitably perceive it, the Apostle establishes an analogy among three very different kinds of relationships: (1) that of a man with Christ, a human being with the divine Savior; (2) that of a woman with a man, or a wife with her husband, one human being with another; and (3) that of the divine Son with the divine Father. In his *Homily 26 on First Corinthians,* John endeavors to sort out these three modes of relationship and distinguish the senses in which Paul's analogy is applicable from the senses in which it breaks down, as is inevitable in any analogy between created and divine realities.

---

in *reg. fus.* 3 (PG 31:916c-17a). Gregory of Nyssa thinks of humankind from the beginning to the end of history as one concrete whole, as David L. Balás explains in "*Plenitudo Humanitatis:* The Unity of Human Nature in the Theology of Gregory of Nyssa," in *Disciplina Nostra: Essays in Memory of Robert F. Evans,* ed. D. F. Winslow (Cambridge, Mass.: Philadelphia Patristic Foundation, 1979), pp. 115-33.

39. See Theodore in Devréesse, *Essai,* p. 14, n. 4; Natalio Fernández Marcos and Angel Sáenz-Badillos, eds., *Theodoreti Cyrensis Quaestiones in Octateuchum: Editio Critica* (Madrid: Textos y estudios Cardenal Cisneros, 1979), pp. 25-27.

Chrysostom presents his reflections on this point in the form of a debate with an imagined Arian opponent who seeks to use 1 Corinthians 11:3 to prove that Christ is inferior to the Father. In the course of this rhetorically constructed argument, the preacher whose usual focus is moral exhortation expresses insights about trinitarian theology that recall Athanasius and the Cappadocians. He first turns the tables on the Arian by using Paul's analogy to support the Nicene position: "For if the man is the head of the woman and the head is of one essence (ὁμοούσιος) with the body, and [if] God is the head of Christ, the Son is of one essence (ὁμοούσιος) with the Father."[40] A text in *Homily 20 on Ephesians* similarly identifies the headship in 1 Corinthians 11:3 with unity both in the Trinity and in marriage: "Paul says elsewhere, 'The head of Christ is God,' and I say that husband and wife are one body in the same way as Christ and the Father are one."[41] John presupposes that as human beings women are of the same essence as men, a point we have seen him make in several other places. He infers that likewise the Son is fully God and is of one essence with the Father.

In the imagined debate over 1 Corinthians 11:3 the preacher then represents his opponent as objecting that the Pauline headship refers not to a difference in οὐσία but to the Son's subjection under the Father. This argument is more difficult to refute since in Late Antique culture it is taken for granted that women are subjected to men. John responds by acknowledging and grappling with the complexities of the theological and exegetical problem.

He first makes a standard Nicene assertion that the Son's subjection pertains to the lowliness of his flesh in his incarnate state. Then he presents the Arian as taking 1 Corinthians 11:3 to mean that as the husband rules the wife, the Father rules the Son, and, what is even more problematic from a Nicene point of view, as Christ rules the man, the Father rules the Son. In reply Chrysostom speaks of the limitations of religious language. He explains that relationships between divine persons cannot be measured in the way relationships between human persons can. So the word "head" cannot have the same meaning in each clause of 1 Corinthians 11:3. Otherwise, he says, various absurdities would follow. "The Father will be as far above the Son as the Son is above us," since the Father is the head of the Son as the Son is the head of the preacher and the men in his audience. (If there are women in his audience, he does not acknowledge their presence at this point. It would only

---

40. *Hom. 26 in 1 Cor.* 2 (PG 61:214).
41. *Hom. 20 in Eph.* 4 (PG 62:140); Catharine P. Roth and David Anderson, trans., *St. John Chrysostom on Marriage and Family Life* (Crestwood, N.Y.: St. Vladimir's Seminary Press, 1986), p. 52.

complicate his argument.) Another interpretation he dismisses as absurd would make women as distant from "us" men as men are from the divine Logos. He would *not* claim that since men bear the divine image and women do not, men hold a godlike position above merely human women. He notes one further absurd reading of 1 Corinthians 11:3, namely, that as the Son is consubstantial with the Father, men are consubstantial with the Son and women with men, which would make all human persons divine just as the persons of the Trinity are divine.[42]

As Chrysostom says a bit later, when the same words are applied to divine and human matters, they mean different things in each case. Yet along with the differences there must be some similarities, otherwise language about God would have no meaning.[43] For example, when speaking of God the "Son," this term means he is of the same essence as the Father and comes from the Father, but it does not mandate the aspects of human generation that involve weakness and are incompatible with the divine. This is a standard anti-Arian point. Likewise, to say that Christ is the head of the Church is to say that the Church is united with him and has its origin from him, though the Church's union with him is more secure and its origination from him more honorable than in cases of merely human headship.[44] Although John does not say so explicitly, this must constitute his reading of the clause, "Christ is the head of man." Of course, in the Ephesians commentary the Church as Bride takes the place of the man in 1 Corinthians 11:3.[45] The issue here is not gender but the divine Savior's relationship to human beings he saves.

However, immediately after he notes the absurdities that follow if "head" is read the same way in each clause of 1 Corinthians 11:3, Chrysostom explores further how the relationship between Father and Son both parallels and differs from the relationship between man and woman. He begins by stating that his imagined Arian interlocutor is wrong to identify headship with rule and subjection as such, because in that case Paul would have used the example of a slave and a master, not that of a wife and a husband. He explains the difference as follows, together with its trinitarian implications.

---

42. *Hom. 26 in 1 Cor.* 2 (PG 61:214).
43. *Hom. 26 in 1 Cor.* 3 (PG 61:215).
44. *Hom. 26 in 1 Cor.* 3 (PG 61:216).
45. *Hom. 20 in Eph.* 3 (PG 62:138-39). In this rhetorically exquisite and theologically suggestive passage John observes that through baptism and the Eucharist Christians are united to Christ just as Eve is united to Adam as bone of his bone and flesh of his flesh, so that in each case the two become one flesh (cf. Gen. 2:23-24).

For though indeed the wife is subordinate to us, yet it is as a wife, as free, as equal in honor. And the Son also, though indeed he became obedient to the Father, yet it was as the Son of God, it was as God. For as the obedience of the Son to the Father is greater than that of human beings to those who have begotten them, so also his freedom is greater. For of course it cannot be that the Son's relations to the Father are greater and more genuine than those among human beings while the Father's relations to the Son are less. For if we marvel that the Son was obedient so as to come even to death, and death on a cross, and if we regard this as a great wonder concerning him, we should also marvel at the Father, that he begot such a Son, not as a slave under subjection, but as one who in freedom obeys and offers advice. For the adviser is not a slave. Yet again when you hear of an adviser, do not take this to mean that the Father is in need, but rather that the Son is equal in honor to the one who has begotten him.[46]

Like Eve in Paradise or Sarah in her ideal marriage to Abraham, the wife in this text is her husband's dignified collaborator. Although she ranks after her husband in hierarchical order, she is his equal, like him a human person endowed with freedom and rationality. Her obedience is not compelled but is a free response offered in love. Similarly, the Son is derived from the Father as second person of the Trinity, yet he is entirely free and equal to his Father. Indeed, because he is God he is more obedient than a merely human partner such as a wife, and interestingly he is also more free. Thus, for John the free obedience of an ideal wife points by analogy to the Son's relationship with his Father, yet the paradoxical union of absolute obedience and absolute freedom in the divine Son surpasses the limits of this human model. Chrysostom then emphasizes the reciprocity between Father and Son as well. The Father is wondrous in begetting a Son who is equal to him and placing him in the role of an adviser, a collaborator he consults as an equal, though he has no actual need for advice. To beget one fully equal to himself, to establish a hierarchical relationship of Father to Son that is immediately and simultaneously constituted as an absolute reciprocity among equals, and to share his place as ultimate first principle with a second person and by implication also a third are acts of ultimate divine humility. John sees this fatherly humility as paralleling the Son's voluntary acceptance of death on the cross.

If 1 Corinthians 11:3 says the husband is the head of the wife just as the Father is the head of the Son, then the Father's sublime humility is the model that the husband is called to follow. His task, then, is to take what is initially a

46. *Hom. 26 in 1 Cor.* 2 (PG 61:214-15).

hierarchical relationship in which his wife is subordinate and owes obedience to him and through his own example and conduct constitute it as a free, dignified, and reciprocal collaboration among equals. Chrysostom's descriptions of the spouses' duties to each other in *Homily 20 on Ephesians* and in later parts of *Homily 26 on First Corinthians* move toward such an understanding. He says that if the husband takes the initiative to love and obey his wife, she will obey him; he further declares that Abraham and Sarah obeyed each other in all things.[47] Significantly, the man, whom he regards as greater and stronger than the woman, bears the primary responsibility in making this work. Unlike some advocates of patriarchal marriage, John does not place the burden of holding the family together on the wife.

Here we see the roots from which can emerge a theology of the human family, and by extension all human community, as an image and likeness of the Holy Trinity. At the beginning of *Homily 20 on Ephesians,* a passage that alludes to Genesis 2:21-24 and 1 Corinthians 11:11-12, there is a lyrical description of how the whole human race is one and all human persons are interdependent because all are derived from a single root like branches of a tree, since Eve is formed from Adam and from them all others spring. Chrysostom concludes that the love between husband and wife and the ties of marriage and kinship are the forces that weld society together.[48] In these two homilies the Antiochene moralist comes close to articulating what theologians today understand as the human vocation of imaging the community of the Trinity. In this context of human unity in diversity and mutual interdependence, love's task is to reconfigure hierarchical structures by lifting the persons below up to the same level as those above them, thus transfiguring these structures into relationships of equal freedom, dignity, mutuality, and reciprocity.

Yet Chrysostom stops short of affirming an unequivocal trinitarian equality and reciprocity in marriage. Immediately after the passage we have quoted from *Homily 26 on First Corinthians* he speaks of how the analogy between human and divine relationships breaks down: "Do not therefore extend the example of the man and the woman to include everything," he says, "For with us the woman is reasonably subjected to the man, since equality of honor causes conflict."[49] In accordance with a Late Antique cultural presupposition, he is unable to believe that among humans a harmonious relationship among equals can truly be possible as it is among the divine persons. If

---

47. *Hom. 20 in Eph.* 6 (PG 62:143-44); *Hom. 26 in 1 Cor.* 6 (PG 61:221, end).
48. PG 62:135-36.
49. PG 61:215.

one human person is not hierarchically subordinated to the other, if one does not exercise authority while the other obeys, he believes that strife and chaos will necessarily follow. "Where there is equal authority," he says elsewhere, "there is never peace. A household cannot be a democracy, ruled by everyone, but the authority must necessarily rest in one person."[50] He believes the same about a city or a nation. As Valerie Karras observes, "he applies monarchist political theory to the question of [women's] submission."[51]

Chrysostom adds that the inapplicability of the trinitarian model is further compounded by the fall.

> For with us the woman is reasonably subjected to the man, since equality of honor causes conflict; and not only because of this, but also because of the deceit that happened in the beginning. For this reason, surely, she did not become subject immediately; nor, when he brought her to the man, did she hear any such thing from God, nor did the man say any such thing to her. He said she was "bone of his bone, and flesh of his flesh" [Gen. 2:23], but he nowhere made mention to her of rule or subjection. But when she used her authority badly and she who had come into being as a helper was found to be a betrayer and ruined everything, then she justly hears thereafter, "your desire will be for your husband" [Gen. 3:16].[52]

Here John summarizes the interpretation of Eve's sin and its consequences that we examined above in his *Homilies* and *Sermons on Genesis*. Again he affirms unity and equality between Adam and Eve in Paradise, though she remains her husband's helper. Her real subjection is a punishment and corrective for her sin, a point underlined here by the contrast between Genesis 2:23, which graphically expresses her unity and continuity of being with the man, and the divine judgment decreed in Genesis 3:16. John then returns to the theme of hierarchy as preventing strife and asserts that God prescribed woman's subjection to man since otherwise man would resent woman for having deceived him and led him into sin, resulting in unmitigated warfare between the sexes. The passage concludes by noting the contrast with God, that is, the Trinity, where one must not imagine any such possibility.[53] Among divine persons equality and harmony coexist, but not, in Chrysostom's view, among human persons. The impossibil-

---

50. *Hom. 20 in Eph.* (PG 62:141); Roth and Anderson, *St. John Chrysostom on Marriage and Family Life*, p. 53.

51. Karras, "Male Domination," p. 135.

52. *Hom. 26 in 1 Cor.* 2 (PG 61:215).

53. *Hom. 26 in 1 Cor.* 2 (PG 61:215).

ity of harmonious equality among humans is at least partly due to sin. One wonders to what extent John could have envisioned a human likeness to genuine trinitarian mutuality as emerging in the relationship between Adam and Eve in Paradise if the fall had not occurred.

Later in the homily, as the exegete interprets 1 Corinthians 11:7-12, he moves still further away from a trinitarian model of marriage. Following Paul, he notes that man is the image of God whereas woman is only the glory of man. As he reads 1 Corinthians 11, he identifies four ways in which men are superior to women:

> The first is that Christ is the head of us [men], and we of the woman [1 Cor. 11:3]; second, that we are the glory of God, but the woman of us [v. 7]; third, that we are not from the woman, but she is from us [v. 8]; fourth, that we are not for her, but she is for us [v. 9].[54]

Here a twenty-first-century reader might find it appropriate to apply some standard rules of patristic exegesis, namely, that difficult verses need to be read in the context of the overarching narrative of the Bible in which God offers love to all humankind without partiality and that, when the "plain" sense of a verse appears morally unworthy of God, one must look for an alternative reading. Moreover, a theologian of today could suggest the anthropological application of a key trinitarian principle that emerged from the long debates of the fourth century, namely, that the origination of one being from another need not mandate the inferiority or subjection of offspring to parent.

Clearly, though this homily contains brilliant insights, some of what it says cannot be pastorally applicable today. Yet it is noteworthy that the moral conclusion Chrysostom draws from the four types of male superiority is to emphasize, on the one hand, that husbands bear great responsibility toward their wives, whom they must treat with profound care and respect. On the other hand, he also emphasizes how wives must obey their husbands completely, even if their husbands batter them. He underlines the principle that each of us is responsible to God for fulfilling our own duties whether or not other people fulfill theirs. Today one could question this on the grounds that family life is communal and that accordingly husbands and wives cannot reasonably be expected to fulfill the duties to each other that Paul prescribes except by mutual consent and cooperation. However, Chrysostom goes on to condemn wife beating severely, comparing it to parricide.[55]

---

54. *Hom. 26 in 1 Cor.* 4 (PG 61:218).
55. *Hom. 26 in 1 Cor.* 4-7 (PG 61:218-22).

Citing 1 Corinthians 11:11-12, he speaks again of the mutual interdependence of men and women. Rhetorically, he uses ideas of male superiority to exhort men to honor women, not to oppress or abuse them.

> Consider that she is a woman, the weak vessel, but you are a man. For because of this you were appointed ruler (ἄρχων) and were given the rank of head, that you might bear the weakness of her who is ruled (ἀρχομένης). Therefore make your rule illustrious; and it will be illustrious when you do not dishonor the one who is ruled. And just as the king appears more majestic to the extent that he shows his viceroy as more majestic, but if he dishonors and disgraces the greatness of that rank he also cuts off not a little of his own glory; so also if you dishonor her who rules with you, you will in no common degree outrage the honor of your rule.[56]

Here Chrysostom observes astutely that honor is social and communal, and that it is increased when shared, not decreased. Yet his appeal to male vanity to move his audience toward his moral and pastoral goals clearly would not work rhetorically with many twenty-first-century audiences. For them the Late Antique assumption that women are weak lacks credibility, and so does the military command structure as a model for understanding marriage, a relationship of love. Yet the goal toward which the preacher directs his ancient Mediterranean male listeners who take for granted their superiority to women appears in context as a laudable one. He ends the homily with a beautiful description of the importance of love and harmony in marriage.

Fourth-century theological anthropology is a work in progress, not a definitive theological synthesis. As Christian discussions of human identity continue, John Chrysostom's insights about the loving transformation of hierarchical structures into relationships of mutuality and the divine persons as the ultimate model for community among human persons may prove invaluable. In his reflections on these themes, Genesis 2:18-24 and 1 Corinthians 11:3-12 play a central role. Although these biblical texts undeniably give rise to exegetical and hermeneutical difficulties, John shows how they can provide an avenue for exploring important aspects of gender and community in human identity. In a context free of Late Antique cultural presuppositions about women's inferiority and the impossibility of egalitarian modes of social organization, today's theologians can speak of human families and communities as called to manifest the image and likeness of the triune God more fully than Chrysostom would have thought possible.

56. *Hom. 26 in 1 Cor.* 7 (PG 61:222).

From "Holy Passion" to Sinful Emotion: Jerome and the Doctrine of *Propassio*

RICHARD A. LAYTON

Writers as diverse as Maximus and Augustine placed emotional attachments at the center of a theory of religious knowledge. Desire could bind the seeker for knowledge with the God who was sought, and the satisfaction of desire simultaneously enlarged the capacity for knowledge. Love, for thinkers such as Maximus and Augustine, was not an instrument for the acquisition of knowledge, but its indispensable condition. As the affections became central to human fulfillment, the classical vocabulary of the emotions inherited by these theorists likewise obtained a new, distinctively Christian cast.

I have profited greatly from this cogent explanation that Robert Wilken has given to the significance of "holy passion" in Christian ethical theory.[1] To acknowledge a small portion of this debt, I would like to examine how anxiety about "sin" similarly refracted Christian appropriation of classical theories of the emotions. The Latin scholar, Jerome, stood at the crossroads between the Greek East and the Latin West, and between the Late Antique and medieval worlds. His introduction into Latin exegesis of a doctrine concerning incipient stirrings of affective response, labeled *propassio,* reverberated with distant echoes in medieval thought. Through Jerome's offices, the concept of *propassio* became a memento of a distortion in human emotional experience embedded in the core of the self. The doctrine of *propassio,* and the

---

1. Robert L. Wilken, "Maximus the Confessor on the Affections in Historical Perspective," in *Asceticism,* ed. V. L. Wimbush and R. Valantasis (New York: Oxford University Press, 1995), pp. 412-23; idem, "Loving God with a Holy Passion," in R. L. Wilken, *Remembering the Christian Past* (Grand Rapids: Eerdmans, 1995), pp. 145-63.

anxiety it entailed, may shed light, even as does the ardent ideal of a holy passion, on the centrality of the emotions to Christian understandings of human identity and fulfillment.

The story begins not with Jerome, but with the Stoics, who identified a class of affects that embraced a spectrum of spontaneous responses that could temporarily disturb psychic balance. This species of a preliminary affect, which they called *propatheia,* performed an important function in the moral psychology of the school.[2] The Stoics were notable among ancient philosophical schools for their insistence that emotions were rational dispositions and for their denial of the origination of the passions in the impulses generated by an irrational component of the human psyche. The Stoics faced a troubling counter-example to this theory: all humans display a number of physical responses that resist rational control, from the blush of embarrassment to the pangs of sexual desire. As Aulus Gellius colorfully described, even a Stoic sage blanched with something like fear during a storm at sea.[3] Gellius's sage, and other Stoics, retorted that these nonrational responses, while psychic affects of a sort, nevertheless differed categorically from genuine emotions. In contrast to a true passion, a *propatheia* represented a transient and unfocused condition without goal-directed deliberation. While such conditions might be unpleasant, and may even initially seem alarming, they did not necessarily inhibit clear rational functioning.[4] *Propatheiai* were epiphenomena that played across the surface features of an individual, and which the well-trained philosopher could dispel. The impulse of genuine emotion, by contrast, stormed the citadels of reason and could not be dispatched by simple rational control.[5] Moreover, the Stoics considered emotions to consist in

---

2. For the origins and function of *propatheia* in Stoic thought, see B. Inwood, *Ethics and Human Action in Early Stoicism* (Oxford: Clarendon, 1985), pp. 175-81; J. Fillion-Lahille, *Le De ira de Sénèque et la philosophie stoïcienne des passions* (Paris: Klincksieck, 1984), pp. 163-69; K. Abel, "Das Propatheia-Theorem: Ein Beitrag zur stoischen Affektenlehre," *Hermes* 111 (1983): 78-97; B. Inwood, "Seneca and Psychological Dualism," in *Passions & Perceptions: Studies in the Hellenistic Philosophy of Mind,* ed. J. Brunschwig and M. C. Nussbaum (Cambridge: Cambridge University Press, 1993), pp. 150-83.

3. Aulus Gellius, *Noctes Atticae* XIX.1.4-8; trans. J. C. Rolfe (LCL; Cambridge: Harvard University Press, 1952).

4. Seneca, *ep.* 57.3-6, describes an occurrence of *propatheia* that he can distinguish from genuine fear. He reports that while passing through a tunnel he felt a "sort of mental shock and confusion" that was dispelled "at the first glimpse of the return of daylight . . . without thought or volition." While this anxiety caused discomfort, it did not impair his reasoning or require conscious suppression by his rational faculties.

5. *Stoicorum veterum fragmenta* 3.377-78.

the mental "assent" of an agent either to obtain a desired end or to avoid an undesirable outcome. The defining mark of a *propatheia* was precisely the absence of this practical dimension.

For the Stoics, the experience of *propatheia* gave vivid expression to the vicissitudes of the human condition but did not constitute a morally relevant psychic event. The evaluation of this type of affect differs dramatically at the end of the career of *propatheia* as a psychological concept. Through the standard compendia of exegesis and systematic theology — the *Glossa Ordinaria* and the *Sentences* of Peter Lombard — this preliminary affective response became part of the "daily bread" of the medieval theological student.[6] As Lombard taught his students, the *propassio* revealed traces, inscribed in the deepest recesses of the self, of the original rebellion of Adam against the divine law.[7] The emotional fluxes of every individual provided a daily reminder of the due punishment of original sin. As an early warning of a soul restive against divine authority, the *propassio* should be monitored vigilantly. Lombard and other Scholastic theologians were scarcely aware of the distance that separated their use of preliminary affective movements from the Stoic concept of

6. See, e.g., *Glossa Ordinaria* (PL 114:94, 169, 488). On the *Glossa Ordinaria,* see M. T. Gibson, "The Place of the *Glossa Ordinaria* in Medieval Exegesis," in *Ad Litteram: Authoritative Texts and Their Medieval Readers,* ed. M. D. Jordan and K. Emery, Jr. (Notre Dame, Ind.: University of Notre Dame Press, 1992), pp. 5-28; B. Smalley, "Glossa Ordinaria," in *Theologische Realenzyklopädie,* ed. Gerhard Krause et al. (Berlin: Walter de Gruyter, 1976-), 13:452-57 (with bibliography). I owe the designation of the *Glossa Ordinaria* as the "daily bread" of the theological student to Beryl Smalley, "Gilbertus Universalis, Bishop of London (1128-1134) and the Problem of the Glossa Ordinaria," *Recherches de théologie ancienne et médiévale* 7 (1935): 235. On the use of *propassio* in medieval exegesis see the texts gathered by D. Odon Lottin, "Les mouvements premiers de l'appetit sensitif de Pierre Lombard à Saint Thomas d'Aquin," in his *Psychologie et morale aux XIIe et XIIIe siècles* (Gembloux: J. Duculot, 1948), 2:493-589.

7. Odon of Ourscamp, *Quaestiones magistri* in Jean Baptist Pitra, ed., *Analecta novissima Spicilegii Solesmensis altera continuatio* (Paris: Roger and Chernowitz, 1885-88), 2:183-84: "Peccavit Adam propassione, non tamen venialiter, sed criminaliter: habuit enim in potestate sua refrenare motus primarios, nos autem non habemus." Odon was a student of Peter Lombard, and the passage attributed to him in this section of Pitra's edition of the *quaestiones* probably derives from lecture notes of Lombard's students. See *Dictionnaire de Spiritualité* 11:628. The sentiment agrees with that of another student of Lombard, Peter of Poitiers, *Sententiarum libri quinque* 2.21 (PL 211:1026b): "quando motus sensualitatis concipit illecebram peccati absque omni cogitationis delectatione; et talis motus est culpa levissima, quia primi motus non sunt in prima hominis potestate, et per generalem confessionem delentur dicendo Confiteor, et a Graecis dicitur *propatheia,* a nobis vero, *propassio.*"

propatheia. In all likelihood, medieval writers depended for the doctrine of *propassio* solely on Jerome, who both introduced the term *propassio* into Latin and set the controlling theoretical framework for its application.

Jerome appropriated the concept of a preliminary affective response as part of his endeavor to make the exegesis of Origen and Didymus the Blind available for a Latin readership.[8] He encountered the *propatheia* no later than his *Commentary on Ephesians,* one of four expositions on the Pauline letters published shortly after his permanent resettlement to Bethlehem in 386.[9] The Pauline commentaries were the scholar's first (successful) effort to produce a biblical commentary under his own authorship, and he depended heavily on Origen to guide him through the difficulties of the epistles.[10] Origen invoked *propatheia* to explain the Apostle's admonition "Be angry (ὀργίζεσθε) and do not sin" (Eph. 4:26). Origen held that this instruction, which Paul cited from the Psalms, conceded that even the perfect would experience an involuntary stimulus to passion, but that the saint must withhold "assent" to the provocation. To secure this interpretation, Origen distinguished between two ways in which one might "become angry":

> Two meanings are indicated by the expression "to become angry" (τῆς ὀργίζεσθαι φωνῆς). One meaning refers to something involuntary, which some have called *propatheia,* which will be an involuntary occurrence even to the perfect when they suffer such mishaps as call forth anger. Another meaning, however, is indicated when the assent is given to the suitability of exacting punishment against the one thought to have committed the injustice, which the Apostle commands us to set aside as being within our free will. Therefore it is clear that it is the first of these meanings in "Be angry and do not sin," which is said instead of "even if you admit anger, do not act upon it."[11]

Following the Stoic theory of the affections, Origen observed a categorical

8. I discuss in detail the use of *propatheia* in the exegesis of Origen and Didymus in R. A. Layton, "*Propatheia:* Origen and Didymus on the Origin of the Passions," *VChr* (forthcoming).

9. For the date of Jerome's Pauline commentaries, see P. Nautin, "La date des commentaires de Jérôme sur les epîtres pauliniennes," *Revue d'Histoire Ecclésiastique* 74 (1979): 5-12.

10. The four commentaries on the Pauline epistles are the earliest exegetical works Jerome published under his own authorship. Jerome, *Abd.,* praef. (CCSL 76:349) mentions as a piece of juvenalia an exposition of the prophet, which he buried in obscurity.

11. Origen, *comm. in Eph.,* frag. XIX.68-75 (*JThS* 3 [1902]: 420).

distinction between an involuntary provocation and a genuine emotion. As an inevitable aspect of the human condition, to which even the "perfect" are subject, the *propatheia* was permitted. Granting "assent" to the stimulus, however, was within the rational capacity of anyone, and consequently a wrongful exercise of reason. This use of the concept is in complete correspondence with the function of *propatheia* in Stoic moral psychology.

In his own comments Jerome relies on Origen, even though he does not employ the term *propassio*:

> The term "anger" *(irae nomen)*, however, is understood in a two-fold sense not only by us, but by the philosophers as well. [It can be understood] either as when we are excited by natural stimuli *(naturalibus stimulis)*, having been provoked by an injury, or when, the impulse having been quieted and the wrath quenched, the mind is able to exercise judgment and nevertheless desires revenge against the person believed to have caused the injury. I judge, therefore, that the first kind of anger is meant here, and a concession is made to us as human beings. So that, even should we be stirred at the appearance of something disgraceful, and it disturbs the tranquility of mind even as some gentle wind, we ought not be tossed about in swelling waves by the force of wrath.[12]

Jerome's purpose is the same as Origen's: to place constraints on the apparent Apostolic permission of anger. Jerome, however, makes a slight, but telling, alteration to Origen in supporting his reading of Paul. Origen placed interpretive emphasis on the verb ὀργίζεσθε to demarcate a frontier in the process of "becoming angry" between passive susceptibility to external stimuli and movements of will subject to one's control. Jerome, by contrast, holds that two separate forms of passion can be derived from the category of "anger" *(irae nomen)*. Where Origen distinguished between two distinct moments in the continuum of emotional response, Jerome distinguishes between two species of anger. Philosophers, as Jerome indicates, differentiated between the heat of fury and the cool calculation of revenge but assigned this distinction to the typology of emotions rather than to separate points in psychological response.[13] Jerome

---

12. Jerome, *Ephes.* 2.4.26a (PL 26:510, Vallarsi, 628). The Migne edition of Jerome's Pauline commentaries in the *Patrologia Latina* reprints the earlier edition of Domenico Vallarsi (Venice, 1769). There were, however, two editions of the Migne (in 1845 and 1884) that varied in pagination, while retaining the Vallarsi page numbers embedded in the text. To reduce confusion, I give here both the 1845 edition of PL and Vallarsi's original pagination.

13. See *Stoicorum veterum fragmenta* 3.395, 398; cf. Basil, *Hom. adv. eos qui*

pays closer attention to the ethical inferences that Origen draws than to the psychological foundations for those conclusions, and misconstrues the relationship posited between an initial stimulus and the structure of a mature emotion.

When he composed his *Commentary on Matthew* in a hasty burst of activity before Easter 398,[14] Jerome again confronted exegetical problems that his predecessors resolved by means of *propatheia*. Arriving at the well-known stricture against committing "adultery in the heart" (Matt. 5:28), Jerome invokes the term *propassio* for the first time:

> There is this difference between *pathos* and *propatheia,* that is, between *passio* and *propassio:* a *passio* is regarded as a fault, but a *propassio* (even though it possesses culpability as a beginning) is not held in blame. Therefore, "whoever sees a woman" and his soul is tickled, has been struck by a *propassio.* If, however, he should consent and produce a disposition *(affectum)* from the thought, even as it is written in David: "they will pass over in the disposition of the heart" (Ps. 72[73]:7), he has crossed from *propassio* to *passio* and does not lack the will to sin, but the opportunity. Whoever sees a woman "for lust" *(ad concupiscendum),* that is, if he has looked upon her that he might lust, he is rightly said "to have committed adultery with her in his heart," as he is disposed to act.[15]

Origen's comments to this verse are now lost, but there is little reason to doubt that Jerome depends here on the Alexandrian exegete.[16] He invokes *propatheia* to restrict the emotional state that constitutes "lust" and thereby to ameliorate the severity of Jesus' command. He exploits the qualifying expression *ad concupiscendum* to differentiate between the spontaneous response to perception and the formulation of an intention.[17] By identifying

---

irascuntur (PG 31:369A). Jerome, *Ephes.* 3.4.31 (PL 26:516, Vallarsi, 636), subsequently distinguishes between θυμός *(furor)* and ὀργή *(ira)* in exactly the same terms: "Furor vero incipiens ira est, et fervescens in animo indignatio. Ira autem est . . . quae furore restincto desiderat ultionem, et eum quem nocuisse putat, vult laedere." These remarks depend as well on Origen, *comm. in Eph.,* Fr. XXII.7-8.

14. See Jerome, *Matt.,* praef.; *epp.* 71.5, 73.10; and E. Bonnard, *Saint Jérôme: Commentaire sur S. Matthieu,* SC 242 (Paris: Éditions du Cerf, 1977), 1:11-14.

15. Jerome, *Matt.* 1.5.28 (CCSL 77:30-31).

16. Jerome, *Matt.* praef., acknowledges using Origen's commentary. Didymus, *Ps.T.* 76.15-17, 252.33-35, also uses the example of seeing a woman "for lust" to illustrate the occurrence of *propatheia*.

17. Cf. Augustine's interpretation of Matt. 5:28: *Serm. dom.* 1.12.33-36 (CCSL 35:35-39). Like Jerome, Augustine identifies three stages that constitute a completed sin: sugges-

two phases of emotional causation, Jerome demonstrates closer fidelity to the concept of *propatheia* than he achieved in the Ephesians commentary.

It is noteworthy, however, that Jerome is ambiguous concerning the culpability of the *propassio*. Assigning liability to *propassio* as a "beginning" could indicate either that in view of a completed "disposition" even the root of that condition is held blameworthy or that the susceptibility to spontaneous responses is itself culpable to some degree. Later in the commentary, Jerome confronts the assertion of the evangelist that Jesus "began to be grieved and to be deeply troubled" (Matt. 26:37) and expressed his fear to his disciples, "I am deeply grieved even to death" (26:38). The emotion of "grief" (λύπη) was one of the four cardinal passions in Stoic theory, the very existence of which was itself culpable in a sage.[18] How could such an affective state be applied to Christ? Jerome again applies the concept *propatheia* to this episode, strongly affirming that Christ's "grief" *(tristis)* refers only to the stage of *propassio* and therefore is not culpable.[19] As applied to Christ, the experience of *propassio* bears no ethical significance. Jerome appears unaware of the possible inconsistency of this declaration with his remarks to Matthew 5:28.

As the *Commentary in Matthew* suggests, Jerome identifies two events that paradigmatically define the experience of *propassio*. In the gospel narrative, Christ's anxiety before his arrest isolates a moment of utmost susceptibility to, and identification with, human emotions.[20] For the life of the saints, Jerome perceives that sexual arousal provides the telltale symptoms of the occurrence of ineradicable affects. Jerome addresses both of these situations in a homily on Psalm 15 (16), probably composed within a few years of the Matthew commentary.[21] Jerome treats the Psalm as a prophetic speech of Christ,

---

tion, delight, and consent. The similarities, however, are superficial. By "suggestion," Augustine refers to an affective movement that includes a prescribed course of action (cf. *Gen. Man.* 2.11.15; *trin.* 12.12.17). The "delight" stage of sin involves a sense of pleasure generated by the anticipation of filling a specific desire, and thus is not comparable to *propatheia*. Scholastic writers in the school of Laon attempted, without success, to harmonize the concept of *propatheia* with Augustine's three-stage system of sin. See Lottin, *Psychologie et morale*, vol. 5, no. 450; *Enarr. in Matt.* (PL 162:1294); *Glossa Ordinaria*, Rom. 6:12 (PL 114:488D-89A).

18. *Stoicorum veterum fragmenta* 3.412-20; Origen, *ser. 92 in Matt.* (GCS 38:205-6).

19. Jerome, *Matt.* 4.26.38-39 (PL 26:197-98), a judgment adopted by medieval exegetes: Paschasius Radbertus, *Matt.* 26.37-38 (CCSL Cont. Med. 56B:307); Peter Lombard, *Sent.* 3.15.6.

20. Jerome, *Matt.* 4.26.38-39. *Tract. psal.* 108 (CCSL 221:366) identifies Christ's experience of *propassio* before his arrest as the conclusive evidence, against Apollinaris, of his possession of a complete human soul. Jerome appropriates this use of *propatheia* in anti-Apollinarian polemic from Didymus, *Ps.T.* 293.6-12.

21. Two series of homilies by Jerome are extant and edited by G. Morin (first series,

and he links verse seven — "I shall bless the Lord who has given me under-standing, even until the night my kidneys have reproved *(increpauerunt)* me" — to Christ's psychic crisis before his arrest.[22] The kidneys metaphorically represent the innermost thoughts of the self, which the divine Word controls, enabling Christ to anticipate and endure his suffering without emotional dis-turbance. Jerome also notes that the "kidneys" can symbolize the generative organs, which produce the seeds or "beginnings of thoughts" *(exordia et principia cogitationum)*. Christ, "whom the Word of God daily instructed, was unable to sin not only in act and word, but even in thought and the be-ginnings of thoughts *(cogitationum exordiis)*, which they call προπάθειας."[23] Jerome here makes explicit the contention that the *propatheia* can be subject to moral evaluation. The *propassio* does not consist of an unfocused affective response, but a "thought" — an incipient, yet practical, mental state directed toward some action. While he studiously preserves Christ's inchoate mental processes from any contact with sin, Jerome also suggests that *propassio,* at least in some circumstances, can be ascribed blame.

The occurrence of *propatheia* in the Psalm homily is loaded with ambi-guity, pointing simultaneously to Christ's triumphant assumption of human nature in its completeness and also to the treacherousness of human emotion. The latter aspect comes to the foreground in Jerome's application of the Psalm to the moral progress of the saints. The Psalmist declares that "*even until the night* my kidneys have reproved me" (emphasis added), and Jerome places weight on this temporal clause. Christ was free from any taint of sin while both waking and sleeping "and remained pure from every apparition of flesh *(carnis phantasmata)*." For this reason, Jerome asserts, "the saints, who desire

---

CCSL 78:3-352; second series, CCSL 78:353-447). The relationship between the two series is not clear, and the increased use of hexaplaric readings and the omission of the doxology in the second series may indicate that these latter were never preached. Morin, CCSL 78:xi, reasonably judges that 401-2 is the most probable date for the first series, a conclusion well supported by a passing reference Jerome makes (CCSL 78:285) to the recovery of churches that the "heretics possessed" twenty years previously. The second series, however, offers no explicit historical references. Nevertheless, the homilies on Psalm 10 and Psalm 83 appear to allude to remarks made to Psalm 9 and Psalm 80 of the first series. Moreover, several homilies of this series include trenchant anti-Origenist comments that would be consis-tent with Jerome's vigorous pursuit of the controversy around the turn of the fifth century. See E. Clark, *The Origenist Controversy: The Cultural Construction of an Early Christian Debate* (Princeton, N.J.: Princeton University Press, 1992), pp. 139-40.

22. Jerome alternates between this form of the text and the Septuagint version, which reads "my reins have instructed *(erudierunt)* me."

23. Jerome, *tract. psal.* 15.7 (CCSL 78:377).

to be like the Lord and teacher, keep complete guard over their hearts, that they might not be overcome, and that not only while waking, but even in sleep, that is, not only in the day but even in the night."[24] Jerome does not elaborate on the goal of emotional self-control in sleep, but he probably refers by *phantasmata* to dreams that stirred sexual arousal in ascetics and caused nocturnal emissions.[25] Conformity of the saint to Christ includes relief from the sexual fantasies that disturb rest, and their occurrence provides unnerving evidence of the gulf that separates the aspirant from Christ's perfect humanity. In linking the experience of dreams to emotional life, Jerome refashions the *propassio* as a leading indicator of the resistance of sexual impulses to rational domination. Jerome bases his reading of this verse on the authority of Origen.[26] It is somewhat surprising, given the frequency of anti-Origenist polemic in the homilies, that Jerome here cites the Alexandrian exegete with apparent approval. Jerome subsequently singled out Origen's reading of Psalm 15:7 for censure on the grounds that it deceptively promised complete control over emotional experience.[27] In the Psalms homilies Jerome's attacks on Origenist theology do not yet prevent him from holding fast to Origen's hope for self-transformation that can extend to the deepest recesses of the self.

In the Psalm homily Jerome suggests that the experience of *propassio* can be inducted into the ascetic endeavor in a way unanticipated by Origen. For Origen, as for the Stoics before him, the concept of *propatheia* enabled a

24. Jerome, *tract. psal.* 15.7 (CCSL 78:377).

25. Cf. Jerome, *Ezech.* 14.47.1-5 (CCSL 75:710); John Cassian, *conf.* 22. Cassian, *Conf.* 12.8 also associates the cessation of sexual dreams with control of the kidneys, citing Ps. 138(139):13. On the evaluation of nocturnal emissions in ascetic practice, see P. Brown, *The Body and Society: Men, Women, and Sexual Renunciation in Early Christianity* (New York: Columbia University Press, 1988), pp. 230-35.

26. On the basis of Jerome, *ep.* 133.3, the identification of *quis alius* with Origen is secure, as Morin, CCSL 78:377 n. 386, recognized.

27. Jerome, *ep.* 133.3, uses the language of *propatheia* to paraphrase Origen's exposition of Ps. 15:7: "he asserts that a holy man, when he arrives at the peak of virtue, will not suffer even in the night those things which are the lot of humanity, or be tickled by any thought of sins" (*nec cogitatione vitiorum aliqua titillari*) (cf. *ep.* 79 discussed below). John Cassian, *conf.* 22.7.1-2, shares Jerome's view: "it is impossible not to sin either through ignorance or carelessness or surprise or thought or forgetfulness or in sleep"; Boniface Ramsey, trans., *John Cassian: The Conferences,* ACW 57 (New York: Paulist Press, 1997), p. 771. By contrast, in the *Ladder of Divine Ascent,* Step 15, John Climacus makes such self-control a sign of genuine chastity: "A sign of real chastity is to be unaffected by the dreams that come with sleep. Equally, a sign of complete sensuality is to be liable to emissions from bad thoughts when one is awake"; C. Luibheid and N. Russell, trans., *John Climacus: The Ladder of Divine Ascent,* CWS (New York: Paulist Press, 1982), p. 172.

distinction between inconsequential and morally relevant affective experiences. Consciousness of an ineradicable susceptibility to sexual desire is integral to this shift, as is further shown by the appeal Jerome makes to *propatheia* in a consolatory letter to Salvina, a widow in the imperial court of Constantinople.[28] Jerome offers her unsolicited advice to preserve her widowhood, counseling Salvina to associate only with other widows and to meditate continuously on Scripture. Salvina should resort frequently to prayer, so that she might "find a shield to repel" the "shafts of evil thoughts" that ever assail the young. Jerome customarily dispenses such counsel to widows and virgins, seeking to instill in them, as Peter Brown notes, an "acute awareness of the sexual dangers of the body."[29] In the letter to this young noblewoman, he also explains the psychological basis for his prescription. "It is impossible," he warns, "for anyone to lack the initial movements of passions, which the Greeks more distinctly call *propatheias,* which we could call *antepassiones* in a literal translation."[30] The most insidious enemy for young female ascetics is their irreducible sexuality, which produces the "suggestions" of sins that "tickle the soul." In addition to the formidable array of biblical witnesses, Jerome also finds that the poet Horace supports his sentiment: "from faults no mortal is wholly free; the best is whoever has but few of them" and "at moles men cavil when they mark fair skins."[31] "All flesh," Jerome warily concludes, "lusts after those things which belong to the flesh and by its allurements draws the soul to partake of deadly pleasures; but it is for us Christians to restrain the desire for sensual pleasure by the stronger love of Christ."[32]

Jerome introduces the term *antepassio* into this mélange of classical poetry, philosophy, and biblical exegesis to provide an etiology of sin — specifically of sexual desire — that would impress upon the young widow the risk

---

28. Jerome, *ep.* 79 (ca. 400). For background to the letter, see S. Rebenich, *Hieronymus und sein Kreis: Prosopographische und sozialgeschichtliche Untersuchungen,* Historia Einzelschriften 72 (Stuttgart: Franz Steiner Verlag, 1992), pp. 121-26.

29. Brown, *Body and Society,* p. 373. Cf. Jerome, *epp.* 54.7, 123.2.

30. This is the only use of the term *antepassiones* I have found; it may suggest that in the letter to Salvina Jerome was still experimenting with translations of the Greek technical terminology.

31. Horace, *sat.* 1.3.68-69, 1.6.66.

32. Jerome, *ep.* 79.9 (CSEL 55:98-99). Cf. Jerome, *tract. psal.* 76.5 (CCSL 78:57): "Turbatus sum, et non sum loquutus (Ps. 76:5[77:4]). Hoc est, quod dicit apostolus 'Sol non occidat super iracundiam vestram' (Eph. 4:26b). Turbatus sum, quasi homo; non sum loquutus, quasi christianus. Iracundia coepit in corde meo, sed iracundiam in verba non protuli." Jerome's citation of Eph. 4:26b is curious since it is 4:26a, "Be angry and do not sin," that is the foundation for Jerome's use of the concept *propatheia.*

she faced.[33] *Propatheiai* are dangerous, and not accidental or spurious events, and actively to be avoided. Prayer, fasting, and other disciplines are ways to control the environments that could produce *propassiones* in an individual. These events are not involuntary responses to external stimuli but traces of the war between flesh and spirit.

Jerome's advice to Salvina foreshadows the ultimate place of *propatheia* in scholastic theology. Rather than insulating some affective responses from blame, Jerome employs the concept to depict a mind unable to subject the body to its benevolent domination. This revision reaches its conclusion in the latest work in which Jerome refers to *propatheia,* his *Commentary on Ezekiel.* The prophet places in the mouth of God a complaint against the people of Israel: "What do you mean circulating this proverb in the land of Israel, 'the fathers have eaten sour grapes and the children's teeth are set on edge'?" (Ezek. 18:2). As Jerome observes, this sarcastic query seems to contradict the solemn admonition elsewhere attributed to God: "I am the Lord your God, I am a jealous God, who will repay the sins of the fathers on the sons until the third and fourth generations" (Exod. 20:5). To reconcile these apparently conflicting proclamations, Jerome resorts to a figurative interpretation of the Exodus text. Some expositors, he notes, refer God's threat of punishment not to the historical nation of Israel, but to the human soul.[34] Jerome explains:

> They say that the "father" is the light prick of the senses and the initial movement of faults; the "son," indeed, if the thought should conceive a sin; "grandsons," if what you have thought or conceived, you should execute in deed; further the "great-grandson," that is the fourth generation, when you not only do what is evil and pernicious, but you glory in your wickedness.[35]

While God does not punish "the first and second pricks of thoughts, which the Greeks call *propatheias,*" Jerome is adamant that this forbearance does not exculpate these "sins." In this complex allegory, Jerome erases the distinction between stages in the development of emotional response in favor of a distinction between sin and its punishment. As equated figuratively with the "fa-

33. Brown (*Body and Society,* pp. 375-76) aptly observes that the "militant" asceticism of Jerome's correspondence is meant to heighten anxiety about the pervasive and ineradicable nature of sexual desire.

34. Jerome likely has Origen in mind, who applied this figurative reading of Exodus to defuse Marcionite criticism of God's "injustice." Cf. Origen, *sel. in Ezek.* 18:1-2 (PG 13:816B-D); *Princ.* 2.5.2.

35. Jerome, *Ezech.* 6.18:2 (CCSL 75:228).

ther," the *propatheia* constitutes a low-grade transgression: sinful enough to constitute impurity, but not enough to merit punishment, at least absent further violations.

Jerome invokes the *propatheia* here to indict all humanity as liable for sin, a theme prominent in his controversy with Pelagius. Jerome's comments on Ezekiel 18 probably predate the open contention with Pelagius by about a year,[36] but links between this commentary and subsequent anti-Pelagian writings suggest that the dispute colors his presentation of *propatheia*. Several prooftexts Jerome collects for the universality of sinfulness in the Ezekiel commentary reappear in his *Dialogue against the Pelagians*.[37] The nearest prologue of the commentary (to book six) employs vitriolic imagery against heretics that Jerome would later deploy against Pelagius in his *Commentary on Jeremiah*.[38] Trenchant criticism of Rufinus's translation of the *Sentences of Sextus*, which Jerome raises in both his anti-Pelagian letter to Ctesiphon and the Jeremiah commentary, appears for the first time in the same book of his exposition of Ezekiel.[39] This pernicious book, Jerome alleges, is read especially by those "who preach *apatheia* and sinlessness."[40] The treatment of *propatheia* in the Ezekiel commentary anticipates Jerome's growing anxiety at the Pelagian threat and may represent the earliest record to his knowledge of Pelagius's teachings.

In his *Commentary on Ezekiel*, Jerome adduces the *propatheia* as a stage in the development of sin and denies any meaningful distinction between *propassio* and rational "assent" to an emotional impulse. Jerome complains that Pelagius teaches that the saints can achieve a complete removal from all emotional states, which Jerome equates with the Stoic doctrine of *apatheia*.[41]

36. Jerome may have completed books IV through VI by autumn of 412. *Ep.* 130 to Demetrias, Jerome's earliest anti-Pelagian writing, cannot be dated before 413. For discussion of dating, see R. F. Evans, *Pelagius: Inquiries and Reappraisals* (New York: Seabury, 1968), pp. 6-8.

37. Jerome, *Pelag.* 2.4.53-60, citing Job 15:14 and Prov. 20:9. In the dialogue, Jerome complains about the quibbles of "your Demosthenes" who corrects the citation of Job 15:14 to "who is free from stain *(a sorde)*" from "who is free from sin *(a peccato)*." The latter form of the text appears in Jerome's paraphrase of the verse in *Ezech.*

38. Cf. Jerome, *Ezech.* 6.prol. with *Ier.* 3.prol.

39. Jerome, *Ezech.* 6.18.5-9 (CCSL 75:236). Cf. Jerome, *Ier.* 4.41 (CCSL 74:210-11); *ep.* 133.3.

40. Jerome, *Ier.* 4.41 (CCSL 74:211). On Jerome's characterization of Pelagius's position as "Stoic," see Evans, *Pelagius*, pp. 43-65; B. R. Rees, *Pelagius: A Reluctant Heretic* (Wolfeboro, N.H.: Boydell & Brewer, 1988), pp. 84-86.

41. Jerome, *ep.* 133.1; *Pelag.* 1.prol.; *Ier.* 4.41.

Although Pelagius's doctrine is hardly Stoic, he does assert that everything can be directed by one's own will, his voluntarism approximating the psychological rationalism that inspired the origins of the *propatheia*.[42] Jerome rebuts this presumption by referring to the numerous mental phenomena that escape rational control. In his letter to Ctesiphon, Jerome asks who can escape the universal feelings of joy, grief and fear.

> Must we not all clap our hands when we are joyful, and shrink at the approach of sorrow? Must not hope always animate us and fear put us in terror? So in one of his Satires the poet Horace, whose words are so weighty, writes: "From faults no mortal is completely free; he is best who has fewest."[43]

These spontaneous reactions are the marks of *propassiones,* and the Horace citation is the same verse Jerome adduces as evidence for *antepassiones* in the letter to Salvina.[44] Jerome appeals to these movements as evidence of the inescapability of sin. Jerome redraws the emotional map in the soul, effacing the boundary crucial in classical ethical theory between affective reaction and emotional state, between a transient event and a disposition to act.

While the impending conflict with Pelagius cast its shadow over the final appearance of the *propatheia* in Jerome's exegesis, this conflict accentuated rather than generated Jerome's redefinition of the concept. Jerome does not integrate the experience of *propassio* into a well-defined moral psychology. He instead invokes it as a potent symbol, initially of the fragility of human mastery over the innermost reaches of emotional life and, eventually, in the Ezekiel commentary, of the illusory nature of such an ideal. At one level, the story of Jerome's *propassio* offers an example of the curious, and ironic, connections between classical and medieval thought. In tying *propassio* to ascetic ideals rather than to Stoic psychology, Jerome bequeathed to medieval exegetes the concept as a *primus motus* of sinful inclinations and a persistent reminder of irrational urges that lurk in the inaccessible recesses of the self. From another perspective, this transformation of the Stoic doctrine points to the same dynamic that informs the theories of the affections in Maximus and

---

42. Jerome, *Pelag.* 1.28 (CCSL 80:35): "Illud vero quod in alio ponis loco: omnes voluntate propria regi, quis Christianorum possit audire?" G. de Plinval (*Pélage: ses écrits, sa vie et sa réforme* [Lausanne: Librairie Payot, 1943], pp. 231-34) includes this citation among the *Testimonia* of Pelagius.

43. Jerome, *ep.* 133.2.

44. Jerome, *ep.* 133.2, also alludes to Horace, *sat.* 1.6.66, "at moles men cavil when they mark fair skins." Cf. Jerome, *Pelag.* 1.23 (CCSL 80:29).

Augustine: the nature of human existence as irreducibly emotional. What is potentially holy is also charged with danger, and Jerome's concept of *propassio* dresses his recognition of peril in the garb of classical vocabulary. While he employs this language, the underlying theory of the affections it expresses is closer to Augustine than it is to Origen.

From Persuasion to Predestination:
Augustine on Freedom in Rational Creatures

J. PATOUT BURNS

A connection between the affirmation of the existence and activity of the
human soul prior to its earthly life and the rejection of both gratuitous divine election and efficacious divine operation of human willing is not only
intuitively evident but also fully worked out in Origen's doctrinal system.
The theory of the fall of the soul into the earthly body explains the differences in initial condition and opportunities of human beings and thus provides a defense of divine justice in the governance of the world. This study
proposes that Augustine's rejection of the fallen soul theory moved him to
elaborate and assert his characteristic doctrines of divine sovereignty over
the created will and of gratuitous predestination of the elect. It will demonstrate correlations between a set of doctrinal positions that Augustine espoused about 417-18, at the height of the Pelagian controversy: the natural
dissimilarity of humans and angels, the terrestrial creation of humanity, the
spontaneous sin of humans without prior temptation, the necessity of a re-
orientation of human willing by an internal, effective operation of the Holy
Spirit, and the revival of a dormant theory of gratuitous divine election. The
spark that ignited this dogmatic conflagration was the final rejection of the
fallen soul theory.

The theory of divine sovereignty over human willing involves a constellation of positions focused on God's governance of the universe and the economy of sin and salvation. To set the context for the elaboration and demonstration of the hypothesis, therefore, a set of general considerations and
Augustine's adaptations of them will first be enumerated.

Some General Principles

First, in the patristic period Christians held a firm belief that God both creates the world and governs its operation. Gnostic Christians challenged this belief by asserting that God controls and perfects the mental or spiritual realm but not the bodily or material one, which had come into being through a failure in the spiritual realm. Most Christians also limited the kind of rule that God exercises in the voluntary order: God respects the exercise of free choice among rational creatures — self-determination being an aspect of the divine image — and allows them to act according to or against God's will and intention. God might intervene historically to provide incentives to good and disincentives to evil, and eschatologically to reward good and punish evil, but he does not obstruct the proper autonomy of the creature.

Second, Christians also believed that the goodness and love of God is generous beyond measure. The original creation of all reality was gracious: God was not naturally impelled to create. God actually cedes some level of control over the creation by giving and respecting voluntary self-determination to creatures. Still, God assists creatures to do good and to break free from the voluntary and natural consequences of their failures. The high point of this generosity was God's voluntarily becoming part of the historical process in the salvific work of Christ.

Third, Christians also believed that God acts with impeccable justice, at least in punishing. God withdraws goodness or denies assistance only when a person refuses to accept it. Suffering must in some sense always be the consequence of sin, preferably of an individual's own refusal of good. Thus even the actual experience of the pain and death attendant upon their animal bodies is assigned to the voluntary fall of humans from an original blessed state. Moreover, Christians tended to believe that God gives assistance equally to all and that differentials in that assistance are based on a person's own actions or efforts, or consequent upon some office or role assigned by God in the historical process of salvation.

Fourth, Christians recognized a weakness in the created order that makes some forms of divine assistance necessary. Beings that are not self-sufficient in their existence can fail to perform properly; because they receive their existence through change, all creatures are unstable in their being and cannot stop changing. Even in their natural state, rational creatures require some form of divine assistance to maintain stable good willing and consistent performing. Fallen humans require additional divine assistance, which is provided through Christ, to counteract mortality, ignorance, and selfish love.

Fifth, in their prayer — if not their theory — Christians thanked God

295

for all the good they do and accepted responsibility — individually or corporately — for their failure and sin. This practice of praise implicitly recognized the divine assistance as a necessary condition or even a sufficient cause of good willing. The degree of recognized dependence on God also limited the creature's right to claim a reward — rather than to qualify for an additional gift — for good actions. The creature may not, however, blame God for failure, either through causing bad willing or through a program of unjustly withholding the assistance necessary for good willing.

General Statements about Augustine

At one time or another in the course of his writings, Augustine affirmed all the general principles that have just been enunciated. Along with most of the Western Christian Church, however, he made some further assumptions that specified the scope and operation of these principles.

First, Augustine believed that some of the rational creatures reject the divine goodness and never return to it. The devils and some humans suffer unendingly as a consequence of their sin.

Second, Augustine believed and gradually came to recognize the implications of the North African assertion that human beings can repent of their sin, receive forgiveness, and fulfill the just commandments of God only through union with Christ, either in the people of Israel or as members of the Christian Church. Thus he believed that the divine operation for the recovery of sinful human beings is limited by the availability of the Christian Church, with its preaching of the moral law and the gospel, with its performance of the rituals of baptism and Eucharist. He believed that this limitation was one that God had actually chosen and intended; he never considered it a consequence, for example, of the Gentiles' refusal to accept Mosaic Law or Christians' failure to fulfill the missionary mandate of Christ. Augustine developed various means of justifying this limitation of divine mercy, including the theory that all souls had sinned either individually or in solidarity with Adam before beginning their individual earthly lives.[1] Thus he believed that God is fully justified in not acting to save all human beings and that the assistance through which God brings some to salvation is undeserved by both those who receive it and those who do not.

Third, Augustine believed in the Christian practice of praise of God for

---

1. Thus, for example, in *lib.* 3.11.32–12.35, 3.20.55-58 (CCSL 29:294.73–296.39, 307.1–309.100).

all the good Christians accomplish. Rigorously pursuing the application of this principle, he asserted that the good willing of the creature is not only supported but at critical junctures actually effected by God. Eventually, he came to assert that God can prevent the creatures from sinning, can turn the creature who has sinned to repentance, can move the creature to will and perform good actions even in the face of opposition, and can even overcome the natural instability of the created will so that a person cannot sin again.

Fourth, Augustine's acceptance of the theses of the limitation of the means of salvation and of praise of God for all the creature's good actions radically undercut the earlier Christian reliance on human freedom of choice and individual responsibility as means of defending divine justice. God — rather than the individual Christian — begins, sustains, and completes the process of conversion and salvation. Although God does in fact have the power to save them, God does not offer the means of salvation to many fallen humans. In such a system, of course, the primal condition of the creature and the creature's individual or corporate responsibility for initial and subsequent failure became critical to the defense of divine justice. Only if the creature originally committed a sin despite the availability of fully adequate assistance would God's withholding of the means necessary for avoiding subsequent sin and damnation be justified. Although the original sin of demons and humans was therefore a key factor in the development of Augustine's thought, he had great difficulty in reaching a satisfactory explanation of the way in which the first sin was committed and individuals participated in its guilt.

Fifth, Augustine's assertion of the inheritance of original guilt was based upon his belief in the limitation of the means of salvation and the deprivations in the conditions into which human beings are born. His explanation of the transmission of this original guilt, however, could not be separated from his understanding of the origin of individual human souls. Though it did develop, however, his position on the origin of human souls never attained satisfactory clarity and stability.

Hypothesis on the Origin of the Soul and the Efficacy of Grace

The correlation between Augustine's understanding of the sin by which humanity fell from its original blessed state and the origin of the human soul is made clear in *De libero arbitrio,* where he first considered the four options for explaining the soul's origin and its coming into the limitations of earthly life.[2] In each instance, he demonstrated that souls fell individually or corporately into either sin or a condition in which sin would regularly eventuate. When he later excluded the theory that the soul had existed in a higher condition and entered the earthly body through individual sin, he lost a preferred manner of explaining its initial sinfulness. The generation of the soul along with the body by the human parents — the traducianist option — would explain the transmission of Adam's sin but not the distinct, spiritual reality of the soul. He explored the power of the concupiscence operative in carnal generation to pollute a soul divinely created for the body. Though he never developed a satisfactory explanation, Augustine clearly recognized the correlation between the soul's origin and its initial sinfulness.

Similarly, Augustine's doctrine of original guilt and moral impotence played the major role in justifying his doctrines of both the gratuity and efficacy of divine assistance. He argued that human beings had lost the capacity for religiously praiseworthy action and all their operations were sinful. First he concluded that none could either initiate or earn God's initiation of the process of salvation. Next he asserted that God must actually move the sinner to repentance, change the sinful dispositions and sustain the convert in good willing. Thus the theory of divine operation of human willing rested on a foundation of original guilt.

Original guilt stands as a middle term linking Augustine's thinking on the soul's origin and the efficacy of grace. A direct correlation between Augustine's thinking on the origin of the soul and divine sovereignty over human willing is not, however, apparent. Both theories developed, as Robert O'Connell's work on the origin of the soul and my own study of operative grace have, I believe, demonstrated. Yet the developments diverged: Augustine never claimed to have solved the question of the soul's origin; he grew increasingly certain of the efficacy of the graces of conversion and perseverance. The chronology of the developments of the two theories, however, suggests that a change in one might have opened the way for the growth of the other.

Robert O'Connell dates Augustine's final abandonment of the theory that souls were created, sinned individually, and thus entered earthly bodies at 417 or 418.[3] I have argued that at just this time — after some twenty years of deliberately avoiding it — Augustine suddenly and adamantly returned to the theory of efficacious grace, which he then vigorously developed until the

---

2. *Lib.* 3.20.55-58 (CCSL 29:307.1–309.100).

3. Robert O'Connell, *The Origin of the Soul in St. Augustine's Later Works* (New York: Fordham University Press, 1987).

end of his life.[4] The historical connection is intriguing; it invites a closer investigation of the dynamics of system development to identify some linking between these two elements.

The hypothesis of this study proposes a connection among the origin or nature of the soul, its mode of sin, and the type of grace by which God achieves its salvation. Two different stages in Augustine's thinking, with intermediary developments, can be clearly distinguished. In his fourth-century writings, Augustine held that human souls were originally created in a nonearthly condition. He distinguished human souls from the spirits of angels and demons only on the basis of their mode of fidelity or sin: angels had spontaneously chosen to remain submissive to God; demons had sinned spontaneously; humans had been persuaded to sin by the demons. Having sinned spontaneously, demons could not be persuaded to repent; just as humans had been tempted to sin, they could be persuaded to repent. Within this context, Augustine developed the concept of a persuasive grace of conversion and a gift of charity that assists the Christian to accomplish the good. Over the next two decades — involving conflict with the Donatists and the Pelagians — Augustine developed a notion of charity or the indwelling of the Holy Spirit that changes the dispositions of the human will. He continued to assert, however, that a sinner must be persuaded to accept this gift. In the second stage, Augustine decided that human souls, unlike angels and demons, were created in an earthly condition. About 417, he recognized and rejected the Origenist theory of the fall of the soul. Once he could distinguish humans from demons by their original condition rather than the mode of their sin, he asserted that humans first sinned spontaneously — like the demons — and were only subsequently tempted. The path opened for Augustine to abandon his earlier system of salvation based upon persuasion; he realized that those who had sinned spontaneously need not, indeed could not, be converted by persuasion. Augustine then introduced an efficacious or coercive grace of conversion, and later of perseverance.

The proof of this hypothesis would support O'Connell's disputed contention that Augustine abandoned the theory on the fall of the soul into the body about 417. The changes in Augustine's interpretation of the sin of Adam and theory of efficacious grace are evident in his texts. The chronology of the latter will be taken as demonstrated. The correlation of these shifts with one another and with the abandonment of the fallen soul hypothesis will then be used to lend plausibility to the chronology that O'Connell proposes for this

4. J. Patout Burns, *The Development of Augustine's Doctrine of Operative Grace* (Paris: Etudes Augustiennes, 1980).

last. The pattern created by the three will also suggest an interpretation of Augustine's religious development.

The First Stage: An Economy of Divine Persuasion

Augustine's theory of divine sovereignty or predestination has four key elements. First, in its original or fallen state the creature requires divine assistance in order to attain its fulfillment. Second, divine power must be able to influence and even determine the functioning of the choices of the creature; the decisions or the intentions of the creature have to be subject to divine control in such a way that God can guarantee and produce their proper functioning. Third, God's operation determining the creature's stable and consistent willing toward good must be gratuitous and unearned by any prior or foreseen merits of the creature. Fourth, God's withholding a determination of the creature's stable and consistent willing toward good must be fully justified by the creature's own choices and actions.

The problem of the instability of the created spirit and the efficacy of the divine assistance afforded it, as well as the justice of God's granting and withholding that assistance, occupied Augustine's attention from the early stages of his thinking through the writing that he left unfinished at his death. The problem of human responsibility, as recounted in the *Confessiones,* was central to his commitment to Manicheism and its eventual rejection. Shortly after his conversion he turned to the problem in the first two books of *De libero arbitrio* and returned to the analysis in the third book after he was made a presbyter in Hippo.[5]

In *De libero arbitrio,* Augustine advanced the firm conviction that created spirits are individually responsible for the adherence to or aversion from the Supreme Good. The good angels never have sinned and never will sin; God assigns them offices in the governance of the universe that are appropriate to the constancy of their minds in adhering to and acting at the direction of the divine wisdom. The evil angels sinned spontaneously; they are held in evil by their own enduring love of self and rejection of God. Humans, whose nature makes them the equals of the other rational spirits, have sinned not spontaneously but through the persuasion of the evil angels; as a consequence, they have been assigned to ruling mortal bodies that are proportionate to their weakened minds and in which their inconstancy does not endanger the good order of the universe. Unlike the demons, those persuaded to

5. *Retr.* i.9.1 (CCSL 57:23.1-11).

evil are not locked in sin; some are humbled by their fallen condition, by the dangers or sufferings of mortal life. Recalled by the ministry of Christ, they are persuaded to repent their sin and to return to willing service of God and apparently to a higher station in the universe.[6] They are upheld in good willing by memory of the sufferings they had endured during their earthly lives, by appreciation of their Savior's generosity and glory, and — if temptation recurs — by the vision of the eternal tortures of the damned.[7] Other humans fix themselves in their rejection of God and join themselves to the demons, whose role in the universe Augustine did not attempt to specify.[8] In analyzing the situation of humans affected by the conditions of mortal life, Augustine argued that ignorance of the good and difficulty in performing it can be overcome, if only gradually. God, moreover, provides various forms of assistance to those who implore help.[9] At this point, Augustine recognized no divine power to determine the willing of creatures and assumed that such assistance as God does provide to a creature's own operation, though it may be gratuitous and unearned, is in response to the efforts of the individual.

In the final sections of *De libero arbitrio*, Augustine considered the vexing questions of human moral impotence, the origin of the souls of Adam's descendants, and the fate of unbaptized infants. Robert O'Connell has suggested that this portion of the treatise was subject to later editing, so that the individual questions are quilted rather than woven together.[10] In each instance, Augustine argued for individual responsibility. If moral impotence is absolute, then it must be the consequence of prior individual failure. If humans retain some power for either doing good or seeking assistance, they are responsible only for their failure to progress. The case of infants who have made no personal decisions during earthly lives must be left to divine justice, which can certainly pronounce the appropriate sentence.[11]

In the other writings of his presbyterate, Augustine demonstrated the

---

6. In his treatment of the redemption in *lib.* 3.10.31, Augustine drew an explicit contrast between the sin of the demons and that of humans. He then explained that humans who had been persuaded by the demons to sin could be persuaded by Christ to repent: "Ita factum est ut neque diabolo per uim eriperetur homo quem nec ipse ui sed persuasione ceperat, et qui juste plus humiliatus est ut seruiret cui ad malum consenserat, juste per eum cui ad bonum consensit liberaretur, quia minus iste in consentiendo quam ille in male suadendo peccauerat" (CCSL 29:294.67-72).

7. *Lib.* 3.25.76 (CCSL 29:320.26–321.62).

8. *Lib.* 3.5.14-16, 3.9.24–12.35 (CCSL 29:283.60–285.133; 289.1–296.39).

9. *Lib.* 3.19.53–20.58 (CCSL 29:306.58–309.100).

10. See O'Connell, *Origin of the Soul*, pp. 45-61.

11. *Lib.* 3.18.50–23.66 (CCSL 29:304.1–314.16).

same commitment to the principle that good and evil lie within the dominion of human free choice. In his commentaries on Paul and in the series of responses to questions that he addressed to fellow clergy, Augustine began to work on the process of persuasion by which humans might be freed from sin and returned to a blessed state. He distinguished four stages in the transition from grief to glory.

First, the moral law — in the heart, the Scripture, or preaching — indicates to a person the good that ought to be done and the punishment that will be suffered for failure to do it. The person who heeds the warning and attempts to do the good discovers resistance in the demands of the mortal body. Moreover, the sinner relies on personal strength rather than divine assistance to perform the good and win a reward, but that strength is inadequate to overcome fleshly desires and customs of self-satisfaction. Under the law, a person actually fails to accomplish the good that ought to be done but recognizes the punishment due for that failure. More importantly, the sinner might acknowledge moral impotence.

Second, the preaching of the gospel of forgiveness and assistance through the ministry of Christ and the Holy Spirit addresses the person facing damnation. A sinner might then abandon reliance on personal strength and choose instead to take refuge in the assistance offered by Christ. This placing of trust in Christ through faith resolves the major problem of self-reliance or pride, the fundamental way in which humans imitate the demons.

Third, to the person who has asked for divine aid, God grants the assistance of the Holy Spirit. The gift of love strengthens the person's intention to do the good, which was conceived in response to the giving of the law, so that the convert actually accomplishes the good. However, the mortal body continues to oppose and resist the soul's good intentions and prevents the perfect performance of the good.

Fourth and finally, by persevering in the effort to do good and repenting the failure to fulfill it, the Christian attains to the glory of heaven where the resistance of the mortal body is removed. The person has surrendered the mind's rebellion against God by submitting to the need for divine assistance. Thus with the mind no longer resisting God and the body no longer resisting the mind, the person is stable in good.[12]

Clearly, Augustine had outlined an economy of salvation based upon persuasion. In each of the steps toward glory, the divine assistance provokes and responds to human choices; it then assists the person's own good inten-

---

12. This schema is set out in *quaest.* 66.3-7 (CCSL 44A:154.86–163.269; *Rom.* 12, CSEL 84:6.17–9.4).

tion. If a person refuses to respond to the law and the preaching of the gospel, then God has no further means to work the person's salvation. God cannot actually control or produce human willing; human negligence or resistance can interrupt the progress at any point and result in ultimate failure.

In the commentaries on the Epistles of Paul that followed *De libero arbitrio*, Augustine also ran up against the two texts from Romans that would provide the foundations for his doctrine of predestination and efficacious divine operation. In the ninth chapter of Romans, Paul turned to the question of God's fidelity to Israel, which was raised by the Jewish rejection of Jesus as Messiah. He argued first that the promise had not been made to Abraham's genetic descendants but to those born in fulfillment of the promise itself. Thus he distinguished Isaac from Ishmael and, in the next generation, Jacob from Esau. Concerning these latter, Paul cites Malachi 1:2-3:

> "I have loved Jacob, but I have hated Esau,"

and elaborates:

> Even before they had been born or had done anything good or bad (so that God's purpose of election might continue, not by works but by his call) she was told, "The elder shall serve the younger." (Rom. 9:11-12)

In its explicit assertion of the gratuity of the divine election and its explicit rejection of individual good or evil deeds as a basis for God's providing assistance, the text seemed to rule out the position on reward and punishment that Augustine had taken in *De libero arbitrio*. As is customary, he tried to find a way of reconciling his established philosophical preference with the scriptural text. First, he argued that Paul excludes works that have already been performed after birth but not actions that are yet to be performed at the time of election. Next, he explained that Paul had excluded the good works that fulfill the moral law because these actually depend upon the prior gift of the Holy Spirit, which strengthens an individual's purpose and actually produces good works. He argued, however, that God does distinguish and choose individuals on the basis of their response to the preaching of the gospel. In this way, those whom God calls according to the promise, the elect, are those whom God foreknows will respond positively to the invitation to believe and seek assistance.[13] Once they have actually accepted the message of Christ and pray for

---

13. *Quaest.* 68.5 (CCSL 44A:180.135–182.172); *Rom.* 52 (CSEL 84:33.19–35.20). See the discussion in Burns, *Development*, pp. 38-39.

God's help, they receive the gift of the Holy Spirit through which their desire to fulfill the moral law becomes effective.[14] Thus by appealing to foreknown faith, Augustine managed to save a crucial role for individual free choice at the beginning of the process of salvation. In this explanation, he not only demonstrated his continuing commitment to human self-determination but continued to hold open a schema in which the affirmation of a life for the soul prior to its entering the earthly body was possible but not necessary for the defense of divine justice, at least not in dealing with adults, who were presumed to have an opportunity to accept or reject God's call during their earthly lives.[15]

The second text from Romans that presented a problem to Augustine follows in Paul's defense of divine justice:

> So it depends not on human will or exertion but on God who shows mercy [or as Augustine's text read: It is not of him who wills or him who runs but of God who has mercy]. (Rom. 9:16)

In his first attempt to deal with this assertion, Augustine explained that human will and exertion are ineffective without the Holy Spirit's assistance.[16] His next effort pointed to the role of faith: because no one can attempt to do good or believe in Christ unless first admonished in the law or called by the gospel, human willing depends upon prior divine calling. God effects human willing, he concluded, in the sense that grace provides the conditions necessary for good choice.[17] This, however, was an unstable position. Under further questioning by his Milanese friend Simplician, Augustine developed a new and startlingly different interpretation of this text.

Simplician posed a number of questions to Augustine, the second of which addressed Romans 9:10-29. The analysis was painstaking: Simplician was Ambrose's hand-picked successor in Milan and had been instrumental in Augustine's own conversion, so he owed him a thorough and careful exposition of the text. In examining Romans 9:16, "it depends not on human will or exertion but on God who shows mercy," Augustine noticed that his earlier explanation allowed the reversal of the Pauline assertion: if God effects human

---

14. In this sense, he interpreted the second foundational text, which will be considered next, *Rom.* 54 (CSEL 84:36.14–39.22).

15. Augustine had already admitted in *De libero arbitrio* that he could not both hold open all four hypotheses on the origin of the soul and deal with the judgment of infants who died without performing good or evil actions during earthly life: *lib.* 3.19.53–21.59, 23.66 (CCSL 29:306.1–310.20, 314.1-16).

16. *Rom.* 54.1 (CSEL 84:36.14-19).

17. *Quaest.* 68.5 (CCSL 44A:180.135–182.172).

willing by providing the conditions necessary for its operation, then human willing completes divine mercy by acting under the favorable conditions. Thus the result would depend upon humans choosing to fulfill a proper, albeit dependent, role; humans could refuse to act and thus frustrate the divine intention. Augustine rejected the explanation immediately: divine mercy cannot wait upon, cannot depend upon human cooperation. For the first time he asserted that God actually produces or effects human cooperation with divine assistance.[18]

Augustine then developed an explanation of the way God causes human cooperation by exploiting the earlier thesis of divine control over the conditions or environment of human decision. A person decides, he observed, in response to the concrete presentation of an invitation; the will is moved by something that is known. The attractiveness of a known object, however, depends upon a person's existing desires and preferences. Because individual dispositions are different, the appeal that provokes one person to consent will leave another unmoved. God, he argued, has an exhaustive knowledge of the dispositions of each heart and adapts the actual preaching of the gospel to the preferences of those who are chosen, so that elect then respond in faith. Although God could certainly find a form of vocation that would correspond to the dispositions of any heart, Augustine opined, those whom God does not elect find themselves addressed in ways that do not move them. Thus the response of faith, upon which forgiveness and the assistance of the Holy Spirit follow, is guaranteed in fact, if not in principle, by the divine control of the environment of human choosing.[19]

This solution is in continuity with Augustine's analysis of human willing in *De libero arbitrio,* in which he recognized that an object had to be presented for willing. There, of course, he had insisted that, although no one could determine what would be presented, a person could accept or reject any given object. Here, in contrast, he argued that certain opportunities will not actually be rejected because of the dispositions of the will and that God, knowing the dispositions of the will, can present such an effective invitation.

In this theory of divine efficacy, the individual dispositions to which the congruous vocation appeals actually differentiate one person from another. Their function, after all, is to explain why a particular call moves one but not another, Jacob but not Esau. Augustine evidently supposed, moreover, that individuals establish these dispositions or orientations by their patterns of choice, prior to encountering the divine call to faith. Thus, Augustine's analy-

18. *Simpl.* 1.2.10-13 (CCSL 44:34.273–38.378).
19. *Simpl.* 1.2.13-14 (CCSL 44:37.345–39.411).

sis presumes that the divine call that separated Jacob from Esau met them as adults already well formed by their individual mentalities. Though Jacob could thank the divine mercy for his conversion, Esau — who was also called — was himself responsible for the dispositions that resulted in his neglect of the divine call. Moreover, Augustine presumed that according to this paradigm, every individual is actually called, though only some are addressed in a way that corresponds to their existing orientation.[20]

The text of Paul's letter focuses on the election of Jacob and the rejection of Esau while they were still in their mother's womb and had done nothing good or bad. Augustine, apparently, was unable — or unwilling — to explain how God might justly deal with such a situation. He simply transformed it into one he could handle through the principles that he had already developed. In these discussions, Augustine was focused on conversion, on the turning of the will from ignorance and weakness to understanding, strength, and good performance. He had not yet addressed the problem of stabilizing the will in good during earthly life, of preventing a person from falling once again after setting out on the path toward God. Through faith, the mind's rebellion against God had been overcome. The resistance of the mortal body was effectively opposed by the good willing of the person, strengthened by the assistance that the Holy Spirit gives to believers. Thus he applied the text of Romans 7, in which Paul addresses the impotence of the will to prevent evil and perform good, to the person who has not yet received God's help.[21] Augustine seems to have presumed that once the mortality of the body was removed in the resurrection of the flesh, then personal consent and the gift of the Spirit would be adequate to insure good willing into eternity, to prevent a subsequent fall into sin.[22]

Augustine's treatise to Simplician marked the end of a decade of intense concern with the questions of human freedom and divine assistance. His belief in the autonomy and responsibility of creatures emerged largely intact: angels and demons fix themselves in good or evil; humans have been persuaded to evil and might be persuaded to return to good through divine operations that Paul had identified as law, gospel, and the gift of love. No one, of course, has a right or claim upon such assistance because — at least in the cases that Augustine was willing to discuss — each individual is personally responsible for falling into sin.

20. *Simpl.* 1.2.13 (CCSL 44:37.345–38.378).

21. *Simpl.* 1.1 (CCSL 44:7-23). See also William Babcock, "Augustine's Interpretation of Romans (A.D. 394-396)," *Augustinian Studies* 10 (1979): 55-74.

22. *Lib.* 3.25.76 (CCSL 29:320.56–321.62) and *Rom.* 12 (CSEL 84:8.12–9.4).

The Intermediate Developments

In the two decades following his response to Simplician, Augustine generally avoided all discussion of divine control over the will. In *De spiritu et littera,* he intentionally turned away from the discussion of the efficacy of motives in conversion.[23] In responding to Coelestius's rebuttal of the use of Romans 9:16 against his own position, Augustine was content to note that divine assistance is necessary to bring good will to performance.[24] After such intense interest in the subject, why was Augustine hesitant to continue exploring the efficacy and the gratuity of the divine assistance that moved individuals to conversion and made their good choices effective in good performance? At least two reasons can be considered. First, the Donatist controversy focused Augustine's attention on the concrete means of salvation: a person had to share the communion of the true Church. Augustine recognized that the preaching of the gospel and participation in the rituals of baptism and Eucharist were not actually accessible to all.[25] His solutions to the problems of human responsibility and divine justice, however, had all presumed the universal availability of the necessary divine assistance. Second, the Pelagian controversy had begun to focus Augustine's attention on the situation of children, particularly those who die without performing any good or evil works through their own volition. He now realized that infants who die unbaptized were condemned, and thus he had to identify a sin committed prior to birth that would justify their punishment.[26]

The theory of inherited guilt required a corresponding explanation of the origin of the soul and its relation to Adam. Augustine knew that he had

23. The discussion begins in *spir. et litt.* 33.57 and continues through 34.60 (CSEL 60:215.16–221.4), where Augustine ends it: "iam si ad illam profunditatem scrutandam quisquam nos coartet, cur illi ita suadeatur ut persuadeatur, illi autem non ita, duo sola occurrent interim quae respondere mihi placeat: *o altitudo diuitiarum!* et: *numquid iniquitas apud deum?* cui responsio ista displicet quaerat doctiores, sed caveat, ne inueniat praesumptores" (CSEL 60:220.26–221.4).

24. The discussion in *perf. jus.* 19.40 (CSEL 42:43.2-4) ends: "non quia hoc sine uoluntate nostra agitur, sed quia uoluntas non implet quod agit, nisi diuinitus adiuuetur."

25. He advanced this argument in *nat. et gr.* 2.2; 4.4 (CSEL 60:234.11–235.7; 235.26–236.6).

26. O'Connell has argued that Augustine was dissatisfied with his first attempt to deal with this question in *De peccatorum meritis et remissione et de baptismo parvulorum,* that he asked Marcellinus to return the treatise, and that he emended it after a major shift in his thinking in 417 (*The Origin of the Soul,* pp. 104-8). For evidence of the return of the book see *ep.* 139.3 (CSEL 44:152.5–153.19).

no scripturally based and polemically useful solution to the problem. He insisted that the four options he had presented in *De libero arbitrio* were open for consideration. In two of these — which were now collapsed into one — the soul existed and personally sinned in a higher condition before it entered the body. Another theory was judged marginally acceptable because it implied the corporeal identity of all souls with that of Adam. Yet Augustine could not exclude the theory most popular outside Africa — that the soul was created fresh and innocent for the newly generated body — which meant that it could be held guilty and punished only for sins committed in earthly life.[27]

In this situation, Augustine was not prepared to advance his theory of the intentional fall of the soul into an earthly body as a means of solving the problems posed to divine justice in the condemnation of unbaptized infants.[28] He may have held the theory within his own mind and heart but judged that presenting it to the African episcopate — much less to the unsympathetic Romans — as a necessary part of the rejection of Pelagian teaching was to invite disaster. Privately holding a view of the sinful fall of the soul into the body as possible while publicly professing his uncertainty on the matter would have permitted Augustine a degree of comfort and assurance in defending a divine justice that condemned some infants before they performed any earthly action and withheld the means necessary for salvation from most adults. At regional and general councils in Africa, he won approval of the doctrine of original sin and moral impotence on scriptural and ecclesiological grounds. The philosophical underpinnings, if they existed, remained unspoken.

The Donatist conflict and initial stages of the Pelagian controversy not only forced the questions of inherited guilt and the origin of the soul but also yielded a major breakthrough in one particular: the role of the Holy Spirit in the transformation of the human will. In his attempts to explain why their otherwise moral actions would not bring to salvation Christians who had rejected the unity of the Church in adhering to a schismatic community, Augustine asserted that intention is constitutive of human action. To perform good actions without loving God and neighbor in the unity of the Church's communion is actually to sin even in those lawful actions. Similarly, in arguing against the Pelagian assertion of the natural power of free choice to do good and avoid evil, Augustine insisted that the first and greatest of the commandments — the love of God for God's own sake — can be fulfilled only

---

27. O'Connell's discussion of this problem is most useful (*Origin of the Soul*, 118-67).

28. He had avoided doing so in *De libero arbitrio* as well.

through the gift of God's own love. The Holy Spirit, he explained, makes human loving truly good; the gift of charity overcomes the disposition of self-love and transforms it into love of God.[29]

Although the indwelling of the Holy Spirit transforms human desiring, in Augustine's explanation it does not violate human freedom and responsibility. The gift of love is given only to those who desire it, who pray to God to liberate them from their captivity to sin and self. Thus as long as belief in the preaching of the gospel remained within the natural power of human willing, dependent upon and even manipulated by the divine call as that may be, human autonomy was not being violated by divine operation.[30] This half-way position, however, would not long endure.

The Second Stage: An Economy of Divine Operation

In 413, Augustine received a memorandum in which was set forth the Origenist theory that the material world was formed for the incarceration and correction of the souls that fell from a spiritual state. He rejected the theory because it contradicted the understanding that he had drawn from the text of Genesis and from Plotinus that the bodily realm had been part of the original goodness of creation.[31] A few years later, he pointed out to Jerome that the theory that asserted that the soul could sin in a higher spiritual condition and thus fall into the body also implied that the soul might sin again once freed from the mortal body and in punishment be returned to earthly life or even consigned to the fires of hell.[32] Thus Augustine was apparently no longer satisfied with the means of stabilizing the soul in goodness that he had worked out two decades earlier in *De libero arbitrio* and *Expositio propositionum ex epistola ad Romanos*. Still, however, he had no scriptural basis for excluding the theory of the fall of the soul.

In 417, however, Augustine realized that the text of Romans 9:11 excluded any theory of the fall of the soul into the body. Paul had asserted that the election pronounced upon Esau and Jacob before birth could not be based on good or evil deeds; Augustine finally recognized that this exclu-

---

29. See Burns, *Development*, pp. 59-63, 111-12.

30. Augustine insisted on this degree of freedom in *spir. et litt.* 33.57–34.60 (CSEL 60:215.16–221.4) cited above, n. 23.

31. *Ad Orosium* 8.9 (PL 42:674). He repeated this objection in a letter to his friend Evodius, *ep.* 164.7.20 (CSEL 44:539.4-19).

32. *Ep.* 166.9.27 (CSEL 44:582.9–584.2).

sion of good and evil deeds implied not simply that God disregarded such actions but that Paul meant to assert that no such deeds existed. Paul had pointed out that the election was prior to birth precisely in order to demonstrate that it could not have been based on individual good or evil deeds. Augustine concluded that this scriptural text clearly asserted that human souls had not existed and acted individually before coming into earthly life.[33] The possibility that individual souls had sinned and thus fallen into earthly bodies was apparently the first element to fall in the general collapse of Augustine's delicately balanced theory of divine operation that persuades human freedom.

Once he had abandoned the one explanation of the origin of the soul that could be used to justify easily differential divine treatment of individuals, Augustine next gave up the notion that humanity had been created in a condition similar to that of the angels, in a spiritual rather than an animal body.[34] In *De Genesi ad litteram,* he explained that Adam and Eve had bodies that were naturally mortal but were preserved from corruption through the tree of life. Had they remained faithful to the divine command, they would have been transformed into incorruptibility without passing through death. Once they sinned and were excluded from access to the tree of life in Paradise, however, their natural mortality became operative. Then, in discussing the creation and fall of humans in *De civitate Dei,* Augustine assumed that angels

---

33. *Serm.* 165.5.6 (PL 38:905). He confidently used Rom. 9:11 to exclude the possibility of sins committed in a higher condition that would merit the fall down into the body. This is thought to have been preached in 417 in Carthage. *pecc. mer.* 2.31.36 (CSEL 42:195.1-7) clearly denies the notion that the soul fell through proper use of free will to live well or evilly and refers to Rom. 9:11. *Ep.* 190.1.4 (CSEL 57:140.10–141.3) rejects the theory with the quotation of Rom. 9:11. *Nat. et gr.* 1.12.15 (CSEL 60:314.22-25) makes the same point by reference to Rom. 9:11; Augustine repeated the assertion in 3.7.9 (CSEL 60:367.16-20) to exclude good works and merits before coming into flesh, with the citation of the text, and then applied it to both good and evil in 3.8.11 (CSEL 60:368.14-29). *Ep.* 202A 4.8 (CSEL 57:306.23–307.12) clearly rejects the notion of a fall into the body, from Origen or Priscillianists or anyone else, relying on Rom. 9:11.

34. Because the chronology of the composition of the various parts of *De Genesi ad litteram* and *De civitate Dei* cannot be securely specified, the sequence of the development cannot be independently established. The basis for abandoning the fallen soul theory is clearly a new insight into Rom. 9:16; this same text plays a key role in *De Genesi ad litteram* 6, where it sets up the shift in the original condition of Adam. The change could also have been facilitated by a realization of the implications of Origen's use of the fallen soul theory to denigrate the earthly realm. This, however, played no role in *De Genesi ad litteram* 3, where Adam is assigned a naturally immortal body like that of the angels and demons.

and demons were naturally immortal while humans were not. Again, the text of Romans 9:11 played a role in the transition.[35]

This shift in the understanding of the original condition of angels, demons, and humans led in turn to a new explanation of their temptation and fall. In *De libero arbitrio*, angels, humans, and demons were seen as equal in nature and differentiated in the roles assigned to them in the universe by reason of their mode of fidelity or sinning: angels set themselves in good; demons set themselves in evil; humans were persuaded to evil and thus might be persuaded back to good. The angels were given rule over the universe as a whole, and the humans over corruptible bodies. The function of the demons in cosmic governance remained unspecified. Two decades later, in *De civitate Dei*, Augustine continued to assert that, though they originally had that divine assistance by which they could have remained in good, the demons had sinned spontaneously. The angels, however, needed an additional divine help that would stabilize them in good willing. Either at the time of their creation or after the fall of the demons, the angels who had preserved themselves in the good will originally given by their creator received an additional assistance that confirms them in good, so that they are assured that they will never fail.[36]

---

35. *Gen. litt.* 3.21.33–22.34 (BA 48:264-68) holds that Adam was made in an immortal body — even though there are problems with food and procreation; 6.9.14 (BA 48:464-66) uses Rom. 9:11 to exclude any merits prior to coming into the body. Then in 6.19.30–29.40 (BA 48:490-508) Augustine explained that the body of Adam was animal rather than spiritual but that it could avoid death; it could die or not die. The function of the tree of life was to prevent the death of the body. However, when sin occurs and results in expulsion from Paradise, the body comes to die. In *civ.* 11.16 (CCSL 48:336.25-28) Augustine supposed that angels and humans are not the same kind of beings, for the angels (and demons) are immortal and the humans are mortal.

36. Augustine asserted that God distinguishes the good angels from those who are going to fall through their own will. In *civ.* 11.13 (CCSL 48:332.1–333.37) the angels might have all been created equal, with no assurance of their remaining in good. Once the demons had fallen, the good angels were given a further assistance by which they knew that they would not fall from the good and the happy life. Alternatively, the good angels might have been created with a fuller happiness that was not given to those who would fall. In *civ.* 12.9 (CCSL 48:363.1–364.72) the distinction between the angels who persevered and those who did not is rooted in a fuller gift from God to the good, though there was certainly a gift of good will to the angels who were going to fall. Either the good angels were originally given a fuller good will or they were given additional assistance by which they persevered. In *lib.* 3.11.32, 3.25.76 (CCSL 29:294.1-18, 320.56–321.62) no such divine influence on the created will had been deemed necessary or even possible. There God simply foreknew the fidelity of the angels. Humans who had recovered from sin were confirmed by the remembrance of their sufferings as a consequence of sin and the vision of the punishment of the

Once the natural equality of humans and angels had been abandoned, Augustine differentiated them not through the mode of their sinning but through the possibility of repentance that the body provided to humans. Humans originally fell spontaneously through a secret sin of pride that, like that of the demons, was unprovoked by any temptation.[37] Humans, unlike the demons, were not however fixed in their evil decision. Instead, Adam and Eve were tempted by the devil to an act of bodily disobedience through which they came to recognize their hidden sin of pride and could thus be moved to repentance. For humans the prohibition of eating of the tree served a function similar to that which Augustine — following Paul — assigned to the Mosaic and moral law: to provoke, expose, and lead to repentance for an underlying sin of pride. The demons' sin of pride was apparently hidden from them, and they were locked in evil.[38] As persuasion lost its role in the fall of humanity, so would Augustine then displace it in the explanation of the redemption.[39]

Augustine promptly gave up the conviction that God should or could respect human autonomy and convert the elect by persuasion. He made a crucial revision of his understanding of the act of faith through which a person repents of the sin of pride, places trust in the promises of the gospel, and thereby comes to receive the Spirit's gift of love. Citing the example of Paul, who was persecuting Christians at the time of his call, Augustine argued that

---

demons. Later, in *corrept.* 11.32 (BA 24:340-42) the good angels are clearly credited with the exercise of free choice that earned the divine operation fixing them in good. They serve as a contrast to elect humans who are preserved in good willing and gratuitously given the perfection of grace in glory.

37. The devils sinned through a sin of pride, and in their hatred of goodness they then tempted humans: *gen. litt.* 11.14.18–16.21 (BA 49:256-64); *civ.* 11.33, 12.6, 14.3 (CCSL 48:353.15-44, 359.1–362.99, 417.41–418.63). The humans also sinned by pride before they were tempted by the demons. In fact that temptation to doubt the goodness of God was possible only in a being that had already fallen from love of God to love of self. The temptation was allowed by God in order to manifest the secret sin: *gen. litt.* 11.5.7, 30.38–31.41 (BA 49:240-41, 292-98); *civ.* 13.20-21, 14.10-13 (CCSL 48:403.1–404.39, 430.1–436.82).

38. Augustine later explained that the demons had fallen irreparably because they had been in a higher state than humans: *c. Iul. op. imp.* 6.22 (PL 45:1553).

39. The change is evident by comparing the two expositions of the process of redemption in *trin.* 4.13.16-17 (CCSL 50:181.1–184.77) and 13.12.16–15.19 (CCSL 50A:402.1–408.33). In the fourth book, Augustine still referred to the consent of humanity to the devil as the basis for the right of which Christ must deprive the devil by his death. In the thirteenth book, however, no mention is made of that persuasion; instead humanity is handed over to the power of the devil as punishment for a prior sin: God withdraws and the instigator of sin marches in.

in causing a person to believe the gospel and to ask for help, God does not appeal to the existing dispositions of the mind, which are in fact evil and opposed to good. Instead, the efficacious call to faith actually reverses the will's orientation and moves a person to abandon an evil way of life and seek a good one. The exterior preaching of the gospel is made effective, he explained, when it is accompanied by an interior teaching that draws — not leads — a person to Christ. The converts do not, of course, believe against their wills; God makes them willing.[40] Having implanted repentance and faith in a sinner, God then grants the gift of the Holy Spirit by which the convert actually loves the good for its own sake and undertakes to fulfill the law of God.[41]

Augustine also changed his explanation of the means by which the human will is finally fixed in good so that the creature may enjoy unending beatitude in security. In the writings prior to his episcopate, he had attributed the stability of the saints in heaven to their remembering the trials of earthly life, their love of Christ the Savior, their vision of the eternal punishment of the demons, and their liberation from bodily mortality. Now he recognized that the created will could be fixed in good only by the operation of the Holy Spirit. This solution to the problem of instability was applied first to the angels.[42] In humans, Augustine balanced two forms of divine operation. As the preaching of the gospel is necessary for conversion but becomes effective only when the Spirit moves the will to respond, so the Spirit's gift of love for God can reach its fullness only when commensurate knowledge of the beloved is bestowed in the vision of God.[43] Secure beatitude will be achieved in heaven.[44]

About a decade later, Augustine was forced to reexamine the issue of divine control over human willing. In response to questions from ascetics in Af-

---

40. The change comes rapidly and completely in *grat. Chr.* 10.11, 14.15, 24.25, 45.49 (CSEL 42:134.17–135.3, 138.5-21, 145.23-25, 161.5-19); *ep.* 194, 3.9-12, 3.15–4.18 (CSEL 57:183.1–186.13, 187.12–190.11); *c. ep. Pel.* 1.19.37, 1.20.38, 2.9.19–10.23 (CSEL 60:454.2-21, 455.15–456.3, 481.5–485.16).

41. For a fuller investigation of this transition, see Burns, *Development*, pp. 135-39.

42. And only gradually. See *civ.* 11.13, 12.9 (CCSL 48:334.20-29, 363.1–364.72); *corrept.* 11.31-32 (BA 24:338-42); *c. Iul. op. imp.* 1.102 (CSEL 85.1:120.6-12).

43. *Spir. et litt.* 36.64 (CSEL 60:224.11–225.15); *perf. jus.* 3.8, 6.14 (CSEL 42:8.2-6, 12.21-23). This solution was retained in *c. ep. Pel.* 3.7.21 (CSEL 60:511.8-26) and *c. Iul.* 4.3.28 (PL 44:752-53).

44. The delay was salutary as well, since the insecurity of Christians during the earthly life helped to prevent a recurrence of the pride that had caused the original downfall of humanity: *corrept.* 13.40 (BA 24:358-62); *perseu.* 8.19, 23.63 (BA 24:636-38, 750-52).

rica and Gaul, he asserted not only that God gives believers the capacity or tendency to love and perform the good required for salvation — a gift that had been bestowed upon Adam and the angels — but that God produces the consistent willing and performance of that good. If, then, a Christian perseveres in good and thus comes to glory, God must be recognized as the true author of that continued good willing. This grace of perseverance, Augustine explained, lies midway between the first and the final grace. In Paradise, Adam had divine assistance by which he could do good and avoid sin; in glory the angels and saints enjoy a divine operation by which they cannot sin or fail; in the Church, the elect — who can sin — are preserved so that they either do not sin or promptly repent and recover from a fall.[45] During earthly life, no one receives the final grace that makes sin impossible; even Christ's humanity was preserved from failure not by the operation of the Holy Spirit but by its union with the divine person.[46] The angels — alone among creatures — actually persevered in good without this special divine operation and thus earned the reward of eternal blessedness, which humans receive as an unmerited gift.[47]

Augustine had fully abandoned the economy of salvation based upon divine persuasion of human freedom. He replaced it with one based upon divine operation that changes the orientation of the person from evil to good, causes repentance and conversion, sustains good willing, and finally fixes the blessed in good by working on the creature's knowledge and love of God.

The Origin of the Soul and Divine Sovereignty over the Will

A schematic summary of the proof of the hypothesis of the dependence of Augustine's doctrine of God's sovereignty over human freedom upon his abandonment of the theory of the sinful fall of the soul into an earthly body will be useful.

The loss of the theory by which humans fall into mortal bodies through a sin of consenting to temptation was the first step, coming about 417. This came as a rejection of Origen's teaching, based on Romans 9:16. Second, since

---

45. For a fuller discussion see Burns, *Development*, pp. 168-75; *Grat.* 15.31–17.33 (BA 24:158-68); *corrept.* 11.31–12.34 (BA 24:338-46); *praed.* 15.31 (BA 24:554-60); *perseu.* 24.67 (BA 24:760-62).

46. *Corrept.* 11.30 (BA 24:334-38). Augustine may have presumed that Christ did not enjoy full human knowledge of God during his earthly life and thus could not receive the fullness of charity.

47. *Perseu.* 7.13-14 (BA 24:626-28).

humans were originally different from angels and demons, they were no longer distinguished by their mode of sinning. Third, since humans and demons did not have to be distinguished by their mode of sinning, the first humans could sin spontaneously rather than in response to temptation. Fourth, since humans had not sinned through persuasion, the economy of their salvation need not be limited to persuasive means. Indeed, human sinners could not be saved through persuasion because they retained no good dispositions to which God could appeal. Fifth, the divine operation of conversion became an interior operation of the Holy Spirit that changed evil dispositions to good and made the convert respond to the preaching of the gospel. Sixth, God preserves Christians who have been elected to glory by persuasive and environmental means so that they do not fail to come to glory. Limited by the continued presence of concupiscence and the absence of a full knowledge of God, the Spirit's operation of charity never becomes so effective as to make sin impossible during earthly life. Seventh, once concupiscence is removed and full knowledge given in glory, love becomes full and the elect cannot sin again. Eighth, since the instability inherent in the created will can be overcome by God's sovereignty over its operation, the problem inherent in the Origenist system can be solved. Ninth, Augustine did not explain why God cannot or does not change the dispositions of demons and convert them from evil to good. Unlike Origen, he assumed that God withheld such assistance from the demons, just as God withholds it from the majority of humans.

Conclusion

Augustine never reached a fully satisfactory understanding of the origin of the soul and the mode of its entering the earthly body. His rejection of one of the possibilities — that the soul had been created in a nonearthly state and fallen by sinning into an earthly body — seems to have provided the impetus for abandoning the autonomy of created freedom and asserting divine sovereignty over the wills of angels and humans. This shift, which O'Connell places in 417, might also help to explain the contrast between Augustine's two decades of reticence on the question of effective grace after the completion of *Ad Simplicianum* in 396 and his adamant insistence upon it beginning in 418. Had he held — though quietly in his own mind rather than exposing it even in his letters — the probability that souls had existed and sinned in a spiritual condition and thus entered earthly life, he would also have been holding open a means of comprehending and explaining divine justice (even if only to himself). If humans could be individually responsible for their fall into earthly life, then the trials of mortal existence could be accounted for not only as justified punishment but as means of moving them to return. If individuals had been persuaded to sin, they might be persuaded to repent. Divine justice could respect the autonomy of the creature in both sin and salvation. Once Augustine had to give up the possibility that humans, particularly infants, were individually responsible for their failure, this means of understanding and explaining the divine justice also had to be abandoned. Once he realized that in Romans 9:11 Paul had explicitly rejected the fallen soul theory, Augustine may have abandoned himself to the incomprehensible divine justice described in the Scriptures and witnessed in the life of the Church. Individual responsibility disappeared from the economy of salvation. All had somehow sinned in Adam in a way he could not articulate, much less establish on scriptural grounds. Some were saved by divine operation that did not wait upon their consent. Others were condemned without even the opportunity to refuse divine assistance.

Once he had himself realized that his quest for understanding of God's ways was futile, Augustine turned with a vengeance upon those who claimed to understand. The bitterness of his attacks on Pelagius and particularly his intemperate railing at Julian of Eclanum may betray his own disappointment. They claimed to uphold and, even worse, to explain human freedom and divine justice. Augustine appears not only frustrated but outraged at their unwillingness to face the problems, such as the suffering and damnation of infants, which he knew he had failed to solve. Robert O'Connell's thesis that the fallen soul hypothesis was abandoned only in 417 may provide a key to understanding Augustine's old age.

Reclaiming Biblical Morality:
Sex and Salvation History in Augustine's
Treatment of the Hebrew Saints

DAVID G. HUNTER

In book three of his *Confessiones,* in the midst of discussing his youthful at-
traction to the Manichees, Augustine noted that one of the Manichean challenges to orthodox Christianity lay in its criticism of the sexual morality of
the Hebrew patriarchs and matriarchs. "Can those be considered righteous,"
the Manichees asked, "who had several wives at the same time and killed people and offered animals in sacrifice?"[1] In response Augustine argued that the
Manichees have confused the eternal and unchanging law of God with the
mutable moral customs of human beings. The Manichees have failed to grasp
that God might have given one command to people in the past, but a different
one to people in the present, "because of a change in historical circumstances" *(pro temporalibus causis).*[2] Although certain sexual acts are contrary
to nature and, therefore, always forbidden — Augustine has in mind sodomy
— other practices, such as polygamy, may merely be contrary to established

---

1. *Conf.* 3.7.12 (BA 13:384); translation in H. Chadwick, trans., *Saint Augustine:
Conf.* (Oxford and New York: Oxford University Press, 1991), p. 43.
2. *Conf.* 3.7.13 (BA 13:386).

This paper originally was delivered at the Thirteenth International Conference on Patristic
Studies, Oxford University, 16-21 August 1999, under the title "The Problem of History in
Augustine's Theology of Marriage." An earlier, and rather different, version was presented
at the symposium, "History, Apocalypse, and the Secular Imagination," held at the University of British Columbia, 18-20 September 1997.

custom. Such acts are not necessarily morally wrong; moreover, when commanded by God, they become positively virtuous. Concluding this line of reasoning, Augustine suggests that whenever God issues a command, it must be obeyed. "A just human society is one which submits to you. But happy are those who know that you are the source of moral precepts. All the acts of your servants are done either to show what present needs require or to prefigure the future."[3]

Augustine's brief discussion of the morality of the patriarchs in the *Confessiones* offers a glimpse of what will gradually become a more significant theme in his work: namely, that the very meaning of human sexual activity can differ according to different historical times and circumstances. My aim here is to sketch the development of Augustine's teaching concerning the sexual history of the human race, particularly in respect to Abraham and the other Hebrew saints. My central argument is that Augustine's thought developed in significant ways as he encountered successive opponents: first, the Manichees, then Jovinian and his followers, and finally Pelagius and the later Pelagians. Each of these new opponents raised different questions about the nature of sex in history, and Augustine's thinking developed in response to that of his adversaries.[4] Nevertheless, there remained a consistent element in Augustine's thought throughout these different controversies, namely, his effort to reclaim the value of Old Testament morality by situating it in the context of salvation history.

Sex and History in Augustine's Anti-Manichean Writings[5]

The issue of sexuality figured into Augustine's anti-Manichean writings from the very start. We find him concerned with the topic, for example, in *De moribus ecclesiae catholicae* and *De moribus manichaeorum*, begun at Rome in

---

3. *Conf.* 3.9.17 (BA 13:396); translated in Chadwick, *Confessions*, p. 48. Cf. 5.14.24 and 6.4.6.

4. For a different look at the late fourth-century Western debates about Abraham, see Elizabeth A. Clark, "Contesting Abraham: The Ascetic Reader and the Politics of Intertextuality," in *The Social World of the First Christians: Essays in Honor of Wayne E. Meeks*, ed. L. Michael White and O. Larry Yarbrough (Minneapolis: Fortress, 1995), pp. 353-65.

5. For an introduction to the anti-Manichean writings of Augustine, primarily from the point of view of the history of scholarship, see the articles of J. Ries, "La Bible chez saint Augustin et chez les manichéens," *Revue des études augustiniennes* 7 (1961): 231-43; 9 (1963): 201-15; 10 (1964): 309-29.

388, shortly after his baptism, and published probably the following year in Africa. In these early writings Augustine attacked the Manichees for their rejection of procreation and defended Catholic Christians for making use of the goods of the world, among them procreation, possessions, and money. For example, he cited Paul's First Letter to the Corinthians, where the Apostle says that "the unbelieving husband is sanctified in the believing wife and the unbelieving wife is sanctified in her believing husband" (7:14). Augustine argued that, if a chaste marital union is capable of sanctifying even unbelievers, and their offspring as well, then Christian marriage certainly cannot be something evil.[6]

Several years later in another anti-Manichean writing, *Contra Adimantum* (ca. 392), Augustine again invoked Paul as well as Jesus to demonstrate that the Old and New Testaments stood in fundamental agreement in their approval of sex and marriage. Augustine cited Matthew 19:3-9, where Jesus appealed to Genesis 1:27 and 2:24 to endorse the permanence of marriage; he also recalled the final verses of Ephesians 5, where the author also quoted Genesis 2:24 and referred the text to the "great mystery" *(sacramentum . . . magnum)* of Christ and the Church. Since both Jesus and Ephesians 5 quote the Old Testament text with approval, Augustine argued, there can be no real contradiction between the Old and New Testaments in regard to marriage: "All things both in the Old and in the New Testament have been written and transmitted by one Spirit."[7]

In these early writings against the Manichees, Augustine steadfastly defended the goodness of marriage and procreation in the Hebrew Scriptures, but we do not yet find any sustained reflection on marriage within the framework of salvation history. To be sure, Augustine was concerned to show the fundamental compatibility of the Old and New Testaments, and this represented an incipient reflection on history. It was not until the later 390s that Augustine began to confront seriously the problem of history and with it the problem of marriage and procreation in God's providential plan. This development can be seen in several writings from this period: the third book of *De doctrina Christiana* (ca. 396), *Contra Faustum manichaeum* (ca. 398), as well as the passage from the *Confessiones* that was mentioned above.

In *De doctrina Christiana* Augustine briefly took up the question of whether the apparently immoral behavior of the Old Testament patriarchs

---

6. 1 Cor. 7:14, cited in *mor.* 1.35.79 (CSEL 90: 85). In *mor.* 2.18.65 (CSEL 90:146-47) Augustine criticized the Manichees for accepting sex while rejecting procreation.

7. *C. Adim.* 3 (CSEL 25/1:121).

should be interpreted both literally and figuratively, or figuratively only.[8] Augustine's general rule of thumb in such cases was that texts that were not conducive to good morals ought to be given a figurative interpretation. The Old Testament saints, however, presented a unique problem. On the one hand, Augustine knew that the literal sense could not simply be jettisoned; the story of Abraham and his descendants was essential to the narrative of salvation history. On the other hand, he clearly believed that their conduct could no longer be taken as a model for the present-day behavior of Christians. Augustine, therefore, had to devote some attention to the literal meaning of the patriarchal narratives and to explain why in this case the literal meaning was true but not to be emulated.

There are several aspects to Augustine's rehabilitation of the *iusti*. He first appeals to the prophetic character of their behavior. Like Hosea, for example, who associated with a prostitute, "the just men of old in the earthly kingdom pictured the heavenly kingdom to themselves and foretold it."[9] Furthermore their conduct was intended only to produce offspring; hence the provision for men to have multiple wives, but not for women to have multiple husbands. Moreover, when the patriarchs and matriarchs engaged in sex, they did so, Augustine insists, without lust, whereas those people who marry today do so only out of a lack of self-restraint, as the apostle Paul teaches.[10] For all these reasons, Augustine concludes, the Old Testament narratives are to be taken figuratively as prophetic in some way, pointing to the end of love of God or of neighbor or both. However, the literal meaning, properly understood, is not to be rejected: "although the reader should not take the actual deeds as models for moral behavior, but should try to understand their figurative meanings. For there are many things which at that time were done out of duty that now can only be done out of lust."[11]

Augustine's reflection on Old Testament morality in *De doctrina Christiana* was an important step forward in the development of his appreciation of the sexual conduct of the patriarchs and its role in salvation history. To a much greater degree than he had previously, Augustine defended the truth of the literal interpretation of the patriarchal marriages, even as he expressed a preference for the figurative reading. Although he still seems somewhat uncomfortable with their conduct, Augustine has now acknowledged its role in the formation of the people of Israel, both literally and prophetically.

8. *Doc. Chr.* 3.10.14–3.22.32 (BA 11/2:254-80).
9. *Doc. Chr.* 3.12.20 (BA 11/2:264); cf. 3.12.18.
10. *Doc. Chr.* 3.18.27 (BA 11/2:272-74).
11. *Doc. Chr.* 3.22.32 (BA 11/2:280).

In *De doctrina Christiana,* however, we do not yet find a full-scale discussion of the place of patriarchal sexuality in the history of salvation. This is the argument that can be found a couple of years later in Augustine's thirty-three books *Contra Faustum manichaeum.* This extensive work, composed shortly after the *Confessiones,* contains a much fuller discussion of the sexual morality of the Hebrew saints than Augustine had previously articulated. Faustus was a Manichean bishop who had criticized the Old Testament Scriptures and repudiated the incarnation. In response to Faustus's attack on the sexual mores of the Old Testament saints, Augustine found an opportunity to develop his thinking on the role of sex and procreation in salvation history.

Faustus had presented a long list of complaints about the sexual immorality rampant in the Old Testament. For example, Abraham was guilty of adultery for his sexual relations with the slave Hagar; Abraham virtually sold his wife Sarah to king Abimelech and to the Egyptian pharaoh in order to profit from them; Lot had incestuous relations with his two daughters; Jacob was the husband of four wives, two of them sisters, and so on. In short, Faustus argued, such scandalous tales are to be rejected by any right-thinking Christian. Either the stories are false, in which case the Old Testament Scriptures are to be rejected as untrue, or the stories are true, in which case the fathers are genuinely guilty of sin. "Choose whichever you please," Faustus taunted, "in either case the crime is detestable, for vicious conduct and falsehood are equally loathsome."[12]

Augustine's initial response to Faustus was to note that there is a difference between the time when the promise was under a veil and the time when the promise was revealed. In the past, that is, in the history of ancient Israel, both the words and the deeds of the patriarchs were prophetic: "The whole kingdom of the Hebrews was like a great prophet, corresponding to the greatness of the Person prophesied."[13] Therefore, in the life of the nation as a whole, as well as in the lives of the individual patriarchs, one can discover a prophecy of the coming of Christ and the Church.[14] For example, in the story of Abraham and Sarah's journey to Egypt, when Abraham pretended that Sarah was his sister — a story that Faustus found particularly offensive since it involved Abraham's virtual sale of his wife to the Egyptian pharaoh — one can find a symbol of the beauty of the Church, which is the bride of Christ in secret. The event also prefigured the secret union of Christ and the human

12. *C. Faust.* 22.5 (CSEL 25/1:595).

13. *C. Faust.* 22.24 (CSEL 25/1:618-19).

14. Augustine's prophetic interpretation of Abraham's behavior continues in *C. Faust.* 22.38-40 (CSEL 25/1:631-34).

soul, which the apostle Paul referred to as the "great mystery of marriage."[15] This reading of history as prophecy is one that Augustine continued to invoke throughout his life. For example, the notion of "prophetic history," as he calls it, was to serve as Augustine's primary interpretive principle when he came to treat the history of humanity in books fifteen through eighteen of *De civitate dei*.[16]

Yet elsewhere in *Contra Faustum*, Augustine offered another, more historical approach to the text. He questioned whether Abraham or the others actually did commit sin. "Sin," Augustine writes, "is any transgression in deed, word, or desire of the eternal law. And the eternal law is the divine order or will of God, which requires the preservation of natural order and forbids the breach of it."[17] In the case of human beings, Augustine argued, the eternal law permits the indulgence of bodily appetite in sexual intercourse, under the guidance of reason, not for the gratification of passion but for the continuance of the human race through the propagation of children. Abraham received a promise from God that he accepted in faith, namely, that he would be the father of many descendants. Since he believed that his wife Sarah was barren, he acted out of obedience to God when he engaged in sex with the slave Hagar and later with his wife Sarah: "He preserved the natural order," Augustine writes, "by seeking in marriage only the birth of a child."[18]

It is clear from *Contra Faustum* that Augustine has two, rather distinct, answers to Faustus's criticisms of the Hebrew saints, both pertaining to the status of marriage in history. On a strictly literal or historical level, procreation was necessary in order to fulfill God's promises to Abraham and to build up the people of God that would lead to Christ. As long as Abraham and the other patriarchs and matriarchs engaged in sex only for procreation, their sexual lives (even their apparent promiscuity) conformed to the divine law; such sexual relations were even necessary for the incarnation. As Augustine wrote slightly later in his response to another Manichee, Secundinus:

---

15. *C. Faust.* 22.38 (CSEL 25/1:632): *magnum coniugii sacramentum.*

16. See *civ.* 16.2 (CSEL 40/2:127) for the expression *prophetica historia.*

17. *C. Faust.* 22.27 (CSEL 25/1:621).

18. *C. Faust.* 22.30 (CSEL 25/1:624). Augustine offers a similar explanation of other forms of sexual behavior, for example, the polygamy of Jacob. Polygamy violates no law of nature, but only custom and legal practice. Since the custom and legal practice of Jacob's day did not forbid polygamy, and since Jacob had intercourse with his four wives only for the procreation of children, his conduct, in Augustine's view, was thoroughly conformable to both divine and human law: *C. Faust.* 22.47 (CSEL 25/1:639-40).

The conjugal duty of the fathers and mothers, such as Abraham and Sarah, should not be judged according to the standards of human society, but according to the dispensation of God. For since it was necessary that Christ come in the flesh, both the marriage of Sarah and the virginity of Mary served to propagate that flesh.[19]

Yet, as we have seen, Augustine also responded to Faustus by appealing to the symbolic character of the biblical story. On the level of symbol or prophecy, the actions of the Old Testament figures foreshadowed the events of the New Testament, particularly the appearance of Christ and the Church. In *De catechizandis rudibus,* composed about the year 400, Augustine succinctly described the prophetic character of the behavior of Abraham and the other Hebrew saints:

Not only the words of these holy men who in point of time preceded the Lord's birth, but also their lives, their wives, their children, and acts were a prophecy of this time, wherein through faith in the passion of Christ the Church is being gathered together from all nations. . . . [In] all these things there were signified spiritual mysteries closely associated with Christ and the Church of which even those saints were members, although they lived before Christ our Lord was born according to the flesh.[20]

The procreative history of ancient Israel was significant to Augustine both because it was historically necessary in order to create the line that led to Christ and because it served as a prophetic foreshadowing of the events of the new dispensation.

Before we move on to the next phase in Augustine's development, it should be noted that *De catechizandis rudibus* was composed about the year 400, sometime after *Contra Faustum* but before the writings on marriage and virginity that will occupy us in the next section.[21] It is significant that *De catechizandis rudibus* was the work in which Augustine first used the language of the "two cities."[22] These terms, which eventually were to provide the theo-

19. *C. Sec.* 22 (CSEL 25/2:940).

20. *Cat. rud.* 19.33 (BA 11/1:162-64); J. P. Christopher, trans., *St. Augustine: The First Catechetical Instruction,* ACW 2 (Westminster, Md.: Newman, 1962), p. 63.

21. *Retract.* 2.14 (CCSL 57:100).

22. *Cat. rud.* 19.31 and 37. See A. Lauras and H. Rondet, "Le thème des deux cités dans l'oeuvre de saint Augustin," in *Études Augustiniennes,* ed. H. Rondet et al. (Paris: Aubier, 1953), pp. 102-5; and the discussion in G. O'Daly, *Augustine's City of God: A Reader's Guide* (Oxford: Clarendon, 1999), pp. 270-72.

logical framework of Augustine's masterwork, *The City of God,* designate those two communities of human beings, the wicked and the just, whose origins can be traced back to the beginning of the human race and whose final separation will occur only at the end of time. Foremost among the citizens of the holy city, Augustine notes, was Abraham:

> And even then, to be sure, there were not wanting just men, to seek God devoutly and vanquish the pride of the devil, citizens of that holy city, who were made whole by the future humility of Christ, their King, revealed to them through the Spirit. Of these, Abraham a devout and faithful servant of God, was chosen that to him might be revealed the mystery of the Son of God *(sacramentum Filii Dei),* so that by imitating his faith all the faithful of all nations in time to come might be called his children.[23]

The emergence of the terminology of the "two cities" in *De catechizandis rudibus* and the placement of Abraham (and his wives and children) within the holy city is significant. It suggests that Augustine had now begun to think of the so-called "Old Testament" not just as a *preparation* for the New, but as a proleptic *participation* in it. Abraham and his descendants, Augustine says, "were made whole by the future humility of Christ . . . revealed to them through the Spirit." It appears that by the time Augustine wrote *De catechizandis rudibus* the sexual conduct of Abraham and the other Hebrew forebears had become something more than just an embarrassment to be explained away by figurative interpretation. It was now an essential aspect of his emerging theology of salvation history.

Sex and History in the Jovinianist Controversy

Around the year 401, shortly after writing *De catechizandis rudibus,* Augustine turned his attention to a new and rather different opponent. In the *Retractationes* Augustine says that it was in response to "the heresy of Jovinian" that he had written the treatise *De bono coniugali* and the companion work, *De sancta virginitate.* About ten years earlier Jovinian had been condemned by a synod at Rome under Pope Siricius and by another at Milan under St. Ambrose. His primary offense was to suggest that married Chris-

---

23. *Cat. rud.* 19.33 (BA 11/1:162); translated in Christopher, *The First Catechetical Instruction,* pp. 62-63, slightly revised.

tians were equal in merit to celibate Christians.[24] Jovinian's work also provoked a bitter response from St. Jerome in Palestine, the notorious *Adversus Jovinianum*. Jerome had spoken so harshly about the defects of the married state that, as Augustine says, it seemed to many that the superiority of celibacy could be maintained only by condemning marriage. Augustine, therefore, entered the controversy in the hope of finding a middle ground between those who deprecated marriage (whether the Manichees or Jerome) and those, like Jovinian, who saw no reason to prefer celibacy.

Augustine's treatise *De bono coniugali* is well-known for its influential teaching on the "three goods" of marriage: the procreation of children, the fidelity of spouses, and the "sacrament" in marriage, that is, its character as an indissoluble bond. Yet for our purposes it is Augustine's discussion of the Old Testament patriarchs and the historical character of Augustine's understanding of sexuality that are most relevant. Several sources say that Jovinian achieved great success by appealing to the example of virtuous married persons from the Hebrew Scriptures. According to Augustine's *Retractationes*, Jovinian had confronted celibate women with the challenge: "Are you better than Sarah, better than Susanna or Anna?" Similarly, Augustine tells us, Jovinian had shattered the celibacy of holy men by comparing them to the fathers and husbands of the Old Testament. Since celibate Christians could not dare to claim that they were superior to the Hebrew patriarchs and matriarchs, Jovinian reasoned, celibacy could not be regarded as superior to marriage.[25]

From Augustine's comments it appears that Jovinian presented Augustine with exactly the opposite problem as had the Manichees. Rather than see the Old Testament saints as examples of sexual degeneracy, Jovinian argued that they were paragons of marital excellence; therefore, sexual activity should be esteemed as highly in the present by Christians as it was in the past by the Hebrew patriarchs and matriarchs. In order to respond to Jovinian, Augustine had to move beyond his earlier anti-Manichean appreciation of the sex lives of the Old Testament saints, a point on which he and Jovinian substantially agreed. In other words, Jovinian's argument forced Augustine to

24. For further discussion of Jovinian and his arguments, see David G. Hunter, "Resistance to the Virginal Ideal in Late-Fourth-Century Rome: The Case of Jovinian," *ThS* 48 (1987): 45-64; idem, "Helvidius, Jovinian, and the Virginity of Mary in Late-Fourth-Century Rome," *JECS* 1 (1993): 47-71.

25. Jovinian's arguments are given by Augustine in the *retr.* 2.22 (CCSL 57:107-8). The centrality of biblical texts to Jovinian's arguments in defense of marriage was also noted by Siricius, *ep.* 7 (PL 20:1170): *novi et veteris Testamenti, ut dixi, continentiam pervertentes, et spiritu diabolico interpretantes.* See also Jerome, *Adversus Jovinianum,* passim.

come to terms with the nature of marriage in the *present* as well as in the *past*. In order to refute Jovinian and to defend the superiority of celibacy over marriage, Augustine had to develop a more differentiated way of interpreting the various meanings of sex and marriage in history. Central to Augustine's new historicization of sexuality was the idea that there are different "sacraments" in different periods of history.

We see this argument developed in *De bono coniugali* in several ways. First, Augustine repeats much of his earlier anti-Manichean argument about the necessity of procreation in ancient Israel in order to produce the line that led to Christ. Now, however, Augustine contrasts this prior period of procreative necessity (i.e., history before Christ) with the present period of history after Christ, when physical procreation is no longer necessary:

> In the earliest times of the human race, in order to propagate the people of God, through which the prince and savior of all peoples might both be prophesied and be born, the saints were obliged to make use of this good of marriage. . . . But now, since the opportunity for spiritual relationship abounds on all sides and for all peoples for entering into a holy and pure association, even they who wish to contract marriage only to have children are to be admonished to practice the greater good of continence.[26]

Augustine argues that there is "a mysterious distinction of times" *(temporum secreta distinctio)*, or, as he calls it in another place, "a diversity of times" *(diversitas temporum)*, that gives different meanings to human choices and actions.[27] In response to historical necessity the Hebrew patriarchs and matriarchs engaged in sex, but they did so only out of duty, in response to a divine command, not out of passion. By contrast, people today no longer have the same need to marry. The last days are near, and the world is already full of people who might become Christian. Therefore, the only reason to marry in the present is, as the apostle Paul teaches, a lack of self-control. Even if there are a few people who marry only in order to have children, Augustine adds, "in these people even the desire for children is carnal, whereas in those people it was spiritual because it was in accord with the sacred mystery *(sacramentum)* of that time."[28]

Augustine's reference to the *sacramentum* of past time leads him imme-

26. *B. coniug.* 9.9 (CSEL 41:200-201).
27. These phrases occur in *b. coniug.* 15.17 (CSEL 41:210) and 16.18 (CSEL 41:212).
28. *B. coniug.* 17.19 (CSEL 41:213): *quia sacramento illius temporis congruebat.*

diately to discuss the history of sexuality from the perspective of its value as a prophetic or sacred sign.[29] Marriages in the past and marriages in the present, he argues, differ not only in their historical purposes (that is, in the necessity or nonnecessity of producing children), but also in their *sacramenta,* that is, in their prophetic or symbolic significance. In the past, for example, polygamy was allowed; today strict monogamy is the norm. For Augustine, the reason for this historical relativity does not lie merely in the different needs of the human race at different points in time. It also derives from the different "sacrament" that marriage possesses in different periods of history: "Just as the sacrament of multiple marriages at that time signified the future multitude that would be subject to God in all the nations of the earth, so the sacrament of single marriages in our day signifies the unity of us all that will one day be subject to God in the one heavenly City."[30]

At the heart of Augustine's argument is the notion that human sexual activity can have different meanings in different phases of salvation history. Marriages, both in the past and in the present, contain within them a transcendent significance, that is, a "sacrament." The primary sacrament of the marriages of the Hebrew dispensation, Augustine suggests, was their promiscuous *multiplicity,* a multiplicity that was fulfilled historically in the spread of the Church among the many nations. In the Christian dispensation, by contrast, the primary sacrament in marriage is an indissoluble *unity.* For Augustine the "sacrament" in Christian marriage lies in the indissoluble bond of unity that exists between spouses and that endures until the death of one or the other.[31] This human bond signifies a unity that will be realized eschatologically in the future City of God. As he writes in *De bono coniugali:* "Out of many souls there will arise a city of people with a single soul and a single heart turned to God. This perfection of our unity will come about after this pilgrimage, when no longer will anyone's thoughts be hidden from another, and no longer will anyone be in conflict with anyone about anything."[32]

29. For an overview of Augustine's use of the term *sacramentum,* see É. Schmitt, *Le mariage chrétien dans l'oeuvre de saint Augustin* (Paris: Études Augustiniennes, 1983), pp. 215-33, and the literature cited there; also idem, "Le 'sacramentum' dans la théologie augustinienne du mariage," *Revue du droit canonique* 42 (1992): 197-213.

30. *B. coniug.* 18.21 (CSEL 41:215).

31. For Augustine this notion of the "sacrament" in marriage is the basis of the Catholic discipline that forbids remarriage after divorce, as well as the canonical prohibition against the ordination of men who have been married more than once. See *b. coniug.* 18.21.

32. *B. coniug.* 18.21 (CSEL 41:214).

In response to the views of Jovinian Augustine appears to have taken his reflections on history and sexuality in a new direction. What began in *Contra Faustum manichaeum* as a defense of the Hebrew saints against the Manichees has become in *De bono coniugali* a way of discriminating between the different values of sex and marriage in the Old and New Testaments. Against Jovinian, Augustine's purpose was less to vindicate the moral stature of the Hebrew saints than it was to depreciate the status of marriage among Christians. There is something of a paradox in Augustine's thought at this point. Marriages in the Christian dispensation are subject to stricter moral standards than marriages in the Old Testament; for example, Christians must adhere to strict monogamy. Moreover, Christian marriages possess a sacrament that is fulfilled eschatologically in the unity of the heavenly city, whereas the marriages of the Old Testament have only a historical fulfillment in the coming of Christ and spread of Christianity. These differences between marriage in the Old Testament and marriage in the New Testament might lead one to suppose that Christian marriages should be esteemed as highly, or even more highly, than the marriages of the Old Testament saints. In other words, Augustine's "sacramental" view of marriage might suggest that Christian marriage should be seen as a prophetic foreshadowing of the eschatological union of Christ and the Church (that is, the *magnum sacramentum*) and, therefore, should be highly valued.[33]

Augustine, however, did not choose to take his thinking any further in the direction of such a sacramental understanding of marriage. In his view the coming of Christ had fundamentally changed the historical conditions under which Christians now participate in marital and sexual life. For the Hebrew patriarchs and matriarchs, procreation was not (as it is for Christians today) motivated simply by a natural desire to produce children to form a succession. "Those people of former times," Augustine noted, "rose above this desire with a much holier attitude of mind, as they looked to have children from their marriages because of Christ, so that the race to which he belonged in the flesh might be set apart from other races. . . . It was, therefore, something of much greater value than the chaste marriages of the faithful of our times."[34] As Augustine saw it, the marriages of Christians no longer play any necessary role in the history of salvation. In the Old Testament, by contrast,

---

33. See the discussion in A.-M. La Bonnardière, "L'interprétation augustinienne du *magnum sacramentum* de Éphés. 5,32," *Recherches Augustiniennes* 12 (1977): 3-45, esp. pp. 30-32. As La Bonnardière notes, Augustine was always reluctant to apply the language of the Eph. 5:32 to any individual Christian marriage.

34. *B. coniug.* 19.22 (CSEL 41:216).

procreation was necessary. The Old Testament saints were motivated not merely by the desire for a natural good, that is, their own children; rather, they pursued the desire for a spiritual good, namely, to produce the physical lineage that would lead to Christ.

Hence it could be argued, as Augustine proceeds to do in *De bono coniugali*, that the patriarchs and matriarchs of the Old Testament should be regarded as superior even to celibate Christians. Abraham, for example, married and engaged in sexual relations only out of obedience to God's command, Augustine suggests. Abraham would gladly have forgone sexual relations if God had commanded him to do so, just as he showed that he was willing to sacrifice his son Isaac at God's command.[35] Such behavior, Augustine insists, demonstrated that Abraham must have possessed the virtue of celibacy or continence as an internal disposition *(habitus),* even if that disposition was not displayed in the external practice of celibacy. Pursuing this line of reasoning Augustine argues that some celibate Christians might actually find it easier to practice celibacy and to renounce sex altogether than to be married and engage in sex in the manner of Abraham, that is, only out of desire to produce children out of religious duty.[36] In such a case, Augustine concludes, the celibate Christian would not be superior to the married saint of the Old Testament, even though in the Christian dispensation celibacy remains preferable to marriage. As Augustine notes in the closing paragraph of *De bono coniugali*, celibate Christians, "although they are not married, are not better than some married persons, namely those holy fathers and mothers in the past, because if they did marry, they would not be as good as those were."[37]

Sex and History in the Pelagian Controversy

Augustine's discussion of the relative virtues of celibate Christians and the married saints of the Old Testament leads us to the final stage in his treatment of sex and marriage in the history of salvation. One of the striking aspects of Augustine's rather optimistic view of the Hebrew saints in *De bono coniugali* is that he never explicitly indicates how it was that Abraham and the other men and women in ancient times managed to achieve such virtuous conduct. Such an omission is all the more surprising, given that by the year

35. See *b. coniug.* 18.22; 23.31; 24.32.
36. *B. coniug.* 22.27.
37. *B. coniug.* 26.35 (CSEL 41:230).

401 Augustine had already developed his distinctive emphasis on the necessity of divine grace to overcome the ingrained tendency of human beings to sin. In *De bono coniugali*, however, Augustine was content simply to assert that the Hebrew patriarchs and matriarchs had possessed the virtues of obedience and continence, without actually discussing how it was that they managed to acquire these virtues.

As time went on, however, Augustine could no longer afford not to address such questions. By the early decades of the fifth century, Augustine had become increasingly explicit about the extent to which Abraham and his descendants shared in the universal human condition of sinfulness, and particularly sexual concupiscence. Conversely, he increasingly noted that it was only by God's grace that the saints of the Old Testament were able to participate in the mysterious history of salvation. There appear to be at least two reasons for Augustine's development in this regard. First, during the first decade of the fifth century his thinking on original sin and its link with sexual concupiscence reached a new degree of clarity as he wrote his *Literal Commentary on Genesis (De Genesi ad litteram)*. Second, he was provoked to emphasize both the problem of sin and the solution of grace as he engaged in debate with Pelagius and, especially, with Pelagius's supporter, bishop Julian of Eclanum.

It has often been noted that *De Genesi ad litteram* marked a decisive turning point in Augustine's view of sexual activity and its relation to the original sin of Adam and Eve.[38] As late as *De bono coniugali* Augustine was undecided on the crucial question of whether Adam and Eve would have reproduced sexually if they had not sinned.[39] By the time Augustine composed Book IX of *De Genesi ad litteram,* sometime before the year 410, he had resolved that God indeed had intended Adam and Eve to have a full bodily life in Paradise and that this life would have included sex and procreation even before the fall. In *De Genesi ad litteram* Augustine argued that it was precisely because Adam and Eve were expected to live forever that they were enjoined to produce companions to fill up the world. Moreover, procreation as a reason for sexual union remains in effect today, Augustine insists, and the origi-

---

38. See, for example, the extensive discussion in Elizabeth A. Clark, "Heresy, Asceticism, Adam, and Eve: Interpretations of Genesis 1–3 in the Later Latin Fathers," in her *Ascetic Piety and Women's Faith: Essays on Late Ancient Christianity* (Lewiston/Queenston: Edwin Mellen, 1986), pp. 353-85; also Susan E. Schreiner, "Eve, the Mother of History: Reaching for the Reality of History in Augustine's Later Exegesis of Genesis," in *Genesis 1–3 in the History of Exegesis: Intrigue in the Garden,* ed. Gregory Robbins (Lewiston/Queenston: Edwin Mellen, 1988), pp. 135-86.

39. Cf. *b. coniug.* 2.2 (CSEL 41:188-90).

nal blessing to "increase and multiply" has not been abrogated, despite the sin and punishment of the human race.[40]

There was, however, another side to Augustine's interpretation of the Genesis story. Once Augustine had begun to think of Adam and Eve as genuinely physical and sexual persons before the fall, he was led to conceive of their sin as having an effect not only on their spirits but also on their bodies. As soon as they disobeyed God's command, Augustine writes, the bodies of Adam and Eve contracted "the deadly disease of death." Moreover, they began to experience something else as well, a phenomenon he describes in the words of Romans 7:23: "I see in my members another law at war with the law of my mind."[41] Sin introduced into their bodies a disordered motion, the "concupiscence of the flesh," that is, a tendency for sexual desire to run contrary to the conscious control of the mind and will. It was the presence of this new movement in their flesh that caused Adam and Eve to experience shame at their nakedness. Although the sin of Adam and Eve in no way involved sexual relations, Augustine argues, the effects of this sin were felt directly as an "animal drive" *(bestialem motum)* in their bodily members, "the same drive that causes animals to desire copulation."[42]

Once Augustine had clarified the fundamental connection between original sin and human sexual desire in this manner, it became increasingly difficult for him to ignore the fact that even the saints of the Old Testament must have experienced — and, indeed, made good use of — this "concupiscence of the flesh." We see this new emphasis already in Books IX and X of *De Genesi ad litteram.* After describing the original condition of Adam and Eve, Augustine goes on to note that because of original sin, all subsequent human beings suffer the effects of concupiscence: "What punishment could have been more deserved than that the body, made to serve the soul, should not be willing to obey every command of the soul, just as the soul herself refused to serve her Lord?"[43] The descendants of Adam and Eve — from Seth to Noah to Abraham and the people of Israel — all produce children by means of this "law of sin in the members 'at war with the law of the mind' (Rom. 7:23), even though virtue overcomes it by the grace of God."[44] "With

40. See *gen. litt.* 9.5-7 (CSEL 28/1:273-76).

41. *Gen. litt.* 9.10 (CSEL 28/1:279).

42. *Gen. litt.* 11.32 (CSEL 28/1:366): *eundem motum, quo fit in pecoribus concumbendi adpetitus.*

43. *Gen. litt.* 9.11 (CSEL 28/1:281); translated in J. H. Taylor, trans., *St. Augustine: The Literal Meaning of Genesis,* ACW 42 (New York: Newman, 1982), p. 83.

44. *Gen. litt.* 9.11 (CSEL 28/1:280); translated in Taylor, *The Literal Meaning of Genesis,* p. 82.

the help of God's grace," Augustine writes, the human soul can overcome the "law of sin in the members of this body of death." Thus the soul "gains a heavenly reward with greater glory, showing how praiseworthy is that obedience which by virtue was able to triumph over the punishment deserved by another's disobedience."[45]

Later, in Book X of *De Genesi ad litteram*, the topic of sexual generation through Abraham arises again in respect to the soul of Christ. Augustine cites Hebrews 7:4-10, which speaks of Abraham and his descendants through Levi ("who was still in the loins of his ancestor Abraham") paying tithes to Melchizedek, a figure of Christ. Commenting on the text, Augustine notes that both Levi and Christ existed in the loins of Abraham, according to the flesh. However, Levi was there "according to carnal concupiscence," whereas Christ was there "only according to corporeal substance." Levi was born of his father Abraham, just as Abraham was born of his father, "namely, through the law in the members 'at war with the law of the mind' and through an invisible concupiscence."[46] Abraham's flesh contained within it both the wound of sin *(vulnus praevaricationis)* and the remedy for that wound, Augustine argues. The "wound" is "the law of the members at war with the law of the mind"; the "remedy" is the body of Christ, "taken from the Virgin without the working of concupiscence."[47]

It is clear from *De Genesi ad litteram* that by the year 410 Augustine had begun to acknowledge explicitly the extent to which Abraham and his descendants were born into the universal condition of sinfulness, precisely because they were born of sexual intercourse. Given this universal "wound" in human nature, the history of the human race would have been nothing other than the history of the propagation of sin had not grace intervened to create a history of salvation. From this point onward, Augustine clearly insisted that the participation of Abraham and the other saints of the Hebrew dispensation in the history of salvation occurred only as a result of the grace of Christ, even though in time they preceded him. During the final decades of his life Augustine was to encounter a new set of opponents whose views of human nature

---

45. *Gen. litt.* 9.11 (CSEL 28/1:281); translated in Taylor, *The Literal Meaning of Genesis*, p. 83.

46. *Gen. litt.* 10.20 (CSEL 28/1:323-24); translated in Taylor, *The Literal Meaning of Genesis*, p. 124.

47. *Gen. litt.* 10.20 (CSEL 28/1:324). For a detailed study of the significance of this text from Romans on Augustine's thought, see M-F. Berrouard, "L'exégèse augustinienne de Rom. 7, 7-25 entre 396 et 418," *Recherches Augustiniennes* 16 (1981): 101-96. The development of Augustine's treatment of Abraham that I am tracing here is, in many respects, parallel to his treatment of the apostle Paul, as traced by Berrouard.

led to a rather different reading of the morality of the patriarchs and matriarchs. In the writings of Pelagius and his disciples Augustine encountered a new challenge to his understanding of sin and grace, one that led him to acknowledge even more explicitly the need of Abraham and his progeny for divine grace.

One of the key elements in Pelagius's own defense of human nature was his use of examples of virtue from the Hebrew Scriptures. The fact that men and women were able to lead righteous lives before the coming of Christ (and even prior to the giving of the Mosaic law) is taken as evidence of the power of human nature to resist sin and acquire virtue. For example, in his *Letter to Demetrias*, Pelagius cited Romans 2:15-16 and noted that there is "a sort of natural sanctity" in the human mind that enables it to discern right from wrong: "It is this law that all have used whom scripture records as having lived in sanctity and having pleased God between the time of Adam and that of Moses." The example of the "righteous Gentiles," as well as that of Abraham and his descendants, is adduced to demonstrate "how great is the good of nature" prior to the giving of the law and the coming of Christ.[48] Similarly, in his note on the same passage in his *Commentary on Romans*, Pelagius observed that "Nature produces a law in [their] heart through the testimony of the conscience. Or: The conscience testifies that it has a law, because, even if the one who sins fears no one else, the conscience is apprehensive when one sins and rejoices when sin is overcome."[49] In Pelagius's view the virtuous conduct of the Hebrew saints was a sign of the integrity of human nature as evidenced in the power of conscience.

In his two books, *De gratia Christi et de peccato originali* (418), Augustine responded directly to Pelagius's idea that nature alone was sufficient to conduce the Old Testament saints to sanctity. Citing 1 Corinthians 15:21-22 ("Just as in Adam all die, so in Christ shall all be made alive") Augustine noted that this means that salvation comes only through Christ.[50] The righteous men and women of ancient times received the grace of God so that they might believe in the incarnation and resurrection, even before the coming of Jesus. Abraham is Augustine's chief example. In John 8:56 Jesus had said that "Abraham desired to see my day, and he saw it and was glad." To Augustine this is sufficient testimony that "Abraham was fully imbued with faith in the

---

48. *Epistula ad Demetriadem* 5 (PL 30:21-22); translated in B. R. Rees, trans., *The Letters of Pelagius and His Followers* (Rochester, N.Y.: Boydell, 1991), p. 40.

49. Theodore de Bruyn, trans., *Pelagius' Commentary on St. Paul's Epistle to the Romans* (Oxford: Clarendon, 1993), p. 73.

50. *Pecc. or.* 2.26.30 (CSEL 42:190).

incarnation."[51] Such faith, Augustine insists, could only be the result of the grace of God, not the product of human nature.

Although Pelagius had clearly raised the question of the source of the righteousness of the Old Testament saints, it was his disciple, Bishop Julian of Eclanum, who steered the Pelagian debate in the direction of issues of sexual morality. For Julian, the sexual activity of Abraham and Sarah became a particular point of contention, precisely because Julian denied that sexual concupiscence was a result of the sin of Adam and Eve. Julian pointed specifically to the sexual activity of Abraham and Sarah as evidence of the goodness of sexual desire. Julian argued that sexual concupiscence could not be regarded as something evil if it was through such desire that God had fulfilled the promise of salvation. In the second book of *De nuptiis et concupiscentia* (ca. 420), we find the following quotation from Julian's initial attack on Augustine: "You have certainly defined as naturally evil this concupiscence without which there is no fertility. Why, then, is it aroused in the elderly by a gift from heaven? Prove now, if you can, that what you see that God bestows as a gift belongs to the work of the devil."[52] Later, in the *Contra Julianum* (ca. 421) Augustine again quotes Julian's opinion that sexual desire "was restored by a gift of God to Abraham and Sarah when their bodies were worn out and all but dead from old age."[53] Finally, in his *Contra secundam Iuliani responsionem opus imperfectum* Augustine again quoted Julian's opinion on the innocence of sexual desire as experienced by Abraham and Sarah: "If the son that God promised them is given to them through concupiscence, then concupiscence is undoubtedly good, since it fulfills God's promise."[54]

In his various responses to Julian Augustine argued that the miraculous gift given to Abraham and Sarah consisted not in their concupiscence, but in their fertility. This we know, he suggests, because they had reached an advanced old age and old age brings with it a loss of fertility, but not necessarily a lessening of desire.[55] Abraham and Sarah, like all human beings, were affected by the concupiscence of the flesh as a result of original sin, but this was something that they needed to overcome with the help of God's grace. Although this concupiscence is something evil, Augustine notes, it can be used

51. *Pecc. or.* 2.27.32 (CSEL 42:191): *quod fide fuerit incarnationis eius inbutus.*

52. *Nupt. et conc.* 2.10.23 (CSEL 42:275); translated in R. J. Teske, trans., *Answer to the Pelagians, II,* The Works of Saint Augustine, Pt. I, v. 24 (Hyde Park, N.Y.: New City Press, 1988), p. 67. The fragments of Julian's four books, *Ad Turbantium,* are edited by L. deConinck in CCSL 88. This and the following quotations are found at CCSL 88:350.

53. *C. Iul.* 3.11.21 (PL 44:712); translated in Teske, *Answer to the Pelagians, II,* p. 350.

54. *C. Iul. imp.* 5.10 (PL 45:1439).

55. *C. Iul.* 3.11.22-23 (PL 44:712-14).

well by human beings when they direct it towards the procreation of children. "Abraham made good use of this evil in marital intercourse, even though this evil was not present in the body of that life which existed in paradise before the sin."[56]

Throughout his anti-Pelagian writings Augustine consistently maintained that the saints of the Old Testament, no less than people today, stood in need of God's assistance to overcome sin. As he wrote in *Contra duas epistulas pelagianorum:* "Whether before the law or in the time of the Old Testament, they were not set free from sins by their own power, for 'accursed are all who put their hope in a human being' (Jer. 17:5) — and they certainly fall under this curse whom the divine psalm describes as people 'who trust in their own power'" (Ps. 49:7).[57] The ancient patriarchs, although they were stewards of the Old Testament "because of the division of the times," were nonetheless the heirs of the New.[58] They too were children of the promise;[59] they too received the power of the Holy Spirit, not merely to assist virtue, but also to bestow it. "Those patriarchs," Augustine writes, "knew how to cry out to the Lord in genuine piety, 'I shall love you, Lord, my strength'" (Ps. 18:2).[60]

Augustine's response to the Pelagians on the salvation of the Old Testament saints added a new dimension to his ongoing reflection on the problem of sexuality and the history of salvation. The shadow of the original sin fell even over the sexual relations of the just. They, too, stood in need of saving grace in order to direct their desires toward the procreation of children. Although Augustine never repudiated his earlier views on the virtue of the Hebrew patriarchs and matriarchs, against Pelagius and his followers he had to emphasize more explicitly than ever that their virtue was the result of divine grace. Such a stance, it would seem, tended to blur the historical distinctions he had developed in his earlier writings, or at least to refocus them. By the later phase of the Pelagian controversy, the crucial historical distinction had become less that of the difference between the Old and New Testaments than that of the time before and after the first sin.

56. *C. Iul. imp.* 5.10 (PL 45:1439).
57. *C. ep. Pel.* 1.7.12 (CSEL 60:32).
58. *C. ep. Pel.* 3.4.6 (CSEL 60:492).
59. *C. ep. Pel.* 3.4.11 (CSEL 60:497-98).
60. *C. ep. Pel.* 3.4.13 (CSEL 60:501).

Augustine, *Sermon* 51:
St. Joseph in Early Christianity

JOSEPH T. LIENHARD, S.J.

The Church of the first millennium showed little interest in Joseph, the husband of Mary. To our knowledge, no Father of the Church ever preached a sermon on Joseph. No feast of St. Joseph was celebrated before A.D. 1000 at the earliest. The Fathers wrote little on Joseph. Indeed, Joseph seems principally to have been an embarrassment, a possible obstacle to the Church's doctrines of the divine paternity of Christ and Mary's perpetual virginity.

Some books of the apocryphal New Testament tried to overcome the perceived difficulty of Joseph's marriage to Mary by making Joseph significantly older than she. They portrayed him as an elderly widower with grown children, thus both protecting the doctrine of Mary's perpetual virginity and accounting for the "brothers and sisters of Jesus" whom the gospels mention. Some Fathers of the Church accepted these legends from the apocryphal books; others set out to depict Joseph in a different way. Commentaries on the gospels were the occasion for speculation on the two different genealogies of Joseph, in Matthew and in Luke, and on other incidents in the gospels in which Joseph is mentioned. Fathers such as Ambrose, Jerome, and Augustine mentioned Joseph in their treatises on virginity and marriage.

Of all the writings of the Fathers that mention Joseph, however, a sermon (51) by Augustine is the closest thing to a treatise on Joseph to survive from the ancient Church. Even this one sermon is spare in what it says about Joseph, but decisive in its teaching. Against the tendencies of the apocryphal gospels and of some of the Fathers who followed those traditions, Augustine set forth two significant doctrines: that Joseph and Mary contracted a true marriage, and that Joseph may rightly be called Jesus' "father." I propose to examine this sermon and its teaching, in light of Augustine's other writings and of other teachings on Joseph from the early Church.

"Joseph" in Augustine's Writings

An electronic search for the name "Joseph" in the corpus of Augustine's writings yields the following results. Augustine used the name "Joseph" 377 times in his authentic writings. Not all instances, of course, are relevant. One is the Jewish historian Josephus.[1] Several are Joseph of Arimathea.[2] About 55% of the remaining instances are references to the Old Testament patriarch. A few more than 150 instances, or about 40% of the total, refer to Joseph the husband of Mary.

Some of these instances are simply citations of gospel texts and not particularly helpful for understanding Augustine's thought on Joseph; but others, clustered in one or another of Augustine's works, indicate places where Augustine was dealing with exegetical or theological problems that involved Joseph. The places where such clusters occur provide a first approach to discerning Augustine's interest in Joseph.

In *Contra Faustum Manichaeum* (397-400) Faustus raises (in book 3) the difficulty of the double genealogy of Joseph, in Matthew's and in Luke's gospels. Augustine answers that Joseph was begotten by one father and adopted by another,[3] a solution that he maintained until near the end of his life, when he read Julius Africanus's *Letter to Aristides* on the double genealogy.[4] In book 23 of the same work, Faustus proposes that the son of David was born of Mary and became Son of God at his baptism. Augustine defends the Catholic teaching that Jesus was Son of God in his divine nature, and writes that Jesus is called son of David either because Mary was also of Davidic descent (citing Rom. 1:3) or because Joseph was Jesus' father in a sense higher than the merely physical.[5]

In *De consensu evangelistarum* (399/400 or 403/5) Augustine worked

1. *Ep.* 199.30.
2. *Cons. Ev.* 3.22.59; *c. Faust.* 20.11; *Tractatus in evangelium Iohannis* 109.2; 120.4; *ser.* 46.
3. *C. Faust.* 3.1-5.
4. Julius Africanus, *Letter to Aristides* (before 240), preserved in Eusebius, *h.e.* 1.7.5-10.
5. *C. Faust.* 23.1-10.

out a more extensive treatment of the exegetical problems that Faustus had raised and mentioned Joseph more than fifty times. In book 2, chapters 1 to 5, Augustine treats the double genealogy and makes two points: Joseph may be called Jesus' father in a higher sense, and the double genealogy is an indication that Joseph was adopted. The different numbers of generations (forty-two in Matthew, seventy-seven in Luke) have a deeper significance, which Augustine gleefully explains.

For about a decade and a half thereafter Augustine seldom mentioned Joseph. Then, beginning in 418, he returned to reflection on Joseph, beginning with *Sermon* 51. The occasion of the sermon may have been Augustine's growing dispute with the Pelagians, since Augustine's teaching in *Sermon* 51 parallels his teaching in *De nuptiis et concupiscentia* (418/19), which he addressed to Count Valerius to refute the charge that the Catholic doctrine of original sin implied a condemnation of marriage. In both works Augustine elaborates his understanding that carnal relations are not essential either to marriage or to fatherhood; both marriage and fatherhood can have a higher sense. Augustine makes the same point in his work *Against Julian* (422). Julian had denied that Mary and Joseph had a true marriage, since they had no carnal relations. Augustine continues to elaborate his understanding of marriage that makes consent, not consummation, its essence.

Finally, in the *Retractationes,* Augustine reconsiders several works in which he had mentioned Joseph. In each case the significant point is that he has read Julius Africanus's *Letter to Aristides* and now accepts Julius's conclusions: the adoption (of which Augustine had already written) was the result of a levirate marriage, and Jacob and Heli (both named as Joseph's father) were uterine half-brothers. In his comments on *Contra Faustum Manichaeum* Augustine indicates that he had read Julius Africanus's account only after writing that work;[6] in fact he must have read it after 419, when he finished the *Quaestiones in Heptateuchum*. He has essentially the same comment in his reviews of *Quaestiones evangeliorum,*[7] *De consensu evangelistarum,*[8] and *Quaestiones in Heptateuchum;*[9] in this last section he refers back explicitly to his review of *Contra Faustum Manichaeum*.

Thus Augustine's interest in Joseph centers on two areas: the exegetical question of Jesus's genealogy and its implications, and the doctrinal questions of the authenticity of Joseph's marriage to Mary and the propriety of

6. *Retr.* 33.
7. Ibid., 38.
8. Ibid., 42.
9. Ibid., 82.

calling Joseph Jesus' father. The latter, doctrinal questions come to the fore in *Sermon* 51.

Sermon 51: Introduction

Internal evidence shows that *Sermon* 51 was preached soon after Christmas. It was preached on a feast day, but one that was also a pagan festival; hence many of the congregation were absent because games were being held in the city. The most likely date is January 1, 418.[10] The sermon is among the longest of Augustine's extant sermons. By a rough estimate, it would have taken close to two hours to preach.

A fine critical edition was made by Pierre-Patrick Verbraken.[11] Two translations into English have been published: by R. G. MacMullen, reprinted in the Nicene and Post-Nicene Fathers,[12] and more recently by Edmund Hill.[13]

Augustine structured the sermon around objections that might be raised to the teachings of the gospels. The structure is this:

1. Introduction: Augustine is preaching after Christmas on a day when games are taking place (1-2)
2. First objection: the birth of Christ from a woman was unnecessary (3-4)
3. Second objection: the gospels are inaccurate (5-15)
   a. Matthew is not credible (5-6)
   b. paraphrase of Matt. 1 (7-10)
   c. inaccuracy: there are 41 generations in Matt. 1, not 42 (11-15)
4. Third objection: the evangelist gives Jesus' genealogy through Joseph, but Joseph was not Jesus' father (16-26)
5. Fourth objection: Matthew and Luke differ on the name of Joseph's father (27-29)
6. Return to the third objection: Joseph was not Jesus' father (30)
7. Fifth objection: Matthew and Luke differ in the number of generations and in the direction in which they list the generations (31-35)

10. *Sermon* MAI 158, preached on Pentecost (June 10), 417, announces this sermon.
11. Pierre-Patrick Verbraken, "Le sermon LI de saint Augustin sur les généalogies du Christ selon Matthieu et selon Luc," *Revue Bénédictine* 91 (1981): 20-45.
12. *Saint Augustin: Homilies on the Gospels,* NPNF, 1st series, vol. 6 (reprinted Grand Rapids: Eerdmans, 1974), pp. 245-59.
13. Saint Augustine, *Sermons,* vol. 3, trans. Edmund Hill, The Works of Saint Augustine: A Translation for the 21st Century, III/3 (Brooklyn, N.Y.: New City Press, 1991), pp. 19-49.

JOSEPH T. LIENHARD, S.J.

Augustine's First Affirmation:
Mary and Joseph Contracted a True Marriage

Augustine writes in *Sermon* 51: "Joseph then was not the less his father, because he knew not the mother of our Lord, as though concupiscence and not conjugal affection constitutes the marriage bond,"[14] thus affirming that Mary and Joseph contracted a true marriage.

In doing so Augustine was defending an expression in the canonical New Testament, and reversing the tendencies of the apocryphal New Testament and the interpretation of several fathers. The Gospel according to Matthew twice calls Mary Joseph's wife[15] and twice calls Joseph Mary's husband.[16] But the apocryphal New Testament, apparently out of doctrinal anxiety, shied away from these terms. The foundational document for this changed attitude was the *Protevangelium of James,* composed ca. 200 or shortly before.[17] According to this work, Mary lives in the temple from the age of three to the age of twelve. Then an angel directs the high priest to assemble all the widowers of the people so that God may designate the one whose wife Mary will be. Joseph is chosen by a miraculous sign, but demurs: he is old and already has two sons. The priest tells Joseph to take Mary under his care; the term "wife," used by the angel, is now abandoned. Only after a threat of punishment does Joseph take Mary "under his care." But as soon as he brings her into his house he leaves on an extended contracting job. The annunciation takes place soon after Joseph leaves. Nine months later, as they are approaching Bethlehem for the census, Joseph asks himself, "How shall I enroll her? As my wife? I am ashamed to do that."[18]

Thus this apocryphon made Joseph the aged and reluctant protector of Mary and not her husband, and it attempted to protect the doctrine of her virginity by presupposing that she entered into the appearance of marriage with a man at least some decades older than she, old enough that he would be ashamed to call her his wife.

Later apocrypha made the relationship of Mary and Joseph only more

14. *Ser.* 51.21 (trans. MacMullen, *Homilies,* 252). Other translations, unless noted, are the author's.

15. Matt. 1:20, 24 (γυνή).

16. Matt. 1:16, 19 (ἀνήρ).

17. Also called the *Book of James.* English translation in Montague Rhodes James, *The Apocryphal New Testament* (Oxford: Clarendon, 1924), 49-65, and E. Hennecke, *New Testament Apocrypha,* ed. W. Schneemelcher, trans. R. McL. Wilson (London: SCM, 1963), 1, pp. 392-401.

18. *Protevangelium of James* 16.2.

bizarre. According to the *Gospel of Ps-Matthew* Joseph was a grandfather when he took Mary under his care and already had grandchildren older than she.[19] The Coptic *History of Joseph the Carpenter* depicts Joseph as an aged widower with six children and even gives a chronology: Joseph married at 40, became a widower at 89, received Mary at 91, and died at 111.[20]

A few Fathers of the Church continued this tradition. Hilary of Poitiers, for example, in his *Commentary on Matthew,* wrote: "Because she was betrothed, she is received as a wife. She is 'known' as such after her childbirth — that is, she advances to receive the name 'wife.' She is 'known' [as wife], but she has no relations [with Joseph]. . . . Whenever there is a question of these two [that is, Jesus and Joseph], she is called rather the mother of Christ [cf. Matt. 2:13, 20; Luke 2:33], because that she was, not the wife of Joseph, for that she was not. . . . Therefore, the betrothed also received the name of wife, and after the childbirth, having been recognized as wife, she is presented only as the mother of Jesus."[21] Maximus of Turin (the second fifth-century bishop of that name) wrote: "Joseph was always the betrothed, but never the husband."[22] A homily by Ps-Origen on Matthew, influential in the West because it was read in the Divine Office until the sixteenth century, also denied that Mary and Joseph had a true marriage.[23] Much closer to Augustine, Julian of Eclanum also denied the true marriage, arguing: "Because there was no intercourse, there was no marriage."[24]

Two Fathers, Ambrose and Augustine, stand out in affirming the true marriage of Mary and Joseph. The affirmation is interesting in itself, but even more interesting for the grounds they give for the affirmation. Both Fathers base their affirmation on the understanding of marriage in Roman law, according to which marriage was constituted by consent, not by consummation, and both Fathers use terms that are drawn from Roman juristic language in their arguments.

Augustine argues this point at some length in *Sermon* 51. The key sen-

---

19. Also called the *Book of the Infancy.* Excerpts in James, *Apocryphal NT,* pp. 70-79, and Hennecke, *NT Apocrypha* 1, pp. 410-13.

20. Also called the *Death of Joseph.* See James, *Apocryphal NT,* 84-86.

21. Hilary, *Mt.* 1.3 (SC 254.96), written in 398.

22. "Sed et venerando illi Ioseph dispensatione coelesti semper sponso, nec umquam marito." Maximus of Turin, *Ser.* 53 (PL 57.639a). This Maximus was bishop from 451 to 465.

23. "Etenim si tibi uxor nominatur, si in desponsatione tibi esse dicitur, non tibi tamen uxor est, sed dei unigeniti electa mater est"; Ps-Origen, *In vigilia natalis Domini* (GCS Origenes 12.242). Cf. CPL 668.

24. "Quia concubitus defuit, nullo modo fuisse coniugium"; quoted by Augustine in *c. Iul.* 5.12.46 (PL 44.810).

tence is the one already quoted: "Joseph then was not the less his father, because he knew not the mother of our Lord, as though concupiscence and not conjugal affection *(caritas coniugalis)* constitutes the marriage bond."[25] Thus what makes a woman a wife is not *libido,* lust, but *caritas coniugalis,* marital love. Augustine demonstrates his point with two arguments, one positive and the other negative. Positively, if a couple follows St. Paul's advice and abstains from relations (1 Cor. 7:29), they do not cease to be husband and wife; by mutual agreement they restrain *concupiscentia carnis,* but not *caritas coniugalis.* Negatively, a man who commits fornication does not thereby contract marriage, whereas a chaste man and woman are husband and wife "because there is no fleshly intercourse, but only the union of hearts between them."[26]

The sort of vocabulary that Augustine uses in the section that follows[27]demonstrates that what he had in mind in writing about marriage was the juridical understanding of marriage from Roman law, according to which marriage was constituted by consent, not by consummation. A classical phrase in Justinian's *Digesta* expresses this understanding concisely: the *Digesta,* quoting Ulpian, has: "it is not intercourse, but consent, that makes a marriage" ("nuptias non concubitus, sed consensus facit").[28] The opposing view, represented by (among others) Julian of Eclanum, that sexual relations constitute marriage, seems to derive not from a different legal tradition (Julian was at least as much a Roman as Augustine was), but from a popular assumption or attitude. The presence of several terms from Roman juridical language in *Sermon* 51.22 points to the source of Augustine's ideas: *tabulae matrimoniales,* marriage contracted *liberorum procreandorum causa,* and *matrimoniale pactum. Tabulae matrimoniales* and its synonym, *tabulae nuptiales,* designated the marriage contract.[29] The usage of such contracts can

25. *Ser.* 51.21 (trans. MacMullen, *Homilies,* p. 252).

26. "Quia non sibi carnaliter miscentur sed cordibus connectuntur." *Ser.* 51.21 (ed. Verbraken, 36; trans. MacMullen, *Homilies,* p. 253).

27. *Ser.* 51.22.

28. *Digesta Iustiniani* 50, 17, 30 (ed. Th. Mommsen [Berlin: Weidmann, 1870], 2: 958).

29. See Adolf Berger, *Encyclopedic Dictionary of Roman Law,* Transactions of the American Philosophical Society, new series, vol. 43, part 2 (Philadelphia: American Philosophical Society, 1953), pp. 728-29 *(tabulae nuptiales* or *matrimoniales).* This volume, and the references it contains, have provided the basis for most of the information on Roman law in this paper. In Roman juristic language, *nuptiae* and *matrimonium* are practically synonyms, whereas *coniugium* does not appear to be a juridical term. *Nuptiae* may be the older term, and more related to the wedding ceremony. "The Roman marriage was a factual relation between man and woman . . . based on *affectio maritalis* (intention to be husband and wife). . . ." Ibid., p. 578.

be traced to the beginning of the Principate. The phrase *liberorum quaeren-dorum* (or *procreandorum*) *causa* was the juridical definition of the purpose of an authentic Roman marriage.[30] Augustine also writes of the *matrimoniale pactum;*[31] *pactum* or *pactio* was the general juristic term for agreement or consent.[32] The view, drawn from Roman jurisprudence, that marriage is constituted by consent, allows Augustine to write of the marriage of Mary and Joseph as a true marriage.

At first glance, the phrase *liberorum procreandorum causa* may seem to militate against Augustine's contention that marriage is constituted by consent. But his point is that marriage is contracted not to satisfy a man's lust but to give a good external appearance. Augustine is quite dramatic at this place in the sermon. He portrays a father handing his daughter over to another man:

> The contract is recited, it's read out in the presence of all the witnesses, and what's read out is "for the sake of procreating children"; and it's called the matrimonial contract. Unless this were what wives are given away and taken for, who with any sense of shame would give away his daughter to another's lust? But to save parents from being ashamed when they give away their daughters, the contract is read out, to make them fathers-in-law, not whoremongers. So what's read out in the contract? "For the sake of procreating children." The father's brow clears, his face is saved when he hears the words of the contract. Let's consider the face of the man who is taking a wife. The husband too should be ashamed to take her on any other terms, if the father is ashamed to give her away on any other terms.[33]

Ambrose's interpretation of marriage is similar. What constitutes a marriage, he writes in his *Commentary on Luke,* is not the loss of virginity but the solemn affirming of the marriage *(coniugii testificatio)* and the celebration of the wedding *(nuptiarum celebratio).*[34] In his work *De institutione*

---

30. "At the registration of citizens the head of a family was asked whether he was living with a wife *liberorum quaerendorum causa.* Hence a woman married in *iustae nuptiae* = *uxor liberorum quaerendorum causa.*" Ibid., p. 563.

31. *Ser.* 51.22.

32. The *Digesta* of Justinian stated that *pactum* or *pactio* was "the agreement and consent of two or more persons concerning the same subject." *Digesta* 2, 14, 1, 2 (ed. Mommsen 1, 62); Berger, *Encyclopedic Dictionary,* p. 614.

33. *Ser.* 51.22 (trans. Hill, *Sermons,* pp. 33-34).

34. "The fact that Scripture often calls her a wife should not disturb you. For it is not the loss of virginity but the solemn affirming of the marriage *(coniugii testificatio)* and

virginis he writes that a marriage is constituted by the *pactio coniugalis,* a synonym for Augustine's term *matrimoniale pactum.*[35]

Thus Augustine (and Ambrose, too), by drawing on the understanding of marriage from Roman law, has given an account of the marriage of Mary and Joseph as a true marriage, and offered an understanding of marriage that finds its essence in a relationship between two persons rather than in corporeal intercourse. The high point of Augustine's teaching is his assertion that a marriage is constituted by *caritas coniugalis,* conjugal love.

Augustine's Second Affirmation:
Joseph May Be Called the Father of Jesus

In his affirmation of Joseph's true fatherhood, Augustine also begins from Scripture, where Luke twice writes of Joseph as Jesus' father.[36] In *Sermon* 51, he writes clearly: "As she was in chastity a mother, so was he in chastity a father. Whoso then says that he ought not to be called a father, because he did not beget his son in the usual way, looks rather to the satisfaction of passion in the procreation of children, and not the natural feeling of affection. What others desire to fulfill in the flesh, he in a more excellent way fulfilled in the spirit."[37]

Other Fathers were hesitant to call Joseph "father." Origen calls Joseph Jesus's foster-father,[38] or says he is called father because of his place in the genealogy of Jesus.[39] Epiphanius of Salamis is far more decisive: "Joseph was in the rank of father . . . but he was not a father. . . . For how could one who did not have relations be his father? This is impossible."[40]

---

the celebration of the wedding *(nuptiarum celebratio)* that is being stated thereby. Then too, no one puts away a woman whom he has not accepted, and thus he who wanted to put her away admitted that he had accepted her." Ambrose, *Luc.* 2.5.

35. "A woman espoused to a man received the name of wife, for when marriage is entered upon, then the title of marriage is acquired. It is not the loss of virginity *(defloratio virginitatis)* but the marriage contract *(pactio coniugalis)* that makes a marriage. Finally, when a maiden is united, then marriage exists ('cum iungitur puella, coniugium est'), not when she is known by union with a man." Ambrose, *De institutione virginis* 6.41 (written in 392).

36. Luke 2:33, 48.

37. *Ser.* 51.26 (trans. MacMullen, *Homilies,* p. 255).

38. *Hom. 16 in Lc.* 16.1.

39. Ibid., 17.1.

40. *Haer.* 51.10.7-8 (GCS Epiphanius 2.262.1-8).

Augustine saw the point differently. He devotes almost one third of *Sermon* 51 to defending Joseph's true fatherhood of Jesus. Since he clearly affirms Mary's perpetual virginity and thus her virginal conception of Jesus, he proposes an understanding of fatherhood that is not merely physical or corporeal. The essence of fatherhood, he will write, consists not in the act of begetting but rather in a relationship between a man and his son.

To establish his first point, that the act of begetting itself is not the essence of fatherhood, Augustine constructs a kind of gradation or scale of fatherhood.[41] The lowest sort of fatherhood is begetting children outside of marriage, in adultery; these children are called "natural children" *(filii naturales)* and are ranked below the offspring of a lawful marriage *(filii coniugales)*. In regard to the work of the flesh, the births of natural children and conjugal children are equal. Some other factor must distinguish them, and that factor is chastity, for the love of a wife is more chaste than that of a concubine ("castior est uxoris caritas"). Following this scale, there exists a third, higher sort of fatherhood, one from which the work of the flesh is absent: namely, adoption. In this instance a man is a father without begetting his son; or rather, parents who adopt children "beget them chastely in the heart, whom they cannot beget in the flesh."[42] We should consider the laws of adoption, Augustine writes: "the will of the one adopting has more rights over the child than the nature of the one who begets him does."[43] Augustine contrasts *natura* and *voluntas,* and finds the latter higher in value. Joseph's fatherly relation to Jesus is of this general sort, but higher still, since the "work of the flesh" was wholly absent from the begetting of Jesus. "For if a man were able to beget children from his wife without intercourse, should he not be more joyful, insofar as she, whom he loves all the more, is more chaste?"[44] he writes.

This argument — admittedly strange to modern perceptions — depends on valuing chastity as a virtue, even within marriage. It is also a way to imagine what, apart from Christian revelation — is unimaginable — fatherhood without intercourse. Augustine's grammar reveals his thought: "if a man were able," *si . . . posset,* an unreal condition. The only instance in which such a thing happened was the conception of Jesus. But that conception, Augustine argues, does not deprive Joseph of true fatherhood, because fatherhood comprises far more than begetting. Or rather, there is a spiritual beget-

41. *Ser.* 51.26.
42. Ibid.
43. Ibid.
44. Ibid.

ting that is superior to physical begetting: "What another man desires to fulfill by the flesh, he fulfilled in a better way, by the spirit."[45]

When he asks what constitutes true fatherhood, Augustine has three answers: paternal authority; natural affection; and marital fidelity, love, and affection. Joseph's paternal authority is demonstrated in the angel's command to him to name the child,[46] and in Jesus' subjection to his parents at Nazareth.[47] Secondly, fatherhood is constituted more perfectly by love than by passion. "Whoever says," Augustine writes, "that 'he should not be called a father, because he did not beget a son in that way,' seeks passion *(libido)* and not the feeling of love *(caritatis affectus)* in begetting children."[48] And finally, wedded love is superior to adultery because a true wife is marked by her feelings of fidelity, of wedlock, and of a love more sincere and more chaste ("affectu fidei, affectu coniugii, affectu sincerioris castiorisque caritatis").[49]

The teaching that Joseph may rightly be called the father of Jesus was not new to Augustine in *Sermon* 51. He had proposed it as early as book 23 of *Contra Faustum Manichaeum,* written just after he was ordained a bishop: Joseph was Mary's husband in affection, and in the intercourse of mind. In Christians' faith, the heart of marriage is not carnal union but the kind of union Christ has with his members.[50] Augustine presents the same argument in *De consensu evangelistarum:* the relation between married persons can be the affection of the mind.[51] And in *De nuptiis et concupiscentia* he writes that the designation "wife" is not untrue simply because carnal relations are absent.[52] Finally, in his first work against Julian of Eclanum, he writes that what constitutes marriage is the "faith of the betrothal."[53]

---

45. Ibid.
46. Ibid., 29.
47. Ibid., 30.
48. Ibid., 26; cf. 25.
49. Ibid., 26.
50. "Non concubitu, sed affectu, non commixtione corporum, sed copulatione, quod est carius, animorum." *C. Faust.* 23.8 (CSEL 25.713).
51. ". . . Posse permanere vocarique coniugium non permixto corporis sexu, sed custodito mentis affectu." *Cons. ev.* 2.1.2 (CSEL 43.82).
52. "Nec perierat nec mendax manserat coniugis appellatio, ubi nec fuerat nec futura erat carnis ulla commixtio." *Nupt. et conc.* 1.11.12 (CSEL 42.224).
53. "Quamquam et tu ipse etiam 'ex desponsionis fide eam nomen coniugis accepisse' fatearis." *C. Iul.* 5.12.48 (PL 44.811). Augustine continues: "He did not think the bond of conjugal faith should be dissolved because the hope of carnal intercourse had been taken away."

Conclusion

Thus Augustine, in his teaching on Joseph, takes a position that attempts both to remain true to scriptural language like the terms "husband" and "father" and also to give a reasonable account of the meaning of that language. Both marriage and fatherhood find the heart of their significance not on the corporeal or physical level, but rather on the level of relationship between persons. I have deliberately avoided the word "Platonic" in describing Augustine's teaching on these points, and also have resisted trying to project what he says about relation in the matter of marriage and fatherhood onto his teaching about the Trinity. Not every assertion that the spiritual is superior to the corporeal had to have Plato as its source; and Augustine himself never relates what he says about Joseph to his doctrine of the Trinity. Augustine's modest contribution to thought about Joseph is just that — modest. But it also shows Augustine at his best: true to the Scriptures, and unwilling to back away from difficult questions that the Scriptures raise or to retreat into fideism. And in this, I believe, he represents the best of the Catholic tradition.

Cyril of Alexandria as Educator

J. DAVID CASSEL

When preparing a sermon, contemporary pastors turn to the shelves of their libraries and find a variety of scriptural translations plus a plethora of commentaries, articles, and sermons concerning the text under consideration. Most of these pastors, having had approximately nineteen years of formal education, experience little or no difficulty reading the scriptural text and the various secondary works at their disposal.[1] The clergy, however, has not always been as well educated as it is today. After Constantine's affirmation of Christianity as the preferred religion of the Roman Empire in the early fourth century, the Church grew rapidly.[2] The centrality of Christianity within the Roman Empire was reaffirmed by Theodosius in the late fourth century when he outlawed pagan practices and declared Christianity to be the only acceptable religion; the growth of the Church continued. One of the side effects of the rapidly increasing numerical growth in the Church was the need for a vast number of new clerics who could administer the sacraments and provide spiritual nurture for the new converts.

It is the goal of this article to examine how this extremely urgent need for new clergy during the late fourth and early fifth centuries affected the church in Alexandria and its archbishop, Cyril.[3] I will make two primary arguments. First, I will suggest that the need for new clergy during this time pe-

---

1. This is assuming that most ordained pastors have had twelve years of public education, four years of college, and three years of seminary training.

2. See Ramsay MacMullen, *Christianizing the Roman Empire (A.D. 100-400)* (New Haven: Yale University Press, 1984).

3. Cyril was archbishop of Alexandria from 412 to 444 C.E.

riod forced the church to recruit and ordain clerics who had not already been educated sufficiently to perform the ecclesiastical tasks required of them. This argument will be based on an examination of the classical educational system as it functioned in the Mediterranean world during the fourth and fifth centuries, a review of the educational requirements for functioning clerics, and an assessment of the capability of the educational system to provide enough adequately educated clerics to fill the needs of the Church. Second, this article will argue that the presence of a large number of undereducated clerics in Alexandria forced Cyril to function as an educator, training those clerics under his care in the science of reading and interpreting literature. Evidence supporting this contention will be drawn from an examination of Cyril's *Commentary on Isaiah*, where the text indicates that Cyril originally presented the material contained in the commentary orally and that his lectures were designed to teach his hearers interpretive skills that directly correspond to those taught by the classical grammarians.

Undereducated New Clerics

The Classical Education System

Before assessing the role Cyril of Alexandria played in educating the clergy under his care, it is necessary to understand the focus and scope of the classical educational system. Several books have been written on this system, including important works by Henri Marrou, Stanley Bonner, M. L. Clarke, and Robert Kaster,[4] but the best portraits of the educational system of that time were painted by ancient sources, such as the rhetorician Quintilian and the grammarian Dionysius Thrax.

Perhaps the most comprehensive description of the classical educational system was written by the Roman rhetorician Quintilian (ca. 35-95 C.E.). Quintilian, being a teacher of rhetoric, wrote his treatise, *Institutio Oratoria*, to describe the various stages in the education of a perfect orator.[5]

4. Henri Marrou, *A History of Education in Antiquity* (London: Sheed and Ward, 1956); Stanley Bonner, *Education in Ancient Rome* (Berkeley: University of California Press, 1977); M. L. Clarke, *Higher Education in the Ancient World* (London: Routledge and Kegan Paul, 1971); Robert Kaster, *Guardians of the Language: The Grammarian and Society in Late Antiquity* (Berkeley: University of California Press, 1988).

5. *Institutio Oratoria,* prol. 2. I am citing Quintilian from the edition by H. E. Butler, *The Institutio Oratoria of Quintilian*, LCL (Cambridge, Mass.: Harvard University Press, 1920-22).

Quintilian argued that the best orator was one who had had a thorough education from his earliest years, and he offered his readers a summary of the kind of educational system that would produce such an orator.[6] In the process of classical education, as Quintilian outlined it, there were three primary steps: (1) in the first stage, the young person learned the rudiments of reading; (2) in the second stage, the lad learned how to read literary texts for and with meaning; and (3) in the final stage, the young man learned how to express himself powerfully and articulately as an orator.

The first stage of a good classical education according to Quintilian occurred during a young boy's earliest years. He suggests that a boy be taught his letters prior to his seventh year and that such learning be made as enjoyable as possible.[7] He says that learning should begin with the names, order, and shape of the letters and proceed to the pronunciation of syllables, words, and finally sentences.[8] Quintilian associates the first stage of a boy's education with the home rather than a public school, and he believes that the best teachers at this stage are either the child's parents or a trained servant known as a pedagogue.[9]

Once a child has mastered the rudiments of reading words and sentences, Quintilian suggests that he move on to the second stage of education in which he will learn how to read and interpret literary texts. Although Quintilian admits that the second stage of a good education could conceivably occur at home under the guidance of a skilled tutor, he is an advocate of public education at this stage in a lad's development since the openness, challenge, and cross-fertilization provided by a public education are preferable to the limited perspective presented by a private tutor.[10] This stage of the educational process was accomplished under the direction of teachers known as grammarians *(grammatici)* whose task according to Quintilian was twofold: (1) to teach students "the art of correct expression" *(recte loquendi scientiam)*; and (2) to teach students how to "interpret the poets" *(poetarum enarrationem).*[11] According to Quintilian, correct reading of a text had to precede interpretation of the text. Correct reading for Quintilian required sev-

---

6. *Institutio Oratoria,* prol. 6-7.

7. Other contemporaries of Quintilian, such as Eratosthenes, suggested that a boy ought to wait until age seven before beginning this initial stage of his education. Henri Marrou believed this to be the more common age for the beginning of a classical education (*History of Education,* p. 143).

8. *Institutio Oratoria* 1.1.12–1.1.17.

9. *Institutio Oratoria* 1.1.8.

10. *Institutio Oratoria* 1.2.9-24.

11. *Institutio Oratoria* 1.4.2.

eral important skills. First, since literary texts at the time were copied without spaces between words and without any form of accents and punctuation,[12] the reader had to learn how to recognize coherent sets of letters and thoughts in order to separate the text into words, phrases, and sentences so that the text could be verbalized correctly.[13] Second, since texts at that time existed only in manuscript form, and were often riddled with copying errors, the reader had to know how to determine whether the apparent errors in the text were errors that had entered the text during its transmission or whether they were part of the original text.[14] Third, the student had to develop skills in identifying and interpreting various literary devices. Quintilian believed that young people should be introduced to the science of language (in order to understand the use of literary tropes), to music (in order to understand meter and rhythm), and to other sciences such as astronomy and philosophy (in order to understand the various allusions to these disciplines within the text).[15] Clearly, this stage of the educational process was designed to move students beyond simple reading skills to a stage in which they were acquainted with subtleties of a text so that they could read with understanding and begin to develop an idea of what it meant to present ideas with clarity and conviction.

When the student completed the second stage of his education, he enrolled in a school of rhetoric where he would learn how to verbalize his thoughts in a manner appropriate for a variety of public situations. The primary method of learning eloquence in oration, argued Quintilian, was to copy the style and method of famous and successful orators of the past.[16] There were, according to Quintilian, several other factors that played a part in producing an accomplished orator such as a proper student-teacher relationship and thorough instruction in the different formal types of orations and their component parts.[17]

---

12. This block format is known as *scriptio continua*.

13. For a thorough examination of the difficulties associated with reading a text that is written in this format, see Harry Gamble, *Books and Readers in the Early Church* (New Haven: Yale University Press, 1995), pp. 203-5.

14. *Institutio Oratoria* 1.4.3. The great Alexandrian critics Zenodotus and Aristarchus developed this textual aspect of literary criticism. For a full explanation of ancient marginal *sigla* see L. D. Reynolds and N. G. Wilson, *Scribes and Scholars: A Guide to the Transmission of Greek and Latin Literature* (Oxford: Oxford University Press, 1974), pp. 10-11.

15. *Institutio Oratoria* 1.4.5.

16. *Institutio Oratoria* 2.1.9-10; 2.5.1.

17. *Institutio Oratoria* 2.10. Quintilian discusses the characteristics of a panegyric in *Institutio Oratoria* 3.7.

Since the second stage of the classical educational system was the most crucial step in the development of the skills of literacy required for reading and interpreting literary texts such as the Bible, it is necessary to examine its component parts in greater detail. The oldest extant source detailing the various skills taught by the grammarians is the *Ars Grammatica*, which was written by Dionysius Thrax.[18] The *Ars Grammatica* is a handbook for grammarians that summarizes the basic elements of what Dionysius calls the science (τέχνη) of reading and analyzing a literary text. For Dionysius, grammar extended far beyond the modern definition that focuses primarily on syntax and morphology. Grammar, in the ancient educational system, encompassed all of the skills needed to understand the meaning of the text. In Dionysius's words: "Grammar is, for the most part, the practical craft of understanding that which has been said by both poets and writers of prose."[19]

Dionysius viewed grammar as a practical science or craft. In saying this, he revealed the ancient conceit that every literary text had a specific meaning that could be ascertained by any diligent reader who practiced certain fundamental principles in the process of reading and analyzing the text. It was the responsibility of the ancient grammarian to teach the students under his care both what these basic principles were and how to use these principles in interpreting literary texts. Dionysius explains that there are six fundamental components of the grammatical analysis of a text:

This craft has six parts: (1) expert reading of the text with its correct accents and punctuation; (2) explication of the poetic tropes which occur in the text; (3) the appropriate definition of both the rare and unusual words and the historical aspects of the text;[20] (4) research into etymolo-

18. Dionysius Thrax lived during the first century B.C.E. There were a number of ancient works that described the scope of the grammarians' task. Some of these have survived only in fragmentary form. See J. E. Dunlap, "Fragments of a Latin Grammar from Egypt," *American Journal of Philology* 61 (1940): 330-43. Many of the latter texts relating to the grammarians were adaptations of or comments on the *Ars Grammatica*. See Alfons Wouters, *The Grammatical Papyri from Graeco-Roman Egypt: Contributions to the Study of the 'Ars Grammatica' in Antiquity* (Brussels: De Koninklijke Academie voor Wetenschappen, Letteren en Schone Kunsten van Belgie, 1979).

19. *Ars Grammatica* 1.1. I am citing Dionysius from the critical edition by Jean Lallot, *La Grammaire de Denys le Thrax* (Paris: Éditions du Centre Nationale de la Recherche Scientifique, 1989).

20. The term Ἱστορία refers to the basic content of the text that may be explained by reference to historical sources or a variety of natural sciences such as geology, biology, or agriculture. Wouters (*Grammatical Papyri*, p. 35) attempts to capture the sense of this term by translating it "subject matter."

gies; (5) reflections on analogies; and (6) the evaluation of the work, which is the most elegant of all the parts of the science. (*Ars Grammatica* 1.4-8)

The most basic aspect of Dionysius's grammatical analysis is expert reading of the text. According to Dionysius, expert reading of the text means "the faultless pronunciation of poetry or prose."[21] Since the text appeared on the page as one continuous block of letters, this was not an easy task, yet no sense could be made of the text until the reader reconstructed and verbalized the word, phrase, and sentence divisions envisioned by the author. Before a student could make such a reconstruction effectively, he had to be taught such things as how to identify the various classifications of words by means of their structure,[22] the principles of syntax, and the general rules of accent and punctuation. The rules of accent and pronunciation coupled with a thorough understanding of the principles of meter were especially crucial in the process of scanning poetry. Once students had developed their skills in dissecting the block of text in front of them into words and phrases and then reconstructing these words and phrases into meaningful sentences, they needed to develop their skills in articulating these sentences and phrases verbally in such a way that their hearers could easily understand the meaning of the text. Effective public reading of a text also required the mastery of several oratorical techniques such as proper breathing and voice modulation. Rigorous mastery of both the skills of reading the text in a meaningful way and verbalization had to be developed before a person could be classified as an expert reader.

The second step in the grammarian's craft was the accurate identification and explication of the various literary devices or tropes used within the text. In order to understand a text correctly students had to be trained to recognize such common literary devices as metaphor, simile, hyperbole, allegory, prosopopoeia, synecdoche, and emphasis and to understand how such devices were used.[23] A good grammatical education according to Dionysius would enable the reader to recognize when the text contained such literary devices and to determine what nuance of meaning the various tropes were meant to convey.

21. *Ars Grammatica* 2.2.

22. This would include training in such matters as the various declension patterns for nouns, the patterns of verb conjugation, and rules for contraction. See Quintilian's *Institutio Oratoria* 1.4.13-29.

23. When a poet, for example, says that love is "a star to every wandering bark," it is only when readers recognize this as a metaphor that they can begin to grasp the meaning of the poem.

Once the text had been expertly read and the various tropes contained in it had been identified, readers faced perhaps the most daunting task of the science of the grammarians. At this point, Dionysius states that they must find the appropriate definition of rare and unusual words[24] and track down the assorted references within the text to other fields of knowledge. Given the ubiquitous presence of dictionaries in the modern world, it is hard to envision the difficulties that faced ancient readers who began to read a book that contained words with which they were unfamiliar. Some wordlists and simple dictionaries were available for frequently read works like the *Iliad* and the *Odyssey,* but, for the most part, readers had few external resources on which to depend for quick and comprehensive summaries of the various possible meanings for unusual words. This meant that it required skill, training, and an excellent memory to parse and define obscure and unusual words. Students were trained to be extremely diligent in their quest for accuracy in their definitions and descriptions of how and why certain words were used in texts.[25]

In order to understand the various historical and scientific allusions within a literary text, the readers had to have both a broad background in various fields of study and a willingness to do research in areas with which they were unfamiliar. A thorough knowledge of history was particularly important. Grammarians realized that when a text such as the *Iliad* discussed the Greek invasion of Troy, the reader had to be familiar with the historical setting in which the altercation between the Greeks and the Trojans arose. The grammarians believed, however, that, in addition to having a good historical background, read-

---

24. There is some disagreement among scholars as to what Dionysius meant by this term (γλωσσῶν). Melempodis, one of the ancient grammarians who annotated an edition of the *Ars Grammatica,* believed that Dionysius meant that students should be familiar with words emerging from the "five dialects of Greek" (i.e., Attic, Doric, Ionic, Aeolic, and koine). See *Grammatici Graeci,* vol. 1, pt. 3: *Scholia in Dionysii Thracis Artem Grammaticam* (Stuttgart: Teubner, 1901), p. 14, lines 13-19. Jean Lallot, however, believes, as I do, that the term refers to rare or unusual words, idioms, or words used in a unique way by a particular author (*La Grammaire de Denys le Thrax,* p. 77).

25. At certain points the grammarians' interest in comparative philology may have been overly pedantic. Seneca skewers such zealous research into the intricacies of language with these words: "The mindset one has when approaching a certain subject makes a great deal of difference. If an individual is going to be a scholar (*grammaticus*) and observes the works of Virgil, he does not read that outstanding passage, *fugit inreparabile tempus* ('time flies away never to be restored') with this attitude: 'Wake up!' Unless we hasten, we shall be left behind. Time drives quickly forward and we are driven forward by it. We are ignorantly hastened along, and, while we are laying out all sorts of plans for the future, we are unconcernedly standing on the edge of many a precipice. Quite to the contrary, he observes how often, when Virgil discusses the swiftness of time, he uses the word *fugit.*" See Seneca, *ep.* 108.

ers needed to be acquainted with other fields such as geography, geology, and meteorology. It would be nearly impossible to understand Xenophon's *Anabasis* without some sense of the geography and geology of Asia Minor. When Xenophon, for example, mentions that people in the region of Cappadocia live in vast underground cities, readers would certainly be better able to understand his reference if they knew that in the area of Cappadocia the rock is primarily volcanic pumice into which tunnels can easily be made. Similarly, knowledge of meteorology and sailing would be necessary to understand why Agamemnon, in Euripides' eponymous play, was willing to sacrifice his daughter to ensure favorable winds. The grammarians knew that literary texts contained allusions drawn from a vast number of other disciplines, and that full comprehension of the meaning of such allusions required accurate knowledge of the discipline from which the allusion was drawn.

Dionysius's fourth stage in the science of interpretation is research into etymologies. According to the grammarians, etymology also included both the explication of archaic words that were included in a text and the development of a matrix of the varied historical usage of a word.[26] By determining how a word was used in previous works of literature, readers could more accurately sense its meaning in its present context.[27]

The fifth element in the grammarians' literary analysis is reflection on the analogies present in the text. Analogy is the process of understanding the meaning of something confusing by comparing it to something about which there is no question.[28] When an obscure idea or word appeared in a text, the reader would look for other parallel or analogous passages in the text that were clearer and might provide clues as to how the original word or idea could best be interpreted. After locating various places in which the same word was used, the reader would compare contextual clues and develop a working definition of the word. Occasionally the reader might be able to develop a definition of the word by comparing the word used in the text under consideration with the same word as it was used in other works of literature.[29]

---

26. See Quintilian, *Institutio Oratoria* 1.6.39-43 and 1.8.15.

27. Donatus used this approach in his *Commentary on the* Andria: "*Eccum* ('here he is!') is used just as *ecce eum* ('lo! him!'); the ancients used to say *eccillum,* which clearly meant *ecce illum* ('lo! that one!'), rarer was their use of *ellum*" (3.3.48).

28. Quintilian, *Institutio Oratoria* 1.6.4.

29. Donatus, the Latin grammarian, used this approach in his commentary on Terence's *Andria* when he encountered an unusual word: "*Appulit* characteristically means to come to the land, that is, to get to shore from the open sea or ocean. See Virgil's *Aeneid,* book III, line 715, where he says, 'after leaving that place God brought me to land *(appulit)* on your coast.'" See Donatus, *Commentary on the* Andria, prol. 1.6.

According to Dionysius, the final stage of the grammarians' science is the evaluation (κρίσις) of the work, which he views as the most elegant of the tasks of the grammarian. What Dionysius means by evaluation is not an assessment of the literary or artistic merit of a text; he means instead the determination of whether a word, passage, or an entire work is spurious or authentic.[30] This skill was considered by the grammarians to be the pinnacle of their craft because it marshaled all of the aspects of grammar (such as analysis of meter, grammatical rules, style, words, allusions, and etymologies) to prove or disprove the authenticity of a particular work or part of that work.[31] In some cases, the evaluation of a text led to simple corrections or emendations such as the insertion of a word that was obviously left out by the scribe who copied the text.[32] In other cases the grammarian had to compare several versions of a text, note the variant readings, and make a suggestion as to which reading was to be preferred.[33] In rare situations, a grammarian might also decide that a particular work that had been attributed to a certain author could not have been written by that individual because of stylistic factors or word usage.

Educational Requirements for Functioning Clerics

As Lucian, the second-century Sophist observed, Christians are people whose lives are centered on a book. According to Lucian, the Christians of his time exhibited an unusual devotion to reading and studying Scripture.[34] Although Peter Brown's contention that literacy was a necessary prerequisite for full participation in Late Antique Christianity is a bit far-fetched, it is certain that the clergy had to be able to read and interpret Scripture.[35] Not only was the reading of Scripture an important spiritual discipline for individual Chris-

---

30. In the scholia to the *Ars Grammatica* it is stated this way: οὐ γὰρ κρίνει, εἰ καλῶς αὐτοῖς γέγραπται ἢ οὐ, ἀλλ᾽ εἰ νόθα ἢ γνήσια (*Grammatici Graeci* 1/3.471, lines 34-35).

31. See *Grammatici Graeci* 1/3.170, lines 6-10 and 1/3.472, lines 19-27.

32. Donatus says, for example, "in this text the *est* is missing. The text should read: *tempus est*" (*Commentary on the* Andria 4.1.7).

33. Donatus makes such an evaluation when he says, "In another recension of the text, this word [*appulit*] has been replaced by *attulit,* but *appulit* is the better reading, for later on [2.6.15] there is a line which reads *animum ad uxorem appulit*" (*Commentary on the* Andria, prol. 1.7).

34. Lucian, *De morte Peregrini* 11-12.

35. Peter Brown, "Christianity and Roman Culture in Late Roman Africa," *Journal of Roman Studies* 63 (1968): 85-95.

tians, the reading and interpretation of Scripture had always taken a central place in worship.[36] In 1 Timothy 4:13 the author urges Timothy to "attend to the public reading of Scripture, to preaching, and to teaching." In the second century, Justin Martyr explained that Christian worship services contained a time when Scripture was read and interpreted.[37] Those who were able to read the Scripture publicly were held in high esteem, and the office of reader became an ecclesiastical office.[38] By the middle of the third century, readers were being appointed to that office.[39] It is clear that the Church believed only those with both the requisite literary skills and spiritual call should be allowed to perform the important task of reading Scripture during public worship. The interpretation of the scriptural text was even more difficult, and this task was entrusted to only well-trained and respected clergy. It would have required all the skills of the grammarians' science to be able to prepare and present an intelligent and edifying homily that would help the less literate church members to understand and apply the moral and spiritual principles found in the text under consideration.

Could the Classical Educational System Supply Enough Clerics for the Church?

Given the need for a large cadre of clerics who could both read and apply the principles taught by the grammarians to the biblical text, this question naturally emerges: Could the classical educational system supply enough thoroughly educated clerics to meet the needs of the Church? Robert Kaster argues convincingly in his book, *Guardians of the Language: The Grammarian and Society in Late Antiquity,* that grammarians were primarily the servants of the upper class. Their role, he posits, was not only to teach young men the skills requisite for command of their language but also to provide a sort of social imprimatur that was expected of everyone belonging to the highest stratum of ancient society.[40] In reviewing the references in ancient literature to grammar-

---

36. Pachomius, in his monastic rule, declared, "If a monk is unable to read, let him go during the first, third, and sixth hours to someone who is able to teach him . . . so that no one is forced to read to him" (*Praecepta* 139-40). See Gamble, *Books and Readers,* pp. 211-14, for a thorough discussion of the place of reading in early Christian worship.

37. *Apol.* 1.67.

38. See Tertullian, *praescr.* 41; and Eusebius, *h.e.* 6.43.11.

39. Hippolytus, *trad. ap.* 12.

40. Kaster, *Guardians,* p. 19, says, "Grammar divides and separates. . . . As a definition of the grammarian's expertise, the phrase could not be bettered, and the definition

ians, he found ample evidence that grammarians took advantage of their role as the gatekeepers to the highest level of society by charging extremely high fees and by expecting their students to supplement such fees with frequent and lavish gifts.[41] Since wealth in antiquity was concentrated primarily in urban centers, the grammarians generally set up their academies in these centers. Such locations severely curtailed the participation of rural youths in this stage of the education process; this led to further exclusivity.[42] The grammarians, Kaster argues, taught relatively small numbers of extremely wealthy students. In fact, it appears that the members of the upper levels of society had a vested interest in making higher education inaccessible to the rest of society. This attitude created a limited number of highly educated, socially elite citizens. It seems highly unlikely that the schools of the grammarians could have produced nearly enough graduates to fill the clerical needs of the Church.

There were, however, other avenues of education open to the *hoi polloi* according to Kaster. He points out that rudimentary literacy training was available to the society in general through what he calls "schools of letters" — public schools that introduced their students to the alphabet, the principles of syllabification, and word structure and taught them how to read and compose simple phrases and sentences.[43] The goal of such schools was to produce graduates who were literate enough to perform the tasks of reading and writing necessary for basic commerce; such schools did not train their students in the science of the grammarians. The graduates of such schools were probably literate enough to read bills of lading and compose bills of sale, but they were hardly capable of the advanced reading and certainly did not possess the literary skills needed for the public reading of and interpretation of Scripture required of the clergy.[44]

Cyril's Role as an Educator

Statistics on the literacy rate among the clergy in Egypt during Cyril's time are difficult to reconstruct, but Ewa Wipzycka has argued that the evidence

---

applies both to the effects of grammar on the language and to its social consequences, distinguishing the educated man from the masses."

41. Kaster, *Guardians*, p. 25.

42. Kaster, *Guardians*, pp. 20-21.

43. Kaster, *Guardians*, p. 24.

44. In his book examining the extent of literacy in the ancient world, William Harris also argues that the vast majority of Church members during this time period were illiterate. See William Harris, *Ancient Literacy* (Cambridge, Mass.: Harvard University Press, 1989), pp. 304-5.

in ancient sources indicates that very few deacons and presbyters during the fourth through the sixth centuries were unable to read.[45] If the classical educational system was unable (or perhaps unwilling) to provide a number of literate candidates for the clergy sufficient to meet the needs of the Church, how were the clergy educated? It seems reasonable to conclude that the Church supplemented whatever rudimentary education their newly recruited clerics had received prior to their commitment to the Church. The Church must have developed some sort of educational program that provided a Christian version of that which was taught by the classical grammarians.[46]

There is ample evidence in his *Commentary on Isaiah* that Cyril spearheaded the educational process in which his clergy were trained to perform the duties expected of them.[47] The style and content of the *Commentary on Isaiah* reveal how Cyril acted in the role of an educator. The style of the commentary indicates that the scriptural expositions in the commentary were originally presented as a series of lectures that Cyril gave to clerics under his supervision. The content of the commentary reinforces its educational objectives since it is clear that Cyril used his lectures to illustrate the various interpretive techniques taught by the grammarians. These lectures, presented to the clergy on a regular basis, provided the opportunity for clerics with little or no formal training in literary interpretation to begin the process of mastering the skills they needed to read and reflect on Scripture in the worship setting.

Evidence That Cyril's Commentary on Isaiah Was Presented Orally

There are many aspects of the style of Cyril's *Commentary on Isaiah* that indicate that it was originally presented as a series of lectures to the clerics un-

---

45. Ewa Wipzycka, "Le degré d'alphabétisation en Égypte byzantine," *Revue des études augustiniennes* 30 (1984): 278-89. See Gamble's discussion of the difficulties associated with developing any meaningful statistics concerning ancient literacy (*Books and Readers,* pp. 2-14).

46. Wipzycka herself ("Le degré d'alphabétisation," pp. 279-86) came to this conclusion in her study of literacy during this period. She suggested that perhaps the only way that a family could hope for a better lifestyle was to provide their children with as much rudimentary education as possible so that they might accepted as clerical candidates whose education would be completed by the Church.

47. The *Commentary on Isaiah* can be found in PG 70.

der his care. Cyril's *Commentary on Isaiah* is typical of patristic commentaries in general in that it is a detailed analysis of the book of Isaiah in which Cyril moves through the text seriatim and offers interpretive comments concerning the text. It is, however, representative of a specific subgenre of patristic commentaries, namely, those that were presented orally as part of the educational process for clergy, transcribed, and then later disseminated in written form as an interpretive resource.[48] The compilation of such oral lectures into written commentary form appears to have been traditional in Alexandria, as is suggested by Didymus the Blind's *Commentary on Zechariah*. The original oral setting of that commentary is clearly evident in the prologue where Didymus says, "pray for me, so that words will be given to me as I open my mouth."[49] Similarly, a variety of internal evidence within Cyril's *Commentary on Isaiah* indicates its original oral character: the titles of the divisions of the commentary, the phrasing Cyril uses throughout the commentary, and his emphasis on the special responsibility of those who are called to teach.

The first evidence of the oral character of Cyril's *Commentary on Isaiah* is found in the headings that have traditionally been associated with the subdivisions in the text. The commentary is divided into five major sections labeled "books" (βιβλία). These sections are, in turn, divided into five or six smaller units. There is nothing unusual about the headings for the subdivisions in Books II, III, and V where they are labeled "volumes" (τόμοι). It is the headings of the subdivisions of Books I and IV that are indicative of the original nature of the text, for they are labeled "orations" (λόγοι).[50] Although the absence of any early manuscripts prohibits categorical conclusions, the unusual and unexplained inclusion of this term as a heading for a literary subdivision is suggestive. The term "volume" as a heading for literary subdivisions is common, but the term "oration" as a literary heading is not documented either in Henry George Liddell and Robert Scott's *A Greek-English Lexicon* or in

---

48. See Paul Parvis's analysis of this subgenre in the context of the commentary genre as a whole: "Theodoret's Commentary on the Epistles of St. Paul," D.Phil. diss., Oxford University, 1975, p. 260.

49. *Commentary on Zechariah* (SC 83:190). Louis Doutreleau, the editor of the *Sources chrétiennes* edition of Didymus's commentary, argues that this commentary was based on a series of lectures presented by Didymus to his students at the catechetical school in Alexandria (*Didymus l'Aveugle: sur Zacharie*, SC 83 [Paris: Éditions du Cerf, 1962], pp. 43-44).

50. The term oration is rare as a heading in patristic literature, but when it is used it refers to a lecture or sermon oriented towards a specific topic (such as those presented by Gregory of Nazianzus).

G. W. H. Lampe's *A Patristic Greek Lexicon.*[51] Given the general rule of textual criticism that scribal emendations are more likely to solve problems than to create them, it seems more likely that "oration" rather than "volume" was the term originally associated with the subdivisions of the commentary.[52] It seems quite probable, therefore, that the use of the term "oration" as the heading of subdivisions within the text indicates that the commentary was originally presented in oral form.

The phrasing and word choice used by Cyril in his *Commentary on Isaiah* also point to the original oral character of the work. One striking aspect of Cyril's phrasing in the commentary is his frequent use of first person pronouns and verb forms, which are, at points, coupled with references to his audience whom he labels as "hearers." For example, when discussing Isaiah 18:2 Cyril says:

> The Greek narrative is pregnant with historical significance, and we will, of necessity, discuss it. We will not, however, exceed the bounds of what likely happened or what is appropriate for Christian preaching. We will, rather, lay out for our hearers (τοῖς ἀκροωμένοις) the meaning of these things. (PG 70:440c)

An additional aspect of Cyril's phrasing in the commentary that indicates its oral character is his use of statements, exhortations, questions, and epithets that are directed at his audience. In describing the two meanings present in Isaiah 51:3, Cyril addresses his audience in this way:

> The word of the holy prophets is always formed from visible things and tangible actions. It contains, however, reference both to things which are tangible and those which are spiritual. Thus when it uses the name Zion, it not only has an earthly referent, you have also received the spiritual referent, which is the church of the living God. (PG 70:1109b)

---

51. Henry George Liddell and Robert Scott, *A Greek-English Lexicon*, rev. and augmented by Henry Stuart Jones (Oxford: Clarendon, 1968); G. W. H. Lampe, ed., *A Patristic Greek Lexicon* (Oxford and New York: Clarendon, 1961). Both Origen's *Commentary on John* and Theodoret's *Commentary on Isaiah* are divided into τόμοι. The term λόγος is used occasionally in classical Greek to refer to narratives such as fables (Plato, *Phaedo* 60d), stories (Thucydides 1.97), or historical accounts (Herodotus 1.184), but there are no references in Lampe or Liddell and Scott where the term is used as a heading for a literary unit.

52. See Bruce Metzger's explanation of this principle in *The Text of the New Testament* (Oxford: Oxford University Press, 1968), pp. 209-10.

When Cyril seems to sense the interest of his hearers is flagging during his interpretation of Isaiah 23:1, he urges them to pay attention with these words:

> Bear with us as we attempt to articulate as clearly as possible those oracles that were given by God concerning Tyre, the history of which we have already explained. (PG 70:520c)

As he reflects on Isaiah 8:4, Cyril seems to wonder whether his audience is following his train of thought. To insure that his hearers understand his point he directly asks them if they know what he is saying: "Do you see how he thus stripped Satan of his spoils and quickly ravaged him?"[53] At various points in his commentary, Cyril adds intensity to his questions by addressing his audience with epithets in the vocative case. When arguing that the Jews are offering an impossible interpretation of Isaiah 7:14 because they fail to recognize the importance of the title Emmanuel, Cyril says: "But what would happen, O most excellent gentlemen, if someone were to ask [the Jews] just who it is that calls Hezekiah Emmanuel?"[54]

A third factor that indicates that Cyril's *Commentary on Isaiah* was originally presented orally to the clergy under Cyril's care is its repeated emphasis on the serious responsibility of those who are called to teach.[55] In his exposition of Isaiah 3:12, for example, Cyril includes a lengthy section in which he scathingly attacks the Jewish teachers for their failures and suggests that Christian teachers should not fall into the same errors:

> Isaiah teaches that these people were dominating them, not as those who would gently help their students progress, but rather as harsh and savage martinets who force their students to adhere to their own perspective and even occasionally drive them away from anything having to do with serious thinking. But this is not at all the perspective of those who are in Christ. Saint Peter, for example, writes to those who are called to be bishops and whose responsibility it is to lead their flock, "not as domineering over those in your charge but being examples to the flock." (PG 70.112c-d)

---

53. PG 70:225a. Cyril repeatedly asks this same question. Cf. PG 70:53b, 56d, 128a, 137a, and 341c. Similarly, Cyril also asks his audience if they hear what he is saying (e.g., PG 70:52a-b).

54. PG 70:204c.

55. In the commentary as a whole, Cyril makes no fewer than forty references to those who are called to teach and their responsibilities.

In a similar vein Cyril articulates the characteristics of a good Christian teacher or cleric in his comments on Isaiah 3:2:

> But I believe that the wise master builder is one who knows how to build up the church spiritually in both correct and blameless rites, who purges those who are deceived of what was falsely labeled as knowledge, and who rebuilds the minds of the believers with true doctrines. Just as St. Paul says in his Epistle to the Corinthians, "According to the grace given to me, like a wise master builder I laid the foundation, and others are building upon it. Let people take care how they build on it." (PG 70:100d-101a)

Certainly Cyril's interest in positive Christian teaching by itself is not a sufficient argument for the oral nature of the text, but when viewed in light of the other evidence, it clearly adds weight to the argument that the text was originally presented orally to the clergy under Cyril's care. The cumulative effect of the evidence, including the use of oration as a subdivision heading and the phrasing Cyril employs throughout the commentary, coupled with his emphasis on the qualities of good Christian teachers, is overwhelming.

Cyril Taught the Skills of Classical Literary Interpretation

Throughout Cyril's expositions on the various passages in Isaiah, there are frequent references to the skills taught by the classical grammarians. Cyril's repetitive allusions to these skills in his lectures would have provided the clerics under his care with both theoretical and practical knowledge of the science of interpretation. An examination of the *Commentary on Isaiah* provides examples in which Cyril introduces and demonstrates each of the six steps outlined in Dionysius's *Ars Grammatica*.

Each of the sections of Cyril's *Commentary on Isaiah* is introduced by a *lemma* that includes the complete text of the verse or verses that Cyril is interpreting. Although there is no evidence that proves that these *lemmata* were included in the original text of the commentary, it seems likely that Cyril began his remarks on a certain passage of Scripture by reading the text aloud. This reading, complete with proper breathing and emphasis, would model the correct manner in which Scripture was to be verbalized in a public setting.

Cyril's demonstration of the second of Dionysius's principles, namely, the explication of the tropes found in the text, occurs frequently in the commentary. He repeatedly indicates that readers cannot understand the intent or deeper meaning of a text unless they understand the stylistic devices (literary tropes, illustrations, allusions, and so on) used by the author to develop the point of the passage. Cyril notes, for example, that readers cannot make sense of Isaiah 9:8-9, an oracle of doom against Jacob and Ephraim, unless they realize that Isaiah is using the literary trope called synecdoche, in which the whole is indicated by reference to one of its component parts (or vice-versa).[56] In other parts of his commentary he identifies various other figures of speech such as prosopopoeia, emphasis, and hyperbole.[57]

The most evident of the steps of Dionysius's approach in the *Commentary on Isaiah* is the explanation of rare words and historical or scientific allusions present in the text. Cyril took great pains throughout his *Commentary on Isaiah* to demonstrate how one should analyze and define the meaning of rare and unusual words. In his reflections on Isaiah 1:8 where the LXX says, "the daughter of Zion will be abandoned (ἐγκαταλειφθήσεται) like a tent in a vineyard," Cyril clarifies the meaning of the word ἐγκαταλειφθήσεται in this way:

> The prophet says that the widely esteemed and famous Zion, namely Jerusalem, will be abandoned (ἐγκαταλειφθήσεται). This means that it will be deserted. (PG 70:17d)

In addition, Cyril frequently pointed out situations in which a common word was being used metaphorically. When Isaiah says in 15:2, "Weep, for all of your heads will be bald," Cyril notes, "This means that dishonor will fall upon one and all, for baldness is symbolic of dishonor" (PG 70:400c).

Throughout his *Commentary on Isaiah,* Cyril also devotes a great deal of time and energy to explaining historical and scientific allusions within the text. He frequently explains the references that Isaiah makes to the history of Judah and Israel. Cyril was convinced that accurate knowledge of the historical situation to which the prophet was referring was crucial for understanding the prophetic text. He says:

> Isaiah prophesies during the reigns of Uzziah, Jotham, Ahaz, and Hezekiah. Let us begin with a brief description of the times of each of them. . . . As we do this, we will find that the prophetic words are fitting and appropriate considering what was taking place at the time. (PG 70:12a)

56. PG 70:260b-c.
57. PG 70:485c and PG 70:372c-73a (prosopopoeia); PG 70:844d (emphasis); PG 70:357c and PG 70:900b-901d (hyperbole).

Not only does Cyril explain references in the text to the history of the Hebrew people, he also explains historical references to the surrounding countries and their customs. He offers, for example, an elaborate history of Greek religious belief and practice to explain the rather obscure reference that Isaiah makes to "sending pledges on the sea" and "letters of papyrus on the water" (Isa. 18:1-2).[58] In a similar way, Cyril clarifies obscure geographical, agricultural, and scientific references within the text. In the realm of geography, Cyril explains that when Isaiah refers to the "Rivers of Ethiopia" (ch. 18), he is referring to the so-called "seven mouths" of the Nile.[59] When Isaiah employs an agricultural metaphor in describing the desolation of Judah as an "abandoned cucumber field" (1:8), Cyril tells his audience that it was the custom of landowners to post guards in the cucumber and melon fields to protect the produce while it was ripening. After the harvest, however, the guards were sent home, and the fields were abandoned to scavengers.[60] When Isaiah makes what appears to be a strange allusion in 1:30 to the shame of the people of Israel making them look like oaks that lose their leaves, Cyril gives his audience a brief lesson in botany. He notes that Isaiah is referring to a type of oak (known today as a live oak) that never loses its foliage.[61]

Cyril's primary use of Dionysius's fourth step, namely, research into etymologies, appears in his comments on Hebrew names. In this vein, he explains that Jashub in Isaiah 7:3 means "a remnant has been brought back" and that Jacob means "one who supplants."[62] In his analysis of the text, Cyril relies

58. See PG 70:440c, which reads: "The meaning of these things which have been said is difficult to understand precisely, for it is pregnant with Greek history which it will be necessary for me to explain. I will not exceed the bounds of that which is appropriate for Christian preaching, but I will lay out for my hearers the traditional meaning of these things."

59. See PG 70:440a, which reads: "Isaiah calls the Seven Mouths, through which the broad and mighty River of Egypt flows to the sea, the 'Rivers of Ethiopia.' He calls the land through which the rivers flow 'Ethiopia'; that same land which is now Alexandria was then known as On. It was, at that time, very densely populated with extremely powerful inhabitants, and it did not extend very far from the River of Egypt."

60. See PG 70:25d-28a, which reads: "The guards, who are placed in the vineyards while the grapes are still bearing fruit, provide the greatest possible protection for them by attacking robbers who want to cut off the grapes. They also drive away every kind of wild animal. This, too, is the custom of the guards or even the owners of the cucumber fields. When the clusters of grapes have been picked and crushed and the cucumbers have been removed from the fields, those who have been guarding the fields are finally sent home, and they abandon their tents. At that point, those who wish to enter the fields are free to do so since their efforts would then be wasted."

61. *Quercus virginiana* or *Quercus agrifolia*.

62. PG 70:196b; PG 70:1081d.

on such etymologies to add insight into the meaning of a passage. When the text of Isaiah 25:6-7 predicts a time of prosperity for Zion and Jerusalem, Cyril makes these comments that relate to the etymology of the names Zion and Jerusalem:

> That the Lord will rule in Zion and Jerusalem . . . points from those things which were seen with the senses to a deeper mystical meaning, for Zion, when translated, means "lifted up" and "watch tower," and Jerusalem means "vision of peace." In truth, both of these titles refer to the Church of Christ which is both lifted up and conspicuous just as if it were situated on a mountain. (PG 70:561a-b)

During the course of his lectures, Cyril often demonstrates how to use the technique of analogy to determine the meaning of problematic words found in Isaiah. For example, with regard to the term "silver" that is used in Isaiah 1:22, where the prophet declares that people's silver will no longer be pure, Cyril refers to Psalm 11(12):6, where the word silver also occurs. By analogy he determines that in Isaiah the term silver must mean "oracles" or "words." Cyril says:

> At one point David in his eloquence sings, "The oracles of the Lord are pure. They are fine silver which has been tested by the fires of the earth." Therefore, the adulterated or completely impure silver is that which originates with the Jews, that is, the words of the Scribes and Pharisees, who are like peddlers who are attempting to water down their wine. (PG 70:52d-53a)

At points, Cyril even makes reference to the use of a word in classical literature or even in Hebrew so that he can help his audience define the same word as it occurs in Scripture. He relies, for example, on both classical Greek and Hebrew sources when he offers a definition of the word "sirens" (σειρῆνες), which is found in the Septuagint rendering of Isaiah 13:21.[63]

Cyril also makes several references in his commentary to the determination of the correct or valid reading of various passages of Isaiah. In most cases, Cyril seems to be conciliatory and offers explanations of how two variant readings could, in fact, mean the same thing. He does so both in reference to Isaiah 5:1, where some texts read "his vineyard" while others read "my vineyard," and Isaiah 9:8, where some texts read "The Lord sent death to Ja-

---

63. PG 70:364d.

cob" while others read "The Lord sent a word to Jacob." When discussing the textual problem in Isaiah 9:8 he remarks:

> The prophet returns here to the intent which he had at the beginning of this section and explains in greater detail about the destruction of Samaria, saying, "the Lord sent death to Jacob. . . ." One must know, however, that the Hebrew recension and several of the Greek translations have inserted the term "word" in place of "death." . . . But what sort of word was it? It was clearly a word condemning their impiety, laying out the penalty for those who had abandoned God to worship the creations of their own hand. He could, therefore, have said either that God sent a "word" or "death," for the force of the argument is not incompatible with either, since both words proceed towards the same goal. (PG 70:260a-b)

In this case, Cyril demonstrates the grammatical principle that the goal or intent of the passage governs which term or terms can or cannot fit into the passage. It must be noted, however, that Cyril seems far less concerned with the determination of an accurate text and the comparison of the readings of the various Greek translations than other ancient commentators on Isaiah, such as Jerome, Theodoret, and Eusebius, are. This could be attributed to the fact that textual criticism and emendation is a task best suited to the study rather than the lecture hall, for textual critics need to work with actual texts spread out before them so that they can diligently compare each successive word and phrase in all of the available texts.

Throughout his *Commentary on Isaiah,* Cyril explains and demonstrates all six of the approaches to literary analysis that Dionysius states are crucial to the science of the grammarians. Given the vast numbers of clerics whose educational background was limited, it seems highly probable that Cyril was using his lectures on Isaiah to teach the skills necessary for reading and interpreting literary texts, particularly the Bible, to the clerics under his care.

Conclusion

During the late third and early fourth centuries, the Church experienced rapid growth. This growth led to an increased demand for clergy who had mastered the skills of reading and interpreting literary texts, particularly the Bible. The classical educational system in place at that time provided the opportunity for such education by means of the schools taught by instructors known as grammarians, whose specialty was teaching the mastery of literary interpretation. It appears, however, that societal and economic factors led to extremely limited enrollment in the schools of the grammarians. For this reason, the pool of people who were educated enough to perform the tasks expected of the clergy was too small to meet the needs of the Church. It is my contention that evidence found in his *Commentary on Isaiah* indicates that Cyril of Alexandria functioned as an educator, lecturing to the clerics under his care about the skills of literary interpretation that were pioneered by the ancient grammarians. In his exposition of the book of Isaiah Cyril both explained the various aspects of literary criticism as taught by the grammarians and offered examples of how each step should be applied to a text.

The Communication of Idioms in Theodoret's *Commentary on Hebrews*

JOSEPH M. HALLMAN

Since the 1960s, there has been a continuous movement of rapprochement between the Oriental Orthodox churches and both the Catholic and Ortho-dox Church.[1] The Oriental churches commonly reject the Christological dog-mas of the Council of Chalcedon promulgated in the fifth century. As early as 1951 in the encyclical *Sempiternus Rex,* Pius XII stated that ancient Christological differences were mostly a matter of terminology. In July 1967, Paul VI, in a statement reminiscent of Justinian and the Second Council of Constantinople, alluded to the Council of Ephesus as the basis of commonal-ity of Christological dogma among the ancient churches, thereby excluding the Nestorians.[2] Later in 1970, he stated the following:

> If we have come to divergent expressions of the central mystery of our faith because of unfortunate circumstances, cultural differences and the

1. I am using the terminology of Ronald Roberson, *The Eastern Christian Churches: A Brief Survey* (Rome: Edizioni Orientalia Christiana, 1995), appendix II, pp. 213-14. The term "Oriental Orthodox churches" refers to five independent ancient groups: Armenian Apostolic, Coptic Orthodox, Ethiopian Orthodox, Syrian Orthodox, and the Malankara Orthodox Syrian Church in India. Together they number about thirty million members.

2. This excludes, of course, the so-called "Nestorian" Christians of the Assyrian Church of the East, but here, too, there is a recent tendency to assign the ancient differ-ences to terminology or to misunderstanding. John Paul II and Mar Dinkha IV, the patri-arch of this church, issued a "Joint Declaration on Christology" in November 1994, stating that their ancient divisions on Christological issues came about in large part because of misunderstandings (*Origins* [Washington, D.C.: CNS Documentary Service], 24,1,402).

difficulty of translating terms worked out with much effort and given precise statement gradually, then research into these doctrinal difficulties must be undertaken again in order to understand what has brought them about and to be able to overcome them in a brotherly way.[3]

I write in the spirit of this last statement. Johnson carefully reviewed similar declarations made by representatives of the Oriental churches and the Catholic Church up to the present time. In his opinion, which is based on statements issued over the past twenty-five years, "the ancient christological dispute between the Oriental Orthodox churches and the Catholic Church has been substantially resolved." The churches have "set aside the old disputes and affirm that their faith is . . . the same."[4]

I have argued previously that the Christological differences that originated in the fifth century among churches, and here I am not excluding the ancient Nestorians, are not only terminological, or based on misunderstanding, but are deeply theological.[5] I believe that the differences in Christology are rooted in two different views of the divine being in the incarnation and that this difference of views is related to the acceptance on the one side of the "communication of idioms" as valid language for the incarnation, and the rejection of this "communication" on the other side either explicitly or implicitly. There are at least two serious issues that were unresolved during the Christological debates, one that is metaphysical (the nature of the incarnate deity) and another that is linguistic (what our language about the incarnate deity signifies). In this paper I will argue that Theodoret of Cyrrhus rejects the communication of idioms because of his "Antiochene" understanding of the divine being as immutable and impassible, and that this is especially evident in his commentary on the Letter to the Hebrews. Further, I will argue that although the communication of idioms is a legitimate part of the Christian tradition, Theodoret's rejection is defensible on historical and theological grounds.

The Communication of Idioms

Those who accept the communication of idioms hold that the attributes of either the human or divine nature can be attributed to Christ because of his

---

3. Cited from Roberson, *Eastern Christian Churches,* p. 215.

4. Roberson, *Eastern Christian Churches,* p. 222.

5. J. M. Hallman, "The Seed of Fire: Divine Suffering in the Christology of Cyril of Alexandria and Nestorius of Constantinople," *JECS* 5.3 (1997): 369-91.

single divine personhood. Hence it is legitimate to say, for example, that "God died on the cross" and "rose from the dead" or that Mary is *Theotokos.* It was the denial of the latter statement that caused the condemnation of Nestorius at Ephesus in 431.

The practice of ascribing human attributes to the Logos occurs sporadically in the tradition prior to the fourth and fifth centuries, when it then became an issue. Both Clement and Origen insist that the divine Logos can neither change nor suffer but, in a few places, do assign these attributes to the Logos.[6] Hence it is somewhat misleading to judge Antiochene theologians such as Nestorius and Theodoret by saying that before the fourth century "there is no trace of hesitation in predicating human attributes of God the Word."[7] Even though early writers such as Ignatius of Antioch attributed suffering to the Logos, it is only when philosophically astute Christians such as Clement and Origen, and in the West Tertullian and Augustine, began to reflect on the implications of their belief in the Word made flesh that the issue emerged more clearly. This came to be the case especially during the Arian and Apollinarian controversies. Although I cannot demonstrate it here, Cyril of Alexandria did not give an adequate theological defense of the "communication of idioms," at least not adequate in the eyes of Antioch, and not adequate in the opinion of this writer.[8] If we attend to one of his latest writings on the subject, *Quod Unus Sit Deus,* one can sense his frustration because of his inability to construct a convincing framework for the *communicatio.*

It is clear that Theodoret did not teach the "two sons." Although he does not use *Theotokos* until after 448 in his letters (four times), and although his constant emphasis is on the duality of attribution, he does accept the unity of the person of Christ from his earliest writings on. I will try to show that in spite of his belief in the unity of person, and because of the development of his "two-natures" terminology evident especially in the commentaries, he did not accept the communication of idioms.

This paper concentrates in some detail on Theodoret's *Commentary on Hebrews* for two reasons: first, it contains many clear examples of Theodoret's use of his two natures understanding of Christ as applied to Scripture; second, it might well be the last scriptural commentary he wrote.[9]

---

6. See my book *The Descent of God: Divine Suffering in History and Theology* (Minneapolis: Augsburg/Fortress, 1991), pp. 36-49.

7. Kevin McNamara, "Theodoret of Cyrus and the Unity of Person in Christ," *Irish Theological Quarterly* 22 (1955): 325.

8. See Hallman, "Seed of Fire," pp. 380-84.

9. This assumes that he commented on Scripture in the order that he gives in Letter

The Commentaries

The dating of Theodoret's work is complicated because of the ambiguity of his own statements about it, and I do not intend to enter into that discussion here. It is quite clear, however, that his commentaries on Scripture were written after the Council of Ephesus and apparently before the *Eranistes* dated in 447-48.[10] Based on internal evidence gleaned from the commentaries themselves, it is fairly easy to decide the order in which they were written, but not the date for each.[11] There is no apparent development of his Christology in the commentaries and no important points of contrast with *Eranistes,* his anti-monophysite dialogue.[12] A more positive way of stating this is that Theodoret's Christology is very consistent throughout his career. The only significant Christological difference between the works written before and after Ephesus is that after the council Theodoret abandons concrete references to the two elements of Christ (God and man) in favor of abstract terminology (the divine, the human, or as God, as man) when referring to the two.[13]

The *Commentary on Hebrews*

One of Theodoret's favorite Christological constructions in this commentary is ὡς θεός and ὡς ἄνθρωπος. He uses the first to assign appropriate attributes to the divinity, the second to assign human things to the humanity. When one examines these interpretations carefully throughout the work, they appear more and more artificial. The "life's blood" of the paradoxical and dramatic combinations of divine and human attributes that result from the incarna-

---

82; it also assumes that he commented on the writings of Paul in order. Obviously, these are not strong reasons in and of themselves.

10. See especially Letters 82 (SC 98:198-204) and 113 (SC 111:56-67).

11. J.-N. Guinot, *L'Exégèse de Théodoret de Cyr* (Paris: Beauchesne, 1995), pp. 43-63. For easy reference see the charts on 62 and 63. Note especially the ambiguity in regard to the commentaries on Paul's letters.

12. Guinot, *Exégèse,* p. 577, n. 46. Regarding his first commentary on the Song of Songs, Guinot writes: "The Christology of Theodoret is well defined at the time of this commentary, and it does not undergo any fundamental modification in what follows" ("La christologie de Théodoret de Cyr dans son Commentaire sur le Cantique," *VChr* 39 [1985]: 266).

13. M. Richard, "Notes sur l'évolution doctrinale de Théodoret," in *Opera Minora* (Turnhout: Brepols, and Leuven: University Press, 1977), vol. 2, pp. 459-81. Several of

tion dries out as Theodoret appropriates the attributes to each nature, rather than to the Logos-subject.[14]

The phrase in Hebrews 1:2 that the Son was "appointed heir of all things" applies to the human, while the phrase that follows immediately, "through whom he created the worlds," applies to the divine.[15] Only the Logos is the "light of glory," and by implication, not the humanity. As God, Christ is always Lord; as man he received the glory that he had as God.[16] That he is now "above the angels" refers to his humanity because as God, he is the creator of the angels. As risen and ascended ἄνθρωπος he is only now come to be "above the angels."[17]

According to Theodoret, Paul teaches that God is ἄτρεπτος τε καὶ ἀναλλοίωτος. This is what it means to say that "they will perish, but you will remain." He also teaches that the divinity is impassible, ἀπαθής. For if divinity suffers, how is it the same? The "sit at my right hand" refers to the humanity, since the divine has an eternal seat.[18]

In commenting on Hebrews 2:7, Theodoret insists that Christ was made lower than the angels only as man, not as God. This saying applies to the human nature, and only before the resurrection and exaltation to God's right hand.[19]

Several passages in Hebrews refer to the priesthood of Christ, and in every single discussion of this topic, Theodoret insists that Christ is our high priest only ὡς ἄνθρωπος, not as God. He is high priest only insofar as he became man and accepted human nature. The divine nature of Christ is present everywhere and in all things. Hence the saying in Hebrews 4:14 that Christ "passed through the heavens" refers only to his human nature. Verse 15, which states that Jesus was "tempted as we are," refers only to the ἄνθρωπος. He accepted our weaknesses as a man. Also on verse 15 Theodoret writes: "As God, Christ the Lord by nature has the kingdom, the eternal throne. . . . As

---

Theodoret's early works are lost, and this also might influence any comparisons between earlier and later writings.

14. Throughout his exegesis, because he is so concerned to uphold divine immutability and impassibility, Theodoret is always decisively dyophysite. See my article "Theodoret's *Eranistes* and Its Aftermath: The Demise of the Christology of Antioch," in *Prayer And Spirituality in the Early Church,* ed. Pauline Allen, Wendy Mayer, and Lawrence Cross (Moorooka, Brisbane: Watson Ferguson & Company, 1999), 2:343-57.

15. PG 82:680a.

16. PG 82:684b. In John 17:5 ("Father, glorify me with the glory which I had with you before the world began") Jesus asks not to receive what he did not have, but to reveal what he had already.

17. PG 82:684b.

18. PG 82:688c-d on Heb. 1:10-12.

19. PG 82:692a-d.

man, however, and as priest and apostle of our confession, he hears 'Sit at my right hand.'"[20]

In spite of the strongly dyophysite nature of Theodoret's Christological exegesis, he does have a sense of unity, which, although it is not new to his work after Ephesus, is certainly present here. On Hebrews 1:3 he writes that the divine Word is joined (συνέζευκται) by human generation to suffering and to time.[21] Christ is God and man in one person (πρόσωπον).[22]

One of the most interesting Christological discussions in the commentary comes at Hebrews 5:7-10, which brings out clearly the problem for Antiochene Christological exegesis generally, and specifically for Theodoret:

> In the days of his flesh, Jesus offered up prayers and supplications, with loud cries and tears, to him who was able to save him from death, and he was heard for his godly fear. Although he was a son, he learned obedience through what he suffered; and being made perfect, he became the source of eternal salvation to all who obey him, being designated by God a high priest after the order of Melchizedek. (Heb. 5:7-10)

Hebrews 5:5 states that Christ "was appointed" as high priest and quotes Psalm 2:7: "You are my son, today I have begotten you," a text which was problematic during the Arian period. For Theodoret, the interpretation is obvious. Because the divine can neither change nor suffer, the "loud cries and tears" cannot come from the divine Logos. Neither can the Logos learn obedience, "be made perfect," or be appointed or designated a high priest.

In his reply to the tenth anathema of Cyril, Theodoret argued that all of these are to be attributed to the human nature of Christ. None can be predicated of the divinity because God the Word does not change (is ἀναλλοίωτος and ἄτρεπτος) and cannot suffer (ἀπαθής).[23] In the Hebrews passage, however, Theodoret states that the divine nature participates (συνεχώρησεν) in the human suffering, and not merely by appearance as in the Gnostic heresies, but truly. This is one of the rare instances where Theodoret is willing to attribute something of the human to the divine nature. Yet he will never directly attribute anything human to the divine subject, the Logos.

20. PG 82:708b-d. For similar passages about the priesthood of Christ, see PG 82:696d, 733a-c, 736a.

21. PG 82:681b. See also PG 82:685a for συνεζευγμένην used in the same way.

22. PG 82:697d. See Guinot, *Exégèse*, p. 874, for other instances of πρόσωπον in Theodoret. It is used only one other time in this commentary, and not in this sense. See PG 82:688b.

23. PG 76:436c-37a.

Theodoret then cites another problematic passage, Matthew 26:39: "Father, if it is possible, let this cup pass from me." Previously, Theodoret insisted that God could not possibly utter these words.[24] They came from the human Jesus. Here, he gives a different explanation. This passage and the phrase "learned obedience through what he suffered" are hyperboles, not meant to be taken literally. Indeed Jesus showed obedience before the passion, not only after it. The sufferings of Christ are also expressed hyperbolically, not only to show the truth of the incarnation but also to confirm what Paul said before, namely, that we have a priest who shares our infirmities and is like us in all things except sin.[25]

The Communication Revisited

I mentioned previously that Theodoret is consistent in holding the unity of the person of Christ. He does not teach the two sons and legitimately defends himself in his letters against this charge by appealing to his corpus. We have seen this in some texts in the *Commentary on Hebrews*. At the same time, Theodoret never uses the communication of idioms, since for him it represents a false way of speaking. As Aloys Grillmeier points out, "he will not make the Logos the common subject of the divine and the human sayings. . . . For him, 'the Logos has suffered' means: the Logos suffered in his divine nature."[26] This is as true for his earlier writings as for his commentaries.

Marijan Mandac[27] suggested that Theodoret had at least a weak doctrine of *communicatio*. Although J.-N. Guinot does not state this explicitly, if I interpret him correctly, he also at least implies it.[28] Since Theodoret had such strong reasons to deny the *communicatio*, and because he is so consistent, I do not see how such an argument is defensible even by implication. To accept the *communicatio* would have been inconsistent for Theodoret. Let us examine the texts used.

24. *Ps.* 21.2 (PG 80:1009b).

25. This discussion is in PG 80:712c-13b.

26. Aloys Grillmeier, S.J., *Christ in Christian Tradition*, trans. John Bowden (Atlanta: John Knox, 1975), 1:493.

27. Marijan Mandac, "L'Union christologique dans les oeuvres de Théodoret antérieures au concile d'Éphèse," *Ephemerides Theologicae Lovanienses* 47 (1971): 64-96. The last six lines of the article argue for a vague sense of the communication of idioms in Theodoret.

28. Guinot, *Exégèse*, pp. 616-18.

Mandac cites Theodoret's response to Cyril's twelfth anathema, which reads:

Whoever does not confess that the Word of God suffered in the flesh and was crucified and tasted death in the flesh, or that he was firstborn from the dead, or was life and living as God, let them be anathema.[29]

Theodoret replies in part that because of the union of the form of the servant with the form of God, the form of God is joined (οἰκειόω, translated by Mandac as *s'est approprié*) to the sufferings.[30] Immediately after this, Theodoret hastens to point out that it is not Christ who suffers, but the man (ἄνθρωπος) who was assumed by the Word. This is hardly the context to argue for even a weak sense of the *communicatio*.

Another passage comes from a pre-Ephesus work of Theodoret on the incarnation, and this text uses the same term, οἰκειόω, to connect human sufferings to the Logos.[31] For Mandac, this is an appropriation of the sufferings of Jesus by the Logos. I believe a better sense of the text is that the Logos, because it is joined to the human, is also joined to human sufferings, but it does not appropriate them to itself in any subjective sense. The divine cannot suffer. For Theodoret, to be joined to suffering does not mean to suffer.

Guinot cites Theodoret's reply to Cyril's twelfth anathema as well and correctly points out that in spite of the use of οἰκειούμενος to connect suffering to the form of God Theodoret never tires of distinguishing between the passible human nature and the impassible divine nature, and that this is obvious in the passage.[32] He cites two other passages using the same term, one from *Questions on Leviticus* 19 (on Lev. 14:51)[33] and one from the *Commentary on Isaiah* (on Isa. 53:3).[34] There is also a comment on Psalm 40:5, which says, "I am the Lamb of God who takes away the sin of the world. [I am] united (οἰκειούμενος) to human suffering."[35]

In other texts, however, the term οἰκειούμενος expresses the unity be-

---

29. PG 76:449b.

30. Mandac, "Union christologique," p. 93.

31. PG 75:1452a.

32. Guinot, *Exégèse*, p. 617.

33. PG 80:324b.

34. SC 315:148.

35. PG 80:1164c. Theodoret also uses οἰκειόω in this way three times in the *Eranistes*. M. de Durand thinks that the imprecision of this term allows both Theodoret and Cyril to use it without agreeing on the communication of idioms, and I believe he is correct. See SC 97:26-27; Guinot, *Exégèse*, p. 616, n. 165.

tween Christ and us because of his humanity, not the unity between the two natures of Christ. In a comment on Hebrews 2:5-8, Christ is οἰκειουμένη τὰ πάσης τῆς φύσεως, joined to our entire nature.[36] One should take into account passages that use the term in this loose way. Once again, I believe that Theodoret is consistent. Christ's connection with other human beings is similar to the connection between the divine and the human natures and should not be construed as being any stronger.

Guinot concludes this discussion by pointing out, once again quite correctly, that for Theodoret the mode of union of the divine and the human natures was ineffable.[37] Nevertheless, whatever it means to think of the union in this apophatic way, it is not even remotely possible that for Theodoret the ineffability of the union could compromise divine impassibility and immutability.

The Theological Issues: Who Is God? What Can Be Said?

If we set aside for the moment the question of Theodoret's orthodoxy, what is at stake here? I believe that there are two issues that were unresolved at the time of the separation of the ancient churches. Beginning with Athanasius, the Alexandrians were convinced that the description of the divine being by Plato and Aristotle as the singular immutable impassible deity was not the only description one needed for the God of Christian faith who became incarnate in Jesus. They were convinced by intuitive religious understanding, rooted ultimately in their soteriology (which was rooted primarily in their intuitive understanding of the Eucharist), that the ultimate subject of attribution in Jesus was the divine Logos, because the incarnation divinized the entire human race. Unless Jesus was God made flesh, and unless the Eucharist is the divine in the form of bread and wine, we are not saved. Nevertheless, they adhered to the Platonic portrait of the divine, thus creating their dilemma. Alexandrians do hold and state repeatedly along with Plato and Aristotle that the perfect divine being can neither change nor suffer.

For Theodoret and for the Antiochenes generally, the God of the philosophers was the God of both Jewish and Christian faith, and unless Antioch could have reconsidered the nature of the deity itself, and reconsidered it philosophically, it simply could not validate the communication of

---

36. PG 82:692a. See also PG 82:360b.
37. Guinot, *Exégèse,* p. 618.

idioms. I believe the same holds true for any contemporary discussion of this issue.

A related point is the manner in which both sides seem to understand the way they attribute human or divine qualities to Christ. Theodoret, as Grillmeier stated above, takes statements of attribution literally as statements of fact. They correspond to reality. Contradictions cannot be accepted, even in religious discourse. Something cannot both be and not be in the same way at the same time in a theology that is logically consistent, as all theology must be. In a striking passage from *Eranistes,* when the monophysite Eranistes says that Christ "underwent the passion impassibly," Theodoret puts into the mouth of the Orthodox person a statement that could have easily come from Athanasius or Cyril:

> And what man in his senses would ever put up with such ridiculous riddles? Who ever heard of an impassible passion . . . ? The impassible has never undergone passion, and what has undergone passion could not possibly be impassible.[38]

The Christological religious discourse of the Alexandrians does admit of apparent contradictions, and the discourse of the communication of idioms is the prime example. Does this mean that ultimately as Christians, we are left with two ways of speaking about the divine being that are at bottom incompatible? Can Antioch and Alexandria ever agree on the proper manner to describe the divine being who is revealed in Christ Jesus?

Grillmeier is critical of Theodoret as having "an incomplete, symmetrical conception of Christ in which the hypostasis of the Logos does not come fully into its own."[39] The choice of the term is a good one, because it brings out what is at stake here. Symmetry is usually considered a virtue, as in logic, architecture, and art, but in the case of the incarnation, according to Grillmeier, apparently not. The asymmetrical view of the incarnate Lord that became Christian orthodoxy is quite possibly the result of the acceptance of the twin axioms of divine impassibility and immutability from philosophy while teaching the communication of idioms from Christian revelation.

An alternative to the permanent incompatibility of these two views is the construction of a revised metaphysical theology that upholds in a consistent manner and without contradiction, that is, symmetrically, a description

---

38. G. H. Ettlinger, *Theodoret of Cyrus: Eranistes* (Oxford: Clarendon, 1975), pp. 218, 30-33.

39. Grillmeier, *Christ,* p. 494.

of the divine being that includes the capacity for change and suffering. I believe that a close examination of the arguments for divine impassibility and immutability in both Plato and Aristotle reveals their weakness. Not only, as Pascal put it, is theirs not the God of Abraham, Isaac, and Jacob; both philosophies of the divine are suspect in their own idiom.

Whether the development of an incarnational view of the deity fits the mood of theology in an age of postmodernity is another question entirely, but perhaps ancient traditions should reject much of postmodernity out of hand. I believe a dialogue that brings these metaphysical and linguistic issues to light might help our ancient Christian traditions come to grips with their Christological differences in a more substantive manner than has occurred over the past twenty-five years.

Romanos's Biblical Interpretation:
Drama, Imagery, and Attention to the Text

JOSEPH W. TRIGG

From the deathless waters that the faithful Samaritan woman
Once discovered, we thirsty ones
Are about to drink. Let us investigate all their channels.
As we recall for a moment the actual words of the Gospel,
So that, wisely, we may see how Christ was that water which
The Samaritan woman once drank,
How from that water she bestowed another water.
Why she did not offer a drink to the one who was thirsty,
    and what stopped her.
The marvelous book
Answers these questions even as it offers us
Joy and redemption.

(Romanos, On the Samaritan Woman, stanza 3)

More or less sixty poems survive from the sixth-century Byzantine poet, Romanos. Most of these are kontakia, in effect, metrical homilies derived from the Syriac *memra*, of which fifty deal with specific biblical texts. Each kontakion has one or more short first stanzas, the *proemium* or *koukoulion*, ending in a refrain, the *ephymnion*. There follow twenty or so longer stanzas, *troparia* or *oikoi*, each ending with the refrain. The first of these, the *irmos*, sets the metrical pattern for the rest. This meter is tonic and syllabic and so has nothing in common with the quantitative meter of classical poetry. The letters beginning each stanza form an acrostic, most commonly τοῦ ταπεινοῦ Ῥωμανοῦ, "by humble Romanos."[1] Although its antecedents are Syriac, this form enabled Romanos to write genuinely popular verse, accessible to the ordinary person, since the classical forms had long since lost their connection with the spoken Greek language. This departure from previous verse forms, combined with his work's literary quality, makes Romanos a pivotal figure in the nearly three-thousand-year history of Greek poetry. We have little reliable information about Romanos himself. He was apparently born at Emesa, in Syria, in the late fifth century and was reputedly of Jewish origin. He settled in Constantinople at the end of the reign of Anastasius I (491-518) and died probably not long after the earthquake of 555, to which he refers.[2] His deep familiarity with the Syriac *Diatessaron* and with works by Ephrem confirms that he was bilingual in Syriac and Greek and effected a creative synthesis between Syriac and Greek traditions.[3]

In the third stanza, quoted above from his hymn *On the Samaritan Woman*, Romanos, conjuring up an image of water spilling in runnels through dusty ground, invites his hearers to join him in investigating their "smallest channels" (literally "veins," φλέβας). These waters, which the woman at the well discovered in the course of her conversation with Jesus, he describes as "deathless," a term that seems to suggest not so much that the waters themselves are immortal but that they confer immortality. He intimates that this investigation will involve a close look at the biblical text since "the marvelous book" (τὸ μεγαλεῖον, ἡ βίβλος) answers our questions about these various channels even as it offers us the "joy and redemption" that are each stanza's refrain. In the following eighteen stanzas we see Romanos going carefully through the biblical text, John 4:5-42, asking at one point, "What then does the book teach?" (9.4.1), and providing, no less than, say, Chrysostom or Augustine, a running interpretation of a passage that had just been read liturgically.[4]

---

1. On the form of the kontakion, see Paul Maas, "Das Kontakion (Mit einem Exkurs über Romanos und Basileios von Seleukeia)," *Byzantinische Zeitschrift* 19 (1910): 285-306; and J. Grosdidier de Matons, *Romanos le Mélode et les origines de la poésie religieuse à Byzance* (Paris: Beauchesne, 1977), pp. 3-156.

2. On Romanos's life, see Grosdidier, *Romanos le Mélode,* pp. 159-98; P. Maas and C. A. Trypanis, *Sancti Romani Melodi Cantica,* vol. 1: *Cantica Genuina* (Oxford: Clarendon, 1963), pp. xv-xx.

3. See William L. Petersen, *The Diatessaron and Ephrem Syrus as Sources of Romanos the Melodist,* CSCO 475 (Louvain: Peeters, 1985). See also Sebastian P. Brock, "From Ephrem to Romanos," *SP* 20 (1989): 139-51; and Lukas van Rompay, "Romanos le Mélode: Un poète syrien à Constantinople," in *Early Christian Poetry: A Collection of Essays,* ed. J. den Boeft and A. Hilhorst (Leiden: Brill, 1993), pp. 283-96.

4. For passages indicating that the lesson commented on had just been read, see Maas, "Das Kontakion," pp. 286-87.

JOSEPH W. TRIGG

Such reverence for the biblical text, expressed in a close attention to its every detail, is typical of Romanos's œuvre. One would have a hard time finding, even among the Fathers, anyone more biblical in his orientation than he is. As already mentioned, fifty of the fifty-nine poems considered genuine by Paul Maas and C. A. Trypanis are effectively commentaries on biblical texts. The other nine are also in their own way thoroughly oriented toward the Bible and permeated by its imagery and language.

In 1910 Paul Maas, in his seminal article, "Das Kontakion," remarked on Romanos's freedom in the formation of biblical material, particularly the way he invents dialogues for biblical characters with only the most meager foundation in the biblical text itself.[5] Thanks to more recent studies by such authors as J. Grosdidier de Matons and William Petersen, we can now more fully appreciate the extent to which Romanos brought to Justinian's Constantinople an artistry and outlook deeply steeped in Syriac as well as Greek approaches to the Bible. As of yet, though, Romanos's biblical interpretation has received relatively little attention. The fullest discussion of Romanos's use of the Bible, as of so many other aspects of his work, is in Grosdidier's magisterial *Romanos le Mélode*. There Grosdidier provides an extensive list of passages in which Romanos interprets an Old Testament incident as a type foreshadowing the life of Christ.[6] He also lists numerous passages where Romanos employs allegory.[7] Thus the parable of the Prodigal Son (Luke 15:11-32) is interpreted symbolically to refer to the reconciliation of a penitent to the Church (Hymn 49), and the parable of the ten drachmas (Luke 15:8-10) is interpreted to refer to Christ's intense concern with the tenth order of spiritual beings (humanity), even though the other nine (the orders of angels) were never lost (Hymn 27).

Grosdidier also points out, though, that what he calls "literal" interpretation, "undoubtedly dependent on the old school of Antioch," as opposed to typology or allegory, is at least as characteristic of Romanos's approach to the Bible. Romanos, according to him, employs such "literal" exegesis in two ways: (1) he clarifies contradictions or obscurities as they arise in the text that he is treating; and (2) he alludes to passages in such a way as to demonstrate their continuing relevance. With the second sort of literal interpretation he

5. Maas, "Das Kontakion," pp. 290-91.

6. Grosdidier, *Romanos le Mélode*, pp. 255-61. See also R. J. Shork, "Typology in the *Kontakia* of Romanos," *SP* 6.4 (1962): 211-20. Alexandros S. Korakides also points out that Romanos has a rich repertoire of types for the Blessed Virgin Mary: Η ΠΕΡΙ ΤΟΥ ΛΟΓΟΥ ΘΕΟΛΟΓΙΑ ΤΩΝ ΚΟΝΤΑΚΙΩΝ ΡΩΜΑΝΟΥ ΤΟΥ ΜΕΛΩΔΟΥ (Athens: Ekdoseis Ionia, 1973), p. 87.

7. Grosdidier, *Romanos le Mélode*, pp. 261-62.

brings to light the new dimension given by Christian revelation to passages in the Old Testament, largely in the Psalms or the prophets, or shows the continuing relevance of passages, more likely in the New Testament, by applying them to himself and his hearers. Grosdidier further points out that Romanos is artful in the way he performs such interpretation, often giving it to the biblical characters themselves. He devotes relatively little space to such interpretation, though, contenting himself with pointing out a few examples.[8] A charming one is when, in his Hymn 1, *On the Nativity,* Romanos has the Magi ask Mary about the presence of Joseph, arguing that her cohabitation with him could give an opening to scandal about her pregnancy. She replies that Joseph is there so that he can testify to his dream (Matt. 1:20-21) and assure the Magi that Mary had conceived by the Holy Spirit (1:18).

Grosdidier also identifies biblical references and occasionally discusses biblical interpretation in his magnificent five-volume edition of fifty-six of Romanos's hymns in Sources chrétiennes.[9] In his introduction to the kontakion he refers to as the *First Hymn on the Resurrection* (Hymn 29 in Maas and Trypanis), he argues that it is a work of remarkable richness in which the author put the best of himself. This is because Romanos adopted the form one finds in his best productions, "like the first hymn on the Nativity, that on the *Temptation of Joseph,* that on the *Beheading of John the Baptist,* a more or less free adaptation of the scriptural text, where as much as possible is left to dialogue, and where the hearer must discern for himself the moral and theological teaching, more mixed in with the drama of the narrative than expressly formulated."[10] I would not necessarily call such interpretation "literal," since I am not sure what literal means, but I would suggest that Romanos's particular gift — I would go so far as to say, his genius — for biblical interpretation shows up most clearly in his ability to bring drama and imagery into direct engagement with the text.

Romanos reveals his delight in drama in his Hymn 11, *On the Gerasene Demoniac,* where in the second stanza he states that we smite the demons when we joyfully enact the comedy (κωμῳδοῦμεν) of their fall and that we make the devil sad when we act out (τραγῳδοῦμεν) in church the triumph over the devils. A particularly effective example of this is the comic subterranean dialogue in his Hymn 14, *On the Raising of Lazarus* (1). There, through much of the poem we listen to Death and Hell bicker and complain as

---

8. Grosdidier, *Romanos le Mélode,* p. 262. The examples are from 7.6; 27.17; 1.10; 32.15 (Maas and Trypanis's numbering).

9. See n. 2 above.

10. Grosdidier, SC 128:355.

Christ's footsteps resound as he approaches Bethany. Similarly, in Hymn 25, *On the Resurrection,* Hell complains of having become a laughingstock. In Hymn 44, *On Joseph's Temptation,* the devil encourages Potiphar's wife to snare Joseph like a fish in a net (stanza 6). As the story unfolds, Romanos presents the steamy domestic drama as a spiritual war, in which the angels take Joseph's part. Romanos's dramatic flair extends, however, far beyond mocking the devil. He has a gift for highlighting the pathos already present in much of biblical narrative. In his Hymn 17, *On Judas,* Romanos, in the persona of the narrator, elaborates on the enormity of Judas's crime:

> When he was readying his treachery, when he was preparing your
>   murder,
>   the one whom you had loved, but who had rejected you,
>   the one whom you had called, but who abandoned you, the one
> who had been crowned but who abused you,
> then you, tenderhearted, long-suffering,
>   wanting to show to the murderer your unspeakable love of
>   humanity,
> you filled the basin, you bent your neck, you became a slave of slaves,
>   and he gave you, redeemer, his feet to wash,
> have mercy, mercy, mercy on us,
>   you who put up with all of us sinners as you wait for us to repent
> (ὁ πάντων ἀνεχόμενος καὶ πάντας ἐκδεχόμενος).
> You washed with water the feet that ran to betray you
>   and nourished with mystic food
>   the enemy of your tenderness, the one who had no part in your
>   eucharistic blessing;
>   you exalted the man who was destitute by your gifts of grace;
>   you caused the wretch to grow by your gifts, you enriched him
>   and made him happy,
> gave him command over demons, alleviation of tribulations he had
>   on his tongue;
>   and in spite of all these things he separated from you, and the
> murderer had no remorse.
> Have mercy, mercy, mercy on us,
>   you who put up with all of us sinners as you wait for us to repent.
>
> (17.2-3)

An even more effective way of achieving pathos is imaginatively entering into a character's thoughts. Thus, in his *Hymn on Abraham,* he adopts the persona of Abraham, who, when he looks with tender love on the beauty of his child, experiences the horror at what he is about to do:

> Alas, pity, your stammering tongue
>   will turn mute under your father's slaughtering hand.
> Your eyelids, it is not Sarah who is going to close them.
> Your rosy lips, now I am going to make them still
> As I fulfill the command of him who gave you to me.
>
> (41.5.4-8)

Another way of enhancing drama is to invent a dialogue between two biblical characters. Thus, in his Hymn 10, *On the Sinful Woman,* Romanos provides for the woman who anoints Jesus with precious ointment not only a passionate soliloquy in which she takes courage from the salvation of Rahab the prostitute in Joshua 2 (stanza 7), but also a lively dialogue with the perfume seller (stanzas 9-11). William L. Petersen has shown that Romanos took the idea, but not the content, for such a dialogue from Ephrem.[11] After she has expressed her willingness to give anything, even her skin and bones, for a precious perfume, the merchant asks her who it is who has so inflamed her passion and whether he is, indeed, worth his best perfume, a question that brings forth the response, "Is he worth it, nothing is worth as much as he is worth!" and the testimony that, although she has not seen him, she has been "wounded by the vision of him whose nature is invisible." In his Hymn 38, *On the Beheading of John the Baptist,* Romanos invents a response on Salome's part to her mother's request that she seek John's head. Before agreeing, Salome expresses reservations, recalling what happened to Jezebel and her family when she compassed the death of Elijah (stanzas 2-9). In the process, of course, Romanos alludes to an Old Testament type. Later on in *On Judas,* he brings in the angels, as if in an invisible gallery, and has them comment on the Last Supper:

> The fiery spirits stood in awe and the invisible choirs were amazed
>   seeing the incomprehensible
>   bend down as a lesson and serve in the dust.
> Gabriel said in alarm:
>   "Holy angels, companions, look and be appalled;
> Peter extends his foot, and he who was born of a virgin mother takes
>   and washes it,

11. Petersen, *The Diatessaron,* pp. 183-84.

and he does not only wash Peter, but Judas along with him.
Have mercy, mercy, mercy on us,
    you who put up with all of us sinners as you wait for us to repent."

                                            (17.7)

In Hymn 32, *On the Ascension*, Romanos dramatizes prosopological exegesis by giving the words of Psalm 24:9, "lift up the gates and open wide the heavenly doors," to the archangels as they prepare for Christ's entry into heaven (32.10.7-8). In Hymn 25 *On the Resurrection*, Romanos makes the point that the resurrection is prophesied in the Old Testament by having the prophets use their own words to greet Christ's harrowing of Hell.

Zephaniah cried with a loud voice to Adam, "This is the one
you have awaited patiently until the day of resurrection, as I told you
    ahead of time."
Then Nahum next announced the good news to the poor, saying,
"He has arisen, blowing on your face and taking away oppression."
And Zechariah, rejoicing, is crying, "Our God, you have come
with your saints"; and David clearly chants his Psalm:
"He has awakened like a mighty man, and as from sleep
The Lord has risen."

                  (25.10, citing Zeph. 3:8; Nah. 2:2;
                        Zech. 14:5; Ps. 78:65)

In these last — and in many cases, as Grosdidier points out — Romanos makes biblical characters themselves the voice of his interpretation.

One may well suspect that Romanos was encouraged to give free rein to his dramatic genius by the conviction that his task was only to bring home to his hearers the great drama of the divine οἰκονομία, the plan of salvation, the plan that has its decisive crisis in the incarnation and resurrection of Christ. This is the plan "for us" that Christ fulfills in his ascension (32, pr I.1). In Romanos, οἰκονομία has not lost the sense it has in Hellenistic grammar, where it can be applied to the "arrangement" of an author's (like Homer's) material in order to enhance drama and pathos. Οἰκονομία as used by patristic writers often describes behavior that we might consider dishonest or manipulative, even if ostensibly well intentioned. Thus, for example, John Chrysostom describes himself as having entered into a pledge with his friend Basil that neither would accept ordination as a priest unless the other did. Basil then accepted the yoke on the understanding that John was also being ordained. However, when he learned that John had actually hidden to avoid ordination, he bitterly reproached him for deception. John, however, argued that his craftiness (τέχνη), was not deception but οἰκονομία and wisdom, since Basil was eminently qualified to be a priest and he, at the time, was not.[12] The οἰκονομία is an expression of the divine φιλανθρωπία, God's "love of humanity," another term with a venerable history in patristic interpretation. Thus, although Romanos warns of the inevitable consequences of sin, his emphasis is consistently on divine mercy and on the accessibility of grace, rather than on judgment. Thus in Hymn 52, *On Repentance,* he takes as his refrain 1 Timothy 2:4, "He who wills all humanity to be saved."

One sees a clear reflection of this attitude in his positive depictions of the sinful woman who anointed Jesus' feet (Hymn 10) or of the Samaritan woman at the well (Hymn 9). Following a homily by Basil of Seleucia, Hymn 45, *On Elijah,* where the refrain celebrates God as "the only lover of humanity" (ὁ μόνος φιλάνθρωπος), engages in an unusual interpretation of the great prophet. Elijah is exasperated by God's immense love of humanity (πολλὴν φιλανθρωπίαν) in the face of "humanity's immense lawlessness" (τὴν πολλὴν τῶν ἀνθρώπων ἀνομίαν) and beseeches God, "be wrathful at those who are now ignoring you, most just judge" (45.1.1-4). The poem shows God so manipulating the prophet's experience that he came to respect God's love for all of humanity.[13] Thus, for example, in order to disabuse him of the notion that Jews must not eat with Gentiles, he guides him to the house of the widow of Zarephath (45.14). Ultimately, Elijah comes to ask God to end the drought he had declared because God in his mercy had persuaded him to do so (45.26). Nonetheless, sensing that Elijah is still too brusque (ἀπότομος) for his purposes, God tells him his intention to remove him from the earth and eventually to descend to earth himself, in his mercy, by becoming a man (45.31). Even apparent sins and misfortunes have their place in the overarching scheme of the divine οἰκονομία. Thus in Hymn 38, *On the Beheading of John the Baptist,* John's death is a part of the divine plan because it enables him to preach in Hades (38, Pr. 2); and in Hymn 30, *On Doubting Thomas,* Thomas's doubt was "planned" (ᾠκονόμησε) by God in order to help us be more certain of the resurrection (30, Pr. 2).

This sense of a plan, grounded in the immense divine mercy, that redeems what would otherwise be sins and disasters does not just apply to bibli-

---

12. See John Chrysostom, *sac.* 1.7.

13. See Basil of Seleucia, Εἰς τὸν ἅγιον Ἠλίαν (PG 85:147-97). Perhaps Basil and, following him, Romanos found the theme of the wrathful prophet complaining about God's mercy for sinners in the story of Jonah, which Romanos celebrated in Hymn 52, *On Repentance* or *Nineveh.*

cal figures but characterizes all of God's dealings with humanity. Thus Romanos states in Hymn 50, *On the Rich Man and Lazarus,* that people suffer as they do because this is a way for them to be cleansed from sin (50.7). In Romanos's great topical Hymn 54, *On Earthquakes and Fires,* he provides an interpretation of recent events in Constantinople — earthquakes followed by a terrible fire associated with the Nika revolt in 532 and Justinian's rebuilding of Hagia Sophia — as expressions of the divine οἰκονομία. In his first stanza Romanos explains how events perceived as human disasters are, in fact, expressions of God's mercy:

> A hospital of souls for those infirm in will he has provided without
>   jealousy,
> he, the only physician of bodies and souls,
> so that those who are ill might request healing from him and receive it.
> For the deliverer hastens to heal everyone's wounds
> and to every entreaty to bestow all favors appropriately,
> but sometimes he withholds his hand from the gift of healing,
> awaking the lazy from their torpor,
> contriving, as a sage, the cure for those who stumble,
> so that he might bestow
> eternal life.
>
> (54.1)

In the course of the hymn Romanos shows the continuity between the way God dealt in sacred history and the way he deals with humanity in the present. He shows how God hid his compassion when Israel sinned in the time of Moses (54.3-4), and he holds up Jesus' dealings with the Canaanite woman (Matt. 15:21-28) as an instance that is ἄγαν οἰκονομικὸν, a good example of οἰκονομία (54.5.1). Inwardly the Lord is loving (φιλάνθρωπος), even if externally he is wrathful (ὀργίλος; 54.5.4), so that he might reward the woman's persistence with eternal life. Having discussed the disasters Constantinople had undergone in his own time, he argues that all these events display the same divine plan. Just as in the past when the temple in Jerusalem had been destroyed and God replaced it with the churches of the Resurrection and of Zion through his servants Constantine and Helena, so now after the destruction of the churches of Hagia Sophia and Hagia Irene he is using Justinian and his consort to rebuild Hagia Sophia with such excellence that it imitates heaven, the throne of God (54.21-23).

If Romanos implicitly commends Justinian's goal to build a church that will be in effect an image of heaven, it is fully consistent with the understanding of imagery we can infer from his poems. We might say that in his gift for dramatic narrative he himself is only imitating the cunning of the divine οἰκονομία. Like the mosaics even then being applied to the walls of Hagia Sophia, his kontakia, many of them on the same subjects, are icons, vivid and lively images of the divine drama. The Old Testament is full of types of the redemption fulfilled by Christ because the divine love of humanity continues to operate in a consistent way. Thus figures in the New Testament look to the Old Testament for encouragement, as when, in Hymn 33, *On Pentecost*, Peter reminds the disciples of the harmless fire in the fiery furnace (Dan. 3:92-94[26-28]) to assure them that the tongues resting on their heads will not burn them (33.11). Sometimes these also provide patterns for behavior, as when Lazarus looks to Job as a model of patience under affliction (Hymn 50, *On The Rich Man and Lazarus*, stanza 8) or when the sinful woman who anoints Jesus with precious ointment finds in Hannah an encouraging example of persistence in prayer being rewarded (Hymn 10, *On the Sinful Woman*, stanza 8).

By the same token, the figures of the New Testament provide further models for us. Thus, in Hymn 31, *Sending Out the Apostles*, Romanos claims that one who sees and imitates (ὁ ὁρῶν καὶ ζηλῶν) the disciples' manner of life (πολιτεία) will be like them (31.2.5). In Hymn 56, *A Prayer of Penitence*, Romanos holds up the tax collector of Luke 18:9-14 and a prostitute, probably the sinful woman of Luke 7:36-50, as models of repentance (56, Pr. 3, and stanza 1). The examples are numerous. Biblical figures can also be models to be avoided, like Judas, who is an image (εἰκών) of betrayal (43.7.6). This process continues in the lives of the saints. In Hymn 58, *On the Forty Martyrs of Sebasteia*, Romaleus, leader of the band, is like Moses, who held up his hands in prayer as the people battled Amalek (58.11). In Hymn 57 on the same topic, the martyrs actually improve on Old Testament models. Although the devil "swindled the protoplast [Adam] with words, them he did not, even with deeds" (57.6.4), and they outdo the wisdom of Solomon, since, unlike them, he was inveigled into idol worship (57.8). That hymn offers Jesus himself as the great object of imitation:

> The martyrs, observing Jesus' sufferings along with his miracles
> and his voluntary death,
> were eager to respond to his sufferings with sufferings and to his death
> with death:
> "If he suffered who was guiltless, how much more should those who
> are guilty.
> If he who did not sin was willing to be crucified,
> let us who were conceived in iniquity [see Ps. 51:5] eagerly suffer."

In Hymn 73, *On Sts. Cosmas and Damian,* one of the few hagiological hymns Grosdidier, if not Maas and Trypanis, considered genuine, Satan complains that just as Christ expelled the demons collectively called "legion" and sent them into pigs, the apostles likewise drove out his soldiers, and now Cosmas and Damian are doing the same thing (73.23). In Hymn 69, *On St. Panteleimon,* another in the same category, Romanos addresses the saint as "imitator of the one who has mercy and graciously provides cures, prizewinner and witness of Christ as God" (69, Pr. 1-3).

In the opening stanza of Hymn 43, *On Joseph,* Romanos concisely explains how the story of Joseph remains a source of salvation because Christ continues to offer salvation through it, and, by implication, through all the stories of the Bible:

> Men, draw salvation from the waters that make the heart glad,
> let us, who thirst for self-restraint, hurry to Joseph's cistern,
> for one who drinks from it will never thirst,
> since a deathless water bubbles up there.
> But how does a deathless water spring up there,
> tell me, from a place entirely dry?
> Christ, who was in Joseph as a type
> making it flow himself, gives us drink as to the Samaritan woman.
> So let us draw water with faith, for he alone,
> our Lord and Savior, is great.
>
> (43.1)

Thus, in that hymn the story of Joseph functions as a type of Christ, who is sold by his nearest and dearest, but it also provides an enduring pattern of behavior for the faithful to imitate. This is because "when he is leading on the good to better conduct, God sketches (ζωγραφεῖ) for you the virtues, just as he traces (στηλογραφεῖ) the vices for you, showing you images (εἰκόνας) of temptation in sleep" (43.2.4-6). God is thus, in effect, an iconographer.

In the final stanza of the hymn *On Joseph* Romanos praises God for providing such lessons for us (43.40.1) and urges his hearers to "imitate Joseph in all things" (43.40.4). Similarly, in his Hymn 6, *On the Epiphany,* Christ tells the hesitant John to baptize him because "I trace (ζωγραφῶ) the form of the church" (6.13.3-4), giving to his disciples and priests the same power to convey the Holy Spirit. One can only call to mind the image of John baptizing Christ in the dome of a Byzantine baptistry, put there to convey the same message. Likewise, in Hymn 9, *On the Samaritan Woman,* she is a person who sketches two images (δύο εἰκόνων ζωγράφος), that of the church and that of

390

Samaria (9.7.1). When she asks Christ his reason for asking her for water, her words "trace a sketch (ὑποσκιογραφοῦσιν) of the font on the well" (9.7.8-9). We should note that this imagery is polyvalent; the well can be Scripture through which Christ gives eternal life by instruction in Christian behavior, or it can be the baptismal font through which the grace of baptism accomplishes much the same thing. In fact, it is both at once. Similarly, in Hymn 13, *On the Miracle of the Loaves and Fishes,* the bread, which generally symbolizes the Eucharist, can also symbolize Jesus' teaching (see especially, 13.6, 9).

One might well expect Romanos as a poet to be a master of drama and imagery, but one might still ask how seriously he engages with the text. As mentioned earlier, Grosdidier pointed out (even if he did not elaborate on) what he called "literal" interpretation in Romanos, an interpretation characterized by questioning the biblical text, sometimes artfully giving such questions to biblical characters themselves. Another example Grosdidier gives is from Hymn 7, *On the Wedding Feast at Cana,* where Romanos, this time in the persona of the narrator, asks the Virgin directly how it is that she knew that her son was capable of doing miracles (7.6.1-4). In his words:

> If you please, venerable Virgin, from which of his miracles did you become aware that your son
> > Could regale them with wine without gathering grapes,
> Even though, according to the inspired author John,
> > He had performed no miracles earlier?

The issue evidently arises because John explicitly states that this was "the first of his signs" (John 2:11). She answers that even before John was born Gabriel had announced the miraculous birth to her (Luke 1:26) and Elizabeth had greeted her as the Mother of God (Luke 1:43). These events, along with others associated with Jesus' nativity, were quite sufficient to convince her that her son could turn water into wine (7.8-9). This is not the first or last time during this hymn that Romanos examines the text of John 2:1-11. Before he deals with Mary's confidence in requesting a miracle, Romanos answers an implicit question: Why did Jesus, the God who honors virginity, who dwelt in a virginal womb and remained a virgin himself, make his first public appearance at a wedding? His response is that Christ, like the Apostle Paul in Hebrews 13:4, wished to honor marriage, without which, as Romanos points out, there would be no virgins (7.1-3). In subsequent stanzas he deals with the issues posed by Jesus' brusque and puzzling response to his mother in John 2:4: "What do you have to do with me, woman? my hour has not yet arrived" (7.11.1-3). Romanos has the Blessed Virgin pose the question directly to her son: "'Now answer, child,' said the entirely chaste mother of Jesus, 'You control the measures of the hours. How do you defer to hours, my son and Lord?'" Jesus answers with what is, in effect, a discourse on the divine οἰκονομία:

> Elevate your mind to my words and know, incorruptible one, what I
>   say. For when out of non-existence
> I assembled heaven and earth and all things,
> Then I could have instantly arranged
>   Everything I called forth,
> But I introduced an appropriate order.
>   Created things were formed in six days,
>   Not because I was insufficiently strong,
> But so that the angelic choir, beholding these things
>   As I made them one by one, might sing this hymn to me,
>   "Glory to you, lord,
>   Who made all things in wisdom."
> Listen closely, venerable lady. I could have redeemed the fallen
>   by another way,
>   Without taking on the form of a poor slave.
> Nonetheless I accepted, first to be conceived
>   And to be born as a man
> And to take milk from your breast, virgin,
>   So that all my faculties grew in an ordered way,
>   Since in me there is nothing disordered.
> So now I want to perform the miracle in an appropriate order
>   Which I have deigned to perform for the salvation of men, I
>   Who made all things in wisdom.
>
> (7.13-14)

Romanos goes on to answer another implicit question, Why it is that Jesus does not directly involve his disciples in doing the miracle but gives orders to the domestic servants? This is so that no one can accuse the disciples of contriving a false miracle and so that they can be credible witnesses (7.17). There is a final implicit question: If this is a "sign," what does it signify? Romanos's answer is that it signifies the transformation of wine into the blood of Christ in the Holy Eucharist (1.20).

Hymn 9, *On the Samaritan Woman at the Well,* also dealing with a pericope in the Gospel of John, is another good example of a poem where Romanos engages closely with the text. In the third stanza, quoted above,

Romanos proposes questions about the symbolism of water, which, he affirms, the Bible itself will answer. In stanza 4, which initiates the actual narrative, he asks why the text presents Christ as tired and thirsty. His answer is that, as God, Christ could not have been tired, but "the Messiah came to enlighten those in darkness. The spring came to the spring to cleanse, not to drink" (9.4.5-7). After more or less paraphrasing the story for six stanzas, Romanos identifies the woman's request in John 4:15, "Sir [or Lord], give me this water," as the point where a turnabout occurs in the narrative (9.10). Having identified the Samaritan woman as an image of the Gentiles, he identifies her former husbands of John 4:18 either as the false gods or the forms of impiety the Gentile church has left behind (9.12). He then describes how she comes to identify Jesus as possibly being the Messiah in John 4:25 and how, having learned of Jesus' identity, she goes to share it with her fellow townspeople. Thus Romanos finds in the Johannine story a striking image of Christian transformation: "She departed and, like a sponge, soaked up life. She departed carrying a jar, she entered carrying God [ἐξῆλθεν ὑδροφόρος, εἰσῆλθε θεοφόρος]" (9.5.8). While one might quibble with Romanos on specific points — the identification of the Samaritan woman with the Gentile church, for example — one can no more deny that his attention to the narrative has repaid him with a genuine insight into the story's meaning than that he uses all his gifts of drama and imagery to exhibit that meaning.

In these and in many more of his kontakia, Romanos pays careful attention to Scripture, questioning it and seeking to learn from it. It is doubtful that Romanos himself thought of such attention as particularly "literal" as opposed to "spiritual" interpretation. Indeed, in both of the kontakia just studied much of the interpretation is, properly speaking, symbolic. Contrary to Grosdidier's impression, such an approach to Scripture seeks, it seems to me, not so much to smooth out difficulties as to gain deeper insight. In Hymn 31, *On Sending Out the Apostles,* Jesus tells the apostles: "So proclaim me to the world, making clear who I am and therefore hating parables and riddles [Οὕτως κηρύξατε με τῷ κόσμῳ, φανεροῦντες ὃ πέλω καὶ μισοῦντες λοιπὸν παραβολὰς καὶ αἰνίγματα]" (31.23.1-3). Such a characterization does not rule out symbolism but implies that the symbolism is not difficult to figure out. In Hymn 34, *On the Last Judgment,* Romanos maintains this attitude even in the face of one of the most obscure books in the Bible, saying that "Daniel has explained everything clearly (σαφῶς) if we examine accurately [ἂν ἀκριβῶς ἐρευνήσωμεν]" (34.6.1). Thus, for Romanos Scripture is not fundamentally esoteric. Even so, in Hymn 36, *On the Annunciation,* when Mary has heard Gabriel interpret Old Testament miracles as types of what is to happen in her case, she tells the angel that she recognizes him as "from above" because he has interpreted the Scripture (34.10-11). Perhaps one might compare Scripture to a great work of art. Certainly, one may gain a good initial impression of the subject of a great painting or poem, but continued close attention will reveal a wealth of detail that greatly enriches one's appreciation and, most likely, subtly modifies one's initial impression. Through such attention, Romanos might well hope to avoid what he took to be the error of the Jews, who read Scripture without understanding it, having it in their hands but not in their hearts (Hymn 21, *On the Infernal Powers* or *On the Crucifixion*, 12). Romanos's strategy is to bring himself into the biblical text and, having done so, to share it with his readers, so that it may be in their hearts as well as in his. We should take him seriously, not simply as a poet, but as an exegete.

The Spirit and the Wheels:
Gregory the Great on Reading Scripture

[15]Now as I looked at the living creatures, I saw a wheel upon the earth beside the living creatures, one for each of the four of them. [16]As for the appearance of the wheels and their construction: their appearance was like the gleaming of a chrysolite; and the four had the same likeness, their construction being as it were a wheel within a wheel. [17]When they went, they went in any of their four directions without turning as they went. [18]The four wheels had rims and they had spokes; and their rims were full of eyes round about. [19]And when the living creatures went, the wheels went beside them; and when the living creatures rose from the earth, the wheels rose. [20]Wherever the spirit would go, they went, and the wheels rose along with them; for the spirit of the living creatures was in the wheels. [21]When those went, these went; and when those stood, these stood; and when those rose from the earth, the wheels rose along with them; for the spirit of the living creatures was in the wheels. (Ezek. 1:15-21, RSV)

"In spite of all their commentaries, the holy doctors, together with all those who could be numbered in their ranks, have never fully interpreted Scripture: human words cannot enclose what the Spirit of God reveals."[1] This

---

1. *Spiritual Canticle,* preface; quoted from Henri de Lubac, *Medieval Exegesis: The Four Senses of Scripture,* trans. Mark Sebanc (Grand Rapids: Eerdmans, 1998-), 1:79-80.

concise formulation of Scripture's inexhaustibility, from John of the Cross's *Spiritual Canticle,* offers an apt entry into a discussion of Gregory the Great's *Homilies on Ezekiel.* Throughout Gregory's sermons one finds evidence of his debt to those "holy doctors" who had preceded him, but, even as he builds on their interpretations, he also presents novel readings.[2] His practice of taking the tradition as the foundation for fresh insights into the divine writings can be seen especially clearly in his construal of the "wheel within a wheel" (Ezek. 1:16), a lengthy meditation[3] on the Bible's unity, its capacity for multiple meanings, and the relationship between reader, sacred text, and Holy Spirit. In recent years Robert Louis Wilken has enlarged our understanding of patristic exegesis, most notably with regard to the Fathers' appreciation of Holy Writ's plenitude and its spiritual senses. In this essay I hope to contribute to this by showing how Gregory's preaching on the "wheel within a wheel" both exemplifies and illuminates the process whereby new vistas on the text appear.

The Exegetical Tradition before Gregory

The first patristic author to comment on Ezekiel 1, Irenaeus of Lyons, makes no specific mention of the "wheel within a wheel." His remarks on the prophet's inaugural vision, directed against the Gnostics, attempt to show both that Ezekiel did not actually behold God, who is inscrutable, and that the faces of the living creatures (lion, man, ox, and eagle) prefigure Matthew, Mark, Luke, and John, and thereby not only demonstrate the inherent agreement between the four evangelists and the Old Testament but also refute those who claim authority for other gospels. In arguing this second point, Irenaeus notes that the countenances and Gospels also correspond to the "four regions of the world" throughout which the Christian community is scattered.[4]

Eusebius of Caesarea appears to pick up on this allusion to the Church's geographic spread when he uses Ezekiel's wheels to explicate Psalm

2. On the way in which Gregory draws on the tradition while also establishing new readings, see my *"What Did Ezekiel See?" Christian Exegesis of Ezekiel's Vision of the Chariot from Irenaeus to Gregory the Great,* forthcoming.

3. All of the sixth sermon and over half of the seventh are devoted to exploration of these topics (*hom. in Ez.* 1.6.1–7.17 [SC 327:196-259]).

4. Irenaeus discusses God's incomprehensibility in *haer.* 4.20.1-11 (SC 100.2:624-68) and refers to Ezekiel 1 in 4.20.8-11. He addresses the fourfold character of the living creatures and the gospel in *haer.* 3.11.7-8 (SC 211:158-70).

76:19 (LXX): "The voice of your thunder was in the wheel (ἐν τῷ τροχῷ)."[5] Because Jesus called James and John "sons of thunder" (Mark 3:17), Eusebius observes, the phrase "the voice of your thunder" points to the evangelical proclamation that has "filled all the world with divine power." When the Psalmist mentions the wheel, it refers to "the ever-changing life of human beings" because, Eusebius concludes, this is what Ezekiel's "wheel within a wheel" signifies.[6]

In a sermon on Psalm 28:3 (LXX) ("The voice of the Lord is upon the waters; the God of glory thunders"), Basil of Caesarea makes moves similar to those of Eusebius. However, by quoting not only Psalm 76:19 and Ezekiel 1:15-16 but also Philippians 3:13, he expressly emphasizes the Good News' advance within the individual. The evangelical voice of thunder is found only in the one "worthy to be called a wheel," who is "straining forward to what lies ahead" and thus is like the wheel beside each living creature (Ezek. 1:15).[7] Both Ambrose and Jerome offer construals of the prophet's vision that are indebted to Basil's, and that likewise train the reader's attention on the gospel's spread in each person.[8] However, Ambrose introduces a new motif that will be central to Gregory the Great's homilies: the prophet's "wheel within a wheel" is a symbol of the two Testaments and their relationship. "*A wheel* was running *within a wheel*," Ambrose observes, "and it was not hindered, the New Testament within the Old. It ran within that through which it was announced."[9]

5. Patristic authors yoke Ezek. 1:15-21 with Ps. 76:19 (LXX) on the basis of common vocabulary that appears in both the Greek and Latin versions. The link between these passages emerges because the Septuagint uses the same Greek word τροχός ("wheel") for the Hebrew term *ofan* in Ezek. 1:15-21 (usually rendered as "wheel") and the Hebrew *galgal* in Ps. 76:19 (often translated as "whirlwind"). This verbal tie is also present in the Latin since it employs *rota* for both Ezekiel's *ofan* and the psalmist's *galgal*. Thus, for early Christian commentators who found τροχός in the Septuagint of Ezek. 1:15-21 and Ps. 76:19, or *rota* in the Latin, the linguistic, and therefore exegetical, relationship between the texts was clear.

6. *Ps.* 76.19 (PG 23:897c-d). Comparable readings of Ps. 76:19 (LXX) appear in works attributed to Athanasius (*exp. Ps.* 76.19 [PG 27:348c-d]) and Cyril of Alexandria (*ps.* 76 [PG 69:1193a-b]).

7. *Hom. in Ps.* 28.3 (PG 29:292b).

8. Ambrose presents this reading in *psal. 118*. 4.27-29 (CSEL 62:80.15–82.4) and *spir.* 3.21.162 (CSEL 79:218.22-32); Jerome in *Ezech.* 1.12 (CCSL 75:16.360–17.372); and *tract. psal.* 76.19 (CCSL 78:60.174–61.201).

9. *Psal. 118*. 4.28-29 (CSEL 62:81.18-20). Jerome includes this motif not only in the passages cited in n. 8, but also in *Ezech.* 1.15-18 (CCSL 75:20.487-88). However, Ambrose's interpretation is earlier, and Jerome is almost certainly dependent upon it.

Gregory the Great's *Homilies 6 and 7 on Ezekiel*

While Gregory shares Eusebius's interest in the gospel's dissemination to the ends of the earth, this notion occupies a relatively minor place in his homilies, and he does not mention it in his exegesis of Ezekiel 1:15-21. Instead, when interpreting the wheels of the prophet's vision, Gregory follows Basil, Ambrose, and Jerome and concentrates on the Good News' growth in the individual. Incorporating Ambrose's insight — the "wheel within a wheel" signifies the Old and New Testaments — he presents an elaborate and nuanced understanding of Scripture's unity and of how the faithful Christian discerns its message.

Gregory begins his exploration of this topic when commenting on Ezekiel 1:15.[10] The single wheel described in this verse denotes Holy Writ because the sacred text, like a wheel, rolls "from every direction to hearers' minds *(ex omni parte ad auditorum mentes)*," proceeding "rightly and humbly" amidst both "adversities and prosperity." Gregory seems to envision the Bible as a wheel, and its spiritual and literal meanings are two points on its circumference, 180 degrees apart. As it moves along, little children *(parvuli)* or those who are spiritually weak receive its lessons through the literal level, while those more advanced (e.g., *docti viri*) learn from its spiritual dimension. Demonstrating that each sense of Scripture has pedagogical value, Gregory presents both a historical and an allegorical commentary on the story of Jacob and Esau.[11] Jesus' miracle at the wedding in Cana also reveals the weight of these two types of signification.[12] That he chose first to fill the empty pots with water — the historical content *(sacrae lectionis historia)* — and then to change this into wine — the spiritual message *(spiritualis intelligentia)* — illustrates the relationship between these two readings of a text. Drawing out the implications of Christ's marvelous deed, Gregory explains that our hearts must first be replenished with the historical interpretation. Only then can *historia* be transformed into the wine of spiritual understanding "through the mystery of allegory *(per allegoriae mysterium)*." Returning to the original imagery from Ezekiel 1:15, he concludes:

> Therefore, the wheel is, as it were, drawn along the ground, since it adapts itself to children by its humble language. Yet it fills adults with spiritual things, as it lifts its orbit to the height and rises from where it was seen be-

---

10. *Hom. in Ez.* 1.6.2 (SC 327:196-98).
11. *Hom. in Ez.* 1.6.2-6 (SC 327:198-202).
12. *Hom. in Ez.* 1.6.7 (SC 327:204).

fore to touch the earth just a little. Truly it edifies in every way, in the same way that a wheel runs through its orbit.[13]

Gregory's description of the wheel as "[touching] the earth just a little," a reference to literal or historical explication, is reminiscent of Jerome's exegesis in his *Commentary on Ezekiel* where the wheels symbolize the Gospels which "touch the earth a little" as they rush to the heights.[14] Gregory adapts his predecessor's language and concepts to speak of Scripture's senses: as the wheel rolls along, the point making contact with the ground, the literal/historical exposition, nourishes neophytes, and when it moves upward in its revolution to the spiritual meaning, it edifies the mature. However, in this homily Gregory is engaging not only established construals of Ezekiel 1, but also a tradition of reflection on the capacity of Holy Writ to benefit both novices and those advanced in the Christian life. In *Confessions* 3.5.9, Augustine characterizes the Bible as "neither open to the proud nor laid bare to mere children; a text lowly to the beginner but, on further reading, of mountainous difficulty and enveloped in mysteries." His remark is not made in the context of commenting on any specific verse but is grounded in his observation that Scripture never fails to feed its readers, whatever their stage of spiritual growth, as long as they approach it with humility.[15] Gregory's innovation lies in recognizing that latent in the received interpretation of Ezekiel's wheels as the Church's sacred writings is a compelling image for the theological insight articulated by Augustine.

Gregory is especially attentive to the details of Ezekiel 1 and thus naturally notices that although the prophet mentions only one wheel in verse 15, in 1:16 he speaks of two: *rota in medio rotae*. The single wheel, Gregory con-

---

13. *Hom. in Ez.* 1.6.7 (11-14)–1.6.8 (1-2) (SC 327:204). Gregory's juxtaposition of remarks about the pedagogical value, even necessity, of *historia* and this image of the adaptable wheel suggests that even the spiritually advanced will alternate between literal and spiritual interpretations (cf. Pier Cesare Bori, "Attualità di un detto antico? 'La sacra Scrittura cresce con chi la legge,'" *Intersezioni* 6 [1986]: 15-49, esp. 23-24), a movement that is consistent with his view that even for the mature, Christian life involves continual cyclical movement from the active life to the contemplative, and back to the active (cf. Carole Straw, *Gregory the Great: Perfection in Imperfection,* Transformation of the Classical Heritage 14 [Berkeley: University of California Press, 1988], p. 189).

14. *Ezech.* 1.15-18 (CCSL 75:20.490-91). In *tract. psal.* 97.3 (CCSL 78:163.66) Jerome seems to make a similar point when he describes Scripture as touching the earth before racing to heaven.

15. *Conf.* 3.5.9 (translation by Henry Chadwick, *Saint Augustine: Confessions* [New York: Oxford University Press, 1991], p. 40). That Augustine considers humility essential to receiving Scripture's lessons is clear from his account of reading the Bible after studying Cicero's *Hortensius*.

cludes, must be the Old Testament,[16] while the "wheel within a wheel" denotes both Testaments and their interdependence:

> In the letter of the Old Testament, the New Testament lay hidden through allegory. . . . Therefore, a "wheel" is "within a wheel," since the New Testament is within the Old. And, as we have often said, what the Old Testament promised, the New Testament showed forth. What the Old announces in secret, the New openly proclaims as revealed. Therefore, the prophecy of the New Testament is the Old Testament, and the exegesis of the Old is the New.[17]

Gregory is clearly dependent upon Ambrose's and Jerome's expositions of the "wheel within a wheel," but he develops what they had articulated in only rudimentary form. They had understood the "wheel within a wheel" to indicate the unity of the two covenants, but neither explained what was involved in this or how it was manifested. Ambrose perhaps gave a hint of the role of each Testament with regard to the other when, in his reading of Psalm 118 (LXX), he wrote, "A *wheel* was running *within a wheel,* and it was not hindered, the New Testament within the Old. It [i.e., the New] ran within that [i.e., the Old] through which it was announced." Nonetheless, his comment still leaves the relationship between the two largely unexplored. Jerome was even more reticent, noting in his interpretation of Psalm 76:19 (LXX) only that "the Old is connected to the New, and the New to the Old." In expanding on these spare statements, Gregory is surely also indebted to Augustine, who sharpened the theological insight latent in the remarks of Ambrose and Jerome by observing that the New Testament is hidden in the Old, while the Old is disclosed in the New.[18] Gregory's contribution to this ongoing theological reflection is, first, to pair Augustine's fuller formulation of the interconnectedness of Old and New Testaments with Ambrose's exegesis of Ezekiel's wheels, and then to build on this in a way that accentuates the distinctive roles of each, not allowing the Old to be swallowed up in the New. In doing this, Gregory draws from Scripture itself an image that illuminates not only its essential oneness but the unique place of each of its parts within the economy of revelation.[19]

16. *Hom. in Ez.* 1.6.10 (SC 327:208-10).

17. *Hom. in Ez.* 1.6.12 (5-6) (SC 327:212).

18. Augustine expresses the basic insight in a variety of ways. See, for example, *civ.* 4.33; 5.18; 16.26. See also de Lubac, *Medieval Exegesis,* 1:245 and 441 nn. 63-65 for other passages.

19. On the use of the "wheel within a wheel" by authors after Gregory, see de Lubac,

That Gregory speaks about the two Testaments first in the past tense (". . . what the Old Testament promised, the New Testament showed forth"), but then shifts to the present (". . . the Old announces . . . the New proclaims") is suggestive of another theological point he stresses in his comments on the prophet's vision. The link between these two divisions of Scripture is not merely forged in the past, though it is that, since the events of Israel's history and their original fulfillment in Christ and his disciples are part of history. It is also continually fashioned in the present as the faithful reader delves into Holy Writ, reading the Old Testament through the New and the New in light of the Old. Although Gregory only hints at this here through the grammar of his statements, he makes clear in his homilies that this ongoing contemporary appropriation of the Bible is central to his purposes.[20]

In his interpretation Gregory not only preserves the singular character of both Testaments but also goes further, splitting each into two segments. On the basis of a variant in the Latin text of Ezekiel 1:15, which suggests that each wheel has four faces, he deduces a fourfold division of the Old and New Testaments into the Law, the Prophets, the Gospels, and Acts and the apostles' sayings.[21] However, while this ensures that the Old Testament is not absorbed into the New, Gregory asserts that these categories are held together by an overarching unity, like the two Testaments themselves, in his exegesis of Ezekiel 1:16: "And there was one likeness of the four (*et una similitudo*

Medieval Exegesis, 1:245-46. Although Gregory underscores the particular function of each Testament, he does not understand them to be on equal footing, and the New Testament's superiority is at least implicit in his comments. For example, that the living creatures, icons of Matthew, Mark, Luke, and John, are introduced before the single wheel of Ezek. 1:15 demonstrates the Gospels' precedence over the Old Testament, and Gregory hints that the prophet had knowledge of this (*hom. in Ez.* 1.6.10 [SC 327:208-10]). Similarly, on the basis of Ezek. 1:17, "And when they went, they did not turn back," he explains that when not understood spiritually, the Old Testament is "turned back on itself" (*hom. in Ez.* 1.6.17 [SC 327:220-22]).

20. See, e.g., *hom. in Ez.* 1.5.1 (SC 327:170) and 2.2.1 (SC 360:92-94) where Gregory specifically mentions the significance of scriptural interpretation for edification and imitation of the saints' virtues.

21. *Hom. in Ez.* 1.6.12 (SC 327:212). The Vulgate of Ezek. 1:15, which Gregory follows here, has *[rota] iuxta animalia habens quatuor facies* (quoted in *hom. in Ez.* 1.6.11 [SC 327:210-12]). The Hebrew behind the Latin *habens quatuor facies* is perplexing; see Walther Zimmerli, *Ezekiel 1: A Commentary on the Book of the Prophet Ezekiel, Chapters 1–24* (Philadelphia: Fortress, 1979), p. 85, verse 15, n. b. Although the Vulgate translation of Ezekiel is from Jerome, in his own *Commentary on Ezekiel,* he renders the participle as *habentia* so that it refers to the living creatures (*animalia*) rather than the wheel (CCSL 75:19.434-35).

ipsarum quatuor)." In the Hebrew and Greek texts, this phrase clearly applies to the one wheel standing beside each of the four living creatures. However, in Gregory's Latin version, it naturally seems to refer back to the wheel's four faces, leading him to conclude that the single likeness symbolizes the fundamental oneness that transcends the Bible's four sections. What the Law foretells, he explains, the Prophets announce. The Gospels recount the fulfillment of these things, while Acts and the apostolic sayings proclaim the worldwide consummation of the evangelical tidings. "Even if the divine pronouncements are given at separate times," he concludes, "they are united in their meaning."[22]

In his seventh homily, Gregory continues to explore the topic of Scripture and its exegesis in the Church. However, when he began this discussion in the previous sermon, he was primarily concerned with the Bible itself and the relationship between its two parts, Old and New Testaments, and its different levels of meaning, literal and spiritual. This is the prominent theme even in those passages where he addresses the reader's role in interpretation. For example, in explaining how the sacred text's literal exposition is suited to the neophyte's abilities, while its spiritual sense nourishes the more advanced, his focus is not the individual but the adaptability of the wheel of Scripture to the varying needs of Christians. In the seventh homily his attention shifts and the notion of Holy Writ's movement within each member of the Body of Christ comes to the fore.

Ezekiel 1:19 describes the coordinated motion of the living creatures and the wheels. On the basis of correlations established in earlier homilies — the creatures signify the saints, and the wheels symbolize the two Testaments — Gregory finds in this verse a portrayal of the interaction between the faithful reader and the divine writings:

> The living creatures proceed when the saints understand from the sacred Scripture how they may lead a moral life. Truly the creatures are lifted up from the earth when the saints raise themselves up in contemplation. And since the more one of the saints advances in the sacred Scripture, the more Scripture advances in him, it is rightly said, "When the living creatures went, the wheels equally went; and when the creatures lifted themselves up from the earth, likewise the wheels lifted themselves up also" (Ezek. 1:19). For the divine pronouncements *(divina eloquia)* grow with the reader: the more deeply someone turns his mind to them, the deeper is his grasp of them. Thus, if the living creatures are not lifted up, the

22. *Hom. in Ez.* 1.6.14 (SC 327:216).

wheels are not elevated. Unless the readers' minds advance to higher things, the divine sayings lie dead, as if on the ground, since they are not understood.[23]

Moreover, when the Bible does not arouse the reader's mind, its wheel stands idle *(otiosa)* "since the living creature [i.e., the reader] is not lifted up from the earth." Yet, the wheel's otiose condition can be transformed by the continually maturing Christian's appropriation of the various dimensions of the divine writings. When she seeks to live a moral life, the wheels begin to roll, keeping pace. Similarly, when the winged creature stretches itself in contemplation, the wheels are lifted up, and he begins to understand Holy Writ in a heavenly rather than earthly way. Gregory describes the height of such a person's apprehension of Scripture: "And the wondrous and ineffable strength *(virtus)* of the sacred text is recognized when the reader's soul is penetrated by heavenly love *(superno amore)*."[24]

Gregory further illuminates the relationship between the reader and the Bible when he presents a unique construal of Ezekiel 1:20: "wherever the spirit went, there, since the spirit went, the wheels also were lifted up equally, following it [i.e., the spirit]."[25] Earlier exegetes had taken this occurrence of *spiritus,* as well as the phrase *spiritus vitae* in the second half of 1:20 and in 1:21, to refer to the Holy Spirit.[26] However, because the first mention of *spiritus* in Ezekiel 1:20 lacks the qualifier *vitae* found later in 1:20 and in 1:21 ("for the spirit of life was in the wheels [*spiritus enim vitae erat in rotis*]"), Gregory assumes that the two are different. For him, *spiritus* (without *vitae*) is "the spirit of the reader *(spiritus legentis)*." Picking up from his comments on Ezekiel 1:19, he understands the wheels to be guided by the *spiritus legentis* insofar as the divine words are raised to whichever of Scripture's senses the reader yearns for. If someone is looking for a passage's historical and moral

23. *Hom. in Ez.* 1.7.8 (SC 327:244). Gregory's exegesis implies that for the faithful reader of Scripture there is continual growth in understanding. On the importance of this for Gregory, see Claude Dagens, *Saint Grégoire le Grand: Culture et expérience chrétiennes* (Paris: Études Augustiniennes, 1977), pp. 69-72; and de Lubac, *Medieval Exegesis,* 2:204-7.

24. *Hom. in Ez.* 1.7.8 (SC 327:244). In *Moralia in Iob* 19.23.36 he presents a somewhat different interpretation of Ezek. 1:19. Here the creatures symbolize preachers and the wheels their hearers. When the preachers set a good example and the audience follows it, then both are lifted up (CCSL 143A:985).

25. *Hom. in Ez.* 1.7.9 (SC 327:246).

26. For example, Ambrose relates Ezekiel's "the spirit of life was in the wheels" to "the word of life" from 1 John to argue that the Holy Spirit, like the Word, is life (*spir.* 1.15.151 [CSEL 79:79]).

explication, "the moral meaning of history follows him."[27] Similarly, if a typological exposition is sought, figurative language is soon recognized; if a contemplative interpretation is desired, the wheels seem to take on wings and ascend so that "the heavenly meaning *(intellegentia caelestis)*" is revealed. Gregory concludes this section by describing the cooperation between the wheels of Holy Writ and the spirit of those who long to comprehend the text: "For the wheels follow the spirit, since the words of sacred speech, as has often been said, grow through understanding *(per intellectum)* in accord with the readers' perception *(sensum legentium)*."[28]

Gregory's conceptions of the Bible, the reader, and their interaction are complex. In the sixth homily, he presented the Old and New Testaments as the wheels of Ezekiel 1:15-16, thereby conveying the idea that Scripture has its own dynamism and discloses levels of meaning proper to each person's capacity as it rolls along. Or, as he puts it in his seventh sermon, the sacred text has power or strength, *virtus,* that is fully apprehended only by the one penetrated by heavenly love. However, he modifies this notion through his exegesis of Ezekiel 1:19-20, claiming, in effect, that Holy Writ's vitality is dependent upon the *spiritus legentis.* Its movement follows the reader's. He adds yet another qualification based on the final phrase in Ezekiel 1:20: "the spirit of life was in the wheels." The Holy Spirit is the *spiritus vitae* "in the wheels," Gregory explains, "since through the divine words we are brought to life by the gift of the Spirit, so that we may fend off deadly works."[29] This Spirit "touches the reader's soul to the observance of patience" and the Bible's wheels follow, as he finds models of steadfastness in the midst of suffering: Moses and Aaron, Samuel, and Jesus.[30] This Spirit "arouses the reader's soul to the study of prophecy," and she discovers the examples of Moses, Stephen, Peter, and Paul, who delivered God's oracles even in the face of danger.[31] Likewise, this Spirit "goads the reader to penitential laments," and Holy Writ presents pictures of David's repentance after Nathan's rebuke, the Publican of Jesus' parable in

---

27. Gregory implies that the historical or literal level of the text is replete with moral instruction, especially in the *exempla* of the various characters (cf. Charles Morel in SC 327:246 n. 1).

28. Gregory does not here entertain the question of what happens when the perception of the reader(s) is antithetical to the Gospel. His failure to raise this issue perhaps derives from the fact that Ezekiel portrays the wheels as filled with "the Spirit of life" and the creatures as moving in harmony with them, which seems to preclude their settling on an exposition counter to the Gospel.

29. *Hom. in Ez.* 1.7.11 (SC 327:250-52).
30. *Hom. in Ez.* 1.7.12 (SC 327:252).
31. *Hom. in Ez.* 1.7.13 (SC 327:252-54).

Luke 18, Peter's tears of sorrow over his denial of Christ, and the conversion of the thief on the cross.[32] Finally, Gregory insists that such divine inspiration is indispensable for apprehending the sacred text's message. While Scripture provides the lamp for our journey, he observes, it is created and so must be illumined by uncreated light. Thus, "the spirit of life was in the wheels" indicates that "the omnipotent God himself fashioned the sayings of the holy Testaments for our salvation, and he himself opened them."[33]

Prior to interpreting the phrase "for the spirit of life was in the wheels," Gregory suggested that appropriating Holy Writ's message involves a collaboration of the reader with the divine writings. Scripture possesses its own dynamism, but its movement and growth in the individual also depend upon the *spiritus legentis,* for its wheels follow the faithful person who seeks its meanings in accord with his capacities. However, with his exegesis of "for the spirit of life was in the wheels," Gregory shows that this symbiotic relationship includes not just two members but three, for the entire process of reading — and indeed of the prior writing — of the Bible is infused with the Holy Spirit's activity. The Spirit of Life works not only in creating the sacred text and opening it up for its human audience but also in animating the reader's spiritual state (as described in the examples of the observance of patience, the study of prophecy, and penitential laments) and in leading him to seek and find those passages that address each condition. This construal of Ezekiel 1:19-21 is original to Gregory and not derived from the earlier exegetical tradition of the vision. Nonetheless, we can see, as we did in his sixth homily, that while expounding these verses he is once more engaging Augustine's remarks in *Confessions* 3.5.9. When Augustine had commented on Holy Writ's adaptability to the different spiritual levels of its audience, explaining that it is "a text lowly to the beginner but, on further reading, of mountainous difficulty and enveloped in mysteries," he also hinted at the way in which the individual's appropriation of the sacred text changes as that person increases in faith: "Yet the Bible was composed in such a way that as beginners mature, its meaning grows with them."[34] Again, Augustine's insight was not tied to any particular passage, but was almost surely based at least in part upon his own experience of becoming proficient in the theological interpretation of Scripture, of learning to understand "the Lord's style of language," as he put it in *Confessions* 9.5.13.[35] The process that Augustine mentions only briefly in

---

32. *Hom. in Ez.* 1.7.14 (SC 327:254).
33. *Hom. in Ez.* 1.7.17 (SC 327:258).
34. Translated by Chadwick, *Confessions,* p. 40.
35. Translated by Chadwick, *Confessions,* p. 163.

Confessions 3.5.9 Gregory explores at length in his seventh homily. His innovation is to recognize that the spirit-filled creatures and wheels of the prophet's vision aptly symbolize this unceasing interaction of God, the Bible, and the faithful reader.[36]

The Mystery of Christ and the Depths of Scripture

In an essay on the unity of the Triduum, Herbert McCabe observes that "mystery concerns what shows itself but does not show itself easily," and "[m]ysteries are not for concealment but for revelation." Moreover, he continues, ". . . as we understand a mystery it enlarges our capacity for understanding."[37] McCabe's remarks illumine the belief, shared by Gregory and other Church Fathers, that the Bible's inexhaustibility is one of its indispensable characteristics. Just as one can never fully fathom the reality of the incarnate Logos, but only penetrate this mystery more deeply as "it enlarges [one's] capacity for understanding," so too with Scripture. As readers grasp its treasures, they are formed to seek and find its still-hidden wealth. This link between Holy Writ and the incarnation is suggested by Ambrose when he comments on the Transfiguration. After quoting 2 Corinthians 3:18 — "[And we all,] with unveiled face, beholding the glory of God, are being changed into [Christ's] likeness . . ." — he asserts, "For your sake, the Word either lessens or grows according to your capabilities."[38] Since the shared purpose of the incarnation and the sacred text is the transformation of humans, the mystery of the Word made flesh is mirrored in the depths of the written Word as its readers are fashioned *in imaginem Christi*.

In his homilies on Ezekiel 1:15-21 Gregory examines this teleological versatility and inexhaustibility of the divine writings. While he starts with previous exegetes' insights — the wheels signify not only the gospel's spread in each person but also the unity of the Testaments — he is not limited by them. Rather, he presses the prophet's vision to disclose its import more and more by exploring these earlier construals in the light of the larger theological tradition and all of the Bible. In so doing, Gregory offers us a way of grasping

36. Dagens, although not mentioning the debt to Augustine, rightly says of Gregory: "n'est-il pas un de ceux qui ont le plus magnifiquement exposé ce principe capital de toute l'herméneutique chrétienne, selon lequel la Parole de Dieu, lué et méditée dans la foi, ne cesse d'approfondir et de renouveler l'intelligence du croyant?" (*Saint Grégoire*, p. 70).

37. Herbert McCabe, "Holy Thursday: The Mystery of Unity," in *God Matters* (Springfield, Ill.: Templegate, 1987), pp. 76-77.

38. *Luc.* 7.12 (CCSL 14:218.135-36).

the synergy among reader, sacred text, and Spirit as he himself enacts this dynamic and symbiotic relationship. Perhaps most important, he invites his audience to join him in the wearying but always sweet search for Scripture's meaning.[39]

39. In *hom. in Ez.* 1.6.1 (SC 327:196), Gregory explains that "the very obscurity of God's speech" is beneficial because it forces one to seek out Scripture's message unceasingly, and the more wearying the search, the sweeter the reward.

The World in the Mirror of Holy Scripture: Maximus the Confessor's Short Hermeneutical Treatise in *Ambiguum ad Joannem* 37

PAUL M. BLOWERS

"For everything is yours, whether the world, or the present, or the future." So says the Apostle Paul in 1 Corinthians 3:22. Such is normally not taken by patristic exegetes as justification for a spiritual interpretation of the Bible, at least not to the extent of a text such as 1 Corinthians 10:11, Paul's statement about ancient biblical events having happened figuratively (τυπικῶς) for our present admonition. Yet the fifth-century ascetic theologian Nilus of Ancyra, for one, favored the former text, 1 Corinthians 3:22. The world, the present, the future are ours. Indeed, says Nilus, "we are the world; we benefit today by interpreting everything that happened yesterday for ourselves."[1] In other words, the lives of the biblical saints are constantly revisited and relived in the virtues and vices of us, the latest inheritors of "the world." So understood, "the world" is the whole intricate cosmos of spiritual meaning that we inhabit — in one simultaneous hermeneutical moment, as it were — with those biblical personages who are our progenitors and exemplars both in faith and in sin. As Douglas Burton-Christie has demonstrated, much of early monastic interpretation is dominated by this fusion of horizons, wherein biblical heroes and contemporary monks are understood as sharing a single mimetic world, fighting one and the same ascetic struggle on a common existential plane.[2]

---

1. Nilus of Ancyra, *ep.* 2.223 (PG 79:316b-17a).
2. See Douglas Burton-Christie, *The Word in the Desert: Scripture and the Quest for*

The great Byzantine theologian Maximus the Confessor (580-662) stands at the end of this early tradition of Greek monastic exegesis and exploits this hermeneutical perspective even more elaborately and philosophically. In two earlier studies I have explored the way in which Maximus parallels the Bible and the created world as mutually analogous — indeed interchangeable — economies of divine revelation.[3] Particularly significant is a long passage in *Ambiguum* 10 where he argues that, just as the world is a kind of "bible" inscribed with the logos of divine meanings, the Bible is itself a kind of "cosmos" constituted of "heaven" and "earth" and of the "things in between," which have to do with "ethical, natural, and theological philosophy."[4] In another text, *Ambiguum* 37, on which I want to expand here, we have in effect a short treatise on biblical hermeneutics, a comprehensive demonstration of how the contemplation of Scripture (θεωρία γραφική) parallels the contemplation of the natural creation (θεωρία φυσική). The Bible is a world all its own, a profoundly sophisticated, intricate, and multi-dimensional constellation of historical data (πράγματα), subtle and profound spiritual typologies, and nuanced symbols that altogether lead the faithful to a progressively more sublime insight into their eschatological destiny.

Ambiguum 37, wherein we find this treatise on scriptural contemplation, actually begins as a concise commentary on a phrase from Gregory Nazianzen's *Oration* 38 on the Nativity of Christ. The specific statement in question comes from a passage in which Gregory is invoking the faithful to identify with every figure in the Nativity narrative and thereby to find a place in the story as participants in the joy over the incarnate Lord shared by shepherds, animals, Magi, angels and archangels, and all heavenly hosts. "Now, I pray you," exhorts Gregory, "receive [the Lord's] Conception, and leap before Him, if not like John in the womb (Luke 1:41), at least like David at the resting of the Ark" (2 Sam. 6:16).[5] Expanding on this statement, Maximus in his turn holds up John the Baptist and King David as exemplars whose peculiar stations in life bespeak their respective roles in modeling the disciplines of ascesis and contemplation. John's profile as a preacher, baptizer, and ancho-

---

Holiness in Early Christian Monasticism (New York: Oxford University Press, 1993), pp. 20-23, 167-70.

3. See Paul Blowers, "The Analogy of Scripture and Cosmos in Maximus the Confessor," *SP* 27, ed. Elizabeth Livingstone (Leuven: Peeters, 1993), pp. 145-49; idem, *Exegesis and Spiritual Pedagogy in Maximus the Confessor: An Investigation of the "Quaestiones ad Thalassium,"* Christianity and Judaism in Antiquity 7 (Notre Dame, Ind.: University of Notre Dame Press, 1991), esp. pp. 104-9, 141-45, 253.

4. Maximus, *ambig.* 10 (PG 91:1129a).

5. Gregory Nazianzen, *or.* 38.17, cited in Maximus, *ambig.* 37 (PG 91:1289d).

rite, yet also as a levitical priest and forerunner of the Word, commends him as an image of repentance and ἀπάθεια, as well as of Gnostic contemplation. David's profile first as shepherd and later as king from the tribe of Judah, and as conqueror of foreign tribes (i.e., the passions), commends him as a venerable image of confession, ascetic practice, and contemplation.[6]

It is in reflecting on the peculiar dignity and status of John the Baptist and King David in their native contexts, and the importance of that status in the broader spiritual scheme of things, that Maximus launches into a detailed exposition of ten different modes (τρόποι) for contemplating the things and persons — the "world" — of Holy Scripture. Before turning to that outline, however, we must note, by way of analogy, that Maximus already in *Ambiguum* 10 had proposed a set of five modes of contemplating the natural world. Accordingly, created beings are to be envisioned — by the use of analytical reason, but with a view to a higher form of contemplation, or θεωρία — in terms of five categories or predicates: (1) essence (οὐσία), the fundamental metaphysical or entitative integrity of beings;[7] (2) motion (κίνησις), the natural movement of beings in relation to their transcendent Cause and End;[8] (3) difference (διαφορά), the variegation of creatures according to their proper physical principles (λόγοι), indicating the salutary diversity within creation;[9] (4) mixture (κρᾶσις), the combination of creaturely will (γνώμη) with the virtues such as enables moral progress; and (5) position (θέσις), the secured moral disposition of creatures in relation to the divine Good.[10] These five modes of contemplation comprehend — in a perspective strongly confuting the Origenist doctrine of the fall, dispersion, and restoration of intellectual beings — the grand economy of divine providence and judgment underlying both the diversification and integration of creation in Christ the

---

6. Maximus, *ambig.* 37 (PG 91:1289d-92a).

7. On Maximus's concept of creaturely being (οὐσία), see most recently Torstein Tollefsen, *The Christocentric Cosmology of St. Maximus the Confessor: A Study of His Metaphysical Principles*, Acta Humaniora 72 (Oslo: Unipub Forlag, 2000), pp. 118-22.

8. On κίνησις and its cosmological import for Maximus, see most notably *ambig.* 7 (PG 91:1072a-77b). See also the studies of Polycarp Sherwood, *The Earlier Ambigua of Maximus the Confessor and His Refutation of Origenism*, Studia Anselmiana 36 (Rome: Herder, 1955), pp. 92-102; Lars Thunberg, *Microcosm and Mediator: The Theological Anthropology of Maximus the Confessor*, 2nd ed. (Chicago: Open Court, 1995), pp. 81-83; and Alain Riou, *Le monde et l'Église selon Maxime le Confesseur*, Théologie historique 22 (Paris: Beauchesne, 1973), pp. 49-54.

9. On διαφορά in Maximus, see Thunberg, *Microcosm and Mediator*, pp. 51-55; cf. Tollefsen, *Christocentric Cosmology*, pp. 126-31.

10. Maximus, *ambig.* 10 (PG 91:1133a-36b).

Logos. More precisely, the first three contemplative modes concern the divine providence that wisely preserves the λόγοι of the universe as a whole and the divine judgment that sustains differentiated individual beings according to those λόγοι. The last two relate to the moral movements of free creatures in that ongoing history wherein they actively pursue assimilation to God.[11]

As Maximus further explains in *Ambiguum* 10, these five basic modes for contemplating the natural world can be variously combined and contracted, in an almost kaleidoscopic way, to yield insights into the unity, diversity, and harmony of the world and to guide the virtuous mind toward that divine wisdom that undergirds the cosmos.[12] For example, in using "position" (the fifth mode) as the primary angle of approach (thus observing the array of creatures in their properly disposed moral status) the full set of five modes reduces to three, as we envision the created world (like the Bible) in terms of "heaven," "earth," and the "things in between," and thereby learn from it "ethical, natural, and theological philosophy."[13] Maximus projects the whole well-ordered creation as one glorious mimetic world whose creatures, both by their ontological predisposition toward God and their virtuous movements in assimilating to God, provide the contemplative and ascetic soul with worthy objects of imitation and prolific resources of spiritual progress. The goal is the "contraction" of the modes of contemplation into a unitary and subtle knowledge of the whole.[14]

We turn, then, to *Ambiguum* 37, and the contemplation of the "world" mirrored in the Bible. Here Maximus proposes a set of ten, rather than five, gradually contracting or ascending modes for contemplating the substance of Scripture:

> Those who are true experts on such mysteries and devoted to the contemplation of the spiritual meanings (πνευματικοὶ λόγοι) contained therein say that the logos of scriptural contemplation (γραφικὴ θεωρία), which is one in general, is, when it expands itself, contemplated in a tenfold (δεκακῶς) manner: by [1] place (τόπος), [2] time (χρόνος), [3] genus (γένος), [4] individual persona (πρόσωπον), [5] dignity (ἀξία) or occupation (ἐπιτήδευμα); by [6] practical (πρακτική), [7] natural (φυσική), and [8] theological (θεολογική) philosophy; by [9] present (ἐνεστώς) and

11. Maximus, *ambig.* 10 (PG 91:1133b).

12. Maximus, *ambig.* 10 (PG 91:1136b-1137c).

13. Maximus, *ambig.* 10 (PG 91:1136c). See also above, n. 4 and the related passage from *ambig.* 10.

14. Maximus, *ambig.* 10 (PG 91:1137a-c).

[10] future (μέλλον), or type (τύπος) and truth (ἀλήθεια). When this logos (of contemplation) contracts itself, it encompasses the initial five into
three tropes (τρόποι); the three into the two; and draws the two into the
one and utterly irreducible logos. In other words, the logos contracts the
first five tropes of time, place, genus, persona, and dignity into the second
three: practical, natural, and theological philosophy. These three it contracts into the next two, which signify present and future. And these last
two are drawn into the perfecting and simple and, as they say, ineffable
logos that comprehends them all. For it is from it (ἐξ οὗ), according to its
procession (κατὰ πρόοδον), that the general decad of tropes for the contemplation of scripture emerges; and it is into it (εἰς ὅν), as comprehensive source (ὡς ἀρχὴ κατὰ περιγραφήν), that this same decad contracts, in
ascending order (ἀνατατικῶς), back into a monad again.[15]

We cannot mistake here Maximus's allegiance to two of his hermeneutical mentors, Origen and Pseudo-Dionysius the Areopagite.[16] Scripture is
once again understood as a vast and diffuse array of data, much of it vulgar
information and crass symbols; and yet underlying the whole is a comprehensive salutary structure (Maximus uses the term εὐταξία) centered on the
unifying spiritual principle (λόγος), better yet the sublime Logos himself,
who holds it all together and establishes the configurative connections that
enable the pious, through ever more sophisticated contemplation, to envision
the unity and harmony of the whole world of Scripture. The language of a
procession/expansion and return/contraction in the cosmic hierarchy clearly
signals the influence of the mature Christian Neoplatonism of the Pseudo-
Areopagite.[17] As Torstein Tollefsen has shown in his recent study of
Maximus's metaphysics, however, the Confessor is less interested in a gradu-

15. Maximus, *ambig.* 37 (PG 91:1293a-c).

16. On Origen's hermeneutical influence on Maximus, see Paul Blowers, "The Anagogical Imagination: Maximus the Confessor and the Legacy of Origenian Hermeneutics,"
in *Origeniana Sexta: Origène et la Bible/Origen and the Bible. Actes du Colloquium
Origenianum Sextum, Chantilly, 30 août — 3 septembre 1993*, ed. Gilles Dorival and Alain
le Boulluec, Bibliotheca Ephemeridum Theologicarum Lovaniensium 118 (Leuven:
Peeters/Leuven University Press, 1995), pp. 639-54. On the Pseudo-Dionysian influence in
Maximus's hermeneutics, see Blowers, *Exegesis and Spiritual Pedagogy,* pp. 107, 111-12,
145-46, 159-60, n. 60.

17. For Maximus's cosmological principle of expansion/contraction, see *ambig.* 10
(PG 91:1177B-80A). On Maximus's quasi-geometric perspective in this section of *ambig.*
37, see Vittorio Croce, *Tradizione e ricerca: Il metodo teologico di san Massimo il Confessore,*
Studia patristica mediolanensia 2 (Milan: Vita e Pensiero, 1974), pp. 60-62.

ated ontological hierarchy as such than in the expansion (διαστολή) of created being (οὐσία) as an unfolding of the fullness of the intercommunion of *particular* creatures.[18] What holds true, then, in the register of his cosmology also obtains in the register of the complex narrative structure of Holy Scripture. The pure analogy between "world" and "text" is made possible by the doctrine of the λόγοι (and τρόποι) of beings.[19] If, in contemplating the physical cosmos, we aspire to a vision of the diverse λόγοι governing the movements of creatures in their peculiar modes (τρόποι) of existence, in Scripture we seek to envision the latent spiritual meanings (λόγοι) of persons and things as evinced through the τρόποι of their symbolically charged motions and actions and mediated to us in the complex "tropes" of scriptural discourse. In both cases we strive toward a vision of the "incarnation" of the divine Logos-Christ in the λόγοι of creation and Scripture, which, more than rendering transparent the unity and harmony of the universe, discloses the *thickening plot* of the drama of God's relation to the world — the mystery of salvation and deification in Jesus Christ.[20]

New with Maximus, it appears, is the attempt to set out a precise scientific scheme of progressive levels of *scriptural* contemplation integrating Aristotelian "categories" and the threefold "philosophical" disciplines of the spiritual life.[21] The doctrine of "categories" (κατηγορίαι) or fundamental predicables of being, variously articulated in Aristotle's logical and metaphysical works,[22] made its way into Byzantine thought for the most part secondhand. Maximus himself probably did not read Aristotle directly. He was doubtless influenced by Leontius of Byzantium (sixth century), whose knowledge of Aristotle was limited precisely to the treatise on *Categoriae*,[23] and quite possibly he had digested Aristotelian teaching on the categories

---

18. See Tollefsen, *Christocentric Cosmology,* pp. 135-38.

19. See Blowers, *Exegesis and Spiritual Pedagogy,* pp. 106-7.

20. On Maximus's doctrines of salvation and deification, see now Jean-Claude Larchet's extensive study, *La divinisation de l'homme selon Maxime le Confesseur* (Paris: Éditions du Cerf, 1996).

21. Though Maximus refers in *ambig.* 37 to the "true experts on such mysteries" in outlining this decad of contemplative modes, I have found no such precise scheme in earlier patristic writers; moreover, it is not uncommon for Maximus, out of sheer humility, to refer to unidentified authorities in entering upon his own speculations on Christian mysteries.

22. Most notably, see *Categoriae* 4-15 (1b-15b); *Analytica posteriora* 1.22 (82b-84b); *Topica* 1.9 (103b); *Metaphysica,* passim.

23. See Klaus Oehler, "Aristotle in Byzantium," *Greek, Roman and Byzantine Studies* 5 (1964): 142-43.

from seventh-century logical compendia and textbooks.[24] Aristotle's basic set of ten categories (as articulated in the *Categoriae* and *Topica*) included essence or "whatness" (τί ἐστι; οὐσία), quantity (τὸ ποσόν), quality (τὸ ποῖον), relation (πρὸς τι), place (τὸ ποῦ), time (τὸ ποτέ), position (τὸ κεῖσθαι), state (τὸ ἔχειν), activity (τὸ ποιεῖν), and passivity (τὸ πάσχειν); in various other works he sometimes subsumed certain of the categories, thus reducing the number.[25] Maximus alludes to a modified version of Aristotle's original set in his cosmological discussions in *Ambiguum* 10.[26] Of the ten modes of scriptural contemplation in the above-quoted passage from *Ambiguum* 37, however, we see a further modification. Under the initial five modes here, the Confessor does include "time" and "place," both of which figure prominently in his cosmology and his exegesis of Scripture; and "genus," though not one of Aristotle's original ten categories, had nonetheless been crucial in the Stagirite's fuller discussions of predication and definition.[27] "Persona," "dignity," and "occupation" indicate Maximus's own preoccupation with particularity and individuality in the consideration of genus.[28] Further on, we shall see how Maximus appropriates other of the Aristotelian categories (viz., "activity" and "passivity") in developing this scheme for the contemplation of Holy Scripture.

The obvious question is: Does this scheme remain in the realm of theory, or does it actually play out in Maximus's exegetical practice? Does he apply the scheme scientifically? In his own exegetical works, especially his long commentary on scriptural difficulties *Ad Thalassium*, Maximus fairly regularly (but never systematically) visits his first five modes: place, time, genus, persona, and dignity or occupation. Place and time intrinsically hold importance in view of the Confessor's larger cosmological interest in these two cate-

---

24. See Tollefsen, *Christocentric Cosmology*, pp. 18-19; also Mossman Roueché, "Byzantine Philosophical Texts of the Seventh Century," *Jahrbuch der österreichischen Byzantinistik* 23 (1974): 61-76; idem, "A Middle Byzantine Handbook of Logical Terminology," *Jahrbuch der österreichischen Byzantinistik* 29 (1980): 71-98.

25. E.g., in *Analytica posteriora* 1.22 (83a), Aristotle drops "position" and "state" and covers them under other categories.

26. Maximus, *ambig.* 10 (PG 91:1181b): Here Maximus mentions essence, quantity, quality, relation, activity, and passivity, and adds movement (κίνησις) and habit (ἕξις) — both of which come under discussion in connection with the "categories" in Aristotle himself.

27. Cf. *Analytica posteriora*, passim; *Topica* 1.5 (102a); *Metaphysica* 5.28 (1024a-b).

28. As Tollefsen argues (*Christocentric Cosmology*, pp. 153-72), Maximus is less interested in individual persons as instantiations of more universal genera than in their individual creaturely being, indeed their personhood.

gories.[29] "Whereness" and "whenness" are absolute conditions of all created beings, the primary boundary markers of the ontological distance (διάστημα) and extension (διάστασις) that separate them from the Uncreated.[30] As Tollefsen notes, Maximus is a thoroughgoing Christian Aristotelian in viewing "place" not as a spatial dimension so much as a being *some*-where, that is, holding "local" status in the movement toward creaturely actualization and deification within the providential, Christocentric order of things.[31] Time, likewise, is less a dimension to be considered in its own right than a *condition* of this creaturely movement.

If contemplating the movements of creatures within the conditions of time and space strikes us *prima facie* as a very different business from reflecting on the actions of characters situated within the times and places of the biblical narratives, we must continue to remember that for Maximus the biblical narratives are simply the peculiar vehicles of the larger "world story," the eschatological epiphany of the Logos-Christ in the λόγοι of the universe. Hence, like all the "categories," designations of place and time in the Bible symbolically give us access to the grand spiritual architecture of the divine economy in global history. As for *place* (τόπος), the sacred topography of the Bible plays an enormous role in conveying the fullness of the revelation. Not just the onomastics of biblical place-names, so important to patristic interpreters in the tradition of Origen,[32] but actual local and geographical considerations can uncover deeper spiritual insights. Subcategories κατὰ τόπον embrace general and particular references to locality: heaven, earth, air, sea, inhabited earth, far limits, countries, islands, cities, temples, villages, fields, mountains, valleys, roads, rivers, deserts, cisterns, threshing floors, vineyards, and the like.[33]

I will cite only two examples, substantive ones at that, of how the contemplation of place factors into his exegesis. In his commentary on Jonah in *Ad Thalassium* 64, Maximus makes much of the different "local" situations in which the prophet finds himself: in Joppa, in the sea, in the whale, and under the shade of the gourd in Nineveh. As Jonah is, from one angle, a figure of the Adamic legacy of human nature, we can envision Joppa (the city by the sea) as the glorious Paradise from which humanity was ultimately plunged into

---

29. See *Capita theologica et oikonomica* 1.68-70 (PG 90:1108c-9a).

30. See *ambig.* 10 (PG 91:1180b-81b); *ambig.* 15 (PG 91:1217c-d); cf. also Tollefsen, *Christocentric Cosmology,* pp. 141-43.

31. Tollefsen, *Christocentric Cosmology,* pp. 140-42.

32. See Blowers, *Exegesis and Spiritual Pedagogy,* pp. 203-11.

33. Maximus, *ambig.* 37 (PG 91:1293c).

the "sea," the "brine of sin."[34] The vivid descriptions of the depths of the abyss in Jonah's lament (Jonah 2:3-7) are prophetic signals of the severe depths of the human fall into darkness and chaos, the nadir of which is the swallowing by the devil himself.[35] Elsewhere, in his brief *Commentary on Psalm 59*, Maximus, like Gregory of Nyssa, takes "Mesopotamia," the "land between the rivers" and the site of some of David's military victories, as symbolic of the soul (so too the situation of all souls in history) flooded on all sides by the invasion of the passions.[36] Here, as throughout Maximus's exegesis, the spiritual history unfolding in the *macrocosm* of creation and Scripture is always paralleled by the spiritual "story" elicited within the *microcosm* of the human soul.

Contemplation of Scripture under the category of *time* (κατὰ χρόνον) scrutinizes every subtle nuance about temporal conditions and verbal tense: "when" (τὸ ποτέ), "was" (τὸ ἦν), "is" (τὸ ἐστι), "will be" (τὸ ἔσται), "before" this or that (τὸ πρὸ τοῦδε), "now" (τὸ παρόν), "after" this or that (τὸ μετὰ τόδε), "in the time of" this or that (τὸ ἐπὶ τοῦδε), "from the beginning of" (ἀπ᾽ ἀρχῆς), "the past," (τὸ παρελθόν) "the future" (τὸ μέλλον), years, seasons, months, weeks, days, nights, and parts of these temporal periods.[37] In *Ad Thalassium* 7, for instance, Maximus addresses the mysterious text from 1 Peter 4:6 concerning the gospel being preached to the dead, who are "judged in the flesh like men, so that they might live in the Spirit like God." He opens his response by observing that "it is customary in Scripture to alter the times and replace them with other times — the future as though it were past, the past as though it were future — and to speak of the 'present' as the time before and after itself." This has led some, Maximus explains, to interpret the "dead" in 1 Peter 4:6 in the *past* tense as those sinners who died before the advent of Christ, and who were addressed by Christ in his descent into Hades; but another hidden possibility (ἐπικεκρυμμένως) — and it is typical of the Confessor to propose multiple legitimate interpretive alternatives — is that the "dead" are those "in the present age" who carry the death of Jesus in their bodies (2 Cor. 4:10) through ascetic mortification.[38] Elsewhere, in *Ad Thalassium* 22, Maximus deals at length with the interrelation between chronological and eschatological "time" in the New Testament. His friend Tha-

---

34. Maximus, *qu. Thal.* 64 (CCSG 22:189.35–91.68).

35. Maximus, *qu. Thal.* 64 (CCSG 22:191.68–93.120).

36. Maximus, *expos. in Ps. 59* (CCSG 23:4.24–5.35); cf. Gregory of Nyssa, *Pss. titt.* (GNO 5:80.24–91.7).

37. Maximus, *ambig.* 37 (PG 91:1293c).

38. Maximus, *qu. Thal.* 7 (CCSG 7:73.1–75.40).

lassius has asked him specifically how Paul could say that God will show us his riches "in the ages to come" (Eph. 2:7) when in 1 Corinthians 10:11 he states that the "end of the ages" has already come upon us. Thoroughly aware of the multifarious language of "ages" (αἰῶνες) in Scripture, Maximus explores a number of different alternative explanations in hopes of showing how chronological and eschatological time are mysteriously "simultaneous" in the economy of Christ.[39]

Contemplation according to *genus* or *kind* (κατὰ γένον) properly divides into considerations of the "general" (καθολικῶς) and the "particular" (ἰδιοτρόπως) in the world of Scripture. "General" categories would embrace the ranks of angels and intellectual essences, the sun and planetary bodies, fire, and the living things of the air, land, or sea, whether they be animals, zoophytes, plants, or minerals.[40] Like his predecessor Evagrius Ponticus, Maximus shows keen interest in the way that various created beings, even the irrational animals, can provide potent images of spiritual disciplines: for example, the monk is called to imitate the sun's alternate changes of position in adjusting to all situations of life with circumspect wisdom; like the soaring eagle the monk must fasten his eyes on the divine radiance of pure light; like the deer he must scale the highest mountains of divine speculation.[41] "Particulars" by genus include appearances in Scripture of specific human nations, races, peoples, languages, tribes, homelands, with or without reference to number.[42] Like Origen and others, Maximus is especially scrupulous about the particular races or tribes in the ancient story of Israel, such as the Philistines, often called simply "foreigners" in the LXX, but so too all the Gentiles who, in their relation to Israel, are analogous to the passions of the soul in relation to ruling reason, needing to be subjugated and ultimately transformed in the service of Christ.[43]

Contemplation by *persona* (κατὰ πρόσωπον) naturally follows in considering individually named angels, archangels, or Seraphim, or other heavenly beings, or else named human personalities (Abraham, Isaac, Jacob, etc.) who appear in Scripture either in a laudable (ἐν ἐπαίνῳ) or culpable (ἐν ψόγῳ) light.[44] Here the anagogical interpretation of personal names is of tre-

---

39. Maximus, *qu. Thal.* 22 (CCSG 7:137-43). For a fuller study of this text, see Paul Blowers, "Realized Eschatology in Maximus the Confessor, *Ad Thalassium 22*," *SP* 37, ed. Elizabeth Livingstone (Leuven: Peeters, 1997), pp. 258-63.

40. Maximus, *ambig.* 37 (PG 91:1293c).

41. Maximus, *Qu. Thal.* 51 (CCSG 7:399.97–403.144).

42. Maximus, *ambig.* 37 (PG 91:1293d).

43. See Maximus, *expos. in Ps. 59* (CCSG 23:17.259–18.269).

44. Maximus, *ambig.* 37 (PG 91:1293d-96a).

mendous significance, as we see in Maximus's excursuses on the different possible spiritual meanings of figures like Zerubbabel[45] and Jonah.[46] The fifth mode accordingly considers the peculiar *dignity* (ἀξία) or *occupation* (ἐπιτήδευμα) of persons or groups of persons in the narratives in which they appear, whether king or kingdom, shepherd or flock, priest or priesthood, farmer, general, architect, or any other designation of profession.[47] As I already noted, this is the special concern of *Ambiguum* 37 in analyzing the unique personages and occupations of John the Baptist and King David.

Old Testament kings are always of special prosopographic interest because of their diverse, sometimes shifty, guises. The foreign King Darius of Persia is allegorized as the "ruling law of nature" in the moral life precisely because he appears in the scriptural story of 1 Esdras (LXX) in good repute (i.e., ἐπαινετῶς), and he cannot, then, like most foreign kings, become a demonic figure or a symbol of vice.[48] Other kings are more slippery characters by comparison since they can appear both laudably and culpably, as instruments of God in some passages and of the Devil in others. Maximus writes in *Ad Thalassium* 26:

The [Christian] gnostic will come to know the significance of all the rest of the kings [in 3 Kings, LXX] through the interpretation of their names, or by their geographic location, or by the common tradition which prevails in those lands, or by the particular customs which are pursued among them, or by the sort of antipathy each has toward Israel. . . . For not all the [foreign] kings are always interpreted in the same way or according to one meaning; rather, they are interpreted *with a view to their underlying utility and prophetic potential* (πρὸς τὴν ὑποκειμένην χρείαν καὶ τῆς προφητείας τὴν δύναμιν). Indeed, Scripture was able to render the "Pharaoh" as the Devil when he sought to destroy Israel, but then again as the law of nature when he served Israel according to the dispensation of Joseph. Through "Joseph" himself Scripture prophetically signified the

45. Maximus, *qu. Thal.* 54 (CCSG 7:443-59); see also Blowers, *Exegesis and Spiritual Pedagogy,* pp. 203-5.

46. Maximus, *qu. Thal.* 64 (CCSG 22:187-229); see also Blowers, *Exegesis and Spiritual Pedagogy,* pp. 206-11; and Carl Laga, "Maximi Confessoris ad Thalassium Quaestio 64," in *After Chalcedon: Studies in Theology and Church History Offered to Professor Albert Van Roey for His Seventieth Birthday,* ed. Carl Laga et al., Orientalia lovaniensia analecta 18 (Leuven: Departement Oriëntalistiek, 1985), pp. 203-15.

47. Maximus, *ambig.* 37 (PG 91:1296b-c).

48. Maximus, *qu. Thal.* 55 (CCSG 7:483.59–485.70); cf. Maximus, *qu. Thal.* 54 (CCSG 7:449.100-138).

divine Logos who was a voluntary servant in human nature and amid our human passions, save only without sin. Likewise the "king of Tyre" is intended to represent the Devil when he waged war on Israel through Sisera, but elsewhere signifies the law of nature when he made peace with David and contributed so much to Solomon for the building of the temple. Each of the kings enumerated in Scripture is interpreted in many different meanings according to their underlying prophetic potential.[49]

Not surprisingly, in view of the long-standing monastic tradition of biblical *exempla,* much of Maximus's exegetical prosopography highlights the virtues (sometimes the vices) of celebrated biblical saints. He devotes much of *Ambiguum* 10, for example, to the profiles of great Old Testament patriarchs who have modeled the disciplines of the spiritual life even before the advent of Christ.[50] Abraham surpassed the senses and through his achievement in asceticism and contemplation "arrived in the divine and blessed land of the knowledge (γνῶσις)" of Christ himself.[51] Like Gregory of Nyssa, Maximus is fascinated with the figure of Moses and the whole theological "iconography" of the Sinai theophany. Moses may have occasionally stumbled in his earlier pursuit of God,[52] but at Sinai, having entered the mysterious cloud of the divine presence (Exod. 19:16-20; 24:12-18; 33:20-23), he ultimately emerged a magnificent image of the Divine (Exod. 34:29-30)[53] and, therefore, worthily appeared flanking the Lord himself at his transfiguration (Matt. 17:1-8 and par.).[54] Maximus also highlights Melchizedek, who intrigued early Jewish and Christian exegetes alike, in view of his unique *dignity* of being "without father or mother or genealogy" and his peculiar *occupation* as a "priest forever" (Gen. 14:18-20; Ps. 109:4, LXX; Heb. 7:3). Given the high estimation of Melchizedek as prefiguring Christ in the writer of Hebrews, Maximus presumes that this great priest (insofar as he was said to be "without beginning of days and end of life," Heb. 7:3) had achieved a knowledge

49. Maximus, *qu. Thal.* 26 (CCSG 7:179.132–181.152). Emphasis added in translation.

50. See Julian Stead, "The Patriarchs as Models of the Christian Life according to St. Maximus the Confessor in the *Ambigua* (1137C-1149C)," *Patristic and Byzantine Review* 15 (1996-97): 141-49.

51. Maximus, *ambig.* 10 (PG 91:1145c-48a; 1200a-b); cf. also *qu. Thal.* 28 (CCSG 7:203.10-21) and *qu. dub.* 39 [III,10] (CCSG 10:32.1–33.34) on Abraham as a visionary of the Holy Trinity.

52. See Maximus, *qu. Thal.* 17 (CCSG 7:111-15).

53. Maximus, *ambig.* 10 (PG 91:1117b-c); see also *ambig.* 10 (PG 91:1148a-49c).

54. Maximus, *ambig.* 10 (PG 91:1160d-69b).

compassing time and eternity and a level of contemplation transcending all material and immaterial being, and as "priest forever" he had already attained an immutable habit of godlike virtue.[55] Drawing upon Origen's principle of spiritually "transposing" (μετάληψις) or internalizing biblical events and persons, Maximus asserts that God provides sufficient grace to every believer "who desires to become a Melchizedek, an Abraham, a Moses, simply to transpose (μεταφέρειν) all the saints into himself, not by exchanging names and places but by imitating their ways of life and their ascetic conduct."[56]

To sum up thus far, the original five modes of scriptural contemplation in Maximus's scheme in *Ambiguum* 37 afford the reader a certain index or register for comprehending the vast array of biblical places, things, persons, and so forth, which fill up the world of Holy Scripture. Yet through deeper investigation — and Maximus explicitly speaks of this contemplative pursuit as one of sublime "research" (ἡ τῆς θεωρίας ἐξέτασις)[57] — these five modes contract into the second three modes of practical (ascetic), natural, and theological philosophy, the three eminent categories of the spiritual life.[58] He further elucidates this in *Ambiguum* 37:

> The logos of Scripture displays all these things (as many as there are included under the original five modes) as constituted of essence (οὐσία), potency (δύναμις), and operation (ἐνέργεια), the primary distinctions about these things: whether overall they move or are moved, whether they act or are acted upon, whether they contemplate or are contemplated, whether they speak or are spoken to, whether they teach or are taught, whether they are heeded or averted, and plainly and concisely, whether by either performing (ποιοῦντα) or being subject to (πάσχοντα) practical,

55. Maximus, *ambig.* 10 (PG 91:1139c-40a, with the full discourse on Melchizedek's exemplary spiritual life extending to 1145b).

56. Maximus, *ambig.* 10 (PG 91:1144a-b; cf. PG 91:1149c-d). On the principle of "transposition" in Maximus and the antecedent tradition, see Blowers, *Exegesis and Spiritual Pedagogy*, pp. 114-17; also Marguerite Harl, Introduction to *Origène: Philocalie, 1-20 sur les Écritures*, SC 302 (Paris: Éditions du Cerf, 1983), pp. 133-35.

57. Maximus, *ambig.* 37 (PG 91:1296b); cf. also *qu. Thal.* 40 (CCSG 7:269.51-53), where he writes: "For all the things (in Scripture) are left for investigation (πρὸς ἐξέτασιν) by the initiate and the mystagogue of the divine realities and meanings and concepts, since we are pleased intellectually wholly by the mode of anagogical interpretation."

58. On these three categories or dimensions of the spiritual life in Maximus's theology, and his obvious dependence on (and correction of) Evagrius, there are substantial studies: see esp. Thunberg, *Microcosm and Mediator*, pp. 332-68; Walther Völker, *Maximus Confessor als Meister des geistlichen Lebens* (Wiesbaden: Franz Steiner, 1965), pp. 236-48.

natural, and theological philosophy, they combine with one another variously so as to initiate us in these three forms of philosophy. In turn each of the things multifariously specified in Scripture is interpreted, with ideas about it gathered through contemplation, either laudably (ἐπαινετῶς) or culpably (ψέκτως), as manifesting principles (λόγοι) of what we are to do or not to do on the basis of that thing, principles of what is natural or unnatural, principles of what is spiritual or unspiritual. For, as I have said, there is a double modality (διττὸς τρόπος) for each scriptural meaning (λόγος) according to the capacity of the one who carries out the research (ἐξέτασις) of contemplation on those meanings intelligently. As a result, through affirmation (θέσις) of the authentic principles, and by denial (ἀφαίρησις) of what we should not do and of unnatural and unspiritual illusions, the pious embrace practical, natural, and theological philosophy, which is the same thing, so to speak, as the love of God (φιλοθεΐα).[59]

In this passage, Maximus reinforces his conviction (already noted above) that the things and persons subject to "scriptural contemplation" stand in a pure analogous relation to the created beings subject to "natural contemplation" or philosophy. This is signaled, first of all, in his reference to the triad of *essence* (οὐσία)–*potency* (δύναμις)–*operation* (ἐνέργεια), appropriated by Maximus from Pseudo-Dionysius and abundantly exploited in his larger cosmology.[60] The things and persons of Scripture, through careful discernment, appear as creatures in a cosmos, ontologically predisposed toward God, having their own unique integrity, and empowered to transcendent ends. Like all beings enjoying essence (οὐσία), their natures (φύσεις) are frontiers of actualization; and the organic interplay among these beings, the configuration of their natural movements and their moral dispositions in relation to one other and to God, furnishes, through the lens of enlightened contemplation, instructive patterns for our own advancement in wisdom and virtue. Interestingly, Maximus also introduces in the passage just quoted the original Aristotelian categories of activity and passivity, identifying the need to discern whether these beings are subjects or objects of motion and activity. This evinces his larger concern for how, in the magnificent network of the world and Scripture, created rational beings are at once self-moving, active agents (morally speaking) and yet passive to the motions of other beings and, more profoundly, to the gracious movement of the God who is both the be-

59. Maximus, *ambig.* 37 (PG 91:1296a-b).
60. On this triad in Maximus, see Sherwood, *Earlier Ambigua,* pp. 103-16; and more recently Tollefsen, *Christocentric Cosmology,* pp. 144-48.

ginning and the end of all creaturely motion.[61] Maximus may well be inspired here by the description of the interworking of the *hierarchia* of divine illumination and deification in Pseudo-Dionysius's *Celestial Hierarchy*, where the Areopagite depicts any hierarchy (specifically here heavenly hierarchies but the same applies to earthly ones) as perfected through "uplifting" (ἀναγωγή) in the imitation of God, such that, in his own words,

> when the hierarchic order lays it on some to be purified and on others to do the purifying, on some to receive illumination and on others to cause illumination, on some to be perfected and on others to bring about perfection, each will actually imitate God in the way suitable to whatever role it has.[62]

Attaining to the panoramic perspective that Maximus describes in *Ambiguum* 37 seems intrinsically to privilege "natural philosophy," the contemplation of nature and of the world of Scripture, as the principal mode or "category" — indeed the very fulcrum — of biblical interpretation. Maximus expressly states here that contemplation (θεωρία) or contemplative "research" (ἐξέτασις) is the means for gathering ideas (ἐπίνοιαι) and sifting out the true λόγοι of beings. Yet he also makes it quite clear that the hermeneutical project is not merely an intellectual vision but a moral and mystagogical venture. The three forms of "philosophy" — contemplation of nature, ascetic praxis, and the mystical discipline of θεολογία proper — mutually co-inhere at every stage in this process of discernment and moral-spiritual *paideusis*. Therein the exegete/visionary is being trained, as Maximus explains, to "affirm" or appropriate principles of pious action, natural contemplation, and mystical vision, and likewise to "deny" or spurn impiety, errant views of the world, and unspiritual illusions. All of this exercises the diligent ultimately in the true goal of interpretation, the religious love of God (φιλοθεΐα) — a point on which Maximus is in full (if unconscious?) agreement with his great predecessor in North Africa, Augustine of Hippo.[63]

A modern critic already biased against patristic "anagogical" interpretation of the Bible might opt to accuse the Confessor, as a monastic exegete, of

---

61. Maximus expresses this notion concisely but substantively in his *cap. theol.* 1.1-12 (PG 90:1084a-87b).

62. Pseudo-Dionysius the Areopagite, *c.h.* 3.2 (PG 3:165b-c), translated by Colm Luibheid, *Pseudo-Dionysius: The Complete Works*, CWS (New York and Mahwah, N.J.: Paulist Press, 1987), p. 154.

63. Augustine expresses this principle concisely in *doc. Chr.* 3.10.15-16.

forcing scriptural truth into these three "categories" of the spiritual life; yet clearly Maximus maintains that scriptural beings/things are genuinely commending them for our instruction,[64] either by actively modeling these three disciplines or else by being found subject to those disciplines. Even if one cannot necessarily discern this for every specific thing or person in the text, it is enough that "they variously combine with each other so as to initiate (εἰσηγοῦνται) us in these three forms of philosophy." Once again we reiterate that, for Maximus, the "world" of Holy Scripture, which we as interpreters inhabit, is a complex, sophisticated, and organic system of *mimesis*. Indeed, Maximus in his own way hints at what has become an important axiom among some postmodern biblical interpreters: the principle that interpretation does not end with the extraction of objective meanings from Scripture but embraces the whole continuum of processing and "performing" the truth in new communal and existential contexts. To recall a hermeneutical paradigm developed by Hans Urs von Balthasar, the late Roman Catholic theologian who was himself so deeply influenced by Maximus the Confessor, the biblical revelation unveils the grand "Theo-Drama" of the interplay of God and the world, more precisely of divine and creaturely freedom — a drama centered in the mystery of Jesus Christ and invoking its "audience" (the Christian faithful) constantly to come "on stage," as it were, as the most recent *dramatis personae*.[65] Respecting more closely Maximus's own idiom, the λόγοι of creation and Scripture hold the key to the deeper plot structure of that cosmic drama, and those faithful souls who join with their exemplars in contemplation and ascesis, in the continuum of *mimesis*, participate vitally in its unfolding eschatological denouement.

So let us turn to the final section of Maximus's short hermeneutical treatise in *Ambiguum* 37, where he demonstrates how the second three contemplative modes or categories (i.e., practical, natural, and theological philosophy) contract into the last two, "present" and "future," which also comprehend the dialectic of "figure" and "truth." Furthermore, this dialectic, at last, gives way to the one sublime Logos, Christ himself.

> And those three forms of philosophy [ethical, natural, theological] are furthermore divided into both present (τὸ παρόν) and future (τὸ

---

64. See Maximus's appeal to 1 Cor. 10:11 in *ambig.* 10 (PG 91:1149b-52b).

65. See Hans Urs von Balthasar, *Theo-Drama: Theological Dramatic Theory*, vol. 1: *Prolegomena*, trans. Graham Harrison (San Francisco: Ignatius, 1988), p. 249; vol. 2: *The Dramatis Personae: Man in God*, trans. Graham Harrison (San Francisco: Ignatius, 1990). There are three subsequent volumes as well in the *Theo-Drama* series.

μέλλον), since they comprehend both shadow (σκιά) and truth (ἀλήθεια), figure (τύπος) and archetype (ἀρχέτυπος). Insofar as it is possible, albeit in a transcendent and sublime way, for humanity, in the present age, attaining to the ultimate measure of virtue and knowledge and wisdom, to reach the knowledge of divine things, it is possible through a figure and an image of archetypes. For actually a figure is the whole truth that we judge to be present now, and an image is also a shadow of the superior Logos. For seeing that the Logos who has created the universe both exists and manifests himself in the universe according to the relation of the present to the future, he is understood as figure and truth; and inasmuch as he transcends present and future, he is understood as transcending figure and truth, by containing nothing that could be considered as contrary. But truth has a contrary: falsehood. So then beyond truth the Logos gathers all things unto himself, since he is man and God, and indeed also beyond all humanity and divinity.[66]

This last elucidation completes Maximus's portrait of the procession and return of divine revelation, and so too the expansion and contraction of the tenfold modes of contemplation. The visionary is returned from the magnificent diversity of creation and Scripture to an exalted and unifying encounter with the Logos himself, who sustains and perfects the revelatory order. We have already made mention of the unmistakable echoes of the symbolic hierarchism of Pseudo-Dionysius in this scheme. The two writers share a deep sense of the "uplifting," or anagogical movement of creatures toward a deifying (indeed ecstatic) vision of the Divine Author of the world and Scripture. Yet I would urge that there is a subtle shift of perspective in Maximus. Some would call it a corrective to the Areopagite's Neoplatonism; Maximus himself probably saw it as more a clarification or adjustment. When Pseudo-Dionysius speaks of the hierarchy of divine illumination that begins with the ranks of heavenly beings and descends down through the orders of the "ecclesiastical hierarchy" on earth, the efficacy of the uplifting of all things toward God is clearly grounded in the vertical ontological arrangement whereby the inferior imitates the superior and is progressively advanced upward by a gracious enlightenment and conversion.[67] Scripture purely parallels that hierarchy in its own resplendent order of symbols descending from the most sublime to the most crass and unseemly earthly symbols of divine

66. Maximus, *ambig.* 37 (PG 91:1296b-d).
67. Cf. *c.h.* 1.2-3 (PG 3:588c-89c); 4.1-6 (PG 3:693b-701b); *d.n.* 1.1-3 (PG 3:120b-24a); 3.1-3 (PG 3:164d-68b); *c.h.* 1.1-4 (PG 3:369d-76c and passim).

truth and back again.[68] Maximus, while drawing upon this symbolic hierarchism to a degree, resists any misconstrual such as would see the anagogical "uplifting" only as an ever more radical intellectual liberation from the symbolic, the securing of the truth over and beyond all its figurative representations. In the text quoted above, he states that the contemplative is indeed led penultimately to the dialectic of "shadow" and "truth," "figure" and "archetype," but the more basic tension remains that of *present giving way to future*. Maximus privileges the progressive *historical* (and *trans-historical*) character of the revelation. The "present," by which he means the whole vast prophetic economy underlying the created world and the world of Scripture, and latent within the λόγοι of all things, has its complement in that "future" where the figures and enigmas of this world gradually and mysteriously unfold before us in all their glory. Beings moving within the created cosmos and in the "cosmos" of biblical narrative are, in effect, a grand cloud of witnesses training us toward that future vision. As Irénée-Henri Dalmais rightly puts it, Maximus's hermeneutic ultimately gives precedence not to the hierarchical antithesis of figure and reality but to the salvation-historical dialectic of preparation and fulfillment.[69] Or as Alain Riou suggests, Maximus has modified the ontological hierarchism of Pseudo-Dionysius with a new vision of the drama of the divine economy centered on the direct action of the Logos:

> Contrary to the Dionysian conception, for Maximus the Deity in his transcendence is no longer rendered remote by the multitude of hierarchical mediations — "all this bureaucracy of light," as Père [M.-D.] Chenu humorously calls it — but the Word bears in himself, without any intermediary, the logos of even the last of created beings.[70]

Indeed, leading the way is the person of the Logos-Christ himself, who indwells and transcends this grand economy, working through the historical dialectic of present and future while himself admitting no such temporal opposition, nor any symbolic opposition of type and archetype. He is, to be sure, the apex of the unity and harmony of the scheme of revelation; but, more important, in his *eschatological* epiphany, the fullness of the mystery of

68. See esp. *c.h.* 2.1-5 (PG 3:136d-45c).

69. Irénée-Henri Dalmais, "La manifestation du Logos dans l'homme et dans l'Église: Typologie anthropologique et typologie ecclésiale d'après *Qu. Thal.* 60 et la *Mystagogie*," in *Maximus Confessor: Actes du symposium sur Maxime le Confesseur, Fribourg, 2-5 septembre 1980*, ed. Felix Heinzer and Christoph von Schönborn, Paradosis 27 (Fribourg: Éditions Universitaires, 1980), p. 21.

70. Riou, *Le monde et l'Église selon Maxime le Confesseur*, p. 58.

his "incarnation" in the λόγοι of all things, he is the pioneer and the guarantor of the diversity and intricacy of that revelation, which, while gradually guiding creatures toward a timeless contemplation of the "monad" of divine truth, can never be simply collapsed into that monad. The decad of modes for contemplating Scripture leads toward a unity of insight into divine truth,[71] yet ultimately that insight protects and preserves the diversity (and historical materiality) of the biblical revelation — and respects its resistance to facile attempts to unlock its secrets. The "scandal" of Scripture, to recall an axiom of Origenian hermeneutics, is precisely that the Holy Spirit has authored a complex and complicated text *for our quickening and benefit.*[72] For Maximus, real vision is granted only to those who delve into the ever thickening plot of the Theo-Drama, who join in the dense cosmic and scriptural "cloud of witnesses" — heavenly and earthly beings, animate and inanimate things — in pressing to unveil the fullness of the mystery of Jesus Christ.

71. Maximus, *ambig.* 37 (PG 91:1293c, 1296d).
72. On the broad ramifications of this principle in patristic exegesis, see Robert Wilken, *"In Dominico Eloquio:* Learning the Lord's Style of Language," *Communio* 24 (1997): 846-66.

Bibliography of Robert Louis Wilken

Compiled by
THOMAS MAMMOSER
REX HILL
and
PAUL M. BLOWERS

Books

1995   *Remembering the Christian Past* (collected essays). Grand Rapids: Eerd-
        mans.

1992   *The Land Called Holy: Palestine in Christian History and Thought.* New
        Haven: Yale University Press.

1984   *The Christians as the Romans Saw Them.* New Haven: Yale University
        Press.

1983   *John Chrysostom and the Jews: Rhetoric and Reality in the Late Fourth
        Century.* The Transformation of the Classical Heritage 4. Berkeley:
        University of California Press.

1978   (with Wayne A. Meeks). *Jews and Christians in Antioch in the First Four
        Centuries of the Common Era.* Sources for Biblical Study 13. Missoula,
        Mont.: Scholars Press.

1971   *Judaism and the Early Christian Mind: A Study of Cyril of Alexandria's
        Exegesis and Theology.* New Haven: Yale University Press.
        The Myth of Christian Beginnings: History's Impact on Belief. Garden
        City, N.Y.: Doubleday. Reprinted by the University of Notre Dame
        Press, 1980.

Edited Works

1979   (with William R. Schoedel). *Early Christian Literature and the Classical Intellectual Tradition: In Honorem Robert M. Grant.* Théologie historique 54. Paris: Éditions Beauchesne.

1975   *Aspects of Wisdom in Judaism and Early Christianity.* Notre Dame, Ind.: University of Notre Dame Press.

Articles and Essays

2000   "What Would Augustine Say? — Pluralism: Is Christianity the Only Path to God?" *Christian History* 19.3 (Issue 67): 41-43.

1999   "Cyril of Alexandria's *Contra Iulianum.*" In *The Limits of Ancient Christianity: Essays on Late Antique Thought and Culture in Honor of Robert Austin Markus,* ed. William E. Klingshirn and Mark Vessey, pp. 42-55. Ann Arbor: University of Michigan Press.

"Gregory VII and the Politics of the Spirit." *First Things,* no. 89: 26-32.

1998   "Arthur Carl Piepkorn (1907-1973): On the 25th Anniversary of His Death" [address delivered to Immanuel Lutheran Church, New York City, 13 December 1998]. *Lutheran Forum* 33: 46-52.

"Foreword" to Henri de Lubac, *Medieval Exegesis,* vol. 1: *The Four Senses of Scripture,* trans. Mark Sebanc, pp. ix-xii. Grand Rapids: Eerdmans.

"In Defense of Allegory." *Modern Theology* 14: 197-212. Reprinted in *Theology and Scriptural Imagination,* ed. L. Gregory Jones and James J. Buckley, pp. 35-50. Oxford: Blackwell.

"Jerusalem: The Christian Holy City." *Judaism* 46: 180-88.

"Prayer and the Work of God: Reflections on the Daily Office and the Prayer of the Heart." *Touchstone: A Journal of Ecumenical Orthodoxy* 11: 11-13.

"Roman Redux" (Interview). *Christian History* 17.1 (Issue 57): 43-44.

"St. Cyril of Alexandria: Biblical Expositor." *Coptic Church Review* 19: 30-41.

1997   "Augustine's City of God Today." In *The Two Cities of God: The Church's Responsibility for the Earthly City,* ed. Carl E. Braaten and Robert W. Jenson, pp. 28-41. Grand Rapids: Eerdmans.

"*In Dominico Eloquio:* Learning the Lord's Style of Language." *Communio* (US) 24: 846-66.

"The Jews as the Christians Saw Them." *First Things,* no. 73: 28-32.

"Leviticus as a Book of the Church." *Consensus* 23: 7-19.

1996   "Grace and the Knowledge of God." In *New Perspectives on Historical Theology: Essays in Memory of John Meyendorff,* ed. Bradley Nassif, pp. 238-49. Grand Rapids: Eerdmans.

"Lutheran Pietism and Catholic Piety." In *The Catholicity of the Reformation,* ed. Carl E. Braaten and Robert W. Jenson, pp. 79-92. Grand Rapids: Eerdmans.

1995   "Loving God with a Holy Passion." In *Remembering the Christian Past* [collected essays of Robert L. Wilken], pp. 145-63. Grand Rapids: Eerdmans.

"Maximus the Confessor on the Affections in Historical Perspective." In *Asceticism,* ed. Vincent Wimbush and Richard Valantasis, pp. 412-23. New York: Oxford University Press.

"Ministry in Lutheran/Orthodox Dialogue." *Lutheran Forum* 29: 34-36.

"Not a Solitary God: The Triune God of the Bible." In *Remembering the Christian Past* [collected essays of Robert L. Wilken], pp. 63-93. Grand Rapids: Eerdmans. Reprinted in revised and expanded form as "The Triune God of the Bible and the Emergence of Orthodoxy." In the *Companion Encyclopedia of Theology,* ed. Peter Byrne and James Leslie Houlden, pp. 187-205. London and New York: Routledge.

"Origen's *Homilies on Leviticus* and *Vayikra Rabbah.*" In *Origeniana Sexta: Origène et La Bible/Origen and the Bible,* ed. Gilles Dorival and Alain Le Boulluec, pp. 81-91. Bibliotheca Ephemeridum theologicarum Lovaniensium 118. Leuven: Leuven University Press/Peeters.

"Serving the One True God." In *Either/Or: The Gospel of Neopaganism,* ed. Carl E. Braaten and Robert W. Jenson, pp. 49-63. Grand Rapids: Eerdmans.

"St. Cyril of Alexandria: The Mystery of Christ in the Bible." *Pro Ecclesia* 4: 454-78.

"The Triune God of the Bible and the Emergence of Orthodoxy." In the *Companion Encyclopedia of Theology,* ed. Peter Byrne and James Leslie Houlden, pp. 187-205. London and New York: Routledge. Revision and expansion of "Not a Solitary God: The Triune God of the Bible." In *Remembering the Christian Past* (1995), pp. 63-93.

1994   "Not a Solitary God: The Triune God of the Bible." *Pro Ecclesia* 3: 36-55.

(with Paul M. Blowers and Jon D. Levenson). "Interpreting the Bible: Three Views" [response to 1993 Pontifical Biblical Commission Report on "The Interpretation of the Bible in the Church"]. *First Things,* no. 45: 40-46. Reprinted as "Three Views from the USA." In *The Interpretation of the Bible in the Church,* ed. James Leslie Houlden, pp. 112-28. London: SCM Press, 1995.

1993   "The Holy Land in Christian Imagination." *Bible Review* 9: 26-33, 53-54.

"*In novissimis diebus:* Biblical Promises, Jewish Hopes, and Early Christian Exegesis." *JECS* 1: 1-19. Reprinted in *Remembering the Christian Past* (1995), pp. 95-119.

"The Lives of the Saints and the Pursuit of Virtue." In *New Visions: Historical and Theological Perspectives on the Jewish-Christian Dialogue,* ed. Val Ambrose McInnes, pp. 55-76. New York: Crossroad. Reprinted in *Remembering the Christian Past* (1995), pp. 121-44.

"Memory and the Christian Intellectual Life." In *Reasoned Faith: Essays on the Interplay of Faith and Reason,* ed. Frank F. Birtel, pp. 141-55. New York: Crossroads. Reprinted in *Remembering the Christian Past* (1995), pp. 165-80.

"No Other Gods." *First Things,* no. 37: 13-18. Reprinted in *Remembering the Christian Past* (1995), pp. 47-62.

"The Pastor as Icon." *Dialog* 32: 19-24.

1992   "Called and Ordained." *Dialog* 31: 149-52.

"Historical Theology." In *A New Handbook of Christian Theology,* ed. D. W. Musser and J. L. Price, pp. 225-29. Nashville: Abingdon.

"Religious Pluralism and Early Christian Thought." *Pro Ecclesia* 1: 89-103. Reprinted in *Remembering the Christian Past* (1995), pp. 25-46.

1991   "The Christian Intellectual Tradition." *First Things,* no. 14: 13-18.

1990   (Correspondence). *First Things,* no. 1: 3.

"Faith and Reason and the Study of Religion." *Thoughtlines* 16.2: 16-24.

"Free Choice and the Divine Will in Greek Christian Commentaries on Paul." In *Paul and the Legacies of Paul,* ed. William S. Babcock, pp. 123-40. Dallas: Southern Methodist University Press.

"Jews, Christians, and the Land of Israel." *First Things,* no. 5: 13-15.

"The Lives of the Saints and the Pursuit of Virtue." *First Things,* no. 8: 45-51.

"Lutheran-Orthodox Dialogue in the United States." *Ecumenical Trends* 19: 68-72.

"The Piety of the Persecutors." *Christian History* 9.3 (Issue 27): 16-19.

1989   "The Image of God: A Neglected Doctrine." *Dialog* 28: 292-96.

"Who Will Speak for the Religious Traditions?" *Journal of the American Academy of Religion* 57: 699-717. Reprinted in *Remembering the Christian Past* (1995), pp. 1-23.

1988   "The Bible and Its Interpreters: Christian Biblical Interpretation." In the *Harper's Bible Commentary,* ed. James L. Mays, pp. 57-64. San Francisco: Harper & Row.

"Byzantine Palestine: A Christian Holy Land." *Biblical Archaeologist* 51: 214-17, 233-37.

"The Durability of Orthodoxy." *Word and World* 8: 124-32.

1987 "Jerusalem, Emperor Julian, and Christian Polemics." In *Jerusalem: City of the Ages,* ed. Alice L. Eckardt, pp. 241-52. Lanham, Md.: University Press of America.

1986 "Early Christian Chiliasm, Jewish Messianism, and the Idea of the Holy Land." *HTR* 79: 298-307. Reprinted in *Christians Among Jews and Gentiles,* ed. George Nickelsburg and George W. MacRae, pp. 298-307. Philadelphia: Fortress.

"From Time Immemorial: Dwellers in the Holy Land." *Christian Century* 103 (July 30–August 6): 678-80.

"Religion, Pluralism and Early Christian Theology." *Interpretation* 40: 379-91.

1985 "The Restoration of Israel in Biblical Prophecy: Christian and Jewish Responses in the Early Byzantine Period." In *To See Ourselves as Others See Us: Christians, Jews, "Others" in Late Antiquity,* ed. Jacob Neusner and Ernest Frerichs, pp. 443-71. Chico, Calif.: Scholars Press.

1984 "Alexandria: A School for Training in Virtue." In *Schools of Thought in the Christian Tradition,* ed. Patrick Henry, pp. 15-30. Philadelphia: Fortress.

1982 "The Resurrection of Jesus and the Doctrine of the Trinity." *Word and World* 2: 17-28.

1981 "The Authenticity of the Fragments of Melito of Sardis on the Sacrifice of Isaac (Genesis 22): Comments on Perler's Edition." In *Überlieferungsgeschichtliche Untersuchungen,* ed. Franz Paschke, pp. 605-8. Berlin: Akademie-Verlag.

"Diversity and Unity in Early Christianity." *Second Century* 1: 101-10.

1980 "The Christians as the Romans (and Greeks) Saw Them." In *Jewish and Christian Self-Definition,* vol. 1: *The Shaping of Christianity in the Second and Third Centuries,* ed. E. P. Sanders, pp. 100-125. Philadelphia: Fortress.

"The Jews and Christian Apologetics after Theodosius I: *Cunctos Populos.*" *HTR* 73: 451-71. Reprinted as "Jerusalem, Emperor Julian, and Christian Polemics." In *Jerusalem: City of the Ages,* ed. Alice L. Eckardt, pp. 241-52. Lanham, Md.: University Press of America, 1987.

(with William R. Schoedel). "Honoring Robert M. Grant." *Criterion* 19: 24-28.

1979   "Introducing the Athanasian Creed." *Currents in Theology and Mission* 6: 4-10.

"Liturgical Piety and the Doctrine of the Trinity." *Dialog* 18: 114-20.

"Pagan Criticism of Christianity: Greek Religion and Christian Faith." In *Early Christian Literature and the Classical Intellectual Tradition: In Honorem Robert M. Grant,* ed. William R. Schoedel and Robert L. Wilken, pp. 117-34. Théologie historique 54. Paris: Éditions Beauchesne.

1976   "The Immortality of the Soul and Christian Hope." *Dialog* 15: 110-17.

"Melito, the Jewish Community at Sardis, and the Sacrifice of Isaac." *ThS* 37: 53-69.

1975   "The Physical Shape of Antioch and Daphne (Literary Evidence)." In the *Society of Biblical Literature: 1975 Papers,* vol. 1, ed. George MacRae, pp. 75-79. Missoula, Mont.: Scholars Press.

"Porphyry's *Philosophy from Oracles* as a Work against Christianity." In the *Society of Biblical Literature: 1975 Papers,* vol. 1, ed. George MacRae, pp. 207-14. Missoula, Mont.: Scholars Press.

"Wisdom and Philosophy in Early Christianity." In *Aspects of Wisdom in Judaism and Early Christianity,* ed. Robert L. Wilken, pp. 143-68. Notre Dame, Ind.: University of Notre Dame Press.

1974   "Tertullian." *Encyclopaedia Britannica,* 15th edition. Chicago: Encyclopaedia Britannica.

1973   "The Making of a Phrase." *Dialog* 12: 174-81.

1972   "The Christianizing of Abraham: The Interpretation of Abraham in Early Christianity." *Concordia Theological Monthly* 43: 723-31.

"The Interpretation of the Baptism of Jesus in the Later Fathers." *SP* 11, part 2, ed. F. L. Cross, pp. 268-77. Berlin: Akademie-Verlag.

"Study of Early Church History." *ChHist* 41: 437-51.

1971   "Collegia, Philosophical Schools, and Theology (Greco-Roman Views of Christianity)." In *The Catacombs and the Colosseum: The Roman Empire as the Setting of Primitive Christianity,* ed. Stephen Benko and John O'Rourke, pp. 268-91. Valley Forge, Pa.: Judson Press.

"Liturgy, Bible and Theology in the Easter Sermons of Gregory of Nyssa." In *Écriture et culture philosophique dans la pensée de Grégorie de Nysse: Actes du colloque de Chevetogne (22-26 septembre 1969),* ed. Marguerite Harl, pp. 127-43. Leiden: Brill.

1970   "Toward a Social Interpretation of Early Christian Apologetics." *ChHist* 39: 437-58.

1969   "Justification by Works: Fate and the Gospel in the Roman Empire." *Concordia Theological Monthly* 40: 379-92.

"Strumming the Theological Harp." *Una Sancta* 26: 37-39.

1968   "Eusebius, Historical Change, and Church Unity." *Una Sancta* 25: 74-83.

"Holiness in the World: The Spirit of Holiness: Basil of Caesarea and Early Christian Spirituality." *Religious Life* 37: 29-39.

"*Insignissima Religio, Certe Licita?* Christianity and Judaism in the Fourth and Fifth Centuries." In *The Impact of the Church upon Its Culture,* ed. Jerald C. Brauer, pp. 39-66. Chicago: University of Chicago Press.

"Speaking Modestly of the Church." *Una Sancta* 25: 52-63.

1967   "A Homeric Cento in Irenaeus, *Adversus Haereses* I,9,4." *VChr* 21: 25-33.

"Judaism in Roman and Christian Society." *Journal of Religion* 47: 313-30. Reprinted in *Origins of Judaism: Religion, History, and Literature in Late Antiquity,* ed. Jacob Neusner, vol. 1: *Normative Judaism.* New York: Garland.

"Scripture and Dogma in the Ancient Church." *Lutheran World* 14: 163-79.

"Tertullian and the Early Christian View of Tradition." *Concordia Theological Monthly* 38: 221-33.

"Testimonia Patrum: Christian Faith, Historical Reason and Jesus." *Una Sancta* 24: 53-59.

"Testimonia Patrum: The Fathers on War." *Una Sancta* 24: 36-43.

"Testimonia Patrum: The Practice of Piety: Basil of Caesarea and the Pastoral Office." *Una Sancta* 24: 76-84.

"Testimonia Patrum: The Rationality of Faith." *Una Sancta* 24: 34-40.

1966   "Exegesis and the History of Theology: Reflections on the Adam-Christ Typology in Cyril of Alexandria." *ChHist* 35: 139-56.

"Is the Old Testament Old?" *Una Sancta* 23: 57-65.

"The Rite of Baptism: Liturgy and Exegesis." *Una Sancta* 23: 43-47.

"Why Only Four Gospels: A Look at the Larger Tradition." *Una Sancta* 23: 49-56.

1965   "Another Look at the 'Spiritual Interpretation' of the Bible." *Una Sancta* 22: 33-37.

"Bucket Brigade: Tradition and Christian Unity." *Una Sancta* 22: 25-31.

"Rites and Rubrics in the Early Church." *Una Sancta* 22: 46-49.

"Tradition, Exegesis and the Christological Controversy." *ChHist* 34: 123-45.

"Who Is Wolfhart Pannenberg?" *Dialog* 4: 140-42.

Reviews

Assmann, Jan. *Moses the Egyptian: The Memory of Egypt in Western Monotheism.* Cambridge, Mass.: Harvard University Press, 1997. *First Things,* no. 95 (1999): 76.

Barnes, Michel R., and Daniel H. Williams, eds. *Arianism after Arius: Essays on the Development of the 4th-Century Trinitarian Conflicts.* Edinburgh: T & T Clark, 1993. *Pro Ecclesia* 5 (1996): 120.

Behr, Charles A. *Aelius Aristides: The Complete Works,* vol. 1: *Orations* I-XVI. Leiden: Brill, 1986. *The Second Century* 7 (1989-90): 185-87.

Benko, Stephen. *Pagan Rome and the Early Christians.* Bloomington: Indiana University Press, 1984. *ThS* 47 (1986): 189-90.

Binns, John. *Ascetics and Ambassadors of Christ: The Monasteries of Palestine, 314-631.* Oxford: Oxford University Press, 1994. *Journal of Religion* 76 (1996): 468-69.

Boswell, John. *Same-Sex Unions in Premodern Europe.* New York: Villard Books, 1994. *Commonweal* 121 (1994): 24-26.

Bray, Gerald Lewis. *Holiness and the Will of God: Perspectives on the Theology of Tertullian.* Atlanta: John Knox, 1980. *Dialog* 21 (1982): 159.

Brent, Allen. *Hippolytus and the Roman Church in the Third Century: Communities in Tension before the Emergence of the Monarch-Bishop.* Leiden: Brill, 1995. *Catholic Historical Review* 83 (1997): 294-95.

Bruce, F. F., et al. *Paganisme — Judaisme — Christianisme.* Paris: Boccard, 1978. *ChHist* 49 (1980): 448-49.

Burtchaell, James. *From Synagogue to Church: Public Services and Offices in the Earliest Christian Communities.* Cambridge: Cambridge University Press, 1992. *First Things,* no. 31 (1993): 52.

Bynum, Caroline Walker. *The Resurrection of the Body in Western Christianity, 200-1336.* New York: Columbia University Press, 1995. *First Things,* no. 56 (1995): 62-64.

Campenhausen, Hans von. *Men Who Shaped the Western Church.* Trans. M. Hoffman. New York: Harper & Row, 1965. *ChHist* 34 (1965): 457-58.

Campenhausen, Hans von. *The Virgin Birth in the Theology of the Ancient Church.* London: SCM Press, 1964. *Una Sancta* 22 (1965): 59-61.

Chènevert, Jacques. *L'église dans le Commentaire d'Origène sur le Cantique des Cantiques.* Brussels: Desclée de Brouwer; Montreal: Bellarmin, 1969. *ThS* 32 (1971): 532-33.

Cooke, Bernard. *Ministry to Word and Sacraments: History and Theology.* Philadelphia: Fortress, 1976. *Dialog* 16 (1977): 230-32.

Davies, W. D. *Gospel and the Land: Early Christianity and Jewish Territorial Doctrine.* Berkeley: University of California Press, 1974. *ChHist* 44 (1975): 242.

Davies, W. D., and Louis Finkelstein. *The Cambridge History of Judaism,* vol. 1: *The Persian Period.* Cambridge: Cambridge University Press, 1984. *Christian Century* 102 (1985): 82.

De Lange, Nicholas. *Origen and the Jews: Studies in Jewish-Christian Relations in Third-Century Palestine.* Cambridge: Cambridge University Press, 1976. *ThS* 38 (1977): 578-79.

Donner, Herbert. *The Mosaic Map of Madaba: An Introductory Guide.* Kampen: Kok Pharos, 1992. *Religious Studies Review* 20 (1994): 242-43.

Duffy, Eamon. *Saints and Sinners: A History of the Popes.* New Haven: Yale University Press, 1997. *Commonweal* 124 (1997): 24-26.

Fiensy, David A. *Prayers Alleged to Be Jewish: An Examination of the Constitutiones Apostolorum.* Brown Judaic Studies 65. Chico, Calif.: Scholars Press, 1985. *Journal of Biblical Literature* 106 (1987): 745-46.

Fitzmyer, Joseph, ed. and trans. *Romans: A New Translation with Introduction and Commentary.* New York: Doubleday, 1993. *First Things,* no. 49 (1995): 77.

Floyd, W. E. G. *Clement of Alexandria's Treatment of the Problem of Evil.* New York: Oxford University Press, 1971. *ThS* 33 (1976): 176-77.

Fowden, Garth. *Empire to Commonwealth: Consequences of Monotheism in Late Antiquity.* Princeton: Princeton University Press, 1993. *Journal of Religion* 75 (1995): 271-72.

Fox, Robin Lane. *Pagans and Christians.* New York: Alfred A. Knopf, 1986. *New York Times Book Review* 92.5 (February 1987): 26; also in *Commonweal* 113 (1986): 154.

Grillmeier, Alois. *Christ in Christian Tradition,* vol. 2, part 4: *The Church of Alexandria with Nubia and Ethiopia after 451.* Trans. Theresia Hainthaler and O. C. Dean, Jr. Louisville: Westminster/John Knox, 1996. *Pro Ecclesia* 6 (1997): 372-74.

Guitton, Jean. *Great Heresies and Church Councils.* Trans. F. D. Wieck. London: Harvill Press; New York: Harper & Row, 1965. *ChHist* 35 (1966): 236-37.

Hebert, A. G. *Apostle and Bishop: A Study of the Gospel, the Ministry and the Church Community.* London: Faber; New York: Seabury, 1964. *ChHist* 33 (1964): 369-70.

Heid, Stephan. *Chiliasmus und Antichrist-Mythos: Eine frühchristliche Kontroverse um das Heilige Land.* Bonn: Borengässer, 1993. *JECS* 5 (1997): 124-25.

Heinemann, Joseph. *Prayer in the Talmud: Forms and Patterns.* Berlin and New York: de Gruyter, 1977. *ThS* 40 (1979): 175-77.

Heither, Theresia, ed. and trans. *Origenes: Commentarii in Epistulam ad Romanos:*

Liber Quintus, Liber Sextus. Freiburg: Herder, 1993. *Religious Studies Review* 20 (1994): 243.

Hengel, Martin. *Judaism and Hellenism,* 2 vols. Trans. John Bowden. Philadelphia: Fortress, 1975. *Christian Century* 92 (1975): 1034-35.

Hudson, Winthrop. *Religion in America.* New York: Charles Scribner's Sons, 1965. *ThS* 27 (1966): 490-93.

Johnson, Luke Timothy. *The Real Jesus: The Misguided Quest for the Historical Jesus and the Truth of the Traditional Gospels.* San Francisco: HarperSanFrancisco, 1996. *Commonweal* 123 (8 March 1996): 19-20.

Kelly, J. N. D. *The Athanasian Creed.* New York: Harper & Row, 1964. *Una Sancta* 23 (1966): 69-74.

Kelly, J. N. D. *A Commentary on the Pastoral Epistles: I Timothy, II Timothy, Titus.* New York: Harper & Row, 1963. *ChHist* 33 (1964): 488-89.

Kelly, J. N. D. *Jerome: His Life, Writings, and Controversies.* New York: Harper & Row; London: Duckworth, 1975. *ChHist* 43 (1976): 376.

King, Archdale Arthur. *Eucharistic Reservation in the Western Church.* New York: Sheed and Ward, 1965. *Una Sancta* 23 (1966): 103-4.

Kinzig, Wolfram. *Novitas Christiana: Die Idee des Fortschritts in der Alten Kirche bis Eusebius.* Göttingen: Vandenhoeck & Ruprecht, 1994. *JThS* N.S. 47 (1996): 271-74.

Klijn, A. F. J., and G. J. Reinink. *Patristic Evidence for Jewish-Christian Sects.* Leiden: Brill, 1973. *ThS* 36 (1975): 538-39.

Kugel, James L., and Rowan A. Greer. *Early Biblical Interpretation.* Philadelphia: Westminster, 1986. *ThS* 48 (1987): 537-38.

LaCocque, André, and Paul Ricoeur, *Thinking Biblically: Exegetical and Hermeneutical Studies.* Trans. David Pelauer. Chicago: University of Chicago Press, 1998. *First Things,* no. 93 (1999): 68.

Lapide, Pinchas E. *Hebrew in the Church.* Trans. Erroll F. Rhodes. Grand Rapids: Eerdmans, 1984. *Journal of Religion* 67 (1987): 126.

Le Boulluec, Alain. *La Notion d'hérésie dans la littérature grecque 2e-3e siècles,* vol. 1: *De Justin à Irénée;* vol. 2: *Clement d'Alexandrie et Origène.* Paris: Études Augustiniennes, 1985. *JThS* 39 (1988): 236-38.

Lieu, Judith, John North, and Tessa Rajak, eds. *The Jews among Pagans and Christians in the Roman Empire.* London and New York: Routledge, 1992. *JThS* N.S. 45 (1994): 290-92.

Malley, William J. *Hellenism and Christianity: The Conflict between Hellenic and Christian Wisdom in the* Contra Galilaeos *of Julian the Apostate and the* Contra Julianum *of St. Cyril of Alexandria.* Rome: Gregorian University, 1978. *ThS* 41 (1980): 410-11.

Markus, Robert. *The End of Ancient Christianity.* Cambridge: Cambridge University Press, 1990. *First Things,* no. 20 (1992): 54-57.

Murray, Robert. *Symbols of Church and Kingdom: A Study in Early Syriac Tradition.* London and New York: Cambridge University Press, 1975. *ThS* 37 (1976): 329-31.

Norris, Frederick W. *The Apostolic Faith: Protestants and Roman Catholics.* Collegeville, Minn.: Liturgical Press, 1992. *First Things,* no. 40 (1994): 46-47.

Pagels, Elaine H. *The Gnostic Paul.* Philadelphia: Fortress, 1975. *Christian Century* 93 (1976): 578-79.

Pelikan, Jaroslav. *The Christian Tradition: A History of the Development of Doctrine,* vol. 1: *The Emergence of the Catholic Tradition, 100-600.* Chicago: University of Chicago Press, 1971. *Saturday Review* 54 (7 August 1971): 26.

Pelikan, Jaroslav. *The Christian Tradition: A History of the Development of Doctrine,* vol. 2: *The Spirit of Eastern Christendom, 600-1700.* Chicago: University of Chicago Press, 1974. *Currents in Theology and Mission* 2 (1975): 298-99.

Pelikan, Jaroslav. *The Excellent Empire: The Fall of Rome and the Triumph of the Church.* San Francisco: Harper & Row, 1987. *ThS* 50 (1989): 204-5.

Peters, Joan. *From Time Immemorial: Dwellers in the Holy Land: The Origins of the Arab-Jewish Conflict over Palestine.* New York: Harper & Row, 1984. *Christian Century* 103 (1986): 678-80.

Petry, Ray C. *A History of Christianity,* vol. 1: *Readings in the History of the Early and Medieval Church.* Englewood Cliffs, N.J.: Prentice-Hall, 1962. *Journal of Religion* 44 (1964): 88-89.

Pollard, T. E. *Johannine Christology and the Early Church.* New York: Cambridge University Press, 1970. *Journal of Biblical Literature* 90 (1971): 362-64.

Quenot, Michel. *The Icon: Window on the Kingdom.* Crestwood, N.Y.: St. Vladimir's Seminary Press, 1991. *Pro Ecclesia* 2 (1993): 122.

Robinson, James M., and Helmut Koester. *Trajectories through Early Christianity.* Philadelphia: Fortress, 1971. *Lutheran World* 19 (1972): 174-75.

Rowland, Christopher. *The Open Heaven: A Study of Apocalyptic in Judaism and Early Christianity.* New York: Crossroad, 1982. *ChHist* 53 (1984): 231.

Ruether, Rosemary R. *Faith and Fratricide: The Theological Roots of Anti-Semitism.* New York: Seabury, 1974. *Anglican Theological Review* 59 (1977): 354-56.

Sanders, E. P. *Paul, the Law, and the Jewish People.* Philadelphia: Fortress, 1983. *Christian Century* 101 (1984): 255-56.

Smith, Jonathan Z. *Drudgery Divine: On the Comparison of Early Christianities and the Religions of Late Antiquity.* Chicago: University of Chicago Press, 1990. *Journal of the American Academy of Religion* 63 (1995): 374-77.

Soloveitchik, Joseph B. *Soloveitchik on Repentance: The Thought and Oral Dis-*

courses. Ed. and trans. Pinchas Peli. Mahwah, N.J.: Paulist Press, 1984. *Christian Century* 102 (1985): 809-10.

Sorabji, Richard, ed. *Philoponus and the Rejection of Aristotelian Science*. Ithaca, N.Y.: Cornell University Press, 1987. *Journal of the American Academy of Religion* 59 (1991): 624-25.

Stancliffe, Clare. *St. Martin and His Hagiographer: History and Miracle in Sulpicius Severus*. Oxford: Oxford University Press, 1983. *American Historical Review* 90 (1985): 913-14.

Torjesen, Karen Jo. *When Women Were Priests: Women's Leadership in the Early Church and the Scandal of Their Subordination in the Rise of Christianity*. San Francisco: HarperSanFrancisco, 1993. *First Things*, no. 43 (1994): 60.

Torrance, Thomas F. *Divine Meaning: Studies in Patristic Hermeneutics*. Edinburgh: T & T Clark, 1995. *ThS* 57 (1996): 743-44.

Van Oort, Johannes. *Jerusalem and Babylon: A Study into Augustine's "City of God" and the Sources of His Doctrine of the Two Cities*. Leiden: Brill, 1991. *Religious Studies Review* 20 (1994): 154.

Van Oort, Johannes, and Ulrich Wickert, eds. *Christliche Exegese zwischen Nicaea und Chalcedon*. Kampen: Kok Pharos, 1992. *JECS* 3 (1995): 228-29.

Vilela, Albano. *La condition collégiale des prêtres au IIIe siècle*. Théologie historique 14. Paris: Éditions Beauchesne, 1971. *ThS* 34 (1973): 502-4.

Von Balthasar, Hans Urs. *Presence and Thought: An Essay on the Religious Philosophy of Gregory of Nyssa*. Trans. Mark Sebanc. San Francisco: Ignatius Press, 1995. *First Things*, no. 63 (1996): 64.

Weltin, E. G. *Athens and Jerusalem: An Interpretive Essay on Christianity and Classical Culture*. Atlanta: Scholars Press, 1987. *Journal of Religion* 69 (1989): 604.

Wickert, Ulrich. *Studien zu den Pauluskommentaren Thedors von Mopsuestia*. Berlin: Alfred Topelmann, 1962. *ChHist* 33 (1964): 97-98.

Wiles, Maurice. *The Making of Christian Doctrine: A Study in the Principles of Early Doctrinal Development*. New York: Cambridge University Press, 1967. *Journal of Religion* 49 (1969): 312-13.

Young, Frances M. *The Use of Sacrificial Ideas in Greek Christian Writers*. Cambridge, Mass.: Philadelphia Patristic Foundation, 1979. *ThS* 43 (1982): 361.